IFIP Advances in Information and Communication Technology   414

Editor-in-Chief

A. Joe Turner, Seneca, SC, USA

Editorial Board

IFIP – The International Federation for Information Processing

IFIP was founded in 1960 under the auspices of UNESCO, following the First World Computer Congress held in Paris the previous year. An umbrella organization for societies working in information processing, IFIP's aim is two-fold: to support information processing within its member countries and to encourage technology transfer to developing nations. As its mission statement clearly states,

> IFIP's mission is to be the leading, truly international, apolitical organization which encourages and assists in the development, exploitation and application of information technology for the benefit of all people.

IFIP is a non-profitmaking organization, run almost solely by 2500 volunteers. It operates through a number of technical committees, which organize events and publications. IFIP's events range from an international congress to local seminars, but the most important are:

- The IFIP World Computer Congress, held every second year;
- Open conferences;
- Working conferences.

The flagship event is the IFIP World Computer Congress, at which both invited and contributed papers are presented. Contributed papers are rigorously refereed and the rejection rate is high.

As with the Congress, participation in the open conferences is open to all and papers may be invited or submitted. Again, submitted papers are stringently refereed.

The working conferences are structured differently. They are usually run by a working group and attendance is small and by invitation only. Their purpose is to create an atmosphere conducive to innovation and development. Refereeing is also rigorous and papers are subjected to extensive group discussion.

Publications arising from IFIP events vary. The papers presented at the IFIP World Computer Congress and at open conferences are published as conference proceedings, while the results of the working conferences are often published as collections of selected and edited papers.

Any national society whose primary activity is about information processing may apply to become a full member of IFIP, although full membership is restricted to one society per country. Full members are entitled to vote at the annual General Assembly, National societies preferring a less committed involvement may apply for associate or corresponding membership. Associate members enjoy the same benefits as full members, but without voting rights. Corresponding members are not represented in IFIP bodies. Affiliated membership is open to non-national societies, and individual and honorary membership schemes are also offered.

Vittal Prabhu   Marco Taisch
Dimitris Kiritsis (Eds.)

Advances in Production Management Systems

Sustainable Production and Service Supply Chains

IFIP WG 5.7 International Conference, APMS 2013
State College, PA, USA, September 9-12, 2013
Proceedings, Part I

 Springer

Volume Editors

Vittal Prabhu
Pennsylvania State University
Marcus Department of Industrial and Manufacturing Engineering
310 Leonhard Building, University Park, PA 16802, USA
E-mail: prabhu@engr.psu.edu

Marco Taisch
Politecnico di Milano
Department of Management, Economics and Industrial Engineering
Piazza Leonardo Da Vinci 32, 20133 Milan, Italy
E-mail: marco.taisch@polimi.it

Dimitris Kiritsis
EPFL, STI-IGM-LICP, ME A1 396, Station 9
1015 Lausanne, Switzerland
E-mail: dimitris.kiritsis@epfl.ch

ISSN 1868-4238   e-ISSN 1868-422X
ISBN 978-3-662-52515-9   e-ISBN 978-3-642-41266-0
DOI 10.1007/978-3-642-41266-0
Springer Heidelberg New York Dordrecht London

CR Subject Classification (1998): J.6, J.1, J.7, H.4, K.4, I.6, I.2, H.1

Typesetting: Camera-ready by author, data conversion by Scientific Publishing Services, Chennai, India

Printed on acid-free paper

Springer is part of Springer Science+Business Media (www.springer.com)

Preface

For the last several years, APMS has been a major event and the official conference of the IFIP Working Group 5.7 on Advances in Production Management Systems, bringing together leading experts from academia, research, and industry. Starting with the first conference in Helsinki in 1990, the conference has become a successful annual event that has been hosted in various parts of the world including Washington (USA, 2005), Wroclaw (Poland, 2006), Linköping (Sweden, 2007), Espoo (Finland, 2008), Bordeaux (France, 2009), Cernobbio (Italy, 2010), Stavanger (Norway, 2011), and Rhodos (Greece, 2012). By returning to the Americas after eight years, we hope to widen the global reach of the Working Group and the APMS conference.

Through an open call for special sessions and papers, APMS 2013 sought contributions in cutting-edge research, as well as insightful advances in industrial practice in key areas of sustainable production and service supply chains, including green manufacturing, sustainability of additive manufacturing processes, advanced control systems, enterprise information systems and integration, sustainable logistics and transportation. The intent of special sessions is to raise visibility on topics of focused interest in a particular scientific or applications area. This year we have planned 15 special sessions which are focused around the theme of the conference. Over 135 papers have been accepted based on blind peer-review. The main review criteria were the paper's contributions to science and industrial practice. Accepted papers of registered participants are included in this volume. This is the first time for APMS conference that full papers have been submitted and reviewed from the outset thereby eliminating the extended abstract stage and allowing for the final proceedings to be available at the time of the conference.

Following the tradition of past APMS conferences, the 6th APMS Doctoral Workshop is planned offering Ph.D. students the opportunity to present, discuss, receive feedback and exchange comments and views on their doctoral research in an inspiring academic community of fellow Ph.D. students, experienced researchers, and professors of the IFIP WG 5.7 community. The Doctoral Workshop will be chaired by Sergio Cavalieri (University of Bergamo).

Two types of awards have been planned for APMS 2013 participants:

- Burbidge Awards for best paper and best presentation
- Doctoral Workshop Award

Approximately 150 participants from across academia, research labs, and industry from 23 countries are expected to attend the APMS 2013 conference. The Scientific Committee consisting of 77 researchers, many of whom are active members of the IFIP WG 5.7, have played key roles in reviewing the papers in a timely manner and providing constructive feedback to authors in revising their manuscripts for the final draft. Papers in this volume are grouped thematically as follows:

- **Part I Sustainable Production:** Enablers for Smart Manufacturing, Social Sustainability in Manufacturing, Intelligent Production Systems and Planning Solutions for Sustainability, Design, Planning and Operation of Manufacturing Networks for Mass Customization and Personalization, Energy Efficient Manufacturing
- **Part II Sustainable Supply Chains:** Sustainability Characterization for Product Assembly and Supply Chain, Interoperability in the Manufacturing and Supply Chain Services, Sustainable Manufacturing and Supply Chain Management for Renewable Energy, Closed Loop Design, Supply Chain Management
- **Part III Sustainable Services:** Service Manufacturing Systems, Art of Balancing Innovation and Efficiency in Service Systems, Simulation Based Training in Production and Operations Management, Modelling of Business and Operational Processes, Servicization,
- **Part IV ICT and Emerging Technologies:** ICT-Enabled Integrated Operations, Sustainable Initiatives in Developing Countries, LCA Methods and Tools, ICT for Manufacturing and Supply Chain Management, Product Design for Sustainable Supply Chains

We hope that the present volume will be of interest to a wide range of researchers and practitioners.

August 2013

Vittal Prabhu
Marco Taisch
Dimitris Kiritsis

Organization

Congress Chairs

Chair

Vittal Prabhu   Penn State University, USA

Co-chairs

Marco Taisch   Politecnico di Milano, Italy
Dimitris Kiritsis   Ecole Polytechnique Fédérale de Lausanne,
                                            Switzerland

APMS 2013 International Advisory Board

Christos Emmanouilidis   ATHENA R.I.C., Greece
Dimitris Kiritsis   EPFL, Switzerland
Vittal Prabhu   Penn State University, USA
Volker Stich   FIR - RWTH Aachen, Germany
Marco Taisch   Politecnico di Milano, Italy
Shigeki Umeda   Musashi University, Japan

APMS 2013 Doctoral Workshop Chair

Sergio Cavalieri   University of Bergamo, Italy

APMS 2013 Local Organizing Committee

Paul Griffin   Penn State University, USA
Ravi Ravindran   Penn State University, USA
Skip Grenoble   Penn State University, USA
Sanjay Joshi   Penn State University, USA
Doug Thomas   Penn State University, USA
Jeep Rattachut Tangsucheeva   Penn State University, USA
Gökan May   Politecnico di Milano Italy) &
                                            Penn State University, USA

Yuncheol Kang   Penn State University, USA
Jinkun Lee   Penn State University, USA

APMS 2013 Conference Secretariat

Penn State Conferences & Institute

Sponsors for APMS 2013

IFIP WG 5.7 Advances in Production Management Systems
Marcus Department of Industrial and Manufacturing Engineering, Penn State
University
The Electro-Optics Center, Penn State University
Center for Supply Chain Research, Penn State University
Enterprise Integration Consortium, Penn State University
Kimberly-Clark Corporation
Intelligent Manufacturing Systems
NABCO, Inc.

International Scientific Committee

Mohammed Reza Alamdari	POLIMI, Italy
Farhad Ameri	Texas State University, USA
Cecilia Berlin	Chalmers, Sweden
Frédérique Biennier	INSA de Lyon, France
Abdelaziz Bouras	Université Lumière Lyon, France
Sergio Cavalieri	University of Bergamo, Italy
Daniele Cerri	POLIMI, Italy
Sila Cetinkaya	Texas A&M University, USA
Qing Chang	Stony Brook University, USA
Hyunbo Cho	Pohang University of Science and Technology, South Korea
Ivanir Costa	Paulista University, Brazil
Christos Emmanouilidis	ATHENA Research & Innovation Centre, Greece
Benoit Eynard	Université de Technologie de Compiègne, France
Peter Falster	Technical University of Denmark
Paola Fantini	POLIMI, Italy
Jan Frick	Stavanger, Norway
Bernard Grabot	National Engineering School of Tarbes (ENIT), France
Jackie Griffin	Northeastern University, USA
Mamun Habib	American International University - Bangladesh (AIUB)
Harinder Jahdev	UMIST, UK
Endris Temam Kerga	POLIMI/CAREL, Italy
Dimitris Kiritsis	EPFL, Switzerland
Gul Kremer	PSU, USA
Boonserm Kulvatunyou	NIST, USA
Minna Lanz	Tampere University of Technology, Finland

Kincho Law	Stanford University, USA
Jan-Peter Lechner	Universität der Bundeswehr Hamburg, Germany
Ming Lim	University of Derby, UK
Gökan May	POLIMI/PSU, Italy
Kai Mertins	Knowledge Raven Management GmbH, Germany
Hajime Mizuyama	AGU, Japan
Mario Mollo	Paulista University, Brazil
Florian Muller	SIEMENS, Germany
Irenilza Naas	Paulista University, Brazil
Drazen Nadoveza	EPFL, Switzerland
Masaru Nakano	Keio University, Japan
Peter Nielsen	Aalborg University, Denmark
Marcelo Okano	VOP Informatica, Brazil
Deise Oliveira	Embrapa Informática Agropecuária, Brazil
Pedro Luiz Oliveira	Paulista University, Brazil
David Opresnik	POLIMI, Italy
Pier Francesco Orrù	Università degli Studi di Cagliari, Italy
Jinwoo Park	Seoul National University, South Korea
Henk-Jan Pels	Eindhoven University of Technology, The Netherlands
Christopher Peters	The Lucrum Group, USA
Giuditta Pezzotta	University of Bergamo, Italy
Selwyn Piramuthu	Warrington College, UK
Golboo Pourabdollahian	POLIMI, Italy; AACHEN, Germany
Borzoo Pourabdollahian	POLIMI, Italy; BIBA, Germany
Daryl John Powell	NTNU, Norway
Vittal Prabhu	PSU, USA
Mario Rapaccini	Florence University, Italy
Jens Riis	Aalborg University, Denmark
Monica Rossi	POLIMI, Italy
Paul Schönsleben	ETHZ, Switzerland
Avraham Shtub	Technion Israel Institute of Technology, Israel
Jaehun Sim	PSU, USA
Riitta Smeds	Aalto University, Finland
Vijay Srinivasan	NIST, USA
Bojan Stahl	POLIMI, Italy
Kathryn E. Stecke	University of Texas, USA
Volker Stich	FIR Aachen, Germany
Jan Ola Strandhagen	SINTEF, Norway
Stanisław Strzelczak	Warsaw University of Technology, Poland
Marco Taisch	POLIMI, Italy
Rattachut Tangsucheeva	PSU, USA

Table of Contents – Part I

Part I: Sustainable Production

Part II: Sustainable Supply Chains

Table of Contents – Part II

Part III: Sustainable Services

Part IV: ICT and Emerging Technologies

Part I
Sustainable Production

Towards an Approach to Identify the Optimal Instant of Time for Information Capturing in Supply Chains

Thorsten Wuest, Dirk Werthmann, and Klaus-Dieter Thoben

Bremer Institut für Produktion und Logistik GmbH (BIBA), Hochschulring 20,
28359 Bremen, Germany
{wue,wdi,tho}@biba.uni-bremen.de

Abstract. Supply chains are becoming increasingly complex and with this development the challenges towards information management increase. The importance of capturing the right, most relevant information in order to avoid having too much information to handle is commonly accepted in industry and academia. But the question not yet sufficiently discussed by industry and academia is: What is the optimal instant of time to capture the relevant information along the process chain? With this paper the authors look into this issue by first analyzing two practical cases, from a transport and a manufacturing perspective. Afterwards, the elements of information captured are shortly elaborated and finally, constraints on the determination of the optimal instant of time for information capturing are elaborated in order to build a foundation for further research. This paper is a first step towards a methodological approach taking on these issues. A short conclusion and outlook summarizes the paper.

Keywords: information management, synchronization, SCM, manufacturing, transport processes, product state.

1   Introduction

In today's ever more complex world, the exchange of information within supply chains is gaining importance e.g. for transparency reasons. Achieving higher transparency, meaning provision of information about future schedules or past events to stakeholders involved, allows process improvements in order to reduce total costs or providing better service levels and a more synchronized supply chain. Finally, the improvement of the processes should increase their efficiency.

Paradigms like the Internet of Things [1] or Cyber Physical Systems [2] highlight the increasing relevance of performing information exchange. Both paradigms are focusing on information creation and information exchange among physical and virtual objects. By using the captured information, decisions could be supported and/or made by computers or humans on how to execute various processes within the supply chain. Those processes can again be executed by either machines and/or humans.

Information management is understood as "the application of management principles to the acquisition, organization, control, dissemination and use of information relevant to the effective operation of organizations of all kinds" [3]. Much of the

V. Prabhu, M. Taisch, and D. Kiritsis (Eds.): APMS 2013, Part I, IFIP AICT 414, pp. 3–12, 2013.

research regarding information management is done in the field of improvement activities within the communication technology, or showing the impact available information has on a supply chain [4; 5; 6]. Identifying relevant information needed for improving specific processes is challenging, but already widely discussed in research and industry [7; 8]. However, experts in the field are aware of this problem. Furthermore, for today's supply chains, the relevant information and the right addressees are mostly known and the stakeholders are supported by various available supporting methods (e.g., Supply Chain Event Management [9]). The related challenge, analyzing the optimal instant of time to capture this relevant information, did not attract that much attention by researchers to this point. The optimal instant of time for information captured within this paper is understood as the point in time along a supply chain process where certain relevant information can be captured in the most efficient way, with regard to cost, technical limitations etc. The authors are aware that the use of the term *optimal* is not a perfect description but in absence of a better, equally brief term decided to use the term optimal throughout this publication. That being said, it is nevertheless essential to look further into this issue in the future, in order to establish an efficient information management and be prepared for growing information needs, e.g. real time-provision of process information. One possible reason why this issue is not yet elaborated on as of today might be that it is either possible to establish the instant of time through common sense or it is not considered relevant when the capturing does take place exactly.

This paper is structured as follows: In order to establish a solid foundation for future research in this area, available and common procedures currently used in practice for identification of the right instant of time for capturing relevant information in supply chains are presented in section two. To take the whole supply chain and the different requirements into account, that section is divided into two sub sections, thus covering manufacturing and transport processes. In section three, the different elements of relevant information captured in supply chains are identified and elaborated on. This is followed by an analysis executed in section four with the goal of categorizing the possible flexibility of information capturing regarding the instant of time. Moreover, restrictions towards the influence of the instant of time towards relevant information are identified. Additionally, a methodology from another domain, possibly related to the identification of the optimal instant of time for capturing information within a supply chain, is briefly introduced. Finally, section five concludes the paper and gives an outlook on future research within this topic.

2   Instant of Time Determination for Information Capturing in Supply Chains

This section focuses on how the optimal instant of time for capturing information is currently determined from a practical (industrial) point of view.

For ease of understanding, the information analyzing the capture of the whole supply chain, is split up into two basic parts, which in the understanding of the authors', best represent the major requirements. These two parts are the production planning and inventory control process, in the following *manufacturing*, and the distribution and logistics process, in the following *transport* [10]. This breakdown is also in accordance with the SCOR model, aggregating *Source* and *Deliver* to transport and *Make* to manufacturing. Therefore, the first sub section looks at industrial manufacturing processes and the second one at transport processes. Finally, the results of both basic processes regarding the information capturing are consolidated.

The overall principles of information management (e.g., [11; 12; 13]) of ensuring the right information is available at the best possible moment (in terms of time, granularity, location and quality) is applicable for all areas of the supply chain. However, the principle does not clearly state when the relevant information should be captured to fulfill these requirements. The approach to capture all measurable information at all times possible is found to be causing more problems than doing good by increasing transparency and productivity (e.g., [7]).

2.1   Instant of Time Determination for Information Capturing in Manufacturing

Information management in manufacturing focuses mostly on how available information should be managed (e.g., [14; 15]) or what existing IM system should be selected to reach the set goals (e.g., [16; 17]).

However, in industrial practice of a manufacturing SME, a more hands-on approach can be found. For this section, the processes of a Tier1 automotive supplier were analyzed. The company produces engine parts subject to high stress during usage with high quality requirements and very little failure tolerance. The processes are automated in most cases, as is the information capturing.

In manufacturing, there is some information which must be known for the following processes to proceed. For example, after machining, the exact geometry (dimensions) has to be available to set the parameters for the following process of milling. Therefore, the instant of time to capture the relevant information (geometry) was determined or at least limited by the previous process (influencing the geometry) and following process requirements.

After milling, the balance is tested and the information captured is deemed ok or not ok. The specific parameters of the individual product are measured but not stored or communicated to another instance. The not ok parts are then separated to be measured again in a machining center where countermeasures are, if possible, directly carried out. These parts then go through a final quality inspection by hand. The instant in time for this information capturing (quality ok / not-ok) was not set time wise but handled flexibly.

Based on this example it was found, that for some information capturing activities, the instant of time is pre-determined by the processes, more specifically the requirements of the following process. However, the information in this case is measured after machining. In an additional process step, it could possibly be derived within the process of machining or directly before milling. So there is at least a small window of flexibility. On other occasions, however, it is handled without a set instant of time.

Overall, it was found, that no systematic approach to determine the optimal instant of time was applied in this use case.

2.2   Instant of Time Determination for Information Capturing in Transport

There are already a lot of studies available that look at the costs and the processes for implementing an information management system for transport processes (e.g. [18]). The benefits of information capturing within transport processes are also explained in a lot of publications (e.g. [19; 20]).

However, to the authors' knowledge, in accordance with the findings in manufacturing, until today there has been no approach found in science and industry for the determination of the optimal instant of time for information capturing within transport processes. In the following, a use case, based on a current research project for transport processes is presented to highlight the current practices. The German research project RFID-based Automotive Network (RAN) (http://www.autoran.de/), focused on improving the automotive supply chains by increasing transparency based on an efficient exchange of information. Therefore, it was necessary to identify the relevant information needed within the supply chain. In this context, one work package has had the task to model all relevant processes within the automotive industry in a generally accepted (by automotive professionals & researchers) manner.

First of all, currently implemented processes were analyzed by modeling the processes using the methodology of Event-driven Process Chain (EDPC). Secondly, these processes were analyzed and generally accepted processes (standard *processes*) were modeled by using the EDPC method again. In total, twelve so-called standard processes were identified: two examples are loading and external transport. The main result of the conducted work was that the modeled processes describe what information is needed within the different standard processes and what information is generated from that. Furthermore, the sequence of the information capturing is described when necessary. Sometimes the sequence was not considered necessary, in which case parallel paths were modeled. By defining processes start and end, borders can be defined in between the necessary information needs to be generated.

In order to draw a conclusion, the instants of time for information capturing in transport processes were not defined precisely within the standard processes, because in most cases there was no generally applicable optimal instant of time for all companies involved within the automotive supply chain. The design of the processes and the determination of the instants of time did not follow a structured approach; it was rather driven by practical experience of the people and experts involved.

As was highlighted in the sections above, there is no structured and methodological approach available today to determine the optimal instant of time to capture relevant information within supply chains.

The question remains: why is that the case? Is there simply no need to determine the optimal instant of time today as it is determined by surrounding processes or requirements by following processes/addresses needing the information?

In order to answer those questions raised above, in the following the elements of captured information in supply chains will be examined, followed by a theoretical discussion on categorization of possibilities to capture relevant information in supply chains. Furthermore, influencing or limiting factors on the determination of the optimal instant of time are briefly presented.

3   Elements of Captured Information in Supply Chains

To be of value, the captured information within the supply chain needs to contain certain elements. Based on the goals of logistics management (Seven-Rights-Definition of Logistics) expresses by Plowman [21], the right goods have to be of the right quantity and quality, in the right location at the right instant of time, and for the right customer for the right costs. Looking at the information captured within the supply chain the element quantity can be derived from the element identity (aggregation of individual products). The element costs and customer cannot be captured on the shop floor or the transport process during the material flow; however, it can later be annotated to the individual product. Based on a supply chain point of view the relevant information elements to be captured are presented in Fig.1.

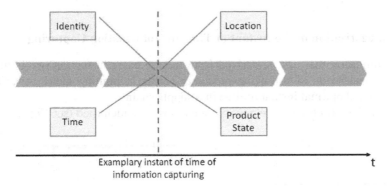

Fig. 1. Elements of information captured

Identity
It is always necessary to link the captured information to a specific object. Therefore, the object has to be identified precisely and uniquely. The identification can take place automatically by scanning a barcode or a RFID transponder or by entering the information manually into an IT system etc.

Time
A time stamp integrated into every event captured is necessary for having unique information. Moreover, the time stamp is necessary to have a precise history of every object being tracked within the supply chain.

Location
Knowing about the location of an object is also very important when generating an event. E.g. information of the current process can be derived from location/time.

Product State

Last but not least, the product state which incorporates various characteristics of a product e.g., quality, dimensions etc. of an object is considered relevant information [22]. Based on the product state's characteristics, the following process steps and their parameters within supply chains can be planned. An example for a state characteristic is the diameter after machining, but also residual stress allocation within a steel disc.

4   Thoughts on Constrains towards the Optimal Instant of Time for Information Capturing

In the following, limitations and pre-set conditions to determine an instant of time for information capturing are presented and, if possible, categorized. This is followed by a short elaboration on external conditions/factors influencing the instant of time for information capturing. In the final sub-section, existing approaches from other domains are presented which could be beneficial when working towards an approach supporting the identification of the optimal instant of time for data capturing in supply chains.

4.1   Categorization of the Instant of Time for Information Capturing

The first limitation that can be derived from the use cases in section two is that requirements and needs of following processes can be a limiting factor towards the determination of optimal instant of time in a supply chain.

Based on those findings three possible scenarios were identified (see Fig. 2.).

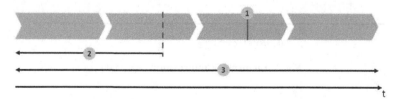

Fig. 2. Categories of Instant of Time capturing

The first category *"fixed"* ((1) in Fig. 2.) describes a case where the capturing of the relevant information has a pre-set instant of time as the relevant information must be captured at a certain instant of time during the process. An example can be a truck leaving the compound. This information can only be captured at that specific instant of time. In manufacturing, this is comparable with the measurement of the temperature at an instant of time during the heat treatment process.

The second category is, when certain flexibility in the determination of the instant of time exists (*"flexible with borders"* (2) in Fig. 2.). In this case the relevant information needs to be captured in a certain area of the process at a certain instant of time, but the execution of the information capturing within the processes is not clearly specified. However, this limitation mostly consists of the instant of time when the considered relevant information (product state) changes before the addressee needs it. An example from manufacturing (section 2.1) would be the described scenario where the geometry must be known before the milling process starts, but the precise instant of time for capturing it is not clearly defined (earliest the moment the geometry changed the last time). Within transport processes an example highlighting this category is when an object is unloaded at a warehouse. The information could be captured, right at that very moment, when the forklift unloads the object from the trailer, but it could also be captured when driving through the gate of the warehouse or when the forklift removes the object.

The third and last category describes the case that the instant of time is absolutely flexible regarding the supply chain processes (*"total flexibility"* (3) in Fig. 2.). This case is a pure theoretical one. When information is relevant within the supply chain, some addressee can only use the information at a certain moment. This addressee is then the limiting factor and this category would fall under category (2). The only theoretical application of this category the authors could think of is the following: an addressee needing to access certain information about the supply chain, but only after the processes are fulfilled and the product is with the customer. This could be within a Product Lifecycle Management (PLM) context or e.g., a governmental agency requiring information for taxation. However, this case will be excluded from further elaboration within this paper.

Another set of categories, influencing the instant of time is how and how often the information capturing takes place within the supply chain. When imaging continuous capturing of information the question for the optimal instant of time becomes obsolete as there is just one long instant of time. If the information capturing is randomized, setting a fixed instant of time would most likely defy the purpose. Categorization on how and how often relevant information can be captured is defined below:

One Time
The relevant information has to be captured once within the process chain. An example is "gate out" if a truck leaves the compound.

Multiple Times
If information has to be captured multiple times throughout a process chain it has to be differentiated between *"regular"*, where information has to be captured at pre-set times e.g., temperature measurements during transport of perishable goods. As the temperature of objects is very inertial, it is necessary to measure the temperature in specific intervals. A second possible characteristic of multiple time information capturing is *"random"*. This can be human or computer triggered events to control the quality of products.

Continuously
Continuous information capturing in a supply chain can be necessary for high value products like diamonds or weapons e.g., through a continuous capturing of the location at all times for security reasons.

A possible instant of time which does not fit directly into these categories is if the instant of time of information capturing is triggered by changing status or state. This could be a Kanban system, where the information is captured once the box is empty. Another example from transport processes could be a truck running late due to traffic congestions and the actual position of the truck does not match the position of where it should be at a specific instant of time (out of synch). An example from manufacturing would be a continuous check of the dimensions and no information is captured (no event) if it is within the tolerance. As soon as the tolerance is reached, the information is captured.

4.2   Influencing Factors for the Instant of Time of Information Capturing

There are a few overarching and predetermined influencing factors for the determination of the optimal instant of time for information capturing in supply chains. Technical restrictions enforce information capturing at a certain instant of time during the process. Other influencing factors can be economic reasons, often strongly connected to technical reasons, limiting the possibilities of information capturing. Information capturing can also be limited by the confidentiality of information during the process. Those factors cannot be influenced but must be taken into account.

Classic limiting factors with a definite instant of time determination are documentation of the transfer of perils and, connected to this, laws or governmental regulations determining when certain information has to be captured in certain industries.

4.3   Existing Approaches for Identification of the Instant of Time for Information Capturing

In this section, an approach with partly similar requirements from another domain will be introduced briefly. However, it has to be understood that this approach does not directly address the issues raised before but rather provides a starting point or lever for the development of an approach with the goal of determining the optimal instant of time for information capturing in supply chains.

Quality Gates are utilized primarily in the product and software development process, [23]. The development of complex products over a time horizon of several years comes with large coordination and synchronization challenges. Therefore, a guideline and a reference process have to be developed to guide the project team through the process. This reference process allows measuring progress and maturity of the project (or the product). Through Quality Gates, the reference process is divided into synchronized process phases [24].

The basic idea of the Quality Gate approach is to determine these process phases and ensure that all defined goals are reached before moving on to the next phase [25]. Thus, the gates are *decision points* where information is captured within a process, which is the basis for a decision concerning further actions [26]. Therefore, the approach to determine the optimal instant of time to install Quality Gates within a process could provide valuable information for the problem at hand.

5   Conclusion and Outlook

The question of how to determine the optimal instant of time to capture the relevant information along supply chain processes is not answered yet. In this paper the authors took a look into this issue by analyzing two practical cases, from a transport and a manufacturing perspective. Afterwards, the elements of information captured were shortly elaborated. Finally, constraints on the determination of the optimal instant of time for information capturing as well as an approach from the domain of software development, Quality Gates, was briefly discussed towards possible overlaps.

In conclusion, it is to be said that the issue is important and deserves more attention from industry and academia. In a next step, the Quality Gate and related approaches will be analyzed further to derive mechanisms which can be applied to develop a generalized approach to determining the optimal instant of time for data capturing in supply chains. Right now, the authors are involved in a study at a major German car manufacturer analyzing this issue. At the same time, similar processes are analyzed at the manufacturing SME in order to ensure that the to-be-developed approach represents the different requirements. In the future, the to-be-developed approach will be evaluated in industrial scenarios and integrated in existing quality frameworks.

Acknowledgement. The authors would like to thank the "Deutsche Forschungsgemeinschaft" for financial support via the funded project "Informationssystem für werkstoffwissenschaftliche Forschungsdaten" (InfoSys) and the Federal Ministry of Economics and Technology, which founded the project "RAN – RFID-based Automotive Network" (Ref. No. 01MA10009) as part of its technology program "AUTONOMIK: Autonomous, simulation-based systems for small and medium-sized enterprises".

References

1. Ashton, K.: That 'Internet of Things' Thing. RFID Journal (July 22, 2009) (retrieved April 8, 2011)
2. Lee, E.A.: Cyber-Physical Systems - Are Computing Foundations Adequate? Position Paper for NSF Workshop on Cyber-Physical Systems: Research Motivation, Techniques and Roadmap, Austin, TX, October 16-17 (2006)
3. Wilson, T.D.: Information management. In: International Encyclopedia of Information and Library Science, pp. 187–196. Routledge, London (1997)
4. Wong, C.Y., McFarlane, D., Ahmad Zaharudin, A., Agarwal, V.: The intelligent product driven supply chain. In: IEEE Int. Conf. on Systems, Man & Cybernetics, vol. 4, p. 6 (2002)
5. Albino, V., Pontrandolfo, P., Scozzi, B.: Analysis of information flows to enhance the coordination of production processes. International Journal of Production Economics 75(1-2), 7–19 (2002)
6. Atzori, L., Iera, A., Morabito, G.: The Internet of Things: A survey. Computer Networks 54(15), 2787–2805 (2010)
7. Jansen-Vullers, M.H., Wortmann, J.C., Beulens, A.J.M.: Application of labels to trace material flows in multi-echelon supply chains. Production Planning & Control 15(3), 303–312 (2004), doi:10.1080/09537280410001697738

8. Zhang, Y., Jiang, P., Huang, G., Qu, T., Zhou, G., Hong, J.: RFID-enabled real-time manufacturing information tracking infrastructure for extended enterprises. Journal of Intelligent Manufacturing 23(6), 2357–2366 (2010), doi:10.1007/s10845-010-0475-3

9. Otto, A.: Supply Chain Event Management: Three perspectives. International Journal of Logistics Management 14(2), 1–13 (2004)

10. Beamon, B.M.: Supply chain design and analysis - Models and methods. International Journal of Production Economics 55(3), 281–294 (1998)

11. Augustin, S.: Information als Wettbewerbsfaktor: Informationslogistik – Herausforderung an das Management. TÜV Media GmbH, Köln (1990)

12. Jehle, E.: Produktionswirtschaft. Verlag Recht und Wirtschaft, Heidelberg (1999)

13. Hoke, G.E.J.: Shoring Up Information Governance with GARP®. Information Management 1(2), 26–31 (2011)

14. Choe, J.-M.: The consideration of cultural differences in the design of information systems. Information & Management 41, 669–684 (2004)

15. Hicks, B.J.: Lean information management: Understanding and eliminating waste. Journal of Information Management 27(4), 233–249 (2007)

16. Beach, R., Muhlemann, A.P., Price, D.H.R., Paterson, A., Sharp, J.A.: The selection of information systems for production management: An evolving problem. International Journal of Production Economics 64, 319–329 (2000)

17. Gunasekaran, A., Ngai, E.W.T.: Information systems in supply chain integration and management. European Journal of Operational Management 159, 269–295 (2004)

18. Hellström, D.: The cost and process of implementing RFID technology to manage and control returnable transport items. International Journal of Logistics: Research and Applications 12(1), 1–21 (2009)

19. McFarlane, D., Yossi, S.: The impact of automatic identification on supply chain operations. International Journal of Logistics Management 14(1), 1–17 (2003)

20. Loebbecke, C., Powell, P.: Competitive advantage from IT in logistics: the integrated transport tracking system. Int. Journal of Information Management 18(1), 17–27 (1998)

21. Plowman, G.E.: Elements of Business Logistics, Stanford (1964)

22. Wuest, T., Irgens, C., Thoben, K.-D.: An approach to quality monitoring in manufacturing using supervised machine learning on product state data. Journal of Intelligent Manufacturing (online first, 2013), doi:10.1007/s10845-013-0761-y

23. Salger, F., Bennicke, M., Engels, G., Lewerentz, C.: Comprehensive Architecture Evaluation and Management in Large Software-Systems. In: Becker, S., Plasil, F., Reussner, R. (eds.) QoSA 2008. LNCS, vol. 5281, pp. 205–219. Springer, Heidelberg (2008)

24. Prefi, T.: Qualitätsmanagement in der Produktentwicklung. In: Pfeifer, T., Schmitt, R. (Hrsg.) Masing Handbuch Qualitätsmanagement. 5. Auflage. Hanser, München (2007)

25. Schmitt, R., Pfeifer, T.: Qualitätsmanagement: Strategie, Methoden, Technik. 4. Auflage, München (2010)

26. Spath, D., Scharer, M., Landwehr, R., Förster, H., Schneider, W.: Tore öffnen - Quality-Gate-Konzept für den Produktentstehungsprozess. QZ - Qualität und Zuverlässigkeit 12 (2001)

Exploring Different Faces of Mass Customization in Manufacturing

Golboo Pourabdollahian, Marco Taisch, and Gamze Tepe

Politecnico di Milano, Piazza Leonardo Da Vinci 32, 20133, Milan, Italy
{golboo.pourabdollahian,marco.taisch}@polimi.it

Abstract. The present research aims at developing a framework to support MC companies in understanding different considerations and issues of mass customization manufacturing (MCM). It introduces crucial aspects of MCM by analyzing existing MC enablers and technologies as well as the trending ones which might be used in future of mass customization manufacturing. The framework is developed in two levels grounding on both literature and practical findings.

Keywords: Mass Customization, Manufacturing.

1   Introduction

Mass customization refers to producing personalized goods and services with an efficiency close to mass production [4,3,6]. A successful implementation of this strategy is based on the accurate design of the entire supply chain. The value chain must be a cooperation oriented network since mass customization primarily aims to satisfy individual needs of customers. Going through literature, "Mass Customization" and particularly MC manufacturing were discussed in numerous articles; but linkages between various manufacturing paradigms, enablers and factors influence MC manufacturing have been rarely covered. This paper aims to present both the current state and the future directions of mass customization manufacturing by integrating data from literature and case studies. Accordingly by analyzing MCM and its different aspects, a conceptual framework will be proposed presenting the main considerations while establishing an accurate MCM system. The framework pictures which factors contribute to the concept and also introduces the different aspects of a successful MCM implementation. The fundamental part of the framework constitutes the exploration of related enablers which address the manufacturing methodologies that are widely debated in the academia as well as enabling technologies which are suggested to be applied. Moreover, the framework includes a future look at the concept of MCM by presenting the cutting edge trends and technologies which are foreseen as potential to align with the manufacturing of mass customized goods.

V. Prabhu, M. Taisch, and D. Kiritsis (Eds.): APMS 2013, Part I, IFIP AICT 414, pp. 13–20, 2013.
© IFIP International Federation for Information Processing 2013

2   Mass Customization in Manufacturing

The implementation of mass customization requires integration of different manufacturing technologies into a structured framework capable of combining human and technological factors [1]. In recent years manufacturing systems have been evolving to satisfy the rapid change of customers' needs and preferences. In this regard several production paradigms, systems, methodologies and enablers for mass customization have been introduced in literature. In this paper we categorize Mass Customization Manufacturing (MCM) enablers in literature into two main categories which will be presented later in the proposed framework: 1) MC operational methodologies 2) MC enabling technologies.

MC operational methodologies refer not only to manufacturing and operational aspects of mass customization implementation but also to organizational and cultural aspects. This category includes methodologies such as lean manufacturing, cellular manufacturing and agile manufacturing. It should be mentioned that a methodology is composed of a set of practices which make it different from the term 'method'. In the context of production, the term 'method' simply corresponds to different aspects of specific techniques that are utilized in a manufacturing methodology. For instance, lean manufacturing, as a methodology, can choose to exploit different production methods whether job production or flow production depending on its needs or other factors. While methods have unidirectional approach which is production-oriented that makes it to focus on a tactical or operational level (maintaining efficiency, etc.), the methodology has a broader perspective that is based on a philosophy at most of the times (customer focus, collaborative mindset, supply chain, etc.).

The second category, MC enabling technologies, refers to subsystems and technologies which facilitate implementation of mass customization. These technologies can be either manufacturing and production technologies or information technologies. Customer-centric vision of mass customization makes it crucial for companies to have a flexible production system and a smooth information flow in company along the supply chain. In this regard, MC enabling technologies such as flexible manufacturing systems (FMS), Reconfigurable manufacturing systems (RMS) and Additive manufacturing technology act as facilitators while pursuing mass customization.

3   Research Methodology and Data Collection

The current study is based on two main types of research methodologies: literature review and empirical findings. Applying these two methodologies enriches the results of this study by combining proposals from academia and literature to real practices of mass customization manufacturing in different industries.

Empirical findings are collected via two types of information sources: primary sources and secondary sources. Regarding primary sources, three mass customization companies operating in three different sectors were analyzed. Required data for each case study were collected via interviews and surveys. Secondary sources for empirical findings include case studies presented in literature. Data were collected through different sources including papers, releases and publications on scientific magazines, official company website, official financial reports, blogs, forums, communities and online sector magazine release. Different practices regarding mass customization manufacturing in these case studies were studied to collect required data and integrate them with data collected from other sources in order to develop the MCM framework. Table 1 illustrates the general information regarding these case studies.

Table 1. Analyzed case studies

Company	Country	Industry	Size	Type of data
A	Italy	Diamond Wires	SME	Primary
B	Switzerland	Kitchen	SME	Primary
C	Italy	Footwear	SME	Primary
D	Finland	Footwear	SME	Secondary
E	UK	Material handling equipment	SME	Secondary

4   Proposed Framework for Mass Customization Manufacturing

Based on the collected data, a conceptual Mass Customization Manufacturing (MCM) framework was developed. The framework aims to visualize the state-of-the art of mass customization manufacturing, to provide a more clear and comprehensive focus on requirement for MC manufacturing, to create a comparison between various manufacturing paradigms and lastly, to explore future trends and direction of the concept.

The framework is developed in two layers. The first layer maps the position of mass customization manufacturing and related factors and requirements (figure 1).

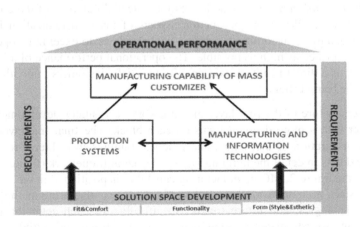

Fig. 1. General MCM framework (first layer of framework)

The initial framework consists of several interdependent building blocks. Interaction of all these blocks leads to operational performance of a MC company. In following a brief description of each block is given.

- *Solution space development* is the beginning point of the framework. It is defined as one of the fundamental capabilities to support a company to implement mass customization successfully [5,7]. In a MC environment it is necessary to identify the idiosyncratic demands of customers and transfer this knowledge into an advantage to create a stable solution space enabling company to adjust the cost and the complexity of customer needs [2]. In this paper three axes of customization namely fit & comfort; functionality and style have been defined for development of a solution space.

- *Requirements* refer to a set of factors demonstrating competitive opportunities and limitations of a MC company. While some of the factors would generate constraints during the implementation of mass customization, some others might enable the company to improve the manufacturing capability and consequently the competence of MC manufacturing. The factors are determined by considering the primary impacts on MC manufacturing related strategies.

- *Production systems and manufacturing / information technologies* are two crucial elements in mass customization manufacturing. A MC manufacturing system must be well designed by applying the appropriate production systems with exploiting suitable technologies to facilitate both flexible production and smooth information flow. Production systems can utilize different types of technologies due to their attributes. A MC manufacturer must be aware of which production system is more suited to its circumstances. Then, different technologies should be examined to find out whether they are applicable in a particular system or not. Production systems and manufacturing technologies determine the existing capability of a mass customizer.

- *Operational performance* addresses the potential outcome of the conceptual framework. When the production aspects of mass customization is considered, a mass customizer's primary goal should be to excel in its operational performance as high as possible. The operational performance of a MC company is a direct result of its capability to satisfy customers' individual needs while being efficient.

The generic nature of the first layer of framework necessitates development of the second layer with a more detailed focus on each block. The final framework is the outcome of integration of theoretical and practical findings from literature and case studies. It exhibits in detail the building blocks of general framework (figure 2).

As shown in figure 2, MC manufacturing capability is positioned in the core of the framework since it stems from three actors of MCM: manufacturing methodologies, enabling technologies, and future trends. Specifically, for each actor the potential enablers of mass customization manufacturing are identified and introduced in the model. Additionally, the requirements are redesigned and illustrated as four main

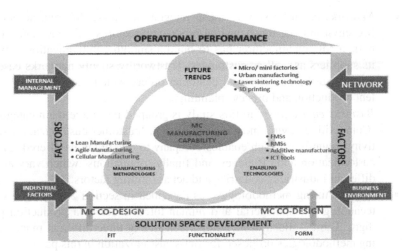

Fig. 2. Final MCM framework (second layer of framework)

factors. In following these four factors along with other building blocks of final framework have been briefly described.

- *Internal management* refers to management issues within an organization which have a significant impact on successful implementation of mass customization. In this paper we have mainly split theses factors into two categories: first, Investment and cost considerations that is a crucial element for mass customization manufacturing. Empirical findings from analyzed case studies highlight the point that MC companies usually face the dilemma of deciding to what extent the automation should be adopted to improve custom manufacturing since most of the technologies require considerable initial costs and efforts. Second category relates to organizational readiness. A company pursuing MC strategy must pay attention to prepare the entire organization for changes towards mass customization considering the fact that usually there is a resistance against change inside of an organization.

- *Industrial factors* play a crucial role in mass customization manufacturing. The state of the art of manufacturing may vary from one industry to the other. While some industries such as electronics and automotive are ground on high-tech solutions for production some other sectors are not pioneers to lead manufacturing. The case of *Levi's* is a well-known example due to its failure to maintain Mass Customization strategy. The company was one of the first customizers at the very beginning of MC implementations. However, it couldn't well establish a proper production system that enables efficient custom jeans manufacturing. One remarkable reason behind the failure was the current technology state of clothing industry that caused Levi's finally to abandon its pursuit of MC. Today rapid advances in computer and manufacturing technologies encourage companies to transform their conventional manufacturing into emerging patterns to answer changing demands.

- *Networks* are necessary to make integration among different actors in a MC environment. Since custom production requires efficiency and timeliness, a MC manufacturer has to build a smooth communication between its suppliers as well as customers. Trustworthy supply networks ease the manufacturing of individual customer orders which necessitate an excellent production and process planning.
- *Business environment* in this study is grouped into three main categories. 'Competitive environment' in the market, 'customer customization sensitivity' regarding which enables company to determine its offered level of customization and efficiency and finally 'regulations' which vary among different industries / countries and act as limiting factors.
- Manufacturing methodologies, as described in section 2, refer to a set of technological, managerial and human force issues of a production paradigm. Table 2 illustrates a comparison among three different manufacturing methodologies proposed for mass customization in this paper.
- *Enabling technologies* refer to manufacturing or information technologies acting as facilitators to pursue mass customization manufacturing. Some notable examples in this regard are: Computer Aided Design (CAD), Computer Aided Manufacturing (CAM), automated handling system (including different types of AGV and conveyors), generic modular mechtronic control, reconfigurable machining system and robotic devices, etc.
- *Future trends* is an important block of MCM framework which can bring competitive advantage to a MC company by implementing innovative and trending technologies in the field of mass customization technologies. Inn this paper trending manufacturing technologies which can support mass customization in terms of manufacturing are divided into three main categories. First category is "micro-factory" which is a new type of small manufacturing system that utilizes less space and reduced consumption of resources as well as energy via downsizing of production processes to have higher throughput. Micro-factories should comprise of extremely precise machining, gripping, and handling units with user friendly interfaces in order to be efficient. Enterprises that are in pursuit of MC manufacturing can gain some substantial advantages from the adoption of micro-factories in terms of shorter process chain, space reduction, quicker response, flexibility, modularity in processes, and cost reduction. Second category relates to "laser sintering technology" which has gained a great attention as an advanced manufacturing process to fabricate products based on electronic data and stimulate new aspects for customization in terms of rapid change and flexibility. Today, laser-dependent technologies shift from being an R&D tool to a promising manufacturing method realizing fabrication of customized products. Finally the third category refers to "3-D printing" which is a manufacturing technique used in Additive manufacturing technology. 3D printing can be used in plenty of fields and it is expected to expand its application in field of mass customization thanks to increasing demand of personalized products.

Table 2. Summarized comparison of different manufacturing methodologies for MC

	Lean Manufacturing	Agile Manufacturing	Cellular Manufacturing/ Group Technology
Characteristics	•ability to respond to competitive pressures with *limited resources* •a collection of *operational techniques* focused on *productive use of resources* •suitable for high and stable demand level • high and stable demand level	•a strategic vision which is capable to adapt continuous and unpredictable change •cooperativeness and synergism -most likely-created with virtual corporations •necessity for *sharing resources&technologies* among companies •an information infrastructure linking constituent partners in a unified electronic network •integration of advanced internet and manufacturing technologies with conventional design& manufacturing techniques	• a philosophical tool to arrange *the product parts into group (product families)* with regards to their *similarities* in terms of design&production process. (GT) • an application of Group Technology in which machines are • traditional cellular layout is appropriate in *medium-variety, medium-volume environments*
Advantages	•elimination of waste •lowering manufacturing cost due to its waste eliminating •quality oriented approach •widespread in many sectors including automotive, electronics, white goods, consumer products manufacturing etc. •focus on preventing breakdowns rather than fixing them	•suitable for unpredictable& dynamic demand with a high degree of mass customization in its products •*proactive adaptation* while FMS is concerned more as a *reactive adaptation* • reduction in set-up time and costs	• standardization of *tooling, fixturing,* and set-ups • reduced *set-up times* and shorter *manufacturing lead times* • reduced *in-process inventory* • shorter *travelling distances* and time • easier *material handling* activities • simplified *process planning* and production *scheduling*
Challenges	•long term commitment to the concept with no short term outcomes •significant transformation is required in the entire company to have a 'Lean Thinking' •dependency on suppliers' efficiency	•skilled labor required to operate different systems •application costs of new technologies •difficulties to distribute the workload among partners •high requirement of an integrated production planning, scheduling and control system •need of instant re-scheduling or re-selection of partners	• difficulty of *part family grouping and cell design* (time-consuming) • in case of a machine breakdown work *stoppage* within the cell •increased *capital investment* •labor resistance (facilitates cross training)
Linkages to MC	•*Torsten et al. (2007):* an empirical study conducted in the furniture industry. 21 out of the 23 respondents mentioned the necessity of the implementation of *lean manufacturing concepts* to support MC.	•*Cho et al.(1996):* agile manufacturing description as "the capability to survive and prosper in a competitive environment of continuous and unexpected change by reacting quickly and effectively to changing markets, driven by *customer-designed products and services*". •*Yang and Li (2002):* MC product manufacturing agility evaluation index system is established with an example of Xi Dian Casting Limited Company. Agility *assessment of an MC manufacture system* is formed by three aspects: *enterprise organization management, products design* and processing *and manufacturing.*	•*Badurdeen (2005):* minicell configuration which divides traditional cells into small multi-stage cells to realize the mass customization manufacturing. •*Akturk and Yayla (2005):* a hybrid model which integrates the cellular manufacturing system design and appropriate technology selection for dynamic market fluctations, or custom products. •*Suzic et al. (2012):* an empirical study applies Group Technology layout into a furniture manufacturer. Particularly, it attempts to transform the business from mass production to mass customization.

5   Conclusion

Mass customization is a strategy which has gained the growing attention of different industries in recent years. One of the critical issues for companies pursuing mass customization is to design their MC manufacturing system. A proper MCM system should focus on flexibility and quick responsiveness to individual customer orders which is based on the balance between pure customization and mass production. The success of customized products manufacturing is dependent on the product and process development which also addresses the importance of balancing basic choice offerings and wide variety of offerings. The proposed MCM framework in this paper is developed based on theoretical and empirical data in order to support companies to follow a successful pursuit of mass customization manufacturing. Collected data from case studies highlight the fact that although the literature links MCM to some production methodologies, described in this paper, but it is less likely to encounter the real practices of these methodologies in enterprises. This is a gap which can be filled by a more efficient knowledge transfer between academia and industry. The presented framework is a general-purpose version without focusing on any specific industry. This was mainly due to the limited samples caused by both the lack of real company cases and the absence of extensive case practices covering manufacturing sides of MC in the literature. However a future work to make a tailored framework for a specific sector would increase the added value of the work and the feasibility of validation phase as well.

References

1. Da Silveira, G., Borenstein, D., Fogliatto, F.S.: Mass customization: Literature review and research directions. International Journal of Production Economics 72(1), 1–13 (2001)
2. Piller, F.T., Tseng, M.M.: Mass Customization Thinking: Moving from Pilot Stage to an Established Business Strategy. In: Handbook of Research in Mass Customization and Personalization, Aachen, Germany (2010)
3. Piller, F.T.: Mass customization: reflection on the state of the concept. International Journal of Flexible Manufacturing System 16(4), 313–334 (2004)
4. Pine, B.J.: Mass Customization - The New Frontier in Business Competition. Harvard Business School Press, Boston (1993)
5. Salvador, F., De Holan, P.M., Piller, F.T.: Cracking the code of mass customi-zation. MIT Sloan Management Review 50(3), 70–79 (2009)
6. Tseng, M.M., Jiao, J.: Mass Customization. In: Handbook of Industrial Engineering, Technology and Operation Management, 3rd edn., Wiley, New York (2001)
7. Von Hippel, E.: User Toolkits for Innovation. Journal of Product Innovation Management (18), 1–28 (2001)

State-Oriented Productivity Analysis in One-of-a-Kind-Production

Florian Tietze[*] and Hermann Lödding

Hamburg University of Technology, Hamburg, Germany
{florian.tietze,loedding}@tuhh.de

Abstract. Traditional productivity analysis has emerged in mass production and cannot be adopted one-to-one on One-of-a-kind production (OKP). Due to the non-repetitive character of the processes in OKP, productivity improvements do not reproduce like in mass production. In addition, preparatory activities such as orientation, material handling and positioning usually consume a lot more time than the actual value-adding activities in OKP. Therefore, OKP requires analysis methods that deliver: 1) a generic working cycle to enable repetitive productivity improvements; 2) activities of personnel in production processes, which include the preparatory activities. We introduce a state-oriented approach for productivity measurement in OKP. With a case study we show how to capture, visualize and evaluate state data of an OKP.

Keywords: one-of-a-kind production, productivity analysis, lean management.

1 Introduction

Methods of lean production facilitate a systematic approach and have enabled large productivity gains primarily in mass production [1]. In one-of-a-kind productions, the use of many methods of lean production is hardly practicable because the processes rarely repeat [2]. The materials, sequence, location, necessary tools as well as the position of parts are changing significantly more often in an OKP. That is why the percentage of manual activities is higher. Analyzing and improving the productivity of these labor-intensive processes is a crucial task for these companies [3].

This paper presents a methodology that enables companies with OKP to analyze the influencing factors of the labor productivity with relatively low effort. The focus is on data collection. This is based on the definition of worker activities, objects and a generic working cycle and enables the aggregation of productivity data across various departments and processes. The analysis of the data allows to compare the different factors of productivity and to prioritize improvement activities. An industrial example shows that the method is suitable to analyze OKP and the influences on the labor productivity in detail. The method claims to be valid for universal OKP, although the case is taken from the maritime industry.

---

[*] Corresponding author.

V. Prabhu, M. Taisch, and D. Kiritsis (Eds.): APMS 2013, Part I, IFIP AICT 414, pp. 21–28, 2013.
© IFIP International Federation for Information Processing 2013

2   One-of-a-Kind Production

Production as well as the assembly can be divided according to different types. In this context, mass production and one-of-a-kind production are the two extremes [4].

Within mass production, products are highly standardized. All relevant information is available from the start of production. As a result of the many repetitions, process improvements lead to high productivity growth.

The OKP with its highly customized product needs a high flexibility of production processes and high reconfigurability of the used equipment. The following organizational principles are typically used [5]: manual production workshop, construction site principle, flexible manufacturing cells. The OKP is characterized by several features [6]: i.e. higher secondary times, long lead times, low transparency of business processes, complex production control and more.

These properties of the OKP lead to low productivity, which is reflected in a different structure of the working time. In mass production, workers spend a huge amount of time directly at the product. In OKP, workers spend an essential time for the acquisition of information and organization of work patterns.

Due to this focus, many methods of lean production cannot be applied directly. Moreover, the lack of transparency as well as the less detailed and not standardized work processes makes it more difficult to analyze the productivity. The various types of manufacturing in the OKP, the parallel processes and the complex production control complicate the prioritization and implementation of improvement activities.

The following section provides an overview of different approaches aiming at the analysis of productivity in industrial companies.

3   Productivity Analysis

A productivity analysis examines a production process normally at defined time intervals to detect productivity potentials [7]. Different approaches for productivity analysis exist:

- Empirical productivity analysis: Productivity indices [8], econometric models [9] and methods of linear programming [10] belong to the empirical productivity analysis. Overall, these approaches are not effective in the OKP, because they provide abstract results based on theoretical assumptions and the heterogeneous causes of lost productivity cannot be identified or associated with the losses.
- Operative methods: Methods-Time Measurement [11], SMED [12] and Primary-Secondary-Analysis [13] provide a high level of detail. However, for the OKP this productivity analyses are limited, because the operations are not sufficiently planned in detail and the processes are repeated rarely.

This overview shows the lack of productivity analysis in OKP, since most of the methods serve rather abstract level and often require high data acquisition and operational effort. Thus, productivity analysis in the OKP has to fulfill the following requirements:

- The productivity analysis must be flexible in different types of production.
- Losses during preparation and other ancillary activities must be included.
- The methodology should enable repeatable productivity gains.
- The results of the analysis should allow prioritization of improvement actions.

4   Concept of a State-Oriented Productivity Analysis

Based on the requirements described for productivity analysis in OKP the procedure
of a state-oriented productivity analysis will be explained. These efficiency or productivity analysis have mainly been applied to machines or interlinked manufacturing
systems [14, 15]. The worker states need to cover the whole time span of paid labor
time to realize a comprehensive analysis. Value-adding tasks as well as non-value-
adding tasks can equally be a source for reduced labor productivity [16]. Fig. 1 shows
the methodology for the productivity management in OKP.

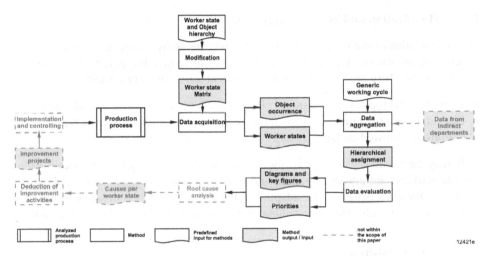

Fig. 1. Methodology for productivity management in OKP

It combines various sub-methods, which are linked with inputs and outputs. The
scope of this paper is limited to the first four sub-methods: Modification, data acquisition, data aggregation and data evaluation. In order to describe the operation of the
methodology, the following section describes the predefined inputs and methods.

4.1   Worker Activity and Object Hierarchy

Mixed production types, few standard activities and higher secondary and setup times
make it difficult to describe the operational procedure in OKP in a standardized way.
Fruehwald developed a method to standardize flexible set-up processes [17]. In this
method, one process step is fully described by combining an object with an activity.

The result is a worker activity and object hierarchy as shown in fig. 2.

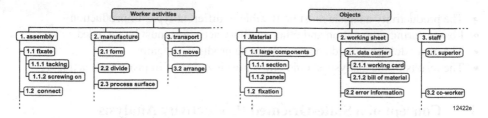

Fig. 2. Example of the worker activity and object hierarchy

The worker activities are clustered in groups and structured with a numerical logic. To identify the worker activities and to minimize the data acquisition effort, each worker activity has an individual number, which implies the main and sub group. The same logic structures the object hierarchy. As a result each unique worker state can be described with a combination of an activity and an object.

4.2   Modification and Worker State Matrix

The combination of the worker activity and object hierarchy is a generic worker activity and object matrix. A plausibility check helps to reduce the potential amount of combinations. There are two reasons for an invalid activity/object combination:

- Technical and logical inconsistency: E.g., it is not possible to screw a colleague.
- Definitive inconsistency: It is invalid to screw a section, because small parts like clamps are screwed on large parts.

It may be necessary to modify the matrix for the data acquisition, because the worker activities are universally valid and have to complement only in special cases. However, the objects have to be adapted to the use case, but it is possible to use generic matrices for industries. The tailored matrix is the input for the data acquisition.

4.3   Data Acquisition

Acquiring time data in OKP is not common, because of the long operation times and low degree of detail of the process descriptions. For the acquisition of above described state data, different approaches have been defined:

- Work sampling measures the frequency of occurrence of certain predefined events by using short-time observations at predetermined times in the investigation area [18]. The results can be aggregated and evaluated statistically.
- Time studies enable a detection of detailed work processes without interrupting the worker. In contrast to work sampling, time study measure actual times.

Prior to the data acquisition, an area has to be selected. Useful criteria are the head count or the repetition frequency of the process due to the large amount of paid working time or rather the potential by gaining repetitive productivity improvements. The observed area and processes determine the data acquisition method: Work samplings are used in manual working shops or productions cells with transparent overview; time studies suit the construction site principle with generic processes, which repeat often. The above described and modified matrix defines the state categories.

To gain efficient productivity improvements the result of the data acquisition has to be combined with a repetitive and generic working cycle.

4.4   Generic Working Cycle

The aim of the generic working cycle is to enable repeatable improvements. As in mass production, repetitions allow an efficient use of improvement activities and lean methods. From the perspective of the worker in an OKP environment the working process can be determined in five steps as shown in fig. 3:

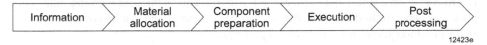

| Information | Material allocation | Component preparation | Execution | Post processing |

12423e

Fig. 3. Generic Working Cycle

At the information phase the worker clarifies the work task and allocates all required information. The next step is to gather necessary materials and tools. During the component preparation phase, the worker sets up machines and builds auxiliary equipment. When everything is prepared, the worker can execute his work. This is the only value-adding activity. At the end the worker has to clean the work area, bring tools back and document results. The single phases of the generic working cycle are defined as operational fields. These fields facilitate a goal-orientated approach to prioritize improvement activities and support the deduction of standard methods.

To gain repetitive productivity improvements, the output from the data acquisition has to be aggregated to the described generic working cycle.

4.5   Data Aggregation

The paid working time consist of different time portions (equation 1). The duration of worker absence consists mainly of times for vacation, training or illness. This information has to be gathered from the corporate data system. The attendance can be recorded with the defined worker state matrix. The classification inside the attendance time is carried out manually and supported by two principles:

- The predefined worker activities have clear classifications specified in the matrix. For example: reading is always in the operation field Information.
- Ambiguous worker activities can be assigned to operation fields by considering the objects. For example: the combination of the worker activity searching and the object engineering drawings is part of the operation field Information; in combination with object drill this worker state belongs to the operation field Material allocation.

If each worker state is classified by these two guidelines, the output from the data acquisition can be aggregated and assigned to the operation fields.

$$T_{paid} = T_{att} + T_{abs} + T_{NR} \tag{1}$$

$$T_{paid} = T_{att} * \sum_{j=1}^{5} OF_j + T_{abs} + T_{NR} \quad \text{with} \quad OF_j = \frac{\sum_{i=1}^{n} s_j}{n} \quad s_j \in OF_j \tag{2}$$

T_{paid}	paid working time [hrs]	T_{abs}	absence time [hrs]
T_{att}	attendance time [hrs]	T_{NR}	not recorded activities [hrs]
OF_j	Portion of all worker states of the operational field j [%]		
s_j	Observation of worker state in the operation field j during work sampling [-]		
j	Index for different operational fields [-]		
n	Number of observations during the work sampling [-]		

If time studies are used, the sum of the worker state durations per operation field plus a term for absence times and not recorded activities equals the paid working time. The work sampling method provides the ratio of worker states and can be converted to the paid time through multiplication with T_{paid} (equation 2).

The result of the data aggregation is a database of all worker states in the observed area. If required, it can be extended with additional information.

4.6 Data Evaluation

The state data needs to be processed and illustrated using key figures and diagrams. The evaluation allows to determine priorities and to deduct methods for operational fields. There are two ways of evaluation:

- Prioritization of the greatest operational field: The combination of worker activities with the greatest portion and most used objects facilitates the prioritization of productivity losses and references for a detailed root analysis.
- Case-based improvement: If a process is recorded with the worker activities state matrix, it is possible to use this as a basis for a standard working description using the generic working cycle.

Key figures and diagrams allow to determine priorities, to derive improvement potentials and standardize work based on worker activity and object hierarchy.

5 Case Study

The proposed method was applied to an OKP at a shipyard. The worker state hierarchy was tailored on the basis of working plans and interviews. The final matrix included 62 different as well as 80 different objects. A plausibility check reduced the number of combinations to round about 1100 different worker states.

Accordingly, the two data acquisition modes were assigned: Work sampling was done for the pre-outfitting and the outfitting at the berth; a time study was conducted at the prefabrication. A recording list with defined fields for activities, objects, time and notes was used and merged with a software tool.

The data acquisition required an effort of two eight-hour days and additional eight hours for tailoring the worker activity and object hierarchy and preparation of the recording lists. The time study described a 3 hours working process. Fig. 4 shows the allocation of the operational fields for the working sample and the time study.

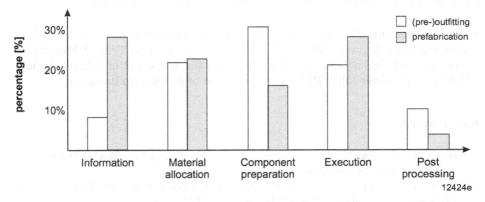

Fig. 4. Allocation to operational fields

As expected the workers spent a big amount of their working time with preparative activities. The evaluation results are not representative, due to of the small amount of samples. However, the case study proves the functionality and practicability of the developed concept especially in different types of production. The evaluation proved the applicability of the worker activity and object hierarchy: Only four worker states out of 87 samples could not be clearly identified and the observer had to ask the worker. All process steps could be described with the worker state matrix.

One challenge is to locate the worker at the construction principle, which was used at the outfitting. In 24% of the samples the worker was not detected in a time frame of one Minute. Also, the distance between the observation points is very long. This problem can be solved by using self reports or auxiliary utilities like location boards.

An evaluation with a significant amount of samples is planned to demonstrate the connection from allocation of the operational fields to productivity potential.

6   Conclusion and Outlook

The paper has introduced a method for a state-oriented productivity analysis in OKP. It combines worker activities and objects with operational fields of a generic working cycle to gain repetitive improvements. With the proposed method, production managers can improve transparency of productivity potentials with low effort.

The case demonstrated the enhanced possibilities of a worker state matrix based on activities and objects. This tool is suitable to describe the work process also in the different production types of OKP in a standardized way.

The ongoing studies at the IPMT include the definition of an accurate sample size for working samples. An improved software demonstrator will further reduce the effort for the data acquisition. In addition, another data acquisition method like self-reports will be adapted for this methods and evaluated.

Furthermore, the evaluation has to be done with further industrial partners to cover different types of productions. A next research step will be to link the distribution of the operational fields with standard optimization. The case showed the high demand on adapted or new improvement methods for OKP especially in the operational fields gathering information and preparing the components and working place.

Acknowledgement. The presented work was done in cooperation with a shipyard within the research project PROSPER, funded by the German Federal Ministry of Economics and Technology (Bundesministerium für Wirtschaft und Technologie - BMWi / Projektträger Jülich PTJ) due to a decision of the German Bundestag.

References

1. Roos, D., Womack, J., Jones, D.: The Machine That Changed the World: The Story of Lean Production. Harper Perennial (1991)
2. Salem, O., Solomon, J., Genaidy, A., Minkarah, I.: Lean Construction: From Theory to Implementation. J. Manage. Eng. 22(4), 168–175 (2006)
3. Ohno, T.: Toyota Production System – Beyond Large-Scale Production. Productivity Press, Cambridge (1988)
4. Gruß, R.: Schlanke Unikatfertigung – Zweistufiges Taktphasenmodell zur Steigerung der Prozesseffizienz in der Unikatfertigung. Gabler Verlag, Wiesbaden (2010)
5. Wiendahl, H.-P.: Betriebsorganisation für Ingenieure. Hanser, Munich (2008)
6. Piller, F.T.: Mass Customization. Wiesbaden (2006)
7. Nebl, T.: Produktivitätsmanagement. Hanser, Munich (2002)
8. Craig, C.E., Harris, R.C.: Total Productivity Measurement at the Firm Level. Sloan Management Review 14(3), 13–29 (1973)
9. Sudit, E.F.: Productivity measurement in industrial operations. European Journal of Operational Research 85(3), 435–453 (1995)
10. Charnes, A., Cooper, W.W., Rhodes, E.: Measuring the efficiency of decision making units. European Journal of Operational Research 2(6), 429–444 (1978)
11. Bokranz, R., Landau, K.: Produktivitätsmanagement von Arbeitssystemen. Schäffer-Poeschel, Stuttgart (2006)
12. Shingo, S.: A Revolution in Manufacturing: The SMED System. Productivity Press, Cambridge (1985)
13. Lotter, B., Spath, D., Baumgartner, P.: Primär-Sekundär-Analyse: Kundennutzenmessung und Kundennutzenorientierung im Unternehmen. Expert Verlag, Renningen (2002)
14. Wiendahl, H.P., Hegenscheidt, M.: Produktivität komplexer Produktionsanlagen. Zeitschrift für Wirtschaftlichen Fabrikbetrieb 96(4), 160–163 (2001)
15. Grando, A., Turco, F.: Modelling plant capacity and productivity: conceptual framework in a single-machine case. Production Planning & Control 16(3), 309–322 (2005)
16. Czumanski, T., Lödding, H.: Integral analysis of labor productivity. In: 45th CIRP Conference on Manufacturing Systems, Procedia CIRP, vol. 3, pp. 55–60 (2012)
17. Frühwald, C.: Analyse und Planung produktionstechnischer Rüstabläufe. VDI-Verlag, Düsseldorf (1990)
18. Simons, B.: Das Multimoment-Zeitmeßverfahren. Univ., Cologne and Dortmund (1987)

A Study on the Effect of Inspection Time on Defect Detection in Visual Inspection

Ryosuke Nakajima[1,*], Keisuke Shida[2], and Toshiyuki Matsumoto[1]

[1] Aoyama Gakuin University, Kanagawa, Japan
d5613005@aoyama.jp, matsumoto@ise.aoyama.ac.jp
[2] Nagaoka University of Technology, Niigata, Japan
shida@kjs.nagaokaut.ac.jp

Abstract. In order to consider the visual inspection utilizing the peripheral vision, this paper examines the inspection times that affect defect detection. The fixation duration and the distance between defect and the fixation point are experimental factors in determining the inspection time. As the result, in case of a large sized defect, the detection rate is high regardless of the fixation duration and the distance between the defect and the fixation point. In case of a small sized defect, when the fixation duration is longer and the distance between the defect and the fixation point is closer, the defect detection rate is higher. Moreover, as the result of conducting multiple linear regression analysis about the experiment factors, it is obtained that judging from standardized partial regression coefficient of factors, higher defect size, less the distance between defect and the fixation point, the higher fixation duration, is proved to improve the defect detection.

Keywords: Visual inspection, Inspection time, Peripheral vision, Effective field of view.

1 Introduction

In order to prevent the escape of defective products into markets, the strict inspection of products is carried out in Japanese manufacturing industries. There are two types of inspections, functional inspection and appearance inspection. In functional inspection, the motion and efficiency of the products is inspected and in appearance inspection, small visual defects like scratch and stain are checked. Automation of functional inspection has advanced whereas the automation of appearance inspection is very difficult and greatly depends on the visual inspection by workers' eyes. Generally, the area which can be processed by the visual stimulus is called field of vision [1]. In the field of vision, the area within $1\sim2[°]$ of the center of the retina is called central visual field and the surrounding area is called peripheral vision. The spatial resolution of the field of vision reduces remarkably when moving far from the center of retina [2]. This is due to the effect of two types of cells in that are distributed in the field of vision. Two different cells distributed un a field of vision have an influence on the human sight, one is a cone cell having the functions to distinguish colors and to view objects clearly in the central visual field. The other is a rod cell having the functions to

V. Prabhu, M. Taisch, and D. Kiritsis (Eds.): APMS 2013, Part I, IFIP AICT 414, pp. 29–39, 2013.

distinguish luminance sensitively and cannot distinguish colors in the peripheral visual [3].

This difference in the distribution of the cells affects the human behavior of searching for something. When humans search for objects, first a wide range is searched using peripheral vision and then the item is searched using the central vision which has high precision. To increase the efficiency of search by reducing the information the eye needs to process. Specifically, low level processes like clustering and detection of properties use peripheral vision and then high level processes like discrimination of object is carried out [4].

However, in actual visual inspection, in order to thoroughly inspect, the central vision is mainly used. This increases the amount of information that needs to be processed and is thought to reduce the work efficiency. In other words, there is the need to use both central and peripheral visions properly and therefore the development of the new visual inspection method that does not only use the central vision, but also the peripheral vision is needed [5]-[9].

In actual visual inspection, the detection of scratches, the stain irregularity in color etc. is necessary and the deciding whether the product is defective or non-defective depends on the size and depth. Furthermore, high-mix, low-volume production is advanced recently and the inspection of various products is necessary which causes other difficulties, for instance, same size scratches can be within the standard for one object but otherwise for another object. Furthermore, the standard is different according to the need of the customer, even though is for the same object. If the defect that is within the standard is decided as the defective product, over kill occurs which causes financial loss, and if the defect that is not within the standard is decided as non-defective, Escape occurs which causes the flow of defective product to markets.

Actually, inspection methods should be changed according to the quality demand of the customer, but in actual visual inspection, single inspection method is continuously used since there is the limit in the inspection time in order to maintain fixed productivities. Therefore, in this study, appropriate inspection method is examined by considering the factors that affects the inspection time.

2   Factors of Affecting the Inspection Time

In visual inspection, the time required to inspect products can be defined using the number of fixation points and the time needed for fixing the fixation points. Normally, the characteristics in the design of the product are used as fixation points, and by fixing these points in order assure that the product is thoroughly inspected. The inspection time increases when the fixation duration of the fixation points and the number of fixation points are increased.

The length of the inspection time depends on the effective visual field range of the peripheral vision and the fact that the effective visual field range widens when the fixation duration increases has been shown [10]. When the effective visual field range widens, the range of inspection in one fixation widens and an increase in the detection rate can be expected. Moreover, when the effective visual field range increases, overlapping area of field of vision also increases and the increase in the detection rate can be expected since the same area is viewed number of times.

Additionally, when the number of fixation points is increased, the probability that the fixation point is placed near the defect increases. Since the distance between the fixation point and the defect is less, the judgment of the defect becomes possible because it is in the field of vision with high spatial resolution and increase in the detection rate can be expected [11].

In this way, both the fixation duration and the number of fixation points can be considered as factors that affect the defect detection, but the relationship between the fixation duration and the number of fixation point has not been clarified. Therefore, when the manager of the production line changes the inspection time, it is difficult whether to increase the fixation duration or to increase the number of fixation points.

Thus, in this study, the effect of fixation duration and the number of fixation points on the defect detection rate for various standards are examined.

3   Experimental Method

3.1   Experimental Task

As the experimental task, the target object which is the black circle of 1cm in an area of A4 size as shown in Fig. 1 is displayed on the monitor (FlexScan SX2462W). By considering the fact that the field of vision of human is horizontally wide [12], the target object is also made horizontally wide. Furthermore, in order to lead inspection by the peripheral vision, the fixation point is placed in the center of the target object and the subject is made to fixation only at the fixation point. In order to make the viewing angle of subjects the same, the stand is placed at 40cm from the monitor where the lower chin of the subject is positioned. The experiment layout is shown in Fig. 2. Furthermore, the brightness of the monitor is 199[cd/m2] and the lighting density calculated from the position of keyboard is 810[lx].

Subjects fixation at the fixation point and inspect the whole target object by the peripheral vision for five different fixation durations, from 0.25sec to 1.25sec, which are decided by the experimenter. If there is not a defect, the subject presses the Space key and the next target object is displayed. If the defect is detected, the subject presses enter key. Furthermore, in order to verify that the subject is inspecting the target using the peripheral vision, the eye movement is monitored using an eye tracker (NAC EMR-9) which is fixed on the subject during the experiment.

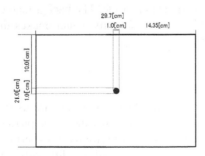

Fig. 1. Target object

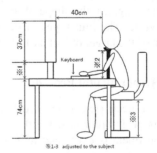

Fig. 2. Experimental layout

3.2   Experimental Factors

3.2.1   Fixation Duration

In order to control the fixation duration of the subject, the display time of the target object is limited. Five sets of display times are used in this experiment, which are 0.25sec, 0.50sec, 0.75sec, 1.00sec and 1.25sec. The reason for fixing the display time of the target work is that, during preliminary experiment, the detection rate for the display time of 0.25sec was 50%. Therefore, if the display time is less than 0.25sec, subjects will not be able to find most of the defects.

3.2.2   Distance between the Defect and the Fixation Point

The target object is divided into thirty six parts (horizontally 6× vertically 6) as shown in Fig.3 and the defect is placed in the center of either one of these parts. As in Fig. 3, the parts are divided in to nine types from a to i, according to the distance from the fixation point. The distance from the fixation point to the center of each part are a: 3.0cm, b: 5.8cm, c: 7.6cm, d: 9.1cm, e: 11.4cm, f: 12.5cm, g: 13.4cm and i: 15.1cm.

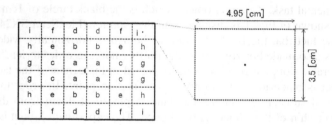

Fig. 3. Target object

3.2.3   Size of the Defect

The sizes of the defects are of four types with diameters of 0.06cm, 0.08cm, 0.10cm, 0.12cm. There are defects of various types in manufacturing industries, for instance, in painting processes, there are point shaped defects like iron powder and line shaped defects caused by threads. However, when the size of the defects become small, the shape of the defect need not be considered and all the defects can be summarized as a circle (point). Specially, in this experiment where small defects that are difficult to detect are targeted, the shape of the defect is fixed as a circle. The background color is set as white. The four types of defects are placed in 36 parts, which makes the total number of the target object as 144 (36 parts × 4 types).

3.3   Experimental Procedure

Fifteen subjects (ten male, five female) from 22 to 24 years of age are used in this experiment. In order to make the subjects get use to the experiment, the procedure of the experiment is explained and they are made to do a preliminary experiment and subjects with corrected eyesight of more than 1.0 are used. Additionally, subjects those who use glasses or contact lens are not used in this experiment, so that there is no effect on the eye camera readings. The proportion of the defect in the experiment is set to 20% and 720 target objects are inspected. This is repeated for the each fixation duration. The reason for setting the defect proportion as 20% is that it was found during the preliminary experiments that there is a tendency of the subjects to use the central vision when the defect proportion increases.

The experiments for the five types of fixation duration were carried out in two days by considering the fatigue of the subjects. The room temperature is set between 18 and 22°C and humidity between 40 and 50%.

4   Experimental Results

4.1   Individual Characteristics of Subject

Using the defect detection rate, the effect of fixation duration and the distance between the fixation point and the defect is examined, but there is the possibility that the individuality of the subject will affect the result. As the result of this experiment, the uniformity of results for various subjects was verified. The defect detection rate is expressed in Eq. (1).

$$the\ defect\ detection\ rate\ [\%] = \frac{the\ number\ of\ detected\ defects}{the\ number\ of\ total\ defects} \times 100 \qquad (1)$$

The defect detection rate of the each subject according to the fixation duration is shown in Fig. 4, from this result it is observed that when the fixation duration increases, the defect detection rate increases for all the subjects, but this tendency is not seen for some of the workers. There were the subjects who had high defect detection rate even if the fixation duration is short. Even if there were differences between the subjects, there is no outlier value for the defect detection rate. Moreover, there is no outlier value in the case of distance between the fixation point and the defect and the size of the defect, therefore, the data of the fifteen subjects were used and examined.

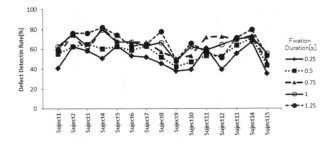

Fig. 4. Defect detection rate of the each subject according to the fixation duration

4.2   Effect of the Fixation Duration and the Distance between the Defect and the Fixation Point on the Defect Detection Rate

The effect of the fixation duration and the distance between the defect and the fixation point on the defect detection rate is shown in Fig. 5a and b, and the effect of the size of the defect on the defect detection is shown in Fig. 5c. The analysis of variance of three-way layout with the fixation duration of the defect (5), the distance between the defect and the fixation point (9) and the size of the defect (4) as factors is executed. As the result, a significant difference of 1% is observed for the main effect of the fixation duration, the distance between the defect and the fixation point and the size of defect. Moreover, the significant difference of 1% is observed for the mutual interaction in which the mutual interaction of the distance between the defect and the fixation point is excluded. The reason for this can be seen when this result is divided according the size of the defect, as shown in Fig. 6a, it can be seen that the effect of the fixation duration and the distance between the defect and the fixation point on the defect detection rate is less when the size of the defect is large. On the other hand, there is the relation between the fixation duration and the distance between the defect and the fixation point as can be shown in Fig. 7. It is confirmed that the defect detection rate is increased when the fixation duration is long and the distance between the defect and the fixation point is short.

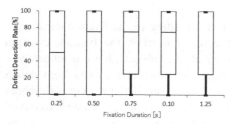

a. Defect detection rate of each fixation duration

b. Defect detection rate of each distance between the defect and the fixation point

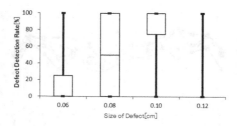

c. Defect detection rate of each size of defect

Fig. 5. Distribution of defect detection rate

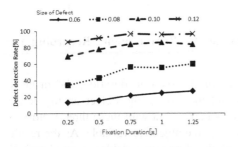

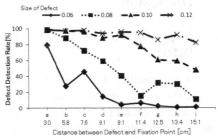

a. Fixation duration and size of defect

b. Distance between fixation point and defect and size of defect

Fig. 6. Interaction between the two factors

Table 1. Analysis of variance

Variation factor	Sum of squares	Flexibility	Mean square	F-number	Decision
Fixation duration of defect (A)	99688.43	4	24922.11	65.49	**
Distance between defect and fixation point (B)	876307.41	8	109538.43	287.84	**
Size of the defect (C)	2152230.56	3	717410.19	1885.17	**
A×B	15090.74	32	471.59	1.24	
A×C	16572.69	12	1381.06	3.63	**
B×C	382677.78	24	15944.91	41.90	**
A×B×C	56581.48	96	589.39	1.55	**
Error	959000.00	2520	380.56		
Total	4558149.07	2699			

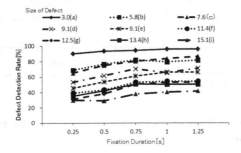

Fig. 7. Relation between the fixation duration and the distance between the defect and the fixation point

5   Discussion

5.1   Inspection Method Corresponding to the Requirements Regarding the Defects

In order to examine the level of the effect of the fixation duration, the distance between the defect and the fixation point and the size of the defect on the defect detection rate, a multiple regression analysis is carried out with these three factors as decision variable and the defect detection rate as the objective variable. As the result, the standard partial regression coefficient of the decision variables is as shown in Table 2, where the coefficient of size of the defect is found to be the biggest. In short, it is seen that the main factor that effect the defect detection rate in the visual inspection is the size of the defect and it reduces in the order of the distance between the fixation point and the defect, and the fixation duration.

This result also supports the fact that there is a significant difference in the mutual interactions including the size of the defect. That is, when the size of the defect is big, the defect detection rate is high and does not depend on the fixation duration or the distance between the defect and the fixation point as shown in Fig. 6. This can be also confirmed through use of the value of the standard regression coefficient of the size of the defect which is 0.7, a high value. On the other hand, for small defects i.e. when the demanding quality standards are high, the fixation duration and the distance between the defect and the fixation point should also be considered.

However, when the fixation duration and the distance between the defect and the fixation point are compared, it is shown that reducing the distance between the defect and the fixation point affects the defect detection rate more than increasing the fixation duration. In other words, if there is the necessity to find small defect and the quality demand of the customer is high, the first measure should be to increase the number of fixation points.

Table 2. Result of multiple regression analysis

Independent variable	Partial regression coefficient	Standard partial regression coefficient	Significant difference (** 1%)
Size of defect	1248.9	0.76	**
Fixation duration	16.2	0.16	**
Distance between defect and fixation point	-4.8	-0.48	**

Decision variable$=0.84$ Adjusted $R^2=0.83$.

5.2   Effect of the Position of the Fixation Point and the Defect on the Defect Detection Rate

The effective field of vision of this experiment is examined. The area that has high defect detection rate is painted with dark color and that with low defect detection rate is colored with light color for each fixation duration. Ten colors are used for each 10% and the result is shown from Fig. 8a to e. As the result, for all fixation duration, the effective field of vision is horizontally wide and the area increases when the fixation duration increases. Generally, the field of vision of humans is horizontally wide [13] and the information inside a horizontal angle of vision of 30° and the vertical angle of vision of 20°can be effectively processed [14]. The angle of vision in this experiment is 21.2°horizontally and 14.8°vertically, which is clearly inside the above said range, but it can be clearly seen that even inside this range of the angle of the vision, the defect detection rate is not uniform.

Furthermore, the shape of the effective field of vision in vertical direction is examined. Corresponding from Fig 8a to e, parts 9 and 10 and parts 27 and 28 were taken for analysis. As the result, instead of the distance of these parts from the fixation point being same, for all the fixation durations there is a difference of an average of 10% in the detection rate and anisotropy is seen for the characteristics of the field of vision in the vertical direction. In other words, the distance between the defect and the fixation point does not affect the detection rate, but there is difference in the detection rate according to the distance between the fixation point and the defect in the horizontal position and the vertical position. This means that it is clear that the position of the defect with regard to the fixation point also causes effect on the detection rate. That is, when fixing the fixation point, it should be considered that not only the distance but also the position in the field of vision causes effect on the defect detection rate.

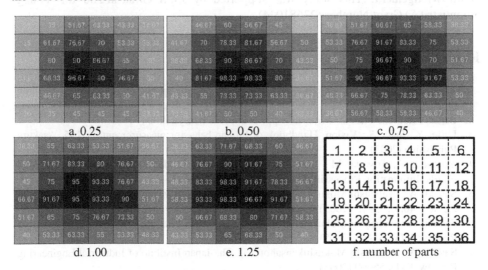

a. 0.25   b. 0.50   c. 0.75

d. 1.00   e. 1.25   f. number of parts

Fig. 8. Relation between the fixation duration and the distance between defect and fixation point

6   Conclusion

Visual inspection is a sensory inspection, in which there is difference in result according to the individuality and the skill of the worker. This has been a major problem in the manufacturing industries where the standardization of the work is required. In addition, there have been various measures like evaluation and training of workers in order to increase the inspection technique, but there have not been any considerable results. Therefore, in this study, the potentiality of human sight mechanism using the peripheral vision was examined, for that, the effect of fixation duration, distance between the defect and the fixation point and the size of the defect on the defect detection rate was examined.

As the result, the effect of the size of the defect was found to be largest and it was shown that in order to find large defects, the number of fixation points could be reduced and the inspection time also would be reduced. On the other hand, while inspecting for small defects, the defect detection rate could be increased by increasing the number of fixation points and reducing the distance between fixation point and the defect which increased as the inspection time. Additionally, it was discovered that while placing a fixation point on the targeted object, not only the distance between the defect and the fixation point had to be considered, but also the position of the defect.

In future studies, the characteristics of the effective field of vision in visual inspection should be examined and also, using the result of this study, the effect of increasing the fixation points and increasing the fixation duration should be tested in actual working lines in the manufacturing industries.

Acknowledgement. This study was supported by JSPS Grant-in-Aid for Young Scientists (A) Grant Number (23681034).

References

1. The Japan Society of applied Physics: Seiri Kougaku, pp. 1–302. Asakura Publishing (1975)
2. Ikeda, M.: Meha Naniwo Miteiruka, pp. 1–289. Heibonsya (2004)
3. Ujiie, Y., Saita, S.: Vision, Handbook of human behavior measurement, p. 165. Asakura Publishing (2003)
4. Yoshida, C., Toyoda, M., Sato, Y.: Vision System Model with Differentiated Visual Fields. Information Processing Society of Japan 33(8), 1032–1040 (1992)
5. Sasaki, A.: Syuhenshi Mokushikensahou (1). The Japan Institute of Industrial Engineering Review 46(4), 65–75 (2005)
6. Sasaki, A.: Syuhenshi Mokushikensahou (2). The Japan Institute of Industrial Engineering Review 46(5), 61–68 (2005)
7. Sasaki, A.: Syuhenshi Mokushikensahou (3). The Japan Institute of Industrial Engineering Review 47(1), 55–60 (2006)
8. Sasaki, A.: Syuhenshi Mokushikensahou (4). The Japan Institute of Industrial Engineering Review 47(2), 53–58 (2006)
9. Sasaki, A.: Syuhenshi Mokushikensahou (5). The Japan Institute of Industrial Engineering Review 47(3), 67–72 (2006)
10. Kumada, T., Kuchinomachi, Y., Saida, S.: The Properties of function Visual Fields on Visual Search: Evidence from Manual Reaction Time and Saccadic Eye movement. The Japanese Journal of Psychonomic Science 14(2), 75–85 (1996)
11. Jacobs, R.J.: Visual resolution and Contour Interaction in the Fovea and Periphery. Vision Research 19(11), 1187–1195 (1979)

12. Chaikin, J.D., Corbin, H.H., Volkmann, J.: Mapping a field of short-time visual search. Science 138, 327–328 (1962)
13. Yamanaka, K., Nakayasu, H., Miyoshi, T., Maeda, K.: A Study of Evaluating Useful Field of View at Visual Recognition Task. The Japan Society of Mechanical Engineers 72(719), 2248–2256 (2006)
14. Hatakeda, T.: Handbook of human behavior measurement, p. 585. Asakura Publishing (2003)

Toward Automated Design for Manufacturing Feedback

Wonmo Kim and Timothy W. Simpson

Department of Industrial & Manufacturing Engineering, The Pennsylvania State University,
University Park, PA 16802 USA
{wzk106,tws8}@psu.edu

Abstract. Iterative loops and rework between design, manufacturing, and testing delay the development lead time for complex products like vehicles. This research focuses on creating an automated design for manufacturing (DFM) feedback system (ADFS) framework that reduces these iterations by providing early, fast, and informative feedback on manufacturability to designers. The proposed ADFS analyzes manufacturability in terms of part geometry with respect to a given set of process capabilities based on DFM guidelines for vehicle manufacturing. In order to increase the fidelity of the search, a heuristic approach to obtain manufacturing process fitness with respect to a part design is introduced. The proposed system framework will help to identify suitable manufacturing processes more quickly as well as provide visual feedback for geometric advice at the feature level with regard to the selected processes.

Keywords: manufacturing assessment system, design for manufacturing, manufacturing feedback.

1   Introduction

1.1   Background

Designing a complex product like a motor vehicle is often delayed due to modifications along with subsequent verifications [1]. These iterative loops between design and testing teams make the whole new product development linger at the design stage. It has been reported that the design process can usually take up to 24 months in North America [2] and 15 to 20 years [3] for military vehicles particularly from the concept initiation to the production phase.

It would be desirable if these iterative loops can be shorten or ultimately, eliminated. If the manufacturing feedback information can be delivered to designers timely by adopting a stand-alone feedback system tool, then it can significantly reduce product lead time, in general, and vehicle development, in particular.

However, so far no manufacturing assessment system (MAS) has been developed that takes multiple manufacturing processes related to vehicle production into account simultaneously [4]. Adopting design for manufacturing (DFM) guidelines into a MAS can be an alternative to respond such difficulty [5]. If geometric features of a design satisfy DFM guidelines of a manufacturing process, then it can be said that the design is manufacturable in terms of the corresponding manufacturing process.

V. Prabhu, M. Taisch, and D. Kiritsis (Eds.): APMS 2013, Part I, IFIP AICT 414, pp. 40–47, 2013.
© IFIP International Federation for Information Processing 2013

Though a design may be judged as manufacturable, some potential hindrances such as visibility issues, fixturing, set-ups, etc. can still occur during the actual manufacturing execution of a design. Those details can only be investigated by the high-level assessment for a particular process. Likewise, an analysis of DFM guidelines alone cannot determine which manufacturing process is the most appropriate to consider. Therefore our goal is to provide feedback information to designers for multiple processes rather than pick a single candidate process.

1.2   Research Objective

A robust systematic framework is needed to feed-forward appropriate manufacturing processes to the next higher-level assessment as well as to provide feedback to designers based on this manufacturability assessment. It is clear that reducing iterative loops requires a stand-alone system in automated fashion to interact with designers in a timely manner. Hence, this research aims to develop an automated DFM feedback system (ADFS) framework to provide early, fast, and informative feedback for manufacturability to designers as well as feed-forward for detailed investigation. There are two main deliverables as objectives:

1. Feed-forward: the ADFS helps determine which manufacturing processes are the most appropriate for the detailed level assessment for more information.
2. Feedback: the ADFS provides geometric advice at the feature level in an intuitive and visual manner.

2   Literature Review

2.1   Manufacturability Assessment System

In the context of concurrent engineering, generating detailed manufacturing feedback in an interactive way is critical in MAS to reduce development time span [6]. With the widespread of CAD systems, studies regarding stand-alone manufacturability assessment tools were also spurred with the support of feature recognition methodology through CAD software [7]. However, those researches were mostly limited to only machining process and concentrated to calculating manufacturing cost by generating adequate process plans [8]. According to Kalpakjian et al. [9], rough statistical analysis of published works shows that approximately 92% of the researches are focusing on the applicability of MAS to machining processes only.

2.2   Utilizing DFM Guidelines

The main benefit of practical use of DFM guidelines is that each guideline of a manufacturing process can serve as one of several criteria, so that they can be also utilized as a source for generating redesign recommendations for failing features. As an example, Jacob et al. [10] present a geometric reasoning methodology by adapting cross-comparisons of geometric features to coded design rules for grinding. When the system recognized salient features, corresponding design rules are invoked to generate manufacturing feasibility decisions automatically. Providing redesign recommendation was implemented as parametric ranges in text format verified by a knowledge base. However, the application was also bound to only single process perspective.

3   Proposed Methodology

3.1   Fast Heuristics

The capability of DFM guidelines enables a "Fast Heuristics" approach that can assess manufacturability without cost estimation analysis. Although calculating manufacturing cost is the most complete measure of manufacturability [9], investigating it is not an easy task in the early stages of design. According to Özbayrak at el. [11], estimating a manufacturing cost for a unit of product design based on activity-based costing approach requires 15+ factors to be considered. Moreover, performing cost estimation becomes worse if there are multiple candidate processes to investigate.

Process Filtering. Therefore, a heuristic filtering approach is proposed that aims to analyze manufacturability faster without losing robustness. In the system shown in Fig. 1, the part geometry extracted from submitted designs will be assessed with respect to a given set of process capabilities collected from the DFM guidelines. Here, those capabilities serve as filters that rule out infeasible manufacturing processes.

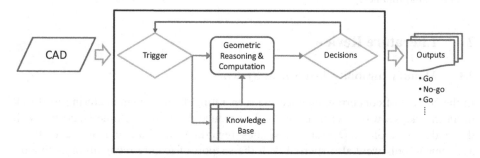

Fig. 1. Filtering system

A different manufacturing process must have its own filter set, as design rules for each manufacturing process are different. When a converted CAD file in XML format comes into the system, a trigger invokes a manufacturing process and its corresponding filter set from the knowledge base. Then each feature's geometry is evaluated against the appropriate filter element in a set. The output database stores "Go"&"No-go" results of every process with respect to a design as well as information of failing features. The system loop iterates until all of the manufacturing processes are analyzed for the submitted design. Through this filtering system framework, it is expected that a series of analyses toward candidate manufacturing processes delivers only suitable manufacturing processes (feed-forward) so that design advice at the feature level can be provided later according to DFM guidelines.

Table 1 shows an example filtering analysis for the bracket shown in Fig. 2. For this preliminary analysis, minimum/maximum section thickness and minimum corner radii allowance are used for the filtering. The reason for the target thickness to be machined (4 in.) is because the machining process removes chunk of raw materials for both sides. For casting, the section thickness limits the width of center and bottom pillars. Also, it is presumed that forging and stamping require fixturing to position the datum B' to the ground. Processes that are grayed out at Table 1 are infeasible processes to manufacture this example part.

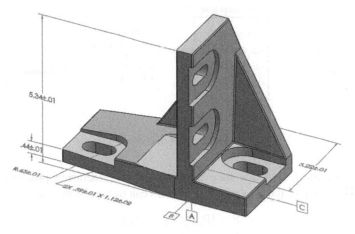

Fig. 2. Example bracket

Table 1. Example filtering 1: manufacturing capabilities of various processes

Process	Target thickness to be machined = 4". For casting processes, 0.394". Minimum corner radii = 0.4"		
	Min Section Thinkness (in.)	Max Section Thinkness (in.)	Minimum corner radii (in.)
Metal Stamping	0.0001	0.79	N/A
Fine-blanking	0.005	0.5	N/A
Draw bending	0.035	0.109	1.5 - 8
Powder Metal	0.06	0.22	No limitation
Forging	No limitation	No limitation	No limitation
Abrasive-Jet Machining	0.005	0.032	0.004
Water-Jet Maching	No limitation	18	No limitation
Electron-Beam Machining	0.001	0.25	No limitation
Laser-Beam Machining	No limitation	0.5	No limitation
Plasma-Arc Cutting	No limitation	1	No limitation
Electroforming	0.001	0.5	No limitation
Metal Injection Molding	No data	0.25	0.015 or 0.5*WT
Machining	No limitation	No limitation	Vary (tool diameter, 1/16")
Wire EDM	No limitation	No limitation	No limitation
Sand mold casting	0.118 (3mm)	No limitation	equal to 0.5*ave. wall thickness
Permanent mold casting	0.079 (2mm)	1.96 (50mm)	equal to 1*ave. wall thickness
Plaster-mold casting	0.039 (1mm)	No limitation	equal to 0.5*ave. wall thickness
Investment casting	0.039 (1mm)	2.95 (75mm)	0.03
Ceramic-mold casting	0.039 (1mm)	No limitation	0.03
Die casting	0.019 (0.5mm)	0.47 (12mm)	equal to 1.5*ave. wall thickness

Process Fitness Function. The filtering process yields a series of "Go" and "No-go" responses for the manufacturing processes that were assessed. To increase the fidelity of the evaluation for the feed-forward, we propose to develop a process fitness (PF)

function that is derived heuristically. If the number of processes in the knowledge base is 16, for example, then the system generates 16 stacks of response data of each process. The fitness will be derived from the statistics of all 16 responses and is presented as percentage value of "Go" proportioned to the total number of filtering attempts. Therefore, each PF provides a capability metric for each manufacturing process with respect to a given design; hence, it can be used to re-sequence filters in a set to derive the feed-forward faster. The modeling of the PF is shown in Fig. 3.

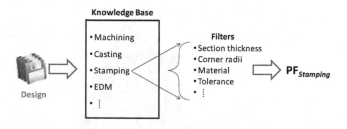

Fig. 3. PF modeling

Suppose that the knowledge base contains 16 manufacturing processes that are available. The group of manufacturing processes can be represented as:

$$P = \{P_1, P_2, P_3, ..., P_{16}\}$$

The number of filters N in a filter set is different among manufacturing processes. A filter F_{ij} of a manufacturing process P_i can be represented as:

$$F = \{F_{i1}, F_{i2}, F_{i3}, ..., F_{ij}\}, \text{ where } i = 1 \text{ to } 16, j = 1 \text{ to } N_i$$

Note that the number of filters is depicted as N_i since it is depends on the ith manufacturing process. Toward any of submitted design D_k, where $k = 1$ to M, performing a filtering analysis with a set of filters F of a manufacturing process P_i bears a response that can be represented as:

$$F_{ij}(D_k) \rightarrow \text{"Go" or "No-go"}$$

Suppose that the system performs filtering analyses for a design D_1 with a designated set of filters for process P_1. After a loop of analyses is performed, the filtering system generates a stack of responses as described in Eq. 1.

$$\begin{bmatrix} F_{11} \\ F_{12} \\ F_{13} \\ \vdots \\ F_{1j} \end{bmatrix} \times [D_1] = \begin{bmatrix} G \\ N \\ G \\ \vdots \\ G \end{bmatrix} \tag{1}$$

Process fitness$PF_i$of process P_i with respect tothe designD_k is derived by:

$$= \frac{\text{total number of Go from } F_{ij} \text{ for a process } P_i \text{ toward a design } D_k}{j}$$

when i = manufacturing process index,1 to 16.

For a group of M designs, the filtering system produces following a response matrix extended from Eq. 1 as follows:

$$\begin{bmatrix} F_{11} \\ F_{12} \\ F_{13} \\ \vdots \\ F_{1j} \end{bmatrix} \times [D_1, D_2, D_3, ..., D_M] = \begin{bmatrix} G & N & G & ... & G \\ N & & & & \\ G & & \ddots & & \vdots \\ \vdots & & & & \\ G & & ... & & N \end{bmatrix} \qquad (2)$$

In this matrix, each column of the response matrix stands for the results from filtering analyses for the $i$thprocess P_i toward a designD_M.

Sequencing Filters. If there is an important feature property that has a small allowance range, then a filtering analysis using that feature geometry would rule out the corresponding manufacturing process frequently. Performing that analysis before any other filters would reduce the number of remaining candidate processes quicker, so that it helps to extract a process faster and increase fidelity of the framework especially for the feed-forward.

If there is enough number of sample designs, it is possible to derive a series of PF values for a process P_i toward M number of designs from the matrix in Eq. 2. From the response matrix, analysis results of a filter F_{ij} toward M number of designs are the jth row of the matrix. The importance of a filter F_{ij} can be simply derived from the proportion of "No-go" responses to the number of all filtering attempts toward M designs as following:

$$\begin{aligned} &\text{Weight of a filter } F_{ij} \\ &= \frac{\text{total number of No-go from } F_{ij} \text{ for a process } P_i \text{ toward } M \text{ designs}}{M} \end{aligned}$$

Instead of counting the number of positive responses, negative responses are collected because the effectiveness of filtering infeasible candidates is the matter; a filter has a higher capability if it rules out the process more often.

3.2   System Framework

The proposed methodology framework for generating automated DFM feedback is presented with two separated phases. At the first phase, collected sample designs are applied to the filtering system to derive filter sequences for manufacturing process in the knowledge base. The information flow of the first phase is presented at Fig. 4.

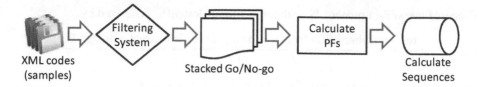

Fig. 4. Phase 1: Derive sequences of filters

When the sequencing is done, the filtering system will be refined by adopting the results from Phase 1 as described in Fig. 5.

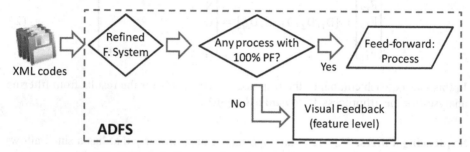

Fig. 5. Phase 2: Generate feed-forward/ feedback outputs

The PF serves as an internal metric in the ADFS. If a manufacturing process obtains 100% of the PF value, then it will be judged as manufacturable in terms of the process and can be passed forward for more detailed assessment. Else, a process with the highest PF will be selected and visual feedback on its failing features will be delivered back to the designer.

4   Closing Remarks

Through the proposed stand-alone ADFS, it is expected that designers can refine their designs for manufacturability from visualized feedback so that iterations can be reduced. Detail development of the visualization feedback is currently ongoing work.

Additionally, there are many research items that can be extended from this research. Although the proposed ADFS is built based on filtering methodology, violating a DFM design rule (i.e., a filter) does not always mean that the design is not manufacturable. In fact, a non-manufacturable design for a selected process may become manufacturable by adding additional processes. In this research, those "superset" of multiple processes and its sequencing are currently not considered. Also, providing dynamic visual geometric recommendations at the feature level would provide richer options that enable designers to "tweak" feature parameters visually on the screen. Along with such techniques, designers can search various parameter options on specific CAD software while it does not hurt the proposed part functionality.

Evaluation of the ADFS is ongoing and will be performed through benchmarking simulation for various design inputs. Any designs revealed as manufacturable (contain

100% PF) will be submitted for detailed evaluation in commercial software (e.g., [12]) so that the decision that ADFS has made can be investigated.

Acknowledgements. We acknowledge support provided by the Defense Advanced Research Projects Agency (DARPA/TTO) under contract HR0011-12-C-0075 iFAB Foundry. Any opinions, findings and conclusions or recommendations expressed in this material are those of the author(s) and do not necessarily reflect the views of DARPA or the U.S. Government.

References

[1] Giffin, M., de Weck, O., Bounova, G., Keller, R., Eckert, C., Clarkson, P.J.: Change Propagation Analysis in Complex Technical Systems. Journal of Mechanical Design 131(8), 081001 (2009)

[2] Morgan, J.M., Liker, J.K.: The Toyota Production Development System. Productivity Press, New York (2006)

[3] LTC Wiedenman, N.: Adaptive Vehicle Make (AVM), from DARPA Tactical Technology Office (January 03, 2013),
http://www.darpa.mil/Our_Work/TTO/Programs/AVM/
Adaptive_Vehicle_Make_Program_Overview (retrieved February 28, 2013)

[4] Shukor, S., Axinte, D.: Manufacturability analysis system: Issues and future trends. International Journal of Production Research 47(5), 1369–1390 (2009)

[5] Gupta, S.K., Nau, D.S.: Systematic approach to analysing the manufacturability of machined parts. Computer-Aided Design 27(5), 323–342 (1995)

[6] McMains, S.: Design for manufacturing feedback at interactive rates. In: ACM Symposium on Solid and Physical Modeling, p. 239. ACM New York, New York (2006)

[7] Pham, D.T.: A concurrent design system for machined parts. Journal of Engineering Manufacture 213(8), 841–846 (1999)

[8] Maropoulos, P., Bramall, D., McKay, K.: Assessing the manufacturability of early product designs using aggregate process models. Journal of Engineering Manufacture 217(9), 1203–1214 (2003)

[9] Kalpakjian, S., Schmid, S.R.: Manufacturing engineering and technology, 4th edn. Prentice-Hall, Inc., Upper Saddle River (2001)

[10] Jacob, D.V., Ramana, K., Rao, P.: Automated manufacturability assessment of rotational parts by grinding. International Journal of Production Research 42(3), 505–519 (2004)

[11] Özbayrak, M., Akgün, M., Türker, A.: Activity-based cost estimation in a push/pull advanced manufacturing system. International Journal of Production Economics 87(1), 49–65 (2004)

[12] aPriori. aPriori, Costing without Complexity, from aPriori (2013),
http://www.apriori.com/ (retrieved March 26, 2013)

Game Theoretical Approach to Supply Chain Microfinance

Jaehun Sim and Vittaldas V. Prabhu

The Harold and Inge Marcus Department of
Industrial and Manufacturing Engineering
310 Leonhard Building
University Park, PA 16802
Jus238@psu.edu, prabhu@engr.psu.edu

Abstract. This paper considers a supply chain microfinance model in which a manufacturer acts as a lender and a raw material supplier as a borrower. Using a game theoretical analysis, the study investigates how investment levels, raw material prices, and profit margins are influenced by loan interest rates under two types of decentralized channel policies: manufacturer Stackelberg and vertical Nash game. In addition, the study shows how the profits of a manufacturer and a supplier are changed under each supply chain channel structure.

Keywords: Game Theory and Supply Chain Microfinance.

1   Introduction

Over the past several years, business leaders have realized that economic growth and success can be enhanced by their efforts toward both environment and social values (Stead et al. 2008). This central concept, corporate sustainability, has become a fundamental principle in the search for sustainable competitive advantages for companies (Savitz and Weber, 2006). For example, global leaders such as Shell, Philips, BASF, and Toyota have incorporated this new concept into their business strategies (Ahn et al. 2008).

Since the success of microfinance institutions (MFIs) in the early 1990s, an effective microfinance program can be considered a corporate sustainability approach for alleviating poverty by offering small amount loans with no collateral requirement to the poor in both developing and developed countries. With the objective of empowering the poor to become self-employed, the microfinance program provides the poor with access to financial and social services in the form of credit opportunities, education, health care, insurance, and savings (Sengupta and Aubuchon, 2008).

Despite their flexibility, MFIs experience difficulty in increasing outreach toward their particular clientele and keeping the sustainability of the institutions at the same time. This difficulty can be attributed to several problems, including high levels of poverty and risk, information asymmetries, incentive incompatibilities, and imperfect enforcement mechanisms (Conning and Udry, 2007). Also, due to the unique features

V. Prabhu, M. Taisch, and D. Kiritsis (Eds.): APMS 2013, Part I, IFIP AICT 414, pp. 48–53, 2013.
© IFIP International Federation for Information Processing 2013

of microfinance, the interest rate is considered to be an important problem because it does not perfectly represent the lender's opportunity costs of loans nor increase the lender's profits, as in a traditional financial market.

To offer a financial sustainability solution, this study incorporates the concept of supply chain finance and proposes the concept of supply chain microfinance to examine the relationships between investment levels, raw material prices, profit margins, and loan interest rates. The basic idea of supply chain microfinance is that the high creditworthiness of a manufacturer can provide a raw material supplier with the low creditworthiness a loan at a low interest rate.

As shown in Figure 1, supply chain microfinance has three players: a bank, a manufacturer, and a supplier. It is assumed that a poor supplier does not have its own financial resources and has little chance to borrower a loan from the bank in order to invest in a project. Even if the supplier obtains a loan, his or her low credit score leads to a high interest rate.

In the supply chain microfinance environment, the high credit score of a manufacturer attracts an investment from a bank with a low interest rate. In turn, the manufacturer lends to the poor supplier at a low interest rate. When the supplier invests in a project with an investment I_M from the manufacturer, the supplier expects a rate of return R_P from the project and repay R_M to the manufacturer. When the manufacturer invests a supplier's project with an investment I_B, the manufacturer expects a rate of return R_M from the supplier and the intangible benefit of corporate social responsibility θ and makes a repayment R_B to the bank.

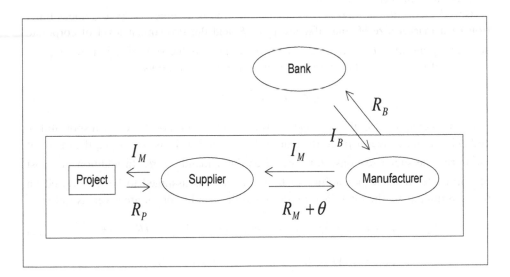

Fig. 1. Basic Model of Supply Chain Microfinance

2   Literature Review

Since the concept of corporate social responsibility has appeared in the early 1960's, corporations have increasingly had to consider environmental and social dimensions as part of their supply chain issues. Despite the growing interest in sustainable supply chain practices, there has not been much research conducted in this regard, compared to conventional supply chain.

Koplin et al. (2007) utilize environmental and social standards at Volkswagen to decrease economic, environmental and social risks throughout the supply chain. Ciliberti et al. (2008) introduce the taxonomy of the logistics social responsibility (LSR) practices based on literature reviews and empirical analysis. Considering a balance between profit and the environment, Fisch and Neo (2008) propose a framework for the design and evaluation of sustainable logistics networks. Guillen and Grossmann (2009) design a sustainable supply chain in the chemical industry under uncertainty in the life cycle inventory.

3   The Game Model

This study considers one supplier and one manufacturer under two sub-problems: manufacturer Stackelberg and vertical Nash game. The modeling approach is similar to Ghosh's approach (Ghosh and Shah, 2012). In this decentralized channel policy, it is assumed that the manufacturer makes decisions on the investment level of corporate social responsibility and the profit margin. On the other hand, the supplier makes a decision on the raw material price.

Based on economic theories, a demand function is assumed to have a linear function of a market size M, manufacture price P, and the investment level of corporate social responsibility I. In addition, the product price is the sum of raw material price s and profit margin m. The demand function is given as follows.

$$q = M - \beta P + \alpha I \tag{1}$$

In this equation, α is the demand coefficient of the corporate social responsibility and β is the influence of price fluctuation on demand. It is assumed that the effort of the corporate social responsibility increases the demand by αI. In addition, the cost of corporate social responsibility such as fair price is assumed to be θI^2. Based on these assumptions, the manufacture profit and the supplier profit are given as follows.

$$\Pi_M = (m - s - c)(M - \beta(s + m) + \alpha I) + IR_M - IR_B - \theta I^2 \tag{2}$$

$$\Pi_S = s(M - \beta(s + m) + \alpha I) + IR_P - IR_M \tag{3}$$

In these equations, c is a production cost, θ is the cost coefficient of corporate social responsibility, R_M is an interest rate of a manufacturer, and R_B is an interest rate of a bank. In the manufacturer Stackelberg, the manufacturer decides the investment level of corporate social responsibility and the product margin in response to the supplier. Then, the supplier decides the raw material price given the investment level and profit margin. In this policy, it is assumed that the manufacturer plays a Stackelberg leader. The optimal investment level, the optimal manufacture margin, the optimal raw material price, and the optimal product price are given as follows.

$$I^* = \frac{M\alpha - c\alpha\beta + 3\alpha^2\theta + 3\beta\theta^2 + 3\beta R_B - 3\beta R_M}{2\alpha^2} \tag{4}$$

$$m^* = \frac{M\alpha + c\alpha\beta + \alpha^2\theta - \beta\theta^2 - \beta R_B + \beta R_M}{2\alpha\beta} \tag{5}$$

$$s^* = -\frac{-M\alpha + c\alpha\beta - \alpha^2\theta - 2\beta\theta^2 - 2\beta R_B + 2\beta R_M}{2\alpha\beta} \tag{6}$$

$$P^* = s^* + m^* = \frac{2M\alpha + 2\alpha^2\theta + \beta\theta^2 + \beta R_B - \beta R_M}{2\alpha\beta} \tag{7}$$

In the vertical Nash game, the supplier chooses the raw material price in response to the investment level and the profit margin, and the manufacturer chooses the investment level and the profit margin in response to the raw material price. In this policy, it is assumed that neither the manufacturer nor the supplier has the power to control the market. The optimal investment level, the optimal profit margin, the optimal raw material price, and the optimal product price are given as follows.

$$s^* = \frac{2M\theta + 2c\beta\theta + \alpha R_B - \alpha R_M}{\alpha^2 - 8\beta\theta} \tag{8}$$

Substituting the value of s^* into the value of m, derive

$$m^* = \frac{c\alpha^2 - 4M\theta - 4c\beta\theta + 2\alpha R_B - 2\alpha R_M}{\alpha^2 - 8\beta\theta} \tag{9}$$

Substituting the value of s^* into the value of I, derive

$$I^* = \frac{-M\alpha + c\alpha\beta + 4\beta R_B - 4\beta R_M}{\alpha^2 - 8\beta\theta} \tag{10}$$

Thus, the optimal product price is

$$P^* = \frac{2(-2M\theta + 2c\alpha\beta + \alpha R_B - \alpha R_M)}{\alpha^2 - 8\beta\theta}$$
(11)

4   Result and Discussion

In this study, the manufacturer Stackelberg and Nash game cases are considered to analyze the impacts of the manufacturer's interest rate. Due to the characteristics of supply chain microfinance, supplier Stackelberg is not considered because the supplier Stackelberg is not reasonable in the microfinance environment in which the manufacturer has more power than the supplier to control the market. For a numerical analysis of manufacturer Stackelberg, the following values are used, M =200, α =0.2, β =0.5, c =6, θ =3.5, R_M =0.2, and R_B =0.1.

As shown in Figure 2, the manufacturer's interest rate has a decreasing effect on the investment level of corporate social responsibility. Conversely, the manufacturer's interest rate has an increasing effect on the profit margin.

The manufacturer's interest rate has a decreasing effect on the supplier's raw material price. Similarly, the manufacturer's interest rate has a decreasing effect on the manufacturer's product price. On the other hand, under the Nash game, the numerical analysis indicates that the interest rates of a manufacturer have little impact on corporate social responsibility, the manufacturer's profit margin, or the raw material cost.

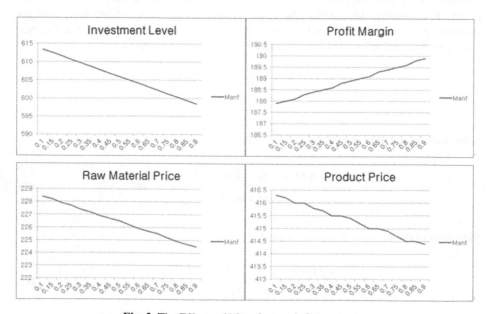

Fig. 2. The Effects of Manufacturer's Interest rates

5   Conclusion

This study investigates the impact of corporate social responsibility on the supply chain microfinance under two decentralized channel policies. The result shows that the manufacturer's interest rate has a positive influence on the manufacturer's margin under manufacturer Stackelberg. In the supply chain microfinance business environment, this study shows that manufacturer Stackelberg is an appropriate model which fully incorporates the characteristics of microfinance. In the future, this study will explicitly model two features; corporate social responsibility and supply risk, to assess how the corporate decreases the supply risk and impacts the sustainable supply chain.

References

1. Ahn, M.J., Meeks, M.: Building a conducive environment for life science-based entrepreneurship and industry clusters. Journal of Commercial Biotechnology 14(1), 20–30 (2008)
2. Ciliberti, F., Pontrandolfo, P., et al.: Investigating corporate social responsibility in supply chains: A SME perspective. Journal of Cleaner Production 16(15), 1579–1588 (2008)
3. Conning, J., Udry, C.: Rural financial markets in developing countries. Handbook of Agricultural Economics 3, 2857–2908 (2007)
4. Fisch, G.G.J., Neo, T.S.P.: Green automotive supply chain for an emerging market. Massachusetts Institute of Technology (2008)
5. Ghosh, D., Shah, J.: A comparative analysis of greening policies across supply chain structures. International Journal of Production Economics 13, 568–583 (2012)
6. GuillénGosálbez, G., Grossmann, I.E.: Optimal design and planning of sustainable chemical supply chains under uncertainty. AIChE Journal 55(1), 99–121 (2009)
7. Koplin, J., Seuring, S., et al.: Incorporating sustainability into supply manage-ment in the automotive industry-The case of the Volkswagen AG. Journal of Cleaner Production 15(11-12), 1053–1062 (2007)
8. Savitz, A.W., Weber, K.: The triple bottom line: How today's best-run companies are achieving economic, social, and environmental success-and how you can too. Jossey-Bass Inc. Pub. (2006)
9. Sengupta, R., Aubuchon, C.P.: The microfinance revolution: An overview. Federal Reserve Bank of St. Louis Review 90(1), 9–30 (2008)
10. Stead, J.G., Stead, W.E.: Sustainable strategic management: An evolutionary perspective. International Journal of Sustainable Strategic Management 1(1), 62–81 (2008)

Surplus Product Donation and Sustainability Strategy: Channels and Challenges for Corporate Product Donations

Md. M. Islam and John Vande Vate

School of Industrial and Systems Engineering
Georgia Institute of Technology

Abstract. Sustainability addresses three aspects of corporate responsibility: economic, environmental and social. Over the years, the operations and supply chain literature has focused on economic and environmental objectives limiting the social agenda to ethical sourcing practices. Yet the disposition of surplus inventories in particular and charitable giving in general are key components of corporate social responsibility. We discuss the channels and challenges for companies' surplus inventory donations and describe why companies should integrate product donations within their overall corporate sustainability strategy.

Keywords: Corporate Philanthropy, Sustainability Strategy, In-kind Donation.

1 Introduction

Sustainability initiatives are now a common component of corporate strategy for large companies. Kiron et al.'s [1] 2012 global survey of 4,000 managers from 113 countries suggests that sustainability related strategies are now competitive necessities for companies and nearly 53% of S&P 500 companies published some form of corporate social responsibility or sustainability report in 2012 [2].

The 1987 World Commission on Environment and Development [3] defines sustainability as "development that meets the needs of the present without compromising the ability of future generations to meet their needs". Most of the management and operations literature has conceptualized sustainability as the interactions among a company's environmental, economic and social goals. Building on this triple bottom line, Carter et al. [4] define sustainable supply chain strategy "as the strategic, transparent integration and achievement of an organization's social, environmental, and economic goals in the systemic coordination of key interorganizational business processes for improving the long-term economic performance of the individual company and its supply chains".

Most corporate sustainability initiatives and academic literature in the area, however, focus exclusively on environmental and economic goals [5]. Ageron et al.'s [6] empirical study finds that most initiatives related to sustainable supply chain are linked to environmental and green practices. Common initiatives

V. Prabhu, M. Taisch, and D. Kiritsis (Eds.): APMS 2013, Part I, IFIP AICT 414, pp. 54–61, 2013.

include waste reduction, energy efficiency enhancements and packaging improvements. For many companies, waste reduction and energy efficiency are the first choices as they reduce environmental impact and cost at the same time.

Increasingly, social and ethical issues are becoming an integral part of companies' supply chain practices. After the damaging revelations implicating the supply chains of major brands such as Nike, Walmart and Disney in questionable social practices in Asia, companies pay close attention to legal and ethical practices in their extended supply chains. Some companies like Natura have already put real teeth in the social aspects of their triple bottom line metrics to the point that these can now drive bonuses and executive compensation to the same extent that financial performance does.

Many large companies work directly with key NGO partners to address specific social issues. For example, Walmart works with a large number of NGOs domestically and internationally to improve working conditions in supplier factories, to promote sustainable farming and to distribute surplus food to food banks in local communities [7].

According to Corporations Encouraging Corporate Philanthropy (CECP), a CEO membership organization of large global companies, U.S. companies donated a total of $19.1 billion in 2011 [8]. Nearly, 64% by value of U.S. companies' total donations is given in-kind, predominantly in the form of surplus or unsalable inventories that manufacturers and retailers donate to NGOs. Surplus product donation can help companies achieve all three aspects of their sustainability goals: environmental, economic and social. It can reduce reportable landfill waste, avoid the operational costs of disposal and advance philanthropic objectives.

This paper relies on literature reviews, formal and informal interviews with practitioners and case studies to explore the structures through which products donated by companies are distributed and used by NGOs in the U.S.. We apply the notion of channels from the marketing[15,16,18] and supply chain literature[17] in describing how NGOs use or distribute donated products to beneficiaries and describe the underlying incentives that shape these channels. This research introduces formal discussion of corporate in-kind donations to the existing body of literature in corporate philanthropy and nonprofit management.

2   Business Case for Product Donations

Companies have limited options for managing surplus or unsalable inventories, each with its own costs and benefits. We discuss the four main options in the following paragraphs.

Return and Reuse. Many retailers return surplus, damaged or unsalable inventories to suppliers who either refurbish and reuse the product or reclaim portions of it for reuse. Return and reuse are often financially impractical for low value goods - the cost of transportation, recovery and refurbishing can exceed the value of the product. Reuse also poses the familiar risks of obsolescence and quality problems.

Liquidation. Companies can sell surplus inventories to liquidators, typically for 10 - 15% of the product's original value. And this small revenue comes with the potentially large risks associated with ceding visibility and control of the product to liquidators. Concerns about the risks to brand reputation and of market cannibalization, for example, generally prevent luxury brands from selling surplus inventories to liquidators.

Disposal. Orderly disposal can be a costly operation as it involves sorting, transportation to landfills, waste handling and processing fees, etc. Disposing significant quantities of surplus inventory can also adversely affect a company's environmental metrics and progress toward its environmental goals.

Donation. Donating surplus products to NGOs is relatively easy and cost efficient. It helps companies fulfill social and philanthropic goals while reducing the operational costs associated with managing surplus inventories. Many product donations are also eligible for enhanced tax benefits under U.S. tax code, section 170(e)(3). However, poorly managed donations can harm donor's reputation, especially if the donated items are sold in the secondary market or used for unethical or inappropriate purposes.

Ross et al.'s [9] recent study on the business benefits of product donation shows that in most cases the low cost recovery from liquidation and high costs of return processing make donating surplus inventories to registered charities the most attractive option.

Table 1 summarizes the benefits, costs and risks associated with the four options discussed here.

3   NGO Motivations for Accepting In-kind Donations

According to a 2012 non-profit sector report by the Urban Institute [13], there are 2.1 million charities in the U.S.. This number has grown significantly over the last decade and has almost doubled since 2001. Total giving by U.S. donors, however, has not increased in as quickly. In fact, adjusting for inflation, total giving has remained essentially flat since 2001 [11] while corporate in-kind giving has increased from 60% in 2009 to 64% in 2011 [8]. A matched dataset of 144 companies' inflation adjusted yearly giving from CECP's survey shows that in-kind giving increased from $7.41 billion to $10.12 billion over the same period.

Most corporate in-kind donations are given in the form of product donations. In-kind donations are helpful to NGOs, but are not nearly as versatile as cash. Product donations can be very specialized and so not appropriate for every NGO's philanthropic mission. Consequently, NGOs face a growing challenge of deciding which in-kind donations to accept and those decisions involve much more than simply determining whether the product is appropriate for the organization's mission.

Many NGOs fear that declining an in-kind donation can adversely impact their relationship with the donor and preclude opportunities to receive more

Table 1. Summary of benefits, costs and risks of disposal methods

Disposal options	Costs & Benefits	Risks
Return or reuse	Significant cost recovery Reverse logistics cost Return processing cost	Product obsolescence Quality issues
Liquidation	Limited cost recovery Easy to do	Risk of brand reputation Market cannibalization
Disposal	Waste processing cost Easy to do	Environmental regulations Reputational effects
Donation	Waste reduction Operational cost savings Tax benefits Potential social impact	Risk to brand reputation Product liability Market cannibalization

valuable donations, including cash donations, in the future. Consequently, fund-raisers try to accept in-kind donations from key donors even when the goods are not particularly well suited to the organization's mission.

Accepting high value in-kind donations increases an NGO's revenue without significantly affecting its administrative expenses and so improves its financial efficiency, the direct program expenses as a fraction of total revenue. A 2011 Forbes article [12] explores how many international NGOs report higher revenues and financial efficiencies by inflating the value of in-kind donations, especially of medical and pharmaceutical donations. Higher revenue and financial efficiency make an NGO look bigger, more important and therefore more attractive to donors.

These incentives can lead NGOs to accept in-kind donations that are not well suited to their needs. This can be especially true for smaller NGOs whose fixed administrative costs for staff salaries and office expenses typically represent a larger portion of total revenues, driving down financial efficiencies and making it difficult to attract donors and, as a consequence, to decline in-kind donations.

4   Channels for Corporate In-kind Donations

Given the motivations for accepting in-kind donations even when they may be poorly suited to the organization's mission, NGOs are often left with the challenge of what to do with the products they've received. Donors generally prohibit an NGO from selling the goods, leaving three main options: Use the goods, share them with other NGOs, or dispose of them. A complicated network of NGO types and donation channels has evolved to help in-kind donations find their way to NGOs that can use them effectively. We describe the salient features of that network in the following paragraphs.

In the simplest case, a company, which we refer to as the *original donor*, donates surplus products to an NGO that distributes them directly to *final beneficiaries*, i.e., to individuals or families in need. In this case, we refer to the NGO as an *end-use organization*[1]. Not all NGOs are end-use organizations. Many simply serve as *Intermediary NGOs* who pass the donation on to other NGOs. This provides corporate donors with a variety of channels for moving in-kind donations to end-use organizations and beneficiaries. Here, we characterize three primary channel categories.

Direct Distribution. The direct distribution channel is the simplest and most familiar: the original donor contributes directly to an end-use NGO, which in turn distributes the goods to final beneficiaries. In response to major natural disasters, for example, companies like Walmart, Target and others donate relief supplies to end-use organizations like the American Red Cross, Salvation Army and others, who distribute the gifts to disaster victims. This model works particularly well when the original donor and the end-use organization have a partnership in place and the donated products are carefully matched to the victims' needs.

Aggregation. When the products aren't well suited to the disaster response or when the donation is made outside the context of a disaster, it can be difficult for a company with a large donation of specialized products to find a single appropriate end-use organization with sufficient scale to manage the entire gift. In this case, a form of intermediary NGO, which we refer to as aggregator NGOs serve as "one stop donation points" for donors. Food banks are a good example. They collect food from various donors and distribute them to smaller food pantries and soup kitchens [14]. NGOs like AmeriCare, Map International and MedShare aggregate medicines and medical supplies donated by various hospitals and corporations and in turn distribute them to partner NGOs or non-profit hospitals nationally and internationally. The aggregation channel is most appropriate for reaching smaller local NGOs with a specific mission, whose limited operational and fund-raising capacity makes it difficult to work directly with large corporations and manage large in-kind donations.

Pass-Through. Often NGOs feel obliged to accept in-kind donations from corporate partners even when these donations are poorly suited to the organization's mission. In these circumstances, NGOs typically look for another more appropriate organization to pass the gift along to. Subsequent NGOs in the chain are similarly motivated to pass it along as each one can, according to the Financial

---

[1] Adopted from AERDO Interagency Gift-in-Kind Standards -2009.

Accounting Standards Board (FASB), also recognize the associated revenue as long as it has the authority to independently decide how it distributes the gift.

Any NGO can participate in the pass through channel and most do. This channel provides a convenient and welcome alternative to sending potentially valuable, but ill-suited donations to the landfill. The loose association of NGOs in this channel makes it difficult to track donations and, for intermediaries to be motivated to participate in the chain, the donor must allow them to determine how the donation is distributed. Consequently, relying on the pass-through channel provides little assurance that the gift will have significant social impact and poses risks that the gift may ultimately be used inappropriately or even irresponsibly.

5 Ensuring Social Impact of Corporate Product Donations

A large and growing share of corporate giving comes in the form of surplus inventory donations. Yet these product donations can prove difficult for NGOs to usefully employ. In the worst case, the product is so ill-suited to legitimate philanthropic needs that it simply passes from NGO to NGO until one finally disposes of it. Along the way it generates tax benefits for the donor and enhances the financial performance of the intermediate NGOs, but produces no social benefit and simply shifts the burden of disposal from the original donor to the final NGO in the chain.

In the best case, surplus inventory donation can help companies achieve significant benefits in all three dimensions of sustainability if they are conceptualized and executed with a larger strategic framework. For example, in 2005, Walmart announced bold steps towards sustainability, when the company decided to run 100% on renewable energy, create zero waste and sell products that help protect environment [10]. Since then, Walmart has taken numerous initiatives to achieve these goals. One initiative, "Fighting Hunger Together" redirects surplus perishable foods to local food banks. The program commits a total of $1.75 billion in food donations between 2010 and 2014 and donated nearly 600 million pounds of food to Feeding America's food bank network by the end of 2012. Perishable foods and produce constitute a significant part of solid waste generated from Walmart's stores and distribution centers in the U.S. and donating it to food banks significantly reduced that waste. According to Walmart's 2012 Global Responsibility Report [7], solid waste from U.S. operations reduced by 80% from 2005.

"Fighting Hunger Together" is not simply a waste reduction initiative. It is part of an integrated sustainability strategy focused on all three pillars of sustainability. In an effort to support the social objectives, Walmart donated nearly $122 million in cash to help food banks strengthen their logistics capacity (e.g. by purchasing refrigerated trucks). Donating to local food banks is also a targeted way to improve Walmart's reputation and relationship with local communities.

Other retailers such as the Home Depot, Guess, Bed, Bath & Beyond donate surplus inventories to local NGOs too. Home Depot's store donation program, "Framing Hopes" has donated over $90 million worth of surplus inventories since 2008. Many store donations programs, however, lack specific focus and are primarily a means for disposing of surplus inventories while generating public recognition. Such donation practices do little or nothing to advance a company's philanthropic agenda and and enhance its social impact.

It is important for companies to use in-kind donations strategically to achieve their specific philanthropic goals. Donating surplus products haphazardly without the benefit of a larger strategic vision is wasteful and potentially risky. Beyond the questionable social impacts, unmanaged product donations can be a source of reputational risk. Unmanaged donations that pass though series of unidentified intermediaries may ultimately be sold in the secondary market or disposed of improperly or worse.

6   Conclusion

Surplus product donation has become a major form of corporate giving in the U.S., valued at billions of dollars each year. Companies can save operational cost, gain tax benefits, re-direct waste from landfills and meet their philanthropic goals though surplus product donations. However, the effectiveness of surplus product donations depends, to a great extent, on the company's effort to integrate it within its overall sustainability strategy. Successful in-kind giving programs require long term partnerships with recipient NGOs and strategic alignment between the NGOs' missions and the donor's philanthropic goals.

Absent this strategic guidance and organizational alignment, in-kind donations are likely to be used as a means to achieve organizational benefits for donors and NGOs, without meeting social needs. It is important that donors understand NGOs' motivations for accepting in-kind donations, the alternative channels of distribution, and the role of donation within sustainability initiatives and the larger corporate sustainability strategy.

References

1. Kiron, D., Kruschwitz, N., Haanaes, K., Velken, I.V.S.: Sustainability Nears a Tipping Point. MIT Sloan Management Review 53(2), 69–74 (2012)
2. Clark, L., Master, D.: 2012 Corporate ESG/Sustainability/Responsibility Reporting - Does It Matter? Governance & Accountability Institute, New York (2012)
3. Brundtland, G.H.: Our Common Future: The World Commission on Environment and Development. Oxford University Press, Oxford (1987)
4. Carter, C.R., Rogers, D.S.: A Framework of Sustainable Supply Chain Management: Moving Toward New Theory. International Journal of Physical Distribution & Logistics Management 38(5), 360–387 (2008)
5. Seuring, S., Muller, M.: From a Literature Review to a Conceptual Framework for Sustainable Supply Chain Management. Journal of Cleaner Production 16, 1699–1710 (2008)

6. Ageron, B., Gunasekaran, A., Spaanzani, A.: Sustainable Supply Management: an Empirical Study. International Journal of Production Economics 140, 168–182 (2012)
7. 2012 Global Responsibility Report, Walmart Stores Inc. (2012), http://corporate.walmart.com/global-responsibility/ environment-sustainability/global-responsibility-report
8. CECP: Giving In Numbers - 2012 Edition, Committee Encouraging Corporate Philanthropy, New York (2012)
9. Ross, J.M., McGiverin-Bohan, K.L.: The Business Case for Product Philanthropy, School of Public and Environmental Affairs, Indiana University, Indiana (2012)
10. Plambeck, E.L.: The Greening of Wal-Mart's Supply Chain. Supply Chain Management Review 11(5) (2007)
11. The Center on Philanthropy at Indiana University: Giving USA 2012 Executive Summary, Giving USA Foundation (2012)
12. Barrett, W.P.: Donated Pills Make Some Charities Look Too Good on Paper. Forbes Magazine (2011)
13. Roeger, K.L., Blackwood, A., Pettijohn, S.L.: The Nonprofit Almanac 2012. Urban Institute Press (2012)
14. Tarasuk, V., Eakin, J.M.: Food Assistance Through Surplus Food: Insights from an Ethnographic Study of Food Bank Work. Agriculture and Human Values 22(2), 177–186 (2005)
15. Bucklin, L.P.: A Theory of Distribution Channel Structure. University of California, Institute of Business and Economic Research (1966)
16. Coughlan, A.T., Birger, W.: On Credible Delegation by Oligopolists: A Discussion of Distribution Channel Management. Management Science 35(2), 226–239 (1989)
17. Cooper, M.C., Lambert, D.M., Pagh, J.D.: Supply Chain Management: More than a New Name for Logistics. International Journal of Logistics Management 8(1) (1997)
18. El-Ansary, A.I., Louis, W.S.: Power Measurement in the Distribution Channel. Journal of Marketing Research, 47–52 (1972)

Social Sustainability: Perspectives on the Role of Manufacturing

Paola Fantini[1], Marco Taisch[2], and Claudio Palasciano[2]

[1] Fondazione Politecnico di Milano,
[2] Politecnico di Milano,
Department of Management, Economics and Industrial Engineering, Milan, Italy
paola.fantini@fondazione.polimi.it,
{marco.taisch,claudio.palasciano}polimi.it

Abstract. The notion of social sustainability has been developed aiming at global growth. Policy makers have elaborated on this concept at regional and country level. Institutions and associations representing the scientific and technological environment have proposed their visions. Enterprises have adopted Corporate Social Responsibility practices. In this context, the role of manufacturing may have appeared so far limited to the specific aspects related to the workplaces. However, a broader perspective can lead to an extended awareness on how manufacturing can contribute to the social sustainability.

Keywords: social sustainability, sustainable manufacturing, human factors.

1   Introduction

The concept of sustainability emerged at the end of the eighties in the World Commission on Environment and Development report, which, instead of assessing the state of natural resources, highlighted possible ways to combine economic growth with environmental and societal issues. In particular, the following definition of sustainable development was provided: 'Development that meets the needs of the present without compromising the ability of future generations to meet their own needs' [1].

The "inter and intra-generational equity, the distribution of power and resources, employment, education, the provision of basic infrastructure and services, freedom, justice, access to influential decision-making fora and general 'capacity-building' have all been identified as important aspects of the development paradigm" according to the literature review on social sustainability examined in [2].

Sustainable development has become one of the main concern for policy makers at national and international level as well as the definition of appropriate frameworks for assessment. The problem of assessing social progress has been addressed in the Stiglitz report [3]: novel approaches have been proposed for measuring quality of life from an objective perspective, considering health, education, personal activities, political voice and governance, social connection, environmental conditions, personal insecurity, economic insecurity, but also from a subjective perspective and including a comprehensive assessment of inequalities.

V. Prabhu, M. Taisch, and D. Kiritsis (Eds.): APMS 2013, Part I, IFIP AICT 414, pp. 62–69, 2013.

This paper illustrates how social objectives and concerns of policy makers have been reflected, interpreted and addressed by the manufacturing industry and propose an extended perspective and a roadmap for further research.

2   State of the Art

As sustainability has been recognized as a global challenge, public authorities, institutions and individuals representing the scientific, technological and industrial environment have started discussing how they should contribute to address this issue.

In [4], the American Association for the Advancement of Science recognized analyses shortfalls of sustainable well-being, identifying a set of topics in which science and technology have a significant role to play. CIRP has proposed a multilevel framework for proactively pursuing competitive sustainable manufacturing, involving industry, public authorities and academia, all the stake-holders at the global, supernational and national level [5], while the most recent trends and research challenges have been clearly outlined in [6].

At the macro level, the main stakeholders further elaborate on the themes of research, innovation and education as the key enablers for shaping the future, frequently adopting a participative approach, based on discussion and public consultations. The European Factory of the Future Research Association [7] has undertaken an open consultation on the proposed research roadmap, which includes several topics tightly related with social sustainability, increasing human achievements in future European manufacturing systems, creating sustainable, safe and attractive workplaces for Europe, creating sustainable care and responsibility for employees and citizens in global supply chains.

On different levels, scientists are developing new theories in order to better support from a theoretical viewpoint the integration of social sustainability in the disciplines and practices of manufacturing. A framework for increasing and assessing sustainability awareness among scientists has been developed as a contribution to better integrate sustainability concepts in production research activities [8].

Corporations have become aware of their environmental and social responsibilities, encouraged by regulators and media. Corporate Social Responsibility (CSR) practices have become more and more common, although often fragmented and disconnected from the business strategy. According to [9], "Addressing social issues by creating shared value will lead to self-sustaining solutions that do not depend on private or government subsides". Each company has to find the way most appropriate to its strategy.

In recent years, following to the well-known trends of globalization, transformation from vertical value chains to open value networks, web 2.0, crowdsourcing, dematerialization, virtualization and so on, management theory has developed new approaches which are more coherent with the emergent business and social landscape, leveraging the human factor along with technology enablers. Some researchers have recommended that management should evolve to foster trust and teamwork; to create a fluid, flexible, customized work community environment; to decompose vertical organizational structures towards inter-intra organizational networks with emergent new roles for facilitators and brokers; to create new exciting, entertaining and challenging workplaces for young people [10]. Others promote a cultural change as the solution to reinforce the companies' commitment towards more innovative ways to manage workforce, in a work-life integrated perspective [11].

Relations between organizational factors, individual psychological status and eventually behaviour have been studied for many years under different perspectives and facets. Although the picture is really complex and often fragmented, evidence of relations between contextual factors and individuals empowerment have been demonstrated [12]. In recent years, analysis on employees wellbeing highlights that more than in the past, individual have to deal with different objectives, desires, expectations and responsibilities, which can be clustered in two main categories of work and life. According to [13], "dual-centric experience" provides "more overall satisfaction, greater work-life balance, and less emotional exhaustion", that organization should take care of employees as whole individuals in order to enhance their wellbeing. Companies that implement policies in this sense, giving support for family responsibilities, improving employee health, leaving more time away from work, pursuing education and training, and supporting voluntarism appear to better perform on the financial side as well. Better performance can be related to the capability to attract and retain employees, to more effective behaviour of more satisfied employees, but also to better reputation of the company. Further studies [14] confirmed that line management support and trust is of the utmost importance to establish good relations with employees and thus subsequently favouring employee wellbeing at work.

In [15], the survey's results suggest that company should "create a workplace environment in which workgroup support takes place on a continuous basis. Moreover, managers should place greater relative emphasis on promoting and developing employees' organizational commitment given its high impact on favourable external representation behaviour. These actions will, ultimately, improve the company's performance."

With the increase of complexity and dynamicity of the business and manufacturing environment, and with automation and information technologies becoming more and more pervasive in the factory and in the supply chain, human intelligence knowledge and expertise is highly appreciated. The human-centricity has become a goal for the design and innovation as "the development of a product requires that always be taken into account the perspective of the people who build, maintain and operate it" [16]. "Meta-design theory emphasizes that future use can never be entirely anticipated at design time, as users shape their environments in response to emerging needs; systems should therefore be designed to adapt to future conditions in the hands of end users", as stated by [17]. This concept stands for end-users in domestic environments as well as for employees in a working environment, where co-designing and "human centerdness" are applied in organizational development settings [18]. According to [7] manufacturing is evolving from being perceived as a production-centric operation to a human-centric business with greater emphasis on workers, suppliers and customers in-the-loop". Manufacturing 2.0 [19]envisions "workers and managers alike given more opportunity for continuous development of skills and competences through novel knowledge-delivery mechanisms". The human centricity paradigms involves inclusion for young and elderly people: "Future enterprises will not only be better equipped for transferring skills to a new generation of workers but also proficient in assisting older workers with better user interfaces, intuitive user-experience-driven workflows and other aids, such as mobile and service robots. Furthermore, Manufacturing 2.0 enterprises would be equipped with interactive e-learning tools to facilitate students, apprentices and new workers gaining understanding of advanced manufacturing operations involving new ICT paradigms" [19].

3   Dimensions of Social Sustainability

Defining social sustainability objectives and their corresponding indicators is a challenging task a) due to the multilevel, multi-stakeholder and multifaceted nature of the addressed themes, b) due to the interaction with environmental, economic and institutional aspects, and, finally c) due to the uncertainty about the beliefs and models to be used as a reference. However, the need to monitor and steer sustainable development has challenged policy makers and the scientific and technological community to develop studies for the definition of applicable assessment methods and tools.

Papers, reports and literature reviews on social sustainability assessment, such as [20], [21], [22], [23], [24], [25], [26] [27], clearly show that priority is given to the definition of appropriate set of indicators as practical means to evaluate and compare performances either at macro and at micro level. However, there is a great fragmentation in the conceptual frameworks, so that different dimensions appear in alternative or intermingled lists, used to collect and group indicators. In general, the following limitations can be observed:

-    lack of conceptual clarity in the definition of the dimensions to be assessed, with frequent confusion between impact categories (i.e. child labour, consume privacy), objectives (i.e. equal opportunities), subjects' implementation of policies (i.e. labour practices, respect of indigenous rights) stakeholders groups (i.e. workers, consumers);
-    shortfall in the identification of the stakeholders;
-    poor awareness and representation of the relationships and inter-linkage among and within the dimensions and the indicators.

In the available schemas indicators have been set in relationship with each of the different dimensions, relevant for manufacturing social sustainability, as illustrated in Figure 1, but the interdependencies among these dimensions have not been explicated.

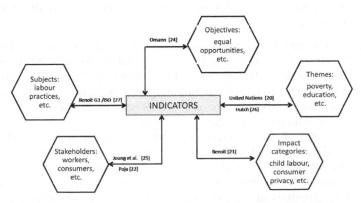

Fig. 1. Dimensions of social sustainability in relationship with indicators

4   Perspectives for Developing a Social Sustainability Roadmap for Manufacturing

Considering the complexity of the subject, in order to overcome the existing issues and better support the progress of social sustainability in manufacturing, a research roadmap is needed. To the authors' judgement, future research will have to thoroughly investigate the complex network of cause-effect relationships and interactions that connect manufacturing and its performances to the sustainability themes, as represented in the simplified schema of Figure 2. In particular, research should address the following topics.

-   The definition of relevant categories for social sustainability to be used in relationship with the manufacturing impact on the different classes of roles and stakeholders. These categories should represent the end-point impact of manufacturing, instantiating the sustainability themes defined by policy makers.
-   The identification of the relevant eco-system roles and stakeholders, considering all the types of interactions that an industrial enterprise directly or indirectly may establish with individuals, associations, private and public institutions. These roles and stakeholders should constitute the mid-point nodes in which to assess the manufacturing impact.
-   The analysis of the effects that manufacturing strategies, policies and practices induce on the eco-system roles, taking into account mutual interactions and interdependencies in the eco-system, and the social and financial implications.

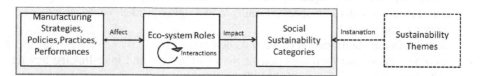

Fig. 2. Manufacturing and Social Sustainability simplified cause-effect relationships

In fact, all the decisions and actions made by manufacturing enterprises create different types of interaction with one or more roles in the eco-systems, even directly or indirectly, by triggering other players' actions and reactions, as illustrated by the following examples.

-   Policies for recruiting, retaining and managing human resources obviously affect internal staff, but also actual or potential candidates for jobs, all their families, other legal entities offering jobs. In addition, policies concerning education/specialization entry levels and training may influence schools and universities to the extent to trigger the creation of special courses, in some cases in collaboration with the manufacturing enterprise.
-   Health, postural, dietary, hygiene programs, screening or caring services offered or incentivized for employees and their families can affect health care systems and contribute to increase health standards in the populations.
-   Environmental monitoring systems set up and managed by a factory may interact with local authorities supervision and contribute to increase safety and security of

the surrounding inhabitants. Furthermore, emergency and disaster recovery plans involving manufacturing staff and equipment might be programmed in collaboration with other institutions and agencies, providing additional environmental and social benefits.

- Procurement policies, supplier evaluation and management can affect local workers, such as service providers' staff employed for ancillary activities in the factories, such as cleaning, packaging, logistics, their health and safety conditions, rights and fair wages as well as the more extensively analysed supply chain employees and their environment, in foreign countries.
- Criteria and procedures for product and service design, marketing and delivery can affect customers health, life style, privacy, but can also impact other roles in the value networks, such as providers for maintenance or application services or end of life operators, who may be favoured, hindered or endangered in their economic and social activities and relationships.
- Involvement and engagement in activities aiming at influencing industrial research, education programs and policies through different forms of association and participation can also shape the future of manufacturing towards more sustainable development.

Manufacturing has traditionally pursued economic, quality, service and flexibility performances. Sustainability objectives have often been superimposed rather than integrated in the corpus of existing theories and practices. Further research is necessary to better understand all the social implications of manufacturing-related processes, decision making, behaviours and the interplay with business and economic results.

To the opinion of the authors, a research roadmap should aim at the definition of a manufacturing sustainability reference model, as the illustrative example of Figure 3, to be used for the analysis, evaluation and revision of the manufacturing theories and practices in order to better assess and improve social sustainability.

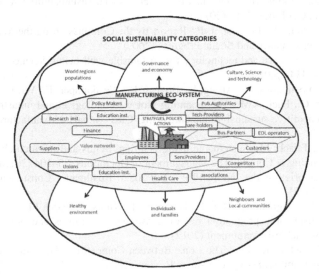

Fig. 3. Dimensions of social sustainability in relationship with indicators

Future research should leverage existing literature from different disciplines, but also evidence from the field, experts judgement, case studies and should address methods and tools to assess and prioritize the types of strategies, policies and actions with higher potential impact on social sustainability categories, as well as viable economic and financial performances. Main achievements should lead to the definition of manufacturing specific policies, indicators frameworks, codes of conducts and principles, guidelines, to support pursuing and assessing social sustainability.

5   Conclusions and Outlook

The knowledge about manufacturing specific current and potential role versus social sustainability is still limited to the main and most evident aspects. Further research is needed to extend the perspective and achieve greater awareness of the different ways in which social sustainability can be pursued through interactions with all the roles and stakeholders of the manufacturing ecosystem.

The authors proposed an approach for a research roadmap that may lead to a reference model, methods and tools to better guide and strengthen the contribution of manufacturing to the global objective of an inclusive and sustainable development.

Acknowledgements. This paper has been developed in the perspective of the research project SO SMART, funded by the European Commission within FP7 (608734).

References

[1] WCED, Our common future: the Bruntland report. Oxford University Press, New York (1987)

[2] Vallance, S., Perkins, H.C., Dixon, J.E.: What is social sustainability? A clarification of concepts. In: Geoforum 2011 (2011)

[3] Stglitz, J.E., Sen, A., Fitoussi, J.-P.: Report by the Commission on the Measurement of Economic Performance and Social Progress (2009)

[4] Holdren, J.P.: Science and technology for sustainable well-being. Science - Published by AAAS, 424–434 (2008)

[5] Jovane, F., Yoshikawa, H., Alting, L., Boer, C.R., Westkamper, E., Williams, D., Tseng, M., Seliger, G., Paci, A.M.: The incoming global technological and industrial revolution towards competitive sustainable manufacturing. CIRP Annals - Manufacturing Technology (2008)

[6] Garetti, M., Taisch, M.: Sustainable manufacturing: trends and research challenges. Production Planning & Control: The Management of Operations, 83–104 (2012)

[7] EFFRA, Factories of the Future PPP - FoF20220 Roadmap - Consultation document, Bruxelles (2012)

[8] Johansson, B., Dagman, A., Rex, E., Nyström, T., Knutson Wedel, M., Stahre, J., Söderberg, R.: Sustainable production research: awareness, masures and development. Intl-Journal-Sustainable-Development (2012)

[9] Porter, M.E., Kramer, M.R.: The Lonk Between Competitive Advantage and Corporate Social Responsibility. Harvard Business Review (2006)

[10] McDonald, P.: It's time for management version 2.0: Six forces redefining the future of modern management. Futures, 797–808 (2011)

[11] Harrington, B., Ladge, J.J.: Present Dynamics and Future Directions for Organizations. Organizational Dynamics, 148–157 (2009)

[12] Siegall, M., Gardner, S.: Contextual factors of psychological empowerment. Personnel Review, 703–722 (2000)

[13] Bourne, K.A., Wilson, F., Lester, S.W., Kickul, J.: Embracing the whole individual: Advantages of a dual-centric perspective of work and life. Business Horizons, 387–398 (2009)

[14] Baptiste, N.R.: Tightening the link between employee wellbeing at work and performance: A new dimension for HRM. Management Decision, 284–309 (2008)

[15] Lages, C.R.: Employees' external representation of their workplace: Key antecedents. Journal of Business Research (2012)

[16] Mavrikios, D., Karabatsou, V., Pappas, M., Chryssolouris, G.: An efficient approach to human motion modeling for the verification of human-centric product design and manufacturing in virtual environments. Robotics and Computer-Integrated Manufacturing, 533–543 (2007)

[17] Maceli, M., Atwood, M.: From Human Factors to Human Actors to Human Crafters. In: iConference, Seattle (2011)

[18] Kronqvist, J., Salmi, A.: Co-Designing (with) Organizations -Human-Centeredness, Participation and Embodiment in Organizational Development (2012)

[19] Majumdar, A., Szigeti, H.: ICT for Manufacturing - The ActionPlanT Vision for Manufacturing 2.0. ActionPlanT (2011)

[20] United Nations, Indicators of Sustainable Development: Guidelines and Methodologies, United Nations, New York (2007)

[21] Benoit-Dorris, C.: Developing Social Sustainability Metrics. In: Roundtable on Social Impacts of the Electronics Sector, Berkeley

[22] Paju, M., Heilala, J., Hentula, M., Heikkila, A., Johansson, B.: Framework and indicators for a sustainable manufacturing mapping methodology. In: Winter Simulation Conference (2010)

[23] Feng, S.C., Joung, C.-B.: An Overview of a Proposed Measurement Infrastructure for Sustainable Manufacturing Metrics. In: The 7th Global Conference on Sustainable Manufacturing (2009)

[24] Omann, I., Spangenberg, J.H.: Assessing Social Sustainability. In: 7th Biennal Conference of the International Society for Ecological Economics, Wien (2002)

[25] Joung, C.B., Carrell, J., Sarkar, P., Feng, S.C.: Categorization of indicators for sustainable manufacturing. Ecological Indicators (2012)

[26] Hutchins, M.J., Sutherland, J.W.: An exploration of mesures of social sustainability and their application to supply chain decisions. Journal of Cleaner Production (2008)

[27] Benoit, C., Vickery-Niederman, G.: Social Sustainability Assessment Literature Review, The Sustainability Consortium, Arizona State University, and University of Arkansas (2011)

Information Flows in Future Advanced Manufacturing Ecosystems

Minna Lanz, Matti Majuri, and Reijo Tuokko

Tampere University of Technology,
Korkeakoulunkatu 10, 33720 Tampere, Finland
{minna.lanz,matti.majuri,reijo.tuokko}@tut.fi
http://www.tut.fi/tte

Abstract. *Manufacturing is the backbone of each and every society, and in order for society to sustain in long run the manufacturing has to be sustainable as well. The sustainability in the field of manufacturing has traditionally been discussed in a sense of operational efficiency and environmental metrics. Rarely the link between individuals working in the company and the efficiency of operations has been established and discussed deeply. This link is information flow that combines both tacit and formal information in a dynamically changing socio-technical environment. In this paper the information flow between individuals in different levels of company hierarchy is utilized as the observation baseline. This paper discusses the information flow within a company and outlines socio-technical challenges needed to solve in order to realize future Advanced Manufacturing Ecosystems.*

Keywords: knowledge management, semantic information, tacit knowledge, systems thinking, social capital, know-how.

1 Introduction

Regarding the information flow two major challenges are identified: content of information and dynamic environment where the information is temporally valid. Today's design and operation control systems produce a variety of data. However, the sheer amount of data that lacks the structure, connectivity and intent cannot be utilized efficiently later on. There is ever the greater need to transfer this unstructured mass of bits and bytes to meaningful information and to human understandable knowledge, as it is understood in the industry. However there are major challenges in understanding the actual content of information flow. Today the information flow should connect the different design departments and activities to be part of the life-time information of a product including its processes and services. For example modern computer-aided design (CAD) tools has made it easier and faster to design products made up of more and more complicated and intricate parts. Without sufficient experience or guidance, todays designer runs the risk of developing product designs that are unnecessarily difficult to produce [14], [12]. Another example of disruptions in information flow

V. Prabhu, M. Taisch, and D. Kiritsis (Eds.): APMS 2013, Part I, IFIP AICT 414, pp. 70–77, 2013.

and/or understanding its content is vividly explained by Redman [16]. He stated that quality errors in manufacturing relating to low quality data may raise costs up to 30%. Furthermore, Redmans study indicates that 8-12% revenue losses occur because of data quality issues. Informally, 40-60% of the expenses in service sector may be consumed as a result of poor data.

It is recognized that environment evolves and changes over the time and the system itself evolves, sometimes unpredictably, during its lifecycle. In recent years changes in the environment have become faster, stronger and harder to predict than ever before. Same time the manufacturing is becoming more decentralized causing challenges in the network level operations management. In order to operate in such dynamic and complex environment best of the both worlds; human intelligence and computers computing power are needed to be combined more sufficient manner. As the unpredictable changes occur, detailed simulations of large systems will become unreliable. Algorithms cannot solve the problems that arise, thus applying human intelligence to solve complex problems or choosing optimal scenario becomes highly important. Paradoxically the current operation strategy has forced human to be the processing unit while computer attempts to make intelligent decision over relatively vague input information. This strategy may improve the effectiveness of manufacturing in limited range of situations but on the other hand it definitely reduces the flexibility and agility of the manufacturing system.

Current engineering and production management methodologies and tools have been created for the old markets where the mass-customization was a norm. The IT-tools for these solutions offer proprietary services and interfaces. This paralyses healthy ecosystem growth, emergence of new start-ups, development and neglects the needs of agile and innovative SMEs. Contemporary tools and services, such as cloud-computing, emphasize on technology in favor of actual industry specific business needs. As a consequence ICT-centric solutions tend to help only in communication, but transfer existing (tedious) work practices in the new media. The current solutions are largely developed from the one perspective respecting the constraints from legacy ICT, not from the modern engineering business processes.

The challenges mentioned above are no doubt look very technical issues. However, technology itself cannot solve the issues. It is very likely that the technology-oriented approach will not be sufficient for the future advanced manufacturing ecosystems. This paper discusses of technical information management, tacit knowledge and system interoperation and relations. By understanding the technical possibilities, social know-how and how human-machine systems interoperate the advanced manufacturing ecosystems can emerge.

2   Considering the Surrounding Systems

2.1   Semantics

The main problem is that the models and documents created with different design and operation management systems are that the documents are meaningless from the knowledge point of view for systems other than their authoring system. The second problem is that the Design Intent is a concept that is not captured by the modern design systems. This raises even bigger challenges for the future manufacturing systems that require this information to provide autonomous reasoning. A case study done in Finnish manufacturing sector highlighted the challenge in capturing the design intent and managing the information flow among various stakeholders [8]. The case study was conducted in a large and globally operating manufacturing company, which possessed large network of subcontractors. The study revealed, that workers personality, human communication, and bureaucracy have a significant effect on what actually gets saved into the information systems, and furthermore what can be retrieved from the system later on. Furthermore the study suggested that the design intent was lost very early from the information content and due to that several important issues were constantly ignored. Different people also have very different ways of doing and understanding things, which may lead to misunderstandings in cooperation.

Knowledge builds on data and/or information that is organized and processed to convey understanding, experience, accumulated learning and expertise. In order to enhance the effectiveness, agility and reactivity of future the manufacturing systems it is needed to look at the detail level; more precisely, where the numbers are coming and how valid those are in given context. On the product design perspective this means that information flow content actually carries the design intent and it can be understood in a context of use. In the manufacturing operations level the simulation results are tied to the given context and are valid in that context. In the recent years industrial standards are being defined in a more computer-readable form, most notably since the emergence of eXtensive Mark-Up Language (XML) -based formats and computing power. XML as a language has number of advantages for developers and implementers. Structural language allows the compilation of specifications, creation of datasets and certain kinds of testing can be performed more easily. However, along the way XML markups have been used as a substitute for modeling the information - a dangerous shortcut that only works in communities that already share a common understanding of the meaning and usage of terms [11], [15].

Knowledge modeling and representation always reflect the view of the modelers on the domain to be modeled, although the ideal should be to initially remain as independent as possible of any purpose or application [17]. More and more information will be retrieved from diverse sources originating from different circumstances and application. Therefore the resultant data are inherently built on different languages and representations that will put high demand on semantic integration solutions. Also, information will be fetched from diverse locations (over the global networks), which will be grounds for extensive use of web technologies. These two basic requirements (semantic integration, access over web) speaks for the adoption of semantic web technologies to describe and integrate (or perhaps rather inter-link) digital content on built environment. Semantic information enables the creation of built-in intelligence into versatile products. Real intelligent functions will be possible to be created based on semantic reasoning algorithms. The difference to "glued" intelligence is significant, because the product and the digital services related to products can utilize more detailed and specific information than traditionally [11].

2.2 Systems Thinking

Centralized systems based on hierarchical data share are giving a way to globally distributed production networks. These networks need to adapt rapidly to the production changes. Due to the resulting larger complexity of heterogeneous interacting components the system can no longer be only guided and controlled based on a human operator. Predicting the future state of dynamic system based on the static and often inaccurate or obsolete models of manufacturing system's state is not reliable or sufficient [10].

According to International Council of Systems Engineering (INCOSE) there is a growing awareness that the revised systems engineering approach is becoming a key to successfully design, develop and sustain the highly complex systems. However the field suffers from the lack of unified principles and models that support a wide range of domains [7]. A shift away from a generic definition and application of systems engineering to a more specifically defined and precise application of systems engineering in diverse domains can thus be expected in the future. The future systems engineering environment will also fully support life cycle perspectives. In many respects, the future of systems engineering can be said to be model-based. A key driver will be the continued evolution of complex, intelligent, global systems that exceed the ability of the humans who design them to comprehend and control all aspects of the systems they are creating. The role of modeling will mature to respond to this need.

2.3 Social Capital

The role of humans in the Factories of the Future will be defined through the stimulation of working environments and conditions that bring about new forms of collaboration and interaction processes among humans, machines and the manufacturing technologies involved. Sustainability of the human capital, in Europe, is subject to the global economic conditions. Age and employment systems need to be adapted, while the societal impact of manufacturing on local environments ought to be taken into account, in terms of energy demands, life quality, natural resources and safety.

Lately, following to the well-known trends of globalization, transformation from vertical value chains to open value networks, web 2.0 and further developments, crowd-sourcing, dematerialization, virtualization etc., management theory has developed new approaches more coherent with the emergent business and social landscape, leveraging the human factor along with technology enablers. However, as the development advances with steady leaps it also causes pressures towards workforce. This pressure comes from dynamic and fast changes in organizational level, new technical solutions requiring faster learning curves and changes in global economy. In the recent years, analysis on employees wellbeing highlights that, more now than in the past, individuals have to deal with different objectives, desires, expectations and responsibilities, which can be clustered in two main categories of work and life. Bourne et al [3] stated that "dual-centric experience more overall satisfaction, greater work-life balance, and less emotional exhaustion", and that organizations should take care of employees as whole individuals in order to enhance their wellbeing.

According to EFFRA [4] manufacturing is evolving from being perceived as a production-centric operation to a human-centric business with greater emphasis on workers, suppliers and customers in-the-loop. ActionPlanT [1] envisions workers and managers alike given more opportunity for continuous development of skills and competences through novel knowledge delivery mechanisms. The human-centricity paradigms involve inclusion for young and elderly people Future enterprises will not only be better equipped for transferring skills to a new generation of workers but also proficient in assisting older workers with better user interfaces, intuitive user-experience-driven workflows and other aids, such as mobile and service robots.

2.4   Technological Advances

According to European Commission communication [5] a digital ecosystem is a self-organizing digital infrastructure aimed at creating a digital environment for networked organizations that supports the cooperation, the knowledge sharing, the development of open and adaptive technologies and evolutionary business models. Boley and Chang [2] proposed definition for a digital ecosystem by terms "open, loosely coupled, domain clustered, demand-driven, self-organizing agent environment", where each agent of each species is proactive and responsive regarding its own benefit/profit but is also responsible to its system. The digital ecosystem approach transposes the concepts to the digital world, reproducing the desirable mechanisms of natural ecosystems.

As several interacting natural ecosystems exist, several digital ecosystems exists due to differentiation and the development of endemic product and services tailored to specific local needs. The key enabling technologies developed within the digital ecosystem research aim at providing a knowledge- and service-oriented infrastructure that supports the spontaneous composition, distribution, evolution and adaptation of ICT-based services. This platform should allow the SME software industry to independently develop (and disseminate on the network) services and software components which will be composed forming complex, evolutive and adopted solutions. These technologies allow the spontaneous development and the cooperative provision of services and solutions, without the need for any keystone player, central coordination or central point of control/failure.

3   Requirements for the Future Advanced Manufacturing Ecosystems

The future advanced manufacturing ecosystems require new and more collaborative approaches, where the technical advantages are understood and accepted, where the social capital is appreciated and utilized and where the interactions of a whole system can be visualized and understood.

As the construction and development of an increasingly artifactual environment continue, little thought has been given to the coherence or compatibility of knowledge between different scientific disciplines. As a result, incompatibilities and contradictions have arisen within that environment, and, most ominously, between it and the surrounding natural environment [18]. Yoshikawa (2008) introduced a term synthesiology. Synthesiology is a term for the theory of integration of scientific and technological knowledge from different disciplines with the needs of society.

McDonald (2011) has recommended that management should evolve to foster trust and teamwork; to create a fluid, flexible, customized work community environment; to decompose vertical organizational structures towards inter-intra organizational networks with emergent new roles for facilitators and brokers; to create new exciting, entertaining and challenging workplaces for young people [13]. Kira et al (2008) emphasize that socially sustainable work organizations are able to both repeat accustomed and devise innovative solutions, and for this reason it is crucial for them to embrace individual stakeholders complexities and encourage them to cultivate it, while at the same time maintaining a holistic view of the organization [9]. Furthermore, Kira et al. [9] suggest that a higher level of collaborative shaping of work (with employee involvement) is highly conducive to sustainable work abilities and development of human resources.

As this paper focuses more on the information flow management in future Manufacturing Ecosystems, the collaboration, motivation and self-organizing interaction between individuals becomes highly important. Fischer [6] summarized well that in interpersonal communication the design intent is mostly casually conveyed and understood based on history, shared experience and circumstances. However, in this modern operation environment each stakeholder has a different context and different understanding of the problem. Communication breakdown occurs when the stakeholders have only little shared context. The message, design intent, gets lost in translation.

4   Summary

All in all the future interoperability among different stakeholders requires more multi-sectoral approach in order to tackle the arisen challenges. The efficient knowledge capture, processing, utilization and reuse as integral part of future product-services requires holistic approach, that includes understanding from following sector:

1. Social and economic sciences (network economics, community buildings, diffusion of knowledge and practices, legal aspects, business and organizational models),
2. System theory, self-organization of complex systems and epistemology
3. Computer science (mainly network architectures, semantic interoperability and formal languages) [5].

Only by adopting the holistic approach in design, operation management and manufacturing the new Advanced Manufacturing Ecosystems can emerge.

References

1. Majumdar, A., Szigeti, H.: ICT FOR MANUFACTURING - The ActionPlanT Vision for Manufacturing 2.0, Factories of the Future 2020 Roadmap. Consultation document. EFFRA - European Factories of the Future Research Association (2012)
2. Boley, H., Chang, E.: Digital Ecosystems: Principles and Semantics. In: IEEE International Conference on Digital Ecosystems and Technologies, Cairns, Australia (2007)
3. Bourne, K., Wilson, F., Lester, S.W., Kickul, J.: Embracing the whole individual: Advantages of a dual-centric perspective of work and life. Business Horizons 52(4), 387–398 (2009)
4. Industrial Advisory Group: Factories of the Future 2020 Roadmap, Consultation document. EFFRA European Factories of the Future Research Association (2012)
5. European Commission: Digital Ecosystems - the enabling technologies and paradigms for fostering endogenous local development, local capacity building and knowledge sharing processes providing tailored and personalized ICT services to citizens and business networks (2013), http://www.digital-ecosystems.org/
6. Fischer, G., Nakakojia, K., Ostwald, J.: Supporting the evolution of design artifacts with representations of context and intent. In: Proceedings of the 1st Conference on Designing Interactive Systems: Processes, Practices, Methods, and Techniques (1995)
7. Anon: Systems Engineering Vision 2020. International Council on Systems Engineering report, INCOSE-TP-2004-004-02 (September 2008)
8. Jarvenpaa, E., Lanz, M., Mela, J., Tuokko, R.: Studying the Information Sources and Flows in a Company - Support for the Development of New Intelligent Systems. In: Proceedings of Flexible Automation and Intelligent Manufacturing (2010)
9. Kira, M., Van Eijnatten, F.M.: Socially Sustainable Work Organizations: A Chaordic Systems Approach. Systems Research and Behavioral Science 25(6), 743–756 (2008)
10. Lanz, M., Nylund, H., Ranta, A., Luostarinen, P., Tuokko, R.: Set-up and first steps on capturing of realistic resource characteristics of an intelligent manufacturing environment. In: Proceedings of Flexible Automation and Intelligent Manufacturing (2010)
11. Lanz, M., Nykanen, O., Aaltonen, J., Ranta, P.A., Koskinen, K.T., Andersson, P.H.: Engineering Intelligence - Product-Service Concepts and Requirements in Industry. In: Proceedings of IEEE International Symposium of Assembly and Manufacturing, ISAM (2013)
12. Lohtander, M., Varis, J.: Collecting manufacturing information in a global distributed manufacturing environment. Mechanika 18(1), 84–88 (2012)
13. McDonald, P.: It's time for management version 2.0: Six forces redefining the future of modern management. Futures of Evolutionary Psychology 43(8), 797–808 (2011)
14. Pulkkinen, A., Rissanen, N., Vainio, V.: PLM state of the practice and future challenges in globally networked manufacturing companies. In: Proceedings of the 1st PDM Forum for Finland-Russia Collaboration, Lappeenranta, April 25-26 (2013)
15. Ray, S.R., Jones, A.: Manufacturing Interoperability. Journal of Intelligent Manufacturing 17, 681–688 (2006)

16. Redman, T.C.: The impact of poor data quality on the typical enterprise. Communications of the ACM 41(2), 79–82 (1998), doi:10.1145/269012.269025
17. Spyns, P., Meersman, R.: Ontology Engineering and (Digital) Business Ecosystems: a case for a Pragmatic Web. IEEE (2007) ISBN 1-4244-0826 831–838
18. Yoshikawa, H.: Synthesiology as sustainability science. Integrated Research System for Sustainability Science 3, 169–170 (2008)

Social Sustainability Challenges for European Manufacturing Industry: Attract, Recruit and Sustain

Cecilia Berlin, Caroline Dedering, Guðbjörg Rist Jónsdóttir, and Johan Stahre

Chalmers University of Technology, Department of Product and Production Development,
Gothenburg, Sweden
{cecilia.berlin,johan.stahre}@chalmers.se,
{carded,gubjorg}@student.chalmers.se

Abstract. The purpose of this paper is to link social sustainability challenges to manufacturing companies, focusing on the upcoming recruitment crisis caused by demographic changes in Europe. The findings are based on literature studies that were validated and reflected upon as the study progressed. The conclusion is that diversity within the manufacturing industry has to be increased in order to expand the pool of possible employees by focusing on three main improvements: providing interesting jobs, work flexibility and an improved image of the industry.

Keywords: Social sustainability, manufacturing industry, demographic change, human resources, recruitment, retention, shared values.

1 Introduction

Manufacturing industries need to take action. The demographic prognosis of Europe for the next two decades will result in an aged population [1], which most likely will mean a recruitment and skills crisis for the industry. In 2020, there will also be a skills gap within the recruitment pool for manufacturing industry [1, 2]. Manufacturing companies are essential to economic growth and sustainability of nations [3, 4], therefore it is crucial that they, in time, become aware of the challenges and take action.

Judging by the current demographic trends in Europe, as shown by the black columns in Figure 1, the current working population (20-55 years) will most likely be replaced by about 20-30 % fewer people. In addition, the health care industry will increasingly be demanding more employees for the caretaking of Europe's aging population [5].

The lack of people to fill the work force will be drastic for manufacturing companies since their recruitment reaches out to a small part of society with limited diversity [6-8]. An illustration of the recruitment pool of possible employees, currently over represented by men aged 35-65 [9-12], is presented in gray in Figure 1. It becomes interesting to examine what other groups in society could be targeted in recruitment, in order to expand the pool.

V. Prabhu, M. Taisch, and D. Kiritsis (Eds.): APMS 2013, Part I, IFIP AICT 414, pp. 78–85, 2013.

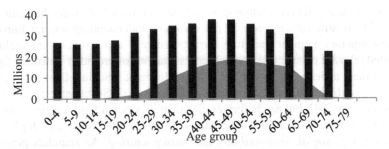

Fig. 1. Age distribution of countries in the European Union [13] – the gray field illustrates the pool of possible employees for manufacturing companies

Top-level industry management as well as societal leaders like the European Commission (via the growth strategy known as *Europe 2020*) have acknowledged these growing problems and the need to formulate socially sustainable strategies to tackle them. This paper presents preparatory efforts (primarily a literature study) for the Coordination and Support Action (CSA) "SO SMART" (Socially Sustainable Manufacturing for the Factories of the Future), which will be funded by the European Commission in 2013. In this paper, different aspects of social sustainability will be explored in relation to what the demographics crisis means for manufacturing companies.

The term Social Sustainability, and the many dimensions it includes, are still being defined. However, most sustainability definitions spring from the World Commission on Environment and Development's (WCED) definition of sustainable development:

"development which meets the needs of the present without comprising the ability for future generations to meet their own needs" [14] .

This definition describes sustainability in broad terms and applies to environmental, economic and social sustainability. The social aspect of sustainability has often been associated with equity among people and equal opportunities [15]. Littig and Griessler have defined social sustainability in relation to work and lifestyle as:

"the freedom to choose at any stage in life between different forms of work (work arrangements, field of work) or lifestyles, while being at all times entitled to individual social security" [15].

That is, all individuals should have the same opportunities for seeking jobs and being accepted in all fields of work, regardless of societal group. As stated earlier, diversity among manufacturing industry employees is lesser than the diversity of society as a whole, resulting in a socially unsustainable industry by this definition.

The question that needs to be asked is therefore: which aspects of social sustainability should manufacturing companies focus on in order to become more resilient to the demographic challenges of 2020?

2   Method

To better understand the concept of Social Sustainability and what it means for manufacturing companies, a multi-stage literature study was carried out. Literature was sought out on many levels, including scientific literature, but since the term Social Sustainability is still taking shape in the common understanding among Europeans, other contemporary popular literature formats, surveys and reports were included if these added relevant perspective, medial representations or provided statistical figures.

Like other aspects of Sustainable Development, Social Sustainability has connotations to the classic inter-generational definition of "Sustainable Development" mentioned earlier [14], but needs further clarification since it has historically been the least defined of the sustainability dimensions. Therefore, the initial search phase used broad terms, e.g. *social, sustainability* and *manufacturing*. As searches progressed, new keywords and keyword combinations were identified (including *Corporate Social Responsibility, attractive jobs*, and *employees + wants/expectations/demands etc.*) and used to refine the literature search towards addressing demographics forecasts and the prognosticated skills gap, and to determine what has been written about the impacts on manufacturing industry. Once collected, literature was categorized into emergent topics and themes in an inductive, qualitative process involving periodic internal validation and reflection by the authors.

This paper reports on a subset of data from the literature search. Starting from the question at the end of the Introduction, the main theme is how manufacturing industries may approach the challenges of the future European demographics, from the perspective of how to recruit and retain personnel. The topics reported on are:

- Social sustainability within companies
- Factors that attract employees to a company and/or job
- What manufacturing companies can improve to attract people
- Examples of social sustainability practices in companies

3   Results and Analysis

Results from the literature study are presented in this chapter organized by identified themes, along with strategies that manufacturing industry may adopt in order to address the upcoming challenges of 2020. The strategies, as identified by the authors, spring from topics listed earlier and include three aspects: starting in the core business; attractive jobs; and the manufacturing industry's image.

3.1   Gaps in the Literature

One aim of the literature study was to identify ways to increase the diversity, and thereby the size, of the recruitment pool for manufacturing industries in Europe, for example by targeting underrepresented groups. Literature was found on a limited range of society groups - primarily young, elderly, women and disabled. Other groups expected by the authors, such as foreign-born, were not represented in the found literature but may still deserve attention. Furthermore, a limited amount of literature was found that was specific to manufacturing industry in Europe. Therefore, the authors have also used literature from the United States on manufacturing industries, as well as literature on other industry types that face similar challenges within Europe.

3.2   Start in the Core Business

For companies to be socially sustainable they have to directly associate social sustainability with their core business [16], thus focusing on their employees instead of e.g. charity work outside the business, which is not value adding for the company [16, 17]. The long-term social impact is the largest when successful social sustainability action is closely associated with core business gains. The company's objective is to create shared values, where both the company and the surrounding society benefit [16]. This is a complicated task, requiring long-term thinking.

3.3   Attractive Jobs

Different societal groups have different "wants", i.e. needs and expectations, when it comes to jobs, as shown in the literature summarized in Table 1. In addition, the table indicates which of those "want-factors" are relevant to manufacturing companies in a contemporary perspective. Some "wants" which were found in available literature can be considered less pressing for manufacturing companies to act upon, since those wants are already fulfilled.

Table 1. What do different societal groups want from a job and is it relevant to manufacturing industry?

Societal Group	Wants identified in literature	Relevant to manufacturing?
Overall	Interesting work [18] Work flexibility [19]	*Relevant:* There is little work flexibility in manufacturing industry [19]
Young	Wages, Job security, Personal growth [20, 21]	*Irrelevant:* Wages and job security in manufacturing are among the highest [22] *Relevant:* Personal growth [23]
Elderly	Sympathetic environment, Ergonomics, Loyalty [20]	*Irrelevant:* Manufacturing companies are now very conscious about work conditions [9]
Women	Work-life balance [24-26]	*Relevant:* Flexibility, see "Overall"
Disabled	Support [27]	*Relevant:* Companies are afraid of hiring disabled workers due to the extra costs and non-suitable work tasks [27]

The literature revealed two main challenges when it comes to attracting workers to manufacturing companies: to offer interesting jobs and to provide work flexibility.

Interesting Job. People want a challenging job that involves interaction with people and a feeling of importance in their working role [20, 21, 28]. In addition, they want opportunities to develop [18] as well as variety, meaning different work tasks. According to the literature, women associate success with having an interesting job according to the definitions above [26].

Flexible Job. Flexibility in the workplace means letting employees have some control over when, where and how much they work [19]. Work-life balance is also about flexibility, but on a higher level, where the job enables parents to take care of their children, by means of flexible work hours [25] but also through parental leave, vacation, and access to child care [19].

3.4   The Manufacturing Industry Image

An important part of attracting a larger recruitment pool is to present a desirable image of working within manufacturing industry. As for today, manufacturing industry has an undeservedly negative reputation, where people understand the importance of the jobs but are not interested in those jobs for themselves. Especially young people have low interest in the jobs since the common perception is that manufacturing is dirty and not well paid, although it is simultaneously considered to be high-tech and require high-skilled workers [12]. Giffi and McNelly [8] argue that high-skilled women working within manufacturing do consider the jobs interesting but other literature [29] suggests that women are struggling with (social) acceptance in male dominated industries, mainly due to a lack of role models. Therefore, to overcome the problem, "good practice" companies ensure that their image is modern and open, by providing real role models and having a female-friendly working environment [6].

3.5   Examples from Different Industries

There are many companies that have already recognized that employee well-being is the key to retaining competent workers within the company, as well as attracting the best ones. Google is famously noted as the most wanted employer in the world today [30], which focuses on keeping work interesting both by adapting tasks to the workers' skills and by encouraging the workers to take on new challenges [31]. Another company that has realized the importance of letting workers develop is Rio Tinto Alcan Iceland (ISAL), an aluminum producer in Iceland. This company has initiated upper secondary level schooling for those of their workers who have only completed primary education. The school is part-time where classes are both during and outside work hours, so the students are still working full time. The aim is to increase the competence, confidence and leadership skills of the workers [32]. Citigroup, an American bank, has seen the benefits of working with internal job mobility [33]. They have therefore created an internal talent market, so when there is a job opening they recruit internally for the right talent, since employees with a broad skillset will make it easier for the company to adapt to changes.

   To increase the involvement of women in the manufacturing workforce, companies have to enable their workers - both men and women - to combine work and family life. For example, the global company Siemens is working with career-and-children combination by offering on-site childcare, support for workers returning from parental leave and elderly care to create a more flexible and attractive workplace [34].

   For manufacturing companies it will not be enough to change the work tasks to attract a broader workforce pool; the work environment and industry image need to be changed with it. Modern manufacturing has come a long way from the stereotypically., dirty and noisy factories - the Volkswagen "Glass factory" in downtown Dresden, Germany, an automotive assembly factory with glass walls and wooden floors [35], is an extreme example of that intentional image change.

When companies have less diversity among their employees than there is in society, they should look into which societal groups are not being represented, and target them especially when recruiting. Deloitte has created a step-by-step approach, summarized below, that is targeted especially at recruiting women, but the steps can be adapted to other groups as well:

- Start at the top of the organization
- Address gender bias head-on
- Create a more flexible work environment
- Foster sponsorship
- Promote personal development
- Build a strong employer brand

4 Discussion and Conclusion

To overcome the foreseen labor crisis due to the rapidly changing demographics of Europe, manufacturing companies need to expand their pool of potential employees. In order to do so, this paper suggests that industry should focus on increasing diversity within their workforce, by reaching out to the societal groups that are currently described as in minority within the industry; primarily women and young people. In order to do so, the image of manufacturing needs to change, to become an attractive career option.

A way of approaching this is shown in Figure 2. The authors would like to stress the importance of starting by improving and integrating Social Sustainability in the core business, *before* working on improving the image. When it comes to attracting workers, work environment and work content has to be improved first, with interesting jobs, more flexibility and more family-friendly working conditions. By anticipating what potential workers want and changing the organization accordingly, companies will attract all groups of society and thereby become more socially sustainable. In this process, long-term thinking is the key, i.e. to always start within the walls of the company by actively supporting, developing and retaining the already recruited workforce. After internal stability has been achieved, it has to be clearly and inclusively communicated to society in order to improve the industry's image (Figure 2).

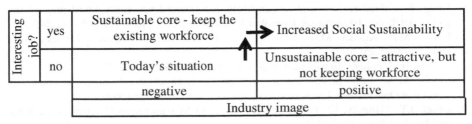

Fig. 2. Matrix of approach for companies; the arrows suggest a progression from today's situation to an ideal, socially sustainable solution to the recruitment challenges

Gaps were also found in the literature regarding societal groups that should be attracted to increase diversity; also, there is a lack of research that specifically examines the European context. The authors see great potential for the aforementioned SO SMART-project to address many of these research and analysis gaps.

When manufacturing has become an attractive career option for people from all groups of society, the manufacturing companies of Europe can commence their journey of social sustainability. Even more importantly, they can then become a sustainable business able to withstand the crisis and remain an attractive source of employment, development and stability for the European labor force.

References

1. Dobbs, R., et al.: The world at work: Jobs, pay and skills for 3.5 billion people. McKinsey Global Institute (2012)
2. Manpower Group, Talent Shortage Survey Report (2011)
3. Manufacturing Institute, Facts About Manufacturing, pp. 1–68 (2011)
4. Mohan, S.: U.S. must revive manufacturing (2008)
5. Christopherson, S.: Childcare and Elderly Care: What Occupational Oppurtunities for Women? In: OECD Labour Market and Social Policy Occasional Papers (1997)
6. Rübsamen-Waigmann, H., et al.: Women in industrial research: A wake up call for European industry. European Commission Directorate-General for Research (2006)
7. Donkin, R.: Employers ignore skills shortages at their peril. The failure to invest in vocational education and training will damage British productivity. In: Financial Times 2006, p. 11. The Financial Times Limited, London (2006)
8. Giffi, C.A., McNelly, J.: Untapped resource; How manufacturers can attract, retain, and advance talented women. Manufacturing Institute, U.S. (2013)
9. Jörn-Henrik, T., Andreas, G., Miczka, S.: The impact of the demographic transition on manufacturing. Journal of Manufacturing Technology Management 18(8), 985–999 (2007)
10. van Ours, J.C., Stoeldraijer, L.: Age, Wage and Productivity in Dutch Manufacturing. De Economist 159(2), 113–137 (2011)
11. Persson, E., Rahm, F.: De yngre drabbas när jobben inom industrin minskar (2005)
12. Giffi, C.A., DeRocco, E.S.: Made in America? What the Public thinks about manufacturing today. Deloitte and The Manufacturing Institute (2010)
13. Eurostat, Population on 1 January by five years age groups and sex, European Commision (2012)
14. World Commission on Environment and Development (WCED), Our common future. Oxford University Press, Oxford (1987)
15. Littig, B., Griessler, E.: Social sustainability: a catchword between political pragmatism and social theory. International Journal of Sustainable Development 8(1), 65–79 (2005)
16. Porter, M.E., Kramer, M.R.: Creating shared value. Harvard Business Review, 1–17 (January-February 2011)
17. Lovins, H.: Employee Engagement is Key to Sustainable Success (2012)
18. Lewis, M.A.: Lean production and sustainable competitive advantage. International Journal of Operations & Production Management 20(8), 959–978 (2000)
19. Bond, J.T., Galinsky, E.: Workplace Flexibility in Manufacturing Companies. Families and Work Institute, USA (2011)

20. Kovach, K.A.: What motivates employees? Workers and supervisors give different answers. Business Horizons 30(5), 58–65 (1987)
21. Zukin, C., Szeltner, M.: Talent Report: What Workers Want in 2012, John J. Heldrich Center for Workforce Development at Rutgers. The State University of New Jersey, New Jersey (2012)
22. Näringsliv, S.: Löner och Löneförmåner (2011), http://www.svensktnaringsliv.se/fragor/fakta_om_loner_och_arbetstid/fola2012/3-loner-och-loneformer_163227.html (April 20, 2013)
23. Langdon, D., Lehrman, R.: The Benefits of Manufacturing Jobs, E.A.S.A. U.S. Department of Commerce, Editor 2012: Washington, DC, USA, p. 10 (2012)
24. Barbulescu, R., Bidwell, M.: Do Women Choose Different Jobs from Men? Mechanisms of Application Segregation in the Market for Managerial Workers. Organization Science, Articles in Advance, 1–20 (2012)
25. Accenture, Defining Success - 2013 Global Research Results (2013)
26. LinkedIn, What do Women Want at Work? Linkedin Corporation (2013)
27. Domzal, C., Houtenville, A., Sharma, R.: Survey of Employer Perspectives on the Employment of People with Disabilities. Technical Report, Prepared under contract to the Office of Disability and Employment Policy U.S. Department of Labor, Editor 2008, McLean (2008)
28. de Lange, A.H., De Witte, H., Notelaers, G.: Should I stay or should I go? Examining longitudinal relations among job resources and work engagement for stayers versus movers. Work & Stress 22(3), 201–223 (2008)
29. Aulin, R., Jingmond, M.: Issues confronting women participation in the construction industry. In: Mwakali, J., Alinaitwe, H. (eds.) Advances in Engineering and Technology - Contribution of Scientific Research in Development, pp. 312–318. Makere University, Uganda Entebbe (2011)
30. Light, J.: Google is No.1 on List Of Desired Employes (2011)
31. Sullivan, J.: A case study of Google recruiting (2005)
32. Guðfinnsdóttir, H.B., Stóriðjuskólinn, G.R.: Jónsdóttir (2013)
33. Buning, N., et al.: Solving the skills crisis. Accenture - Journal of High-Performance Business (March 2011)
34. Siemens. How to balance family and career (2013), http://www.siemens.com/sustainability/en/core-topics/employees/references/family-and-career.htm (cited April 12, 2013)
35. Glaeserne Manufaktur. A Car Factory in the Centre of Town (2011), http://www.glaesernemanufaktur.de/en/idea (May 10, 2013)

Energy-Efficiency Concept for the Manufacturing Industry

Volker Stich, Niklas Hering, Christian Paul Starick, and Ulrich Brandenburg

Institute for Industrial Management at RWTH Aachen University, Pontdriesch 14/16,
52062 Aachen, Germany
{Volker.Stich,Niklas.Hering,Christian.Starick,
Ulrich.Brandenburg}@fir.rwth-aachen.de

Abstract. Depletion of fossil energy sources, rising energy prices and govern-ment regulation coerces manufacturing companies to foster their energy-efficiency. Among others, Information and communication technologies (ICT) are considered to be major enablers for improving the energy-efficiency. In this paper a concept for energy-efficiency based on an Event-driven Architecture (EDA) using Complex-Event-Processing (CEP) is presented that supports the integration of sensor data from the shop-floor level into the company's decision support systems. Finally, a use-case for implementing the proposed concept in a real production environment is presented.

Keywords: Energy-Efficiency, Real-Time Capability, Event-driven Architecture, Complex Event Processing, Production Planning and Scheduling.

1 Introduction

The so-called "energy concept 2050" of the German Federal Government calls for a complete change of the German energy supply. The ambition is to establish one of the most sustainable and energy-efficient economies. By the year 2020 the proportion of renewable energy sources such as wind, solar and water power should account for up to 35% of the German energy mix [1]. The manufacturing industry is one of the big-gest consumers of primary energy (31%) and one of the largest emitters of CO_2 [2]. Although energy intensity has declined within the European Union over the last 30 years there is still an unrealized long-term energy efficiency economical potential in the industry sector of almost 60 per cent [3]. Among others, Information and Commu-nication Technologies (ICT) play an important role for measurement, control and improvement of energy efficiency in manufacturing [4], [5]. ICT that is relevant for energy efficiency include Supervisory Control And Data Acquisition Systems (SCADA), Manufacturing Execution Systems (MES), Energy Management Systems (EMS) and Enterprise Resource Planning (ERP) Systems. However, the problem in manufacturing companies is how to use ICT and seamlessly integrate it into their production system.

V. Prabhu, M. Taisch, and D. Kiritsis (Eds.): APMS 2013, Part I, IFIP AICT 414, pp. 86–93, 2013.
© IFIP International Federation for Information Processing 2013

The EU research project "Sense&React" aims at providing support for manufacturing companies to implement an ICT-infrastructure that feeds decision support systems to increase energy-efficiency. Therefore, role-specific aggregated information from various sources is provided to employees in manufacturing environments using a factory wide sensing and ICT end-to-end infrastructure. Among other things, a real-time optimisation method for energy efficiency shall be developed. [6]

In this paper, a detailed energy efficiency concept is presented. It acts as a conceptual framework that will support companies to analyse their production state regarding energy efficiency, providing them with detailed information about deviations from their targets (e.g. energy plan), and provide information regarding energy efficiency for production planning and control.

2   State-of-the-Art: Real-Time Capable Information Integration for Supporting Energy Efficiency in the Manufacturing Industry

As a first rough definition energy-efficiency can be expressed as the ratio between the useful output of a process and the energy input into a process [7]. The term energy efficiency is closely related to the term of energy productivity. Reinhart et al. define an increase in energy productivity as producing the same amount of products in the right time, with the right quality consuming less energy [8]. For companies of the manufacturing industry consuming less energy always means to reduce costs. Basically energy costs for manufacturing companies comprise of two components [9]:

- **Basic energy price**: Based on the total amount of energy consumed and measured in kilowatt-hours.
- **Price for peak demand** (price per kilowatt): Calculated based on the monthly (sometimes yearly) highest peak demand.

Therefore, in order to reduce energy costs and increase energy-efficiency, companies need a profound knowledge about their energy consumption in real-time. To realize the compliance of hard time constraints in technical processes, so called 'real-time systems' define today's information processing. Fleisch et al. [10] refer to a further development of production and logistics, containing ubiquitous computing and information systems. The 'Internet of Things' is a concrete approach for the realization of decentralized and completely integrated data handling [10]. To enable an autonomous data exchange between goods among themselves and with their environment, embedded systems are combined with Radio Frequency Identification (RFID) and sensor technology [10]. Within defined ranges, so called 'smart players' as self-contained and communication capable objects are able to make decisions and initiate activities independently [11]. This leads to a decentralization of the control of the material flow and to a need of low communication depth. The Electronic Product Code (EPC) and its related information services (EPCIS) are part of the implementation of the 'Internet of Things' [11].

Another important factor in providing information about production processes is sensing technology. Its significant developments as well as communication technology have become a relevant part in production systems. Whereas to today the use of wireless technology has mainly been limited to production monitoring and production system performance measurement applications [12] now a new generation of sensors is prevailing. Its characteristics are embeddable size devices, the possibility of wireless and untethered mode of operation, so called smart items and the Wireless Sensor Networks (WSNs). These networks are much acclaimed for many purposes and will be used in a variety of contexts [13]. Because of the demanding industrial requirements, security reasons and high degree of availability the integration of wireless IT technologies at shop floor level is often impeded [14], but by multi-channel communication interferences can be alleviated. With it parallel transmissions over different channels are enabled and the network throughput is improved [13]. To gain real-time visibility and traceability at the shop-floor level RFID technologies offer the capability of automatic and accurate object data capturing [15]. Therefore the management of the shop-floor and also the management of work-in-progress (WIP) can continuously be improved [16]. To master the challenge of the authentication management procedure a shared key between entities is needed. As one solution, a common key between two nodes can be generated which uses the secret key of one node and the identity of the other [17]. Also considerable is an innovation called push technology which can be a big support for shop-floor monitoring and training. The software client gets necessary information automatically without manual searching in data lists [18]. Moreover, mobile asset tracking and indoors localization sensing technologies have become popular. Their ranges of application are workforce productivity analysis, workforce training and safety monitoring. For outdoor environments and personnel tracking e. g. movable video camera systems have been proposed and pointed out the constraints when using vision-based tracking systems such as visual clutter or occluding and moving obstacles [19]. As analyses on human based assembly systems have shown, human operators are contemplated as major flexibility enablers because of their ability to react directly with changing products and market situations [20]. Hence it must be a key objective to integrate the human workers flexibly in the process, create the right conditions for them and allow them to perform different tasks. Bar code identification has been a proven, low cost and reliable technology and is extensively used for a long time now. But Radio Frequency Identification technology could prevail over the last decades because of the barcode's visual contact requirement and its inability of real time updates and of tracking single items [21].

3   Approach for an Energy-Efficiency Concept for the Discrete Manufacturing Industry

In order to use ICT and sensor networks (and therefore improve energy-efficiency) the concept of event-driven architectures (EDA) has gained acceptance as a new architectural paradigm for dealing with event streams produced by continuously data-emitting sensor networks [22], [23], [24]. Each event therefore contains general metadata (event ID, event-timestamp, event type, event occurrence number), and event-specific information such as sensor ID and data [25]. Due to the steadily increasing amount of available data it is necessary to detect patterns within a cloud of data. Complex event processing (CEP) is an event processing model introduced by Luckham [26] that can be used to identify those patterns of events that are significant for the application domain [22].

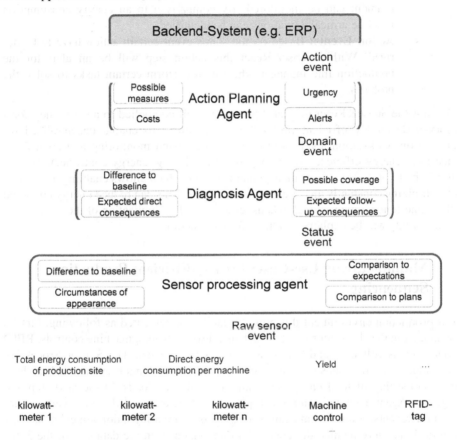

Fig. 1. Structural event model using CEP for energy-efficiency adapted from [22]

Fig. 1 illustrates the structural event model that is used for implementing the energy-efficiency concept in the manufacturing industry. It comprises of four hierarchical layered event types significant for the production environment [22]:

- **Raw Sensor Events:** Data collected from shop-floor sensor devices such as kilowatt-meters, machine-controls, or RFID tags attached to loading equipment. Problems often occur due to technical difficulties such as unreliable readings so the data has to be cleaned and pre-processed. Examples for raw sensor events are load curves of machines.
- **Domain Events:** In a next step the cleaned data has to be mapped to domain concepts. In a production system the load curves of the

individual machines (Raw sensor event) can be synthesized to an overall load curve of the production system. Therefore, in this context examples of domain concepts are production events characterized by total energy consumption or work-in-progress.

- **Status Events:** Within this diagnosis step the domain events are synthesized to status events. Therewith, the overall state of the physical environment can be monitored. By comparison to an energy consumption baseline critical deviations can be identified.
- **Action Events:** Based on the status event certain action have to be derived. Within Sense&React this action step will be an alert for the production line manager who might perform certain tasks to solve the problem.

Within the Sense&React project this concept will be applied to a case-study for a factory-wide energy efficient production. The aim is to enable decentralized re-planning on workstation level and to realize centralized monitoring and controlling concerning energy efficiency on management level (e. g. energy controller). The result will be to provide a power management system, which allows enabling, document and optimizing constantly an efficient use of energy. This can reduce energy costs and at the same time climate critical exhaust emissions. The application of the concept for the case-study will be explained in the following section.

4   Manufacturing Use-Case: Energy-Efficient Production Sequencing

For a production environment this concept can be implemented as following. Firstly, raw data from the shop-floor sensors such as kilowatt-meters, machine controls, RFID readers etc. is collected and raw sensor events are created. The Sensor Processing Agent cleans the raw sensor events[1] and maps them to domain events such as load curves consisting of total energy consumption and peak loads. In the next step, the Diagnosis Agent executes continuous queries on the stream of domain events to derive status events. Status events can be derived by comparing a domain event such as the total load curve against the energy baseline taken from the database of the ERP-system. Then, an action alert is created in this case an Alert Event containing a visualization of the detected deviation from the energy plan. A context-sensitive distribution of the Alert Event to a production line manager is also part of the Sense&React Integrated System illustrated by Fig. 2. The production line manager then manipulates the order sequence under consideration of e.g. delivery dates, availability of material taken from the ERP-system. The integrated backlog processing prioritizes orders to meet the planned delivery dates. The system schedules orders under consideration of restrictions such as conflicting targets (e.g. energy-efficiency vs. delivery time) or the limited availability of resources.

---

[1] Filtering algorithms can be a source of support by dividing the useable data collected from shop-floor sensors from noise and measurement errors.

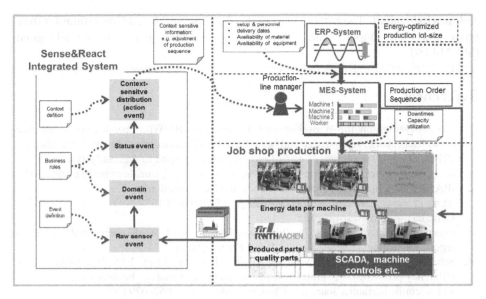

Fig. 2. Model of the energy-flexible Production sequencing

5   Outlook and Further Research

The control and exact prediction of the energy consumption of production processes under cost and purchasing aspects will become an important component of production planning and control in the near future. The main issues in this context are: Dispatching of energy-intensive orders in periods of lower energy costs and consideration of variable energy prices; short and middle term forecasting of energy consumption; support of seasonal purchase of energy; prevention of cost intensive overload scenarios (exceeding the contracted quantity of energy); directed manipulation of load curves; collection and consolidation of energy consumption data and continuous comparison with planned load curves.

The proposed concept provides a support for manufacturing industries to integrate energy relevant data information from sensors and in-process measurements into the planning systems. The use-case presented in this paper will be realized in the demonstration plant at the RWTH Aachen Campus Cluster Logistics which offers a real manufacturing plant for demonstration purposes. The demonstration plant is open to the public so interested companies can adapt the approach easily. The benefit for manufacturing companies will the ability to reduce energy costs. This can be done reducing total energy consumption as well as smoothing load profiles and avoiding peak load penalties. Additionally, the concept of CEP can easily be adapted to various kinds of optimization problems that require real-time information from the shop-floor. Further research has to focus on determining quantitative relations between production and energy-related targets for a given production setting e.g. a job shop production. Determining these interdependencies will help companies to act proactively upon the increasing uncertainty caused by energy-price and supply volatility by choosing the right energy-tariffs and adapting their production planning and control.

Acknowledgement. The authors wish to thank the Sense&React Consortium for their input and their support. The Sense&React project is funded by the EU grant FP7-314350.

References

1. Bundesministerium für Wirtschaft und Technologie (BMWi). Energiekonzept für eine umweltschonende, zuverlässige und bezahlbare Energieversorgung. Report (September 28, 2010), http://www.bmu.de/fileadmin/bmu-import/files/pdfs/allgemein/application/pdf/energiekonzept_bundesregierung.pdf
2. IEA. Tracking Industrial, Energy Efficiency and CO2 Emissions, http://www.iea.org/textbase/nppdf/free/2007/tracking_emissions.pdf
3. International Energy Agency, World Energy Outlook 2012, World energy outlook special report, International Energy Agency, Paris, France (2012)
4. Schönsleben, P., Bunse, K., Vodicka, M., Brüllhart, M., Ernst, F.O.: Integrating energy efficiency performance in production management - gap analysis between industrial needs and scientific literature. Journal of Cleaner Production 19, 667–679 (2011)
5. May, G., Taisch, M., Stahl, B., Sadr, V.: Toward Energy Efficient Manufacturing: A Study on Practices and Viewpoint of the Industry. In: Emmanouilidis, C., Taisch, M., Kiritsis, D. (eds.) Advances in Production Management Systems. IFIP AICT, vol. 397, pp. 1–8. Springer, Heidelberg (2013)
6. Sense&React project homepage (March 19, 2013), http://www.sense-react.eu/
7. Kuhlmann, F., Amende, M.: EPC-Informationsservices (EPCIS) und Umsetzung im EPC-Showcase. Konzept und Anwendung des EPCIS im EPCglobal-Netzwerk. Hg. v. GS1 Germany GmbH. GS1 Germany GmbH (2009) (in German)
8. Reinhart, G., Geiger, F., Karl, F., Wiedmann, M.: Handlungsfelder zur Realisierung energieeffizienter Produktionsplanung und -steuerung. ZWF 106(9), 596–600 (2011) (in German)
9. Erlach, K., Westkämper, E. (eds.): Energiewertstrom: Der Weg zur energieeffizienten Fabrik. Fraunhofer Verl. Stuttgart (2009) (in German)
10. Fleisch, E., Christ, O., Dierkes, M.: The Business Vision of the Internet of Things. In: Fleisch, E., Mattern, F. (Hrsg.) Das Internet der Dinge. Ubiquitous Computing und RFID in der Praxis: Visionen, Technologien, Anwendungen, Handlungsanleitungen, pp. 3–37. Springer, Berlin (2005) (in German)
11. Bottani, E., Rizzi, A.: Economical assessment of the impact of RFID technology and EPC system on the fast-moving consumer goods supply chain. International Journal of Production Economics 112(2), 548–569 (2008)
12. Zhou, S., Ling, W., Peng, Z.: An RFID-based remote monitoring system for enterprise internal production management. International Journal of Advanced Manufacturing Technology 33(7-8), 837–844 (2007)
13. Incel, O.D.: A survey on multi-channel communication in wireless sensor networks. Computer Networks 55(13), 3081–3099 (2011)
14. Chryssolouris, G.: Manufacturing Systems. Theory and Practice, 2nd edn. Springer, New York (2006)
15. Chalasani, S., Boppana, R.: Data Architectures for RFID Transactions. IEEE Transactions on Industrial Informatics 3(3), 246–257 (2007)

16. Huang, G.Q., Zhang, Y.F., Chen, X., Newman, S.T.: RFID-enabled real-time Wireless Manufacturing for adaptive assembly planning and control. Journal of Intelligent Manufacturing 19(6), 701–713 (2008)

17. Fanian, A., Berenjkoub, M., Saidi, H., Gulliver, T.A.: A high performance and intrinsically secure key establishment protocol for wireless sensor networks. Computer Networks 55(8), 1849–1863 (2011)

18. Makris, S., Michalos, G., Chryssolouris, G.: A Pushlet-Based Wireless Information Environment for Mobile Operators in Human Based Assembly Lines. In: 7th International Conference on Digital Enterprise Technology (DET 2011), Athens, Greece, pp. 622–631 (2011)

19. Teizer, J., Vela, P.A.: Personnel tracking on construction sites using video cameras. Advanced Engineering Informatics 23(4), 452–462 (2009)

20. Feldmann, K., Slama, S.: Highly Flexible Assembly. Scope and Justification. Annals of the CIRP 50(2), 489–499 (2001)

21. Stankovski, S., Lazarevic, M., Ostojic, G., Cosic, I., Puric, R.: RFID technology in product/part tracking during the whole life cycle. Assembly Automation 29(4), 364–370 (2009)

22. Dunkel, J.: On Complex Event Processing for Sensor Networks. In: International Symposium on Autonomous Decentralized Systems, ISADS 2009, pp. 1–6 (2009)

23. Bruns, R., Dunkel, J.: Event-Driven Architecture. Softwarearchitektur für ereignisgesteuerte Geschäftsprozesse. Springer, Heidelberg (2010)

24. Michelson, B.M.: Event-Driven Architecture Overview. Event-Driven SOA is just part of the EDA story, Boston (2006)

25. Dunkel, J., Bruns, R., Pawlowski, O.: Complex Event Processing in Sensor-based Decision Support Systems. In: Nag, B. (Hg.) Intelligent Systems in Operations, pp. 64--79. IGI Global (2010)

26. Luckham, D.: The power of events. An introduction to complex event processing in distributed enterprise systems, 3rd print. Addison-Wesley, Boston (2005), Online verfügbar unter http://www.worldcat.org/oclc/255701022

Attacking the Critical Parts in Product Development

Marin Platform – Building Flexible Structural Elements for Boats

Bjørnar Henriksen and Carl Christian Røstad

SINTEF Technology and Society, 7465 Trondheim, Norway
{bjornar.henriksen,carl.c.rostad}@sintef.no

Abstract. The product cycle is changing, where time legs are shorter, high volume- and cash cow-phases fading. Rapid product introduction and customization are keywords, and often associated with modularization. The objective is to create a flexible product design, not requiring changes in the overall product design every time a new variant is introduced. This has been a feasible strategy for manufacturers of small boats in high-cost countries where an incremental development process is well suited for modularization. However, also more radical innovations are needed, not only change modules and product configurations but also have to develop new product platforms. We then have to deal with the critical, resource demanding processes. This conceptual paper describes how boat builders take modularization to a higher lever by attacking the critical parts in product development, i.e. the structural elements of boats.

Keywords: Innovation, modularization, product development, leisureboat.

1 Introduction

At an IMS (Intelligent Manufacturing System) meeting in Zurich in 2007, leading academics and industrialists identified four major drivers for change [1]; globalization of manufacturing; extended enterprises; digital business; and innovation. The financial crisis that hit global markets from 2008 reinforced this picture. We have seen how tough market conditions are met by enterprises that try to gain new market shares by surpassing the customer's expectations, innovate and constantly establishing new market standards. The product cycle is changing, time legs are shorter, high volume- and cash cow-phases fading. Consequently the initial innovative- and product development phases of the product life cycle are getting more and more important. Companies need to find ways to reduce costs and/or gain good money in these initial stages.

The above changes are reflected in recent manufacturing paradigms such as "mass customization" introduced by Stan Davis [2]. He describes mass customization as when a large number of customers could be reached as in industrial "mass production", but at the same time be treated as in customized markets like craft production. However, product differentiation has normally resulted in higher prices than standardized products [3]. This is also the situation in the leisure boat industry (and related industries) where it has been difficult to get a higher price from more innovative and

V. Prabhu, M. Taisch, and D. Kiritsis (Eds.): APMS 2013, Part I, IFIP AICT 414, pp. 94–102, 2013.

customized products then the competitors. As a consequence strategies based on cus-tomization, frequent product introduction and innovations must be based on resource effective product development and production.

Modularity is a key to achieve low cost mass customization as products built around modular architectures can be more easily varied without adding too much complexity to the manufacturing system [4]. A modular design strategy reduces prod-uct costs by partitioning some functions in a product architecture into component designs that will be used in common across product models or reused in future archi-tectures. Standardized modules allow for mass-customized products to achieve the low cost and consistent quality associated with repetitive manufacturing [5].

It is very resource demanding to develop a completely new boat model. Instead of searching for "an optimal design for an optimal product," the objective should be to create a flexible product design, allowing product variations without requiring changes in the overall product design every time a new variant is introduced. Howev-er, even though module-based design is an efficient way of reducing product devel-opment costs, the steps for the initial overall product architecture and platforms, might be found very resource-demanding. For boat builders these costs are often re-lated to the hull-development, inner liner and structural elements. Focusing on these critical parts in the product development process could reduce time and resources thus enabling competitive prices for customized and innovative products.

The purpose of this conceptual paper is to illustrate how modularization could be the key for more effective (time and resources) product development and production of boats, when focusing on the critical parts of the boats – the structural elements.

The paper is based on a R&D project involving manufacturers of leisure boats and boats for the professional markets. The project is at an early stage and so far the activ-ities have mainly been to develop hypothesis, challenges, and how to approach them in concrete contexts. The project is closely related to what is happening in the compa-nies (case studies) and the researchers aim to participate in the product development processes in order to improve them through action research. Literature studies have also been important for the project (and this paper) at this early stage.

Section 2 presents theoretical perspectives on innovation and modularization. Sec-tion 3 presents the R&D-project while Section 4 focuses is a discussions around major challenges in the project and how they are approached. Section 5 concludes.

2   Theoretical Perspectives

2.1   Innovation and Innovation Management Concepts

Innovation has been defined as the process of making changes in something estab-lished by introducing something new [6]. In an ever-changing economic landscape, innovation has become a key competitive factor in manufacturing. Continuous im-provement and incremental change is not enough - companies also need to be part of major changes. Innovation is no less important in manufacturing than any other sec-tion of industry. Innovation in manufacturing can be either radical or incremental, but where most organizations are involved in both types of innovations [7] .

Arthur D. Little, describe five innovation management concepts on how innovations could be dealt with depending on strategic contexts [8]. *Customer-based Innovation* is about profoundly involving and engaging customers to create innovative solutions. In contrast to traditional innovation, *Frugal Innovation* have their basis from lower-income, emerging markets, which are then transferred and adapted into the more developed markets. *Proactive Business Model Innovation* focuses on developing mechanisms enabling the generation of new, innovative business models. In *High Speed/LowRisk Innovation* further development of approaches and tools to drive fast, de-risked product and service innovation are focused. *Integrated Innovation* is about taking innovation approaches from New Product Development (NPD) such as idea management, stage gates and portfolio optimization, and applying them consistently as an integral part of business strategy. [9]

2.2   Modularization Enabler for Efficient Product Development

Modularity allows part of the product to be made in volume as standard modules while product distinctiveness is achieved through combinations or modifications of modules [11]. Modularization could bridge the advantages of: (1) standardization and rationalization, (2) customization and flexibility, and (3) reducing complexity [10].

The cost effects through reduced product development lead time and volume effects from standardization are important, but there are also revenue aspects of modularization: With a modular product platform structure, a set of building blocks (modules) is created with which, through different combinations, a great number of final products can be built. Parts of the product that strategically should vary to satisfy customer needs are well defined and separated from the parts of the product that should be kept as common units. In this way, many variants of final products can be handled without increasing a company's internal complexity.

Parallel development activities are possible once the interfaces between the modules have been defined, and subsequent work conforms to the established interface specifications [14]. This reduces overall development time and resource requirements by eliminating the time-consuming redesigns when component interfaces are not fully defined and standardized during component development processes [13].

2.3   Functional Approach to Modularization

By breaking a complex product structure into smaller, manageable units, a company can regain control of the product and the product-related activities. Modularity aims at increasing efficiency by reducing complexity. We often find module-based design within incremental product development, where e.g. not all innovations or "novelties" are introduced at the same time. However, to exploit the benefits of modular product development, it is crucial to have modularization in mind from the start of the design process, and not only as an afterthought when all components are developed. If modularity is identified and exploited in the initial conceptual or reverse engineering effort, the immediate product design reaps benefits in several strategically important areas.

Modularity has often been about splitting up products systematically in logical/practical units and parts. Today modularization based on functionality is a common approach and methods have been introduced to cut out a module from function structures using module heuristics [14]. These methods such as Modular Function Deployment (MFD™), identify modules from a functional model of a product, create rough geometric layouts and group products into families based on function [12]. Rather than a fixed product platform upon which derivative products are created through substitution of add-on modules, this approach permits the platform itself to be one of several possible options. After comparing function structures for common and unique functions, rules are applied to determine possible modules. This "inverse" process defines possible architectures. This approach increase the flexibility as it also represents a modularization of the basic platform [16].

A systematic approach needs knowledge from people that knows customer demands, service requirements, and from those producing the products. Concurrent engineering could be a key to mobilize and capture this knowledge [15]. An important part of the knowledge of the company is embedded in the products and reusing modules knowledge saves time and money. Also reuse of engineering specifications, testing, process engineering etc, may lead to the desired effects by blurring the boundary between knowledge management and traditional modularization [17].

3   Marin Platform – The R&D Project

Marin Platform is a 4-year R&D project started in 2012. The overall objective of is to radically improve the product development process focusing on the critical and resource demanding phases related to the structural elements of the boat. The project aims to define the premises and solutions for a flexible structural platform. Focus is on design for manufacturing (DfM) and how to involve the operators (craftsmen) in improvement and development.

The project has four Norwegian industrial partners: two SMEs manufacturing leisure boats, one large partner in the professional market and one SME supplying boatbuilders. The SME boat-builders operate in different markets, where one is making GRP boats in the high- end markets for speedboats 24-33 feet. The other makes GRP and aluminum utility-boats in the same size-range. They both want to use the project as an enabler for product configuring for new markets, especially the professional market for smaller boats. The large partner is a world leading company producing advanced lifeboats, davits and a range of different products for, rescue, marine service and military markets. One of the main objectives for this company is to come up with better DfM. The SME supplier is a key actor in the boatbuilding industry as it is the biggest and most important supplier of their products in the Scandinavian boatbuilding industry. The company is within the mechanical engineering industry, but still has many of the same characteristics of craft manufacturing as the other partners.

SINTEF is project coordinator and two other research partners are also contributing to the action research, The University of Agder and Inventas. The project is co-financed by The Norwegian Research Council.

4   The Key Areas of Research

4.1   Customization and Product Development

Craft manufacturing industries such as the Norwegian leisure boat industry has been characterized by small-scale production and high levels of customization. With limited resources for R&D and investments the development processes have been incremental where changes have been carefully introduced in new or modified products. Today, the need for "news" and more radical product innovations rocks this picture.

An advantage of craft manufacturing is the involvement of the persons actually making the product, but also by the customers and has resulted in high quality and a high degree of customization. However, the extensive use of tacit knowledge when it comes to sharing design requirements and good practice, and standardization.

Marin Platform has used MFD methodologies to define customer requirements as a starting point for the innovation- and product development- process. These requirements are then prioritized and extracted into a design brief describing the new concepts, setting the direction for the product development. Figure 1 illustrates the conceptual model describing how customization trigger the process for developing module based design, flexible structural platforms and module based production.

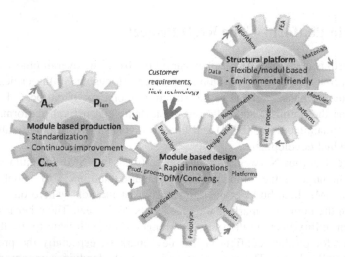

Fig. 1. The conceptual model of Marin Platform

At the early stages of the product development process it is important to check out the business effects of the customer requirements and new concepts. Marin Platform has conducted BEEM (BEEM: Business Effect Evaluation Methodology)-analyses in all companies to get an early picture of expected effects on; customer value; (internal) cost/efficiency; growth (new revenue streams); sustainability [18]. BEEM is based on workshops involving people from technical departments, production, market/business, and to some extent also external people (customers, suppliers and consultaints). Table 1 illustrates effects on cost described by one of the companies.

Table 1. BEEM   Marin Platform, excerpt cost effects

Business outcome - Structural platform	Weight 1=low, 6= high	Stay even Score=1	Significant advance Score=3	True tech. break-through Score=9	Company target	Primary risk(s)
Cost reduction associated with materials and optimation of laminate (hull, deck etc osv)	6	20% average reduction all models	40% average reduction all models	60% average reduction all models	40% average reduction all models	* To finance a complete redesign
Reduced number of components new models, right use of materials (aluminum, stainless etc)	5	0 %	10 %	40 %	20 %	* loose "design"-signaturen * Being to much product-oriented
Increase reuse of components new design	4	20 %	30 %	75 %	30 %	* Being to much product-oriented * Finance the initial change
More efficient variant handling/tailoring	6	0% cost reduction customer handling	20% cost reduction customer handling	45% cost reduction customer handling	35% cost reduction customer handling	* Communication to customer * Coordination sales-production etc
Reduced development "soft" cost hull (software/drawing/spec/calculating)	5	0 %	20 %	50 %	30 %	* Unable to develop calculation-modules * Education of personel
Reduced development "hard" cost. hull (physical)	6	0 %	20 %	50 %	30 %	* Not able to develop dynamic mould * Theoretical basis for new mould
Number of platform-variants from each mould	6	1 platform-variant	2 platform-variants	10 platform-variants	3 platform-variants	* Not able to develop dynamic mould
Reduction in resources used for CE-cetification new models	4	same as today	30% reduction in resources used	70% reduction in resources used	50% reduction in resources used	* More and more complex standards * Lack of competence at authorities

4.2   Flexible Structural Platform as the Basis

The product development of leisureboats has been characterized by a lack of well-defined phases, roles, resource control, documentations etc. The product development is so resource demanding that even the prototype has to be sold to a customer. The (first) customer is often highly involved in the development process making design freeze to an irrelevant term and could overshadow the general customer requirements.

One of the consequences of this diffuse process is that the required structural elements have been added to the design at a very late stage - sometimes as "trial and error". Even though the result of this process has been boats of high quality, the products could be even better with another approach to the structural solutions. For certain a more resource efficient way to develop them is needed.

One of the ways Marin Platform aim to improve the product development process is to introduce more systematic approaches such as MFD. MFD has the following basic steps: (1) design requirements, (2) identification of functions that fulfill the demands and their corresponding technical solutions, (3) technical solutions are analyzed regarding their reasons for being modules, (4) module concepts are then generated and the interface relations of the modules derived are evaluated. In the final step, (5) a specification is established for each module.

For boats and other complex marine products there are to a standards and requirements issued by regulatory bodies (EU-standards), classification agencies or key customers that could limit modularity options within critical areas such as interfaces/connections of modules. However, these requirements when captured in the initial step (1) of the MFD process could also indicate options in functionality and modules.

Table 2 illustrates design requirements for a boat that is to be designed and developed both for the leisure- and professional market (rescue boat).

Structural elements are critical in the development of boats and Marin Platform focus on how structures could be developed more efficiently and be the premises for the rest of the product development. The idea is that once the basic requirements of the boats are defined (Table 2) and described in the design brief, the structural performance should quickly be developed through structural modules. Structural modules could be; (part of) inner liners; stringers; windows/doorframes etc. Research activities in Marin Platform will conduct stress-strength analysis of these elements to understand how they could represent modules in flexible structural platforms. It requires extensive data collection, testing and simulations to develop algorithms/models for different configurations and structural platforms.

Table 2. Excerpt design requirements

Customer/market requirements	Weight 1=low, 10=high	Basic functionality	Mould for different configurations: define basic principles, geometry	Common solution for pentry and toilet with other products/areas	Common solution: benches, tables etc	Fixing/interfaces: flexibility vs. Robustness	Structural modules - flexibility across models and fields	Technologies for surveillance of quality,service needs etc	Materials, coating adjustable for different climate and conditions	Equipment for survival	Driverless technologies	Navigation, communication	Flexible driveline	Ergonomy/HSE/smartness	Speed/seaworthiness	Quality/durability	Design/coolness
			7	7	5	9	9	9	8	7	5	5	7	7	9	8	8
MOB 6-10 meters: wateriet for the range	9		o	o	o	o	o		o		o		o		o	o	o
Freefall 16-21 meters	4		o	o	o	o	o	o	o			o		o	o	o	
MOB: 22-36 persons	8			o	o		o			o				o			
Freefall: 16-40 persons	3					o			o				o				
Configurable for: cruise, cargo and tankers, as well as police/amb./military/etc. and	9		o	o	o	o	o	o	o	o	o	o	o			o	o
Quality (doc) according to North see/Solas	9		o				o	o	o					o	o	o	o
Transparent production process	5																
Alternative material: alum. GRP..	5		o	o	o	o	o	o	o			o	o	o	o		
Good interfaces with davit-upgradable	8		o			o											
Flexible solutions for production (capacity)	7			o	o	o	o			o		o	o	o			
Certified before customer takeover	7		o			o	o	o	o					o			
Technologi vs robustness	5			o	o	o		o	o		o		o				o
Solutions for surveillance/self-testing	7									o	o	o		o			
Easy to operate	9						o				o		o				
Effective testprogram	3									o	o	o	o		o		
Be used in different climat zones	8			o	o	o		o	o	o	o	o		o	o	o	
Produced in Europe	5		o							o	o	o		o	o	o	o
"Safety" feeling for people/passengers	4			o	o		o			o	o	o		o	o		

4.3   Module Based Design and Production

The structural platform defined through structural modules represents the "room to maneuver" for the rest of the module based design process. The basic design requirements are taken into account in the structural platform, and the rest of the modularization process will focus on optimization of modules and functionality for example through the MFD-steps.

The modularization represents to some extent constraints for the customization but could also give a clearer picture of the opportunities and choices for customers. The positive effects on product development time and -cost are expected to more than offset the negative effects. However, to realize and exploit business effects described in the BEEM exercise, Marin Platform also involves production and other functional units in the conceptual model for product development (Figure 1). This implies standardization of processes but also continuous improvement. Concurrent engineering is a key for a broad and structured involvement [15]:

- increased role of manufacturing process design in product design decisions
- formation of cross-functional teams to accomplish the development process
- focus on the customer during the development process
- use of lead time as a source of competitive advantage

A significant part of concurrent engineering is that the individual employee is given much more say in the overall design process due to its collaborative nature. Modularization is also important for the people in the production since it to a large extent is about DfM and standardization of production. Knowledge about these aspects will often be found at the shop floor.

5 Conclusion

Innovations and high speed product development is more and more important in manufacturing industries. Customization and flexibility have for many companies been the strategic response to challenging competitive situations. Modularization has been launched as an enabler for customization and resource effective product development and production. These ideas and strategies have also been adapted by boat builders that have traditionally been characterized by craftsmanship.

Marin Platform is a 4-year research project where boat builders and suppliers together with research institutes focus on the critical parts in product development – the structural elements. The project aims to develop modules that could "easily" be put together into different structural platform for boats. This is difficult as it requires research in fields such as material technology, hydrodynamics, and dynamic stress-strength analysis.

There is a risk for not finding the "right" answers, but also for not being able to develop prototypes and physical manifestations of the research. The research project started in 2012 and so far the activities have mainly been preliminary analysis. However, this initial phase has already shown that we are on the right track where modularization is important for customization and mass customization strategies. We are also more confident that to optimize the effects of modularization we have to attack the most critical and difficult parts in the product development, which for the boat builders are the structural elements.

References

1. O'Sullivan, D., Rolstadås, A., Filos, E.: Global education in manufacturing strategy. Journal of Intelligent manufacturing 22(5), 663–674 (2011)
2. Davis, S.: Future Perfect. Addison-Wesley, Reading (1987)
3. Du, X., Tseng, M.M.: Characterizing CustomerValue for Product Customization. In: Proceedings of the 1999 ASME Design Engineering Technical Conference, Las Vegas (1999)
4. Ulrich, K.T., Eppinger, S.D.: Product Design and Development. McGraw-Hill, New York (1995)
5. Duray, R., Ward, P.T., Milligan, G.W., Berry, W.L.: Approaches to mass customization: configurations and empirical validation. Journal of Operations Management 18, 605–625 (2000)
6. Fagerberg, J., Mowery, D.C., Nelson, R.R.: The Oxford handbook of innovation. University Press, London (2005)
7. Christensen, C.M.: The innovator's dilemma. Harvard Business School Press, Boston (1997)

8. Eagar, R., van Oene, F., Boulton, C., Roos, D., and Dekeyser, C.: The future of innovation management: The next 10 years. Prism 1. Arthur D. Little (2011), http://www.adlittle.com/prism-articles.html?&no_cache=1&view=379

9. Hart, S.J.: New product development. In: Baker, J.M., Hart, S.J. (eds.) The Marketing Book, 6th edn. Elsevier, UK (2008)

10. Ericsson, A., Erixon, G.: Controlling Design Variants: Modular Product Platforms. ASME Press, NY (1999)

11. Duray, R.: Mass Customizers use of inventory, planning techniques and channel management. Production Planning & Control 15(4), 412–421 (2004)

12. Ericsson, A., Erixon, G.: Controlling Design Variants: Modular Product Platforms. ASME Press, NY (1999)

13. Sanchez, R.: Using modularity to manage the interactions of technical and industrial design. Design Management Journal 2, 8 (2002)

14. Stone, R.B.: A heuristic method for identifying modules for product architectures. A heuristic method for identifying modules for product architectures. Design Studies 21, 5–31 (2000)

15. Jo, H.H., Parsaei, H.R., Sullivan, W.G.: Principles of concurrent engineering. In: Concurrent Engineering: Contemporary Issues and Modern Design Tools, pp. 3–23. Chapman and Hall, New York (1993)

16. Dahmus, J.B., Gonzales-Zugasti, J.P., Otto, K.N.: Modular product architecture. Design Studies 22(5), 409–425 (2001)

17. Sanchez, R., Mahoney, J.T.: Modularity, Flexibility, and Knowledge Management in Product and Organization Design. IEEE Engineering Management Review. Reprint from Strategic Management 17 (1996); special issue December. John Wiley & Sons Limited

18. Henriksen, B., Røstad, C.C.: Evaluating and Prioritizing Projects – Setting Targets. The Business Effect Evaluation Methodology BEEM. International Journal of Managing Projects in Business 3(2), 275–291 (2010)

Chance Constrained Programming Model for Stochastic Profit–Oriented Disassembly Line Balancing in the Presence of Hazardous Parts

Mohand Lounes Bentaha, Olga Battaïa, and Alexandre Dolgui

École Nationale Supérieure des Mines, EMSE-FAYOL,
CNRS UMR6158, LIMOS, F–42023 Saint–Étienne, France
{bentaha,battaia,dolgui}@emse.fr

Abstract. A Stochastic Partial profit–oriented Disassembly Line Balancing Problem (SP–DLBP) in the presence of hazardous parts is considered. The goal is to assign disassembly tasks of the best selected disassembly alternative to a sequence of workstations while respecting precedence and cycle time constraints. An AND/OR graph is used to model the disassembly alternatives and the precedence relations among tasks. Task times are assumed independent random variables with known normal probability distributions. Cycle time constraints are to be satisfied with at least a certain probability level fixed by the decision maker. The objective is to maximize the profit produced by the line. It is computed as the difference between the positive revenue generated by retrieved parts and the line operation cost considered as negative revenue. The line cost includes the workstations operation costs as well as additional costs of workstations handling hazardous parts of End of Life (EOL) product. To deal with uncertainties, a Chance Constrained Programming formulation is developed.

Keywords: Sustainable Manufacturing, Product Recovery, Disassembly, Line Design, Cone and Chance Constrained Programming, Interior–point Algorithm.

1 Introduction

Disassembly lines play a key role in the selective separation of parts and materials of EOL products. The success of the product recovery depends partially on the economical efficiency of such lines. However, their design presents a complex optimization problem requiring adapted mathematical tools to obtain efficient solutions.

A first study on disassembly line considering task failures was presented by Güngör and Gupta [6]. Later, the deterministic version of the Disassembly Line Balancing Problem (DLBP) was studied in [10,11,12,13]. Several performance criteria were considered including minimization of the number of stations needed and variation in idle times between the stations of the line. The following solution methods were developed and compared: exhaustive search, genetic algorithm, ant

V. Prabhu, M. Taisch, and D. Kiritsis (Eds.): APMS 2013, Part I, IFIP AICT 414, pp. 103–110, 2013.

colony metaheuristics, a greedy algorithm, greedy/hill–climbing and greedy/2–optimal hybrid heuristics. Altekin et al. [3] defined and solved the profit–oriented DLBP. The problem was modeled via a mixed–integer programming formulation and its solution simultaneously determined the number of stations and cycle time along with the assignment of the tasks to the stations. Upper and lower bounding schemes were also developed. Koc et al. [7] proposed two exact (MIP and DP) formulations to solve DLBP with the objective of minimizing the number of stations. They used an AND/OR graph to model EOL product data and showed that the use of such a graph allowed obtaining better solutions in comparison with a single precedence diagram. Altekin and Akkan [2] considered task–failure driven rebalancing of disassembly lines. A mixed–integer programming based predictive–reactive approach was proposed. In the first step, a predictive balance was created and then, in the second step, given a task failure, the tasks of the disassembled product with that task failure were reselected and re–assigned to the stations. Agrawal and Tiwari [1] considered the case of a mixed–model U–shaped disassembly line with stochastic task times. They proposed a collaborative ant colony optimization technique to simultaneously determine the sequencing of the models and assign the tasks to the stations.

The literature exposed above shows that no adequate mathematical model taking into account simultaneously the stochasticity of disassembly task times, the partial disassembly and maximizing the profit produced by the line can be found. To fill this gap, this paper aims to provide such a model where some of disassembled parts are considered hazardous and require a particular treatment incurring a supplementary cost. An adapted solution method to find efficient design solutions is presented. The paper is organized as follows. Section 2 presents the problem formulation. Section 3 describes the solution method. Section 4 analyzes the numerical experiments. Conclusions are given in Section 5.

2   Problem Statement

The SP–DLBP aims to assign a set of disassembly tasks, $I = \{1, 2, \ldots, N\}, N \in \mathbb{N}^*$ to an ordered sequence of workstations, $J = \{1, 2, \ldots, M\}, M \in \mathbb{N}^*$ under precedence relationships constraints among tasks. Cycle time ($C_0 > 0$) limitation at each station is satisfied with a certain probability level fixed by the decision maker. Task times are assumed mutually independent random variables with known normal probability distributions, i.e. $t_i(\tilde{\xi}) \rightsquigarrow \mathcal{N}(\mu_i, \sigma_i), t_i(\tilde{\xi}) > 0, i \in I$; the random variables are modeled by a random vector $\tilde{\xi} = (\tilde{t}_1, \tilde{t}_2, \ldots, \tilde{t}_N)$ varying over a set $\Xi \subset \mathbb{R}_+^N$ given a probability space $(\Xi, \mathcal{F}, P)$ introduced by $\tilde{\xi}$. A disassembly task $i \in H \subset I$ is called hazardous if its execution generates a hazardous subassembly or component. All possible alternatives for disassembly process and precedence relationships among tasks and subassemblies are modeled by an AND/OR graph [5]. An example for such a graph is given in Fig. 1. To simplify the graph, without information loss, subassemblies with one component are not shown. Each subassembly of single type EOL product to be disassembled is represented by a node $A_k, k \in K = \{0, 1, \ldots, K\}, K \in \mathbb{N}$ in the graph and each

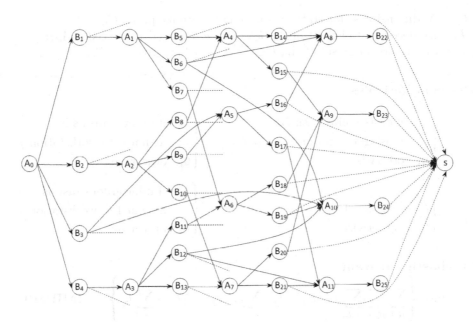

Fig. 1. AND/OR graph of the piston and connecting rod

disassembly task gives a node $B_i, i \in I$. Two types of arcs define the precedence relations between the subassemblies and tasks: AND–type and OR–type arcs. For instance, if a disassembly task generates two sub–assemblies, or more, then it is related to these subassemblies by AND–type arcs. If, for a given subassembly, one or more disassembly tasks can be performed, but only one must be selected, this subassembly is related to these disassembly tasks by OR–type arcs. In order to consider the case of partial disassembly, where the product is not necessarily disassembled till obtaining single parts, a dummy task s is introduced into the precedence graph as a sink node, as illustrated in Fig. 1. Since the case of partial disassembly is considered, not all existing tasks have to be assigned. The level of the disassembly depends on the profit generated by the corresponding line. The recycling or reuse of certain parts or subassemblies bring its benefit while the line cost is considered as a negative revenue. This cost includes two components: the cost of workstations used and additional cost entailed by the treatment of hazardous parts. For the problem defined, the following stochastic Mixed Integer Program with Joined Probabilistic Constraints (MIPJPC) has been developed.

Parameters

H: Hazardous disassembly tasks' index set;

L: Parts' index set: $L = \{1, 2, \ldots, \mathsf{L}\}$, $\mathsf{L} \in \mathbb{N}^*$;

r_ℓ: Revenue generated by part $\ell, \ell \in L$;

L_i: Set of retrieved parts by the execution of disassembly task $B_i, i \in I$;

F_c: Fixed cost per unit time of operating workstations, $F_c > 0$;

C_h: Additional cost for stations handling hazardous parts, $C_h > 0$;

P_k: Predecessors index set of A_k, $k \in K$, *i.e.* $P_k = \{i \mid B_i \text{ precedes } A_k\}$;

S_k: Successors index set of A_k, $k \in K$, $S_k = \{i \mid A_k \text{ precedes } B_i\}$.

Decision Variables

$$x_{ij} = \begin{cases} 1, & \text{if disassembly task } B_i \\ & \text{is assigned to workstation } j; \\ 0, & \text{otherwise.} \end{cases} \qquad x_{sj} = \begin{cases} 1, & \text{if dummy task s is} \\ & \text{assigned to workstation } j; \\ 0, & \text{otherwise.} \end{cases}$$

$$z_j = \begin{cases} C_0, & \text{if } x_{sj} = 1; \\ 0, & \text{otherwise.} \end{cases} \qquad h_j = \begin{cases} 1, & \text{if a hazardous task is} \\ & \text{assigned to workstation } j; \\ 0, & \text{otherwise.} \end{cases}$$

Stochastic Program

$$\max \left\{ \sum_{i \in I} \sum_{j \in J} \sum_{\ell \in L_i} r_\ell \cdot x_{ij} - F_c \cdot \sum_{j \in J} j \cdot z_j - C_0 C_h \cdot \sum_{j \in J} h_j \right\} \qquad \textbf{(MIPJPC)}$$

s.t.

$$z_j = C_0 \cdot x_{sj}, \forall j \in J \tag{1}$$

$$\sum_{i \in S_0} \sum_{j \in J} x_{ij} = 1 \tag{2}$$

$$\sum_{j \in J} x_{ij} \leqslant 1, \forall i \in I \tag{3}$$

$$\sum_{i \in S_k} \sum_{j \in J} x_{ij} \leqslant \sum_{i \in P_k} \sum_{j \in J} x_{ij}, \forall k \in K \backslash \{0\} \tag{4}$$

$$\sum_{i \in S_k} x_{iv} \leqslant \sum_{i \in P_k} \sum_{j=1}^{v} x_{ij}, \forall k \in K \backslash \{0\}, \forall v \in J \tag{5}$$

$$\sum_{j \in J} x_{sj} = 1 \tag{6}$$

$$\sum_{j \in J} j \cdot x_{ij} \leqslant \sum_{j \in J} j \cdot x_{sj}, \forall i \in I \tag{7}$$

$$h_j \geqslant x_{ij}, \forall j \in J, \forall i \in H \tag{8}$$

$$P\left(\sum_{i \in I} t_i(\tilde{\xi}) \cdot x_{ij} \leqslant C_0, \forall j \in J \right) \geqslant 1 - \alpha \tag{9}$$

$$z_j \geqslant 0, \forall j \in J \tag{10}$$

$$x_{sj}, x_{ij}, h_j \in \{0, 1\}, \forall i \in I, \forall j \in J \tag{11}$$

The terms of the objective function represent respectively the earned profit of retrieved parts, the cost of operating workstations and the additional cost for handling hazardous parts. If the dummy task s is assigned to workstation j, which defines the number of processed stations, then $\sum_{j \in J} j \cdot z_j = j \cdot C_0$ and workstations operating cost becomes $j \cdot (F_c \cdot C_0)$. Constraints (1) ensure the value of z_j to be C_0 when the dummy task s is assigned to station j. Constraint (2) imposes the selection of only one disassembly task (OR–successor) to begin the disassembly process. Constraint set (3) indicates that a task is to be assigned to at most one workstation. Constraints (4) ensure that only one OR–successor is selected. Constraint set (5) defines the precedence relations among tasks. Constraint (6) imposes the assignment of the dummy task s to one station. Constraints (7) ensure that all the disassembly tasks are assigned to lower or equal–indexed workstations than the one to which s is assigned. Constraints (8) ensure the value of h_j to be 1 if at least one hazardous task is assigned to a workstation j. Constraints (9) enforce the station operating time to remain within the cycle time, for all opened workstations, with a probability at least $(1 - \alpha)$ determined by the decision maker. Finally, sets (10)–(11) represent the trivial constraints.

3   Solution Method

Let $(1 - \alpha) = \bar{\alpha}$. Sine disassembly task times are assumed mutually independent random variables with known normal probability distributions, then:

$$P\left(\sum_{i \in I} t_i(\tilde{\xi}) \cdot x_{ij} \leqslant C_0, \forall j \in J\right) \geqslant \bar{\alpha} \iff \prod_{j \in J} P\left(\sum_{i \in I} t_i(\tilde{\xi}) \cdot x_{ij} \leqslant C_0\right) \geqslant \bar{\alpha}$$

$$\iff \prod_{j \in J} P\left(\sum_{i \in I} t_i(\tilde{\xi}) \cdot x_{ij} \leqslant C_0\right) \geqslant \bar{\alpha}^{1 = \sum_{j \in J} y_j}, y_j \geqslant 0, \forall j \in J$$

$$\iff P\left(\sum_{i \in I} t_i(\tilde{\xi}) \cdot x_{ij} \leqslant C_0\right) \geqslant \bar{\alpha}^{y_j}, \forall j \in J, \sum_{j \in J} y_j = 1.$$

$$P\left(\sum_{i \in I} t_i(\tilde{\xi}) \cdot x_{ij} \leqslant C_0\right) \geqslant \bar{\alpha}^{y_j}, \forall j \in J$$

$$\iff P\left(\frac{\sum_{i \in I} t_i(\tilde{\xi}) \cdot x_{ij} - \sum_{i \in I} \mu_i \cdot x_{ij}}{\sqrt{\sum_{i \in I} \sigma_i^2 \cdot x_{ij}}} \leqslant \frac{C_0 - \sum_{i \in I} \mu_i \cdot x_{ij}}{\sqrt{\sum_{i \in I} \sigma_i^2 \cdot x_{ij}}}\right) \geqslant \bar{\alpha}^{y_j}$$

$$\iff P\left(Z_j \leqslant \frac{C_0 - \sum_{i \in I} \mu_i \cdot x_{ij}}{\sqrt{\sum_{i \in I} \sigma_i^2 \cdot x_{ij}}}\right) \geqslant \bar{\alpha}^{y_j}, Z_j \rightsquigarrow \mathcal{N}(0,1), \forall j \in J$$

$$\iff \sum_{i \in I} \mu_i \cdot x_{ij} + \Phi^{-1}(\bar{\alpha}^{y_j}) \cdot \sqrt{\sum_{i \in I} \sigma_i^2 \cdot x_{ij}} \leqslant C_0, \forall j \in J \tag{12}$$

Let $(v, w) \in \mathbb{R} \times \mathbb{R}^{l-1}$; the unit second–order convex cone of dimension l is defined as $\mathcal{Q}^l = \left\{ \begin{pmatrix} w \\ v \end{pmatrix} \middle| v \geqslant \|w\| \right\}$ where $\|\cdot\|$ refers to the standard Euclidean norm. Since $\alpha < 50\%$, which is justified by the fact that α represents the risk and mostly

$\alpha \leqslant 10\%$, we have $\Phi^{-1}(\bar{\alpha}^{y_j}) > 0$, and since $x_{ij} \in \{0,1\} \iff x_{ij}^2 \in \{0,1\}$, then, inequality (12) is a second–order cone constraint of dimension $l = \mathsf{N} + 1$:

$$\sum_{i \in I} \mu_i \cdot x_{ij} + \Phi^{-1}(\bar{\alpha}^{y_j}) \cdot \sqrt{\sum_{i \in I} \sigma_i^2 \cdot x_{ij}} \leqslant C_0, \forall j \in J$$

$$\iff \mu^\mathsf{T} \cdot x_j + \Phi^{-1}(\bar{\alpha}^{y_j}) \cdot \|\Sigma^{\frac{1}{2}} \cdot x_j\| \leqslant C_0, \forall j \in J$$

$$\iff \|\Sigma^{\frac{1}{2}} \cdot x_j\| \leqslant \frac{1}{\Phi^{-1}(\bar{\alpha}^{y_j})} \cdot \left(C_0 - \mu^\mathsf{T} \cdot x_j\right), \forall j \in J$$

$$\iff \left\{ \left(\frac{\Sigma^{\frac{1}{2}}}{\frac{-\mu^\mathsf{T}}{\Phi^{-1}(\bar{\alpha}^{y_j})}} \right) x_j + \left(\frac{\mathbf{0}}{\frac{C_0}{\Phi^{-1}(\bar{\alpha}^{y_j})}} \right) \right\} \in \mathcal{Q}^{\mathsf{N}+1}, \forall j \in J$$

where $\mu = (\mu_1, \dots, \mu_\mathsf{N}), x_j = (x_{1j}, \dots, x_{\mathsf{N}j})^\mathsf{T}, \forall j \in J, \Sigma^{\frac{1}{2}} = \begin{pmatrix} \sigma_1 & & \mathbf{0} \\ & \ddots & \\ \mathbf{0} & & \sigma_\mathsf{N} \end{pmatrix}$ is a

diagonal matrix and $\Phi^{-1}(\cdot)$ is the inverse of the standard normal cumulative distribution function $\Phi(\cdot)$.

Let x be a vector of the decision variables x_{ij}, x_{sj}, h_j, z_j and $X = \{x|$ constraints $(1) - (8), (10) - (11)$ are satisfied$\}$. The Second Order Cone Mixed Integer Program given below represents an equivalent version of problem (**MIPJPC**) [4].

$$\max \left\{ \sum_{i \in I} \sum_{j \in J} \sum_{l \in L_i} r_l \cdot x_{ij} - F_c \cdot \sum_{j \in J} j \cdot z_j - C_0 C_h \cdot \sum_{j \in J} h_j \right\} \qquad \text{(SOCMIP)}$$

s.t.

$$x \in X$$

$$v_j \leqslant \frac{1}{\Phi^{-1}\left(\bar{\alpha}^{\frac{1}{\mathsf{M}}}\right)} \cdot \left(C_0 - \mu^\mathsf{T} \cdot x_j\right), \forall j \in J$$

$$w_{ij} \geqslant \sigma_i \cdot x_{ij}, \forall i \in I, \forall j \in J$$

$$v_j \geqslant \|w_j\|, \forall j \in J$$

$$v_j \geqslant 0, \ w_{ij} \geqslant 0, \forall i \in I, \forall j \in J$$

where $v_j, w_{ij}, \forall i \in I, \forall j \in J$ are intermediate variables, $w_j = (w_{1j}, \dots, w_{\mathsf{N}j})^\mathsf{T}$, $\forall j \in J$. We consider the case where cycle time constraint is to be satisfied with the same probability for each station of the line, *i.e.* $y_j = \frac{1}{|J|} = \frac{1}{\mathsf{M}}, \forall j \in J$. The resulted (**SOCMIP**) is then solved using the interior point algorithm [14] of CPLEX 12.4.

4   Numerical Results

The program (**SOCMIP**) was implemented in Microsoft Visual C++ 2008 and ILOG CPLEX 12.4 was used to solve the model on a PC with Intel(R) Core(TM)

Table 1. Problem instances and obtained results

	N	K, L	arcs	AND–relations			M	C_0	obj.	tasks	stat.	H–stat.	CPU time
				0	1	2							
MJKL11	37	22, 33	76	4	27	6	3	40	20	7	3	1	0.50
L99a	30	18, 28	60	2	26	2	3	50	75	7	3	1	0.03
BBD13	25	11, 27	49	4	18	3	2	120	640	3	2	0	0.05
KSE09	23	13, 20	47	4	14	5	2	20	53	4	2	0	0.05
L99b	20	13, 23	41	5	9	6	3	10	72	7	3	1	0.22
BBD12	10	5, 12	18	3	6	1	2	0.51	18.39	2	2	1	0.05

i5–2400 CPU 3.10 GHz and 8Go RAM. It has been applied to the problem instance illustrated in Fig. 1 and to 5 available in the literature benchmark problems containing process alternatives for disassembly. The names of the problem instances were respectively composed of the first letters of authors' names and year of publication, *i.e.* BBD12 [5], KSE09 [7], L99a and L99b from [8], MJKL11 [9]. BBD13 corresponds to the piston and connecting rod product instance, see Fig. 1. The input data for each problem instance is given in Table 1. The columns 'AND–relations' report the number of disassembly tasks with no successor in column 0, with one AND–type arc in column 1, and with two AND–type arcs in column 2, column 'arcs' gives the total number of AND–type and OR–type arcs.

The interior–point algorithm of CPLEX was applied to each instance for $\alpha = 10\%$. Cost of operating workstations F_c was fixed to 5 and cost for stations handling hazardous parts $C_h = 3$ for all instances. The results obtained are also presented in Table 1 where columns 'obj., tasks, stat., H–stat., CPU time' report respectively the optimal profit of the line, the number of selected tasks, the number of opened stations, the number of hazardous stations and solution time in seconds. All instances were solved in less than 1 second.

5   Conclusion

In this paper, partial profit–oriented disassembly line balancing problem in the presence of hazardous parts was studied under uncertainty. A second–order cone mixed integer program was developed. Disassembly task times were assumed mutually independent random variables with known normal probability distributions, where cycle time constraints were to be jointly satisfied with at least a probability level fixed by the decision maker. To solve the problem, the interior point algorithm and CPLEX solver were used. The solution method was evaluated on a set of 6 problem instances taken from the literature. All instances were solved in less than 1 second.

Our future objective is to develop an exact solution algorithm for the problem considered based on branch & cut method and compare it to interior point CPLEX algorithm.

References

1. Agrawal, S., Tiwari, M.K.: A collaborative ant colony algorithm to stochastic mixed–model U–shaped disassembly line balancing and sequencing problem. International Journal of Production Research 46(6), 1405–1429 (2006)
2. Altekin, F.T., Akkan, C.: Task–failure–driven rebalancing of disassembly lines. International Journal of Production Research 50(18), 4955–4976 (2011)
3. Altekin, F.T., Kandiller, L., Ozdemirel, N.E.: Profit–oriented disassembly line balancing. International Journal of Production Research 46(10), 2675–2693 (2008)
4. Atamtürk, A., Narayanan, V.: Conic mixed–integer rounding cuts. Math. Program. 122, 1–20 (2010)
5. Bentaha, M.L., Battaïa, O., Dolgui, A.: A stochastic formulation of the disassembly line balancing problem. In: Emmanouilidis, C., Taisch, M., Kiritsis, D. (eds.) APMS 2012. IFIP AICT, vol. 397, pp. 397–404. Springer, Heidelberg (2013)
6. Güngör, A., Gupta, S.M.: A solution approach to the disassembly line balancing problem in the presence of task failures. International Journal of Production Research 39(7), 1427–1467 (2001)
7. Koc, A., Sabuncuoglu, I., Erel, E.: Two exact formulations for disassembly line balancing problems with task precedence diagram construction using an AND/OR graph. IIE Transactions 41(10), 866–881 (2009)
8. Lambert, A.J.D.: Linear programming in disassembly/clustering sequence generation. Computers & Industrial Engineering 36(4), 723–738 (1999)
9. Ma, Y.S., Jun, H.B., Kim, H.W., Lee, D.H.: Disassembly process planning algorithms for end–of–life product recovery and environmentally conscious disposal. International Journal of Production Research 49(23), 7007–7027 (2011)
10. Mcgovern, S.M., Gupta, S.M.: Combinatorial optimization analysis of the unary NP–complete disassembly line balancing problem. International Journal of Production Research 45(18-19), 4485–4511 (2007)
11. McGovern, S.M., Gupta, S.M.: Ant colony optimization for disassembly sequencing with multiple objectives. The International Journal of Advanced Manufacturing Technology 30(5-6), 481–496 (2006)
12. McGovern, S.M., Gupta, S.M.: A balancing method and genetic algorithm for disassembly line balancing. European Journal of Operational Research 179(3), 692–708 (2007)
13. McGovern, S.M., Gupta, S.M.: The Disassembly Line, Balancing and Modeling, 2011th edn. McGraw-Hill Companies, New York (2011)
14. Nesterov, Y.E., Nemirovski, A.S.: Interior–Point Polynomial Algorithms in Convex Programming. Society for Industrial and Applied Mathematics (1994)

From EcoDesign to Industrial Metabolism: Redefinition of Sustainable Innovation and Competitive Sustainability

Stig Brink Taps, Thomas Ditlev Brunø, and Kjeld Nielsen

Department of Mechanical and Manufacturing Engineering, Aalborg University, Denmark
taps@m-tech.aau.dk

Abstract. Successful enterprises are distinguished by their sustainable development reliant on their ability to learn and develop innovative solutions. Recyclability (material and product design) and recycling (process design) emerge as new paradigm for sustainable competitiveness.

The paper makes a critical evaluation of the most commonly tools and techniques in use and suggests a redefinition of the concept of EcoDesign by integrating End-of-Life activities to gain industrial metabolism. This approach takes a broader innovation perspective, necessary to construct a sustainable innovation community with material balance of the system. The paper suggests a modular approach as generator for integrating embedded firm specific elements into a renewal networked supply chain.

Keywords: Sustainable innovation, Radical change, EcoDesign, Industrial metabolism, Modularity.

1 Introduction

It was Schumpeter [7] who first describes the dynamic pattern in which innovative firms unseat established firms through an innovation process he called "creative destruction" an insisted that disequilibrium was the driven force of capitalism. In significant hostile competitive environments forced by dramatic changes in technological and economic global infrastructures, firms are seeking new competitive edges. Since Taylor's [9] seminal work, the global engineering community has produced endless methodologies with the focus on operational efficiencies to gain cost advantages. But these advantages run out of competitiveness because firms are similar in their exploitation of methodologies advancing incremental improvement only in products, processes, and services. The increasing global hostile battlefield on cost advantages has recently been enlarged by incumbent firms desperately seeking profit opportunities by moving their cost curve from established market to developing markets such as China, India and similar.

But there is not much new dynamic innovation as business driver by pulling existence production technologies to emergent markets to gain continuous improvement of exiting products and processes based on lower cost of wages, materials, manufacturing, maintenance etc. The key to survival are founded in capitalizing on the

V. Prabhu, M. Taisch, and D. Kiritsis (Eds.): APMS 2013, Part I, IFIP AICT 414, pp. 111–118, 2013.

changing nature of market. Those managers, who are able to perceive trends and weak signals where others see only noise or chaos, that reposition their firms proactively and change the way, they think about products, technologies, processes and business models, will develop competencies to survival funded on innovative competiveness that rivals will be hard-pressed to match.

The ongoing process of creative destruction of the economic structure, from price competition to dynamic innovation founded on new competences in knowledge, innovation, and learning as core aspects within a global structured network of actors, networks and institutions, transforms dramatically the socioeconomic landscape. Further, an era of abundant raw materials, cheap energy, and limitless sinks for waste disposal is running out, making increase pressure from legislators, customers and networks to improve environmental performance.

To improve environmental performance foresight managers must focus on reducing the life cycle impacts of products through technological innovation and outdate practices and technologies from the price competition era.

The paper is conceptual attempting to evaluate from a critical stance common approaches applied to gain sustainable innovation. It serves the purpose to identify critical parts as driver of competitive sustainability and of providing a holistic approach on sustainability. The rest of this paper is organized around three key questions: (a) Is EcoDesign a driving force to radical change (b) Is Cradle-to-cradle a driving force to radical change (c) and how can a generator be constructed to gain industrial metabolism.

2   The Battle of Innovation Approach

Weizsaecker [11] reported that global waste account on more than half of the world's GNP and much of this is from inefficiency in design. It is an enormous challenge for society to change this waste disaster which has taking the rise in firms reactively respond to ecological environment.

Most managers, especially in operations, focus on the constraint that environmental regulation imposes on product and or process designs. The traditional approach to product design is that materials, assembly, and distribution cost are minimized instead of optimizing life-cycle performance which includes maintenance, reuse, and disposal issues.

Sustainability is a systemic concept which derives from understanding the entire cycle of products, from raw material extraction to final disposition. Figure 1 illustrates a typical material product life cycle and shows some alternatives at its end-of-life phase [5]. The main flow (product life cycle) is composed of the following phases: raw material extraction, primary industry, manufacturing, usage and product discarding at its end-of-life. The secondary flow is related to the different end-of-life strategies: reuse, remanufacturing and recycling.

EcoDesign can be seen by systematic integration of creativity, innovation and environmental responsibility into the design process across the product life cycle from cradle to grave (industrial eco innovation). McDonough [4] argue for a fundamental conceptual shift away from current industrial system designs toward a "cradle-to-cradle" system which design industrial systems to be commercially productive, socially beneficial, and ecologically intelligent (industrial metabolism innovation).

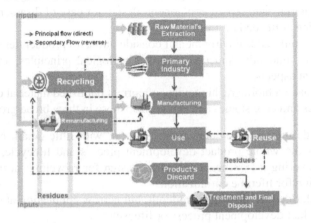

Fig. 1. Material product life cycle [5]

Metabolism innovation and eco-innovation coves the spectrum of levels of innovation from incremental to radical. Stevels [8] advocates four main levels of innovation:

1. Level (incremental): Incremental or small, progressive improvement to existing products.
2. Level (re-design or green limits): Major re-design of existing products but limited the level of improvement that is technically feasible).
3. Level (functional or product alternatives): New products or service concepts to satisfy the same functional need e.g. teleconferencing as an alternative to travel.
4. Level (systems): Design for sustainable society.

In the following section these two innovation approaches are outlined, and their ability as driving force to radically change the innovation process from an efficiency focus into to an effectiveness focus is evaluated.

2.1   EcoDesign as Driving Force to Radical Change

Today, nearly all processes and approaches related to the integration of environmental considerations in product design are grouped under the term EcoDesign. The most common approach used for EcoDesign is life-cycle analysis (LCA). It involves taking simultaneously into account the environmental impacts in the selection of raw materials, the manufacturing, the manufacturing process, the storage and transportation phase, usage, and final disposal and van Hemel [10] include proper recycling. The aim is to find a new way for developing products where the environmental aspects are given the same status as functionality, durability, cost, time-to-market, aesthetic, ergonomics and quality [5].

Hill [2] proposes that the following self-evident EcoDesign axioms should be considered and reduced at all stages along the product life cycle: manufacture without producing hazardous waste; use clean technologies; reduce product chemical emissions; reduce product energy consumption; use non-hazardous recyclable materials; use recycled materials and reused component; design for ease of disassembly; product reuse or recycling at the end of life.

These axioms only adds environmental considerations to product design but do not incorporate more innovative practices, employ ecological principles, and encompass social and ethical aspects.

Knight [3], made a bibliographic review of current published material on EcoDesign tools, techniques and case studies and categorized those in three broad groups:

1. Guidelines: defined as: providing broad support, with little detail, but applicable either across the whole product development process and lifecycle, e.g. ISO/TR 14062, or covering a significant area, e.g. design for recycling; design for disassembly; design for lifetime optimization.
2. Checklists: defined as: providing in-depth, but narrow application at selected stages of the product development process or lifecycle.
3. Analytical tools: Defined as: providing detailed and/or systematic analysis at specific stages of either the product development process or lifecycle e.g. eco-indicators; environmental effect analysis; environmental impact assessment; life cycle assessment; material, energy and toxicity matrix; life cycle cost analysis.

The range of tools and techniques applicable and in use seems to be linked to level 1 and level 2 in the innovation process, whereas when the challenge is systematic integration of creativity, innovation and environmental responsibility into new product concepts and productions systems application of LCA is becoming too complicated.

Based on literature analysis and current EcoDesign experiences van Hemel [10] clustered 33 EcoDesign principles, possible solutions to improve the environmental profile of a product system, taking all the stages of its life cycle into consideration, into eight EcoDesign strategies illustrated in Table 1. He clustered the strategies into two: the 'evolutionary' approach; and the 'revolutionary' approach. The incremental approach deals with a straightforward process of incorporating environmental principles into the design process while been largely technological focused. The innovative approach aims to develop new products, services and scenarios that enhance sustainable Lifestyles. Van Hemel [10] investigated 77 Dutch SME's use of EcoDesign principles for improving the environmental profile of products and concluded that all of these were incremental with a clear technological focus.

Schischke [7] found in their investigation of EcoDesign in SME operating in the electrical and electronic sector that these firms rarely implement EcoDesign in the product development process. Stevels [8] argue that EcoDesign is in a situation in which there is a kind of "saturation", enhanced by increasing legislation, easy technical improvements have been realized, limiting the potential of further competitiveness, and 'green' has turned out to be part of total functionality value. Bhamra [1] concludes in his investigation of EcoDesign models that little is understood or practiced with most EcoDesign theory because it is incremental in nature.

Table 1. EcoDesign strategies and principles [10]

EcoDesign strategies	EcoDesign principles
1. Selection of low-impact materials	Clean materials, Renewable content materials, Recycled materials
2. Reduction of materials usage	Reduction in weight, Reduction in volume
3. Optimization of production techniques	Clean production techniques, Fewer production steps, Low/clean energy consumption, Less production waste, Few/clean production consumables
4. Optimization of distribution system	Less/clean reusable packaging, Energy-efficient transport mode, Energy-efficient logistics
5. Reduction of impact during use	Low energy consumption, Clean energy source, Few consumables need, Clean consumables, No waste of energy/consumables
6. Optimization of initial lifetime	High reliability and durability, Easy maintenance and repair, Modular/adaptable product structure, Classic Design, Strong product-user relation
7. Optimization of end of life	Reuse of product, Remanufacture/refurbishment, Recycling of materials, Safe incineration (with energy recovery), Safe disposal of product remains
8. New concept development	Shift to service provision, Shared product use, Integration of functions, Functional optimization

2.2 Cradle-to-Cradle as Driving Force to Radical Change

Design for sustainable society (Level 4 of innovation) demand optimizing life-cycle performance, re-designing products and services based on re-thinking and new thinking with connection to life style change. This concept proposes the transformation of products and their associated material flows such that they form a supportive relationship with ecological systems and future economic growth The goal is not to minimize the cradle-to-grave linear material flow, but to generate closed-loop cyclical industrial systems that turn materials into two distinct metabolisms: the biological metabolism and the technical metabolism.

Three tools or instruments of industrial metabolism are most commonly applied. Ecological footprint; environmental life cycle assessment; and industrial ecosystems. The ecological footprint is a physical material and energy flow measure to and from a specific economy (country, region, land). Life cycle assessment has become the most widely used tool of practical environmental policy and industrial management. The cradle-to-cradle approach is an industrial ecosystem that alerts policy makers and managers to the importance of integration production, consumption and recycling activities and processes into a one local system.

On the firm level the cradle-to-cradle approach has growing attention in both in-dustry and academics. It is claimed to be a science and value based vision of industri-al systems to be commercially productive, socially beneficial, and ecologically intelligent [4]. Based on the 12 Principles of Green Engineering, designers and engi-neers can optimize products, processes, and systems.The principles are visionary guidelines to designer of industrial systems and not a defined conceptual approach including practical applications and tools. The focus is almost entirely on the physical flows of matter and energy in both the Product-Life-Cycle and the End-of Life-Cycle.

Comparing those 12 Design principles with the 8 EcoDesign strategies previously investigated it seems reasonably that the tools and applications to be used in the Prod-uct Life Cycle might be similar such as pollution prevention, cleaner production, re-cycling and waste management, environmental management system such as ISO14001 standard and EU Eco-Management and Audition Scheme that follow the quality management system philosophy of continuous improvement. There are no radical changes in the ways EcoDesign and Cradle-to-Cradle is implemented in the Product Life Cycle. It remains incrementally innovation based on the same set of beliefs, norms and standard practiced by the EcoDesign community.

3   Modularity as Open Innovation Generator

The material life cycle in the industrial ecosystem is at network of material cycles based on cooperation and linkages between different firms. These actors adapt to their surroundings with technologies, combustion and incineration techniques, production techniques, waste treatment techniques and other technical infrastructure for material cycles that are in a certain local industrial system. To function as an integrated sus-tainable supply chain working together up-streams in the product chain, but also down-stream requires the need to think holistic in the whole industrial ecosystem, and not just on those links which belong to its own sphere of legal responsibility.

Reuse, Remanufacturing, and recycling as end-of-life strategies, have addressed relatively little attention in the research community. It has earlier been presented the hierarchy of end-of-life strategies focuses on using simple product characteristics to make end-of-life strategy decisions (Figure 2). Strategies higher in the hierarchy mi-nimize the environmental impact.

The most critical discipline is the design for disassembly. The aims is to design a product that can be readily dismantled at the end of it life and thus optimize the reuse, remanufacturing or recycling of materials, components and sub-assemblies. Driven by the economic imperative cost minimization, the simple and most cost effective as-sembly technique may result in a product that turns out to be exceeding difficult to disassemble. But product design designed with disassembly in mind very often proves to be more profitable, with economic benefits arising from: high quality image, mod-ular design, upgrading of products, reduces components, reduced parts and materials inventories and fewer joints and connectors. Further, manufactures can benefit from generating a continuing revenue stream from the original materials by refurbishing their products.

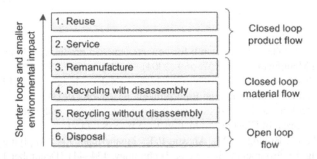

Fig. 2. Hierarchy of End-of-life strategies

The whole system is proposed to be understood as a modular system where each and every firm is a module whose structural elements are powerfully connected among themselves and relatively weekly connected to elements in other units. Each module consist of firm specific elements organized in its own way and with embedded knowledge infrastructure, integration of cleaner technologies, production systems, standards, planning procedures, worker skills and belief on sustainable initiatives. Modularity becomes the integration generator of modules by organizing the interdependencies among Product-Life-Cycle and End-of-Life initiatives so the socio-technical system function as an integrated whole. Transition to a sustainable system is founded on the configuration and alignment of heterogeneous elements and processes from each module into the renewal of an integrated networked supply chain. This broader innovation system perspective recognizes the need to radically new ways of organizing the socio-technical system instead of implementing isolated sustainable technologies into self-contain communities.

In emergent economies the collision between rapidly growing demand and a stable or diminishing stock of material supply will be the biggest challenge because industries depend on renewable resources The evolving focus on the industrial metabolism is a catalyst for a new round of creative destruction that offers unprecedented opportunities to foresight managers to rethink their prevailing views about strategy, technology, and markets.

4   Conclusion

The critical perspective on approached and means most popular in sustainable communities show these are isolated to the firm specific level and minimizing the volume, velocity and toxicity of the material flow system. The aim is to improve incrementally the performance of existing product and processes.

The industrial metabolism approach broader the problem of sustainable innovation by including the whole system perspective. This perspective calls for integration among embedded firm specific activities to form a renewal networked supply chain.

The paper proposes a modular approach as generator for development of a sustainable system taking account on both the social, economic and environmental elements. This multi-level perspective is evolving in the literature but much more work has to be done to improve its application into sustainable communities.

References

1. Bhamra, T.A.: Ecodesign: the search for new strategies in productdevelopment. Journal of Engineering Manufacture 218, 557–569 (2004)
2. Hill, B.: Industry's integration of environmental product design. In: IEEE International Symposium on Electronics and the Environment, pp. 64–68 (1993)
3. Knight, P., Jenkins, J.O.: Adopting and applying eco-design techniques: a practitioners perspective. Journal of Cleaner Production 17, 549–558 (2009)
4. McDonough, W., Braungart, M., Anasta, P.T., Zimmerman, J.B.: Applying the Principles of Egineering. Environmental Science & Technology, 434–441 (December 1, 2003)
5. Pigosso, D., Zanette, C.A., Evelyn, T., Filho, A.G., Ometto, A.R., Rozenfeld, H.: Ecodesign methods focused on remanufacturing. Journal of Cleaner Production 18(1), 21–31 (2010)
6. Schischke, K., Mueller, J., Reichl, H.: Ecodesign in European small and medium sized enterprises of the electrical and electronics sector. In: Proceedings of the IEEE International Symposium of Electronics and the Environment, Art. No. 1650067, pp. 233–238 (2006)
7. Schumpeter, J.: The Theory of Economic Development. Harvard University Press, Cambridge (1934)
8. Stevels, A.: Moving Companies towards Sustainability Through Eco-Design: Condition for Success. Journal of Sustainable Product Design 3 (October 1997)
9. Taylor, F.W.: The Principle of Scientific Management. Harper & Brothers, New York (1911)
10. Van Hemel, C.G., Brezet, J.C.: Ecodesign; A promising approach to sustainable production and consumption. United Nations Environmental Programme, Paris (1997)
11. von Weizsaecker, E., Lovins, A.B., Lovins, L.H.: Factor Four-doubling wealth halving resources. The New Report to the Club of Rome. Earthscan, London (1997)

Resource-Efficient Production Planning through Flexibility Measurements in Value Creation Systems

Sven Rogalski[*], Hendro Wicaksono, and Konstantin Krahtov

Institute for Information Management in Engineering, Karlsruhe Institute of Technology,
Karlsruhe, Germany
{sven.rogalski,hendro.wicaksono,konstantin.krahtov}@kit.edu

Abstract. For years, manufacturing companies have faced an increasingly complex and rapidly changing market environment which is the result of, if nothing else, higher customer individualization. This particularly concerns SME's, whose competitiveness is increasingly dependent on the early identification of new customer and market requirements and their ability to dynamically respond to these in an adequate fashion. In order to meet the high standards demanded of the planning quality and planning safety with ever increasing complexity and the continuous reduction of the planning time available, SME-compatible IT technologies are needed for the simulation of complex manufacturing relations. The following article addresses this problem and in-troduces the method set ecoFLEX, which enables the simulation of targeted and dynamic alignment of existing plant structures, resources and value-added processes with new production requirements. Unlike digital factory planning tools, a complete picture of the specific plant situation is not required, as will be illustrated by selected case studies from the medium sized production sector.

Keywords: Flexibility Measurement, Manufacturing Systems, Resource Efficiency, Production Planning and Control.

1 Introduction

The transition of modern industrial nations from a post-industrial to an information orientated society has gained considerable momentum in recent years. Global integration due to the explosive spread of modern communication technologies, especially with the advent of the Internet in the early 90s, resulted in an unprecedented level of transparency and integration of national and international markets. This led on the one hand to the development of new markets, while on the other hand, pushed competitors from low-wage countries into the established markets of developed countries, whose influence in their own markets is slowly disappearing [1]. This places new demands on the flexibility and adaptability of companies to successfully master the ever-changing, complex strategic and operational requirements in this turbulent market environment [2] [3].

---

[*] Corresponding author.

V. Prabhu, M. Taisch, and D. Kiritsis (Eds.): APMS 2013, Part I, IFIP AICT 414, pp. 119–126, 2013.

One approach to dealing with the increased requirements of this environment is the product- and resource-based networking of companies in the form of individual value-creation systems, attuned to manufacturing targets. Their goal is to balance the high uncertainty in planning, induced by the turbulent operational field, on an inter-company level through the appropriate configuration of the network. However, the information acquisition and processing of value-creation planning is already very time consuming and complicated, even at a corporate level [4] [5].

In this climate it is apparent that a company's information management is gradual-ly becoming a key competitive advantage and its importance will undoubtedly contin-ue to increase significantly. While the CIO was once purely responsible for the technical provision of data, it now holds the most responsibility for an enterprise's innovation. The effective and efficient management of information is thus largely co-decisive in the quick and effective performance of innovation processes and thus crucial for economic success [6] [7].

Despite the rapid increase in importance and value of information, the IT landscapes of many companies are still stuck in the past. While large companies struggle to align their systems and processes with the new conditions, small and medium-sized enter-prises often lack integrated systems. This applies particularly to the production, which must actively contribute to securing long-term corporate success. The use of IT takes over the tasks of planning, design, monitoring and controlling of information through-out the product manufacturing. However, there is a lack of effective and efficient in-formation management, especially for SME, which collects and evaluates information from existing ERP, CRM, SCM or digital factory planning systems, in order to inte-grate the flexibility and adaptability requirements for its own value creation while taking into account the customer and supplier processes [2] [5].

To master the complexity of the competing requirements of the demanded flexibility and adaptability along with the cost, time and quality goals in the product manufactur-ing, new information technology tools are needed. These must ensure the integration of existing IT solutions in the production environment of companies in order to allow the systematic and mutually manageable information processing for both strategic plan-ning and operations. Such tools can be grouped under the generic term "Digital Facto-ry" and allow the planning, simulation and optimization of products, processes and their associated use of energy, material, personnel and equipment [5] [8]. However, companies make different demands on the degree of detail of the simulations, the ex-pense for the construction of simulation models, the evaluate options and depth of integration with other systems to avoid redundant work. It is particularly difficult for companies to incorporate the system and product life cycle aspects into their economic goals within their product, process and resource planning, to find the best possible degree of flexibility and resource efficiency for its own value creation [9] [4] [5].

2   State of the Art

Leading digital factory planning and simulation tools offer an extensive range of functions for simulation, which can calculate complex and especially dynamic busi-ness processes in order to make mathematically safe business decisions. They are also suitable for the geometric and functional planning of factory layouts, whose production processes can also be planned and optimized in 2D and 3D. This allows for the visualization, simulation and analysis of the technical elements of production with their respective space requirements, but also physically available production area, the prescribed height and weight loads as well as the material and transportation flows in conjunction with the required manufacturing manpower [5] [10] [11]. Significant obstacles are in particular the high acquisition costs for the usage of such systems which threaten a positive cost-benefit ratio. Also their high training costs, due to their high complexity mean that they find little acceptance. Smaller factory planning tools are indeed cheaper than the market leader, but generally inadequately cover many specific planning problems. Further simulations are therefore mainly performed manually and are supported by self-developed software extensions or often by MS Excel. Especially critical here is the dependence of the planning results on the subjective factors involved in planning which often only restrictedly survey the impact of decisions and their consequences. Thus, there are significant weaknesses in the design, dimensioning and personnel allocation of production facilities, based on economic uncertainty and the current overcapacity [5].

In the relevant literature there are various approaches that are isolated from the typical digital factory planning tools, through which attempts are made to evaluate flexibility and adaptability of production [5]. The disadvantage of these approaches and assessment procedures, however, is their lack of prevalence in industry as they relate to restricted areas of concern and do not allow cross-analysis. Reasons for this are on the one hand, the unsolved problem of a generally applicable measurement and evaluation of the flexibility and adaptability.

3   Flexibility Measurements with ecoFLEX

Against this background, the flexibility assessment toolbox ecoFLEX was developed. This, thanks to its generically built interface, allows for easy integration with existing IT systems for strategic and operational production planning. This enables extensive information gathering and data processing, through the integrated evaluation methods and analysis algorithms for various planning and control tasks (Figure 1). Via the provided functionality for flexibility analysis, existing weaknesses in the design, dimensioning and staff assignment of production assessed in the context of economic uncertainty and potential capacity fluctuations can be evaluated, so that an economic balance between the prevailing planning uncertainties and the required degree of flexibility in production can be assured. Quantifiable parameters can be calculated with ecoFLEX by using existing resource information and their cost-, time and application dependencies, as for example from ERP-systems. Beyond the state of the art and research, this enables objective flexibility analysis on different levels of value creation systems (Network, factory, workplace, etc.).

Due to the fact that calculation parameters, which can be determined for different types of production systems, form the basis of the flexibility evaluation methodology, it can be applied in different sectors. Its customization to different evaluation challenges requires little effort and thus contributes most to the user acceptance of SME. The reason for this is the production network model, which allows the presentation of evaluation-relevant and existing production objects in an abstracted way and that ensures the logical, level-related gathering and structuring of the needed flexibility parameters. This enables the identification of flexibility-related dependencies between single production objects, so that flexibility deficits can be allocated to the responsible unit. The conceptual set-up is graphically represented in the figure 1.

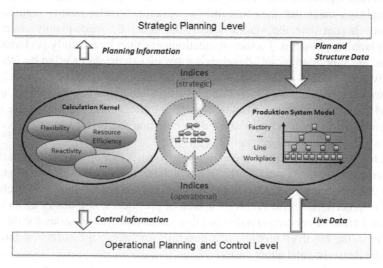

Fig. 1. Overview of the ecoFLEX approach (according to [2])

4   Application Experience with ecoFLEX

The usefulness of the Flexibility Assessment Toolbox ecoFLEX has already been proven many times in practice. The basis for this was the previously presented implementation of the evaluation mechanisms as a software tool. An example of the associated benefits and advantages will be shown using the example of a medium-sized automotive supplier for assembly technology. There, two assembly lines, together with workplaces have been investigated, where a total of nine different products for roof mounting are manufactured for the automotive industry. One of these products is available in two variants.

Due to the remarkable scope of analysis and the emerging findings, only the findings obtained with ecoFLEX in Assembly Line 1 will be discussed in this paper. Through the analysis with ecoFLEX, the production volume that allows the production to run economically was determined for the first time. This corresponded to the production numbers of at least 1,286 pieces (break-even amount) and a maximum of 5,596 pieces (maximum production), based on a work week and a defined product mix ratio (see Figure 2, top left).

All deviations above or below this volume range will inevitably lead to a loss of revenue. Such a break-even analysis was not possible before, because despite a directed material flow, this was discontinuous, which meant that there was a buffer in the form of crates and rolling racks at each work station. In addition, the personnel were not necessarily tied to a specific workplace, but could change between different ones (but not all). This allowed for buffers upstream the product stage to be depleted and replenished to a certain degree. In addition, there were also scattered cycles in the material flow that occurred whenever intermediate products did not meet the prescribed quality standards and were therefore sent back to workplaces upstream for rework. This resulted in a very high complexity and consequently a lack of transparency in production-related dependencies in the production planning of the company, so that resource planning was dependent on a so-called "gut feeling".

This "gut feeling" was also of great importance in the strategic planning of resources. Similarly so for the consideration of the conversion of Assembly Line 1, where the company's production planning found "suspected" flexibility deficits and thus wanted to improve the corresponding sub-optimal work processes. The focus was on the manual riveting workplace of the line (see figure 2, workplace 0060), which could be occupied by up to two operators and which processed the intermediate products from the Assembly Line. According to planning, this workplace should be replaced with an automated workplace (a riveting robot), where the necessary investment costs would be € 100,000. The analysis of this proposed line reconstruction was done by calculating the so-called ecoFLEX index. This index, which represents a flexibility index for a particular factory object, gives information about the manufacturing flexibility in a value-creation system in a simple form. It is not very useful when considered in isolation, but only when compared with the ecoFLEX indices of other factory objects in the scenarios to be examined. Thus, with larger deviations in the indices in the form of "outliers", existing flexibility discrepancies in a value creation system can be detected very quickly and the corresponding factory objects can be classified.

This confirms the aforementioned example of the proposed procurement of a riveting robot to replace the manual workplace 0060. This led, as shown in the flexibility investigation, to a significant increase in the ecoFLEX index from 79.95% to 94.38%, due to a significant increase in productivity, resulting from reduced scrap and reduced process times. Although this looked very promising at first glance, such a measure would have led to a local flexibility surplus which could not be totally exhausted by the assembly line. Worse still, from the perspective of the assembly line, this measure would have resulted in flexibility losses as a result of high investment costs for the conversion of the line, which would've increased the break-even volume to 1,441 units per week, whereas the maximum production rate could only be able to be increased to 48 units per week. These new findings led to the procurement of the planned riveting robot being discarded. Unexpectedly for the production planner, the real flexibility bottleneck in line 1 was at the workplace 0065, which emerged from the ecoFLEX index calculated (see Figure 2, left side).

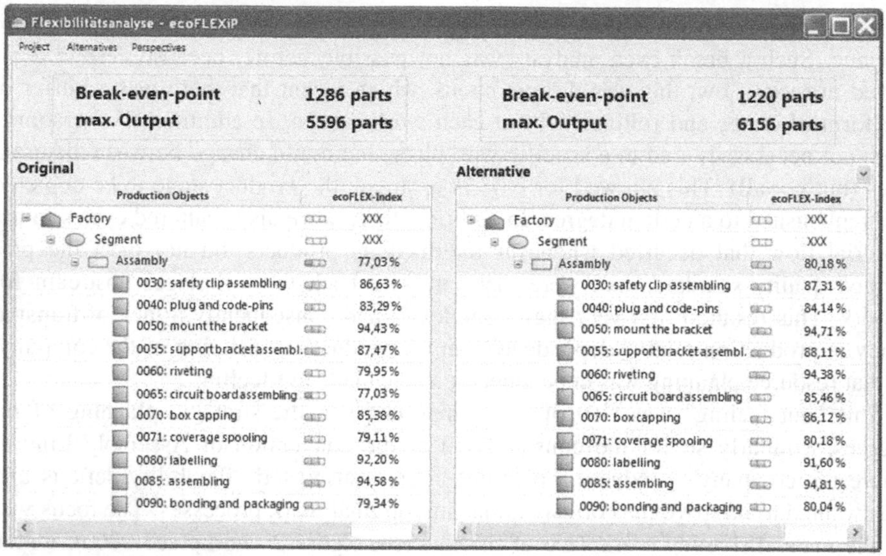

Fig. 2. Analysis of manufacturing flexibility with ecoFLEX

It was found that the operations carried out at this workplace did not have to be exclusively done by specially trained workers, but instead there was the possibility to decouple work operations to allow for different tasks to be done by semi-skilled personnel. This resulted in the skilled work force being freed up for other tasks. To achieve this, only the existing workplace 0065 had to be extended by an additional work bench and buffer storage. Through this an increase in the ecoFLEX index from 77.03% to 80.18% resulted for the entire line 1, which brought a clear improvement of manufacturing flexibility for the line. Expressed in terms of production numbers, this means a reduced break-even quantity of 1,220 pieces, as well as an increased maximum production of 6,156 pieces per workweek (see Figure 2, top right).

As part of these studies it was also found that the dimensioning of the workplaces 0050 and 0085 were chosen as too big in the former planning phase. This is illustrated by the ecoFLEX indices of over 94%, which as op-posed to workplace 0065 deviate greatly from the average of all ecoFLEX indices (see Figure 2, left panel). The result is a flexibility surplus, which causes avoidable additional costs through the acquisition of both workplaces. This finding was surprising for the production management, which made it clear that it can sometimes be useful to check the so-called "gut feeling" with the appropriate IT tools.

Another consideration made in this context with the ecoFLEX analysis was the assessment of potential outsourcing in order to be able to meet, if necessary, short-term demand spikes that exceed the maximum possible production rate of 6,156 pieces per week. The production management was clear in this case that the work done at workplace 0065 could be outsourced to a production supplier, but lacked a clear overview of the associated chances and risks for Assembly Line 1. In this way, in-house, operations-related production costs of 6.31 € occur for the carrying out of special assembly process at workplace 0065 (see Figure 3, right panel). The outsourcing of the process to an external third party would mean an increase in the company operations-related costs to 7.35 € (see Figure 3, right panel), which are based on the production service costs and logistics costs. Due to the increased variable production costs within the Assembly Line 1, the break-even volume increased to 1,573 pieces per work week, but thereby also increasing the maximum production volume to 7,920 pieces per week.

Fig. 3. Outsourcing Analysis with ecoFLEX

The ecoFLEX investigations provided important insights for the production planning of the company, as it was now clear that workplace 0065 represented a flexibility bottleneck that could be solved as described above by the easily accessible process improvement measures, significantly increasing the total flexibility and output rates (6156 units per week) of the assembly line (see Figure 2, top right). To meet sudden demand levels that exceed the existing capacity of the line, there is the possibility of using a production service provider, creating an additional flexibility buffer of 1,764 pieces per week, which can be retrieved when needed with a lead time of approximately three weeks.

5   Summary

The ecoFLEX investigations provided important insights for the production planning of the company, as it was now clear that workplace 0065 represented a flexibility bottleneck that could be solved as described above by the easily accessible process improvement measures, significantly increasing the total flexibility and output rates (6,156 units per week) of the assembly line (see Figure 2, top right). To meet sudden demand levels that exceed the existing capacity of the line, there is the possibility of using a production service provider, creating an additional flexibility buffer of 1,764 pieces per week, which can be retrieved when needed with a lead time of approximately three weeks.

On this basis, cost-driven flexibility and capacity weaknesses in the complete plant structure are quickly identified and solved through both operational and strategic measures. Taking into account the total efficiency of the production, strategic production changes can be quickly simulated by a simple integration of existing expertise of the company's own production planning and control. Thus, unnecessary additional costs due to inefficiencies in resource usage or senseless adjustments to the production infrastructure, such as construction and reconstruction of production facilities are avoided, creating financial flexibility for future investments.

A recent coupling of ecoFLEX with a 3D Visualisation and simulation solution allowed an immersive virtual reality of the production facilities. Production planners now have the opportunity to examine in detail the inefficiencies in resource allocation identified with ecoFLEX in the virtual plant models and to develop alternative solutions that would otherwise only be possible using a real object. With the help of the virtual image of the production and the simulation of processes, it is possible to test different strategies of dealing with their impact on the entire system.

References

1. Ehrlenspiel, K.: Integrierte Produktentwicklung: Denkabläufe, Methodeneinsatz, Zusammenarbeit. Karl HanserVerlag, München (2003)
2. Rogalski, S., Wicaksono, H.: Handling Resource Efficiency in Production of Small and Medium sized Enterprises. In: 18th International Conference on Engineering, Technology and Innovation (ICE 2012), Munich, Germany, June 18-20 (2012)
3. Loeffler, C., Westkämper, E., Unger, K.: Änderungsdynamik und Varianz im Automobilbau Analyse der Produktvarianz und deren Auswirkung auf die Produktion. Wtwerkstattstechnik Online 3, 99–104 (2011)
4. Reinhart, G., von Bredow, M.: Bewertung von Kunden-Lieferanten-Beziehungen in der Automobilindustrie. ZWF Zeitschrift für Wirtschaftlichen Fabrikbetrieb 12, 832–836 (2008)
5. Rogalski, S.: Factory design and process optimisation with flexibility measurements in industrial production. International Journal of Production Research, 1--12 (2012)
6. Maass, W.: Elektronische Wissensmärkte: Handel von Information und Wissen über digitale Netze. GablerVerlag (2009)
7. Schwinn, K.: Informationsmanagementprozesse im Unternehmen. In: Daten-und Informations-qualität, pp. 260–276 (2011)
8. Bracht, U., Geckler, D., Wenzel, S.: Digitale Fabrik Methoden und Beispiele. Springer, Heidelberg (2011)
9. Kunst, S.: Wirtschaftlichkeit der Virtual Reality Technologie. VdmVerlag Dr. Müller, Saarbrücken (2007)
10. Kohler, U.: Methodik zur kontinuierlichen und kostenorientierten Planung produktionstechnischer Systeme. Herbert Utz Verlag, München (2007)
11. Westkämper, E.: Digital Manufacturing in the Global ERA. Digital Enterprise Technology, Part 1, 3–14 (2007)

Modeling Energy Performance of Manufacturing Systems Using Gi/M/1 Queues

Hyun Woo Jeon and Vittaldas V. Prabhu

The Harold and Inge Marcus Department of Industrial and Manufacturing Engineering,
Pennsylvania State University, University Park, PA 16802, USA
albert.jeon@psu.edu,
prabhu@engr.psu.edu

Abstract. Energy expended in a discrete manufacturing system can be saved by turning idle machines off. Utilizing this idea, previous research has contributed preliminary models in which mainly M/M/1 machines are considered. To generalize existing approaches, this paper proposes a new energy model based on a Gi/M/1 queueing network. To start, a simulation model is built with Gi/M/1 machines. The proposed model is then built by fitting each GED (Generalized Erlang Distribution) to the observed first two moments of simulated interarrival times of all machines. Consumed energy is calculated separately by the proposed and simulation models, and, in the comparison between two estimations, the proposed method shows at most 4% different energy estimation from simulated values, suggesting that the proposed approach is promising for the energy analysis about a Gi/M/1 queueing network.

Keywords: Energy Aware Model, Gi/M/1, Queueing, Distribution Fitting.

1 Introduction

1.1 Motivation and Previous Research

Energy demand by the U.S. industrial sector accounted for more than 30% of the total U.S. energy demand, and electricity consumption of the sector took up about 10% of the total demand in 2010 [1]. The American electricity price for industrial consumption has continuously increased since 1990, and there remains an acute need to monitor industrial/manufacturing facilities to find a way of saving energy [2]. In the light of this observation, one noteworthy research contribution implies that 30–85% of energy in machining is spent at a constant rate [3]. Since it suggests that the significant amount of energy is wasted for machine idling, research works have been conducted to save energy by turning idle systems off especially in the DPM (Dynamic Power Management) field [4]. Thus DPM is grounded in theory, but there are inherent limitations in their applicability to manufacturing: First, each microprocessor state in DPM does not correspond well to that of a machine [4], [5]. Second, while electrical signals in DPM can be freely created and discarded among processors, physical parts in manufacturing cannot. Hence there has been difficulty in applying DPM theories

V. Prabhu, M. Taisch, and D. Kiritsis (Eds.): APMS 2013, Part I, IFIP AICT 414, pp. 127–134, 2013.

directly to manufacturing. On the other hand in manufacturing research, power and energy analysis has relied on the approaches which focus on a short span of time in machining. The traditional method has limitations in observing long run properties of energy consumption by machines [6]. One analysis, to address the problem, takes the idle state into consideration, but it still depends on coarse textbook tables for important parameters [7]. In more recent literature, the focus is on energy optimization of a unit machining process, but the methods are still unable to analyze energy consumption of yearlong machining [8], [9]. Queueing theory models, in consideration of described problems, can be alternatives to previous research since they can include working and idling states in the long run [10], [11]. However queueing based models in [10], [11] also have limitations in that they assume only M/M/1 systems or the restricted machine states. As a consequence, we need to improve existing queueing models in order to take more general types of manufacturing systems into accounts.

1.2   Contribution and Organization

The main contribution of this paper is the development of an extended energy aware model of machining. A machine network, in this paper, consists of multiple machines, and each machine has renewal arrivals and exponential processing times (Gi/M/1) to allow more generality. Dealing with renewal interarrivals, we assume that the first two moments of the arrival distribution are known, and the distribution fitting is performed to generate the arrival flow following the two moments. For machine states, total five states are included: setup, tool change, cutting, nominal power idling, and low power idling. Thus this research aims to provide a more general energy analysis than previous models described earlier in [10], [11].

The rest of this paper is organized as follows: After the machine states and the energy control policy are defined, a brief experiment is introduced to measure energy/power parameters of a milling machine in Section 2. Then in Section 3, the distribution fitting method with two moments is described. Section 4 introduces simulation experiments, and examines the comparison between the result by the proposed method and that by the simulation experiments. The conclusion and future research directions are detailed in Section 5.

2   Energy Performance Model

2.1   Machine States, Power Consumption Levels, and Energy Policy

Generally, machine states are defined as working, nominal power idling, and low power idling states [10], but this research regards the working state as the combined state of setup, tool change, and cutting. Thus we define five machine states, and power consumption level W of each state is as follows:

- Setup: Generic machine state of waking-up with W_S
- Tool Change: State for tool (cutter) changing with W_T
- Cutting: State of air or material cutting with W_C

- Nominal Power Idling: Idle state whose duration is less than τ with W_N
- Low Power Idling: Idle state whose duration is greater than or equal to τ with W_L

For the energy policy, machines are assumed to enter the low power idling state if the current idle duration is greater than the time threshold τ. Otherwise machines stay in the nominal power idling state during idling [10], [11].

2.2   Power Data and Experiment

Power data was collected in the experiment with a Haas VF3 milling machine. Six cuts were made on the steel block in 6 x 4 inches size, and depth of cut and contact surface (full/half) in each pass varied. Power and processing times were collected as in Figure 1 and Table 1, and data values of Table 1 are averaged during each machine state.

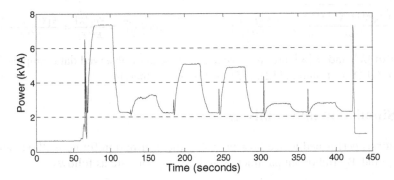

Fig. 1. Power Data (Haas VF3 Milling Machine)

Table 1. Averaged Power Data (kVA)

Pass No.	Machine State				
	Off	Idle	Cutting (time)	Setup (time)	Tool Change (time)
1	0.63	0.99	5.24 (57 secs)	1.89 (5 secs)	3.25 (1 sec)
2	-	-	2.78 (58 secs)	-	-
3	-	-	3.81 (59 secs)	-	-
4	-	-	3.72 (57 secs)	-	-
5	-	-	2.54 (57 secs)	-	-
6	-	-	2.56 (58 secs)	-	-

2.3   Theoretical Model of Consumed Energy Amount

The consumed energy for a unit time under the energy policy is written as [10], [11],

$$E[Energy] = \left\{ \begin{array}{l} W_S P_S + W_T P_T + W_C P_C + W_N P_N + W_L P_L \\ where\ P_X\ is\ probability\ in\ state\ X \end{array} \right\} \tag{1}$$

3   Distribution Fitting with Two Moments

$P(X > \tau)$ and $P(X \leq \tau)$ of the arrival process are important parameters in our energy analysis since the two parameters are used in calculating $P_N: P(X < \tau)P(idle)$ and $P_L: P(X \geq \tau)P(idle)$ in (1) [11]. Thus we need to have the probability distribution function from which the two probabilities can be calculated, and the distribution has to be fitted to the first two moments. For this approach, any single machine in a network is decomposed as an independent system, and GED (Generalized Erlang Distribution) is fitted to each machine's arrival flow [12], [13], [14], [15]. Using GED for fitting has two advantages: First, it allows us to consider relatively regular interarrivals with less coefficient of variation $(C_X < 1)$. Second, GED is easier to treat than other probability distributions as seen in its probability density distribution:

$$f(t) = p\mu^{k-1}\frac{t^{k-2}}{(k-2)!}e^{-\mu t} + (1-p)\mu^k\frac{t^{k-1}}{(k-1)!}e^{-\mu t} \; for \; t \geq 0 \tag{2}$$

$$p = \frac{kc_X^2 - \sqrt{k(1+c_X^2)-k^2c_X^2}}{1+c_X^2}, \mu = \frac{k-p}{E[X]}, \frac{1}{k} \leq C_X^2 < \frac{1}{k-1}, and \; C_X^2 = \frac{Var[X]}{E^2[X]} = \frac{E[X^2]-E^2[X]}{E^2[X]} \tag{3}$$

where $Var[X]$ and $E[X]$ are the variance and mean of observed data samples. More details of GED are found in [12], [15], and literature therein.

4   Simulation and Analysis

Simulation is performed to see how precisely the distribution fitting method can estimate P_N and P_L. Important parameters and assumptions are as follows:

- Scenario 1: Two machines in a row
- Scenario 2: Typical COMS manufacturing fab. [16]
- Utilization of Machine i $(\rho_i = \lambda_i/\mu_i)$: 0.5 or 0.8
- Cutting, Setup, and Tool Change Rates: Table 1
- Arrival Rate λ_i of Machine i: Number of arrivals per a time unit
- Processing Rate μ_i: Reciprocal of total sum of cutting, setup, and tool change time
- Arrival Distribution: Normal distribution with parameters in Table 2 and 3
- Processing Distribution: Exponential for Cutting, Setup, and Tool Change
- Queueing Model: Gi/M/1 as approximation
- Power Consumption (kVA) : W_S, W_T, W_C, W_N, W_L from Table 1
- Simulation Software: Simio V4.68

4.1   Scenario 1: Two Machines in Serial Line

Table 2 gives good estimations of P_N and P_L by fitting. Since the method is based on first two moments, normal arrivals would have been ideal subjects with symmetry and unimodal in their density. This also explains the smaller difference (F-S) of Machine 1 than of Machine 2 since arrivals to Machine 1 appear more normal than Machine 2's. It seems that there is no apparent relationship between F-S and utilization ρ.

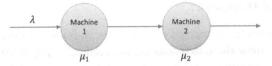

Fig. 2. Scenario 1 (Two Machines in Serial Line)

Table 2. Probabilities of Nominal / Low Power Idling States (Scenario 1)

| | | $\rho = 0.5, interarrival\ mean = 2.1, \sigma = 1.05$ | | | | | | $\rho = 0.8, interarrival\ mean = 1.31, \sigma = 0.66$ | | | | |
| | | Prob.(Low) | | | Prob.(Nominal) | | | Prob.(Low) | | | Prob.(Nominal) | | |
M	τ	Fit	Sim.	F-S	Fit	Sim.	F-S	Fit	Sim.	F-S	Fit	Sim.	F-S
	0.7	0.48	0.47	0.01	0.02	0.03	-0.01	0.19	0.18	0.01	0.01	0.02	-0.01
	1.4	0.37	0.37	0.00	0.13	0.13	0.00	0.15	0.14	0.01	0.05	0.06	-0.01
1	2.1	0.22	0.23	0.00	0.28	0.27	0.01	0.09	0.08	0.01	0.11	0.12	-0.01
	2.8	0.11	0.11	0.00	0.39	0.39	0.00	0.05	0.04	0.01	0.15	0.16	-0.01
	3.5	0.05	0.03	0.01	0.45	0.47	-0.01	0.02	0.01	0.01	0.18	0.19	-0.01
	0.7	0.43	0.47	-0.04	0.06	0.03	0.04	0.15	0.20	-0.05	0.04	0.01	0.03
	1.4	0.31	0.40	-0.09	0.18	0.10	0.08	0.11	0.17	-0.06	0.08	0.04	0.04
2	2.1	0.21	0.30	-0.09	0.29	0.20	0.09	0.08	0.13	-0.06	0.11	0.08	0.03
	2.8	0.13	0.20	-0.07	0.36	0.29	0.07	0.05	0.10	-0.05	0.14	0.11	0.03
	3.5	0.08	0.13	-0.05	0.42	0.37	0.05	0.03	0.08	-0.04	0.15	0.13	0.02

4.2   Scenario 2: CMOS Manufacturing Fab.

Contrary to the previous result in Table 2, P_N and P_L of Etching in Table 3 show slightly larger difference with the max F-S of 0.16 than those of Deposition and Lithography. In the next subsection, it is shown and analyzed how different energy estimations are made between simulation and proposed models based on probabilities in Tables 2 and 3.

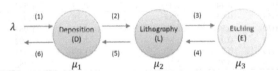

Fig. 3. Typical CMOS Manufacturing System

Table 3. Probabilities of Nominal / Low Power Idling States (Scenario 2)

| | | $\rho = 0.5, interarrival\ mean = 4.2, \sigma = 1.4$ | | | | | | $\rho = 0.8, interarrival\ mean = 2.63, \sigma = 0.88$ | | | | |
| | | Prob.(Low) | | | Prob.(Nominal) | | | Prob.(Low) | | | Prob.(Nominal) | | |
M	τ	Fit	Sim.	F-S	Fit	Sim.	F-S	Fit	Sim.	F-S	Fit	Sim.	F-S
	0.44	0.43	0.48	-0.04	0.07	0.03	0.04	0.17	0.19	-0.02	0.03	0.01	0.02
	0.88	0.31	0.40	-0.08	0.19	0.10	0.08	0.12	0.16	-0.04	0.08	0.05	0.03
D	1.31	0.21	0.29	-0.09	0.29	0.21	0.08	0.08	0.12	-0.04	0.12	0.09	0.03
	1.75	0.13	0.19	-0.06	0.37	0.31	0.06	0.05	0.08	-0.03	0.15	0.13	0.02
	2.19	0.08	0.10	-0.02	0.42	0.41	0.02	0.03	0.05	-0.02	0.17	0.16	0.01
	0.44	0.41	0.44	-0.03	0.08	0.04	0.04	0.15	0.18	-0.03	0.04	0.02	0.02
	0.88	0.30	0.36	-0.06	0.19	0.12	0.07	0.11	0.15	-0.04	0.08	0.05	0.03
L	1.31	0.20	0.29	-0.09	0.29	0.19	0.10	0.07	0.11	-0.04	0.11	0.08	0.03
	1.75	0.13	0.22	-0.09	0.36	0.27	0.10	0.05	0.09	-0.04	0.14	0.11	0.03
	2.19	0.08	0.16	-0.08	0.41	0.33	0.08	0.03	0.07	-0.03	0.15	0.13	0.02
	0.88	0.69	0.72	-0.03	0.05	0.03	0.03	0.48	0.56	-0.08	0.11	0.03	0.08
	1.75	0.51	0.61	-0.10	0.23	0.13	0.10	0.35	0.50	-0.15	0.24	0.09	0.15
E	2.63	0.32	0.44	-0.12	0.42	0.30	0.12	0.24	0.40	-0.16	0.35	0.19	0.16
	3.50	0.18	0.25	-0.07	0.57	0.49	0.07	0.16	0.30	-0.15	0.43	0.28	0.15
	4.38	0.09	0.13	-0.04	0.65	0.62	0.03	0.10	0.22	-0.12	0.49	0.37	0.12

4.3   Analysis and Discussion

From simulated parameters, expected energy demands for a unit time are calculated in this section by (1). Since these demands are the product of power consumption levels (W_X: X is any machine state) and the time proportion at each state (P_X), the resulting energy consumption between fitting and simulation depends on P_N and P_L as given in Tables 4 and 5.

Table 4. Expected Energy Consumption for a Unit Time (Scenario 1)

ρ	Machine 1 (kVA*min)			Machine 2 (kVA*min)		
	Fit	Sim.	Diff.(%)	Fit	Sim.	Diff.(%)
	2.793	2.805	-0.41	1.714	1.692	1.30
	2.832	2.841	-0.30	1.755	1.717	2.20
0.5	2.886	2.892	-0.21	1.793	1.753	2.30
	2.926	2.933	-0.25	1.821	1.788	1.88
	2.949	2.962	-0.44	1.840	1.813	1.47
	4.084	4.100	-0.40	2.342	2.283	2.56
	4.099	4.117	-0.42	2.356	2.294	2.70
0.8	4.121	4.137	-0.39	2.368	2.307	2.66
	4.137	4.153	-0.38	2.377	2.317	2.56
	4.146	4.162	-0.37	2.383	2.327	2.40

Table 5. Expected Energy Consumption for a Unit Time (Scenario 2)

ρ	Deposition (kVA*min)			Lithography (kVA*min)			Etching (kVA*min)		
	Fit	Sim.	Diff.(%)	Fit	Sim.	Diff.(%)	Fit	Sim.	Diff.(%)
	2.811	2.790	0.75	1.720	1.722	-0.16	1.429	1.413	1.11
0.5 (D, L)	2.853	2.817	1.27	1.760	1.750	0.58	1.492	1.451	2.74
0.25 (E)	2.892	2.855	1.27	1.795	1.776	1.07	1.561	1.511	3.17
	2.920	2.893	0.95	1.821	1.803	1.01	1.612	1.581	1.93
	2.939	2.926	0.44	1.838	1.824	0.77	1.643	1.625	1.08
	4.092	4.058	0.85	2.343	2.313	1.29	1.917	1.885	1.66
0.8 (D, L)	4.109	4.070	0.97	2.357	2.325	1.39	1.963	1.909	2.76
0.4 (E)	4.124	4.084	0.97	2.368	2.337	1.36	2.002	1.942	3.00
	4.135	4.099	0.87	2.377	2.346	1.33	2.031	1.977	2.68
	4.142	4.110	0.77	2.383	2.353	1.26	2.052	2.008	2.11

Energy demands of Scenario 1 are shown in Table 4. As P_N and P_L of fitting and simulation show quite close values, the largest difference is less than 3% in energy consumption. This agreement is also observed in Table 5 of Scenario 2. Although the largest difference 3.17% between simulated and estimated values is seen with Etching process, this value does not seem to be very large in that we just used the first and second moments E[X] and E[X²] of observed arrival times to estimate the arrival flow. Since the difference of P_N and P_L in Table 3 between simulated and estimated values is relatively greater than others, this is also expected difference. As a consequence, both tables are suggesting that the proposed method provides quite accurate estimations about the total spent energy on the machine network. In order to show the good fits between observed and fitted interarrival times, Figures 4 and 5 are added below. Both figures illustrate the histogram of observed data and pdf (probability density function) for Deposition and Etching processes respectively when the machine utilization 0.8 is considered.

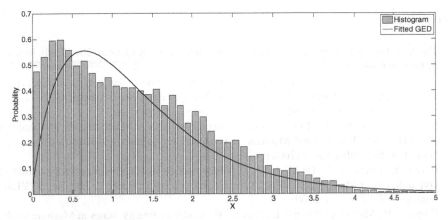

Fig. 4. Simulated Interarrival Histogram and pdf of Deposition (Scenario 2, Rho = 0.8)

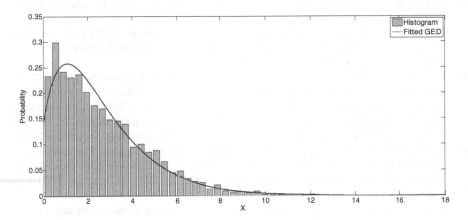

Fig. 5. Simulated Interarrival Histogram and pdf of Etching (Scenario 2, Rho = 0.8)

5   Conclusion and Future Research

This research proposes the method of estimating the energy amount of a manufacturing facility with machines in a network under the energy policy. Especially this approach aims at Gi/M/1 machines rather than M/M/1 systems for allowing more generality. To validate estimated values by the method, simulation is conducted, and the simulated result is compared with that of our approach. Consequently, it is shown that the proposed method gives, even at the worst case, only 4% different estimation. For further research, other queueing models such as the Gi/G/1 need to be investigated with the percentile fitting method for considering more general distributions, since the proposed strategy of fitting is based on exponential service times.

References

1. The U.S. Energy Information Administration: Annual Energy Outlook 2012 Early Release Reference Case (2012),
   `http://www.eia.gov/pressroom/presentations/howard_01232012.pdf`
2. The U.S. Energy Information Administration: Average retail price of electricity,
   `http://www.eia.gov/electricity/data.cfm#sales`
3. Dahmus, J.B., Gutowski, T.G.: An Environmental Analysis of Machining. In: Proceedings of 2004 ASME International Mechanical Engineering Congress and RD&D Expo, Anaheim, CA, November 13-19 (2004)
4. Benini, L., Bogliolo, A., De Micheli, G.: A Survey of Design Techniques for System-level Dynamic Power Management. IEEE Transactions on Very Large Scale Integration (VLSI) Systems 8(3), 299–316 (2000)
5. Frigerio, N., Matta, A., Ferrero, L., Rusina, F.: Modeling Energy States in Machine Tools: An Automata Based Approach. In: Proceedings of 20th CIRP International Conference on Life Cycle Engineering, Singapore (2013)
6. Kalpakjian, S.: Manufacturing Engineering and Technology, 3rd edn. Addison-Wesley Publishing Company (1995)
7. Overcash, M., Twomey, J.: Unit Process Life Cycle Inventory (UPLCI)–A Structured Framework to Complete Product Life Cycle Studies. In: Leveraging Technology for a Sustainable World, pp. 1–4. Springer, Heidelberg (2012)
8. Yan, J., Li, L.: Multi-Objective Optimization of Milling Parameters – The Trade-Offs between Energy, Production Rate and Cutting Quality. Journal of Cleaner Production (2013)
9. Calvanese, M.L., Altertlli, P., Matta, A., Taisch, M.: Analysis of Energy Consumption in CNC Machining Centers and Determination of Optimal Cutting Conditions. In: Proceedings of 20th CIRP International Conference on Life Cycle Engineering, Singapore (2013)
10. Prabhu, V.V., Jeon, H.W., Taisch, M.: Simulation Modelling of Energy Dynamics in Discrete Manufacturing Systems. In: Borangiu, T., Thomas, A., Trentesaux, D. (eds.) Service Orientation in Holonic and Multi Agent, SCI, vol. 472, pp. 293–311. Springer, Heidelberg (2013)
11. Prabhu, V.V., Jeon, H.W., Taisch, M.: Modeling green factory physics—An analytical approach. In: Proceeding of 2012 IEEE International Conference on Automation Science and Engineering (CASE), pp. 46–51 (2012)
12. Whitt, W.: Approximating a Point Process by a Renewal Process, I: Two Basic Methods. Operations Research 30(1), 125–147 (1982)
13. Whitt, W.: The Queueing Network Analyzer. The Bell System Technical Journal 62(9), 2779–2815 (1983)
14. Kuehn, P.J.: Approximate Analysis of General Queueing Networks by Decomposition. IEEE Transactions on Communications Com-27(1), 113–126 (1979)
15. Tijms, H.C.: Stochastic Models – An Algorithmic Approach. Wiley Series in Probability and Mathematical Statistics (1994)
16. Jaeger, R.C.: Introduction to Microelectronic Fabrication, 2nd edn., vol. V. Prentice Hall (2002) ISBN 0-201-44494-7

Modeling of Energy-Efficient Factories
with Flow System Theory

Hendrik Hopf and Egon Müller

Department of Factory Planning and Factory Management
Institute of Industrial Sciences and Factory Systems
Chemnitz University of Technology
Chemnitz, Saxony, 09107, Germany
{hendrik.hopf,egon.mueller}@mb.tu-chemnitz.de

Abstract. Energy and resource efficiency have become important objectives for industrial processes. They are taking more and more impact on the competitiveness of companies. Therefore, energy-efficient factory systems are needed in terms of sustainable production. Thus, new or improved models, methods and tools focusing energy efficiency are necessary. In this paper, the "Flow System Theory", as a tool for modeling technical systems and processes, is presented. It is extended in order to describe the energy flow systems of factories. This is supposed to be the basis for systematic modeling of energy-efficient factory systems.

Keywords: Energy Efficiency, Factory Modeling, Energy Flow Systems.

1   Introduction

Increasing demand for raw materials and the depletion of non-renewable resources lead to scarcity and uncertain availability of resources. Raw material and energy prices continue to rise in the future. Climate policy objectives such as the reduction of global CO_2 emissions and the expansion of renewable energy should counteract these developments. Besides cost, time and quality, energy and resource efficiency are more and more considered in business activities. It is not only an environmental contribution due to political, social and ecological challenges [1]. These objectives influence increasingly the competitiveness. The industrial sector causes about 30% of the energy consumption in Germany, whereas the most of it is used for process heat and mechanical energy [2]. By improving energy efficiency, direct cost savings and indirect environmental benefit can be achieved [3]. The saving potential through more efficient use of energy is estimated in different studies with 20 - 30% for industry, but it varies from company to company [4]. It should be noted that energy efficiency is recognized as an essential tool for energy savings. However, for instance, the "World Energy Outlook 2012" emphasizes that this potential is not yet exhausted [5].

In consequence, more research and development are necessary to design energy-efficient systems and processes.

V. Prabhu, M. Taisch, and D. Kiritsis (Eds.): APMS 2013, Part I, IFIP AICT 414, pp. 135–142, 2013.

2   Methodical Planning of Energy-Efficient Factories

The energy-efficient factory has become a new type of factory. It focuses on the manufacture of goods and services by minimal energy use and it emphasizes the energy flow [6]. Therefore, it includes energy-optimized systems and processes which are treated in their entirety with the complex coherences. Closed energy cycles of the factory contribute to the minimization of energy losses [7]. The energy-efficient factory is an active participant of the energy conversion chain. In addition, this factory integrates holistically the objective energy efficiency in the structural and procedural organization through Energy Management.

For the above-mentioned reasons, there are new requirements which lead to numerous new energy-related planning contents and volumes in different fields of action (e.g. building, building services or manufacturing) [8]. In this way, the complexity of this discipline rises. Therefore, there is a demand for new or improved models, methods and tools to support the planning participants.

For designing energy-efficient factories, a few scientific approaches have been developed in the last time.

The planning method for manufacturing processes in automobile industry by Engelmann concentrates the factory planning process on energy-related activities and includes action approaches (efficiency factor, reduced losses, recovery, substitution, dimensioning and mode of operation) for improving energy efficiency [9]. These approaches are expanded by including "sensitization" by Reinema et al. [10]. The "EnergyBlocks" planning methodology by Weinert et al. predicts the energy consumption of production systems basing on energy profiles of different operating states [11]. The "Peripheral Model" structures the systems of a factory according to the dependence on the production program, whereby the energy consumption can be traced to its origin backwards from the peripheral processes to the main processes [8]. The model for sustainable factories by Despeisse et al. aims at the interactions between manufacturing operations, supporting facilities and building with the help of material, energy and waste flows [12].

Besides, there are further methods and tools such as "Cumulative Energy Demand" [13], "Life Cycle Assessment" [14], "Material Flow Analysis" [15] or "Material Flow Cost Accounting" [16] which are not originally developed for factory planning, but can be used for specific activities (e.g. for analysis or evaluation). Energy flow visualization tools like Sankey diagrams support planning tasks, too. A popular example is also the "Energy Value Stream Mapping" (EVSM). It integrates energy aspects like energy key figures and design recommendations in the primary Value Stream Mapping [17-20]. The EVSM is a tool for energy-oriented analyzing and optimization of business processes and chains. However, the EVSM is not suitable for designing systems because of the specific principles of the Value Stream Mapping (e.g. process analysis based on a snapshot).

As a result, it was found that it is hardly possible to model factory systems with its elements, relations, items etc. considering energy efficiency with the help of existing methods and tools.

3   Modeling with Flow System Theory

In factory planning the factory is interpreted as factory system through system theory approaches. Complex totalities and coherences are described with the help of systems thinking [21]. In general, the factory is a sociotechnical system including humans and technology. In this paper, the technical systems are focused. These systems are artificial constructions that are created to fulfill a specific purpose [22]. In the case of factories, this means the production of goods.

The "Flow System Theory" is a tool for modeling technical systems and processes [23-25]. Hereby, the factory as an entire system combines particular flow systems. They are mainly separated by the flow items material, information, energy as well as persons and capital. The flow systems consist of individual flow system elements (e.g. machines or facilities) which are passed by the flow items. Meanwhile, flow functions such as the basic functions transform, transport and store are executed as well as changes of property or state of the flow items or flow system elements are caused [25]. Thus, the Flow System Theory offers a suitable basis for describing the factory system with its elements, functions, relations and items. Therefore, in the following, this approach will be extended in order to describe energy flow systems of factories.

4   Extension of Energy Flow Systems

4.1   Energy Flow Items, Functions, System Elements and Structures

In general, terms of energy are specified by physical (e.g. anergy, exergy or forms of energy) technical (e.g. energy consumption, energy losses or waste heat) or economical (e.g. primary or secondary energy) aspects [26]. On the one hand, flow items of energy flow systems can be described by the energy forms such as mechanical energy or heat energy. On the other hand, energy carriers such as electricity, compressed air or water can be used. This means that these mediums are allocated to the energy flow although they belong to the material flow by system theory approaches. However, due to the good measurability of the energy carriers, it is an acceptable solution which is also often used in practice (e.g. metering of consumption by Energy Management).

The basic functions of system theory are usable for energy flow systems, too. Transform converts qualitatively and / or quantitatively the input into the output, while transport and store do not change the objects themselves, but moves them through space and time [22]. Based on that, specific technical functions of energy flows such as energy provision / input, generation, conversion, storage, transportation / distribution, utilization, recovery and emission / output are derived (based on [26-30]). The flow functions are connected as chains or cycles.

The necessary technologies (e.g. generation or storage system) are derived from the flow items and the flow functions. The energy-relevant systems of the factory are classified in these types of technologies. In addition, these systems act as the so called flow system elements of the energy flow. It should be noted that the elements belong to different flow systems. This condition allows describing the object with its different functions. For example, primarily, a manufacturing machine is a part of the material flow, but it is also an energy consumer in the energy flow and an information-processing computer in the information flow. Thus, the system includes several major and minor functions. Furthermore, it is important to remember that each process and each flow system element needs energy for its performance. Therefore the material and information flows are always connected to energy flows [25]. Thus, the different flow systems are linked with each other through the flow system elements.

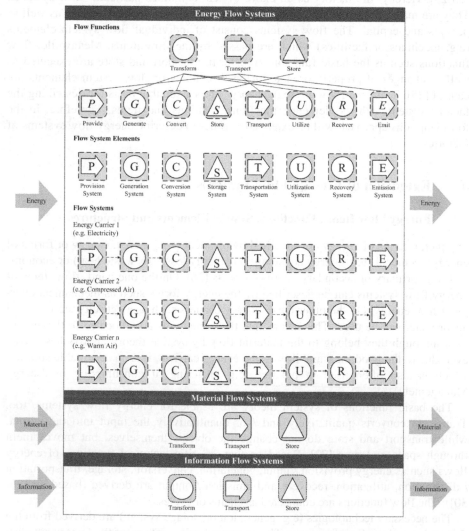

Fig. 1. Energy Flow Systems as Extension to [25]

The flow items pass the flow system elements one after another which results in a chain of functions (processes). By this, the flow system elements are connected with each other in space and time. Different structures of flow systems are derived from that fact. In general, an energy conversion chain starts with the input of a source and ends with the output of a drain. Meanwhile, various transformation, transportation and storage steps are processed. The energy chains differ in the energy carrier and the structure of the factory system. For example, compressed air is usually generated in-house whereas electricity comes mainly from outside. In context of energy efficiency, closed energy cycles (e.g. by energy recovery) are preferred. By this, the energy losses are minimized.

4.2   Energy Flow Systems

The classification of the energy flow systems belongs to the flow items. Therefore, basing on the necessary energy forms, the energy carriers of the processes are determined. The principle flow system from provision to emission can be set up for every energy carrier. However, it is also possible to separate the energy flow systems by energy forms (for physical description) or classes such as solids, liquids or gases. Figure 1 summarizes the energy flow functions, system elements and systems.

5   Use Case

The application of the Flow System Theory for modeling energy flow systems of a factory is illustrated in this section. The "Experimental and Digital Factory" (EDF) [31] is chosen as a simplified example. The EDF consists of various manufacturing, logistics and information systems of an item-based production. For example, figure 2 shows an assembly machine which needs electricity and compressed air and generates waste heat as byproduct. Therefore, different facilities such as the supply of electricity and compressed air as well as room lighting and heating are necessary for the operation of the machine and the other production systems. The structures of the flow systems are derived from the connection between the output of sources (e.g. air compressor) and the input of drains (e.g. tank) of the several energy flows.

The electricity is delivered in the building and distributed in several areas by distribution boxes. The compressed air and heat generation is in the same building but outside the production area. The room heat is provided by wall and ceiling radiators. The waste heat of machines and facilities has to be added, too. The interchange of warm and cold air between the building and its environment happens through the building envelope as well as through doors, gates and windows. In this case, the room is declared as energy user as drain of the generation of heat. However, it is also a heat converter, transporter and storage.

As an extension, by adding quantitative key figures (e.g. energy consumption per time period), inputs and outputs (balancing) as well as capacities and demands can be compared (not shown in figure 2). Hereby, weak spots such as bulk consumers as well as under-/overcapacities can be identified.

For example, facilities such as building services are often oversized because of multiple safety factors. Moreover, in practice, there is often no adaption of the energy infrastructure after changing the production processes. However, this is very important to optimize the energy infrastructure like reducing energy losses by avoiding converting processes or oversized systems (e.g. transformers or compressors). These facts are important indicators for the energy efficiency-oriented determination of functions, dimensioning, structuring and designing of factory systems.

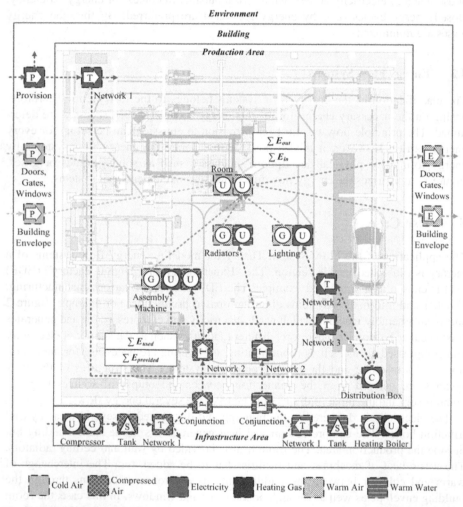

Fig. 2. Qualitative Model of the Energy Flow Systems of the Experimental and Digital Factory

As a result, the modeled factory creates transparency of the energy flow systems. It is the basis for the energy efficiency-oriented planning, analyzing and optimizing of the factory. Furthermore, other planning tools and methods such as energy flow visualizations with Sankey diagrams can build on it.

6   Summary

Sustainable production depends on energy and resource-efficient factory systems. Therefore, adequate models, methods and tools are necessary for factory planning. In this paper, the extension of the "Flow System Theory" and the qualitative description of energy flow systems are presented. As a result, the presented approach offers a suitable basis for the description of factory systems with their elements, relations and items. This is supposed to be the starting point for systematic modeling of energy-efficient factory systems and for further planning, analyzing and optimization activities. Currently, the energy-relevant key figures are specified and evaluated for the quantitative modeling of factory systems (see also [32]). Further on, the approach is tested and validated in other practical use cases.

Acknowledgements. The Cluster of Excellence "Energy-Efficient Product and Process Innovation in Production Engineering" (eniPROD®) is funded by the European Union (European Regional Development Fund) and the Free State of Saxony.

References

1. Nyhuis, P.: Ressourceneffizienz im Fokus. wt Werkstattstechnik Online 101, 179 (2011)
2. Federal Ministry of Economics and Technology: Energiedaten – nationale und internationale Entwicklung,
   http://www.bmwi.de/DE/Themen/Energie/energiedaten.html
3. Jeon, H.W., Prabhu, V.V.: Modeling Green Fabs – A Queuing Theory Approach for Evaluating Energy Performance. In: Emmanouilidis, C., Taisch, M., Kiritsis, D. (eds.) APMS 2012, Part I. IFIP AICT, vol. 397, pp. 41–48. Springer, Heidelberg (2013)
4. Hesselbach, J.: Energie- und klimaeffiziente Produktion – Grundlagen, Leitlinien und Praxisbeispiele. Vieweg+Teubner, Wiesbaden (2012)
5. International Energy Agency: World Energy Outlook 2012, – Executive Summary (2012),
   http://www.worldenergyoutlook.org/publications/weo-2012/
6. Wirth, S., Schenk, M., Müller, E.: Fabrikarten, Fabriktypen und ihre Entwicklungsetappen. ZWF Zeitschrift für wirtschaftlichen Fabrikbetrieb 106, 799–802 (2011)
7. Neugebauer, R.: Forschung für die Produktion in Deutschland – Maximale Wertschöpfung aus minimalen Ressourceneinsatz. In: 3. Kongress Ressourceneffiziente Produktion, Leipzig (2013)
8. Müller, E., Engelmann, J., Löffler, T., Strauch, J.: Energieeffiziente Fabriken planen und betreiben. Springer, Heidelberg (2009)
9. Engelmann, J.: Methoden und Werkzeuge zur Planung und Gestaltung energieeffizienter Fabriken. TU Chemnitz, Chemnitz (2009)
10. Reinema, C., Schulze, C.P., Nyhuis, P.: Energieeffiziente Fabriken – Ein Vorgehen zur integralen Gestaltung. wt Werkstattstechnik Online 101, 249–252 (2011)

11. Weinert, N., Chiotellis, S., Seliger, G.: Methodology for planning and operating energy-efficient production systems. CIRP Annals – Manufacturing Technology 60, 41–44 (2011)
12. Despeisse, M., Ball, P.D., Evans, S., Levers, A.: Industrial ecology at factory level – a conceptual model. Journal of Cleaner Production 31, 30–39 (2012)
13. The Association of German Engineers (VDI): VDI 4600: Cumulative energy demand (KEA) – Terms, definitions, methods of calculation. Beuth, Berlin (2012)
14. International Organization for Standardization: ISO 14040: Environmental management – Life cycle assessment – Principles and framework (2009)
15. Tschandl, M., Posch, A.: Integriertes Umweltcontrolling – Von der Stoffstromanalyse zum Bewertungs- und Informationssystem. Gabler, Wiesbaden (2012)
16. International Organization for Standardization: ISO 14051: Environmental management – Material flow cost accounting – General framework (2011)
17. Erlach, K., Westkämper, E.: Energiewertstrom – Der Weg zur energieeffizienten Fabrik. Fraunhofer, Stuttgart (2009)
18. Reinhart, G., Karl, F., Krebs, P., Maier, T., Niehues, K., Niehues, M., Reinhardt, S.: Energiewertstromdesign – Ein wichtiger Bestandteil zum Erhöhen der Energieproduktivität. wt Werkstattstechnik Online 101, 253–260 (2011)
19. Bogdanski, G., Schönemann, M., Thiede, S., Andrew, S., Herrmann, C.: An Extended Energy Value Stream Approach Applied on the Electronics Industry. In: Emmanouilidis, C., Taisch, M., Kiritsis, D. (eds.) APMS 2012, Part I. IFIP AICT, vol. 397, pp. 65–72. Springer, Heidelberg (2013)
20. Schillig, R., Stock, T., Müller, E.: Energiewertstromanalyse – Eine Methode zur Optimierung von Wertströmen in Bezug auf den Zeit- und den Energieeinsatz. ZWF Zeitschrift für Wirtschaftlichen Fabrikbetrieb 108, 20–26 (2013)
21. Haberfellner, R., de Weck, O., Fricke, E., Vössner, S.: Systems Engineering – Grundlagen und Anwendung. Orell Füssli Verlag (2012)
22. Ropohl, G.: Allgemeine Technologie – Eine Systemtheorie der Technik. Universitätsverlag Karlsruhe, Karlsruhe (2009)
23. Wirth, S.: Flexible Fertigungssysteme – Gestaltung u. Anwendung in d. Teilefertigung. VEB Verlag Technik, Berlin (1989)
24. Wirth, S., Näser, P., Ackermann, J.: Vom Fertigungsplatz zur Kompetenzzelle - Voraussetzung für den Aufbau kompetenzzellenbasierter Netze. ZWF Zeitschrift für Wirtschaftlichen Fabrikbetrieb 98, 78–83 (2003)
25. Schenk, M., Wirth, S.: Fabrikplanung und Fabrikbetrieb – Methoden für die wandlungsfähige und vernetzte Fabrik. Springer, Heidelberg (2004)
26. The Association of German Engineers (VDI): VDI 4661: Energetic characteristics – Definitions – terms – methodology. Beuth, Berlin (2003)
27. Crastan, V.: Elektrische Energieversorgung 1 – Netzelemente, Modellierung, stationäres Verhalten, Bemessung, Schalt- und Schutztechnik. Springer, Heidelberg (2012)
28. Rebhan, E.: Energiehandbuch – Gewinnung, Wandlung und Nutzung von Energie. Springer, Heidelberg (2002)
29. Rudolph, M., Wagner, U.: Energieanwendungstechnik – Wege und Techniken zur effizienteren Energienutzung. Springer, Heidelberg (2008)
30. The Association of German Engineers (VDI): VDI 4602 Part 1: Energy management – Terms and definitions. Beuth, Berlin (2007)
31. Horbach, S., Ackermann, J., Müller, E., Schütze, J.: Building Blocks for Adaptable Factory Systems. Robot. Cim.-Int. Manuf. 27, 735–740 (2011)
32. Hopf, H., Müller, E.: Visualization of Energy – Energy Cards create Transparency for Energy-Efficient Factories and Processes. In: Proceedings of 23rd International Conference on Flexible Automation and Intelligent Manufacturing (FAIM), Porto (2013)

Agile Planning Processes

Ralph Riedel, David Jentsch, Sebastian Horbach,
Joerg Ackermann, and Egon Müller

Chemnitz University of Technology, Department of Factory Planning
and Factory Management, Chemnitz, Germany
{ralph.riedel,david.jentsch,sebastian.horbach,
joerg.ackermann,egon.mueller}@mb.tu-chemnitz.de

Abstract. The paper explores the requirements and support systems for agile planning processes. It reviews therefore traditional planning processes and proposes a new model based on agile principles. The novel planning model is employed to frame a component-based planning approach and its application in a planning manual.

Keywords: Agility, component-based planning, planning methods.

1 Introduction

Production systems are decisive for the competitiveness of industrial enterprises and major characteristics of these systems are determined during their planning phase. Both, production systems and production system planning are embedded in a dynamic and complex environment, which is shaped by tremendous changes like higher market dynamics and the awareness for scarce resources. New system characteristics like modularity and adaptability [1] are needed in response. Together with further trends e.g. in IT, resulting production systems become more and more complex and less predictable.

Resulting challenges cannot be met with the traditional planning approaches. New methods are required to cope with uncertainty, dynamics and complexity [2]. Agile principles were developed for software development to meet exactly these challenges. This paper absorbs these agile principles and transfers them to the process of production system planning.

The remainder of the paper is organized as follows: The following chapter briefly summarizes production systems in general, the particularities of production system planning, as well as agile principles. Concluding requirements for new planning approaches are derived. The third chapter provides the novel agile planning model. This is followed by the description of a concrete idea of realization, the modular planning methodology and of a supportive tool, the interactive planning manual. The paper concludes with directions for further research.

V. Prabhu, M. Taisch, and D. Kiritsis (Eds.): APMS 2013, Part I, IFIP AICT 414, pp. 143–150, 2013.

2   Theoretical Background

2.1   Production Systems

The notion of production systems is based on general systems theory [3] and the fundamental views on systems [4]: the structural, hierarchical and functional perspective [5]. The structure includes people, technology and organization, while the hierarchy denotes several layers from the individual workplace up to the network of production facilities [6]. The function highlights that the system transforms inputs into value added outputs due to an open system border and processes (operational, management and supportive processes).

2.2   Production System Planning

The core task of production system planning, namely factory planning [7], is the design, dimensioning, realization and ramp-up of production sites [8]. Due to its uniqueness, production system planning is usually executed as a project and is primarily oriented on the business objective of ensuring a strong competitiveness [9]. There is a high degree of uncertainty in early stages of the planning process whereas this decreases throughout the planning project. Therefore, a systematic procedure is recommended in order to cope with the existing complexity [8]. A common generic procedure for problem solving is the systems engineering method, which consists of the steps (1) searching for and setting goals, (2) searching for solutions and (3) selecting a suitable solution [10]. Most of the phase models for production system planning are based on this logic.

The majority of methods used in production system planning can be characterized as analytical, which qualifies them for deterministic and static situations as well as for long-term planning cycles [11]. The usage of these methods follows a simple stimulus-response scheme (problem – method – solution) which does not reflect the actual understanding of a problem [12]. Therefore, conventional planning principles are more and more limited in a complex and turbulent environment.

Production systems (and also planning systems) can be described with typical characteristics from general systems theory: They are *emergent*, i.e. the behavior of the system can be predicted from the behavior of the single elements, which are the different protagonists and stakeholders in a planning project. They are *cross-linked*, i.e. the particular elements (protagonists, activities, decisions) are dependent on each other. They are *contingent*, i.e. the relations between the particular elements cannot be determined a priori but emerge in the course of execution. They are *open*, i.e. there is an exchange with the relevant environment, which in turn can be characterized as fuzzy and dynamic. They are *complex*, i.e. a huge amount of elements and relations and their dynamics lead to a high amount of possible alternatives for behavior (high variety). They are *self-referential*, i.e. the behavior of the system has effects on the system itself. They are *(partly) autonomous*, i.e. the system can independently make decisions regarding its own activities.

2.3   Agility and Advanced Planning Methods

Agile principles emerged first in software development projects and were established to overcome the traditional plan driven methods, e.g. the waterfall model or the spiral model [13, 14]. The agile principles are documented in the Agile Manifesto [15] (see also [14, 16]) and comprise values like "Individuals and interactions are more important than processes and tools" or "Responding to change is more important than following a plan". Agile methods can be characterized as follows [14, 17]:

- Iterative: they deliver full functionality from the very beginning and then change it with each new release
- Incremental: the system is partitioned into small subsystems by functionality and new functionality is added with each new release
- Self-organizing: the development team has the autonomy to organize itself
- Emergent: technology and requirements emerge throughout the development process

Augustine et al. [13] characterize the agile approach as an "overall humanistic problem solving approach", which assumes that all members are skilled and valuable stakeholders relying on the collective ability of autonomous teams as the basic problem-solving mechanism and minimizing up-front planning. The adaptability to changing conditions is stressed instead. Agility does not mean that there is no planning. Conversely, there is no detailed pre-determination of the whole project activities at the beginning. Planning is done phase by phase and is understood as a continuous process, which adapts to the ever changing situation [18].

2.4   Implications and Requirements for Planning Processes

The process of production system planning can be defined as a problem solving process for complex, ill-defined problems. Typical characteristics of such problem situations are a small amount of transparency, multiple and contradictory objectives, a vast number of interrelated influencing factors, fuzziness and uncertainty. As a result, it is hardly possible to oversee all relevant factors, interrelations and the problem as a whole from the very beginning. A clear picture can be developed only when working on the problem and when gaining more and more knowledge about the situation and about the system.

A central requirement from this discussion is that planning processes and the underlying activity sequences must be able to cope with insecure and incomplete information and goal definitions. Further information is gained in the course of working on the planning project. With more and more detailed information, the activity plan as well as used methods and tools can be concretized. Furthermore, a common issue is the unreflected usage of methods and tools ("methodism"). Solving this problem requires the evaluation of the suitability of methods for each situation and to allow necessary adoptions.

3   Agile Planning Model

3.1   Process Model

For the subject area of production systems planning, which is characterized by a high degree of complexity and dynamics, it is barely possible to determine all necessary steps and activities in advance in a detailed manner. It is rather necessary to adapt the planning procedure to the actual situation. Therefore, the planning of activities becomes more and more accurate when eligible information becomes available in the course of the project execution. The activity plan itself cannot be considered as finalized but needs to be adapted during the whole project. This procedure is known as "planning on the road" or as "planning construction site" [19, 20]. Transferring this principle to production system planning relates back to the agile approaches and the resulting procedure is displayed in figure 1 [cf. 21].

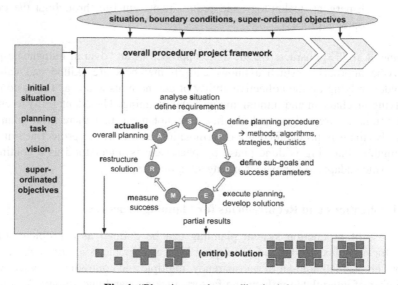

Fig. 1. "Planning on the road"-principle

Based on a problem definition, objectives and a vision for the planning project are developed. Hereby it has to be considered that objectives may change during project execution due to external developments or due to knowledge gained as the project progresses. Then a framework is defined based on objectives and identified boundary conditions. The expected result is specified as far as possible. For the execution, this framework needs to be detailed – but only as far as reliable information allows. Activities which are close to the point of time when the planning is carried out can be specified better than activities with a greater temporal distance.

This is followed by executing the project, whereas – following the procedure of a continuous improvement process – the following steps are processed in terms of several iterations:

- Analysis of the situation, i.e. of environment, requirements, goals, actual results, system behavior and system performance etc.
- Fixation of an appropriate procedure/ development of an activity plan for the next steps; hereby the procedure is concretized stepwise while executing the planning project
- Definition of sub-goals consistent with the overall goals of the project
- Execution of the activities, i.e. of particular planning steps
- Evaluation of results, based on pre-defined success criteria
- Restructuring of the entire solution/ concept, based on the insights gained whilst performing the activities
- Actualization of the overall planning procedure

The advantage of this procedure is that intermediate results can be gained, which are tangible, and the results can be evaluated against initially defined goals. At the same time, internal and external dynamics are considered due to the iterations. Therefore, the project planning as well as the whole planning project can be labeled as evolutionary. The effects of the proposed procedure are shown in figure 2.

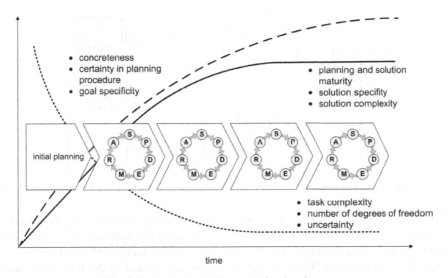

Fig. 2. Project and solution maturity development

On the one hand the uncertainty might be rather high at the beginning of a planning project. On the other hand the degrees of freedom for the later solution and the possibilities for variations are high as well. This is equivalent to a high degree of complexity [22]. Therefore, the concreteness and specificity of goals needs to be low in order to allow enough degrees of freedom for planning activities and for the later solution. This corresponds to a high degree of internal variety which fulfills the "law of requisite variety" by Ashby [23]. With an increasing degree of maturity, i.e. progress in the planning project, uncertainty is reduced, and the complexity of the task and internal variety are decreasing. As a consequence, the degrees of freedom for activities and for the solution are reduced. However, the complexity of the solution increases because intermediate solutions and sub-systems as well as their interrelations are fixed.

The described model could be summarized as reference on how agile planning processes are designed. This leaves a gap on the actual planning content which is further elaborated in the next section.

3.2   Component-Based Planning as Content Model

One possibility to model the planning content can be found in component-based planning, dating back to the 1970s, when Wirth and Zeidler [24] developed the vision of functional elements (components) in a modular system allowing for combination of components and their reuse across planning projects. This line of thought yielded two analytical classes: *planning components* and the particular elements of the production system: the *object components* (e.g. technology). Jentsch et al. [25] showed in this respect a strong dominance of object components in the planning literature, while planning components are less developed. We will therefore focus on planning components further on.

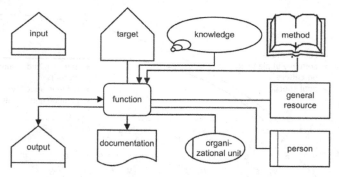

Fig. 3. General model of a planning component displayed as a function diagram (based on [26])

The concept of planning components was significantly enhanced by King-Kordi and Näser [26, 27] with the perspective of socio-technical systems and yielded the following views: The target view pertains to specific and measurable goals of a component or its deployment. Tasks or operations are represented in the functional view. A function utilizes tangible and intagible resources (people, knowledge, machinery etc.) summarized with the resource view. The structural view refers to different hierarchical layers of the production system. Finally, the yield view summarizes the (potential) output of a system in terms of products or services. Planning components can be further detailed based on this view concept (see figure 3). This generic model of a planning component distinguishes further kinds of resources such as methods and particular knowledge, which is necessary to fulfill the planning function.

The outlined component model enables the modularization of the planning process. Hence, planning components provide the generic building block to fill agile planning processes with required tasks. This could be done either with a blank-sheet-approach in every project or building upon the documentation of prior experience. The next section follows the second suggestion and introduces a way to access experience structured in a component-oriented manner.

3.3 Interactive Planning Manual

The general idea of the interactive planning manual is to support on the one hand inexperienced project members with a pool of completed planning processes. Here, the user may check e. g. how to use a specific planning tool. On the other hand, the component oriented structure allows for a simple reuse of particular building blocks by integrating them into a new planning project. Users receive consequently a bridge between task specific knowledge and its application during the planning process.

The manual follows a modular structure enabling for example the classification of the planning problem in order to find in a library suitable building blocks or combinations of them as planning processes. Further modules allow for definition of new components and processes as well as the tracking of project progress. Further details are given by Jentsch et al. [25]. The manual was implemented in a standard enterprise content management system and is currently being prepared for a laboratory test with students utilizing the manual during a long-term case study on production system planning. The test is intended to yield further insights in system acceptance and its suitability for agile planning processes.

4   Conclusion and Outlook

The dynamics of the environment and the complexity of modern production systems induce the requirement to reconsider planning methods. The combination of these observations with a modern understanding of human problem solving yields a new approach towards planning the production systems of the future.

However, the conceptual work on planning processes does not stand alone. There are conceptual synergies to component-based planning and those synergies will be further investigated by means of laboratory tests in the near future.

References

1. Zaeh, M.F., Moeller, N., Vogl, W.: Symbiosis of Changeable and Virtual Production – The Emperor's New Clothes or Key Factor for Future Success? In: CARV 2005, pp. 3–10. Utz, München (2005)
2. Riedel, R., Mueller, E.: Integrating Planning and Operations, Technology and People in Industrial Engineering. In: Spath, D., Ilg, R., Krause, T. (eds.) Proceedings of the 21st International Conference on Production Research (ICPR), Stuttgart (2011)
3. von Bertalanffy, L.: An Outline of General Systems Theory. The British Journal for the Philosophy of Science I, 134–165 (1950)
4. Ropohl, G.: Allgemeine Technologie - Eine Systemtheorie der Technik. Universitätsverlag Kalsruhe, Karlsruhe (2009)
5. Bellgran, M., Säfsten, K.: Production Development. Springer, London (2010)

6. Jentsch, D., Riedel, R., Günther, L., Müller, E.: Strategic Capabilities as Enablers for Innovation in Production Systems. In: Spath, D., Ilg, R., Krause, T. (eds.) Proceedings of the 21st International Conference on Production Research (ICPR), Stuttgart (2011)
7. Schenk, M., Wirth, S., Müller, E.: Factory Planning Manual: Situation-Driven Production Facility Planning. Springer (2009)
8. Hernández Morales, R.: Systematik der Wandlungsfähigkeit in der Fabrikplanung. VDI Verlag, Düsseldorf (2003)
9. Schmigalla, H.: Fabrikplanung: Begriffe und Zusammenhänge. Hanser Verlag, München (1995)
10. Haberfellner, R., Nagel, P., Becker, M.: Systems Engineering. Orell Füssli (2002)
11. Dombrowski, U., Hennersdorf, S.: Methoden- und Werkzeug-Matching zur Planung innovativer Fabriken: Von Betriebszielen zu innovativen Fabrikstrukturen. wt Werkstattstechnik Online 100, 234–241 (2008)
12. Dörner, D.: Problemlösen als Informationsverarbeitung. Kohlhammer, Stuttgart (1987)
13. Augustine, S., Payne, B., Sencindiver, F., Woodcock, S.: Agile projectmanagement. Communications of the ACM 48, 85–89 (2005)
14. Lindvall, M., Basili, V.R., Boehm, B., Costa, P., Dangle, K., Shull, F., Tesoriero, R., Williams, L., Zelkowitz, M.V.: Empirical Findings in Agile Methods. In: Wells, D., Williams, L. (eds.) XP/Agile Universe 2002. LNCS, vol. 2418, pp. 197–207. Springer, Heidelberg (2002)
15. Manifesto for Agile Software Development, http://agilemanifesto.org/
16. Boehm, B.: Get ready for agile methods, with care. Computer 35, 64–69 (2002)
17. Pfleeger, S.L.: Software Engineering: Theory and Practice. Prentice Hall, Upper Saddle River (1998)
18. Gernert, C.: Agiles Projektmanagement: Risikogesteuerte Softwareentwicklung. Hanser, München (2003)
19. von der Weth, R.: Die Sinnlichkeit des Wissens und die Weisheit der Dinge. In: Sachse, P., Weber, W.G. (eds.) Zur Psychologie der Tätigkeit, pp. 87–100. Huber, Bern (2006)
20. von der Weth, R.: Management der Komplexität. Ressourcenorientiertes Handeln in der Praxis. Huber, Bern (2001)
21. Riedel, R.: Systemische Fabrikbetriebsplanung auf Basis eines kybernetisch - soziotechnischen Modells. Chemnitz (2012)
22. Malik, F.: Strategie des Managements komplexer Systeme: Ein Beitrag zur Management-Kybernetik evolutionärer Systeme. Haupt, Bern (2006)
23. Ashby, W.R.: An introduction to cybernetics. Chapman & Hall, London (1956)
24. Wirth, S., Zeidler, H.: Untersuchungen zur Entwicklung und Anwendung von Bausteinen in der technologischen Betriebsprojektierung unter besonderer Berücksichtigung ihrer Schnittparameter (1974)
25. Jentsch, D., Horbach, S., Ackermann, J., Mueller, E.: Towards an Interactive Planning Manual for Production Networks. In: XVII Summer School "Francesco Turco", Venice (2012),
   http://www.summerschool-aidi.it/images/paper2012/3.6.pdf
26. King-Kordi, A.: Methodik zur bausteinbasierten Planung und Organisation von verfahrenstechnischen Produktionssystemen (2010)
27. Näser, P.: Component based planning of manufacturing plants. In: 3rd Annual Conference on Systems Engineering Research, pp. 393–402. Stevens Institute of Technology, Hoboken (2005)

Multi-stage Parallel Machines and Lot-Streaming Scheduling Problems – A Case Study for Solar Cell Industry

Hi-Shih Wang[1], Li-Chih Wang[1], Tzu-Li Chen[2],
Yin-Yann Chen[3], and Chen-Yang Cheng[1,*]

[1] Department of Industrial Engineering and Enterprise information, Tunghai University
Taichung 40704, Taiwan, ROC
chengcy@thu.edu.tw
[2] Department of Information Management, Fu Jen Catholic University
New Taipei City 24205, Taiwan, ROC
[3] Department of Industrial Management, National Formosa University
Yunlin County 632, Taiwan, ROC

Abstract. This research focuses on a parallel machines scheduling problem considering lot streaming which is similar to the traditional hybrid flow shop scheduling (HFS). In a typical HFS with parallel machines problem, the allocation of machine resources for each order should be determined in advance. In addition, the size of each sublot is splited by parallel machines configuration. However, allocation of machine resources, sublot size and lot sequence are highly mutual influence. If allocation of machine resources has been determined, adjustment on production sequence is unable to reduce production makespan. Without splitting a given job into sublots, the production scheduling cannot have overlapping of successive operations in multi-stage parallel machines environment thereby contributing to the best production scheduling. Therefore, this research motivated from a solar cell industry is going to explore these issues. The multi-stage and parallel-machines scheduling problem in the solar cell industry simultaneously considers the optimal sublot size, sublot sequence, parallel machines sublot scheduling and machine configurations through dynamically allocating all sublot to parallel machines. We formulate this problem as a mixed integer linear programming (MILP) model considering the practical characteristics including parallel machines, dedicated machines, sequence-independent setup time, and sequence-dependent setup time. A hybrid-coded particle swarm optimization (HCPSO) is developed to find a near-optimal solution. At the end of this study, the result of this research will compare with the optimization method of mixed integer linear programming and case study.

Keywords: Hybrid flow shop scheduling, particle swarm optimization, solar cell industry, lot streaming.

---

* Corresponding author.

V. Prabhu, M. Taisch, and D. Kiritsis (Eds.): APMS 2013, Part I, IFIP AICT 414, pp. 151–158, 2013.
© IFIP International Federation for Information Processing 2013

1   Introduction

Lately, many countries have focused their research and development efforts on sustainable energies such as wind, tidal, and solar energies. Among these, solar energy has attracted the greatest attention. Solar cell manufacturing follows the hybrid flow shop (HFS) mode, which is a flow shop mode incorporated with multiple processes and parallel machines. [1,2] proposed a flow shop mixed mode that consists of flow shop scheduling (FSS) and parallel machine scheduling (PMS)[3].

Initially, HFS could only match a single machine for one order. Later on, Chen and Lee (1999)[4] proposed a production environment wherein one order could plan mutiple machines (multiprocessor task) (Fig. 1.), and wherein a series of studies follows the same assumption that configure only when the machine resources for each order is known. In this same enviroment, [5] planned the allocation of machines for each order and worked out an optimal production sequence configured by various scheduling algorithms.

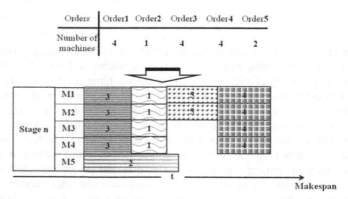

Fig. 1. Schematic diagram showing a single order being assigned to multiple machines (machine configuration is known)

The production environment nowadays is constantly changing, thereby generating more complicated environments. Therefore, the production environment has no way of finding an optimal scheduling combination through sequence adjustment in an existing machine configuration. Recently, the heated solar cell industry has been classified as an architecture of parallel machine resource in an HFS environment in academic research, but they are not identical. As a result, the configuration pattern of parallel machine for this order is not clear among line managers. Thus, the production sequence has to be planned using traditional dispatching rules such as the earliest due date, which cannot provide an optimal schedule plan. Hence, [6] created a schedule plan with an unknown machine configuration and order production to extend the HFS environment. Each order can plan a maximum number of machines in the process, and the number of machines is subject to dynamic adjustment. This plan proposes a scheduling solution for this problem and gives proper assessment to solve such kinds of production problems.

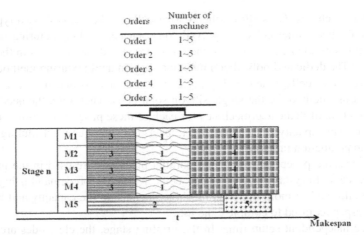

Fig. 2. Schematic diagram showing a single order being assigned to multiple machines (machine configuration is unknown)

Methods such as lot splitting have been developed and introduced into the manufacturing industry to shorten time of completion. Literature suggests that lot splitting can provide better performance ([7],[8]). With respect to the production architecture of parallel machine resource in an HFS environment, studies have paid little attention to variable lot splitting. Therefore, the current study proposes an actual instance-crystal silicon solar cell industry based on the architecture of HFS production to consider process properties such as parallel machine, special machine, setup time, etc., and to solve scheduling issues through the particle swarm optimization (PSO) with the batch, batch size, and sequence of order as unknown variables.

The aim of this research is to determine the job production sequence, number of sublots, and which machines these sublots should be assigned to. This study employs the production scheduling of crystalline silicon solar cells as a case study that focuses on the four characteristics to establish a suitable product planning and reduce the makespan time. The characteristics include parallel processing, dedicated machines, sequence-independent setup time, and sequence-dependent setup time. Due the computational complexity of the model, A hybrid-coded particle swarm optimization algorithm (HCPSO) was used to design to obtain the near-optimal scheduling configuration. Our preliminary computational study shows that the developed HCPSO not only provides good quality solutions within a reasonable amount of time but also outperforms the classic branch and bound method and the current heuristic practiced by the case company. The rest of the paper is organized as follows; Section 2 defines the multi-stage and parallel-machine scheduling problem in the solar cell industry; Section 3 develops a hybrid coded PSO algorithm to obtain the near-optimal solution; Section 4 addresses the excellent performance of the HCPSO algorithm through the computational study and Section 5 finally presents the concluding remarks.

2   Hybrid Flow Shop Scheduling for Solar Cell Manufacturing

The manufacturing of crystal silicon solar cells comprises six processes, and each process has its practical characteristics that influence the production schedule. The production characteristics are detailed below:

1. Dedicated machines: Crystalline silicon solar cells are basically of two types: single-crystal silicon solar cells and polysilicon solar cells. Manufacturing machines of both types of solar cells are the same. However, the difference lies in the texturing stage. The dedicated polysilicon machines use an acid texturing method for the polysilicon solar cells, whereas the single silicon dedicated machines use an alkaline texturing method for the single silicon solar cells. Therefore, the need for different numbers of dedicated machines for each of these processes is obvious due to the variance in capacity. This difference impacts the subsequent scheduling method in the job production process.
2. Parallel machine processing: Identical parallel machines are used in the manufacturing process of crystalline silicon solar cells. When the job demand is high, a job must be allocated to more than one machine, increasing the capacity and reducing the makespan required to complete the job.
3. Sequence independent setup time: In the printing stage, the electrodes are printed on both sides of the silicon that is used to collect and conduct the current flow. Depending on customers' requirements, different densities of printing designs are available. Because a few order can have the similarity design, the print setup are almost necessary for all kinds of orders, which is referred to as sequence independent setup time.
4. Sequence dependent setup time: Due to the number of electrodes on the surface, the crystalline silicon solar cell can be categorized as: 2 busbars and 3 busbars. In the testing stage, the measurement probe must be adjusted according to the number of electrodes in both busbar types. Therefore, the probe adjustment time will be affected by the job sequence, which influences the setup time. This is referred to as sequence dependent setup time. Setting the optimal production sequence to reduce the number of setups and shorten the overall completion time is the key focus of this restriction.

3   Hybrid-Coded Particle Swarm Optimization Algorithm

In this section, a novel hybrid-coded particle swarm optimization algorithm (HCPSO) is designed to find the near-optimal solution through the evolutionary process because of the computational complexity of the proposed MILP model. The details of the elements are described as follows.

1. Particle Representation

The decision of HFS problems must simultaneously determine the batch numbers and size of each manufacturing order and the batch sequence for all manufacturing orders in each stage. There are two parts in the HCPSO which is different from the traditional PSO. The first part called the master (the numbers and size of batch) particle, indicates the batch numbers of the each order and the each batch size. For each particle within first part, there exists a second part called the slave (batch sequence) particle, indicates the batch sequence decision using batch-based encoding.

2. Generate an Initial Population

In our HCPSO implementation, the initial population of master and slave particle is randomly generated.

3. Initialize the Value of *Cr*

In PSO, the parameters w, r_1, r_2 are critical factors influencing the convergence level of the algorithm (Naka et al., 2003).The research in this paper displaces the random numbers of r 1 and r 2 with the *Cr*, which makes its convergence level better (Chuang et al., 2008b; Sun et al., 2011b). The equation to calculate *Cr* is as follows:

$$Cr(n + 1) = k \times Cr(n) \times (1 - Cr(n)) \tag{1}$$

In Eq. (1), $Cr(n)$ represents the *Cr* of the n time; k represents the driving parameter, controlling the oscillation of *Cr*. When initializing $Cr(0)$, the $Cr(0)$ generated by random numbers can not equal $\{0, 0.25, 0.5, 0.75, 1\}$ and k must equal to 4.

4. Update the Inertia Weight

Appropriate inertia weights enable a particle to have exploration capability in the initial period and better exploitation capability in the final period. A higher inertia weight implies larger incremental changes in velocity per iteration, and thus the exploration of new search areas for better solution. However, a smaller inertia weight signifies less variation in velocity, providing slower change in terms of fine tuning a local search. Therefore, it would be better that the searching process should start with a high inertia weight for global exploration, with the inertia weight decreasing to facilitate finer local explorations in later iterations. The equation to update the inertia weight adopted in this paper is proposed by Fan and Chiu (2007), nonlinearly decreasing weight method. In this equation, t is the iteration number; $w(t)$ is the inertia weight of the t iteration.

$$w(t) = \left(\frac{2}{t}\right)^{0.3} \tag{2}$$

5. Calculate the Fitness Value

Based on the known the numbers, size and sequence of batch, this step precedes the forward capacity allocation to calculate the fitness values (makespan) of all the particles.

6. Update Particle Best (*pBset*)

The *pBest* is the best position of each particle in its own searching process. During the iterations, the particle's fitness evaluation is compared with *pBest*. If the current value is better than *pBest*, then set *pBest* value equal to the current value.

7. Update Global Best (*gBset*)

Compare fitness evaluation with the population's overall previous best, *gBest*. If the current value is better than *gBest*, then update the current particle's value to *gBest*.

8. Update Cr, Velocity and Position of the Particle

Assuming that the search space is D-dimensional, the i-th particle of the swarm is represented by a D-dimensional vector $X_i = (X_{i1}, X_{i2}, \dots, X_{iD})$ and the position change (velocity) of the i-th particle is $V_i = (V_{i1}, V_{i2}, \dots, V_{iD})$. The best particle of the swarm, that is, the particle with the best objective function value, is denoted by $gBest$. The best previous position of the i-th particle in its own searching trajectory is recorded and represented as $pBest$. This paper adopts the Eq.(3) to update the Cr and the velocities and positions of the particles are manipulated according to the following equations (the superscript t denotes the iteration):

$$
\begin{aligned}
V_{id}(t+1) &= w \times V_{id}(t) + c_1 \times Cr(n) \times \big(pbest_{id}(t) - X_{id}(t)\big) \\
&+ c_2 \times (1 - Cr(n)) \times \big(gbest_d(t) - X_{id}(t)\big)
\end{aligned}
\tag{3}
$$

$$
X_{id}(t+1) = X_{id}(t) + V_{id}(t+1)
\tag{4}
$$

where $i = 1, 2, y, N$, and N is the size of the population; w is the inertia weight which was developed to better control exploration and exploitation; c_1 and c_2 are two positive constants, called the cognitive and social parameters respectively; and $Cr(n)$ represents the Cr of the n time, as stated in 3. Eq. (3) is used to determine the i-th particle's new velocity, at each iteration, while Eq. (4) provides the new position of the i-th particle, adding its new velocity to its current position.

9. Determine Whether the Same Optimal Solution of the Population Which Iterates n Times Exists

If yes, execute 10 and precede the boundary search. If not, skip to 11.

10. Boundary Search

The boundary search aims to prevent that the current solution falls into the local optimum and enable it to avoid being a regional solution, and in turn to find the global optimum. The boundary search is to generate new particles for each dimension by random. The amount is 10% of the population, with which displace the worst 10% of the original population.

11. To Decide whether the Designated Times of Iteration Are Reached

The termination criterion of the HCPSO algorithm proposed in this paper is that when the number of iteration exceeds the designated maximum iteration times, terminate the algorithm. If it is not reached, return to 4.

4   Computational Study

We test objective value for HCPSO algorithm. The objective values of all problems are shown in Table 1. From this table, we can observe that the value of average solution for HCPSO. This shows that the proposed HCPSO algorithm can find the near-optimal solution. In the large samples (from problem #6 to problem # 9), the developed HCPSO algorithm still generates better solutions for the large samples in the reasonable time. Consequently, from above analysis, our results claim that the proposed HCPSO algorithm not only provides the near-optimal solutions irrespective of the size of the sample data, it also generates the better solutions for any samples in which MILP algorithm cannot found any feasible solutions.

Table 1. The objective value for B&B

Problem Number	Problem Size (order,machine,stage)	Min. Solution	Average Solution	Max. Solution
1	(3, 3, 4)	46512	46767.6	46800
2	(3, 5, 4)	36000	37555.6	38448
3	(5 3, 4)	72000	72064.8	72648
4	(5, 5, 6)	60480	60761	61020
5	(5, 8, 6)	42120	42288.6	42480
6	(10, 8, 6)	78552	81453	82980
7	(10 10, 6)	66960	74760.6	78084
8	(20, 10, 8)	131439	135654.6	143280
9	(20, 15, 10)	106740	117176.4	128016

5   Summary

This paper presents a multi-stage and parallel-machine scheduling problem which is similar to the traditional hybrid flow shop scheduling (HFS) in the solar cell industry. The multi-stage and parallel-machines scheduling problem simultaneously determines order production sequence, multiprocessor task scheduling and optimal machine configuration through dynamically allocating all jobs to multiple machines under the minimization of the maximum makespan. A mixed integer linear programming model has been proposed, in consideration of many practical characteristics including hybrid flow shop, parallel machine system, specified machines, sequence-independent setup time, and sequence-dependent setup time. Because of the computational complexity, a hybrid approach based on the variable neighborhood search and particle swarm optimization (HCPSO) is developed to obtain the near-optimal solution. The computational study shows that the proposed algorithm could be more suitable and efficient for solving large size problems than the conventional B&B algorithm. Moreover, HCPSO also has better improvement than the current heuristic practiced by the case company based on realistic data. For the future research, other heuristic algorithm can be developed to efficiently attack large-scale instances and compare with the proposed algorithm.

References

1. Salvador, M.S.: A solution to a special class of flow shop scheduling problems. In: Elmaghraby, S.E. (ed.) Symposium on the Theory of Scheduling and its Applications. LNEMS, vol. 86, pp. 83–91. Springer, Heidelberg (1973)

2. Salvador, M.S. (ed.): A solution to a special class of flow shop scheduling problems. Symposium on the theory of scheduling and its applications. Case Western Reserve University (1972)
3. Ruiz, R., Vázquez-Rodríguez, J.A.: The hybrid flow shop scheduling problem. European Journal of Operational Research 205(1), 1–18 (2010)
4. Chen, J., Lee, C.-Y.: General Multiprocessor Task Scheduling. Naval Research Logistics 64(1), 57–74 (1999)
5. Engin, O., Ceran, G., Yilmaz, M.K.: An efficient genetic algorithmnext term for previous termhybrid flow shop scheduling with multiprocessor task problemsnext term. Applied Soft Computing 11(3), 3056–3065 (2011)
6. Chuang, M.-C.: A genetic algorithm for multi-stage parallel machines scheduling problems – A case study for solar Cell industry. Tunghai University, Taichung (2011)
7. Ranga, V.R., Fu, H., Duncan, K.H.F., Jack, C.H.: Lot streaming in multistage production systems. International Journal of Production Economics 66(2), 199–211 (2000)
8. Zhang, W., Yin, C., Liu, J., Linn, R.J.: Multi-job lot streaming to minimize the mean completion time in m-1 hybrid flowshops. International Journal of Production Economics 96, 189–200 (2005)

An Exact Method for the Assembly Line Re-balancing Problem

Fatme Makssoud, Olga Battaïa, and Alexandre Dolgui

LIMOS, École des Mines de Saint-Étienne, France
{makssoud,battaia,dolgui}@emse.fr

Abstract. In this paper, we propose a mathematical optimisation model to solve the simple assembly line rebalancing problem. This problem arises when an existing assembly line has to be rebalanced in order to meet new production requirements. In this paper, a Mixed Integer Program is proposed for solving this problem with the objective to minimize the number of changes in the initial line. The computational experiments show the efficacy of the proposed method.

Keywords: Balancing and rebalancing of assembly lines, Binary integer programming.

1 Introduction and Related Literature

The assembly line consists of a number of consecutive workstations. Products are assembled by means of the successive execution of tasks in workstations as shown in Figure 1.

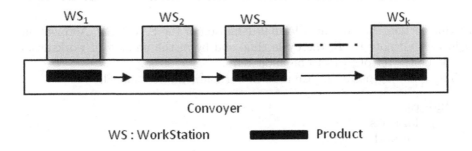

Fig. 1. Assembly line

The most known formulation of the Simple Assembly Line Balancing Problem (SALBP) aims to find a minimal number of workstations required for assigning a given set V of tasks taking into account precedence and cycle time constraints. The precedence constraints are given by a directed acyclic graph $G = (V, E)$ over

V. Prabhu, M. Taisch, and D. Kiritsis (Eds.): APMS 2013, Part I, IFIP AICT 414, pp. 159–166, 2013.

this set of tasks, where each edge $(i, j) \in E$ indicates that task i is an immediate predecessor of task j and therefore has to be assigned to a prior or the same workstation as task j.

Each task $j \in V$ is also characterized by its time, t_j. The sum of task times of the tasks assigned to the same workstation has to not exceed a given cycle time denoted by T_0. This problem is known to be NP-hard. Even if it was introduced in the literature almost 60 years ago [10], many recent studies still address it [2,3,7,9,11].

However, because of frequent changes in the product characteristics and demand, the problem that arises more frequently than initial line balancing problem is how to reassign the set of the tasks in order to meet new production requirements while minimize the number of modifications to be done in the initial line. We call this problem Simple Assembly Line Rebalancing Problem (SALReBP) and propose an exact method to solve it. Indeed, until now rebalancing problems for production lines have been principally addressed by means of approximate methods. Heuristics and genetic algorithms were used for solving stochastic assembly line rebalancing problem by Gamberini et al. [5,4]. For the case of a vehicle assembly line, three heuristic methods have been developed by Grangeon et al. [6]. A COMSOAL based heuristic for re-balancing of assembly lines that determines a fixed task sequence for a number of different cycle times was proposed by Agpak [1].

The remainder of this paper is organized as follows. A formal definition of the SALReBP is presented in the next section. The linearization of the model proposed is described in Section 3. An illustrative example is given in Section 4. A computational study is presented in Section 5 and concluding remarks are given in Section 6.

2 Formal Problem Definition and Mathematical Model

In this section, we present a formal definition of the SALReBP. As mentioned before, we denote by T_0 the cycle time and by m the number of workstations. Let V be the set of tasks to be allocated.

The following notations are used in our mathematical model:

- Indices:
  i, j for tasks,
  k for workstations.

- Parameters:
  V the new set of tasks, $j \in V$,
  t_j the processing time of task j, $j \in V$,
  $M = \{1, 2, ..., m\}$ is the set of workstations in the existing line,
  $L = \{1, 2, ..., l\}$ is the set of workstations in the new line, where l is an upper bound on the number of workstations for new line.
  $Q(j)$ is the interval of workstations in the upgraded line, where task $j \in V$

can be assigned. It is calculated using the precedence constraints.

- Decision variables:
  $x_{jk}^* = 1$ if task $j \in V^* \subset V$ is assigned to workstation k in the initial config-uration, 0 otherwise. Set V^* contains tasks j such that for $x_{jk}^* = 1, k \in Q(j)$; $x_{jk}^* = 0$ for all $k > m$, constraint 7 in model (1) - (7);

  $y_{jk} = 1$ if task $j \in \cap V$ is assigned to workstation k in the new solution, 0 otherwise; $y_{jk} = 0$ for all $k \notin Q(j)$, constraint 6 in model (1) - (7).

The following model is used for the presented assembly line rebalancing prob-lem. The objective function (1) consists in minimizing changes in the existing task assignment. Constraint (2) guarantees that every task j is assigned to one and only one workstation. Constraint (3) imposes the precedence constraints. Constraint (4) ensures that the total duration of the tasks assigned to worksta-tion j does not exceed cycle time. Constraint (5) deals with the impossibility of executing certain tasks at the same workstation. Constraint (6) ensures that the variables outside intervals $Q(j)$ are set to 0.

$$Minimize \sum_{j \in V^*} \sum_{k \in L} | x_{jk}^* - y_{jk} | \tag{1}$$

$$\sum_{k \in Q(j)} y_{jk} = 1, \forall j \in V \tag{2}$$

$$\sum_{k \in L} k y_{ik} \leq \sum_{k \in L} k y_{jk}, \forall (i, j) \in A \tag{3}$$

$$\sum_{j \in V} t_j y_{jk} \leq T_0, \forall k \in L \tag{4}$$

$$y_{ik} + y_{jk} \leq 1, \forall \{i, j\} \in E, \forall k \in L \tag{5}$$

$$y_{jk} = 0, \forall j \in V, \forall k \notin Q(j) \tag{6}$$

$$x_{jk}^* = 0, \forall j \in V, \forall k > m \tag{7}$$

3   Linearization of the Model

In the following, we propose a method to linearize the proposed model.

Lemma 1. Let $x, y, z \in \{0, 1\}$. Then the following logical expression

$$if \ x = 1 \ and \ y = 1, \ then \ z = 1$$

can be modeled as follows:

$$x + y \leq z + 1.$$

Lemma 2. Let $x, y \in \{0, 1\}$. Then the following non-linear expression

$$z := \mid x - y \mid$$

can be linearized using the following inequalities

$$x + y \leq (1 - z) + 1,$$
$$x + (1 - y) \leq z + 1,$$
$$(1 - x) + y \leq z + 1,$$
$$(1 - x) + (1 - y) \leq (1 - z) + 1,$$

It is evident to see that $z \in \{0, 1\}$. Moreover, only four following cases are possible:

if $x = 1$ and $y = 1$; then $z = 0$,

if $x = 1$ and $y = 0$; then $z = 1$,

if $x = 0$ and $y = 1$; then $z = 1$,

if $x = 0$ and $y = 0$; then $z = 0$.

Applying for these four cases Lemma 1, we obtain the necessary inequalities. To linearize the problem (1) - (5), we introduce a new variable $z_{jk} := \mid x^*_{jk} - y_{jk} \mid$. Using Lemma 2, we obtain:

$$Minimize \sum_{j \in V^*} \sum_{k \in L} z_{jk} \tag{8}$$

$$\sum_{k \in Q(j)} y_{jk} = 1, \forall j \in V \tag{9}$$

$$\sum_{k \in L} k y_{ik} \leq \sum_{k \in L} k y_{jk}, \forall (i, j) \in A \tag{10}$$

$$\sum_{j \in V} t_j y_{jk} \leq T_0, \forall k \in L \tag{11}$$

$$y_{ik} + y_{jk} \leq 1, \forall \{i, j\} \in E, \forall k \in L \tag{12}$$

$$y_{jk} = 0, \forall j \in V, \forall k \notin Q(j) \tag{13}$$

$$x^*_{jk} = 0, \forall j \in V, \forall k > m \tag{14}$$

$$x^*_{jk} + y_{jk} \leq (1 - z_{jk}) + 1, \forall j \in V, \forall k \in L \tag{15}$$

$$x^*_{jk} + (1 - y_{jk}) \leq z_{jk} + 1, \forall j \in V, \forall k \in L \tag{16}$$

$$(1 - x^*_{jk}) + y_{jk} \leq z_{jk} + 1, \forall j \in V, \forall k \in L \qquad (17)$$

$$(1 - x^*_{jk}) + (1 - y_{jk}) \leq (1 - z_{jk}) + 1, \forall j \in V, \forall k \in L \qquad (18)$$

4   Illustrative Example

Let us consider the following case study. The initial assembly line is given in Figure 2. This line has to be rebalanced for a modified product where the following tasks {14, 19, 23, 28, 29} have been deleted and new tasks {31, 32, 33, 34, 35} have been introduced. The task times of all tasks are reported in Table 1. The precedence constraints to be respected are given in Figure 3. Exclusion constraints are:

{{1, 4}, {1, 17}, {1, 20}, {2, 11}, {3, 24}, {3, 7}, {4, 15}, {5, 22}, {6, 24}, {8, 21}, {9, 22}, {10, 15}, {11, 31}, {12, 13}, {12, 20}, {13, 28}, {15, 17}, {16, 17}, {22, 26}, {30, 33}, {31, 32}} and the cycle time $T_0 = 100$.

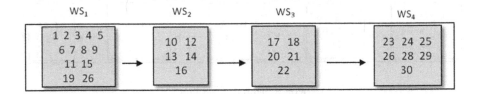

Fig. 2. Initial line

Table 1. Set of tasks V and their times

Task	Time (s)	Task	Time (s)	Task	Time (s)	Task	Time (s)	Task	Time (s)
1	0.93	7	0.68	13	0.64	21	0.78	30	0.91
2	1.06	8	0.16	15	0.09	22	0.64	31	0.72
3	0.68	9	0.68	16	0.17	24	0.09	32	0.15
4	0.16	10	0.16	17	0.09	25	0.17	33	0.19
5	0.68	11	1	18	0.12	26	0.09	34	0.33
6	0.16	12	0.78	20	1	27	0.12	35	0.97

The optimal solution was obtained in 0.36 second and consists to reassign the following tasks: {2, 4, 10, 12, 21, 31, 32, 33, 34, 35}, they are shown in bold in Figure 4 that illustrates the rebalanced line.

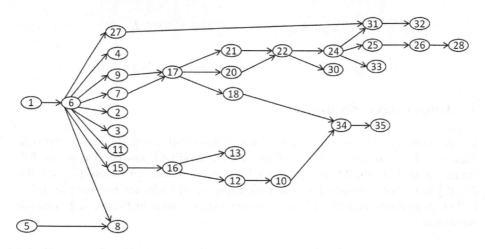

Fig. 3. The new precedence diagram

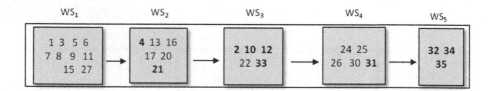

Fig. 4. Rebalanced line

Table 2. Results for rebalancing :25% Objective function

Instance tasks number	Changed	Time(s)	Instance tasks number	Changed	Time(s)	Instance tasks number	Changed	Time(s)
1	22	0.45	15	4	0.07	29	17	1.6
2	22	0.42	16	14	0.92	30	13	1.62
3	8	0.12	17	6	0.51	31	10	0.98
4	12	0.04	18	11	0.1	32	21	0.12
5	13	0.96	19	12	0.2	33	13	0.31
6	10	0.15	20	5	0.74	34	13	0.07
7	10	0.09	21	23	0.09	35	24	0.99
8	14	1.49	22	21	0.12	36	11	0.32
9	16	0.93	23	19	0.12	37	14	0.10
10	9	0.09	24	4	0.68	38	12	1.23
11	24	0.07	25	13	0.43	39	17	0.18
12	13	0.12	26	10	0.14	40	10	0.17
13	11	0.6	27	12	0.1	41	12	0.17
14	22	0.04	28	4	0.06	42	15	0.87

5   Computational Results

The proposed method was evaluated on a dataset that consists of 42 instance problems of 25 tasks each. For each initial problem, 3 versions of the modified product were generated: (1) by changing 25% of tasks (five tasks deleted and five added); (2) by changing 50% of tasks (five tasks deleted and eight added); (3) by changing 75% of tasks (five tasks deleted and fourteen added).

The computational results are respectively presented in Tables 2-4, where the values of the objective function indicating how many tasks were reassigned and

Table 3. Results for rebalancing :50% Objective function

Instance number	tasks Changed	Time(s)	Instance number	tasks Changed	Time(s)	Instance number	tasks Changed	Time(s)
1	23	0.2	15	6	0.45	29	21	0.51
2	27	0.54	16	14	0.18	30	13	0.18
3	14	1.04	17	5	0.29	31	10	1.07
4	13	0.4	18	15	0.2	32	20	0.24
5	21	0.29	19	12	0.07	33	15	0.14
6	12	0.51	20	5	0.18	34	16	0.12
7	11	0.12	21	23	1.31	35	24	0.29
8	14	0.37	22	20	0.14	36	15	0.14
9	18	0.67	23	20	0.23	37	15	0.18
10	12	0.92	24	4	0.21	38	15	0.31
11	24	0.1	25	12	0.1	39	18	0.2
12	14	0.2	26	11	0.09	40	10	0.17
13	14	0.59	27	13	0.17	41	13	0.6
14	22	0.18	28	10	0.98	42	17	0.53

Table 4. Results for rebalancing :75% Objective function

Instance number	tasks Changed	Time(s)	Instance number	tasks Changed	Time(s)	Instance number	tasks Changed	Time(s)
1	23	1.07	15	12	0.29	29	27	0.45
2	23	0.85	16	20	0.23	30	18	0.14
3	16	0.96	17	5	0.39	31	16	0.23
4	19	1.09	18	20	0.21	32	26	0.18
5	27	1.35	19	18	0.14	33	21	0.93
6	18	0.63	20	11	0.2	34	22	0.26
7	15	0.18	21	29	0.24	35	29	0.45
8	20	0.45	22	26	0.12	36	21	0.43
9	24	0.59	23	26	0.18	37	21	0.35
10	17	0.15	24	9	1.06	38	21	0.74
11	30	0.1	25	18	0.1	39	23	0.28
12	20	0.32	26	17	0.15	40	16	0.17
13	19	0.99	27	18	0.34	41	19	0.23
14	27	0.12	28	16	1.13	42	22	1.02

the solution time are given. Experiments were carried out on PC Intel(R), 2.20 GHz, with 8 Go RAM. The model was coded in C++ with ILOG CPLEX 12.4.

6   Conclusion

The problem of assembly line rebalancing was addressed. We have presented a mathematical optimization model that aims at minimizing the number of changes in the initial line. On the basis of an industrial case study, it was shown that the model proposed can be successfully applied in real world environment. The experimentation revealed that the model is capable of solving problems with up to 40 tasks in the precedence diagram.

The further research will undertake a more comprehensive computational experiment in order to evaluate the problem's size limit for which the exact method can be applied and to propose efficient heuristic or metaheuristic methods to obtain sub-optimal solutions for such problems.

References

1. Agpak, K.: An approach to find task sequence for re-balancing of assembly lines. Assembly Automation 30(4), 378–387 (2010)
2. Battaïa, O., Dolgui, A.: A taxonomy of line balancing problems and their solution approaches. International Journal of Production Economics 142, 259–277 (2013)
3. Bautista, J., Pereira, J.: A dynamic programming based heuristic for the assembly line balancing problem. European Journal of Operational Research 194(3), 787–794 (2009)
4. Gamberini, R., Gebennini, E., Grassi, A., Regattieri, A.: A multiple single-pass heuristic algorithm solving the stochastic assembly line rebalancing problem. International Journal of Production Research 47(8), 2141–2164 (2009)
5. Gamberini, R., Grassi, A., Rimini, B.: A new multi-objective heuristic algorithm for solving the stochastic assembly line re-balancing problem. International Journal of Production Economics 102(2), 226–243 (2006)
6. Grangeon, N., Leclaire, P., Norre, S.: Heuristics for the re-balancing of a vehicle assembly line. International Journal of Production Research 49(22), 6609–6628 (2011)
7. Kilincci, O.: Firing sequences backward algorithm for simple assembly line balancing problem of type 1. Computers &Industrial Engineering 60(4), 830–839 (2011)
8. Patterson, J.H., Albracht, J.J.: Technical NoteAssembly-Line Balancing: Zero-One Programming with Fibonacci Search. Operations Research 23(1), 166–172 (1975)
9. Pastor, R., Ferrer, L.: An improved mathematical program to solve the simple assembly line balancing problem. International Journal of Production Research 47(11), 2943–2959 (2009)
10. Salveson, M.E.: The assembly line balancing problem. Journal of Industrial Engineering 6(3), 18–25 (1955)
11. Sewell, E.C., Jacobson, S.H.: A branch, bound, and remember algorithm for the simple assembly line balancing problem. INFORMS Journal on Computing (2011), doi: 10.1287/ijoc.1110.0462

Green Factory Planning

Framework and Modules for a Flexible Approach

Florian Mueller[1], Alessandro Cannata[1], Bojan Stahl[2], Marco Taisch[2],
Sebastian Thiede[3], and Christoph Herrmann[3]

[1] Siemens AG Corporate Technology, CT PPC PPO IFP, München, Germany
{muellerflorian.ext,alessandro.cannata}@siemens.com
[2] Departimento di Ingegneria Gestionale, Politecnico di Milano, Milan, Italy
{bojan.stahl,marco.taisch}@polimi.it
[3] Institute of Machine Tools and Production Technology,
Technische Universität Braunschweig, IWF, Braunschweig, Germany
{s.thiede,c.herrmann}@tu-braunschweig.de

Abstract. Planning green factories implies increased complexity depending on specific planning requirements and contradictory planning targets; these aspects challenge present methods and tool for factory planning. To properly face these challenges with limited time and resources (typical of planning projects) , a factory planning approach that particularly addresses green has to be adaptable to specific cases and aligned with the green vision of the factory. This paper proposes a modular Green Factory Planning and describes its main components. The conceptual elements for a framework and a planning process are presented and differences in methods and tool applications are described in comparison to established approaches. The method and tools are combined to planning modules, linked with a clear information flow as well as responsibility definition. A use case for a typical module that specifically considers energy consumption shows the potential of green as integrated vision for factory planning.

Keywords: Factory Planning, Green Factory Planning, Energy Efficiency, Sustainable Factory, Modular Planning.

1   Motivation

The scarcity of resources and the use-related environmental impact of production created a new ecological challenge with economic impacts for industrial companies. Starting with the reactive measures for the end use of products (i.e. recycling) the awareness for resource consumption moved into more proactive consideration within product design, production operation and also factory planning. This challenged existing principles and approaches and required new ways of thinking.

The term 'green' is often used for exploitation of energy and resource efficient production. Even if there is no widely accepted definition of 'green' and 'green factory' available, the common understanding is to provide more economical value with minimized effects on the ecological surrounding. Definitions like 'sustainability' [1],

V. Prabhu, M. Taisch, and D. Kiritsis (Eds.): APMS 2013, Part I, IFIP AICT 414, pp. 167–174, 2013.

'eco-efficiency' [2] or 'green production' [3] are considered in this paper to create an individually applicable framework and vision for green factory planning.

Hence 'green' as planning target should be identified individually within several borders (e.g. ROI accepted, environmental influences considered) to achieve company wide acceptance. Existing factory planning approaches that consider the effect on the environment are mainly focused on energy efficiency as defined in formula (1):

$$\frac{\text{Net production value}}{\text{primary energy consumption}} = \frac{€}{\text{kWh}} \tag{1}$$

From the descriptive point of view, green measures and methods are added to standardized establish factory planning approaches, e.g. Mueller et al. [4] uses the standard process of factory planning by the German society of engineers (VDI) [5]. 'Green' is seen as add-on to a general planning process and is mainly executed by applying a list of different measures to improve energy efficiency. Interactions of several measures to improve energy efficiency are not integrated in the planning task but need to be calculated iteratively. An alignment of all planning activities to this goal is missing.

On top, several other trends like lean production, transformation ability or IT integration changed the approach factory planning is executed [6]. Additional targets increased complexity and required expertise for the factory planner, while the available time and resources for factory planning projects decreased because of increased speed of market change. To overcome this, standardized step-by-step factory planning approaches were redesigned to be more case specific and adaptable to changing requirements. By making planning activities modular, planning time can reduced by parallelized work among different disciplines (e.g. production planner and architect) and the focus on most important activities for the specific case [7].

2   Overview Green Factory Planning

Industrial challenges, i.e. 'green' as fully integrated in factory planning and a modular planning approach, led to the definition of 'Green Factory Planning' described here. This research was developed within the framework of the European research project 'EMC²-Factory' (www.emc2-factory). The authors argue that we cannot address challenges of green factory planning by solely adding energy efficiency as additional goal to existing planning approaches, because synergies from energy perspective are weakly addressed. A green factory for automotive with highly automated processes is different from a train production with mainly manual processes for example, because the energy consumption of the equipment is more relevant in the automotive case.. Moreover, every factory has its own main distinguishing drivers for energy efficiency (e.g. dimensioning of machines or TBS optimization). Consequently, each factory should be planned uniquely, by selecting and addressing its specific energy drivers.

A first attempt for an adaptable planning process considering environmental aspects has been done [8]. Effects of factory elements are linked with their effects on the environment, so an overview of interactions among each other is provided.

Nevertheless, the approach is focused on impact evaluation and has no broad view on other planning aspects. The execution of other planning tasks is not extensively addressed. A comprehensive factory planning consists of four components (see Fig. 1) as suggested from the comparison of several planning approaches (see for example [9]):

1. A clear vision and a framework, where underlying targets of factory planning project are defined and the content and decisions for the factory planning are distinguished. The framework links management with planning activities and aligns the whole process to general fields of action.
2. The planning process, that provides the general order of planning tasks (e.g. detailed definition after rough definition), the decision making flow and project management integration. In most approaches a straightforward step by step process is used. But to ensure green integration and adaptability to specific cases, a process based on independent modules with guided interactions among them has been chosen. For the content of planning environmental-conscious, some planning tasks have to be redefined, integrated and conducted by different planning disciplines. Timeframe and methods for evaluation and decision making have to be rethought.
3. Definition and description of applicable methods that can be used to fulfill the planning tasks. Within these components the work is performed, information generated and responsibilities defined.
4. Tools that support the execution of planning methods. Especially in data processing, decision preparation and evaluation of alternatives the use of tools, from highly sophisticated software up to simple checklists, is recommended.

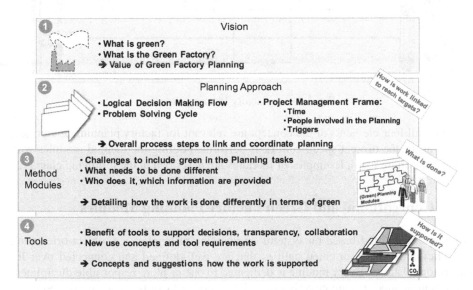

Fig. 1. Elements of Green Factory Planning

The framework and vision bring general guidance and specific planning targets while the process defines the order of method modules (timeline) and its information input-output relations. To ensure case-specificity and adaptability, the work that needs to be performed during factory planning is encapsulated into planning modules.

To identify the modules that need to be conducted specifically 'green', a target planning method based on a factory morphology is developed (1) (see overview in Fig. 2). The target definition is mandatory to set clear targets and decide on green/conventional modules. Objective factory features are analyzed with subjective planning targets to prioritize the most relevant drivers for energy efficiency. Based on the prioritization, factory-specific green modules can be chosen (2). To allow for an integrated perspective during the multi-disciplinary factory planning, a methodic evaluation is continuously provided for every decision that needs to be made (3). The evaluation is based on a layer visualization concept, that represents energy and production related indicators (e.g. temperature, consumed energy) with a multi-perspective view on the layout to make the high variety of interacting aspects visible. The planning modules are linked to a logical timeline (4) considering the involvement of different experts (5). A detailed description of prioritization and the work flow is given in [10].

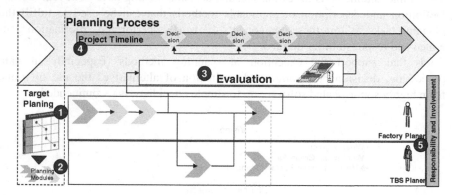

Fig. 2. Green Factory Planning Process

While all four elements of the concept are relevant for factory planning and project organization, the project-specific work is performed during the method modules with use of supporting tools. Examples of modules are described in the following chapter.

3   Conventional and Green Factory Planning Modules

Modules are defined based on systems engineering principles, e.g. object-orientation [7]. They are activity oriented entities that are well-defined and connected over information relations. Every module is dedicated to one or more responsible disciplines. The planning modules are covering descriptions of tasks to be done and the proceeding how to do, a set of possible tools to support and the people that need to be involved in the module. To make modules independently usable for different disciplines involved in the Green Factory Planning, interactions between the planning modules are defined over a clear information flow with input-output restrictions.

To be comprehensive, the factory planning process considers green planning modules or conventional planning modules. Conventional planning modules cover tasks that are not as relevant for establishing a green factory in the specific case; hence they are done with methods and tools that don't have an additional focus on 'green'. Green modules on the other hand can combine or extend several tasks of conventional modules (e.g. layout planning and planning of technical building services), because interactions among these tasks are important for the overall green factory performance.

3.1   Conventional Planning Modules from Green Perspective

Planning modules are based on a sum of tasks that is necessary to ensure an overall green factory and integrate supporting tools into the proceeding. The factory planning tasks vary between different planning approaches, for Green Factory Planning several conventional modules were identified as considerable, see [11], [12] and [13]. For example:

- Target Definition and Production Scenario Generation
- Process Planning, Machine Selection and Capacity Planning
- Material Flow Planning, Transport and Production Systems Planning
- Information Planning and Worker Planning
- Area and Layout Planning
- Building Planning and Technical Build Service Planning

For every module, a variety of methods and tools exists for the disciplines dealing with the tasks to perform them. Traditionally, activities are performed nearly independently apart from the fact that information generated in earlier tasks (e.g. process and machine planning) is used from other disciplines in later tasks. With that approach, a lot of effort is required to adjust outcomes of different planning modules and generate an overall factory view. Locally optimized factory items are the result. The modular green factory planning process instead needs to take the integrated green perspective on the overall factory into account and perform modules differently when they are relevant for green performance instead.

Every planning task and module was analyzed regarding green aspects that are not covered sufficiently in the existing modules. For every activity were aspects identified, that allow an influence on the green performance of the factory part that is planned. This can be aspects that are already considered in the methods and tools for the planning module (e.g. takt time), but get another dimension when environmental impacts are considered. Beyond that, aspects like the interaction between technical building services, building and production are not appropriately considered during the planning activity so they need to be included or emphasized. Table 1 gives an overview of some planning modules with additional aspects in terms of 'green' and the aspects, where 'green' has to be included as relevant performance driver.

Criteria that are considered in the established planning modules are still relevant, but might become less important depending on the green planning case. Methods and tools that support the work within the modules need to ensure, that 'green' as well as conventional aspects are covered, otherwise green factors planning will be just a theoretical concept. To make this possible, established criteria with no influence on 'green' (not mentioned in table 1) could be methodically linked to the green aspects.

Table 1. Excerpt of planning modules and additional criteria for 'green'

	Planning Modules						
	Target Definition and Production Scenario Generation	Process Planning	Machine Selection and Capacity Planning	Material Flow Planning and Transport Systems Planning	Information and Worker Planning	Area and Layout Planning	Building and Technical Building Services Planning
Aspects in traditional planning, where environmental perspective needs to be included	Product Requirements and quantities	Production sequence planning	Degree of automization	Takt time	Manufacturing IT Systems	dimensions	building design
	Make or Buy	Technology Trends	Investment Cost	transport (volume; -ability)	Production control	infrastructure; storage areas	building materials
	Motivation and vision	Cost, quality	Supplier selection	material flow		material and resource supply	windows; doors
	Planning Targets	Usability	product specificiations	hub/dock concept		Lean production	dimensions
	Risks and opportunities			means of transportation			tubes and grids
	Project organization			Production planning			HVAC
Green aspects, that need to be focused/included additionally	Environmental boundaries (regulations, public pressure/ focus)	Energy carriers and environmental impacts (e.g. emissions)	TCO, LCA	Energy/ Building/ TBS interactions	Green Awareness	EHS (Fire protection)/ Environmental Imact zones (AOE storage)	centralised / decentralised (dependant/indep endant from machines)
	Green Targets and Strategy	(energy) generation and consumption	equipment components and operationa parameters	Green transportation ideas	Green IT	interactions of TBS, Building, transport and Production line	supply and disposal areas and infrastructure
	Concept for Energy Management	information flow	materials	Sensors + Controls; Metering concept	Energy (Data) Management	zoning	on-site generation, re-use of energy, integration of renewables
	Energy data gathering	Recycling and waste management	Energy supply concepts	load curves		area usage efficiency	(roof) shape, orientation
	Highest impact drivers, selection of priorities	Environment and building requirements	dimension/ capacities	drive and speed of transport			Green building guidelines
		energy mix and energy cost					Insulation, heat emissions

3.2   Green Planning Modules

From this analysis, green modules can be generated in three ways: First, they can be additional tasks that are not covered at the moment. These tasks become important, because factory elements might have major importance for the green factory, but they are not explicitly planned during factory planning in established approaches. An example would be a module for Energy Supply Planning that deals with the challenges of integrating renewable energies, security of energy supplies and on-site generation.

Second, some tasks have to be combined to ensure the interactions among factory entities for the purpose of green modules. Green modules are described based on the comparison of traditional method and tools with additional interactions and influences in terms of 'green'. These additional aspects of factory planning tasks result in new modules and requirements for supporting tools, because energy-related information has to be included, processed and evaluated in an integrated way. The difference between established modules (see [12] and [13]) and these green planning modules is the degree of information to be processed and the consideration of additional aspects.

Layout Planning in terms of 'green' has to be done not just in consideration of machine area use, storage requirements and transport ways but also considering zones (e.g. temperature, compressed air supply, lighting) with its interactions to building and technical building services. In the layout, machine dimensions are carefully considered, causing district heating or ventilation during operations. So the dimensioning and capacities of machine influence energy efficiency of the overall factory over its interactions with the layout. Therefore, more experts from different areas have to participate in terms of 'green' and green layout planning has to be interactive, communicative and visually representative considering additional influences. Planning methods like IntuPlan   [14] or planning tables are not prepared for these requirements.

The third possibility for green modules is the integration of green aspects within the methods and tools of established modules. If the tasks and activities have no major connection to the performance of other modules (considering the total factory) it is sufficient to slightly adjust the planning module to ensure the relevance of green aspects. Taken the target definition as example, requirements have to be analyzed and the planning targets need to be defined as established, adding the environmental aspects to the methods and tools. As already described above, clear goals for the green factory have to be defined and linked to the features of the factory to identify the green planning modules. Nevertheless the conventional methods and outcomes are still relevant, so target planning changes to green target planning by extending the existing modules with the green aspects.

To make full use of the green modules in Green Factory Planning the input-output relations, the information environment and the method need to be clearly defined and described in a standardized profile. Especially the data processing and information generation has to coordinated, so that new conflicts that might appear (e.g. between lean – fast transport systems – and 'green' – energy efficient transport) can be solved with the overall factory competitiveness in mind.

4   Conclusion and Outlook

The paper described an approach for Green Factory Planning that is adaptable to specific cases and includes research results on green methods and tools. The approach is modular to pick the green planning modules that contribute the most to the green factory vision based on a mandatory target definition method. The additional aspects of green panning modules have been analyzed, described and the three possibilities to generate green planning modules presented.

Further research is required to ensure that all additional criteria are considered in the green modules. Some tools and methods have to be developed or detailed, to establish a common planning language among different disciplines involved in the planning. In addition, the flexible combination of green modules and conventional modules to a comprehensive planning process that integrates the green factory vision and the framework has to be detailed and reviewed within industry cases.

Further methods from academia could be included to address some challenges that occur due to the additional green aspects. For this, collaboration among the EMC²-Factory consortium and the research communities is pursued. Green planning modules can be changed or adopted easily, because they are well-defined and encapsulated from each other, but linked over input-output information.

Acknowledgements. This research is partially funded by the European Commission in the 7th Framework research project EMC²-Factory (www.emc2-factory.eu).

References

1. Brundtlandt Comission, Our Common Future. United Nations World Commission on Environment and Development (WCED). Oxford University Press, Oxford (1987)
2. World Business Council of Sustainable Development (WBCSD), Changing Course: A Global Business Perspective on Development and the Environment. MIT Press, Cambridge (1992)
3. Hart, S.L.: How green production might sustain the world. Northwestern Environmental Journal 10, 4–14 (1994)
4. Müller, E., Engelmann, J., Löffler, T., Strauch, J.: Energieeffiziente Fabriken planen und betreiben. Springer, Berlin (2009)
5. Verein Deutscher Ingenieure, VDI5200:2009: Factory Planning – planning procedures. Beuth Verlag, Berlin (2009)
6. Wirth, S., Schenk, M., Müller, E.: Fabrikarten, Fabriktypen und ihre Entwicklungsetappen. ZWF Zeitschrift für Wirtschaftlichen Fabrikbetrieb 106(11), 799–802 (2011)
7. Bergholz, M.-A.: Objektorientierte Fabrikplanung. Shaker, Aachen (2005)
8. Chen, D., Heyer, S., Seliger, G., Kjellberg, T.: Integrating sustainability within the factory planning process. Paper presented at the 62nd CIRP General Assembly, Hongkong, China, August 19-25 (2012)
9. Hennersdorf, S., Dombrowski, U.: Algorithm for Choosing Factory Planning Methods and Tools. In: Katalinic, B. (ed.) DAAAM International Scientific Book, pp. 45–52. DAAAM International, Vienna (2009)
10. Müller, F., Cannata, A., Okur, A., Thiede, S., Herrmann, C.: Classification of factories from a green perspective: initial guidance and drivers for 'Green Factory Planning'. Paper presented at the 10th Global Conference of Sustainable Manufacturing, Istanbul, Turkey, October 31-November 02 (2012)
11. Felix, H.: Unternehmens- und Fabrikplanung: Planungsprozesse, Leistungen und Beziehungen. Fachbuchverlag Leipzig, Leipzig (1998)
12. Chen, D.: Information Management for the factory planning process. Dissertation, KTH Stockholm, Sweden (2009)
13. Nöcker, J.C.: Zustandsbasierte Fabrikplanung. Apprimus Verlag, Aachen (2012)
14. Tröger, S., Berndt, M., Müller, F., Jentsch, D., Riedel, R., Müller, E.: 3D-Kommunikation in der Fabrikplanung. ZWF Zeitschrift für Wirtschaftlichen Fabrikbetrieb 107(9), 632–636 (2012)

Sustainability Evaluation of Mass Customization

Thomas Ditlev Brunø, Kjeld Nielsen, Stig Brink Taps, and Kaj A. Jørgensen

Department of Mechanical and Manufacturing Engineering, Aalborg University, Denmark
tdp@m-tech.aau.dk

Abstract. This paper addresses the issue whether the concepts mass customization and sustainability are fundamentally compatible by asking the question: can a mass customized product be sustainable? Some factors indicate that mass customized products are less sustainable than standardized products; however other factors suggest the opposite. This paper explores these factors during three life cycle phases for a product: Production, Use and End of Life. It is concluded that there is not an unambiguous causal relationship between mass customization and sustainability; however several factors unique to mass customized products are essential to consider during product development.

Keywords: mass customization, sustainability, remanufacturing.

1   Introduction

Mass customization (MC), popularized by Pine et al. have proven a successful business strategy in various industries markets and for several different product types [10]. Mass customization is different from mass production in several different ways, including product design and production to sales and marketing and fit with customer needs.

Sustainable development is defined by the Brundtland Commission as "a development that meets the needs of the present without compromising the ability of future generations to meet their own needs" [4]. Sustainable development includes three dimensions: the environmental, economic and social dimensions [4]. However, in this study it is chosen to focus on the environmental dimension of sustainability.

Sustainability is a concept that is gaining more and more attention, and companies are experiencing a greater demand for sustainable products. Several concepts are applied to achieve greater sustainability in product design and manufacturing. Among these is Eco-design, which is a concept that attempts to integrate environmental aspects into the product development process thereby creating products with lower negative environmental impacts and thus more environmentally sustainable products. Since mass customizing companies, just like every other company, will have to consider sustainability, it is relevant to consider how mass customized products are different from mass produced products in a sustainability perspective.

V. Prabhu, M. Taisch, and D. Kiritsis (Eds.): APMS 2013, Part I, IFIP AICT 414, pp. 175–182, 2013.
© IFIP International Federation for Information Processing 2013

2   Research Method

The research objective of this paper is to identify mechanisms in mass customization, which can yield mass customized products more sustainable or less sustainable compared to traditionally mass produced products. The research question is: "How can the elements of mass customization influence the environmental sustainability of a product?" To answer this question, it must first be clarified which elements of mass customization are addressed in this context. Secondly the concept of environmental sustainability must be clarified. Finally the interrelations between these two concepts are identified and analyzed. To structure this analysis, the interrelations are grouped according to the product life cycle. Rose [11] presented a generic product lifecycle, which is illustrated in figure 1.

Fig. 1. Generic representation of a product life cycle (Rose, 2000)

The first stage, materials extraction and processing, is not expected to have strong relations to whether a product is mass produced or mass customized and this stage is thus disregarded in this paper. Furthermore, the manufacturing and assembly stages are joined into one stage. The analysis is thus divided into the following phases of a product lifecycle: 1) Production, 2) Use and 3) End of Life. For each of these phases, mass customization and mass production products are compared.

Within the first two areas, production and use, the analyses are structured on basis of concepts which are characteristic for mass customization production and products. More specifically, the factors described by Berman [2] and Maccarthy [8] have been reviewed and those which were found to have relevance for this study have been included: 1) Product Modularity, 2) Process Variety, 3) Distribution Channels, 4) Improved fit with customer needs & 5) Product functionality customization.

Furthermore, concepts which have their origin in sustainability research have been identified through literature studies. The concept of reducing energy consumption, which is essential in eco design as well as life cycle thinking [6], is included as well. In the End of life stage, a number of end of life strategies identified by [11] are included in the elements which are analyzed: 1) Energy efficiency, 2) Reuse, 3) Service, 4) Remanufacturing, 5) Recycling and disposal. In the following, the elements presented above and their relations will be analyzed.

3   Analysis

3.1   Production

Modularity is usually considered a key enabler for efficient mass customization [10] and thus most producers of mass customized durables apply modular product architectures. Ulrich et al. describe modular product architecture as the opposite of an integral architecture [12]. The advantages of an integral architecture are usually that the performance of a product can be improved compared to a modular product. In this context, the performance could among other things be properties like size and weight. It is generally acknowledged to be good practice in EcoDesign to minimize usage of material resources in manufacturing [7]. Since mass customized products are usually modular and following the arguments from Ulrich et al. [12], it could be expected that more material resources are necessary to produce those compared to mass produced products, since modular products cannot be optimized with regards to weight and thereby material usage as mass produced products. This is assuming that the mass produced product is optimized for minimum material resource usage by applying integral product architecture. Hence, mass customized products may have a greater environmental impact during production due to a higher material usage.

In relation to process variety, mass customization requires much higher process flexibility compared to mass production due to the higher product variety and subsequently process variety [2]. The fact that many more different manufacturing processes are necessary to product customized products compared to standard products makes it more difficult to optimize the processes with respect to energy and material consumption. Hence the fact that the process variety is higher in mass customization may imply a greater environmental impact than mass production.

An element of mass customization which differentiates it significantly from mass production is the distribution channels. In mass production, a finished product may be distributed through several tiers of distributors before being purchased and taken to the final customer. In contrast to this, mass customized products are produced for one specific customer and are thus possible to distribute directly from producer to end customer. This could serve as an argument for mass customization to have both a higher and lower environmental impact compared to mass production in relation to distribution.

The argument for a higher environmental impact would be that each product is distributed individually from manufacturer to customer, which would require more packaging and presumably more energy, since each product would take more space compared to a larger number of similar standard products, which could be packaged and distributed together. The argument for a lower environmental impact would be that the product does not travel through multiple tiers of suppliers and thus is expected to have a shorter route from producer to consumer which could again be expected to consume less energy and fewer emissions.

Finally, to be able to deliver a mass customized product to the customer within an acceptable time, it can be beneficial to produce the product closer to the customer than for mass produced products. The reason for this is that mass produced products can be produced geographically far away from the customer, but given they are standard products, they can be kept in stock close to the end customer. This is of course not possible for customized products and this distribution strategy is thus not feasible for mass customization. This is a reason why mass customized products are more likely to be produced close to the end customer than mass produced products and as a consequence the product has to travel a shorter distance from producer to end customer yielding lower energy consumption in the distribution.

3.2   Use

When a customer chooses to purchase a mass customized product, this will most likely provide an improved fit between the product's properties and the customer's needs [2], compared to purchasing a standard product.

For certain groups of mass produced products, the purchase price is so low that consumers do not hesitate to dispose a nearly unused product if it does not meet the customer's needs and purchase a replacement, assuming that it will better fit the needs. However, this will likely produce extra negative environmental impacts, since the product reaches its end-of-life before it has worn out. One example of this from the apparel industry is presented by Hethorn et al. [5]. Much apparel is so inexpensive that many customers purchase clothing which may not fit. Clothes that do not fit are unlikely to be worn by the customer, and the resources for producing those clothes are thus wasted, and the resources for producing clothes for that customer, from an overall perspective, could be reduced.

Creating products that have a better fit with the customers' needs could thus reduce the waste that is produced by manufacturing products that are never used. Mass customization presents an opportunity to do just that, since the better fit that customers achieve by choosing a mass customized product would logically reduce the probability that the product is not used and that the resources used for manufacturing it are thus wasted. This goes not only for apparel but for other product types as well which have a cost low enough for customers not to hesitate disposing even an unused product if it does not fit their needs. Hence the mechanism that mass customization provides a better fit introduces an opportunity that mass customization products could reduce the type of waste presented above.

In relation to production it was described above that integral product architecture would usually yield a greater potential for optimizing the product with respect to performance compared to modular product architecture. One other aspect where this is relevant in relation to environmental impact is the energy efficiency, which obviously is only relevant for those durables that consume either electricity or other energy sources. Given that most mass customized products are modular; this is another mechanism that could render mass customized products less environmentally sustainable than mass produced products which have the potential of being more optimized for energy consumption than mass customized products.

There is however an argument which could counter this mechanism. Applying modular product architecture, most companies would attempt to establish modules which are standardized across multiple products. This would then imply that the company due to the larger volume could, invest larger sums in optimizing that particular module thus potentially achieving greater energy efficiency than a mass produced product, given that module is was is produced in larger numbers than individual mass produced variants.

3.3   End of Life

Rose [11] presented the hierarchy of end-of-life (EOL) strategies which is illustrated in figure 2. Generally, in order to minimize the environmental impact at product end of life, strategies higher in the hierarchy should be chosen. Strategies 1-5 are so called closed loop strategies [1], and are preferable to open loop strategies (6), since they make use of the value and resources already added to the raw materials [11]. End-of-life in this context is defined as the point in time where the original user does no longer wish to use the product for whatever reason.

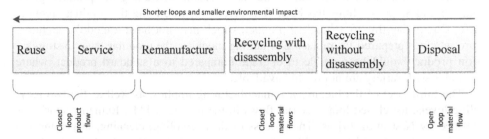

Fig. 2. Hierarchy of End-of-life strategies from [11]

The EOL strategy reuse implies that the product at EOL is obtained and used by a new user without modifying or refurbishing the product. This strategy implies no consumption of resources and makes it unnecessary to manufacture a new product thus reducing the resources needed to fulfill the customers' needs. Considering this strategy in relation to mass customization presents a critical issue: Since mass customized products are tailored to an individual customer's requirements, it is unlikely that the product's properties will fit an entirely different customer's requirements, since those requirements would need to be uniform. For example it is unlikely that for example a T-shirt customized with some personal information, e.g. a photo or a name would be worn by someone else than the original buyer. Hence we can conclude that there is potential complication in designing a mass customized product that can be "reused" in their original form. There are however mechanisms which can counter this issue. If mass customization of a product is achieved by designing a self-customizing product as presented by Alhstrom et al. [1], a new user of the product would simply re-configure or re-personalize the product to meet the new requirements. Hence, it cannot be unambiguously concluded that mass customized products cannot be re-used and therefore be optimal in relation to their EOL environmental impact.

If a product is to be replaced due to "wear and tear", i.e. the product is somehow worn or defective and thus cannot be reused, which is the preferred EOL strategy according to the hierarchy, the strategy "service" should be considered [11]. In this strategy, the life of a product is extended by repairing or servicing the product thus pushing the time where a new product will have to be manufactured to fulfill a user's needs. There is no apparent and strong relation between this strategy and mass customization, however the variety of parts included in the product may cause some issues if spare parts are necessary. This would be the case if the parts, which are to be replaced to repair the product, are custom fabricated, as opposed to a customized product assembled from standard components. If a custom fabricated component is required for repairing or servicing the product, this would likely be more expensive than repairing a product using standard components, since the spare part would need to be manufactured specifically for that product which would likely introduce higher logistical costs as well as a problem regarding the identification of specifications for manufacturing that specific part. Many mass customization products are designed using modular product architecture to be able to efficiently manufacture custom products. The nature of a modular product would likely enable upgrading the product, given that upgrading possibilities has been considered when defining the product architecture. Comparing this to a standard product, which may not have a modular architecture which is prepared for replacing or adding modules, the modular mass customization product would be possible to upgrade compared to a standard product, where modules with variety are not readily available.

The third level of the hierarchy, remanufacturing implies, as well as the two recycling levels, the closed loop material flows in the hierarchy [11]. Remanufacturing is defined by Nasr et al. [9] as: The process of disassembling, cleaning, inspecting, repairing, replacing, and reassembling the components of a part or product in order to return it to "as-new" condition. As described above, many mass customized products will have modular product architecture. Modular products can generally be expected to be more appropriate for disassembling compared to integral products [3]. It should be noted in this context, that this relationship is based on the product architecture (modularity) and not the customization of the product. Hence this relationship can also be applicable for standard products given they are based on a modular architecture.

Many mass customized products are configured using configurator software and a specific configuration can be traced to a specific customer. This implies that the manufacturer is likely to have knowledge of exactly which customers do have a product that can be taken back for remanufacturing thus enabling companies to provide incentives to the customer for returning and EOL product. Using remanufacturing as an EOL strategy for mass customized products, products can be disassembled into modules which are stored and reassembled to new products configured to match a new customer's requirements. As for the service EOL strategy, custom fabricated components complicate this strategy since it may not be possible to remanufacture these and hence must be recycled, which is less desirable. It can thus be concluded that remanufacturing is likely to be a good EOL strategy given the mass customized product is not self-reconfiguring and does not contain custom fabricated components.

In levels 4 and 5, EOL strategies are less desirable than the strategies where the entire product is reused, however preferable to disposal. Mass customized products are often modular and thus easier to disassemble than standard products which are more likely to be non-modular. This is of course relevant for the "Recycling with disassembly" EOL strategy. Furthermore, modular product architecture will enable concentrating certain material fractions in certain modules which will likely increase the recyclability.

4   Analysis of Results and Implications

The results of the analyses performed in section 3 are summarized in figure 3. As it can be seen from this figure there are several relations between the elements of mass customization and environmental sustainability that indicate that mass customization does have an effect on the sustainability of a product. In figure 3, the boxes above the dashed line represent concepts which are typically addressed by researchers and practitioners within mass customization, whereas the boxes below the line represent the elements of sustainability that were found to have a relation to mass customization.

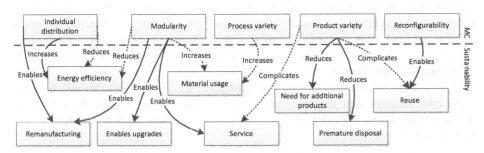

Fig. 3. The relations between mass customization and sustainability

The dotted arrows from the mass customization concepts to the sustainability concepts represent the identified relationships where mass customization potentially has a negative influence on sustainability compared to mass production. The solid lines are opposite and represent relationships where mass customization can be expected to be more sustainable than mass production. Eight positive relationships and six negative relationships were identified; however these numbers cannot be used for concluding that mass customization is more sustainable than mass production, since these relations are not unambiguously quantifiable, since they can only be quantified for specific products, as different products will have different environmental impacts. What is also interesting is that not several single elements of mass customization potentially have both negative and positive effects on sustainability compared to mass production. One example of this is the individual distribution, which can have both negative and positive impact on the energy efficiency during distribution.

This finally implies that the assessment of whether mass customized products are more or less sustainable than similar mass produced products will depend entirely on individual studies. Consider two completely different products; an automobile and a piece of clothing. The environmental impact profiles of these two products are completely different. The automobile will consume much more energy throughout the use phase of its lifecycle than consumed during product phase, whereas a piece of clothing will consume no energy during its lifecycle. Furthermore, an automobile is much more likely to be serviced to extend its life cycle and to be reused when its original purchaser disposes of it. Hence, the difference between mass customized and mass produced products will vary greatly between these two groups of products.

From the results of the analysis in section 3 there is no indication that mass customization should have the potential to be less sustainable than mass production. The results presented can thus be used as guidelines for how to address sustainability issues in mass customization by pointing out areas where mass customization is different from other business strategies, thereby assisting in tailoring strategies for becoming more sustainable.

5   Conclusion

It can be concluded that there are indeed many elements of mass customization which can influence the environmental sustainability of a product if it is compared to a similar mass produced product. However, since there are both factors which contribute more sustainable and less sustainable products, a universal conclusion cannot be drawn for all mass customized products. It can thus be concluded that mass customization it not either sustainable or unsustainable, but has indeed the potential to contribute to sustainability.

The work presented in this paper is a qualitative study to explore the links between mass customization and sustainability. Further research could analyze these relations using a quantitative approach for specific product types to analyze the relations in specific cases.

References

1. Ahlstrom, P., Westbrook, R.: Implications of Mass Customization for Operations Management: An Exploratory Survey. International Journal of Operations & Production Management 19, 262–275 (1999)
2. Berman, B.: Should Your Firm Adopt a Mass Customization Strategy? Bus. Horiz. 45, 51–60 (2002)
3. Bogue, R.: Design for Disassembly: A Critical Twenty-First Century Discipline. Assem. Autom. 27, 285–289 (2007)
4. Brundtland, G.H.: World Commission on Environment and Development. Our Common Future (1987)
5. Hethorn, J., Ulasewicz, C.: Sustainable fashion: Why now. Fairchild Publications, Inc., New York (2008)
6. Kørnøv, L., Lund, H., Remmen, A.: Tools for a sustainable development. Institut for Samfundsudvikling og Planlægning. Aalborg Universitet (2005)
7. Luttropp, C., Lagerstedt, J.: EcoDesign and the Ten Golden Rules: Generic Advice for Merging Environmental Aspects into Product Development. J. Clean. Prod. 14, 1396–1408 (2006)
8. Maccarthy, B.: Understanding Customization in Mass Customization. IEE Seminar Digests, 1 (2003)
9. Nasr, N., Thurston, M.: Remanufacturing: A Key Enabler to Sustainable Product Systems. In: Proceedings of LCE. 13th CIRP International Conference in Life Cycle Engineering, pp. 15–18 (2006)
10. Pine, B.J.: Mass customization: The new frontier in business competition. Harvard Business School Press (1993)
11. Rose, C.M.: Design for environment: A method for formulating product end-of-life strategies. In: Design for Environment: A Method for Formulating Product End-of-Life Strategies. Stanford University (2000)
12. Ulrich, K.T., Eppinger, S.D.: Product design and development. McGraw-Hill, New York (2004)

Methodology for Internal Traceability Support in Foundry Manufacturing

Rhythm Suren Wadhwa

Høgskolen I Gjøvik, 2802, Gjøvik, Norway

Abstract. Appropriate description and implementation of internal part traceability in manufacturing is a complex task. Accurate and real-time traceability from a part, or a part feature, to a manufacture, storage, or transport issue is essential to efficient and high-quality operations. With the increasing amount of machine status and product quality information coming from the manufacturing lines, certain questions arise. When there is a problem with the process or product quality what information can be utilized to enable effective traceability to the foundry batch lot? Also, what aggregate information values are needed to enable real-time problem solutions? In this paper a systems-based approach is used to propose a method to define and implement internal part traceability in two participating foundries.

Keywords: Foundry Traceability, Foundry Process Automation, Internal Traceability.

1   Introduction

Similar to existing *flexibility* definitions[1]; *traceability* in literature also results in a number of definitions   and its types and its applications being in areas ranging from part recall, part-liability-prevention, process improvement, logistic applications etc. Traceability in the context described in this work, can be defined, as the ability to retain and trace the identification of the part, its originating melt batch and value added operations [2]. The two industrial implementation discussed relates to the traceability in a passive sense [3]. Traceability in the passive sense helps in providing visibility to which melt batch do the parts come from, where the items are and their respective dispositions.

There has been very limited academic literature published in the area of foundry traceability, and almost non-existing in traceability related to data collection supporting manufacturing control plan, and hence the novelty of this paper. Vedel-Smith et al. presented a methodology for enabling traceability cast iron foundries by part number marking on individual castings [4]. Arabatzis et al. described the issue of traceability in aluminium foundry [5].   The paper rest of the paper is organized as follows : Section 2 describes the usage requirements of internal traceability system for iron foundry. Section 3 describes the methodology for iron foundry traceability. The described methodology and the data collection activity can be extended to the capture

V. Prabhu, M. Taisch, and D. Kiritsis (Eds.): APMS 2013, Part I, IFIP AICT 414, pp. 183–190, 2013.
© IFIP International Federation for Information Processing 2013

data from processes (see process sequence in the Appendix) through the entire foundry manufacturing enterprise. The methodology and procedure were applied to an iron foundry business described as case study I and were also found applicable to an aerospace foundry business described as case study II. Section 4 presents the conclusions.

2 Usage Requirements for Internal Traceability System in an Iron Foundry

The Implementation of a traceability system in the manufacturing process is a complex task. Several problems exist at different stages throughout the process. In order to achieve traceability goals the manufacturing firms should focus both on internal plant traceability. Determination of the usage requirements of the traceability system is the first step in implementing the system. Each manufacturing sub-process should determine their traceability plan based on the driving factors like the regulatory need, business need and the customer preferences. Relational database management system could be used to implement internal traceability system by each process step. All batch manufacturing information should be recorded in a centralized database system and only relevant lot/batch information should be passed on to the next link in the process. Additional information can be requested by the authorized users (such as regulatory agencies) in case of a part non-conformance. This additional information should be provided in a timely manner.

Below is a proposal for a standard traceability procedure which contains the following elements:

• *Users:* People (at some level of the organization and with certain limitations) who are able to input and extract data from the system.
• *Actors:* An actor is a person or organization that plays a role in one or more interactions with the system.
• *Associations*: An association exists whenever an actor is involved with an interaction in the traceability system procedure.
• *System boundary:* The boundary indicates the scope of the system.

The following procedures and use case actors are proposed for iron foundry traceability systems:

Process Traceability: The foundry should be able to record the raw material batch, metal composition, the complete manufacturing process of the part including automated machining and the handling processes used by them internally in the facility.

Machine Status Traceability: The operator working on the part should be able to record (depending on the downstream and final customer requirements) the manufacturing processes and parameters used in the system. Depending on the machine it may include heat lot number, metal batch number, holding time etc.

Authentication Support: The manufacturing system and its users must be able to use the data stored in the system to authenticate their claims based on the complete data set.

Customer Regulations Compliance: Using the traceability system, the manufacturing system actors should be able to retrieve data to show that the manufacturing processes comply with the customer requirements.

Company Integrity Protection: The system users must be able to protect the integrity of their company through the traceability in the system. For example, if the part is claimed to be produced under controlled process parameters the system should support traceability to those parameter values.

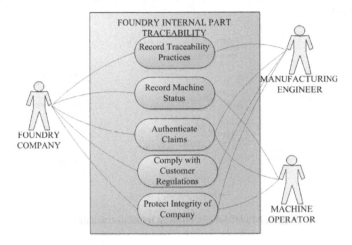

Fig. 1. General usage requirements for an iron foundry process

3   Methodology for Iron Foundry Traceability

The following methodology is described from the perspective of a part's journey in the foundry internal manufacturing process. The main purpose of the methodology is to enable quick identification, collection and integration of traceability data using automation enablers following the parts journey in a manufacturing facility. [12] The methodology can be extended and applied to the entire enterprise.

Step 1: Investigate the system and build the functional model
At this stage the model builder identifies the characteristics and operations of the system under investigation. Through a variety of methods available for this purpose, such as: interviews with stakeholders, a walk-through the system, use of company's operating manuals etc. The primary task is to identify the operating rules. The next step is to translate these operating rules into a series of IDEF diagrams. The main

objective of this step is to develop a complete functional model of the system under investigation. The IDEF modules are assembled in hierarchical fashion so more details can be shown at lower levels. The resulting functional model forms the basis for identifying the data requirements.

The Functional (IDEF0) Model

The IDEF0 functional modelling methods are designed to model the decisions, actions and activities of the system.[125] The methodology permits a system to be described as completely as desired. A series of standard IDEF0 functional model diagrams for the system elements in sand casting flexible automation cell were developed which were suitable to Jøtul. (selective details disclosed on request) For example, the figure below shows one of the standard IDEF0 functional model diagrams that describes the requirements to develop inetrnal traceability at the flexible automation cell.

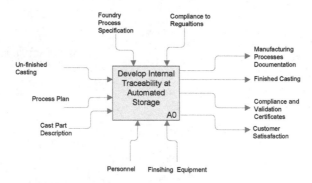

Fig. 2. Model for developing internal traceability

Although IDEF0 models are good at providing an initial view of activity development it is unable to describe the integration among various components. Based on the traceability information requirements, a foundry manufacturer, for example, is supposed to develop a control plan with all process details and raw materials along with the tools being used. The control plan is to be approved by the customer by means of technical audit. This control plan becomes the basis on which quality system is developed. A control plan also gives various values of parameters within which it needs to be controlled, frequency of checks, composition of the melt, sand properties, core sand properties, recycling metal properties, recycling sand properties, critical dimensions, reference surface, mechanical properties, and any other special customer requirements. This eventually leads to process control, which is the basis for product consistency.

Step 2: Build the reference model of the system

The reference data model's purpose was to describe the integration among various components such as parts, resources, and the manufacturing logic into a single system to describe the flexible automation cell database implementation conceptually.

The reference data model shows the major entities with their attributes and relationships. For a relational DBMS (database management system), each entity in the reference model becomes a table and each attribute becomes a column. Primary (PK) and foreign keys (FK) are declared for each relationship.

Everytime a part transformation (*finishing, rework or scrap*) takes place, the resulting dispositions are recorded. The information regarding the part handling (picking and placing) position and orientation using various grippers is also recorded.

Step 3: Collect and store data

The internal database to this finishing cell is required to maintain information about the operations performed on the part, the operation outcome and automated storage entry/exit movement date and time, the operator, machining status, outcome of the machining process, and the time of movement out from the automated storage. By utilizing the relational database design, the developed model can store, manage, and retrieve cast part processing data and make it available to the plant-wide ERP system. As long as all the relevant information is recorded in the local database of the cell the retrieval of all necessary information in the production process becomes easier. In appropriate manufacturing environments, it is possible to link data tables directly to the data sources, such the robots, the vision system, etc. via standard protocols.

Step 4: Validate and handle non-conformances

A quality assurance plan should be developed which ensures the data quality and personnel assigned who monitor the system and establish a process to maintain the quality of data stored and the equipment. Any non-conformance should be submitted to the appropriate non-conformance authority for part disposition.

Case Study I

A series of IDEF diagrams were created to support the implementation of part traceability at an automated cell at company 1 (a commercial product cast iron foundry manufacturer). The foundry wanted to look into automating traceability data collection at the CNC finishing and thereby reducing the manual handling of heavy parts with flash on its edges.

Fig. 3. Cast iron parts with flash on the edges

A series of standard IDEF0 functional model diagrams for the system elements in sand casting flexible automation cell were developed which were suitable to the manufacturing needs. The manufacturing automation installation consists of the following modules: (1) the vision module, (2) the robot module (3) the robot end effecter part handling module (4)   the automated storage lift, (5) the CNC machine (6) RFID tags placed on the (7) part family fixtures. When there is an order from ERP system to meet a request downstream, the HMI requests the bin selection from storage lift. When the requested bin is available at the exit of the lift the robot receives a signal notifying that the bin is in place under the vision system, and notifies the camera through PLC, to take the picture. The position and orientation of the part/fixture is transferred to the robot via the PLC, which then proceeds to orient the gripper accordingly to pick the part. Different grippers and configuration for part pick-up and delivery position to the basket were programmed by the foundry engineers to make them available for possible use. After the part is loaded by the robot on the CNC the delivery of the part on the fixture is confirmed by the inductive sensors located on the fixture. The part is located on the fixture via rotation and sliding locators. A sliding locator ensures that the variation in part linear dimensions during the casting process is properly compensated. If the part is in the correct position the clamps are activated and the machining starts.

Step 2 and Step 3
The entity-relationship (E-R) technique was used to develop the internal traceability database model for the automation cell. The E-R model is represented in terms of entities in the manufacturing environment, the relationship among the entities and their attributes. [16] The implementation of the database, the human-machine software interface and its performance testing was conducted by an external vendor and is proprietary on request. A control plan was developed for use at the automation cell by the manufacturing engineers under the supervision of the Quality director at the company. Initial validation of the installed automation cell was done internally in the company. Due to company's reorganization and facility layout restructuring, any further validation of the cell could not be conducted.

Case Study II
Case company 2 is an aerospace metalcasting components manufacturer with lifelong data traceability requirements. (Selective details disclosed on request) At the manufacturer, the process starts when an operator loads a part into a fixture and puts it on the incoming conveyor line. The operator then keys in the part number and serial number using the HMI. This will send the message to the machining center and CMM for the process that is required for the loaded part or parts. The Fanuc robot then comes to the incoming conveyor and retrieves a pallet, moves it to the CMM for a pre-alignment part offset location. This information is then sent to the machining center, the Fanuc robot moves the pallet from the CMM to the machining center, and the machining cycle starts.

After the machining is finished the Fanuc robot moves the pallet from the machining center to the blow-off clean booth. The robot then moves the part back to the CMM for the inspection process. After the part inspection is, finished the data is sent to a database, it moves the pallet to the correct outgoing conveyor, and the process starts over for the next part.

4 Conclusions

From the literature it is apparent that the use of traceability data is not limited to crisis situations, where defective products need to be identified and recalled, and situations where evidence needs to be provided. It is very clear to many authors that the necessity for traceability exists throughout a variety of manufacturing businesses whether it is a foundry or an aerospace manufacturer. The methodology could be generalized and applied to the case of an aerospace manufacturer, as the data collection process supporting traceability remains the same but the regulatory requirements on data storage may be longer, for example 50-60 years or longer, as compared to the short term requirements in commercial product manufacturing foundries. There is a wealth of data present in the new automated systems and it can be used to provide the status of each component in the system as well as the condition of the systems components. From the business side of the organization the data can be fed to an internal database and determine if the performance of the manufacturing operations is in line with the planed output and to know the quality of the parts as they come off the end of the line. The data is valuable and can be utilized for as many of the process indicators that are possible. As the processes are developed, the traceability element will need to be part of the design. This type of innovation will keep the organization on the leading edge of the competition.

References

[1] Wadhwa, R.S.: Flexibility in manufacturingautomation: A living lab case study of Norwegian metalcasting SMEs. Journal of Manufacturing Systems (2012)
[2] Fisk, G., Chandran, R.: Tracing and recalling products. Harvard Business Review, 90–96 (November-December 1975)
[3] Florence, D., Queree, C.: Traceability—Problem or Opportunity. Logistics Information Management 6(4), 3–8 (1993)
[4] Vedel-Smith, N.K., Lenau, T.A.: Casting traceability with direct part marking using reconfigurable pin-type tooling based on paraffin-graphite actuators. Journal of Manufacturing Systems (2012)
[5] Aarbatzia, T.: Elval pilot aluminum casting traceability supported by CIMOSA. Computers in Industry (1995)
[6] Vokura, R.J., O'Leary-Kelly, S.W.: A review of empirical research on manufacturing flexibility. Journal of Operations Management 18, 485–501 (2000)
[7] EN ISO 9001, Section 4.8
[8] Chow, H., Choy, K., Lee, W., Lau, K.C.: Design of an RFID case based resource management system for warehouse operations. Expert Systems with Applications 30, 561–576 (2006)

[9] McFarlane, D., Sarma, S., Chirn, J.L.: Auto ID systems and intelligent Manufacturing control. Engineering Applications with Artificial Intelligence 15, 365–376 (2003)

[10] Wadhwa, R.S., Lien, T.K.: Manufacturing automation for environmentally sustainable foundries. In: CIRP LCE (April 2013)

[11] Kim, H.M., Fox, M.S., Grüninger, M.: An ontology for quality management enabling quality problem identification and tracing. BT Technology Journal 17(4), 131–140 (1999)

Appendix

An Iron Foundry Process Sequence

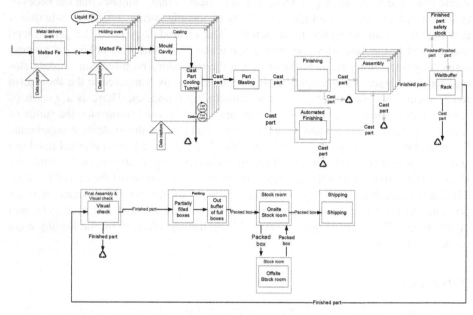

Assessment of Process Robustness for Mass Customization

Kjeld Nielsen and Thomas Ditlev Brunø

Department of Mechanical and Manufacturing Engineering, Aalborg University, Denmark
kni@m-tech.aau.dk

Abstract. In mass customization, the capability Robust Process Design defined as the ability to reuse or recombine existing organizational and value-chain resources is essential to deliver a high variety cost effectively. We argue that there is a need for methods which can assess a company's process robustness and their capability to develop it. Through literature study and analysis of robust process design characteristics a number of metrics are described which can be used for assessment. The metrics are evaluated and analyzed to be applied as KPI's to help MC companies prioritize efforts in business improvement.

Keywords: Robust Process Design, Mass Customization, Flexibility.

1   Introduction

In any company it is essential to offer products which match the needs and desires of customers to achieve sales and profit. This is true for mass producers as well as mass customizers; however in mass customization this issue is somewhat more complex than mass production due to a much higher variety and a more complex product structure. As pointed out by Salvador et al., mass customizers need three fundamental capabilities to be successful: 1) Solution Space Development – Identifying the attributes along which customer needs diverge, 2) Robust Process Design – Reusing or recombining existing organizational and value chain resources to fulfill a stream of differentiated customer needs and 3) Choice Navigation – Supporting customers in identifying their own solutions while minimizing complexity and the burden of choice [3], [7].

In order for companies to be able to establish themselves as mass customizers or for existing mass customizer to improve performance, it is proposed that a set of methods for assessing the three capabilities is developed. In this paper, the focus is solely on the capabilities for Robust Process Design. The research question for this paper is: *What metrics can be used to assess capabilities for robust process design and how can these be determined?*

The research question is sought answered through first defining robust process design, and in overall terms, what should be assessed. Then a literature review is conducted to identify related metrics already defined in literature. These metrics are evaluated, whether they are descriptive in relation to the robustness of processes, and

V. Prabhu, M. Taisch, and D. Kiritsis (Eds.): APMS 2013, Part I, IFIP AICT 414, pp. 191–198, 2013.

a final set of metrics is developed. The metrics developed is a preliminary set of metrics, and should be regarded as an assessment framework which will need further validation and refinement in order to be applied in practice.

2   Robust Process Design

The capability robust process design is defined by Salvador et al. [7] as *"Reusing or recombining existing organizational and value chain resources to fulfill a stream of differentiated customer needs"*. Hence this capability is related primarily to the capabilities of the manufacturing system, and its ability to manufacture a variety of products. The robustness of the processes, both on a detailed level as well as on enterprise level can be perceived as the ability to adapt to manufacturing a variation of products efficiently, both in terms of time and in terms of cost. However, the robustness of the processes can be interpreted in two different ways:

- The ability to manufacture a variety of products within a fixed solution space, i.e. the current product portfolio / variety – *Robustness towards existing variety*
- The ability to adapt the manufacturing system to accommodate new variety, e.g. when the solution space changes due to new product options - *robustness towards new variety* This has a close relation to solution space development.

Both dimensions of the capability are relevant and critical to MC success; however they are not necessarily correlated. For example would a purely manual production be highly flexible towards new variety compared to a highly specialized and automated production, whereas the latter would probably be more efficient in manufacturing a predefined variety. Hence in order to assess the robustness of processes, we will need to distinguish between these two dimensions.

A study by Wildemann [8] investigated the ratio between product variety and manufacturing unit costs for different manufacturing technologies. This study found that for factories with conventional manufacturing technologies, doubling the variety would imply an increase in unit costs of 20-35%. Flexible automated and segmented plants however would only increase unit costs by 10-15% when doubling the variety. This indicates that there are great differences between the costs of increasing variety. The goal of robust process design is to minimize this ratio, so that increasing variety increases unit costs as little as possible. In the following, the existing literature addressing metrics for process robustness will be reviewed.

3   Literature Review

It is generally acknowledged that a late differentiation point or customer decoupling point is an enabler for an efficient MC production. Martin & Ishii [4] defined the

Differentiation Point Index (DPI) as a measure of how postponed the variant creation is in a manufacturing process:

$$DPI = \frac{\sum_{i=1}^{n} d_i v_i a_i}{n d_1 v_n \sum_{i=1}^{n} a_i}$$

v_i: #of different exiting in process i
n: number of processes
v_n: final number of varieties offered
d_i: average throughput time from process i to sale
d_1: average throughput time from beginning production to sale
a_i: value added at process i

Similarly the Setup index (SI) was introduced by Martin and Ishii [4] as a measure of how the setup costs contribute to the overall manufacturing costs. The SI metric is defined as:

$$SI = \frac{\sum_{i=1}^{n} v_i c_i}{\sum_{j=i}^{v_n} C_j}$$

v_i: #of different exiting in process i
n: number of processes
v_n: final number of varieties offered
C_j: Total cost of Jth product
c_i: cost of setup at process i

Blecker et al. [1] argue that capacity utilization (CU) is an important metric for mass customization and the definition from Mueller [5] is adopted as:

$$CU = \frac{Processing\ time}{Processing\ time + idle\ time}$$

The CU metric can be calculated for process or aggregated factory level, but in either case, a higher CU would imply a more efficient manufacturing setup implying lower manufacturing costs.

Blecker et al. also defines a production process commonality (PPC) metric, which indicated to what extent manufacturing processes are common to all product variants manufactured. The metric is defined as:

$$PPC = \frac{Number\ of\ common\ production\ processes}{Number\ of\ all\ production\ processes}$$

A delivery time reliability (DTR) metric was further introduced by Blecker et al. [1]. This is relevant as a high DTR will indicate a robust system able to deliver the necessary variety of products. The metric is defined as:

$$DTR = \frac{Agreed\ delivery\ time}{Actual\ delivery\ time}.$$

Pine [6] argued that a key metric for Mass Customization production is the work-in process turnover (WIPT), which indicates the value of goods in the manufacturing system compared to sales for a given period:

$$WIPT = \frac{Sales}{Work\ in\ process}$$

Daaboul et al [2] also introduced a number of metrics for mass customization. The Customization Process Indicator (CPI) indicates the relationship between the actual manufacturing time of a customized product and the time a customer is willing to wait for a custom product:

$$CPI = \frac{Total\ time\ for\ customization\ process}{Max\ allowed\ time\ for\ customziation\ process}$$

The metric Quality of Order Reception (QOR) indicates how well the production performs in terms of on time delivery and the defect rate [2]:

$$QOR = \frac{\#\ of\ orders\ delivered\ on\ time\ \cap\ \#\ of\ orders\ with\ zero\ defects}{total\ \#\ of\ orders}$$

Finally the Order Delay Time (ODT) indicates how fast a manufacturer is able to deliver a customized product:

$$ODT = Time\ elapsed\ between\ order\ placement\ and\ order\ reception$$

The metrics defined in literature to some extent all support the assessment of process robustness, however in different ways, and not necessarily towards both existing variety and new variety. In the following section, it will be evaluated which metrics can support the assessment of process robustness.

4   Metrics for Process Robustness Assessment

4.1   Robustness towards Existing Variety

Two of the metrics found in literature are related to standardization of the manufacturing processes; those are differentiation Point Index (DPI) and production process commonality (PPC). PPC gives an indication of to what extent manufacturing processes for different processes are common and DPI indicates the postponement of variants and on the other hand how many manufacturing processes have to change due to product variety. The most postponed manufacturing setup is expected to support highly robust manufacturing processes and therefore a very good indicator of robust process design. Because of that the DPI metric is chosen.

The Setup Index (SI) addresses the cost of setup of manufacturing processes compared to the total cost of a product. Since a high setup cost would be an indicator of a low robustness, this indicator can contribute to the assessment of process robustness.

In the literature review, three different metrics were identified which are related to time performance of the manufacturing system, i.e. the delivery time reliability (DTR), Quality of Order Reception (QOR) and the Order Delay Time (ODT),

Customization Process Indicator (CPI). Although these metrics are not direct indicators of process robustness, it is expected that highly robust manufacturing processes will have a good time performance and good performance within these metrics will indicate robust processes. The metrics QOR and DTR however are very similar, and it is thus chosen only to include the QOR metric since it not only takes into account delivery performance but also quality of the product.

The metrics Capacity Utilization (CU) and work-in process turnover (WIPT) are considered important metrics which can indicate the state of a manufacturing system; however they are not considered essential in relation to assessing process robustness and are thus not included in the final set of metrics.

In addition to the metrics identified in literature we propose two additional metrics for process robustness which are defined below:

The metric Number of different modules manufactured per process (NMP) gives a measure of the average number of modules manufactured in the different manufacturing processes:

$$NMP = \frac{\sum_{i=1}^{n} m_i}{n} \qquad \begin{array}{l} m_i \text{: \# of different modules manufactured at process i} \\ n \text{: : \# of different processes} \end{array}$$

A higher NMP will indicate robust processes, since each process will be able to manufacture more different modules and thus a higher number of end variants.

The metric Degree of manual labor (DML) can be used as an indirect indicator of process robustness, since a low need for manual processing will indicate that the non-manual manufacturing processes are able to supply a high variety. The DML metric is defined as:

$$DML = \frac{\sum_{i=1}^{n} \frac{lc_i}{tc_i}}{n} \qquad \begin{array}{l} lc_i \text{: labour cost for manucaturing product i} \\ tc_i \text{: total cost of manufacturing product i} \\ n \text{: \# of different products} \end{array}$$

4.2   Robustness towards New Variety

Only the SI metrics found in the literature were considered good measures of process robustness towards new variety and is chosen as metrics which could be useful in assessment of robust process design. This metric however is not considered sufficient for assessing the robustness towards introduction of new variety and hence four additional metrics are proposed:

Process variety increase (PVI) indicates how much the variety of manufacturing processes increases when a new product option or product is introduced in the manufacturing system. The PVI metric, calculated as an average during a period in time, is defined as:

$$PVI = \frac{\sum_{i=1}^{n} p_i}{n} \qquad \begin{array}{l} p_i \text{: \# of new processes introduced for product option i} \\ n \text{: \# of new product options in the period} \end{array}$$

A low PVI will indicate a high robustness since this implies that few new processes need to be introduced when a product option is introduced and thus that the existing processes can accommodate new product variety.

In addition to the PVI metric the Capacity expense (CAPEX) increase when introducing a new option (CAPIV) is introduced. This is done since a high PVI does not necessarily come a high cost, given a new process is implemented on existing flexible equipment. The CAPIV metric, also calculated as an average over a period of time, is defined as:

$$CAPVI = \frac{\sum_{i=1}^{n} capi_i}{n}$$

$capi_i$: Percentual CAPEX increase from introducing product option i

n: #of new product options in the period

The time and cost to introduce new product variety are also important metrics to assess process robustness, since robust processes will imply low cost and fast introduction of new product variety. The metrics Time to introduce a new option in the manufacturing system (TIV) and Cost of introducing a new option in the manufacturing system (CIV) are thus defined as:

$$TIV = \frac{\sum_{i=1}^{n} ti_i}{n}$$

ti_i: time from product design finish to manufacturing system ready

n: #of new product options in the period

$$CIV = \frac{\sum_{i=1}^{n} ci_i}{n} \quad ci_i: \text{cost of introducing product option i}$$
$$\text{n: #of new product options in the period}$$

5   Conclusion

In order to support the development of production in mass customization, metrics are needed in order to assess the robustness of processes. To establish these metrics, relevant literature was reviewed and several applicable metrics were identified. Further metrics were defined in areas where no sufficient metrics could be identified in literature. The following list compiles the metrics identified in literature and newly defined metrics within the two areas robustness towards existing variety and robustness towards new variety:

Metrics identified in the literature
- Differentiation Point Index (DPI)
- Setup Index is the cost of setup of manufacturing processes (SI)
- Quality of Order Reception (QOR)
- Number of different modules manufactured per process (NMP)

Newly defined metrics
- Number of different modules manufactured per process (NMP)
- Degree of manual labour (DML)
- Percentage point increase in process variety (PVI)
- Capacity expense increase when introducing a new option (CAPIV)
- Time to introduce a new option in the manufacturing system (TIV)
- Cost of introducing a new option in the manufacturing system (CIV)

The reason why new metrics were introduced is that the metrics identified in literature were found insufficient for a number of purposes. In relation to process robustness towards existing variety, the metrics NMP and DML were introduced because the existing metrics focused on the robustness of a manufacturing system as a whole. The new metrics seek to assess the robustness on individual process level. The four new metrics PVI, CAPIV, TIV and CIV were introduced simply because no existing metrics were found in literature supporting the assessment of process robustness towards new variety.

It is the intention that these metrics can be used to in MC companies for different purposes. One purpose is benchmarking against "best practice" mass customizers, in order to identify areas with the greatest potential for improvement. Another purpose is to use these metrics as key performance indicators which are continually calculated to monitor performance to continuously improve. In relation to research in mass customization it is the intention to apply these metrics in different types of mass customization companies to analyze what distinguishes successful mass customizers.

It is evident that the application of these metrics poses certain requirements related to data availability and quality. However, most MC companies already have systems in place which are very likely to contain the data required for calculating the metrics presented in this paper.

As mentioned in the introduction, robust process design is one of three fundamental capabilities for successful mass customizers; the other two solution space development and choice navigation. There are strong relations between these three capabilities, and phenomena experienced in a company cannot necessarily be attributed to only one capability, and as such, the metrics defined in this paper can also be influenced by other factors than the robust process design capability.

When research of identifying existing metrics with further literature review and defining metrics for all three capabilities has been finalized, the future research should establish the links between all three capabilities. Furthermore, the relations between metrics performance and specific methods should be addressed so that an assessment could point out not only what a company should do to improve but also how.

References

1. Blecker, T., Abdelkafi, N., Kaluza, B., et al.: Variety Steering Concept for Mass Customization. Munich Personal RePEc Archive (2003)
2. Daaboul, J., Da Cunha, C., Bernard, A., et al.: Design for Mass Customization: Product Variety vs. Process Variety. CIRP Annals-Manufacturing Technology 60, 169–174 (2011)

3. Lyons, A.C., Mondragon, A.E.C., Piller, F., et al.: Mass Customisation: A Strategy for Customer-Centric Enterprises. Customer-Driven Supply Chains, 71–94 (2012)
4. Martin, M.V., Ishii, K.: Design for Variety: Development of Complexity Indices and Design Charts, pp. 14–17 (1997)
5. Müller, V.: Konzeptionelle gestaltung des operativen produktionscontrolling unter berücksichtigung von differenzierten organisationsformen der teilefertigung. Shaker (2001)
6. Pine, B.J.: Mass customization: The new frontier in business competition. Harvard Business School Press, Boston (1993)
7. Salvador, F., Forza, C.: Configuring Products to Address the Customization-Responsiveness Squeeze: A Survey of Management Issues and Opportunities. International Journal or Production Economics 91, 273–291 (2004)
8. Wildemann, H.: Das just-in-Time-Konzept: Produktion Und Zulieferung Auf Abruf, 5. Aufl., München (2001)

Conception of Technology Chains in Battery Production

Achim Kampker, Heiner Hans Heimes, Christian Sesterheim, and Marc Schmidt

Laboratory for Machine Tools and Production Engineering (WZL), RWTH Aachen University,
Steinbachstraße 19, 52074 Aachen, Germany

Abstract. Mainly activated by the ambitious global political targets in terms of electrification of transport, the demand for lithium-ion cells will rise strongly in the coming years. Currently, the request is slowed down by the high prices of battery cells. The production process of battery cells is characterized by very heterogeneous areas of expertise in the various process steps. This complicates the economic design of the whole production process considerably and leads to a focusing of the plant engineers to their original core issues. Therefore this article engages at this point and provides a methodology to support the production planner along the entire production planning process. After defining the requirements for the production line, the singular performance of technological alternatives, their suitability for the product as well as the interplay of alternatives are checked. Within in the focus of this paper, all steps are shown in context to lithium-ion-cells. Nevertheless, the presented methodology has a generic approach and can therefore also been used for other production processes.

1 Introduction and Motivation

In august 2007 the European Union published a postulation on cutting down about 40% on CO_2 emissions in comparison to the year 1990. In Germany, this demand initiated the "Nationaler Entwicklungsplan Elektromobilität" (National Development Plan for Electric Mobility) in the year 2009. This plan includes the ambitious goal to get one million electric vehicles on the streets in 2020. Although the goal currently has been reduced to about 600.000 vehicles, the demand for Lithium-Ion-Cells will rise in the next years. However, not only Germany is a driving force for this trend. Also the Chinese government pursues ambitious plans by claiming that up to 500.000 hybrid and pure electric vehicles will drive in China in the year 2015. In 2020 there shall be a vast production volume of about 5 million vehicles per year. Today the predicted growth is slowed down by the complex and disruptive technology change from internal combustion engines to electric engines as well as by the high prices of electric vehicles. The battery is a significant factor of the pricing, concerning that 60% of the production costs and 40% of the overall costs can be tracked down to the battery. Regarding very low priced vehicles these figures can rise, so that the battery costs outrun the value of the residual vehicle. Comparing the worldwide goals and potentials with the cost structure of electric vehicles, it is obvious that a reduction of costs is indispensable. A potential approach for reducing costs in battery production is the reduction of the costs of production by a more structured conception of the technology chain.

V. Prabhu, M. Taisch, and D. Kiritsis (Eds.): APMS 2013, Part I, IFIP AICT 414, pp. 199–209, 2013.

An internal study of the Laboratory for Machine Tools and Production Engineering points out that only a few of more than 200 national and international machine and plant engineering companies are able to cover several process steps due to their competences. In fact a plurality of specialists serve the value added chain of the cell production. By doing so, they apply their competences in a partial process on the battery production. The operator of a lithium-ion-cell production is challenged by the identification of national and international machine and plant engineering companies for every process step. He has to instruct these specialists, which production technology has to be used, and connect all machines and plants to an economic overall process. There has to be a methodology conceived in order to support this decision-making process and systematically design technology chains. This would lead to more balanced investments over the different process steps and so reduce the overall costs.

To present this approach, the article is structured as follows. First, the existing approaches and their weaknesses are discussed. This is followed by the presentation of the structure of our new methodology. Based on this, we show how the methodology was used at our institute. The article ends with a conclusion.

2   Existing Approaches

The evaluation of the existing approaches and their weaknesses, as follows, is based on a set of criteria. The approach generates one or more technology chains out of a set of previous identified technologies (criteria 1). This should include assembly processes (criteria 2). Based on the identified production technologies, production resources can be assigned to them (criteria 3). The interactions and influences between technologies and production resources have to be taken into account, in order to guarantee an optimal adjustment. Not only interactions between neighbored, but between all technologies and production resources should be considered (criteria 4). A cross-company consideration of technologies and production resources is important as well (criteria 5). In order to guarantee global competitive and economic technology chains, an evaluation of the technology chains is important. THADEN states that, time, costs and quality are especially relevant for process performance evaluation. [1] SCHUH sees the degree of maturity of a technology significant for the technological-strategic success of a company. [2] In addition flexibility should be taken into account (criteria 6).

FALLBÖHMER`s approach does not consider interactions and influences between all technologies. His approach only considers neighbored technologies. The focus of FALLBÖHMER`s approach is on production technologies only, production resources are being left out. [3] Assembly processes are not discussed, as well. The approach P.A.R.T. developed by VAN HOUTEN states, that work steps create conditions by which the following step is measured. The consideration of the influences on not neighbored technologies is being left out, as well as assembly processes and cross-company consideration. VAN HOUTEN focusses only on machining. [4] The identification of disruptive technologies is the focus of KOSTOFF`s approach. [5] The generation of a technology chain is not discussed. The approach leaves out interactions and influences between not neighbored technologies.

3   Structure of the Method

The methodology consists of four main steps. The first one defines the requirements with regard to the product and the process. Then the general performance of technological alternatives for the different process steps gets determined. In the last step before the final conception, the suitability for the product as well as the interplay of the alternatives is checked. All these information are represented through three, so-called, technology values which show how high the performance of one alternative is for the certain case. At least these values were aggregated to an overall technology value. This rate determines than the final choice of the technologies.

3.1   Definition of the Product and Process Characteristics

At the beginning, all favored product and process characteristics are specified. Then the technology chain gets designed with this information. The phase is divided in to three steps. First, the product characteristics are defined and then recorded in a product profile. Afterwards a process profile is defined, which is used to create an ideal profile including all requirements on the production technologies.

In order to ascertain the favored product characteristics, all customer requirements relevant to the application and their influences on the product characteristics have to be defined. Thereto the correlation matrix is used (cp. Fig. 1). The product characteristics are arranged in groups on the horizontal axis. The vertical axis on the left side represents the relevant costumer requirements derived from the product specification sheets. They are completed with two additional columns. In the first column, the target course of a characteristic is displayed by arrows. The second column is used to consider the diverging relevance of different costumer requirements due to a variable weighting. In dependence on the QFD-process-matrices this weighting is multiplied with the strength of the correlations and a higher sum results for every single product characteristic. Every field in the matrix represents the relation between a costumer requirement and a product characteristic. Two pieces of information can be recorded. At first, this is the strength of the relation, illustrated by the "House of Quality"-symbolism and their numerical value, considering a weak relation with one point, a medium relation with three points and a strong relation with nine. The correlation matrix distinguishes from the "House of Quality" by the second information, which can be recorded in every field. That is what the target course is. The target course can be distinct in the form minimize, maximize or specify and shows how a specific product characteristic can clearly fulfill the customer requirements. After recording all information, the weighting can be used to specify on which product characteristic the operator has to focus on, in order to fulfill the customer requirements as much as possible. Therefore, the product profile is created by assigning a weighting to every product characteristic. For example, it is not directly apparent how a costumer requirement for a high performance cell influences the production process. However, the correlation matrix shows that this type of cell requires a low coating thickness. This parameter can easily be matched with the performance characteristics of a production machine. (cp. Fig. 1)

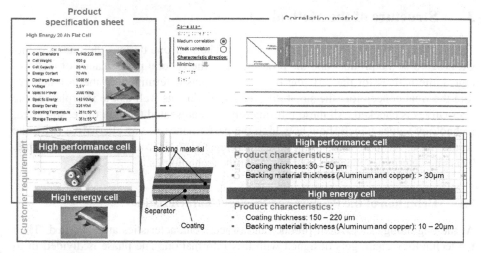

Fig. 1. Definition of the product characteristics

Subsequent the process profile is defined. Thereto the crucial characteristics have to be defined. The most important process characteristics are maturity, flexibility, costs, time and quality according to the relevant literature of KLOCKE, THADEN and BECKER.

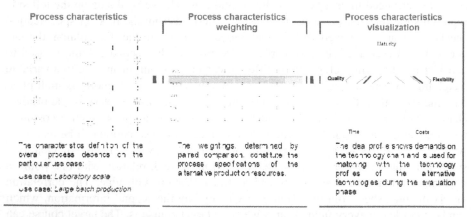

Fig. 2. Definition of the overall process characteristics

In order to these process characteristics all possible specifications are defined. Due to conflicts of goals between the different dimensions, the use of a paired comparison is recommended. The methodology operator can ponder which process characteristic is the most important to him. For the generation of the ideal profile it is necessary to normalize the sum to a value of five. It has to be mentioned that the values more outside represent a better performance. Later this profile is being used to match the customer's ideas with the performance of the production resource's.

3.2   Identification and Evaluation of Production Resources

After defining the requirements of the operator in the correlation matrix (product) and the ideal profile (process) in the first phase, the attention is now on the production process. Thereto the steps "value added chain conception" and afterwards "identification and evaluation of technological alternatives" are necessary.

In the methodology two procedures can be used for the designing of the value added chain. KLOCKE states, that a technology chain is a combination of production processes in a defined order to produce a product. In doing so, every production process's task is to create or change one or more product characteristic. After each production process the work piece of the product can be stated in an intermediate stage. The focus on those intermediate stages is very important for the generation of the value added chains, as interfaces between the processes can be depicted. The initial state, produced by a technology n, has to match with an input state, produced by technology $n+1$. This procedure enables a continuous process. When the states are defined, the production technologies for each step have to be chosen. [6] Based on the analysis of known technology chains, there are four classes of technologies: the shaping, form changing, feature changing and joining technology. They can be sorted in to classes orientated to the DIN8580 [7].

FALLBÖHMER's methodology states an alternative approach. His methodology is based on a strong informational connection between product and technology. During the product's rough planning and the ascertainment of the functional product features, the designing engineer confers with the technology planer. Just after comparing the product requirements with the production resource's potentials, the detailed planning starts and non-functional product features are being designed. [8] Both procedures enable the operator to design the value added chain with a minimal effort due to a systematical approach. This is the basis for the identification of alternative production processes along the entire process chain. [9]

Based on the designed value added chain, alternative production processes have to be identified. Therefor the technology monitoring developed by SCHUH is used. [10] In case of the production of a Lithium-Ion-Cell it has been executed for every process step. Overall 128 alternatives from mixing to the final quality check have been identified. The gathered information has been recorded in the morphological box (cp. fig. 4. left side).

Now, the technology evaluation is used to evaluate the identified alternatives based on a plurality of criteria and match them with the ideal profile. The highest technology value is assigned to the alternative technology with the best match to the ideal profile. The criteria are formed by the process characteristics maturity, flexibility, costs, time and quality again. Each criteria itself contains sub-criteria. The singular technology evaluations are summarized based on the process characteristics, in radar charts. The axes of that radar chart are formed by the five process characteristics. The first technology value, used for the selection of the production resources, is calculated with this data and the formula shown in Fig. 4. on the right side.

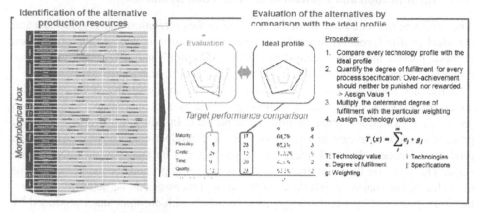

Fig. 3. Identification and evaluation of the production resources

3.3   Identification of Interdependences

In the next step, the focus moves from unique technologies to their connections with the product and with other production resources. These two poles are processed successively. Each area of tension delivers one further technology value.

The connections between technologies and product properties are shown in the technology map. All investigated technology variants noticed in the morphological box are entered into this map and ordered according to their appearance in the value chain.

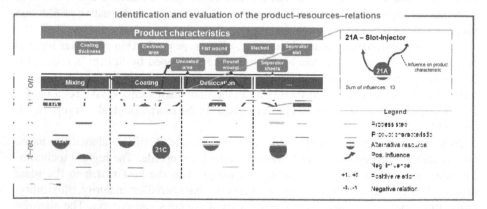

Fig. 4. Identification of product interdependences

Technology variants, which can be used in the first production step, are entered into the first column, technology variants, which can be used in the second production step, are entered into the second column and so on. In this way, all technology alternatives noticed in the morphological box are entered into the map. Afterwards, the identified technology properties are filled into the row above the different process steps. Finally, the connections between technology and product are drawn in as arrows. They start at the technologies (drawn as circles) and end at the product properties (drawn as grey rectangles). Positive connections are drawn in blue and negative in red. Each arrow possesses an edge weight which is divided into three classes (weak – 1, medium – 2, strong – 3). Positive and negative connections are differentiated by the sign. For those connections two examples between product properties and production alternatives are presented below:

- High coating thickness on cathode side – Application tool slot die
  Quality +3: There is no risk of contact between the die and the surface of substrate. The process stability is guaranteed. The greater material flow is adjustable by the pump settings. Although the die chamber and the exit slot can be designed for a greater material flow.
- Enclosure made of aluminum foil – Filling under vacuum
  Quality +3: In order to the elastic properties, the pouch cell puffs out under vacuum conditions. After raising the pressure, the cell has its starting volume. Through the constant change of pressure it comes to the suction effect. The suction effect improves the inclusion of electrolyte in a strong way.

The technology map is primarily used for the visualization and comprehension of the search results. After the completion of the technology map, the identified connections between technology and product are calculated by using the impact matrix. The impact matrix is an n x m-Matrix (n technologies, m properties). The technologies are entered into the rows and the properties into the columns. The user has to fill out the matrix with the intensities of the connections (including signs). These intensities have to be evaluated and added up to the sum of influence. Through scaling (value between one and five) the sum of influence, the second technology value is generated.

After evaluating the suitability of the technologies with regard to the product, the suitability of the different technologies has to be evaluated. Problems at the several process interfaces and with the designing of production facilities should be minimized. Therefore, the technology interdependencies have to be visualized by entering these interdependencies into the so-called technology map. The technology map includes all technological variants. Alternative technologies are entered among each other and technologies, which follow one another in the value chain, are entered next to each other. Technologies are drawn as circles and interdependencies are drawn as arrows. An arrow between technology A and technology B means, that A has an influence on B. The intensities of the interdependencies are characterized by values at the arrowheads. -1, -2, -3 (with increasing intensity) are used for negative interdependencies and +1, +2, +3 (with increasing intensity) are used for positive interdependencies. To facilitate an understanding of the different interdependencies two examples are listed below:

- Slitting with laser cutting – Separation with laser cutting
  Time +3: The use of laser cutting during the slitting process allows the determination of a final edge, so that the second laser must only finalize three edges in the separation process. This procedure saves time.

- Conventional mixer – Coating knife

  Quality -1: The conventional mixer tends to build agglomerates which are, in case of the use of a coating knife, especially dangerous for the quality of the coating. The reason is that they get stuck between the knife and surface of the ground material which influences the material flow permanently and leads to strips in the coating.

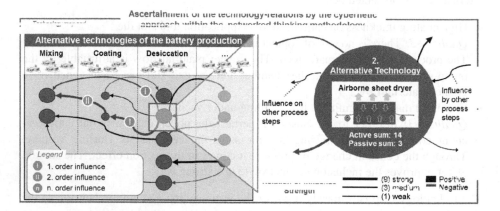

Fig. 5. Identification of interdependences 2

After the visualization of the interdependencies by using the technology map, the interdependencies are entered into the so-called impact matrix. These data are evaluated by the help of the methods of networked thinking [11] and generate a further technology value. The evaluation of the technological interdependencies is carried out separately for each process property (costs, quality, flexibility ...) and generates different subtotals. Taking account to the weights of the properties, these subtotals generate the last technology value.

3.4 Selection of Production Technologies

The final stage of technology chain development is the linking of the evaluated technology variants and the creation of a production technology chain, which fulfills the specifications of the product and process profile. Therefore, the generated technology values are combined to one value. With regard to the properties of the technology chain, preferences are defined. Depending on the preferences, the generated technology values influence this value differently. These preferences are defined at macro-level, while the preferences mentioned in the previous chapter are defined at micro-level. The technology schedule helps to decide, which aspects of technology are more important than others. Therefore, these different technology chains can be selected:

- Normal technology chain
- High-performance technology chain

- Customer-oriented technology chain
- Homogeneous technology chain
- Individual technology chain

The normal technology chain assesses the three components of technology evaluation equally. With regard to the final evaluation value, the three generated technology values have the same influence-coefficient (performance-factor). If there are special preferences, one of the other technology chains should be chosen. (cp. Fig. 7)

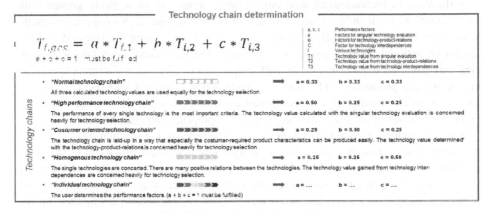

Fig. 6. Types of technology chains

After choosing the type of technology chain, the final technology value has to be generated for each technology alternative. With regard to the considered process step, the technology alternative with the highest value has to be chosen. If several alternatives have the same value, the adjacent process steps and possible complications also have to be inspected.

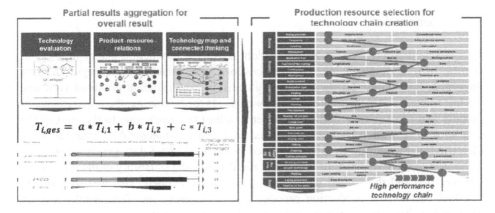

Fig. 7. Selection of production resources

4   Case Study

For the scientific verification of this methodology, it was used to build the laboratory production in the Laboratory for Machine Tools and Production Engineering. In such a production, flexibility and quality criteria need special attention because it should be possible to produce many different types of cells and they must have a high quality to carry out meaningful measurements. Due to the ease of manufacturability and the wide application, a flat pouch cell by type "High Performance" was selected. The identification of technological alternatives was carried out in working groups with representatives from industry and research. For the singular technology assessment, tests were carried out in partner companies, many experts were interviewed and the results of national research projects were used. The identification of interdependencies was based on expert interviews with employees of plant manufacturers specializing in battery production. The resulting technology chain corresponded to a large extent to previous expectations. Combinations that are not possible because of technical reasons were avoided effectively and the appropriate alternatives for the application were highlighted in almost all cases. As it turned out, the problem was to collect the needed input data, because there are only a few machinery and plant engineering companies, who address the production of lithium-ion cells directly and therefore have a sound knowledge and experience. Furthermore many companies are not pleased passing their knowledge to a research institute. The fear of losing their knowledge, and therefore their competitive advantage to a competitor, as well as the very stringent requirements of cell producers, inhibit an exchange of industry and research. The dialogue to cell producers is even worse. They almost make no information available. So there are no experiences from a running production and therefore the only input data comes from machinery and plant engineering companies. This is why the input data can be considered in a way uncertain. By a validation, together with a cell producer, this uncertainty could be significantly reduced.

5   Conclusion

This article presents a methodology, which assists the production planer in the conception of technology chains. The methodology is separated in four steps. The first three give information for the technology decision from different points of view and the last one generates the final technology chain. In the beginning, the requirements of process and product were defined in order to adjust the production to the aims of the customer. The value chain was designed and 128 technological alternatives were identified and evaluated by a standardized procedure. These data generated the first technology value. With regard to the specific product, the suitability of the procedures was verified and the second technology value was generated. The next step was to consider the holistic production process and to eliminate interface problems at an early stage. Therefore, interdependencies between and within the several process steps were exposed and classified. These interdependencies generated (with the help of networked thinking) the third technology value. The final step was to decide which technology value is the most important one. At least the technologies with the highest value were chosen.

References

1. Thaden, C.: Prozessorientierte Unternehmensplanung - Ein Konzept zur Planung und Budgetierung in einer prozessorientierten Unternehmung: Hammer, Patrick, Tanja Hammer, Matthias Knoop, Julius Mittenzwei, Georg Steinbach u. Michael Teltscher, p. 40. GRIN Verlag GbR (2008)
2. Schuh, G., Klappert, S.: Technologiemanagement: Handbuch Produktion und Management 2, p. 10. Springer (2011)
3. Fallböhmer, M.: Generieren alternativer Technologieketten in frühen Phasen der Produktentwicklung, p. 14. Shaker, Aachen (2000)
4. Van Houten, F.: PART: A Computer AidedProcessPlanning System. Dissertation, p. 83. University Twente, Enschede (2001)
5. Kostoff, R., Boylan, R., Simons, G.: Disruptive technology roadmaps. Technological Forecasting and Social Change 71(1-2), 141–159 (2004)
6. Klocke, F., Wegner, H., Willms, H.: Strategien der integrierten Technologieplanung. Industrie Management (19), 63 (2003)
7. DIN 8580, 1987: Fertigungsverfahren
8. Fallböhmer, M.: Generieren alternativer Technologieketten in frühen Phasen der Produktentwicklung, p. 38. Shaker, Aachen (2000)
9. Kampker, A., Burggraf, P., Deutskens, C., Heimes, H., Schmidt, M.: Process alternatives in the battery production, p. 1. IEEE, Piscataway (2012)
10. Schuh, G., Klappert, S.: Technologiemanagement: Handbuch Produktion und Management 2, pp. 93–98. Springer (2011)
11. Vester, F.: Die Kunst vernetzt zu denken. Ideen und Werkzeuge für einen neuen Umgang mit Komplexität; ein Bericht an den Club of Rome, 3rd edn. Deutscher Taschenbuchverlag (dtv, 33077), Munich (2003)

Towards a Knowledge-Intensive Framework for Top-Down Design Context Definition

Nicolas Petrazoller*, Frédéric Demoly, Samuel Deniaud, and Samuel Gomes

IRTES-M3M,
Université de Technologie de Belfort-Montbéliard (UTBM),
90010 Belfort Cedex, France
{nicolas.petrazoller,frederic.demoly,samuel.deniaud,samuel.gomes}@utbm.fr

Abstract. This paper presents a skeleton-based modeling approach enabling the definition of a knowledge-intensive design context at the beginning of the embodiment design stage. The research introduces an analogy to the incubator concept by creating a suitable support along the design phase including CAD modeling. The main objective of the proposed approach is to integrate engineering information and knowledge in the early phases of the product development process in a top-down and seamless manner so as to provide a knowledge-based design context for designers. The fact of including a design context in the embodiment design phase will assist designers to make better-informed decisions and therefore linking *what* (technical entities and engineering data), *why* (rationale) and *how* (processes and functions). The concept of design incubator will be defined according to its function, behavior and structure (i.e. skeleton entities, functional surfaces, design spaces, parameters, knowledge and design requirements). The proposed design incubator ensures the knowledge delivery and engineering support at the right time. A case study has been carried out to demonstrate the developed method.

Keywords: Assembly modeling, Skeleton-based modeling, Top-down assembly design, Proactive engineering, Design context definition, Knowledge-intensive design.

1 Introduction

Nowadays the globalized competitive context requires companies to deliver new products which are more innovative, more efficient with shorter lead time and optimized costs in order to fulfill customer's requirements. Designing such systems requires a phase of architectural design, lead by product architects, which must take into account a growing number of constraints (increased reliability, sustainability, reduced environmental impact, etc.). In addition, since product development includes a large amount of viewpoints [7], product architects have a global view on the system to be developed, especially on functional, structural, behavioral, geometric and physical aspects.

---

* Corresponding author.

V. Prabhu, M. Taisch, and D. Kiritsis (Eds.): APMS 2013, Part I, IFIP AICT 414, pp. 210–218, 2013.
© IFIP International Federation for Information Processing 2013

In a context of large scale company with many stakeholders working collaboratively and remotely on the same product, the definition of a design context to assist designers on their collaborative design work is important and critical. Based on previous research works related to assembly design – such as proactive design for assembly and skeleton-based modeling approaches ([8] [9] [10]) –, the main objective of this paper is to propose a proactive top-down modeling approach of design layout elements based on an analogical reasoning approach with incubator in the embodiment design stage. Here, incubator is composed of several layers of engineering information and knowledge (i.e. skeleton entities, functional surfaces, design spaces, parameters, knowledge and requirements to name a few), in order to support designers activity with a well-defined design context. For instance, the flow of engineering information and knowledge, which is required to convert product architect intents into design support elements for designers, can be seen with the analogy of an incubator (i.e. knowledge-intensive and living design context) offering an optimal environment to an embryo (i.e. design concept) until its complete development (i.e. detailed design). This novel approach will support designers by integrating engineering information and knowledge in embodiment design stage, so that designers have all needed inputs and associated procedures to define geometry. Compared to previous research efforts in this field [9], this approach will introduce new technical entities to already defined assembly skeletons, such as interface skeletons and functional surfaces in a top-down and proactive manner.

Built on this, section 2 reviews some previous works in the field of layout modeling, assembly modeling, and geometric skeleton-based modeling. In Section 3, a terminology of the design incubator concept is proposed and the overall approach is presented. Then section 4 discusses about the deployement of the approach through a mechanical assembly. Finally, conclusions and future work are addressed.

2   Related Works

This section states a brief overview of published research works on layout modeling, assembly modeling, and geometric skeleton-based modeling issues, so as to provide the foundation of the proposed approach.

The design phase of a product is composed of several stages [15] from the identification of customer needs to the detailed definition of the product. The approach of this paper will focus on the embodiment design stage of the product, in which layout design has a very important role to play [3]. The using of layout elements composed of geometry and engineering information needed to design permits to support designers and offers the possibility to exchange design data with other teams. From the literature, many attempts have been made to carry out various aspects of the layout design, such as the determination of kinematics constraints between functional components [12], the assessment of design scenarios [11], the deployment of tools based to carry out collaborative design activities among multi-disciplinary teams[2], the capture of all the feasible designs to find an optimal geometry with integration of user-defined constraints

[13], the development of full comprehensive models for spatial constraints and in particular for free-space requirements [18] and even the analysis of interferences between product components [4].

Literature has provided numerous published research works about Design for assembly (DFA) which seems to be the most investigated component of Design for (DFX). First published contributions introduced heuristic rules and design guidelines as qualitative evaluation ([1] [16] [14] [19]). More recently, Stone et al. introduced a conceptual DFA method using a functional basis and heuristic rules [17], and a DFA approach has been initiated based on System Modeling Language (SysML) in the PLM context considering an assembly oriented product structure based on preliminary assembly sequence [5]. Furthermore, recent research efforts in proactive DFA have proven that the early generation of admissible assembly sequences during conceptual design stages can be created in order to provide an appropriate contextual support for assembly design and modeling phases ([6] [8]), even for the geometric definition in a top-down way [9].

3   Proposed Approach

This section presents the proposed approach which introduces the design incubator concept. Design incubator provides a knowledge-intensive and living support to designers by defining layout product geometry at the beginning of the embodiment design phase. Such analogical reasoning will enable the introduction of a novel paradigm in CAD modeling stage.

3.1   Terminology

Based on the SKeLeton geometry-based Assembly Context Definition (SKL-ACD) approach [9], new geometric elements are introduced and defined so as to clarify the structure of the design incubator (Fig. 1):

- Assembly skeleton entity: This entity is a support for the product modeling phase (line, point, etc.) and can be considered as the first geometric elements to which the designers can allocate and define part volume and geometry.
- Skeleton interface entity: This entity describes some geometric boundaries (circle, square, etc.) which is used to build a functional surface and is supported by an assembly skeleton entity (line, plane, etc.).
- Functional surface entity: Functional surfaces are determined from the kinematic relations and product functionalities. They are limited in space by contours (i.e. skeleton interface entities)
- Design space: Design spaces are used to represent product components in a layout. Their location and orientation in space is represented by a local coordinate frame, to which a simple geometry (cylinder, cube, etc.) is attached [4]
- Design incubator: Design incubator is a set of geometric entities (skeleton assembly entities, skeleton interface entities, design spaces, parameters), knowledge and requirements which are linked formally and semantically.

Fig. 1 presents an UML class diagram of the design incubator concept.

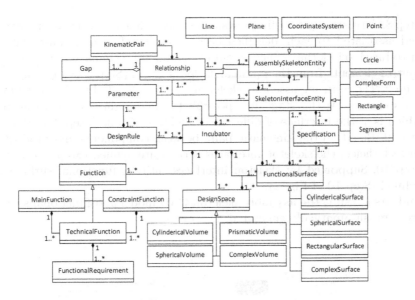

Fig. 1. UML class diagram of the incubator concept

3.2   Overall Methodology Description

Based on the SKL-ACD approach[9], an enriched flow chart is introduced to describe the proposed approach in a more detailed view (Fig. 2). An explanation of the different steps of the method is visible below:

- Start: Starting from the early defined assembly sequence generated by the ASDA algorithm and product relational information (contact and precedence information) embedded in graphs and matrices, the product architect defines kinematics/technological pairs in the directed graph;
- Steps 1 and 2. The product structure is automatically generated and assembly skeleton places are assigned inside (Steps 1 and 2 of Fig. 2);
- Steps 3 and 4. Based on these relationships, assembly constraints are automatically defined and geometric skeleton entities can be generated in order to provide interface control elements for assembly modeling (Steps 3 and 4 of Fig. 2);
- Step 5. The product architect introduces new assembly constraints between the generated geometric skeleton entities, consistent with previously defined kinematic and technological pairs (Step 5 of Fig. 2); A new graph, called skeleton graph, built upon these constraints, is defined by skeleton entities and their related assembly constraints;
- Step 6. This graph is simplified later on by the generalization and the concatenation of skeleton elements into a minimal skeleton graph (Step 6 of Fig. 2);
- Step 7. Based on this minimal skeleton graph and the early-defined assembly sequence, this step allows the structuring and regrouping of skeleton elements in assembly skeletons (Step 7 of Fig. 2);

- Step 8. An assembly coordinate system is then defined for each assembly layer and associated to each identified base part. Therefore new constraints are introduced to link the defined assembly coordinate systems with the interface control elements from the minimal skeleton graph (Step 8 of Fig. 2);
- Step 2. The resulting assembly skeletons can be allocated to the initial product structure. At this stage, it is possible to assign rights to a skeleton entity which is at the interface of different assembly skeletons (Step 2 of Fig. 2);
- Step 9. Based on the kinematic pairs between components and product architect choice, the skeleton interfaces entities are defined (Step 9 of Fig. 2);
- Step 10. Supported by skeleton interfaces entities, functional surfaces are defined (Step 10 of Fig. 2);
- End: As a result, the assembly skeleton CAD model and functional surfaces are semi-automatically generated.

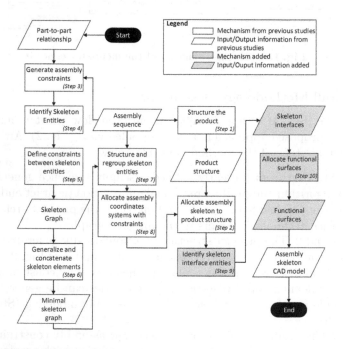

Fig. 2. Enriched flowchart of the proposed approach

4 Case Study

In this section, the proposed approach is illustrated with a mechanical system composed of 3 parts. Each step of the method are described for a better understanding (Fig. 3).

4.1 Determination of the Skeleton Minimal Graph (Step 3 to 6 of Fig. 2)

The product architect starts by defining the kinematic pairs between each parts. Based on the kinematic pairs, the skeleton entities and position constraints between each parts are deducted. At this point, to facilitate the management of the skeleton entities, it is possible to simplify the proposed skeleton graph by generalize and concatenate skeleton entities (Fig. 3).

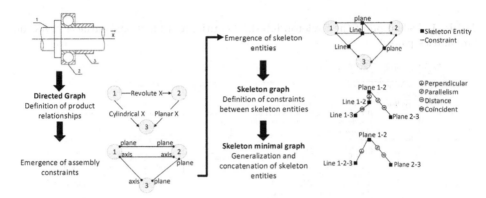

Fig. 3. Definition process of a minimal skeleton model

4.2 Introduction of an Assembly Coordinate System (Step 7 to 8 of Fig. 2)

Based on the minimal skeleton graph of the previous step, an assembly coordinate system is introduced. Each skeleton entities are linked to this new assembly coordinate system by the intermediate of geometrical constraints. Then, the geometrical constraints are concatenated (Fig. 4).

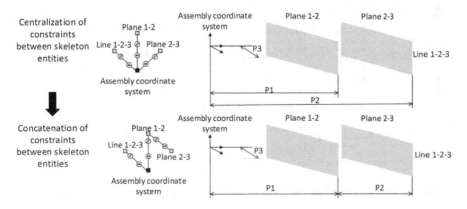

Fig. 4. Impact of the introduction of an assembly coordinate system in the minimal skeleton model

4.3 Allocation of Skeleton Interface Entities and Functional Surfaces (Step 9 to 10 of Fig. 2)

Based on previous steps and Table 1, the skeleton interface entities are defined and associated to a skeleton entity. Then, it is possible to concatenate the skeleton interface entities in order to simplify the design environment. Finally, after this simplification, the functional surface are deduced from the skeleton interface entities (Fig. 5).

Table 1. Definition of the Skeleton interface entities and functional surfaces based on kinematics pairs

Kinematic Pair	SKL Entity	SKL Interface Entity	Position	Functional surface
Rigid	Coordinate system	non-determined form	To be defined	To be defined
Revolute	Line, Plane	2 Circles for the plane contact 1 circle for the rotational guidance 1 segment for the rotational guidance non-determined form	Plan to be defined Line	1 disk inside the plane 1 cylindrical surface perpendicular to the plane
Prismatic	Line, Plane	non-determined form 1 segment	Plan Line	non-dertermined form perpendicular to the plane
Screw	Line, Plane	1 circle for stoping the thread 1 circle for the rotational guidance 1 segment for the rotational guidance	Plan to be defined Line	1 disk inside the plane 1 cylindrical surface perpendicular to the plane
Cylindrical	Line	1 circle for the rotational guidance 1 segment for the rotational guidance	To be defined Line	1 cylindrical surface cocident with the axis
Spherical	Point	1 circle	to be defined	1 sphere with the center cocident with the point
Planar	Plane	non-determined form for the contact	Plan	non-dertermined form inside the plane
Point-contact	Point, Plane	non-determined form for the contact	Plan	non-dertermined form inside the plane
Line-contact	Line, Plane	non-determined form for the contact	Plan	non-dertermined form inside the plane
Curve-contact	Curve	1 circle 1 segment	To be defined Line	1 cylindrical surface cocident with the curve

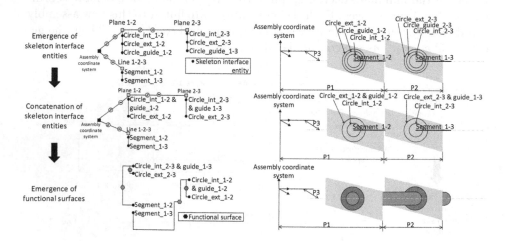

Fig. 5. Generation of the functional surfaces from skeleton interface entities

5   Conclusions and Future Work

In this paper, a method to define a design context in the early phase of the design development process has been presented. The current issue of the paper is to allocate further information to the assembly skeleton model such as skeleton interfaces and functional surfaces. Defining functional surface allocation based on skeleton modeling will permit a better understanding of "what to design" by designers. To illustrate the feasibility and the relevance of the proposed approach, a use case has been carried out. Finally, four main issues demand further research: the allocation of design space, the incorporation of knowledge; adding requirements; and create a link between the method and PLM softwares.

Acknowledgments. The research activity is part of the INGéPROD (Productiveness for Product-Process Engineering in a Design Chain context), which has been funded by French Automotive Cluster Pôle de Compétitivité Véhicule du Futur. The authors would like to thank General Electric for this collaboration and all the financial supports of this research and technology program: DRIRE de Franche-Comté, Communauté dAgglomération du Pays de Montbéliard, Conseil Général du Doubs and Conseil Régional de Franche-Comté.

References

1. Andreasen, M.M., Kahler, S., Lund, T.: Design for assembly. IFS Publications Ltd., Springer, Verlag, UK (1983)
2. Bai, Y.W., Chen, Z.N., Bin, H.Z., Hu, J.: Collaborative design in product development based on product layout model. Robotics and Computer-Integrated Manufacturing 21, 55–65 (2005)
3. Chen, X., Gao, S., Yang, Y., Zhang, S.: Multi-level assembly model for top-down design of mechanical products. Computer-Aided Design 44, 1033–1048 (2012)
4. Csabai, A., Stroud, I., Xirouchakis, P.C.: Container spaces and functional features for top-down 3D layout design. Computer-Aided Design 34, 1011–1035 (2002)
5. Demoly, F., Gomes, S., Eynard, B., Sagot, J.C.: Towards a design for assembly approach based on SysML paradigm and PLM systems. In: Proc. Second CIRP Int. Conf. Assem. Technol. Syst. (CATS), Toronto, Canada, September 21-23, pp. 100–113 (2008)
6. Demoly, F., Gomes, S., Eynard, B., Rivest, L., Sagot, J.C.: Assembly-oriented product structure based on preliminary assembly process engineering. In: Proc. Int. Conf. Eng. Des., ICED 2009, Stanford, CA, USA, August 24-27 (2009)
7. Demoly, F., Monticolo, D., Eynard, B., Rivest, L., Gomes, S.: Multiple viewpoint modelling framework enabling integrated product process design. International Journal on Interactive Design and Manufacturing 4, 269–280 (2010)
8. Demoly, F., Yan, X.-T., Eynard, B., Rivest, L., Gomes, S.: An Assembly oriented design framework for product structure engineering and assembly sequence planning. Robotics and Computer-Integrated Manufacturing 27, 33–46 (2011)
9. Demoly, F., Toussaint, L., Eynard, B., Kiritsis, D., Gomes, S.: Geometric skeleton computation enabling concurrent product engineering and assembly sequence planning. Computer-Aided Design 43, 1654–1673 (2011)

10. Demoly, F., Yan, X.-T., Eynard, B., Kiritsis, D., Gomes, S.: Integrated product relationships management: a model to enable concurrent product design and assembly sequence planning. Journal of Engineering Design 23, 544–561 (2012)
11. Gane, V., Haymaker, J.: Design Scenarios: Enabling transparent parametric design spaces 6, 618–640 (2012)
12. Kim, K.J., Sacks, E., Joskowicz, L.: Kinematic analysis of spatial fixed-axis higher pairs using configuration space 6, 279–291 (2001)
13. Li, C.G., Li, C.L., Liu, Y., Huang, Y.: A new C-space method to automate the layout design of injection mould cooling system 6, 811–823 (2012)
14. Miyakawa, S., Shigemura, T.: The Hitachi assemblability evaluation method (AREM). In: Proc. Jpn. Soc. Mech. Eng., Conf. Manuf. Syst. Environlooking Toward 21st Century, pp. 277–282 (1990)
15. Pahl, G., Beitz, W.: Engineering design, a systematic approach, 2nd edn., p. 544. Springer, London (1996)
16. Redford, A., Chal, J.: Design for assembly principles and practice. McGraw-Hill Inc., England (1994)
17. Stone, R., McAdams, D., Kayyalethekkel, V.J.: A product architecture-based conceptual DFA technique. Design Studies 25, 301–325 (2004)
18. Theodosiou, G., Sapidis, N.S.: Information of layout constraints for product lifecycle management: a solid-modelling approach 6, 549–564 (2003)
19. Yamagiwa, Y.: An assembly ease evaluation method for product engineers: DAC. Tech. Jpn. 21 (1988)

A Novel Framework for Technological Evolution within Product Architecture

Yannick Chapuis*, Frédéric Demoly, and Samuel Gomes

IRTES-M3M,
Université de Technologie de Belfort-Montbéliard (UTBM),
90010 Belfort Cedex, France
{yannick.chapuis,frederic.demoly,samuel.gomes}@utbm.fr

Abstract. Nowadays, products are increasingly complex mostly in the area of high value-added products such as airplanes, oil rigs, digger or central power generation. More generally, these products are more complex due to successive and concatenation of innovations introductions while products constraints needs a capitalization of all developed technologies. This paper introduces a novel framework for technological evolution/introduction within product architecture in order to assess and manage product family and modular architecture to personalize and customize products. This framework is based on a medical analogy to walk through customer need recognition, product portfolio, and new technological introduction in all product lifecycle. To be proactive, this challenge highlight the need to capitalize knowledge and lesson learned on the past, present and future of the product architecture and technology used in today's products based on innovative processes. More than one part, a technology is characterized by resources needed by this artifact in order to answer to an added function, new requirements, or added services. So a methodology will be proposed to tackle this challenge to be innovative in product design.

Keywords: Product architecture, Technology impact, Technology introduction, Proactive engineering, Complex product.

1 Introduction

Nowadays, numerous design processes are proposed in literature to develop a product answering to customers' needs while guaranteeing cost and delay. This step is in accordance with PLM (Product Life Cycle) strategy which proposes an integrated management of all lifecycle data [20][4]. Moreover, linked to globalization of large scaled companies [24], delocalization of business actors leads to make the engineering more collaborative [11]. In addition to this collaborative engineering, productivity has forced engineering to reduce design times, improve responsiveness and thus spent a sequential cycle to said integrated concurrent engineering or even proactive [16][22]. In such acceleration, the design process

---

* Corresponding author.

V. Prabhu, M. Taisch, and D. Kiritsis (Eds.): APMS 2013, Part I, IFIP AICT 414, pp. 219–226, 2013.

for X [2] have emerged and proven. Despite these good intentions, the very large and competitive market, forcing company's product with high value and long life cycle such as oil platforms, digger, and airplane or energy production plant meet each offer. This requirement highlights the need for each company, each to be agile and therefore take into account the variability of the product [1] compared to variability of demand [12] and therefore the one to the other [21]. In addition, all of these processes must be applied to methods such as the waterfall model [17], the classic V-cycle [8] or even the iterative method [23]. In many cases, the R&D department is separated from operational service, this difference is at the origin of many shortcomings in the design of new products. Indeed, efforts to link the process of design and the innovative process are still numerous. From 'Black Box Model' of Schumpeter [19], where is the market which ask to companies to develop new products with innovation to Kline and Rosenberg model [13] where is the design process is addressed and directive, some models finer and complex, are still unable to aggregate the creativity and design. According with definition of 'Frascati manual' (1993) one innovation covers new products and new processes or technological modification of them. One innovation is done when it is introduce to the market. At the opposite of the invention, innovation induces social change, progressive or radical, and use. In the same view with Kline and Rosenberg [13], Design process is a sub-process of innovative process, and design process is a succession of stem from needs identification to specification book (destined to manufacturing phase).

2   Overall Methodology Descriptions

2.1   Multi-aspect Positioning

In accordance with ISEA framework (Fig. 1) where different aspects linked to technological introduction were described, authors propose a new method

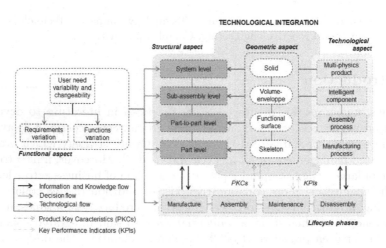

Fig. 1. ISEA Framework [3]

(Fig. 2) which allows technological transplantation seen in [3]. One can note this framework deals with several aspects, there is no knowledge notion because it is included in each aspect (engineering knowledge management). First of all, it is necessary to understand and to manage the state of art of the current product. This work, in the frame of an application, must be guaranteed not to miss out different aspects proposed in (Fig. 2).

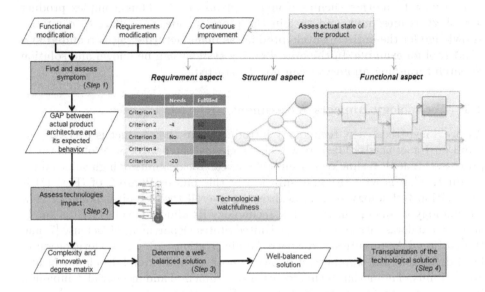

Fig. 2. Method for new technological integration

2.2 Symptoms Research: Semiology

Semiology is particularly used in the medical area but also in geography or cinema. Indeed, this science which studies signs in the medical area, studies symptoms of a disease, the way to capitalize it and to propose a diagnosis. Make a diagnosis need before this step to detect a disease through some elements. These elements are, in product design frame, a change or limitation of requirements, a dysfunction, function not integrated, a service not included or more generally, a product improvement. So the first activity of this method is trigger by one or several aforementioned. The limitation requirements are the easier to visualize. Indeed, by a feedback on products already introduced in markets, it is easy to assess components capacities already developed and integrated. Thus a matrix is allowing the realization of multi-criterions viewing of the customer expectations compared to product capacities. In the way of a non-capacity, it is possible to check more precisely limiting components and to propose a new technology, a new component (assembly or sub-assembly) to answer customer needs. All triggering elements can also directly affect the structural aspect. A customer can, expressly request a specific component, sub-assembly, assembly or a system for its maintenance globalization for example. It is possible to assess the product tree extent in order to measure and manage product options and interactions between products. Finally, it is possible to customize and personalize a functional point of view to ensure the better offer to clients. It is necessary to assess the margin between several models ('Black Box Model') and customer requirements. Generally, this step consists in having a product overview on complete and global product architecture. Furthermore, this kind of catch permits to trace impacts from a view to another such as Königs explains in [14]. Thus, complex product semiology is presented, and to join the proactive idea, an effort to capitalize knowledge for the entire lifecycle product as manufacturing [5], is required in a PLM tool for example. In this way, limiting systems can be known and solution research furnishing an answer can now be started.

2.3   Technology Impacts Assessment

As previously seen, new technology introduction in the product is necessary to fulfill customer needs. These new technologies can be part of a set of innovative processes. Indeed, technological surveillance can tackle limits of high value added product. That is why the first sub-step in this phase (Phase 2 of (Fig. 1)) is to position technology in a scale from an overall technological point of view (technology versus maturity). This Technology Readiness Level (TRL) is amply accepted and was introduced by the United States Department of Defense [7] and the National Aeronautics and Space Administration. After a modernization of level definitions and numbers, it allows to position and extend development and applicability of numerous technologies in governmental and industrial companies. In this case, main steps of this model are Fundamental research (1, 2), Applied research (3), Experimental development (4, 5), Prototype (6, 7) and Industrial development (8, 9).

   This common scale permits to understand the state of a technology, assess the risk with this choose but the assessment of this technology in a complex product is difficult. In fact the point of view of the technology readiness level is centered in the technology (in its maturity). Nowadays, it is important to express this point of view in the complex product to assess the impact of the technology in the architecture. The majority of technologies are developed in companies whose need it, it is important to introduce this technology and so on, to be innovative, to measure the adaptation of this technology in two companies and, two products. Therefore the concept of donor and recipient (as in the medical area) is introduced. Since technology integration issues in product design covers conceptual and detailed design stages, the proposed analogy is made at various abstraction levels (related to the complexity level of the technology) and according to the origin of technology area. As such, (Table 1) presents three distinct technological introductions based on medicine experience: graft, transplant and establishment. For each introduction scenario, some properties have been added in order to know if the proposed integration requires particular attention to the relationships with existing product components and related stakeholders for both sides (i.e. receiver and donor). Another relevant property is the initial

Table 1. Analogy of medical transplantation

Properties	Graft	Transplant	Establishment
With relationship	○	●	●
Same domain	●	●	○
Medical analogy	Cells	Kidney	Pacemaker
Engineering Examples	Standard part replacement	Car fuel switching	Added service inclusion

domain of the technology which must be incorporated. For instance, graft and transplant are processed within the same domain, whereas establishment is carried out in another one in order to fulfill the novel requirements. In that precise case relationship property can be illustrated with kinematic pairs, energy flows, information flows, etc. Finally a mechanical engineering example is introduced. Following the targeting between donor and recipient, it is possible to estimate the variation between developed and integrated technology into the product from new technology. This variation can be modeled by a technology S curve (Fig. 4) [9] [15] which shows the potential benefit of a technology introduced compared with a technology already developed. However, a concept not developed in the new technology integration may need some resources with technological dependences which could be cons indication of treatment for a person. These necessary resources need a modeling in a black box model [10]. Thus, the dependencies of materials, energy, flow information can be modeled and therefore focus on the presence or absence of a system for co-integration of technology. When electric technology was introduced in the automotive area, the modification of technology has required many changes in the product architecture. For example, for the same model from thermal engine to all electrical motor the system linked to the engine could be removed (tank, fuel pump ...) while some binds to the

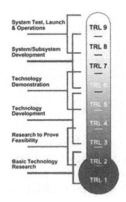

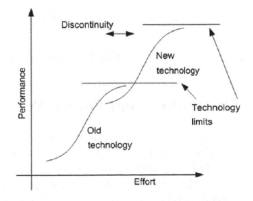

Fig. 3. Technology Readiness Level [7]

Fig. 4. Technology S curve [9] [15]

electric motor system were introduced (battery, calculator ...). This famous example of a high abstraction level illustrates the dependence of some technological resources available in a product. For example, the notion of co-system is highlighted. It is therefore necessary to model all product architecture based on the technology used but also to ensure the traceability of resources linked to technology as part of a next improvement.

2.4   Well-Balanced Solution and Optimization

This final step before grafting [3] by geometric modeling issues in a top-down manner [6], is necessary to validate and weigh each technological solution used. This optimization phase of the overall product compared to a criterion (dependent of the current limit of the product but also the needs of the client) is based on fuzzy logic (Fig. 5) [18] [25]. This tool is the receptacle of all previous data (donor data, technological maturity, potential benefits ...), but also the brain in which reasoning is built to compare and decide the best possible solutions in relation to elements of the overall process beginning. This tool will also make available the functional block in which the co-integrated systems hinterland. This gives up the context modeling.

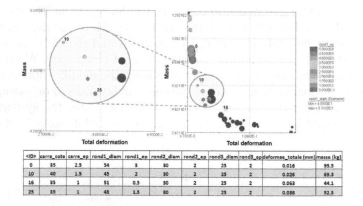

<ID>	carre_cote	carre_ep	rond1_diam	rond1_ep	rond2_diam	rond2_ep	rond3_diam	rond3_ep	deformee_totale (mm)	masse (kg)
0	85	2.5	54	3	80	2	25	2	0.016	95.5
10	40	1.5	45	2	80	2	25	2	0.025	69.3
16	85	1	51	0.5	80	2	25	2	0.063	44.1
25	85	1	48	1.5	80	2	25	2	0.038	52.3

Fig. 5. Fuzzy logic optimization

3   Conclusions and Future Work

In this paper, authors proposed a method to take into account the earlier as possible the technological introduction in product design with a lifecycle point of view. This consideration is necessary in order to achieve innovative process to improve the product and to be able to be more competitive. Finally, different issues needs furthers research as criterion of technologies resources, tree learning occurs through the technological knowledge, fuzzy agent matrix to trade off the well balance of solutions. And in the more distant future, architecture is able to learn all technological links with associated system in the product and vision board quantitative change of entry criteria in relation to overall suitability.

Acknowledgments. The research activity is part of the INGéPROD (Productiveness for Product-Process Engineering in a Design Chain context), which has been funded by French Automotive Cluster Pôle de Compétitivité Véhicule du Futur. The authors would like to thank General Electric for this collaboration and all the financial supports of this research and technology program: DRIRE de Franche-Comté, Communauté dAgglomération du Pays de Montbéliard, Conseil Général du Doubs and Conseil Régional de Franche-Comté.

References

1. Agard, B.: Contribution à une méthodologie de conception de produits forte diversite. Laboratoire GILCO 'Gestion Industrielle Logistique et COnception', Grenoble, Institut National Polytechnique De Grenoble. Thése de Doctorat (2002)
2. Baxter, D., Gao, J., Case, K., Harding, J., Young, B., Cochrane, S., Dani, S.: A framework to integrate design knowledge reuse and requirements management in engineering design. Robotics and Computer-Integrated Manufacturing 24(4), 585–593 (2008)
3. Chapuis, Y., Demoly, F., Gomes, S.: Towards an approach to integrate technological evolution into product design. In: International Conference on Engineering Design (2013)
4. CIMdata Incorporated. PLM Market Growth in 2008 'A Mid-Year Look in 2009-Weathering the Storm'. White Paper (August 2009)
5. Demoly, F., Troussier, N., Eynard, B., Falgarone, H., Fricero, B., Gomes, S.: Proactive assembly oriented design approach based on the deployment of functional requirements. Journal of Computing Information and Science in Engineering 11(1), 014501-1 (2011)
6. Demoly, F., Toussaint, L., Eynard, B., Kiritsis, D., Gomes, S.: Geometric skeleton computation enabling concurrent product engineering and assembly sequence planning. Computer-Aided Design 43(12), 1654–1673 (2011)
7. DOD.: Defense Acquisition Guidebook (2006)
8. Forsberg, K., Mooz, H.: The Relationship of System Engineering to the Project Cycle. National Council for Systems Engineering (NCOSE), Chattanooga, Tennessee (1991)
9. Foster, R.N.: Innovation: The Attacker's Advantage. Summit Books, New York (1986)
10. Han, X., Xie, W., Fu, Z., Luo, W.: Nonlinear systems identification using dynamic multi-time scale neural networks. Neurocomputing 74(17), 3428–3439 (2011)
11. Jagdev, H.S., Browne, J.: The extended enterprise-a context for manufacturing. Production Planning and Control 9, 216–229 (1998)
12. Kerbrat, O., Mognol, P., Hascoet, J.Y.: Manufacturing complexity evaluation at the design stage for both machining and layered manufacturing. CIRP Journal of Manufacturing Science and Technology 2(3), 208–215 (2010)
13. Kline, S., Rosenberg, N.: An overview of innovation. In: Landau, R. (ed.) The Positive Sum Strategy. Harnessing Technology for Economic Growth, pp. 275–306 (1986)

14. Königs, S.F., Beier, G., Figge, A., Stark, R.: Traceability in Systems Engineering - Review of industrial practices, state-of-the-art technologies and new research solutions. Advanced Engineering Informatics 26(4), 924–940 (2012)
15. Nikula, U., Jurvanen, C., Gotel, O., Gause, D.C.: Empirical validation of the Classic Change Curve on a software technology change project. Information and Software Technology 52(6), 680–696 (2010)
16. Prasad, B., Morenc, R.S., Rangan, R.M.: Information Management for Concurrent Engineering: Research Issues. Concurrent Engineering 1(1), 3–20 (1993)
17. Royce, W.W.: Managing the Development of Large Software Systems. In: IEEE WESCON 26 (1970)
18. Saridakis, K.M., Dentsoras, A.J.: Integration of fuzzy logic, genetic algorithms and neural networks in collaborative parametric design. Advanced Engineering Informatics 20(4), 379–399 (2006)
19. Schumpeter, J.: Business Cycles: a Theoretical, Historical and Statistical Analysis of the Capitalist Process (1939)
20. Stark, J.: Product Lifecycle Management: 21st Century Paradigm for Product Realisation. Springer London Ltd., London (2004) ISBN: 978-1852338107
21. Tang, D., Qian, X.: Product lifecycle management for automotive development focusing on supplier integration. Computers in Industry 59(2-3), 288–295 (2008)
22. Tichkiewitch, S.: De la CFAO á la conception integree. Hermes, Paris (1994) ISBN 0298-0924
23. Whitten, J.L., Bentley, L.D., Dittman, K.C.: Systems Analysis and Design Methods. Irwin/McGraw-Hill (2004) ISBN: 025619906X
24. Willaert, S.S.A., de Graaf, R., Minderhoud, S.: Collaborative engineering: A case study of Concurrent Engineering in a wider context. Journal of Engineering and Technology Management 15(1), 87–109 (1998)
25. Yadav, O.P., Singh, N., Chinnam, R.B., Goel, P.S.: A fuzzy logic based approach to reliability improvement estimation during product development. Reliability Engineering & System Safety 80(1), 63–74 (2003)

A Production-State Based Approach for Energy Flow Simulation in Manufacturing Systems

Marco Taisch[1], Bojan Stahl[1], Federica Vaccari[1], and Andrea Cataldo[2]

[1] Politecnico di Milano, Department of Management, Economics and Industrial Engineering, Milan, Italy
{marco.taisch,bojan.stahl}@polimi.it,
{federica.vaccari}@mail.polimi.it
[2] Institute of Industrial Technology and Automation National Research Council, Milan, Italy
{andrea.cataldo}@itia.it

Abstract. Energy Efficiency plays a major role in manufacturing being one of the largest consumers and offering opportunities for cost-savings and improvements. Simulation is an established tool for optimizing manufacturing systems. The paper shows a new production-state based approach for integrating material flow and energy consumption in commercial discrete-event simulation software. Besides typical investigation of production assets, also technical building services as one potential major source for energy consumption are taken into account. The approach considers TBS as energy demand requirements from assets and does not require modeling the behavior of TBS systems. Hence, robust simulation results can be achieved by much faster modeling time.

Keywords: eco-factory, energy efficiency, sustainable manufacturing, simulation.

1 Introduction

Energy efficiency in manufacturing has raised the attention of research and industry for quite a while. With a consumption of primary energy sources of ca. 30% and 36% of CO2 emission, the manufacturing sector is a promising area for reduction and optimization potential [1]. Gains in energy efficiency have been tackled from various directions including process and technology optimization, identification of barriers and support of drivers, development of adequate performance measures, and development of supporting tools and methodologies.

Especially quantitative and qualitative tools and methodologies can support decision-makers and stakeholders in gathering information, enlarging perspectives, providing ideas and solutions for improving energy efficiency in production systems. Simulation has been identified as a promising tool to address energy efficiency investigations appropriately in research as well industry.

V. Prabhu, M. Taisch, and D. Kiritsis (Eds.): APMS 2013, Part I, IFIP AICT 414, pp. 227–234, 2013.

2   State of Research

A remarkable progress has been done in the modeling and simulation of energy efficiency related aspects in manufacturing in the past 5 years. Simulation and modeling is seen as a core information and communication technology in manufacturing towards the next decade [2]. The usefulness of Discrete-Event-Simulation (DES) in manufacturing application is nowadays undisputable and has been demonstrated in various studies [3], hence diverse commercial simulators like Arena, FlexSim, Plant-Simulation, Anylogic, just to name a few, support the planning and optimization of manufacturing systems. But the implementation of energy related functions or indicators or other environmental-oriented functions within commercial simulators is not realized yet, although recent empirical studies have shown that companies see the combination of simulation enhanced by the empirical perspective as a supporting methodology [4] and requirements for future eco-oriented factories claim the same issue [5].

Approaches for including energy flows into material flow simulation are merely dependent on two issues: the first one is programming and coding work if the software allows it dependent on the modeling approach chosen, the second one is the scope of the simulation model. Standard simulation tools concentrate on production asset objects like machines, conveyors, robots, handling systems etc. Since the total energy consumption of a production system is not only dependent on production assets but also periphery systems like compressed air and steam generation as well as central technical building services (TBS) such as HVAC, the scope of the model from production assets via periphery systems to central TBS can have a significant impact on the simulation results. A detailed overview and comparison of existing simulation approaches taking into account energy flows is presented in [6].

Using the PlantSimulation software, Schulz and Jungnickel contribute by combining two different approaches [7]: the calculation of energy consumption associated to each manufacturing state of the production system assets starting from the power profile as proposed by Kulus et al. [8] and the calculation of energy consumption associated to the power profile of each process step as proposed by Putz et al. [9]. The approach is very detailed and gives the user a very good estimation of the real system performance. However, in order to apply the simulation tool and to build the model, detailed information in form of power profiles are required to feed the model. Usually that kind of information is difficult to get since it requires additional measurement activity directly at the production asset of the different energy carriers like electricity and air.

The aim of this paper is to present an approach which suggests the inclusion of periphery systems in the modeling without the reproduction of the TBS behavior but consideration as energy demand requirements from the assets. This approach is supposed to deliver robust and sufficient results with much faster modeling time.

3   Concept Development

Integrating energy consideration in DES requires enlarging the system of investigation in order to get a comprehensive view of the energy consumption of a production system. In a production system energy consumers can be divided twofold: consumers which are directly and indirectly involved in the production. Direct consumers are referred to as production assets. Production assets are machines, robots, working stations, conveyors, transport systems, storages, buffers etc. They are comprised by all elements which foster the material flow and manufacturing processes directly. Indirect consumers are referred to as technical building services (TBS). TBS are units which enable the production conditions, either by servicing production assets with the right form and quantity of energy or by keeping the production environment in the required condition. The first one is referred to as periphery system, whereas the second one is referred to as central TBS. Since the periphery system are connected to the production assets, the following model for DES will consider both production assets and periphery systems in the modeling approach.

The challenge is to integrate periphery systems, which are typical continuous systems, in a discrete event environment. Within the current state of the art, two approaches have been chosen to integrate periphery systems into DES simulation: the first approach is connecting two different software environments, i.e. a discrete-event-simulator with specialized software for TBS design. This approach tries to reach the highest level of detail and highest granularity of the model built, however large challenges occur in combining the two different models and programming a suitable interface. Another approach is to model both production assets and periphery systems in one software environment. While this approach has been proved to be feasible and applicable, it puts some rigid constraints on the application. First, the simulation environment has to be able to cope with discrete and continuous flows simultaneously. Most commercial and in industry used software do not support this requirement. Second, both production asset and periphery system behavior needs to be modeled in detail, which puts high demands on modeler skills. Third, the efficiency of the approach concerning requested information and output from the simulation compared to modeling effort can be questioned. The intention of this paper is based on previous work in this field, to derive an approach which enables a fast integration of periphery system into discrete event simulation while maintaining short modeling time, easy application in industry and foremost robust results.

The production assets pass through different productive states during their operation cycle. The power requirements of each state are satisfied by different energy carriers and can be constant or not, according to the type of process and part to be worked. The production assets modelled in this work are exemplarily machines, conveyors and robots, to which a specific power profile can be associated. Each profile results from the approximation to the closest polynomial function for each state applying the EnergyBlocks methodology [10]. The integral of the approximated power profile [kW] calculated along the state interval given by the simulation, provides the calculations of the energy consumptions [kWh] for each entity.

The machine behaviour has been modelled through their productive states. The considered states for the machine are: off, idle -divided in blocking and starvation-working, set-up and failure. From the energy point of view, there exist also the states ramp-up and ramp-down, which are not productive states but which can imply peaks in the power profile and may have an   impact on the energy consumption of a machine. The energy consumption associated to the peaks has been considered adding the correspondent value to the energy consumptions calculations coming from the simulation. Assuming that the interval and the extension of the peak are known and that the peak cannot be interrupted by other events, the energy calculation is done independently from the simulation environment. Instead of being calculated gaining from the simulation the real duration associated to the peak, the peak energy consumption value is calculated multiplying ¾ the peak extension for the known peak duration. As a matter of fact, for the reason that the peaks present a cusp shape and that calculating the peak energy consumption as the product of the peak extension for the duration would overestimate it, ¾ the peak extension has been used as a realistic estimation of the area included under the peak function.

The model has not differentiated where the energy requirements satisfaction of the production assets come from; they could be due to direct electricity feeding or they could come from the periphery system provision through the energy carriers. For each entity the energy consumption calculation is performed considering the equivalent electrical energy consumption for each of the different carrier feeding the equipment. For a machine which receives in input electricity and compressed air, the energy consumption calculation will be performed calculating the sum of the electrical energy consumption and the equivalent electrical energy consumption consumed by the periphery system which feed the machine with compressed air.

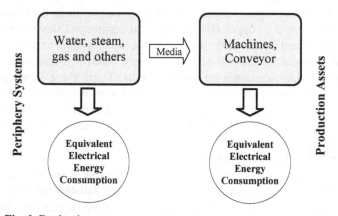

Fig. 1. Production assets and periphery systems energy requirements

The periphery system chosen to be integrated in the model was the compressed air system. It is called by the production assets in specific states -the working and the set-up- which need the power coming from the compressed air system for the pneumatic components. The energy consumption associated to the compressed air system has three different consumption ways: the energy provided by the periphery system to the production asset, necessary to satisfy the power requirements of the pneumatic components; the energy required to bring the compressed air system at operational level, filling tanks and pipes; the energy associated to the losses in the compressor and inside the system itself.

The modelling of the compressed air requirements of the production assets both in terms of power and of associated compressed air has been based on thermodynamic laws. Starting from the calculation of the mechanical work to compress a litre of air passing to the electrical energy consumed by the compressor and arriving then to the calculation of the amount of air required by each single production asset as the equations below show.

$$W = C_v * T * \left(1 - \left(\frac{p_2}{p_1}\right)^{\frac{\gamma-1}{\gamma}}\right) * M_m$$

$$E = \frac{W}{\eta}$$

$$V_1 = V_2 * \left(\frac{p_2}{p_1}\right)^{\frac{1}{\gamma}}$$

The energy consumption has been then calculated multiplying the energy required to compress one litre of air with the compressed air demand of production assets. Assuming uniform distributed compressed air consumption and energy consumption, dividing them for the value of the processing time for the specific asset and product, it has been possible then to calculate the air consumption per time unit and the power requirements, data required in order to calculate the real time consumption of air and of energy inside the simulation model. The real time calculations inside the model have been needed by the fact that the failures are stochastic events which affect the duration of other states which cannot be considered fixed; furthermore different products can require different power levels and different processing times, making clear why real time calculations are necessary.

The deployment phase has been represented by the translation of the conceptual models in the discrete event simulation software Tecnomatix PlantSimulation. The model performed the calculations of the energy consumed by the production assets real time at three different levels: the production state level, the production assets level and the manufacturing system level. These energy consumption calculations have considered also the energy consumptions coming from the compressed air system as described above.

4   Application

The model developed has been assessed in a case study represented by an automated line for the filling of sacks with powders. The automated manufacturing system is composed by two parallel lines, a line for the processing of three types of sacks and a line for the processing of the pallet.

The entities of the system have been customized with the data related to the processing/set-up times, the availability, the speed and the length for the conveyors, the electrical power, the power coming from the compressed air system and the associated consumption of air. Three different tests have been performed on the line used as a case study in order to validate the model and to see its application. The different tests have been performed using KPIs articulated at different levels of analysis and dealing with different dimensions – production, economic and energy.

The first test has dealt with the assessment of different parts sequencing: random, big batches and small batches. As it could be easily predictable, the big batches solution has represented the best trade-off of production and energy performances, a result which represented also a validation for the model developed. The simulations have been conducted over a total production of 90 parts, divided in the three tests as the table shows.

Table 1. Part distribution

Strategy	Part Type 1	Part Type 2	Part Type 3
Random	17%	33%	50%
Big batches	15	30	45
Small batches	5	10	15

While the manufacturing performances remained constant, the energy ones have been shown to change: having big batches represents the best solution in terms of total energy consumption.

Table 2. Consumption and emissions based on batch sizes

Strategy	Total Energy Consumption [kWh]	CO_2 Emissions [Kg]
Random	4,005	2,127
Big batches	3,675	1,951
Small batches	3,692	1,961

The big batches solution represents the most valuable solution also from the point of view of the energy efficiency performances, meant in terms of energy efficiency (process output/energy input), SEC (1/energy efficiency) and eco-efficiency (parts produced/environmental influence).

The second test conducted dealt with the assessment of the reduction of the processing time for the bottleneck. The reduction of the processing times even implying more energy consumed, assures the best trade-off with the parts produced. The performances have been assessed changing the processing times of the bottleneck, respectively decreasing it by 10% and 20%.

Table 3. Altering process times

Processing Time	Processing Time (P1) [s]	Processing Time (P2) [s]	Processing Time (P3) [s]
AS-IS	4,00	8,00	9,60
-10%	3,60	7,20	8,64
-20%	3,20	6,40	7,68

In this scenario the happening of the failures cannot be forecasted, the outputs are not deterministic and are represented by the average values. The decrease in the processing time of the bottleneck increased the flow rate and decreased the throughput time of the entire manufacturing system. Nevertheless, it did not cause significant changes in the total energy consumption of the manufacturing system, decreasing instead the energy consumption of the bottleneck. The following table shows the global results in terms of manufacturing and energy consumption.

Table 4. Consumptions for altering process times

Processing Time	Flow Rate [pallet /month]	Total Energy Consumption [kWh]	Total Air Consumption [l]
AS-IS	18619	13991,665	4242139,590
-10%	18610	13967,169	4073167,231
-20%	18702	13990,639	3925761,366

Finally, the third test has dealt with the doubling of the bottleneck station, bringing to the conclusion that a slightly improvement of the productive performances lead to a worsening of the energy ones, as the table below, reporting the energy efficiency performances, shows.

Table 5. Results for doubling bottleneck

	Energy efficiency	SEC	Eco-efficiency
AS-IS	1,331	0,751	2,506
TO-BE	1,324	0,755	2,493

5 Summary and Outlook

The aim of the paper is to highlight the opportunity of using discrete-event simulation with material flow simulation as a standard tool in manufacturing and enrich it with taking into consideration energy consumption. The approach is based on production-states of the production assets and has shown that implementing energy measures is possible and can lead to a widened decision sense. The approach has shown the usefulness of the equivalent energy consumption, which allows also the detailed planning, sizing, and consideration of periphery systems within material flow simulation without modelling the detailed behaviour of the TBS but including it in the energy demand requirements of the assets. The enlarged provision of information for the user from the environmental perspective point of view might be an opportunity for considering green issues in production system optimization.

Acknowledgements. The results were developed within the research project EMC2 Factory (Eco Manufactured transportation means from Clean and Competitive Factory) funded by the European Commission within FP7 (285363).

References

1. Interntional Energy Agency, Worldwide Trends in Energy Use and Efficiency, Key Insights from IEA Indicator Analysis (2008),
   http://www.iea.org/publications/freepublications/
   publication/Indicators_2008-1.pdf
2. Taisch, M., Stahl, B., Tavola, G.: ICT in Manufacturing: Trends and Challenges for 2020 – An European View. In: Proceedings of the IEEE 10th International Conference on industrial Informatics, Beijing, July 25-27, pp. 941–946 (2012)
3. Jahangirian, M., Eldabi, T., Naseer, A., Stergioulas, L.K., Young, T.: Simulation in manufacturing and business: A review. European Journal of Operational Research 203, 1–13 (2010)
4. May, G., Taisch, M., Stahl, B., Sadr, V.: Toward Energy Efficient Manufacturing: A Study on Practices and Viewpoint of the Industry. In: Emmanouilidis, C., Taisch, M., Kiritsis, D. (eds.) Competitive Manufacturing for Innovative Products and Services (2012)
5. Taisch, M., Stahl, B.: Requirements analysis and definition for eco-factories: the case of EMC2. In: Emmanouilidis, C., Taisch, M., Kiritsis, D. (eds.) Competitive Manufacturing for Innovative Products and Services (2012)
6. Thiede, S.: Energy efficiency in manufacturing systems. Dissertation TU Braunschweig (2012)
7. Schulz, S., Jungnickel, F.: A General Approach to Simulating Energy Flow in Production Plants via Plant Simulation. In: Seliger, G., Kilic, S.E. (eds.) Proceedings of the 10th Global Conference of Sustainable Manufacturing, Towards Implementing Sustainability, pp. 724–729 (2012)
8. Kulus, D., Wolff, D., Ungerland, S.: Simulating Energy Consumption in the Automotive Industry. Use Cases of Discrete Event Simulation. Springer, Berlin (2012)
9. Putz, M., Schlegel, A., Lorenz, S., Schulz, S., Franz, E.: Gekoppelte Simulation von Material- und Energieflüssen in der Automobilfertigung. In: 14. Tage des Betriebs- und Systemingenieurs, Chemnitz, pp. 134–145 (2011)
10. Weinert, N., Chiotellis, S., Seliger, G.: Methodology for planning and operating energy-efficient production systems. CIRP Annals – Manufacturing Technology 60, 41–44 (2011)

Sustainability Enhancement through Environmental Impacts Evaluation

Matteo Mario Savino and Antonio Mazza

University of Sannio, Department of Engineering, Piazza Roma 21, 82100 Benevento, Italy
{matteo.savino,antonio.mazza}@unisannio.it

Abstract. The work is aimed to propose an approach toward the evaluation of environmental impacts enhancing sustainability and the process of environmental assessment in an optic of sustainable development. A set of environmental aspects applicable to a firm activity to define the overall environmental impact are selected and processed through a fuzzy approach aimed to reduce subjective judgments. The procedure is based on a vectorial graph allowing to organize data and define a structured data analysis. An action research conducted in a genetic research center is conducted to evaluate the effectiveness of the proposed approach.

Keywords: Sustainability, Environmental impacts, Fuzzy techniques.

1   Introduction

Environmental Impact Assessment (EIA) is an efficient method for preserving natural resources and protecting the environment. Therefore, most developed countries have introduced EIA into their regulations and the consequent approval of all projects [8]. An EIA can be a useful tool to promote the goals of sustainable development as the process includes assessments of the effects of a project development and includes local opinion and knowledge [15]. Too often in the past, development projects have taken place in developing countries without EIA studies or conscious efforts to predict and mitigate adverse environmental impacts [2]. Nowadays, the trend toward industrial sustainability is observed in many matters requiring a shift in managerial and methodological approaches [10]. Despite criticism, the influence on decision making still maintains its importance as a criterion of effectiveness of the EIA system because of its valuable attributes - quantifiability with descriptive statistics and understandability to involved parties [11].

The work presents a methical approach to enhance sustainability and environmental assessment process. It selects a set of environmental aspects which can be applied to a firm activity, defining its overall environmental impact. This is done thorough a fuzzy approach aimed to reduce subjective judgments rising along multi criteria processes. The procedure is based on a vectorial graph allowing to organize data and define a structured data analysis.

The work is organized in five sections: after a literature review on sustainability, environmental management approaches and application fields of fuzzy techniques, the

V. Prabhu, M. Taisch, and D. Kiritsis (Eds.): APMS 2013, Part I, IFIP AICT 414, pp. 235–242, 2013.

third section shows the methodical proposal for the sustainability environmental assessment, the fourth section describes the action research conducted in a genetic research center and its main results while the last section deals with conclusions.

2   Literature Review

-Sustainability and Environmental Management Systems

The term "sustainable development" was coined by the IUCŃs 1980 World Conservation Strategy stating that "for development to be sustainable it must take account of social and ecological factors, as well as economic ones" [12]. In this sense, environmental sustainability can be considered one of the three pillars of sustainable development, together with social and economic one [22]. White and Nobel [24] examined the strategic environmental assessment (SEA) sustainability relationship over the past decade, focusing in particular on the incorporation of sustainability in SEA while Apolloni and Savino [1] analyzed the motivations that can lead Small and Medium Enterprises to implement an Environmental Management System.

The progress of improving sustainability can be evaluated by a set of appropriate environmental sustainability indicators with reasonable target values [23]. Fischer and Gazzola [9] or Bond et al. [4] identified effective sustainability assessments involving procedural, substantive, transactive and normative elements. Manzini et al. [16] developed a model for assessing the environmental sustainability of energy projects not only integrating environmental sustainability indicators over the lifetime of the project but also taking into account the influenced area by the local energy project. Moldan et al. [17] pointed out the attention toward different approaches and types of indicators developed for the assessment of environmental sustainability to set targets and then "measuring" the distance to a target to get the appropriate information on the current state or trend. On the same line, Caniato et al. [7] developed a research aimed at identifying the drivers that push companies to adopt "green" practices, the different practices that can be used to improve environmental sustainability, and the environmental Key Performance Indicators (KPI) measured by fashion companies. Cai et al. [6] explored the role of information technology (IT) for energy and environmental sustainability for its crucial role in the energy consumption and environmental related issues while Petrini and Pozzebon [20] managed sustainability with the support of business intelligence.

-Fuzzy Approaches for Environmental Assessment

Over the last years several approaches based on fuzzy logic have been developed to assess environmental impacts, indicating the potential of fuzzy logic in this field [19]. As an example, Peche and Rodriguez [19] presented a fuzzy procedure specifically developed to control and minimize the inconsistencies that arise from the available information on environmental impacts while Blanco et al. [3] developed an EIA computational application based on fuzzy logic, which takes into account either the quantitative or the qualitative assessments of each environmental impact. Similarly, Larimian et al. [14] proposed a model to achieve environmental sustainability using a fuzzy Analytic Hierarchy Process (AHP) to prioritize environmental factors. A fuzzy decision aid model for environmental performance assessment in waste recycling is developed by Nasiri and Huang [18] while Kaya and Kahraman [13] proposed an environmental impact assessment methodology based on an integrated fuzzy AHP–ELECTRE approach where weights of the assessment criteria are determined by a fuzzy AHP procedure. In general terms, applications of fuzzy techniques can also be found with reference to maintenance [21], [5] or economy [25].

3   Methodological Proposal

A multi decision problem is featured by different and relevant aspects where multiple objectives can be involved. A new methodology has been proposed aimed to overcome the limits of common techniques in order to obtain a fair and objective evaluation of such goals. Fuzzy logic has been applied to a vectorial graph which represents a tool of simple applicability providing at the same time useful information in visual form. Such method allows the auditor to identify from a qualitative and quantitative point of view the most critical environmental aspect for the organization and together the industrial activities involved in such aspect.

As shown in Fig. 1, the graph is organized in two levels of nodes: the first level represents the firm activities which can be in [1,N] interval while the second one represents the environmental aspects in [1,M] interval. Eight environmental impacts has been selected: (i) fuel consumption, (ii) water consumption, (iii) power consumption, (iv) air pollution, (v) special wastes, (vi) smell, (vii) noise and (viii) dangerous materials.

Arches link the two levels of nodes indicating that a given activity generates an impact on one or more environmental aspects. In Fig. 1, the third activity generates impact over the fifth, sixth and eight environmental aspect. In addition, a four position vector can be associated to each arch indicating the (i) legislation compliance -LC, (ii) impact entity –IE on the basis of detectability, dangerousness and importance, (iii) control degree –CD according to type of control and reaction capability, and (iv) territorial sensitivity –TS considering territorial context and claims frequency: {LC, IE, CD, TS}.

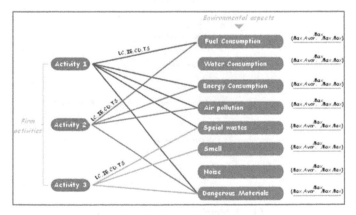

Fig. 1. Vectorial graph

As an example, Impact Entity is based on the following three parameters: (1) Consistency of the impact-C, (2) Dangerousness -D and (3) Degree of Detectability -DD. C assumes the following values according to some conditions related to consistency: 1 - negligible, 2 – low, 3 – medium, 4 – high. D is the dangerousness toward environment and health assuming values: 1 – no dangerousness, 2 – dangerous , 3 – very dangerous, 4 – extremely dangerous. Finally, DD can assume values 1 in case of immediate and simple detectability, 2 in case of detectability performed by proper instruments, 3 in case of detectability through bio-chemical analysis and 4 in case of impossible detectability. The value IE is obtained by the average of these three parameters.

The four position vector is filled for each activity and its corresponding environmental aspects; for this reason, to each second level node, i.e. the environmental impact, an impact matrix [nx4] can be associated according to the number of n ($n<=N$) activities linked to the environmental impact. The matrix is elaborated to obtain an overall vector referred to the environmental impact, i.e. $\{max[LC],$ $average[IE]^{\max[IE]}, max[CD], max[TS]\}$. Elevating to its maximum value the average of IE favors the accountability of dangerousness within the process of impact evaluation. LC, CD and TS are evaluated on a [1, 4] scale for IE a fuzzy set on a [1, 4^4] scale is used.

The final evaluation of the environmental impact is performed considering the overall vector. Values of the first, third and last column are compared to a [1, 4] scale indicating possible corrective actions to be planned and the respective timing: 1) Not necessary actions, 2) Long/Medium term actions, 3) Short term actions, 4) Urgent actions. On the other hand, the second value of the overall vector is evaluated according to a triangular or trapezoidal fuzzy function by the use of Matlab, a mathematical software. A flow diagram summarizing the methodology is shown in Fig. 2.

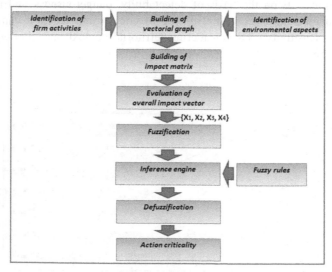

Fig. 2. Methodology flow diagram

According to the selected environmental aspects and the firm activities to be investigated, the corresponding vectorial graph is built through whom it is possible to obtain the impact matrix. Values of relative overall impact vector are processed by a classical fuzzy process made of a fuzzyfication step, an inference engine according to fuzzy rules and a de-fuzzyfication step. Such process allows to define the criticality of the selected activity with respect to the environmental aspects.

4   Application Case and Results

Proposed methodology has been validated on field in a genetic research center. For simplicity and according to environmental assessment, in the present work the analysis has been focused on two firm activities, i.e. (1) animal breeding and (2) laboratories, and six environemenatal impacts, as shown in Fig. 3.

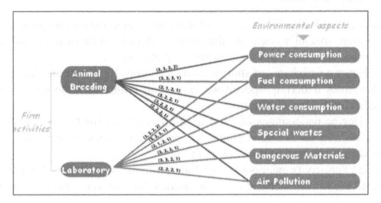

Fig. 3. Vectorial graph – Application case

Each activity has been related to the environment aspect filling the respective impact vector to define values LC, IE CD and TS. The vector has been processed by a fuzzy analysis through the use of fuzzy rules and functions, as shown in Fig. 4.

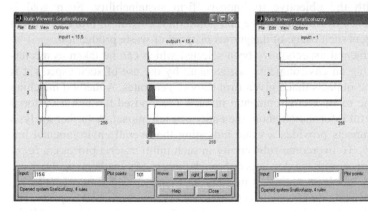

Fig. 4. Fuzzy rules implemented thorough a mathematical solver

Values LC, CD and TS are compared to a [1, 4] scale as stated in the previous section. Concerning fuzzy value IE, it has been decided to interpret the outcomes as follows:

- *IE* ∈ [0,2]: no necessary interventions;
- *IE* ∈]2,4]: long/medium term interventions are necessary;
- *IE* ∈]4,27]: short term interventions are necessary;
- *IE* ∈]27,256]: urgent interventions are necessary.

Values have been set through a tuning performed in accordance to firm management on the basis of the possible outcomes. More in details, short term and urgent interventions have been preferred defining not balanced value intervals for IE.

For the specific case study, the analysis of the de-fuzzyfied overall impact vector allowed to state the following:

- Legislation compliance necessitates of short term interventions for power and fuel consumption, special wastes and dangerous materials while of long/medium term interventions for water consumption and air pollution;
- Impact Entity necessitates of short term interventions for power and fuel consumption, dangerous materials, special wastes and air pollution while no interventions are needed for water consumption;
- Control Degree necessitates of short term interventions for fuel consumption and of long/medium term interventions for power and water consumption, special wastes, dangerous materials and air pollution;
- Territorial Sensitivity necessitates of long/medium interventions for power consumption while no interventions are needed for the remaining environmental aspects.

5   Conclusions

The present work defines a methodological proposal for the evaluation of environmental impacts with the objective to improve firm sustainability. Such goal is achieved with reference to resource usage and pollution reduction in order to prevent environmental impacts such usage of dangerous material or waste production.

A set of environmental aspects have been selected which can be taken as a reference while conducting an environmental assessment; by the use of such aspects it is possible to define the impacts that a given firm activity generates. A method matching the activities and the relative environmental impacts is proposed through a vectorial graph providing useful information about the entity of each impact. A further analysis of these multiple impacts provides a value indicating the overall environmental impact of each activity. To overcome subjectivity in such multi criteria process, a fuzzy technique has been proposed and developed through the use of a mathematical solver.

The methodology has been validated in a real test case considering a genetic research center and focusing on two main activities and six environmental impacts. The analysis has allowed to define intervention area of the firm with respect to some lacks in terms of environmental aspects which the procedure has allowed to highlight. Together with intervention area, the methodology has provided a timing of corrective actions to be performed to front weak aspects emerged during the analysis. The support provided by fuzzy set theory application allows to reduce and overcome uncertainties and subjectivity in the values assignment procedure which can be found in other models.

In general terms, such methodology is well suited to be used in a wider environmental management system where in accordance to actual regulations a certification process is sometimes necessary. It can provide a strong support to a criticality analysis of environmental aspects, focusing on intervention area and defining corrective actions ad respective timing through a fair and objective analysis.

References

1. Apolloni, S., Savino, M.M.: Environmental plant optimization in small sized enterprises through an operative framework. International Journal of Operations and Quantitative Management 13(2), 95–113 (2007)
2. Appiah-Opoku, S.: Environmental impact assessment in developing countries: the case of Ghana. Environmental Impact Assessment Review 21(1), 59–71 (2001)
3. Blanco, A., Delgado, M., Martín-Ramos, J.M., Polo, M.P.: AIEIA: software for fuzzy environmental impact assessment. Expert System Applications 36, 9135–9149 (2009)
4. Bond, A., Morrison-Saunders, A., Howitt, R.: Framework for comparing and evaluating sustainability assessment practice. In: Sustainability Assessment: Pluralism, Practice and Progress, ch. 8, pp. 117–131. Routledge, London (2012)
5. Brun, A., Savino, M.M., Riccio, C.: Integrated system for maintenance and safety management through FMECA principles and fuzzy inference engine. European Journal of Industrial Engineering 5(2), 132–169 (2011)
6. Cai, S., Chen, X., Bose, I.: Exploring the role of IT for environmental sustainability in China: An empirical analysis. International Journal of Production Economics (in press, 2013)
7. Caniato, F., Caridi, M., Crippa, L., Moretto, A.: Environmental sustainability in fashion supply chains: An exploratory case based research. International Journal of Production Economics 135(2), 659–670 (2012)
8. Environmental Protection Agency, Environmental Impact Assessment Guidelines (2007), http://www.epa.qld.gov.au/environmental_management/impact_as sessment/environmental_impact_assessment_guidelines/ (July 24, 2008)
9. Fischer, T.B., Gazzola, P.: SEA effectiveness criteria - equally valid in all countries? The case of Italy. Environmental Impact Assessment Review 26(4), 396–409 (2006)
10. Garetti, M., Taisch, M.: Sustainable manufacturing: trends and research challenges. Production Planning & Control 23, 83–104 (2012)
11. Heinma, K., Poder, T.: Effectiveness of Environmental Impact Assessment system in Estonia. Environmental Impact Assessment Review 30(4), 272–277 (2010)
12. IUCN, UNEP, WWF, World Conservation Strategy, International Union for the Conservation of Nature, Gland (1980)
13. Kaya, T., Kahraman, C.: An integrated fuzzy AHP–ELECTRE methodology for environmental impact assessment. Expert Systems with Applications 38(7), 8553–8562 (2011)

14. Larimian, T., Sadat Saeideh Zarabadi, Z., Sadeghi, A.: Developing a fuzzy AHP model to evaluate environmental sustainability from the perspective of Secured by Design scheme - A case study. Sustainable Cities and Society 7, 25–36 (2013)
15. Lee, N., George, C.: Environmental assessment in developing and transitional countries, pp. 1–12. Wiley (2000)
16. Manzini, F., Islas, J., Macías, P.: Model for evaluating the environmental sustainability of energy projects. Technological Forecasting and Social Change 78(6), 931–944 (2011)
17. Moldan, B., Janoušková, S., Hák, T.: How to understand and measure environmental sustainability: Indicators and targets. Ecological Indicators 17, 4–13 (2012)
18. Nasiri, F., Huang, G.: A fuzzy decision aid model for environmental performance assessment in waste recycling. Environmental Modelling & Software 23(6), 677–689 (2008)
19. Peche, R., Rodriguez, E.: Environmental impact assessment by means of a procedure based on fuzzy logic: A practical application. Environmental Impact Assessment Review 31(2), 87–96 (2011)
20. Petrini, M., Pozzebon, M.: Managing sustainability with the support of business intelligence: Integrating socio-environmental indicators and organizational context. The Journal of Strategic Information Systems 18(4), 178–191 (2009)
21. Savino, M.M., Mazza, A.: A model for the optimization of maintenance costs through fuzzy techniques. In: 5th International Conference on Software, Knowledge Information, Industrial Management and Applications, art. no. 6159579 (2011)
22. UN, Report of the World Summit on Sustainable Development, Johannesburg, South Africa, United Nations, New York (2002)
23. Walmsley, J.J.: Framework for measuring sustainable development in catchment system. Environmental Management 29, 195–206 (2002)
24. White, L., Nobel, B.F.: Strategic environmental assessment for sustainability: A review of a decade of academic research. Environmental Impact Assessment Review (2012) (in press)
25. Yadav, D., Singh, S.R., Kumari, R., Kumar, D.: Effects of learning on optimal lot size and profit in fuzzy environment. International Journal of Operations and Quantitative Management 18(2), 145–158 (2012)

A Queuing Approach for Energy Supply
in Manufacturing Facilities

Lucio Zavanella, Ivan Ferretti, Simone Zanoni, and Laura Bettoni

Department of Mechanical and Industrial Engineering
Università degli Studi di Brescia,
via Branze, 38, I-25123, Brescia, Italy
{zavanell,ivan.ferretti,zanoni,laura.bettoni}@ing.unibs.it

Abstract. Nowadays increasing energy efficiency is one of the main objectives of manufacturing systems so as to remain competitive despite of the foreseen increase in energy prices for the next years. We propose a novel queuing-based model for the appreciation of the energy consumption on a company base, so as to optimize the total energy costs due to electricity utilization.

We propose an analytical model based on the extension of the $M^{[x]}/M/\infty$ model where arrivals of the queuing model represent the statistical distribution of switch-on of a generic set of machines and departures represent statistical distribution of the resources switch-off. This model can be easily used to assess and establish the contract with the energy supplier under optimal parameters of contractual power, based on its tariff components. Numerical examples are offered to show the applicability of the proposed model.

Keywords: energy efficiency, Energy-aware models.

1   Introduction

Manufacturing systems are usually organized in multiple departments and in many of them there are multiple machines and each machine has its own electricity demand pattern over time. This energy requirement is usually different from machine to machine and it depends on the power of the machine and on the relative duration of the different states (idle, standby, load level, machining parameters, maximum speed) determined by different product routings which encompass it. The practical problem lies on the fact that a company does not have access to endless amounts of electricity, or that it is already subject to a contract with the supplier, which generally provides a maximum level of supply which, when exceeded, determine substantial penalties to the user.

For this reason, the objective is to create a model, of simple use, able to assist energy managers who, thanks to the model itself, may simulate different production scenarios under different electricity supply contracts, so as to minimize the expected costs. In particular, the application of the model may lead to the calculation of the following performance indices:

V. Prabhu, M. Taisch, and D. Kiritsis (Eds.): APMS 2013, Part I, IFIP AICT 414, pp. 243–248, 2013.

- probability of exceeding a specific level of power requirement;
- expected average-power requirement;
- economic evaluation and comparison of different electricity supply contracts.

Dietmair and Verl [1] introduced a generic method so as to model the energy consumption behavior of machines based on a statistical discrete event formulation. The parameter information, required to characterize the discrete events, can be obtained by a small number of simple measurements or by a degree of uncertainty from the machine and component documentation.

Bruzzone et al. [2] proposed the integration of an EAS module (energy-aware scheduling), within an advanced planning and scheduling (APS) system, incorporating a model to control the shop-floor power peak for a given detailed schedule; unavailability of the actual machine tool power profile and idle-state energy consumption require to assume constant mean power demand for each job. The goal of EAS is to optimize the given schedule from the viewpoint of the energy consumption, while keeping the given assignment and sequencing fixed. The problem is discussed by minimizing the shop-floor power peak, while limiting the possible worsening of the two scheduling objectives (tardiness and makespan minimization), modeling it as a Mixed Integer Programming (MIP) problem.

He et al. [3] proposed a modeling method of task-oriented energy consumption for machining manufacturing system. The energy consumption characteristics, driven by task flow in machining manufacturing system, are analyzed, thus describing how energy consumption dynamically depends on the flexibility and variability of task flow in production processes. The results show a valuable insight of energy consumption in machining manufacturing system, so as to make robust decisions on the potential for improving energy efficiency.

Prabhu et al. [4] proposed a queuing models to predict energy savings in serial production lines, where idling machines are switched to a lower power state in serial production lines consisting of machines with Poisson arrival and exponential service time.

Prabhu and Jeon [5] extended their previous model and generalize the energy aware queuing model to a re-entrant structure. Moreover, an application to a semiconductor factory is presented.

The paper is organized as follows: section 2 presents the system and the main assumptions. In Section 3, a model and the energy cost function are presented. In Section 4 a numerical example is offered. Section 5 summarizes the paper content, describing possible future research directions.

2   The System

One of the most important managerial actions to reduce energy costs is the proper fitting of the energy supply contracts with the plant requirements. In particular, these contracts generally provide the maximum thresholds that, when exceeded, require the payment of penalties. For example, in the electricity contract there is a threshold for the maximum power contemporary required by the loads, also defined as "contractual power". The problem faced in this paper is to determine the appropriate contractual power considering the variability in electricity usage (given by stochastic distribution of loads switch on and switch off), which is generally not predictable a priori. A simple model is then proposed, derived from queuing theory, which allows to model adequately the variability of the electrical energy consumption and to suggest the contractual power more correct, adopting a probabilistic approach to the economic optimization.

Queuing theory is capable of providing models (and consequent insights) able to predict the system behavior when jobs, i.e. system customers, ask for providing services at a randomly occurring demand. In a queuing model, entities (data, parts, jobs, etc.) arrive at the system and require for some form of service (operations, machining, assembly processes, etc.). Due to demand variability and service capability, a queue is formed. The idea is to model the variability in electricity usage by a queuing system, where the entities are represented by the power devices of the department considered. In particular, the distribution of arrivals describes the devices activation, while the distribution of services describes their shutdown. Given the random nature of the two distributions, two exponential distributions may be considered. Obviously, this assumption is valid in departments where the consumption of these devices is not easy to be predicted. Thus, the arrival and the service rates of the queuing system are expressed as power per unit of time. In such a queuing system, the average number of entities in the system is a strategic information to assess the contractual power. The queuing system defined is depicted in the following figure.

Fig. 1. The system considered in the analysis

In order to obtain tractable models, it is assumed that the arrival process and the service process are stationary. Figure 2 shows how the electric power required by a generic machine is variable (for reference see He et al, 2012) because, in general, power varies with respect to the states in which the machine is (e.g., state of heating, pressing state, stand-by). In order to simplify the problem, it may be useful to define the required power as constant, as shown below. In the next section the queuing model proposed is presented.

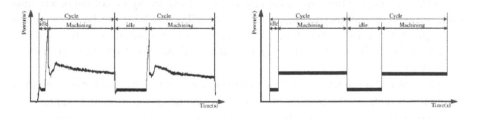

Fig. 2. Variation of the required power according to the machine states

3   Model

The model of the queuing theory proposed for the solution of the problem investigated is $M^{[x]}/M/\infty$. In particular, we assume, in addition to the assumption that the arrival stream fits a Poisson process, that the actual number of entities in any arriving module is a random variable X, which takes on the value k with probability w_k, where k is a positive integer. Because the Poisson process models the arrival of one - and only one - entity per arrival event, we consider a bulk input. This assumption models the simultaneous activation of multiple devices or the activation of a device at different power levels.

Moreover, we assume infinite service capacity, because every device is activated instantly (i.e., no queue is allowed).

After the definition of the birth-death process and the equations governing the system, using a generating function approach (Gross and al., 2008), it is possible to calculate the average number of entities in the system $L = \sum_{i=0}^{X}(i \cdot p_i)$. This performance index is the average power required. Following, we show the rate balance equations related to the states 0-1 and the states 1-2:

$$\lambda \sum_{k=1}^{X} w_k p_0 = \mu p_1 \quad \rightarrow \quad p_1 = \frac{\lambda}{\mu} p_0 \tag{1}$$

$$\lambda \sum_{k=1}^{X} w_k p_1 + \lambda(1 - w_1) p_0 = \mu p_2 \tag{2}$$

Using the Little's law and assuming infinite service capacity, the average waiting time in the system is:

$$W = \frac{1}{\mu} \tag{3}$$

In the industrial context, the power required by the department, or company, is always satisfied by the supplier of the electric power, even if the power required exceeds the predetermined contractual power. Whenever the power required exceeds the contractual threshold, the consumer will be subjected to a penalty. The objective of the analysis proposed is to verify in which cases it may be convenient to pay penalties instead of having a greater contractual power and vice versa.

In order to compare the cost of energy, in case of exceeding or not the power threshold, the following objective function is defined. The model is not based on energy consumption, but on the probability of being in a given state, thus requiring power at a given level. Thus, the following formulae will be based on these probability distributions.

In particular, the objective function (expressed as a rate €/h) is composed by three parts: the first is the evaluation of the cost below the threshold, while the second is the evaluation of the cost above the threshold and the third part is the cost proportional to the threshold chosen:

$$EEC(P) = \sum_{i=0}^{P} p_i \cdot \alpha \cdot i + \sum_{i=P+1}^{Pmax} p_i \cdot [\alpha \cdot P + \beta \cdot (i - P)] + \gamma \cdot P \tag{4}$$

where:

- α is the energy cost below the threshold [€/kWh]
- β is the energy cost above the threshold [€/kWh]
- γ is the energy cost related to the threshold [(€/kW)(1/h)]
- P is the threshold (contractual power supply) [kW]
- P_{max} is the maximum power beyond the threshold [kW]
- p_i is the probability of requiring a power level equal to i

4   Numerical Analysis

So as to study the behavior of the model, a numerical analysis was carried out to investigate how the model parameters influence the optimal solution of the energy model. The scenario considered consists of a production system with machine tools with a required power that can be represented by four different batch sizes with linearly increasing probability distribution. The arrival rate is equal to 10 kW/h (e.g., 10 events of 1 kW per hour), while the service rate is 35 kW/h (the arrival and service rates have been obtained by a fitting analysis of the statistical data of the real profile of power consumption in a basic shop floor).

Given a particular energy supply contract with α =0.2 [€/kWh], β=0.3 [€/kWh], γ=0.05 [(€/kW)(1/h)], the average power required is equal to 12.99 kW. Thus, a first option could be to set a contractual power at 13 [kW]: according to the formulae listed above, the expected hourly energy cost is equal to 3.77 [€/h].

Alternative options could be to adopt a supply contract larger than the average, e.g. 20 kW, or a supply contract smaller than the average, e.g. 10 kW.

According to the formulae shown in the previous section, the expected hourly energy cost for the supply contract with 20 kW is equal to 3.92 [€/h], while for the supply contract with 10 kW is equal to 3.74 [€/h]. Thus, in this case it is preferable to operate with a smaller power contract and pay the penalties, due to the probability of exceeding the contract power.

5   Conclusion

This work faced the problem of the electrical energy supply contract in an industrial environment. The main objective is to properly adjust the contractual power in a manufacturing system composed by several electrical resources and analyze the power consumption probability distribution applying queuing theory. The electrical power demand has been viewed as a physical user (client) that requests access to a system (electrical network) for a certain period of time (thus resulting in the consumption).

The mathematical model of a $M^{[x]}/M/\infty$ queue fits this case and it helps in capturing the dynamics of the system. Moreover, using synthetic formulae with probability functions it is possible to look for the most convenient electrical supply contract, given a set of offer available from the suppliers.

References

1. Dietmair, A., Verl, A.: A generic energy consumption model for decision making and energy efficiency optimisation in manufacturing. International Journal of Sustainable Engineering 2(2), 123–133 (2009)
2. Bruzzone, A.A.G., Anghinolfi, D., Paolucci, M., Tonelli, F.: Energy-aware scheduling for improving manufacturing process sustainability: A mathematical model for flexible flow shops. CIRP Annals - Manufacturing Technology 61(1), 459–462 (2012)
3. He, Y., Bo Liu, B., Zhang, X., Gao, H., Liu, X.: A modeling method of task-oriented energy consumption for machining manufacturing system. Journal of Cleaner Production 23(1), 167–174 (2012)
4. Prabhu, V.V., Jeon, H.W., Taisch, M.: Modeling Green Factory Physics – An Analytical Approach. In: 8th IEEE International Conference on Automation Science and Engineering, Seoul, Korea, August 20-24 (2012)
5. Jeon, H.W., Prabhu, V.V.: Modeling Green Fabs – A Queuing Theory Approach for Evaluating Energy Performance. In: Emmanouilidis, C., Taisch, M., Kiritsis, D. (eds.) APMS 2013. IFIP AICT, vol. 397, pp. 41–48. Springer, Heidelberg (2013)

Efficient Energy Performance Indicators for Different Level of Production Organizations in Manufacturing Companies

Hendro Wicaksono, Tim Belzner, and Jivka Ovtcharova

Institute for Information Management in Engineering, Karlsruhe Institute of Technology,
Karlsruhe, Germany
{hendro.wicaksono,jivka.ovtcharova}@kit.edu,
tim.belzner@kit.edu

Abstract. Demands for lower CO2 emissions due to the climate change and the rising of energy prices force manufacturing companies to deal with the energy issue. Energy management, where one of the tasks is energy efficiency evaluation, can help the companies to overcome the issue. This paper presents holistic metric to evaluate the energy efficiency in manufacturing companies, which considers the different organization level of production, such as machine or equipment level, production line level, and factory level. As the size of the scope and the number of observed factors vary, the metric provide flexible criteria to select relevant variables. The developed metric could be used to simulate and to compare energy efficiency of different production facilities, lines, and factories in a single company. The metric is an instrument to recognize how energy (in) efficient is a production system, so that adjustments may be made in the planning and management to achieve the energy savings.

1   Introduction

The global climate change, which is caused by the increase of CO2-emmisions, is a crucial issue in 21st century. Every sector including manufacturing is demanded to reduce the CO2-emissions. One of the important measures to achieve this is to use the energy more efficiently. However this is not an easy task. Demands on various and customized products have made the manufacturing processes more complex. The processes are often very energy intensive and therefore expensive. In order to minimize expenses in production, energy consumption has to be regulated.

The corporate energy management is designed to support companies in this task. Energy management defines the sum of all processes and measures which are developed and implemented to ensure minimal energy consumption by given demand [1]. An energy management system (EnMS) is a systematic way to define the energy flows and as a basis for decision for investments to improve energy efficiency. Through an EnMS, the energy policy, planning, implementation and operation, monitoring and measurement, control and correction, internal audits, as well as a regular management review are designed and executed [2]. The standard ISO 50001 describes

V. Prabhu, M. Taisch, and D. Kiritsis (Eds.): APMS 2013, Part I, IFIP AICT 414, pp. 249–256, 2013.
© IFIP International Federation for Information Processing 2013

the requirements for EnMS for industrial companies. Energy management systems that are built according to this standard can either be integrated into existing systems or implemented independently. The standard is based on the PDCA cycle (Plan-Do-Check-Act), where continuous improvement is possible [3]. This paper presents the development of energy performance indicators (EPI) to help the manufacturing companies in "Check" phase of the cycle. The indicators are used to measure energy efficiency degree of different levels of production organization in a single manufacturing company, namely machine or production facility, production line, and factory. The indicators provide a flexibility that allows the selection of relevant variables and definition of the observation system.

In section 2 we present our analysis result on the existing energy efficiency measurement concepts and identify their advantages and deficiencies. Section 3 describes the first necessary step to calculate the energy efficiency metric namely the modeling the system boundaries and components. In section 4 we list the factor influencing the figure calculations. And then, we demonstrate the calculation of the figures for different levels of production organization in section 5.

2   Related Work

Figures to measure energy efficiency can be classified into absolute and relative figures. Absolute figures consider only the output values, whereas relative figures take into account the dependency of the output value with the given input. Further categories of energy efficiency figures are classification and relational figures. Classification figures represent the energy consumption portion of smaller part to the bigger part of a system. Relational figures describe the energy consumption based on cause-effect relation, for instance, energy consumption per produced product piece [4]. German Engineer Association (VDI) introduced technical figures related to energy evaluation namely energetic efficiency degree, utilization ratio, and specific energy demand [5]. The energy requirements relative to the amount of product depends very much on the type and quality of the product. For example production of a car requires more energy than a lamp. An approach that solves this problem is energy efficiency figure presented with the equation (1) [6].

$$Energy\ Efficiency \left[\frac{€}{MWh}\right] = \frac{Net\ production\ value\ [€]}{Primary\ Energy\ Use\ [MWh]} \tag{1}$$

This energy-efficiency measure also allows a comparison of systems that produce completely different products and can be applied in the machine level as well as in the factory level, even if different products with different quantities or qualities are produced.

Some metric systems have been developed to evaluate the energy efficiency for entire industry sectors. The Energy Performance Indicator (EPI) from Energy Star considers the energy efficiency at the factory level. The data are reported by the participating companies each year and then can be compared in a tool. It is not possible to evaluate energy efficiency in operation level, since production process and equipment change very quickly. To ensure comparability between different factories, separated benchmarking for different industrial sectors is created, for instance, for automotive industry [7], glass manufacturing [8], and cement industry [9-10]. The Energy Star EPI is a good tool to evaluate the energy efficiency to compare different factories in the same industry sector. However, in order to determine cause-effect relation, the concept is not suitable. The Odyssee Energy Efficiency Index (ODEX) is an index that determines energy efficiency progress in the main sectors (industry, transport, households) and the overall economy (all consumers) [11]. ODEX is designed to track developments of energy efficiency over time in the industry. It is not able to compare individual companies or factories. The International Energy Agency (IEA) developed MEEP (Measure(s) of Energy Efficiency Performance) consisting four types of figures that differ in their potential applications [12]. The fourth MEEP figure is interesting, since it can be estimated, how energy efficient is a factory or an entire industry sector. However, this figure cannot be applied at the machine level.

3   System Modeling

To develop energy efficiency metric for a single manufacturing company, first it is important to define the system boundaries and a model that covers the different organization levels of production. In our work we extend the UPN model [13] to UPNT model and consider the machine, production line and factory level. The basic elements of the UPNT model are energy conversion (U), production (P), ancillary (N), and transport (T) facilities. Only through the interaction of these facilities the production processes are conducted.

Energy conversion facilities convert energy and deliver it in a processed form to the other systems (N, T, P). Examples of energy conversion facilities include tranformators, air compressors, steam generators, power plants etc. If an energy conversion facility is connected to internal energy network, where other sources including the ones from utility companies are connected, mix-costs from different sources is resulted in the network. Fig. 1 illustrates the method to calculate the mix-costs in the company's internal energy network.

Ancillary facilities provide the necessary conditions to achieve an unobstructed production. They serve the production directly or operating condition generally. Ancillary facilities include lighting, HVAC systems, coolant pumps, exhaust systems, etc. Facilities that are not located directly in production, such as kitchen appliances in the canteen are also considered as ancillary facilities. In principle, the transport facilities are included as ancillary facilities. However, they differ, because instead of being directly used by production facilities, they transport products to the next process step. It is very important, in particular, if the manufacturing company has different sites.

Production facilities are the most important entities in the production, because they are used to manufacture the product. Based on the efforts in production process that executed by production facilities, the customers pay the production costs and the manufacturers earn the money. However, the production facilities depend on functioning conversion, ancillary and transport facilities to work.

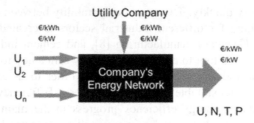

Fig. 1. Method for calculating energy costs in company's internal energy network

4   Influencing Factors on the Figures

As the basic in calculating energy efficiency degree, we use the ratio of output-input (effort) that is expressed with equation (2):

$$Efficiency = \frac{output}{input} \qquad (2)$$

There are many factors that are considered influencing the input and output in our energy flow model. We consider the following factors influencing the production outputs that are used as the numerator in calculating the efficiency.

- *Product quantity and characteristics.* The influencing factors are not only product quantity, but also the qualitative characteristics of the products. Both of the influencing factors should be integrated as a unified parameter.
- *Generated added value.* The generated added value may not be known for each stage of production directly. It can be calculated by considering the values of incoming to outgoing products.
- *Output Energy.* The output of conversion facility is directly the amount of generated energy that is delivered in the production.
- *Distance traveled between production facilities.* Transport facilities are needed to carry the products or materials between production facilities. It is not an adding value, since it does not change the product value.

The following list presents the factors that are taken into account in our work affecting the energy effort to manufacture products and determine the denominator in calculating the energy efficiency.

- *Energy demand or consumption.* The energy demand corresponds to the energy effort in executing a production process. It also can be easily measured. It is calculated through a certain time as integral of power over time.
- *Energy form.* Various energy forms have different characteristics, application areas, and costs.
- *Energy price.* The energy price takes into account all costs incurred in the generation of every form of energy.
- *Energy peak load.* The energy peak load plays role in the costs incurred in providing the energy to the company. It corresponds to which amount of power should be provided to the company in a certain time, in order to ensure that the production activities are still running properly.

- *Emission certificate efforts.* Companies are demanded to get emission certificate because of the pollution and climate change issue. The costs to achieve emission certificate is considered in the calculation.

5   Calculation Model and Results

In the section we describe the developed methods to calculate the energy efficiency figures or Energy Performance Indicators (EPI) on machine, production line, and factory level. The calculations are based on the main principal as described by the equation (2).

The main function of production facilities or machines is to create a new product or product part from source materials. As mentioned before, it is not appropriate to consider only product for evaluating energy efficiency. The solution is through considering also values generated by the production facilities. For example, if particleboard manufactured from waste wood, the value is greater than when they are produced from fresh wood. Fig. 2 depicts the energy flow model for machine level. From it can be seen, that the inputs of a production facility is made up from direct and an indirect ones. The direct inputs are from the energy and load supplied by utility companies or conversion facilities. The indirect inputs are generated due to the fact that the production facility receives the outputs of ancillary and transportation facility. The energy cost of a production facility is also ascribed from the output of the connected ancillary and transport facilities. The inputs of a production facility include proportion of used energy and load cost from ancillary and transport facilities, energy provided by conversion facilities, and energy form. Equation (3) calculates the energy performance index on machine/production facility level. The ratio α_i can be defined by the energy modeler or estimated for some kinds of facilities such as lighting and heating.

On the production line level, the efficiency calculation is in principle the same as at the machine level, but with extended system boundary. It includes other ancillary and conversion facilities, which are not considered at machine level. Fig. 3 illustrates this relationship. Other facilities that are taken into account cannot be defined in general way. They must be decided individually. A question that leads to the decision, for example: Which facilities should be shut down if the entire production line is shut down? Such as facilities are for instance lighting systems or IT facilities for production line monitoring. Analogue to the equation (3), equation (4) computes the energy performance index for production line level.

Similar to machine and production line level, the energy performance indicator on factory level is calculated with expanded system boundary. Only ancillary facilities that are used by production processes are considered in the calculation. The energy efforts of facilities belonging to other business departments such as sales, logistics is not taken into account. But social rooms, canteen etc. are taken in to consideration, since they are used by the production personnel. Similar to line level, for the factory level the system boundary is widened again including those considered conversion and ancillary facilities.

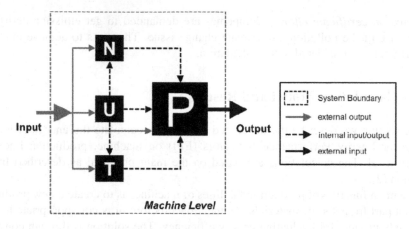

Fig. 2. Energy flow model for machine level

$$EPI_k = \frac{V_k}{P_k + \sum_{i=1}^{m} \alpha_i A_i + \sum_{j=1}^{n} T_j}$$ (3)

where

	V_k	=	output value generated by production facility k [€]
	P_k	=	input of production facility k [€]
	α_i	=	ratio of use inputted ancillary facility = [0,1].
	A_i	=	inputted ancillary facility I [€]
	T_j	=	used transport facility j [€]

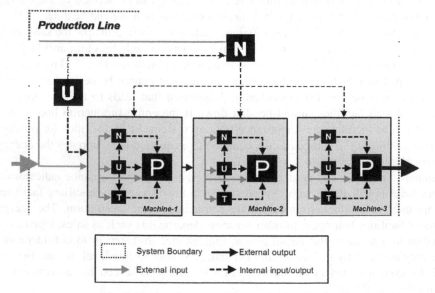

Fig. 3. Energy flow model for production line level

$$EPI_l = \frac{V_l}{\sum_k^p P_k + \sum_{i=1}^m \alpha_i A_i + \sum_{j=1}^n T_j + \sum_v^q A_v} \qquad (4)$$

The EPI is applied in a stainless steel manufacturer. Table 1 shows examples of the calculation results in machine and production line levels. The entities having EPI less than one means that energy costs exceed the supply and therefore should not occur. Otherwise, it would be an alarm signal, because the process is extremely inefficient. Higher values are conceivable when a process generates a lot of values and /or require very little energy. A value greater than one does not automatically make a positive contribution margin, as there are other costs in addition to the energy costs. However, this is not the objective of the EPIs. Rather, they should provide a comparison of different alternatives in the choice of equipment to be used. As shown in table 1, the EPI can benchmark the energy efficiency of different machines, e.g. ovens, pressers, turning machines. It also shows the comparison of three production lines L1, L2, L3, which L3 is the most energy efficient production line.

Table 1. EPI calculation results in stainless steel production

Description	EPI
M: Oven	21,0 — 30,3 – 49,6
M: Presser (1x) and Drop hammer (2x)	11,4 - 21,0 – 21,9
M: Turning machine (3x)	10,5 – 20,9 – 32,6
M: Boring Machine and CNC machine	15,7- 17,7
M: Ring roller(2x)	15,5 – 18,9
L1: Oven (EPI = 21,0), Drop hammer (EPI = 21,9), Ring-rolling (EPI = 15,5)	19,5
L2: Oven (EPI = 49,6), Presser (EPI = 11,4), Ring-roller (EPI = 18,9), Rolling- machine (EPI = 21,7)	19,3
L3: Oven (EPI = 30, 3), Drop hammer (EPI = 21,0), Rolling machine (EPI = 20,9),	21,3

6   Conclusions

So far, institutions and researchers has been developing energy performance indicators (EPI), which are used to measure and benchmark energy performance of different companies belonging to particular branch. This paper presents an approach to calculate EPI in a single manufacturing company. The EPI represents the ratio of total energy usage to the generated production value in different organization levels in production system, such as machine, production line, and factory level.

The energy flow involving the production, ancillary, transport, and conversion facilities in the company should be defined first to perform EPI calculation. The energy flow is modeled based on extended UPN-Model. It considers also the external energy sources from utility companies. The energy flow model is mainly used to calculate the costs of input and output energy. We demonstrated the energy flow model for different levels of production organization. In this paper, we list the factors influencing the energy inputs and outputs. The formulas to calculate the EPI for different levels are also illustrated. Furthermore we present some results of the EPI application in a stainless steel manufacturer.

By using the developed EPI, production planners or facility managers are able to simulate and compare different production and facility configurations, in order to find the most energy efficient ones. However, the developed EPI is exclusively used for evaluating energy efficiencies within the companies. The EPI itself cannot be used directly for measuring the economic performance. Nevertheless, there is a strong relation of the EPI to other conventional metrics. The EPI may use the conventional metrics, such as total cost and cycle time to calculate the net production value and energy effort.

References

1. Deutsche Energie-Agentur: Energiemanagement (2012), http://www.industrie-energieeffizienz.de/energiemanagement.html (accessed on April 2, 2012)
2. Kahlenborn, W., Kabisch, S., Klein, J., Richter, I., Schürmann, S.: DIN EN 16001: Energy Management Systems in Practice - A Guide for Companies and Organisations. Bundesministerium für Umwelt., Naturschutz und Reaktorsicherheit, Berlin, Germany (2010)
3. Milgram, L., Spector, A., Treger, M.: Plan, Do, Check, Act: The Deming or Shewhart Cycle. In: Managing Smart. vol. 25. Gulf Professional Publishing (1999)
4. Kals, J.: Betriebliches Energiemanagement - Eine Einführung. Verlag W. Kohlhammer, Stuttgart (2010)
5. Verein Deutscher Ingenieure (VDI): Energeticcharacteristics: definitions – terms – methodology. Beuth Verlag GmbH, Düsseldorf (2003)
6. Müller, E., Engelmann, J., Löffler, T., Strauch, J.: Energieeffiziente Fabriken planen und betreiben. Springer (2009)
7. Boyd, G.: Development of a Performance-Based Industrial Energy Efficiency Indicator for Automobile Assembly Plants. Technical Report, Argonne National Laboratory, Decision and Information Sciences Division, Chicago (2005)
8. Boyd, G.: Development of a Performance-based Industrial Energy Efficiency Indicator for Glass Manufacturing Plants. Technical Report, Duke University, Department of Economics, Durham, North Carolina (2009)
9. Boyd, G.: Development of a Performance-based Industrial Energy Efficiency Indicator for Cement Manufacturing Plants. Technical Report, Argonne National Laboratory, Decision and Information Sciences Division, Chicago (2006)
10. Boyd, G., Zhang, G.: Measuring Improvement in the Energy Performance of the U.S. Cement Industry. Technical Report, Duke University, Department of Economics, Durham, North Carolina (2011)
11. European Energy Efficiency: Analysis of ODYSSEE indicators. Technical Report. Department of Energy & Climate Change, London (2012)
12. Tanaka, K.: Assessing Measures of Energy Efficiency Performance and their Application in Industry. Technical Report, International Energy Agency (IEA), Paris, France (2008)
13. Fünfgeld, C.: Energiekosten im Betrieb. Solar Promotion. GmbH-Verlag, Munich (2000)

Energy Related Key Performance Indicators – State of the Art, Gaps and Industrial Needs

Gökan May[1,2], Marco Taisch[1], Vittaldas V. Prabhu[2], and Ilaria Barletta[1]

[1] Politecnico di Milano, Department of Management, Economics and Industrial Engineering,
Piazza Leonardo da Vinci 32, Milano, 20133, Italy
[2] Pennsylvania State University, Marcus Department of Industrial and Manufacturing
Engineering, University Park, PA 16802, USA
{gokan.may,marco.taisch}@polimi.it, gokan.may@psu.edu,
prabhu@engr.psu.edu

Abstract. Better monitoring and control of energy consumption and effective use of performance indicators are of utmost important for achieving improved energy efficiency performance in manufacturing for current and future enterprises. This paper aims at analyzing the current state of the art on energy related production performance indicators to derive research gaps and industrial needs in the area. The research has been conducted as preliminary step before a comprehensive effort in which the authors suggest a new methodology to develop energy related key performance indicators. Therefore, the study resulted in a clearer understanding and synthesis of the research field, gaps in scientific literature and industrial needs, hence guiding further research.

Keywords: Energy efficiency, key performance indicator, energy management, sustainable manufacturing, research activities.

1 Introduction

Manufacturing has changed its focus and approaches from pure cost to quality, productivity and delivery performance in the last several decades. Currently, energy efficiency has gained significant attention from both academia and the industry due to the environmental and economic impacts associated with consumption of energy. Global warming and climate change, scarcity of resources, unsecured energy supply in conjunction with global strategies and policies such as Europe's 2020 strategy constitute the main global drivers of energy efficient manufacturing whereas industrial drivers comprise rising and volatile energy prices, ever-stricter legislations, customer demand and awareness as well as competitiveness that could be achieved through improvement in energy efficiency (May et al., 2012a).

Thus, manufacturing firms must put more efforts on in-depth analysis of energy and resource performance within their manufacturing processes and facilities. In this regard, energy efficiency monitoring is of paramount importance for effective energy management since it supports decision-makers in identifying opportunities for improvement and in recording the impacts of their decisions on energy use. For

V. Prabhu, M. Taisch, and D. Kiritsis (Eds.): APMS 2013, Part I, IFIP AICT 414, pp. 257–267, 2013.

effective monitoring, performance indicators are necessary beyond measurement of data to evaluate energy efficiency performances.

In this vein, performance indicators play a significant role in evaluating the efficiency and effectiveness of manufacturing systems. KPI intelligence is essential for effective energy management in manufacturing since it supports energy related decision making. However, existing knowledge on energy related production performance indicators is limited and a thorough analysis of the literature is currently missing. Therefore, this study aims at analyzing the current state of research regarding energy related key performance indicators in manufacturing to find out the gaps and future research needs in the area. This analysis was carried out as preliminary to a further research that the authors have been carrying out to create a model for developing energy related production performance indicators.

To this end, this research is conducted to provide KPI knowledge in manufacturing with respect to energy efficiency. This scope has been identified by a preliminary research carried out in May et al. (2012a), which includes critical review of the literature on energy efficient manufacturing and an industrial survey complemented by interviews, carried out to highlight the gaps between theory and practice, as well as the importance of different aspects in integrating energy efficiency in manufacturing.

The paper is structured as follows. Theoretical background on the research area is provided in section 2 which precedes the research methodology and framework. In section 4, existing research studies are classified. Next, research gaps and industrial needs are derived in section 5 and consequently section 6 concludes along with an overview of further research and frameworks derived based on this particular study.

2   Theoretical Background

Traditional performance measures considered in manufacturing include factors such as quality, cost, delivery time and safety. Therefore, it is essential to investigate the impact of integrating energy efficiency as another performance dimension in manufacturing on traditional performances. Furthermore, since different performances are measured through indicators, identification and assessment of suitable KPIs for these performance measures is also necessary.

In this regard, measuring the energy efficiency performance of equipment, processes, factories and whole companies is a first step to effective energy management in manufacturing. The energy-related information allows the assessment of the optimization potential and improvements of energy efficiency measures, before and after their implementation. Thus, it is important to provide knowledge that highlights the overall state of the factory and its performance regarding energy consumption. In this sense, KPIs mainly serve as a measure to decide whether a system is working as it is designed for and to define progress towards a defined target value.

Regarding energy efficiency measurement, the development and application of energy related indicators depend on the purpose for which they will be applied There is no singular energy efficiency indicator that can be applied in every situation and it changes according to the decision to make or decision tool to be applied. Therefore, different measures of energy efficiency performances have been applied to manufacturing energy use. For this reason, many scholars focused on measuring energy efficiency performances [e.g. (Feng and Joung, 2011), (Tanaka, 2008)]. Feng and Joung (2011) proposed a sustainable manufacturing measurement infrastructure and Tanaka (2008) explored different ways to measure energy efficiency performance. In his analysis, Tanaka excludes the economic indices and focuses on indices that are possibly used in policy processes for a specific industry sector. He proposes the use of thermal energy efficiency of equipment, energy consumption intensity, absolute amount of energy consumption and diffusion rates of energy efficient facilities of equipment as measures of energy efficiency performance. These measures can be used for comparisons between plants and countries, policy-making and also for evaluation of policy measures but it is important to know for sure how the indicators are computed (Tanaka 2008).

Measuring the energy consumption of a process enables assessing the optimization potentials and supports visualizing verifiable benefits from improvement measures. Consequently, it is essential for all the manufacturing companies to count on a reliable system to address energy efficiency in production management and the performance after energy efficiency improvements. Performance indicators are necessary beyond measurement of data to evaluate energy efficiency performances. Thus, several energy efficiency indicators have been developed and applied for different purposes [e.g. (Ramirez et al., 2006), (Patterson, 1996)]. These indicators represent supply efficiency and energy consumption. Mostly, the relationship between energy used for an output and the output itself presented in ratios from these KPIs. There are economic and physical indicators depending on the description of the output (Ang, 2006). Economic indicators for energy efficiency are often used on an aggregated level, for instance, to compare different sectors or countries. Physical indicators are more suitable to analyze specific processes (Phylipsen et al., 1997). Besides, Patterson (1996) proposed four groups of indicators: thermodynamic, physical-thermodynamic, economic-thermodynamic, and economic.

Phylipsen considers that economic indicators are useful at an aggregated level (entire economy or industrial sector) and physical indicators for giving insight into manufacturing processes (Phylipsen, Blok and Worrell 1997). This last statement is also confirmed by Worrell that shows in his study for the iron and steel industry, that using physical indicators improves comparability between countries and provides more information regarding intrasectoral structural changes while economic indicators are not very useful for analyzing changes in the production structure of an industry (Worrell, Price, et al. 1997). Nevertheless, the more common indicators for measuring energy efficiency are Energy intensity (EI) defined as the ratio of energy consumption to a monetary value and Specific energy consumption (SEC) defined as the ratio of energy consumption to units (Ramirez, et al. 2006, Neelis, et al. 2007). Regarding the energy consumption, it can be defined and measured in many ways such as demand for primary carriers, net available energy, purchase energy, etc. (Phylipsen, Blok and Worrell 1997).

In addition, some researchers propose indicators to measure energy efficiency across plants and among countries. Aguirre proposes the use of energy-production signatures (EPPs) to measure relative industrial energy efficiency across plants. These EPSs relates total energy consumption to production output and can be used for proactive benchmarking and diagnostic purposes leading to improvements in energy consumption for individual companies. As well, the results show that the proposed methodology identifies energy and production inefficiencies within a manufacturing segment (Aguirre, et al. 2011). Meanwhile, Zhou develops an approach for monitoring energy efficiency trends over time in a country or comparing the economy-wide energy efficiency performance among countries. The proposed approach uses the Shephard distance function to define an energy efficiency index and applies the stochastic frontier analysis (SFA) technique to estimate the index (Zhou, Ang and Zhou 2012).

To conclude, proper methods for measuring energy efficiency are essential to enhance decision making of manufacturing companies by energy efficiency aspects. Thus, measuring the energy efficiency performance on different levels (i.e. machine, process and plant) is a first step to effective energy management in manufacturing. Implementation of an appropriate KPI and monitoring system is of paramount importance for enhanced energy management in a manufacturing plant since it supports energy related decision making.

3   Research Methodology and Framework

In this study, first step concerned investigating research areas in sustainable manufacturing and highlighting the role and place of energy related key performance indicators in a global view. Figure 1 below thus provides the result of such an analysis as a diagram.

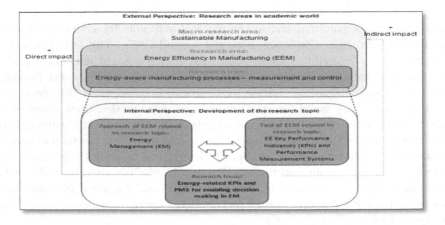

Fig. 1. Research area and focus

In Figure 2, the main approach and elements of the literature review and gap analysis are highlighted.

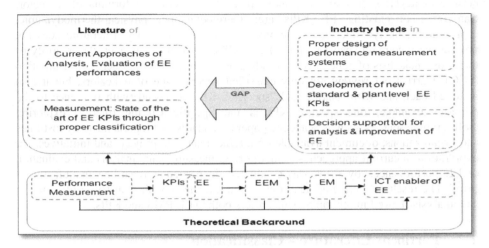

Fig. 2. Literature review and gap analysis

Theoretical background, placed at the bottom of the figure, provides the essential energy themes regarding energy efficiency performance, concerning topics of *Performance Measurement, Key Performance Indicators, Energy Efficiency, Energy Efficiency in Manufacturing, Energy Management, and ICT as enabler of Energy Efficiency.* Figure 2 thus shows current relations between the different topics within theoretical background and GAP in the figure is the conclusive output of bibliographic review. According to information collected from literature and from rising needs, it formerly highlights the existing problems through research gaps.

In the analysis of literature, a careful overview of EE KPIs has been conducted. Their state of the art has been classified through proper dimensions of classification.

Table 1 shows the three dimensions used for classification of EE KPIs, and the relations between attributes of these dimensions. In this regard, a state of the art study on energy efficiency KPIs has been conducted ranging from sector and national level, to machine and process level.

Table 1. Dimensions used for classification of energy related KPIs

Aggregation Level	Decisional Level	Scale
Aggregated	Strategic	Enterprise
		Site
Disaggregated	Tactical	Work Center
Process/Appliance	Operational	Work Unit

As seen in Table 1, scope of EE KPIs is as wider as possible. Furthermore, all *categories* of EE KPIs already existing into literature were explored and differences between categories depend on quantity present in calculation formula of indicator. Categories of existing EE KPIs are: thermodynamic, physical-thermodynamic, economic-thermodynamic, economic-physical, and eco-efficiency. Literature does not provide very comprehensive review of EE KPIs. As a matter of fact, the majority of them just make lists of general type of indicators, such as Specific Energy Consumption (SEC). Carried out review not only classified general type of indicators, but it also matched each one with relating and "specific" KPIs reviewed (with reference to the previous example, one specific KPI is the Specific Cutting Energy) exploring bibliographic sources such as academic papers, standards and reports made by institutes and organizations, document available on internet related to projects and initiatives. An exploration of current approaches to monitoring, measurement, analysis and evaluation of EE performances by firms was conducted, in particular regarding manufacturing firms. The result of bibliographical review and interviews with industry resulted in the gap analysis showed in section 5, which refers both to EE PMS and KPIs.

4   Pertinent Literature – Classification

The pertinent literature have been analyzed and classified based on the dimensions developed specifically to understand the contribution to the content discussed in this study. In particular:

— The particular section of this study, for which the concerning work from literature (represented by the single row of the matrix) has made a contribution, is represented by the dimension "dim i" ($1 \leq i \leq 5$) which constitutes the single column of the matrix;
— The importance of the contribution from the source for a particular section is represented in the matrix cell through a circle in grayscale. A darker color indicates higher importance of the contribution of the concerning work from literature.

The dimensions in the column are defined as follows:

- Dim 1: Literature to identify the research focus
- Dim 2: Literature for theoretical background
- Dim 3: Literature to define state of the energy related KPIs
- Dim 4: Literature that contributes to gap analysis and/or future trends
- Dim 5: Literature to support the development of a new KPI methodology

The circles are defined based on criteria developed to balance quality and extent of the information provided. Each source may be associated to different columns with circles of different colors, depending on the extent of the contribution made.

- White circle - marginal contribution; Gray circle - modest contribution; Black circle - decisive contribution

Pertinent literature included relevant papers published in the last 15 years and important documents of related organizations such as IEA, EC, CECIMO, etc. The analysis concerned more than 100 papers and a summary of the list is shown in Table 2 below (The whole list is not presented in this paper due to page limit).

Table 2. Classification of pertinent literature

Reference	Dim 1	Dim 2	Dim 3	Dim 4	Dim 5
(Ang, 2006)			○	○	
(Artley, Ellison e Kennedy, 2001)		○			○
(Azapagic & Perdan, 2000)	○				
(Bourne, Mills, Wilcox, et al., 2000)		○			
(Boyd, Dutrow, et al., 2008)			○		
(Braglia, Zanoni, & Zavanella, 2003)				○	
(Bunse, Vodicka, Schönsleben, Brülhart, & Ernst, 2011)				●	
Chryssolouris (2006)		○			
(Diakaki C., 2006)		○			
(Eichhammer W. , 2004)	○				
(Erlach, 2010)		○			
(Groot, 2011)	○				
(Gutowski, Dahmus, & Thiriez, 2006)					●
(Hendrik & Verfaillie, 2000)			○		
(Kannan & Boie, 2003)				○	
(Ishikuma, 2011)	○				
(Karnouskos, Colombo, Lastra, & Popescu, 2009)				●	
(May et. al, 2012a)	●	○		○	
(May et al., 2012b)			○		○
(Muchiri & Pintelon, 2008)					○
(Najmi, Rigas, & Fan., 2005)		○			
(Neely, 1999)		○			
(Patterson, 1996)		○	●		
(Phylipsen, Blok, & Worrell, 1997)		○			
(Worrell, Price, et al. 1997)		○	○		
(Prindle, 2010)			○		
(Rahimifard, Seow, & Childs, 2010)				○	
Reich-Weiser et al. (2008)			○		
(Slizyte & Bakanauskiene, 2007)		○			○
(Sutherland, 2008)	○				
(Tanaka, 2008)			○		
(Tyteca, 2002)			○		
(Van Gorp, 2005)			○		
(Veleva & Ellenbecker, 2001)			○	○	
(Yildirim, 2007)					○

5   Research Gaps and Industrial Needs

As mentioned in section 3, thorough review of the literature and interviews with the industry guided us to research gaps and industry needs with respect to energy efficiency performance indicators and performance measurement systems as highlighted in Figure 3.

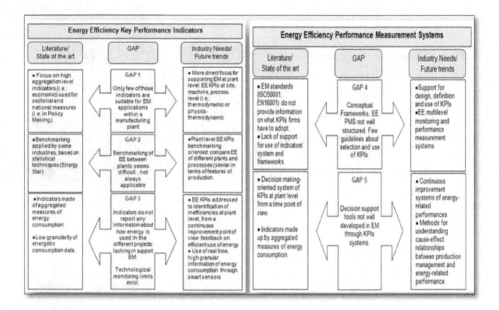

Fig. 3. Gaps and industrial needs

6   Conclusion and Future Work

In this research, we thoroughly analyzed the pertinent literature and industrial needs regarding energy related production performance indicators and came up with two main frameworks, first one highlighting the role of KPIs in an overall view of energy management and a second framework that guided a new methodology for developing KPIs to close the gaps identified. Thus, Figure 4 below is the framework that presents an overview of energy management in production and relationships between its different components.

Besides, a second framework has been derived based on the gaps identified in this research and led us to a further work in which the authors developed a new methodology to develop energy related production performance indicators based on the identified gaps.

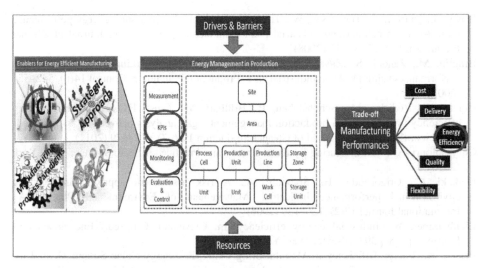

Fig. 4. Energy Management in Production and role of KPIs

Finally, some basic research motives for our further works have emerged:

- KPI model to create appropriate energy efficiency measures to be used in the different levels (e.g. tool, equipment, process and plant level) of a manufacturing facility. The main focus in this part will be on the machine level to change the traditional time based view to energy based view
- Set of guidelines for effective design and use of Energy related KPIs in manufacturing facilities to improve energy efficiency
- An approach to increase the visibility and transparency of energy related KPIs in a manufacturing facility, facilitating ICT as an enabling factor. This approach is expected to provide a decision support mechanism for enhanced energy management and hence support improvement of energy related performances

References

Aguirre, F., Villalobos, J.R., Phelan, P.E., Pacheco, R.: Assessing the relative efficiency of energy use among similar manufacturing industries. International Journal of Energy Research 35(6), 477–488 (2011)

Ang, B.W.: Monitoring changes in economy-wide energy efficiency: From energy-gdp ratio to composite efficiency index. Hong Kong Editorial Board meeting presentations. Energy Policy 34(5), 574–582 (2006)

Artley, W., Ellison, D.J., Kennedy, B.: The performance based management handbook (2001)

Azapagic, A., Perdan, S.: Indicators of sustainable development for industry: a general framework. Process Safety and Environmental Protection 78, 244–246 (2000)

Bourne, M., Mills, J., Wilcox, M., Neely, A., Platts, K.: Designing, implementing and updating performance measurement systems. International Journal of Operations & Production Management 20(7), 754–771 (2000)

Boyd, G., Dutrow, E., Tunnessen, W.: The evolution of the "energy star" energy performance indicator for benchmarking industrial plant manufacturing energy use. Journal of Cleaner Production 16(6), 709–715 (2008)

Braglia, M., Zanoni, S., Zavanella, L.: Measuring and benchmarking productive systems performances using DEA: an industrial case. Production Planning & Control 14(6), 542–554 (2003)

Bunse, K., Vodicka, M., Schönsleben, P., Brülhart, M., Ernst, F.O.: Integrating energy efficiency performance in production management - gap analysis between industrial needs and scientific literature. Journal of Cleaner Production 19(6-7), 667–679 (2011)

Chryssolouris, G.: Manufacturing Systems: Theory and Practice, 3rd edn. Springer, New York (2006)

Diakaki, C., Grigoroudis, E., Stabouli, M.: A risk assessment approach in selecting environmental performance indicators. Management of Environmental Quality: An International Journal 17(2), 126–139 (2006)

Eichhammer, W.: Industrial energy efficiency. In: Cleveland, C.J. (ed.) Encyclopedia of Energy, pp. 383–393. Elsevier, New York (2004)

Erlach, K.: Energy Efficiency in Manufacturing Using the Energy Value Stream Method for building an energy efficient factory. In: International Conference on Advances in Production Management Systems, APMS 2010, Cernobbio, Italy (2010)

Feng, S.C., Joung, C.B.: An overview of a proposed measurement infrastructure for sustainable manufacturing. In: Proceedings of the 7th Global Conference on Sustainable Manufacturing (2009)

Groot, H.V.: Energy saving by firms: decisionmaking, barriers and policies. Energy Economics 23, 717–740 (2011)

Gutowski, T., Dahmus, J., Thiriez, A.: Electrical Energy Requirements for Manufacturing Processes. In: 13th CIRP International Conference on Life Cycle Engineering (2006)

Verfaillie, H.A., Bidwell, R.: Measuring eco-efficiency: A guide to reporting company performance. Technical report, World Business Council for Sustainable Development (2000)

Ishikuma, T.: International Standardization for Low-Carbon Society - Status of Energy Efficiency and Environmental Guidelines –. In: SICE Annual Conference 2011. Waseda University, Tokyo, Japan (2011)

Kannan, R., Boie, W.: Energy management practices in SME - case study of a bakery in Germany. Energy Conversion and Management 44(6), 945–959 (2003)

Karnouskos, S., Colombo, A.W., Lastra, J.L.M., Popescu, C.: Towards the Energy Efficient Future Factory. In: 7th IEEE International Conference on Industrial Informatics. IEEE, Piscataway (2009)

May, G., Taisch, M., Stahl, B., Sadr, V.: Toward Energy Efficient Manufacturing: A Study on Practices and Viewpoint of the Industry. In: Emmanouilidis, C., Taisch, M., Kiritsis, D. (eds.) APMS 2012. IFIP AICT, vol. 397, pp. 1–8. Springer, Heidelberg (2013a)

May, G., Taisch, M., Geoghegan, K., Beccaris, M.: Improving Energy Efficiency in Manufacturing via KPI Intelligence Based on Plant Integration. In: 10th Global Conference on Sustainable Manufacturing, Istanbul, Turkey (2012b) ISBN-978-605-63463-1-6

Muchiri, P., Pintelon, L.: Performance measurement using overall equipment effectiveness: literature review and practical application discussion. Int. Journal of Production Research (2008)

Najmi, M., Rigas, J., Fan, I.S.: A framework to revieperformance measurement systems. Business Process Management Journal 11(2), 109–122 (2005)

Neely, A.: The performance measurement revolution: why now and what next. International Journal of Operations & Production Management 19(2), 205–228 (1999)

Neelis, M., Ramirez, A., Patel, M., Farla, J., Boonekamp, P., Blok, K.: Energy efficiency developments in the Dutch energy-intensive manufacturing industry, 1980-2003. Energy Policy 35(12), 6112–6131 (2007)

Patterson, M.G.: What is energy efficiency? Concepts, indicators and methodological issues. Energy Policy 24(5), 377–390 (1996)

Phylipsen, G.J.M., Blok, K., Worrell, E.: International comparisons of energy efficiency-Methodologies for the manufacturing industry. Energy Policy 25(7-9), 715–725 (1997)

Prindle, W.R.: From shop floor to top floor: Best practices in energy efficiency. Technical report, Pew Center on Global Climate Change (2010)

Rahimifard, S., Seow, Y., Childs, T.: Minimising embodied product energy to support energy efficient manufacturing. CIRP Annals - Manufacturing Technology 59(1), 25–28 (2010)

Ramirez, C.A., Blok, K., Neelis, M., Patel, M.K.: Adding apples and oranges: The monitoring of energy efficiency in the Dutch food industry. Energy Policy 34(14), 1720–1735 (2006)

Reich-Weiser, C., Vijayaraghavan, A., Dornfeld, D.A.: Metrics for sustainable manufacturing. Technical report, UC Berkeley: Laboratory for Manufacturing and Sustainability (2008)

Slizyte, A., Bakanauskiene, I.: Designing performance measurement system in organization. Journal of Business Logistic 43, 135–148 (2007)

Sutherland, J.R.: Challenges for the manufacturing enterprise to achieve sustainable development. In: Manufacturing Systems and Technologies for the New Frontier. The 41st CIRP Conference on Manufacturing Systems, pp. 15–18 (2008)

Tanaka, K.: Assessment of energy efficiency performance measures in industry and their application for policy. Energy Policy 36, 2887–2902 (2008)

Tyteca, D.: Business organisational response to environmental challenges: performance measurement and reporting (2002)

Van Gorp, J.C.: Using key performance indicators to manage energy costs. Strategic Planning for Energy and the Environment 25(2), 9–25 (2005)

Veleva, V., Ellenbecker, M.: Indicators of sustainable production: framework and methodology. Journal of Cleaner Production 9, 519–549 (2001)

Worrell, E., Price, L., Martin, N., Farla, J., Schaeffer, R.: Energy intensity in the iron and steel industry: a comparison of phys. and econ. indicators. Energy Policy 25(7-9), 727–744 (1997)

Yildirim, M.B.: Operational methods for minimization of energy consumption of manufacturing equipment. Wichita State University (2007), http://soar.wichita.edu/dspace/handle/10057/3435

Zhou, P., Ang, B.W., Zhou, D.Q.: Measuring economy-wide energy efficiency performance: a parametric frontier approach. Applied Energy 90(1), 196–200 (2012)

A Model Based Continuous Improvement Methodology for Sustainable Manufacturing

Sanjay Jain[1], Gordon Shao[2], Alexander Brodsky[3], and Frank Riddick[2]

[1] George Washington University, Washington, DC, USA
jain@email.gwu.edu
[2] National Institute of Standards and Technology, Gaithersburg, MD, USA
{guodong.shao,frank.riddick}@nist.gov
[3] George Mason University, Fairfax, VA, USA
brodsky@gmu.edu

Abstract. This paper proposes a model based continuous improvement methodology to support efforts to achieve sustainable manufacturing, i.e., to increase efficiency and reduce environmental impact of manufacturing systems. Past efforts have provided guidance at a high level or with a focus on products. This paper focuses on supporting efforts for manufacturing, in particular, at the factory level. A framework is proposed to support the methodology by facilitating application of optimization and simulation models for sustainable manufacturing.

Keywords: Environment, energy, metrics, optimization, simulation, sustainable manufacturing.

1   Introduction

The global competition coupled with difficult world economic situation continues to push manufacturers to improve efficiency. There is also an increasing recognition of the need for sustainable manufacturing. Sustainable manufacturing includes efforts to reduce energy consumed, increase material efficiency (i.e., reduce material used per unit output), reduce water use, and reduce waste and emissions at manufacturing facilities.

Advancements in computing technology over recent years allow employing realistic optimization and simulation models to support manufacturing decision making. Technology for tracking of plant floor activities has further enabled the use of optimization and simulation models.

The confluence of the need for improving efficiency, reducing the use of earth's resources, and rapidly improving technology has motivated the proposal of a model-based continuous improvement methodology and an associated framework for its use. The methodology is of a generic nature similar to the various continuous improvement methodologies including Deming's Plan-Do-Check-Act (PDCA) cycle. A domain specific infrastructure is required to implement the methodology.

Application of modeling and analysis techniques in general requires specialized skills that are usually not available in manufacturing environment. Successful

V. Prabhu, M. Taisch, and D. Kiritsis (Eds.): APMS 2013, Part I, IFIP AICT 414, pp. 268–277, 2013.

implementation of the methodology hence requires an infrastructure that facilitates application of modeling and analysis for strategic and tactical manufacturing decisions. This paper proposes a framework for sustainability modeling and optimization that will provide the integrating infrastructure for developing models to improve the sustainability aspects of a manufacturing facility using the proposed methodology.

The next section reviews related prior efforts. Section 3 presents the methodology, while section 4 presents the proposed framework. The execution of the methodology using the framework is discussed in section 5. Section 6 concludes the paper.

2   Related Efforts

There have been multiple efforts for application of optimization and simulation models to improve sustainable manufacturing. Only a few relevant examples are mentioned here due to paper length constraints. Vergnano et al. (2012) utilized a mixed-integer linear programming model to optimize the schedule for a robotic manufacturing system leading to reduced energy consumption. Bi and Wang (2012) reduced the energy consumption of a selected machine tool through optimization of the process parameters. Taplin et al. (2006) utilized simulation to evaluate different options for improving the sustainability performance of a metal casting company. The sustainability metrics included amount of scrap, dross, and carbon dioxide emissions. Zhou et al (2011) utilized a simulation model together with a response surface methodology to identify the optimal solution with respect to green sustainable development measures including energy/resource conservation and environmental emission/pollution. The reported efforts employ significant expertise for developing and applying optimization and simulation models. There is a need for developing an infrastructure that facilitates such application.

Smith and Ball (2012) point out that most of the recent reported efforts in the area of sustainable manufacturing are at a high level, and thus there is limited guidance for improving sustainability at the factory level. They provide guidelines to analyze material, energy, and waste flows in a factory and use a quantitative spreadsheet model to identify improvements. The provided spreadsheet models facilitate Pareto analysis by assets and by flows to identify key areas for improvement. Improvement opportunities are evaluated using the quantitative and qualitative information gathered. Selected improvements are implemented using standard project management techniques. We are motivated by similar goals and propose a methodology and supporting infrastructure that allows application of advanced optimization and simulation models.

3   Model Based Continuous Improvement Methodology

The methodology is identified as "model based" as the analysis of current operations and improvements makes extensive use of various types of models including optimization and simulation. It is further identified as "continuous improvement" as it uses an iterative procedure employing an increasingly rich set of models to support successive improvements. This allows taking a leap beyond the typical process of ad-hoc models that end up as "shelf-ware" after a study. The proposed methodology can be executed for a manufacturing facility using the following steps as shown in figure 1.

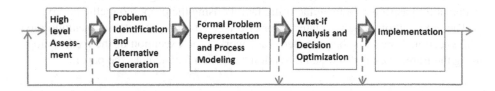

Fig. 1. Model Based Continuous Improvement Methodology

High Level Assessment: This step is aimed at upfront identifying the area where the improved planning effort should be focused on. This step will focus on a high level assessment of the major opportunities for improvements using identified metrics. In manufacturing applications, this step may be referred to as "factory level assessment." For example, based on comparison with other facilities of similar nature, this step may identify that the largest improvement opportunity for improving sustainability of a facility is via reducing its energy consumption. This assumes that the facility has a system in place for collecting a number of different metrics and for comparing them with other facilities.

Problem Identification and Alternative Generation: This step includes the collection of data and analysis for narrowing down the area targeted for improvement effort and development of an improvement plan. The collected data relevant to the narrowed down area will help identify the problem specifically. Alternatives may be generated based on experience and knowledge of the team. The team may suggest policy, procedure, process, and/or equipment modifications to achieve desired improvements. If the factory level assessment identified reducing energy consumption as the primary focus, this step may narrow that down to reducing energy consumption in heating and cooling of the facility based on comparison with other uses of energy and potential reductions. Subsequently alternatives for the purpose may be generated including, adding insulation to the building, adding thermal enclosures around manufacturing equipment that generate large amounts of heat, and improving efficiency of HVAC systems.

Formal Data Representation and Process Modeling: This step involves representation of the manufacturing process and facility data using proposed structures that allow capturing the current state to develop a better understanding of the underlying phenomenon and causal relationships. Once the requisite data is represented using proposed structures, it can be used to generate optimization and/or simulation models of the areas of interest of the manufacturing system. The simulation modeling part of this step can be viewed as equivalent to the "AS-IS" modeling of the process re-engineering efforts. Continuing the energy consumption reduction example, a simulation model of the manufacturing facility with representative product volumes processed through equipment of interest will allow verification of the ranges of amounts of generated heat. The heat generated from manufacturing equipment can then be used in the heat flow calculations to estimate the heating, ventilation and cooling (HVAC) energy demand and compared against recorded values. This ensures that the AS-IS model has captured the relevant major factors and serves to validate the simulation model for the next step. The insights gained at this step may uncover a problem that needs to be addressed first leading to a loop back to problem identification step as shown in figure 1.

What-If Analysis and Decision Optimization: This step will involve development of optimization and simulation models for generation and evaluation of the improvement alternatives respectively. The evaluation will include use of metrics generated by the models and business metrics such as return on investment. Optimization models may be used to develop proposed solutions to achieve the desired goals. Alternatives may also be generated by the decision makers and analysts based on the past experience and the increased understanding and insights gained through the development and use of simulation models of the current processes. For example, optimization may be used to determine the combination of available options that will best achieve the sought for energy reduction. It may identify the proportion of products to be produced using alternative processes such that the generated heat is minimized.

Simulation models can be used to evaluate "what-if" alternatives generated by decision makers and analysts. They can also be used to validate the alternatives generated by the optimization models since more often than not the optimization models cannot take all the realistic factors into account.

The analysis at this step may determine that none of the proposed alternatives provide a desired return and result in a loopback to the problem identification step.

Implementation: This step involves implementing the improvement plan validated via simulation in the previous step. For the discussed example, it may involve changing parameters in the production scheduling system such that desired proportion of products flows through the alternative processes.

The methodology is generic and can be applied to different domains though it has been explained above with respect to the manufacturing environment. Implementation of the methodology is challenging and requires high expertise with large time and effort particularly for the modeling and analysis steps. The challenges can be significantly reduced through the use of an infrastructure that facilitates development of models appropriate to the domain. The framework described in the next section is aimed at providing just such an infrastructure.

4   Framework for Sustainability Modeling and Optimization

The proposed framework for sustainability modeling and optimization (SMO) provides an integrating infrastructure for capabilities needed for development of models of manufacturing that include sustainability aspects. It is comprised of four major components described below. The framework will support a test-bed that will utilize commercial-off-the-shelf (COTS) simulation and optimization tools to support sustainability analysis of factories (see Lee et al., 2013 for the test-bed concept).

4.1   Sustainable Manufacturing Maturity Model (SM3)

The sustainable manufacturing maturity model (SM3) will be used to support the "high level assessment" step of the methodology, i.e., to conduct the factory level assessment to gauge the current sustainability performance possibly against a set of defined levels and determine the improvement opportunities using the next level of maturity as the target. An initial version of the model is show in figure 2. The first and second levels assess the ability of organization to capture standard metrics for energy use, material efficiency, and corporate carbon footprint. Levels III and IV assess and guide the factory's journey to improved sustainability. Clearly, this approach has to address the major challenge of identifying the best in class. Further work is in progress to develop alternate approaches.

Level	Criteria
IV	Metrics among best in class
III	Metrics halfway to the best in class from base values
II	Metrics base values captured using standard methods
I	Environmental Management System implemented & audited
0	Status quo

Fig. 2. An initial version of Sustainability Manufacturing Maturity Model

4.2   Sustainable Process Description Model (SPDM)

A unified sustainable process description model will be developed to support the "Model" step of the methodology, i.e., for creating a formal representation that captures the factory information and sustainability objectives needed to develop models of alternative solutions to the problem (Shao et al., 2012). Figure 3 presents the current concept of the description model.

Initially diverse manufacturing processes and industrial scenarios will be examined to identify most appropriate modeling methods/tools/ languages, and to specify the process representation requirements. A representation will be designed to address the research challenges of (1) providing a generic mechanism to represent the diverse manufacturing scenarios, and (2) supporting taxonomies and metrics for representation of unit manufacturing and assembly processes. Specifically, the process representation will be designed to include process structure and data model to describe input and output resources, sustainability data, and hierarchical composition of processes.

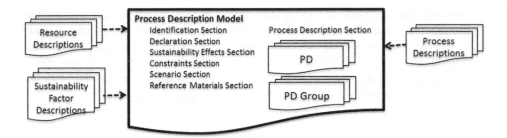

Fig. 3. Concept of Sustainability Process Description Model

4.3   Sustainable Process Analytical Formalism (SPAF)

A process analytics formalism will be used to support the "Check" step of the methodology, i.e., for "what-if" analysis and decision optimization. The formalism and associated procedures will automatically translate the analytical representation into a formal optimization model that can be executed using commercial optimization software. The formalism will be designed to include process analytics model to define control variables, express metrics computation, and define constraints that completely characterize a set of process alternatives. A prototype system for translating the analytical representation to a formal optimization model has been implemented (Shao et al. 2013).

The range of problems faced by industry in improving sustainability will be studied to define model scope and answer questions. The research challenge here is the development of sound and complete methods to automatically transform decision optimization questions posed against the sustainable process analytical representation into formal optimization models. These machine-generated models will then be solved by COTS optimization tools selected for the proposed test-bed.

4.4   Support Tools

Support tools and procedures may be used to facilitate various steps. In particular, they include translators that may be used to generate optimization/simulation models that can be executed using COTS software.

Figure 4 shows the integration of components of framework to facilitate sustainability modeling and optimization by human decision makers and analysts. The maturity model will help identify the improvement opportunities areas that can be delved into to identify specific objectives for an improvement initiative and associated constraints. The understanding of the problem can help develop a conceptual model of the factors involved that in turn guides the data to be collected to further analyze the problem. The conceptual model of the problem may be formally represented using the description model. Support tools may use the description model representation to generate simulation models that can be executed using commercial simulation software. The simulation models can be used to study the problem.

Once the data is represented in the description model, support tools can be used to facilitate representation of optimization problem using the formalism. Again, support tools can be used to execute the optimization using commercial optimization and analysis tools.

The results from the simulation and optimization models can be presented to the human decision makers and analysts to help guide the decision making.

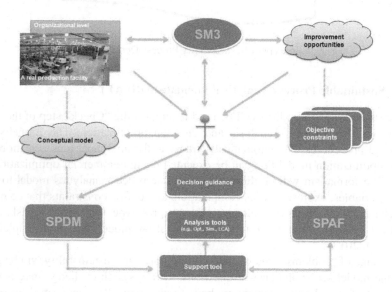

Fig. 4. Framework for Sustainability Modeling and Optimization for Decision Guidance

5   Methodology Execution Using SMO Framework

The execution of the methodology can be facilitated, indeed enabled, through the use of the framework as shown in figure 5. The first step, high level assessment, will be supported by the maturity model component of the framework. The maturity model will help a manufacturing facility identify the metric that offers the opportunity for most improvement. The metrics may include energy use, material efficiency, and carbon footprint. The next step of problem identification and alternative generation will then focus on the metrics identified via the high level assessment. This step will require collection of data to identify the relevant operations within the factory that have a large impact on the selected metric.

To prepare for formal analysis and optimization modeling, defined case scenarios need to be formally described, and data collected for the defined case scenarios need to be formally represented. Further, decision variables need to be modeled in a way so that their values can be automatically instantiated, i.e., assigned using the appropriate data items. The formal representation and process modeling step will be supported by the description model and the formalism components of the framework. The collected data is represented using the description model. The structures in the description model may identify other relevant data needed for process modeling and thus prompt correct and complete data collection. The formalism supports these by representing process analytics expression such as mathematical specification for metrics, constraints, and objectives; and enabling the formulation of what-if analysis and decision optimization queries.

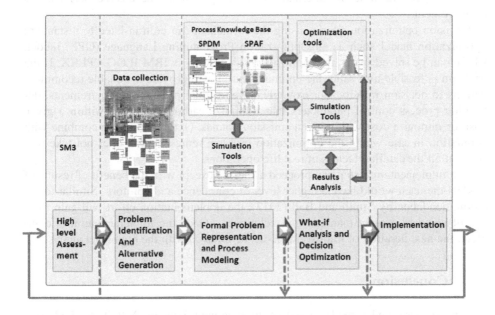

Fig. 5. Methodology execution using SMO framework

The description model representation also provides sustainability indicators and metrics for the formalism representation of the problem through the framework support tools. The support tools in the framework are then used to generate simulation models of the current state of the factory in COTS simulation software. The simulation models are used to develop further understanding of issues surrounding the problem. In some cases sufficient understanding may exist to move to the next step quickly while in others a number of simulation runs may be executed to understand the key factors that impact the metrics of interest. Queries using the formalism also facilitate the understanding of the problem at this stage. Users may query the system for questions ranging from simple ones such as the process for a particular product to more complex ones such as the percentage contribution to energy use by a particular product flow at particular equipment.

The what-if analysis and decision optimization step of the methodology is supported by the framework using the description model and the formalism representations, support tools, and COTS simulation and optimization tools. Two kinds of queries using the formalism are used at this step: what-if analysis queries and decision optimization queries. Different answers to what-if analysis allow decision makers to compare and assess changes before they happen; users can see how different changes would affect various aspects of the outcome. For example, given certain settings of a process' controls and input, total carbon emission and costs can be estimated before investing in a new machine tool. If all variables in the expressions can be instantiated through computation using the data given, What-if analysis queries using the formalism allow computation and simulation representing different alternatives and analysis of outputs to determine the alternatives that help achieve the desired performance improvement.

Decision optimization queries using the formalism can be translated to a standard optimization model such as an Optimization Programming Language (OPL) model, which can be solved using an optimization solver such as IBM ILOG CPLEX. If the problem is feasible and valid, the optimal solution will provide actionable recommendations to decision makers. For example, given certain production requirements, determine process control parameters that minimize carbon emissions within a given cost, or minimize cost within given emission bounds. Optimization can combine with simulation in case where the optimization problem representation does not take into account all the detailed factors of real life operations.

The implementation step can proceed as before except with the benefit of results of models the team would have a higher level of confidence and comfort. Similar to the recommendation by Smith and Ball (2012), the implementation effort will gain from use of standard project management techniques. Once the implementation is complete, the next iteration of improvement can be initiated with the high level analysis.

6   Conclusion

This paper described a model based continuous improvement (MBCI) methodology that can be utilized by manufacturers for supporting their movement towards improved sustainability. The model based nature of the methodology allows manufacturers to evaluate alternative approaches in virtual mode, i.e., using computer models, and this provides a more efficient approach than the traditional plan-do-check-act improvement cycle. The efficiency comes from avoiding the time and expense of a real life pilot of a selected alternative for its evaluation and instead allowing evaluation of multiple alternatives via rapid modeling. The paper also proposed a framework for Sustainability Modeling and Optimization to provide an integrated set of capabilities for modeling and optimization of manufacturing systems. The paper further discussed how the implementation of the MBCI methodology can be enabled by the framework.

7   Disclaimer

A number of software products are identified in context in this paper. This does not imply a recommendation or endorsement of the software products by the authors or NIST, nor does it imply that such software products are necessarily the best available for the purpose.

References

1. Bi, Z.M., Wang, L.: Energy Modeling of Machine Tools for Optimization of Machine Se-tups. IEEE Transactions on Automation Science and Engineering 9(3), 607–613 (2012)
2. Lee, Y.-T.T., Lee, J.Y., Riddick, F., Libes, D., Kibira, D.: Interoperability for Virtual Manu-facturing Systems. International Journal of Internet Manufacturing and Services (forthcom-ing, 2013)
3. Shao, G., Riddick, F., Lee, J.Y., Campanelli, M., Kim, D.B., Lee, Y.T.: A Framework for the Interoperability of Sustainable Manufacturing Process Analysis Applications. In: 2012 Winter Simulation Conference. IEEE, Piscataway,
   http://informs-sim.org/wsc12papers/includes/files/con334.pdf
4. Shao, G., Westbrook, D., Brodsky, A.: A Prototype Web-Based User Interface for Sustaina-bility Modeling and Optimization. NIST Interagency/Internal Report (NISTIR) – 7850 (2013), http://www.nist.gov/customcf/get_pdf.cfm?pub_id=909618
5. Smith, L., Ball, P.: Steps towards sustainable manufacturing through modelling material, energy and waste flows. Intl. Journal of Production Economics 140(1), 227–238 (2012)
6. Taplin, D.M.R., Spedding, T.A., Khoo, H.H.: Use of simulation and modelling to develop a sustainable production system. Sustainable Development 14(3), 149–161 (2006)
7. Vergnano, A., Thorstensson, C., Lennartson, B., Falkman, P., Pellicciari, M., Leali, F., Bill-er, S.R.: Modeling and Optimization of Energy Consumption in Cooperative Multi-Robot Systems. IEEE Trans. on Automation Science and Engg. 9(2), 423–428 (2012)
8. Zhou, M., Pan, Y., Chen, Z., Yang, W., Li, B.: Simulation based analysis for selection and evaluation of green manufacturing strategies. In: 8th International Conference on Service Systems and Service Management (ICSSSM 2011), pp. 1–6 (2011)

Part II
Sustainable Supply Chains

An Information Reporting Web Service Framework for Integration of Gate-to-Gate Process-to-Energy Metrics

Lewis John McGibbney[*], Mark Peng, and Kincho Law

Civil and Environmental Engineering, Stanford University, Stanford, CA, USA
{lewis2,mvpeng,law}@stanford.edu

Abstract. Modern day manufacturing is required to respond to many facets of dynamic change including consumer and technological trending, increasing levels of legislation, fluctuation of competitor market strategy and total available market based on domestic and international trading conditions amongst others. High up on the supply chain agenda and a topic of continually increasing importance is energy efficiency. This paper presents an information reporting service framework for gate-to-gate[1] (G2G) process-to-energy[2] (P2E) metrics. Our use case focuses on obtaining energy performance information associated with welding robots used in assembly process.

Keywords: sustainable manufacturing, automotive, assembly, energy, metrics, reporting.

1 Introduction

This paper builds upon advances in research within resource efficiency assessments and energy metrics for product assembly process and equipment. We introduce an information service framework focused on enabling fine grained reporting of energy efficiency from G2G processes within a product assembly plant. The novel aspects of our approach lie in facilitation of ontology development for the manufacturing domain and integration of information between processes and components, enabling capturing of energy metrics. In this paper, we use welding robots as a demonstrative example to illustrate the information service framework. Welding is a process which is energy intensive involving melting joining metals. Manufacturing processes typically involve many robots and they can be used for multiple welding or other assembly activities, each of which would require varying degrees of energy usage. We highlight the Hybrid Laser GMAW (Gas Metal Arc Welding) activity as one involving a considerable amount of energy usage and therefore well suited for P2E analysis and reporting of energy metrics. This application scenario is both difficult to monitor

---

[*] Corresponding author.

[1] G2G is defined as one particular variant within manufacturing life-cycle assessment, looking at only the factory level processes in the production chain [6].

[2] P2E metrics refer to energy properties and values associated with the physical G2G processes.

V. Prabhu, M. Taisch, and D. Kiritsis (Eds.): APMS 2013, Part I, IFIP AICT 414, pp. 281–288, 2013.
© IFIP International Federation for Information Processing 2013

and challenging to infer energy efficiency from, and thus presents an excellent area to study in an attempt to drive information integration within a product assembly plant.

2   Utilizing Integration of Process Information as an Energy Efficiency Improvement Mechanism

Fundamentally, sustainable manufacturing promotes the use of value-added processes and integration of design and process controls into intelligent manufacturing operations. In this context, integration of process information across the supply chain is a key factor in improving manufacturing energy metrics.

A growing amount of comprehensive product assembly literature acts as a direct knowledge base for us to utilize in an attempt to assimilate G2G energy consumption to output data which can be used within energy efficiency improvement.

2.1   Formal Representation of Gate-to-Gate Manufacturing and Assembly Knowledge Sources

The core focus of addressing energy efficiency has now shifted to industry driven reporting models involving the computation of G2G energy efficiency at various levels of the product assembly processes. By addressing energy consumption at G2G processes we can "…measure, monitor, and improve energy and material efficiency across …production networks [6]." One of the key tasks is to integrate information from separate physical entities within the product assembly process. The basic issue is to find common characteristics among the processes as complex queries cannot be answered by any single data source alone. Table 1 enlists examples of equipment(s) and/or process(es) (with physical entities relating to welding shown in bold.) with the intention of building relationships between equipment and/or components.

Table 1. Common characteristics between assembly process data sources

Equipment/Process Name	Equipment/Process Characteristics
Product Assembly Process	Assembly of components: Tasks involve parts fitting, **joining**, etc. and related sub processes
Joining Process	An aspect of the product assembly process for joining-specific parts: Tasks involve adhesives bonding, **welding**, mechanical fastening, etc.
Material Handling Equipment	Moving materials and components within a plant: Equipment includes materials handling and other **robots**, belt/roller conveyors, chutes, etc.
Automobile Manufacturing Process	Vehicle Body Production: Tasks include painting, fitting and trimming, **door assembly**, etc. Chassis Production: Tasks include under carriage assembly, **frame assembly**, etc.

We adopt a formal methodology for developing a (machine processable) representation of the above equipment/process domains with the purpose of enabling inference. In this study, individual ontology is constructed based on observation of an
automotive assembly plant and from relevant literature sources [1-6]. We use Protégé[3]
to develop ontological representations of the knowledge sources (from Table 1),
building a graph structure which links resources to properties. As an example, Figure
1 shows the class associations for the automobile assembly ontology for representing
the automobile manufacturing process as described in Table 1.

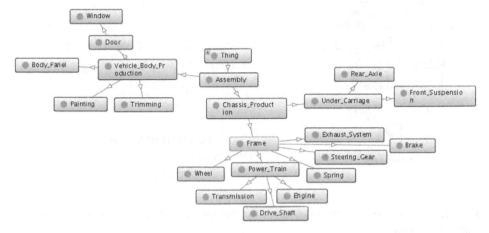

Fig. 1. Automobile Assembly Ontology Class and Properties

The ontology development process involves identifying the natural hierarchical
structure found within (e.g. automobile) production line assembly. Figure 1 represents
one of many domain ontologies developed where individual elements at each level
represent physical 'things'. Predicate relationships (linkages) are introduced to make
physical connections between elements hence exposing relationships between manufacturing components. Figure 2 depicts an ontology development process which semi-
automates partial aggregation and persistence of the target knowledge sources as
ontology graphs. Existing knowledge sources, such as the equipment and processes
identified in Table 1, are first run through a content transformation process implemented using Apache Any23[4]. As existing process and equipment domain information is heterogeneous in nature, it is essential to first identify the content MIMEType[5].
The information is then validated and useful content (such as specific names, types of
equipment and processes) extracted. It is then further filtered to remove discrepancies
and unwanted relationships. Finally, the RDF/XML data are serialized in triples format for persistent storage in Fuseki[6] and for queries using SPARQL[7]. It should be

---

[3] http://protege.stanford.edu
[4] http://any23.apache.org
[5] http://www.iana.org/assignments/media-types
[6] http://jena.apache.org
[7] http://www.w3.org/TR/rdf-sparql-query/

noted that we transform knowledge sources to the RDF/XML format not because it is the only solution, but because it gives structure to both the representation, and retrieval of information within the target domain. It should further be noted that the generated RDF/XML[8] streams still require some degree of human quality assessment and control such as checking for missing, incorrect and/or inconsistent relationships. Triples relations (as illustrated in the description of Figure 4 as the result of the query in Figure 3) can be produced using the development process in Figure 2.

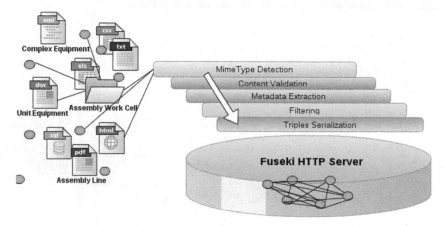

Fig. 2. Aggregation and Representation of Product Assembly Equipment and Process Knowledge Sources

2.2 Linking Product Assembly Processes and Equipment with Energy Consumption Metrics

As well as making clear internal associative relationships between elements from within a single knowledge domain, we also leverage the ability to associate elements between domains. For example if we consider that welding (as a parent process including many sub processes) is most commonly associated with the assembly process domain, we can associate welding with elements within the joining process domain such as specific welding techniques (Hybrid Laser GMAW), or particular manufacturing processes such as body panel or chassis under carriage assembly from within the automobile manufacturing domain. We adopt a methodology, referred to as the open world assumption[9] (where everything relates to everything else unless explicitly stated not to). This greatly enhances the possible integration, sharing and integration of knowledge within G2G activities.

We use energy efficiency calculation methods and deploy them as services which can be instantiated depending directly upon the output of queries we can now execute over the underlying data within Fuseki. The next section explores example structured queries which can be executed over the RDF/XML data providing detail on the

---

[8] http://www.w3.org/TR/rdf-syntax-grammar/
[9] http://bit.ly/134dYCj

powerful and verbose granularity relating to G2G process energy metrics which can be obtained by carefully crafted queries.

2.3   Querying Assembly Process Ontology/Information Resources

It is logical to assume that the calculation relating to energy metrics will also change based on user requirements, consequently affecting varying process artifacts and manufacturing equipment. Subsequently it becomes extremely important that the underlying ontologies persisted within Fuseki are rich in both property associations and data type values which can in turn be used as input for the calculations. Additional examples of data associated with equipment may include "U – *The Voltage of welding power source (Volts)*", "I – *Peak current in welding power source (Amps)*", "$\mathit{\Delta t_a}$ - *arc time (sec)*", etc. SPARQL 1.1 Query Language provides many useful mechanisms for executing queries to obtain results that are expressive and sufficient to be used as input parameters for the energy calculators.

The DESCRIBE query is an informative query mechanism which returns a single result RDF graph containing RDF data about resources. This suits many requirements within our example application as extremely verbose results can be obtained enabling us to manipulate and structure them as input for the calculators. The following example shown in Figure 3 asks the query service to describe any instance of a single *MaterialsHandlingEquipment* variable, which matches the following criteria:

- it is a subclass of a welding robot equipment, and
- executes welding as a process, and
- executes Hybrid Laser GMAW as a specific joining process, and
- is involved in the body panel manufacturing process.

```
DESCRIBE ?MaterialsHandlingEquipment
WHERE {
  ?MaterialsHandlingEquipment
     rdfs:subClassOf    MaterialHandlingEquipment:Welding_Robot.
  ?MaterialsHandlingEquipment
     MaterialHandlingEquipment:executesAssemblyProcess AssemblyProcess:Weld.
  ?MaterialsHandlingEquipment
     MaterialHandlingEquipment:executesJoiningProcess JoiningProcess: Hybrid_Lazer_Gas_Metal_Arc_Weld.
  ?MaterialsHandlingEquipment
     MaterialHandlingEquipment:involvedInManufactureOf AutomobileManufacturing:Body_Panel.
}
```

Fig. 3. A SPARQL query describing the Hybrid Laser GMAW process

Dependent upon how comprehensively annotated the underlying ontology graph is, we receive varying resource description results (which in this case) relate to a Hybrid Laser GMAW robot including a long list of accompanying sub components, their data properties and relations. Figure 4 shows a snippet of the results for the query presented in Figure 3. (Note that the results have been summarized. Typically result streams contain many resources.)

```
"http://eil.stanford.edu:443/svn/eil-repo/Users/Lewis/ontology/MaterialHandlingEquipment.owl
   #Hybrid_Lazer_Gas_Metal_Arc_Welding_Robot" : {
 "http://www.w3.org/2000/01/rdf-schema#subClassOf" : [ {
  "type" : "uri" ,
  "value" : "http://eil.stanford.edu:443/svn/eil-repo/Users/Lewis/ontology/
   MaterialHandlingEquipment.owl#Welding_Robot"
 }
 ] ,
 "http://www.w3.org/2000/01/rdf-schema#comment" : [ {
  "type" : "literal" ,
  "value" : "A robotic laser welding system consists of a servo-controlled, multi-axis mechanical arm,...
  "datatype" : "http://www.w3.org/2001/XMLSchema#string"
 }
 ] ,
 "http://www.w3.org/1999/02/22-rdf-syntax-ns#type" : [ {
  "type" : "uri" ,
  "value" : "http://www.w3.org/2002/07/owl#Class"
 }
 ] ,
 ...
}
```

Fig. 4. A snippet taken from extensive output from a DESCRIBE SPARQL query

An example of triples semantics from the query result can be seen in Figure 4. The result snippet in Figure 4 explains that the single *MaterialsHandlingEquipment* variable requested within the query is a Hybrid Laser GMAW Robot, whose parent is Welding Robot, and has a comment "A robot laser welding system consists of a servo...", and within the RDF/XML ontology it was obtained from "is of" type Class.

3 Information Service Framework for Gate-to-Gate Process-to-Energy Reporting

This section details the information service framework, consolidating the ontology, knowledge and resources (such as calculation methods) into a comprehensive user-oriented workflow. On the left of Figure 5 (in the blue area), Users are presented with a query form where they are required to submit stored structured SPARQL queries to initialize the reporting framework. In addition to browser oriented interaction, the framework also supports SRARQL Over HTTP (SOH), a server independent, SPARQL 1.1 compliant protocol offered to systems (such as Fuseki) with HTTP access. Finally, we provide a SPARQL endpoint which can be consumed by other HTTP clients. Moving clockwise, requests are sent to an HTTP servlet contained within a communication layer, which coordinates Fuseki queries and responses. Upon processing the query, Fuseki sends a result stream back to the HTTP servlet as an object containing n fields directly dependent upon the result of the DESCRIBE query (e.g. Figures 3 and 4). Again moving clockwise, the result stream is then read into another servlet which, based upon the particular input parameters, coordinates the appropriate communication to the energy calculators which take the form of (web) services (shown in powder blue). Services are executed on the basis of parameters being present in the results stream, with the returned data (post calculation) being numeric in nature and representing various energy efficiency criteria. Figure 5 shows both an overview of the framework as well as examples of the consumable services made available through the calculations such as required energy, processing energy lost, unit equipment energy efficiency, theoretically required energy, amongst others.

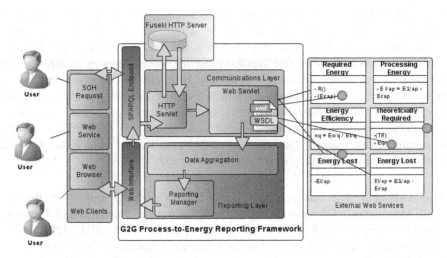

Fig. 5. An Information Reporting Web Service Framework for Integration of G2G P2E Data

The numeric output is communicated back to the web servlet before being sent to the reporting layer (red) where aggregation, sorting and processing occurs. Finally a reporting manager formats and presents reports as consumable PDF's using the popular Apache PDFBox[10].

4   Summary and Discussion

In this paper we present an information service framework for G2G P2E reporting, with illustrative examples for automobile assembly processes. The work builds upon extensive prior research from within the field [1-6] to establish resource efficiency assessments and energy metrics for product assembly processes and equipment. In essence, the novelty of energy metrics reporting in this manner is facilitated by an ontology development methodology based on integration of heterogeneous information. Building on our representation methodology, we present an example of the framework execution relating specifically to energy reporting for the Hybrid Laser GMAW process. This example exposes an architectural overview of our framework as well as a simple functional implementation. We indicate how in the future our framework can be adapted to advance the inference of equipment and process energy efficiency based on improved reporting of energy metrics.

P2E reporting is a concept which has seen a lot of interest as we strive to infer more from energy metrics relating to G2G product manufacturing equipment and assembly processes. It is widely recognized that plethora of data relating to many domains is both widely available and that it can and should be used to drive energy efficiency across such domains. Structuring of manufacturing data and inter-domain information integration not only offers the ability to execute federated queries relating to process

---

[10] http://pdfbox.apache.org

and equipment knowledge from heterogeneous sources, but also provides enhanced opportunity to drive information integration within the manufacturing assembly processes and supply chain. It is important for sustainable manufacturing to move towards making better use of fine grained reporting mechanisms in an effort to improve process and equipment energy efficiency. It should also be noted that there is significant benefit to receive direction from the industry on better reporting tools such as energy calculators, performance metrics and benchmarking statistics, etc. for assessing performance within supply chain and manufacturing as a whole. The automobile manufacturing industry has seen promising progress in these areas, however transparent reporting technologies should be further embraced.

Acknowledgment. The authors would like to acknowledge the supports by the Sustainable Manufacturing Program at the National Institute of Standards and Technology (NIST), Cooperative Research Agreement Number #70NANB12H273. Mark Peng is partially supported by an National Science Foundation (NSF) REU Grant #IIS-0811460. Certain commercial products may have been identified in this paper. These products were used only for demonstration purposes. This use does not imply approval or endorsement by NIST, NSF or Stanford University, nor does it imply that these products are necessarily the best for the purpose. Any opinions, findings, and conclusions or recommendations expressed in this paper are those of the authors and do not necessarily reflect the views NIST or NSF.

References

1. Boyd, G.A.: Development of a Performance-based Industrial Energy Efficiency Indicator for Automobile Assembly Plants. Decision and Information Sciences Division, Argonne National Laboratory (2005)
2. Boyd, G.A.: Estimating Plat Level Manufacturing Energy Efficiency with Stochastic Frontier regression. The Energy Journal 29(2), 23–44 (2008)
3. Boyd, G.A.: Assessing Improvement in the Energy Efficiency of U.S. Auto Assembly Plants. Working Paper EE 10-01 (2010)
4. Gatlitsky, C., Worrell, E.: Energy Efficiency Improvement and Cost Saving Opportunities for the Vehicle Assembly Industry, An ENERGY STAR®Guide for Energy. Environmental Energy Technologies Division, Ernest Orlando Lawrence Berkley National Laboratory (2008)
5. Greene, W.H.: The Econometric Approach to Efficiency Analysis. In: The Measurement of Productive Efficiency: Techniques and Applications, pp. 68–119. Oxford University Press, N.Y. (1993)
6. Rachuri, S.: 2013 El Program: Sustainable Manufacturing. Lifecycle Engineering Group, Systems Integration Division, National Institute for Standards and Technology (2013), http://www.nist.gov/el/msid/lifecycle/upload/sustainmanufacturing.pdf

The Reverse Logistics Technology and Development Trend of Retired Home Appliances

Xin Zhao[*], Yonggao Fu, Jiaqi Hu, Ling Wang, and Meiling Deng

China National Electric Apparatus Research Institute Co., Ltd.,
Guangzhou, China
{zhaox,fuyg,wangl}@cei1958.com,
zhx075@126.com

Abstract. This paper has introduced the status of retired home appliances reverse logistics industry in China , elaborated the key technologies which need to be focused on to enhance the development level of reverse logistics industry, including product   life cycle information tracing technology , retired product quality detection technology , inventory optimization control technology, to build efficient reverse logistics information system and lead the industry to develop in the direction of informationization and standardization.

Keywords: retired appliance, reverse logistics, development trends.

1   Introduction

China is the world's biggest home appliance manufacturing country, has a huge number of home appliances ownership. According to data from the National Bureau of Statistics, our country's social ownership of TV sets, refrigerators, air conditioners, washing machines, computers reached 1.5 billion units in 2011. Faster product replacement product life cycle has been reduced each year due to end-of-life , out of substandard products returned loss is growing at a phenomenal rate. Because of the faster product update speed, shorter product life cycle, the loss caused by discarded, obsolete, unqualified products return is growing at an alarming rate each year.On the other hand, as people's environmental awareness is growing, the government   began to require manufacturers to be responsible for the whole process of the product life cycle with legislation, especially in the recycling of waste product."Waste electrical and electronic product recycling management regulation " has formally implemented from the year of 2011, this regulation improves the threshold of waste electrical and electronic products industry, makes the responsibilities of production enterprise , sales enterprise , recycling enterprise, handling enterprise clear. The implementation of this regulation has the significance of the milestone type on the development of the recycling of waste electrical and electronic products industry. Reverse logistics

---

[*] Corresponding author.

V. Prabhu, M. Taisch, and D. Kiritsis (Eds.): APMS 2013, Part I, IFIP AICT 414, pp. 289–293, 2013.
© IFIP International Federation for Information Processing 2013

is still a new industry in China, but it can reduce costs, improve the economic efficiency of enterprises, enhance their competitive advantage, improve the living environment of mankind, promote sustainable development, these advantages has attracted the attention of enterprises , so the retired home appliances reverse logistics industry has developed rapidly [1] .

2   The Development Status of Reverse Logistics Technology

The research for retired home appliances reverse logistics in china focuses on the following aspects: [2] (1)reverse logistics network design research, which mainly studies network structure characteristics and the construction of model of reverse logistics ; (2)inventory control and management research, which discusses how to the process inventory management of recycled products efficiently and economically ; (3) the effective application of forecasting and decision technology in reverse logistics research ,which discusses effective treatment of forecasting and decision technology on uncertainty ,complexity and other factors which exist in the reverse logistics; (4) reverse Logistics Information System research , which analyses the structural characteristics of the reverse logistics system, studies the building of reverse logistics information system.

Above research is basically limited to the theoretical level of mathematical modeling. As for how discarded home appliances characterize, identify and trace the full life cycle information, and how to realize the quality inspection and judgment of retired appliances quickly, to supervise the recycling process effectively, to build reverse logistics management information system are still a lack of systematic research.

2.1   The Classification and Labeling of Product

Due to the models, specifications of home appliance products circulating on the market are different at present, if just only trace the information of retired home appliances, it is more cumbersome, so the relevant government departments should study and define the encoding rules in the design, using and maintenance and other stages of the life cycle of home appliances, establish a special classification and coding system.

2.2   Recovery and Inventory

At present, the waste home appliances recycling channels are still not perfect, which can be divided into three categories: First, the individual small traders purchase from door to door or at street, which is the most common way to recovery; Second, the home appliances flea market or sales, recycling enterprises purchase and recover, including the successful home appliances enterprise's recovery; Third, organs and institutions trade unified, but this is a very small proportion. It should be based on the existing home appliances products (refrigerators, air conditioners, televisions, computers, washing machines) sales logistics platform and multidimensional recycling (contains a variety of recycled sources, such as scrap, return, fund management, etc.) network system to analyze the characteristics of reverse logistics in different ways, to determine the basic operation mode and technical requirements of reverse logistics.

Due to the connection and operation of reverse logistics is uncertain, it should build reverse logistics inventory control model which is suitable for home appliance recycling enterprise. First, considering the time and space factors impact on the overall cost of recycling , the analysis of the quantity drive and time drive mechanism in the recycling enterprise inventory management under the environment of uncertainty sources of quantity and quality . Second , as the demand of home appliance is fuzzy in the reverse logistics , it should through the analysis of the distribution processes of key materials, establishing fuzzy environment multicycle inventory control model , proposing inventory control strategy of the manufacturing enterprises under different conditions , to achieve effective coordination of inventory materials in reverse logistics system between the main enterprise. [3]

2.3   Dismantling

To improve the enterprises' efficiency of dismantling, it should accord to the national retirement products, key product disassembly information label specification, to develop the monitoring and control system of information collection system and dismantling process, to realize the identification,   collection and data analysis of the EX-warehouse and warehouse information of outbound products and inventory products, real-time tracking of enterprise internal operation, to provide technical means for government regulation.

Combining with the status , and under scientific planning, to promote the area construction of facilities for central treatment of waste electric and electronic products, improve the standardization processing capacity, site selection should be coordinated the planning of urban development, environmental protection, land and so on, should straighten out the dismantling households, sorting and dismantling field and other non-standard processing units, enter the centralized treatment plant which is planed and built by government within a definite time, implement unified management. [4]

2.4   Remanufacturing

China is home appliance consumption and production power country, electric and electronic products resources consumption of which is larger. Remanufacturing is refers to through the necessary disassembly, such as repair and replacement of parts, to recover the waste products such as the new process, which can effectively realize the recycling of resources, reduce unnecessary waste. Faced with limited resources and waste disposal capacity, remanufacturing as a senior form of product recycling, can effectively achieve the comprehensive target of optimization utilization of resources, environmental protection and economic sustainable development, has attached great importance to by the government and enterprises, become one of the most effective way to realize sustainable development.[5]

3   Policy and Measure

China has carried out the law of "Cleaner Production Promotion Law of the People's Republic of China", according to the Decree 551 of the State Council of the People's Republic of China, since January 1, 2011, "The Management Regulations of recycling of waste electrical and electronic products", has also went into effect.

Guangdong Province for example, by the end of 2015, we forecast that the institutional mechanisms of recycling of waste electrical and electronic products in Guangdong Province are basically perfect, the construction of enterprises with centralized treatment of the four areas, such as the Pearl River Delta, Eastern Guangdong, Western Guangdong, Northern Guangdong, etc. The recycling network and unified norms regulatory system which covers urban and rural are basically established. [6]

Guangdong Province has carried out some specific measures as follows:

1. Focus on strengthening the layout guide, and to build a large-scale centralized processing system, and to promote the cleaner production.

Implement national policies related to subsidies, improve the subsidy audit procedures, and transfer on time the subsidy funds, to speed up dismantling company capital return. Implement the preferential policies of corporate income tax of the comprehensive utilization of resources; provide the processing enterprises tax incentives of the operating income in accordance with the regulations.

Promote the use of recycling technology recommended by "China Resources Comprehensive Utilization Technology Policy", encourage the waste electrical and electronic products processing enterprises to adopt advanced technology and equipment, and conduct the upgrading of technological improvements and dismantling production line. Pursue the cleaner production audits; increase the resource recycling efficiency and the level of environmental pollution prevention and treatment, to build a cleaner production and park. Construct the renewable resources comprehensive utilization information Center, Technology Center, and Key Laboratory in each province, actively organize the development and application of the dismantling of waste electrical and electronic products and the new processes, new technology, new equipment of Pollution prevention.

2. Depending on the construction of network, to build industrialized recycling system and to encourage resource utilization.

Establish a network which covers the communication and exchange of province-wide waste electrical and electronic product recycling information, for the convenience of strengthening the exchange and feedback of information between enterprises. Authorities, organizations and enterprises should inform specific recycling enterprises of fixed asset retirement details, ensuring that electrical and electronic products can be delivered uniformly to qualified enterprises for its recycling and dismantling.

Support Waste electric and electronic products processing enterprises to establish cooperation with manufacturing enterprises, importers, distributors and recycling enterprises, in an endeavor to jointly build a recycling industry chain between the upstream and downstream industries on the manufacturing, recycling , processing, and utilization of electrical and electronic products. Through the ordered links of the industry chain and the construction of renewable resources utilization system, improve the rate and levels of resource recovery.

3. By means of strengthening the supervision and management, improve and standardize the unified regulatory system, to ensure the harmlessness.

Strengthen and standardize the management of channels of recycling and circulation of waste electrical and electronic products, and gradually establish a unified and standardized, fair and orderly recycling and circulation order, with clear division. Establish the system of evidence record, filing, registration and management for the waste electrical and electronic product recycling, in order to regulate the auditing of amount of recycling and processing and the fund subsidy program.

Strictly supervise the recycling, transportation ,storage and dismantling processes of waste electrical and electronic products, standardize the environmental behavior of dismantling and recycling process of waste electrical and electronic products. Crushing and sorting components, parts with toxic and hazardous substances should be conducted in the closed facilities. Waste gas, dust and other pollutants should be collected and purified , to ensure that it reaches the discharge standards.

4   Summary

The benign development of reverse logistics of waste electrical and electronic product has caused great attention of the national, so individuals, enterprises , and government need to cooperate . Recycling and re-manufacturing not only reduces the cost of home appliances, but also solves the environmental problems caused by the accumulation of dangerous dismantling .It has an extremely important significance for the sustainable development of the economy. [7] In the technical method of reverse logistics applications, RFID and smart inventory have broad prospects, so the environmental and economic value can be increased by enhancing the efforts of application.

References

1. Gan, W.-H.: Reverse logistics. Peking University Press (2012)
2. Huang, Z.-Q.: The reverse Logistics Management. Zhejiang University Press (2010)
3. Dai, Y., Ma, Z.-J.: The recycling system and management mechanism of waste home appliances (2010)
4. Yam, J.: The research of reverse logistics network site optimization strategy. China Social and Sciences Press (2011)
5. Yu, O.-D.: The production logistics simulation of the home appliances remanufacturing. Logistics Technology (2009)
6. Environmental protection bureau of Guangdong Province compiled. Audit manual of waste electrical and electronic products dismantling situation (2013)
7. The national development and reform commission resource conservation and environmental protection department compiled. Research and Practice on Waste Electrical and Electronic Product Recovery Processing (2012)

Warehousing Sustainability Standards Development

Richard Bank[1] and Richard Murphy[2]

[1] Sustainable Supply Chain Foundation (SSCF), Washington DC, USA
rbank@sustainable-scf.org
[2] IWLA and Murphy Warehouse Company, Minneapolis, MN
RMurphy@MurphyWarehouse.com

Abstract. Warehousing, traditionally, is concerned only with the storage and distribution of products or work-in-process (WIP). However, the role of warehouses has evolved to also provide manufacturing, assembly, and other value-added services. In that sense, warehouses and their operations play an important role in sustainable supply chain. However, sustainability improvement in warehousing has not been receiving much attention. This paper describes the motivations to develop sustainability standards for warehousing and introduces an effort recently started by industry to develop these standards. The paper is a starting point to define uniform sustainability metrics, measurements, and guidelines for the warehouse industry. It discusses future development directions and existing works that can form the basis for expanding the warehousing sustainability standards. Although there are no specific metrics and guidelines for warehousing operations in the existing works, we discuss they may be the basis for further development of such warehousing sustainability standards.

Keywords: Supply Chain, Sustainability, Warehousing, Logistics.

1   Motivation

Sustainability improvement in warehousing has not been receiving much attention in spite of significant interests to increase efficiencies and sustainability of supply chain logistics[1]. However, there are reasons to pay more attention to this area of industrial activity. This section describes the reasons from the economic, operational, and sustainability perspectives.

1.1   Economic Perspective

Warehousing plays an important role in supply chain from the economic perspective. According to [1], supply chain logistics, which comprise inbound and outbound

---

[1] Supply chain logistics is a subfield of the supply chain management and refers to supply chain operations that deal with the storage, distribution, and transportation of product and work-in-process. Warehousing in turn is commonly known among supply chain practitioners as a kind of operations dealing primarily with storage and distribution; however, warehousing has evolved to also provide manufacturing, assembly, and other value-added services.

V. Prabhu, M. Taisch, and D. Kiritsis (Eds.): APMS 2013, Part I, IFIP AICT 414, pp. 294–301, 2013.
© IFIP International Federation for Information Processing 2013

warehousing and transportation, account for more than $1.28 trillion or 8.5% of the 2011 US GDP. In addition, [13-14] indicate that warehousing business alone was worth $120 billion in 2011 (roughly 10% of the total supply chain logistics). It is also the fastest growing segment of supply chain logistics industry. Since 1996, the compound annual growth rate of the segment is at 10.3% while in 2011 it grew three times the US GDP growth [14].

Qualitatively, warehousing, as part of the supply chain, plays an important role as suggested by the survey of more than 700 CEOs conducted by Accenture and United Nation Global Compact in 2010. The survey data reported: "96% of the CEOs indicated that sustainability should be integrated into all aspects of strategy and operations while 88% of them singled out the supply chain as an area of specific importance" [6].

Studies have also suggested that supply chain sustainability performance improvements positively impact other business operations. These types of business operation improvements have been described in the supply chain management study entitled "Why a Sustainable Supply Chain is Good Business" published by Accenture [6]. A joint study by five industry organizations also points out other promising aspects associated with sustainable supply chain management [7-8]. The study indicates that supply chain is a place where return-on-investment (ROI) on sustainability can be expected. The study also shows that organizations that engaged in sustainability with supply chain members saw a 21% increase in sustainable supply chain effectiveness.

1.2   Operational Perspective

Warehousing plays an important role in manufacturing from the operational perspective. This is evident from the fact that manufacturers, distributors, and retailers have shifted more activities to the warehouse [2]. According to [16], automotive, grocery, and high tech/computers industry have been using third-party warehousing service providers (or contract warehousing service providers) extensively. In addition, the Reinventing American Manufacturing report [27] identified the increase in distribution efficiency as one of the five key technology advances to transform US manufacturing.

Traditionally, warehouses provide flexibility and agility in the supply chain by providing flexible spaces (pay-per-use) to store large buffers of inventory (with low turnover rate). In fact, warehouses play an even larger role in maintaining the flexibility and agility, as manufacturing cycle time reduces, product life cycle shortens, and product mix and customization increase. This is commonly known as logistics postponement strategy [28]. According to studies in [2, 12], warehouses provide several value-added services including packaging, labeling, marking, testing, assembly, manufacturing, maintenance, and recycling to name a few, in addition to simply storing and distributing product or WIP. These services or activities are better performed at the warehouse because it allows for parts (including packaging materials) and products to be more efficiently shipped and managed (e.g., it is more economical to first ship an unassembled product to warehouses at distribution points which then assemble and ship to local customer as unassembled products typically use less shipping space than when they are already assembled). In addition, the large number of warehouses allows parts and products to reach customer (point-of-consumption) quicker (higher responsiveness). For example, warehousing supports just-in-time production that requires more frequent shipments in smaller batches. Warehouse value-added service is also advantageous for customized products. Fig. 1 shows the final product customization occurring inside a Murphy Inc.'s warehouse where the manufacturer supplies products in standard configurations (to multiple warehouses across the country) which are more economical to ship.

Fig. 1. Product customization at warehouses

1.3   Sustainability Perspective

The following are the economic and operational perspectives of warehousing that result in warehousing playing significant role in the product manufacturing carbon footprint and the need to increase sustainability considerations in warehousing operations:

1. More activities are occurring inside the warehouse leading to higher energy and material consumptions.
2. More automation has been used inside the warehouse to achieve greater efficiency and agility [26] leading to higher energy consumption.
3. The number of warehouses is growing. This can lead to more energy consumption across warehouses even if volume is unchanged.
4. Concentration of new warehouses in urban areas that are closer to points of consumption [15] and stringent urban waste and emission regulations lead to the need for more sustainable warehousing operations in those new warehouses.

Although there is no specific accounting of warehousing sustainability contribution, its significance can be inferred from the supply chain logistics contribution as a whole. For example, studies undertaken by manufacturers in [3-5] showed that, depending on the industry, supply chain logistics produces between 26 to over 50 percent of Green House Gas (GHG). One may estimate the warehousing GHG contribution as proportional to the economic value.

In conclusion: Although sustainability improvements can benefit warehousing operations both from the economic and operational perspectives, there has been little effort so far to establish sustainability metrics, guidelines and practices for warehousing operation. The Sustainable Logistics Initiative (SLI) is a recently established industry initiative to address this void. The next section introduces SLI, which so far has developed a set of sustainability metrics and a software tool for sustainability characterization. The following section reviews related supply chain sustainability efforts and discusses how their results may be used as the basis to expand SLI.

2   Sustainable Logistics Initiative (SLI)

Sustainable Logistics Initiative (SLI) is a sustainability program developed and administered by the International Warehouse Logistics Association (IWLA) in conjunction with the Sustainable Supply Chain Foundation (SSCF), which acts as a third-party neutral verifier. The program enables IWLA warehousing service provider members to demonstrate to their customers and to the public that their facilities' environmental efforts are helping to make the supply chain more sustainable [21-22]. The key drivers for the SLI are: improving financial results, assisting the customer to meet sustainability requirements, meeting request for proposal (RFP) sustainability criteria, demonstrating environmental stewardship as a responsible corporate citizen, and showing corporate pride for current and potential employees. SLI participants, through an independent verifier and a software tool, can use SLI metrics to establish each facility's baseline and target sustainability performances for annual improvement. SLI currently uses four environmental metrics (1 to 4 below) and two social responsibility metrics (5 and 6) as shown below.

1. Electrical usage: Metric = KWH of electricity / sq.ft. / operational hours or FTE hours (annual)
2. Recycling: Metric = annual lbs. or tons of paper, cardboard, plastic and wood packaging waste / sq.ft.
3. Liquid Fuel Usage: Metric = annual propane BTUs used / number of forklift hours
4. Water consumption: Metric = gallon / sq.ft. / FTE hours
5. Employee Safety: Metric = OSHA 300 Total Recordable Incident Rate (TRIR)
6. Community Service: Metric = facility community service participation

IWLA and SSCF have shared interest to enrich SLI's metrics and measurement capabilities related to energy and material consumptions. Possible enrichments include additional energy and material performance metrics, their measurement guidelines, and performance improvement best practices. Such enrichments are critical to the environment and bottom lines of warehousing companies and their supply chain partners. Next section discusses possible development directions and existing works that can be the basis for such developments.

3   Directions for Warehousing Sustainability Standards Development

3.1   Develop Warehousing-Specific Energy Management Guidelines

Warehousing-specific energy management guidelines can be developed based on the ISO 50000 series[2] of standards [9-11]. ISO 50001 defines basic terminology and a plan-do-check-act procedure for managing energy performance in an organization. ISO 50006 provides a guideline for specifying performance indicators, data collection methods, measurement time period, and energy measurement baseline. ISO 50015, currently in committee draft stage, specifies the verification and validation guidelines for energy performance measurement. In other words, ISO 50000 series is a horizontal/industry-neutral standard, and each industry or organization needs to come up with its own specifics. For example, no specific metrics, e.g., for warehousing operations, are identified in these standards. In addition, specific guidelines for setting and normalizing performance baselines over a period of operation are needed for different types of warehouses performing different operations over different periods. Such guidelines provide the implementable details for the routine and non-routine adjustments - two important concepts defined in ISO 50015 that are necessary for an effective energy performance improvement program. These guidelines can also be extended to cover other types of resources, such as material and water.

3.2   Develop New Metrics

The repository of sustainable manufacturing indicators (SMIR) created at the National Institute of Standards and Technology (NIST) [17] is a useful resource to expand the SLI metrics. It documents sustainability indicators[3] for various types of resources from various industries. For example, a recent discussion with IWLA members has indicated that natural gas should also be considered as part of the energy consumption metrics. To address this requirement, more precise metrics than those currently defined in SLI could be developed based on the energy intensity indicator documented in SMIR. The energy intensity indicator allows the respective metric to consider all energy types consumed. SMIR includes over one hundred and thirty indicators covering five categories: environmental stewardship, economic growth, social well-being, technological advancement, and performance management. It is a reference resource when expanding the coverage of SLI metrics.

---

[2] ISO 14000 series provide similar information for environmental management system.

[3] Term 'indicator' can be viewed as more general/abstract than the term 'metrics'. For example, energy intensity indicator refers to a kind or collection of sustainability performance measurement. On the other hand, energy intensity metrics refers to a sustainability performance measure that is specific, e.g., to car manufacturing (an energy intensity metrics maybe BTU/per car), a warehousing operation (an energy intensity metrics maybe as defined in #1 in section 2).

3.3   Develop Industry Benchmarks

Sustainability metrics typically only allow for internal benchmarking of sustainability performances over different periods of time or different internal facilities. External benchmarking between companies allow for companies to determine how they perform as compared to peers. Companies can use the benchmarking outcomes to decide whether and where to invest in sustainability improvements. However, data privacy is typically a concern. Approaches used in the EPA Energy STAR programs for automotive assembly plants and for warehouses can be the basis for cross-facility benchmarking [19-20]. However, the Energy STAR for warehouses characterize warehouses as buildings (as opposed to manufacturing plants) and only categorizes warehouses into dry vs. refrigerated [18, 20]. As we discussed earlier, warehouses are involved in a wide variety of activities. Hence, the current characterization and categorization may be insufficient. Further studies about warehouse characteristics to categorize them into comparable groups and to identify independent, predictive variables are necessary.

The Automotive Industry Action Group (AIAG) also has an ongoing project to apply the Energy STAR methods to different kinds of automotive manufacturing plants. These plants, such as engines, transmission, and even part manufacturing plants, are heterogeneous in their activities similar to those of warehouses. Lessons learned from this effort will be leveraged within the SLI.

3.4   Develop Theoretical Minimum Quantification Model

Current practices and guidelines for energy management and other sustainability management, such as in ISO 50000 series, only establish baselines and identify opportunities for performance improvements based on energy consumption within a particular time period. The assumption is that areas with high energy consumption provide greater opportunity for energy performance improvement. However, this is not an energy saving opportunity in an absolute value, because in the area where both the energy consumption and energy efficiency are high, the opportunity for improvement is, indeed, low. A better indicator for an energy performance improvement opportunity is the energy efficiency. To quantify the energy efficiency of a warehousing operation or process, it is necessary to develop a theoretical minimum energy quantification model for the activity or process. Cullen et al. [24] is an exemplary effort which utilized the notion of theoretical minimum to reduce energy consumption in steel and aluminum supply chains. Theoretical minimum may be established coarsely at the facility level as well as more specific at the process level. With theoretical minimums, companies can identify a gap with their actual consumption. Large gaps may indicate leaks/wastes or poor performance of equipment or systems. Best practice guidelines can be adopted from the energy efficiency measures identified in [25] or developed to minimize those gaps.

3.5   Connect with Other Nodes in the Supply Chain

The EPA SMARTWay program assists and encourages fuel efficiency and emission reduction specifically in freight companies [23]. The program provides tools to support three freight company roles in the supply chain: the *shipper, carrier,* and *logistics provider*. Because the tools connect the fuel efficiency data from one role to another, they allow companies in each role to choose partners based on their efficiency data. Since the tools only consider transportation, SLI may add a warehousing provider tool to include energy efficiency related to warehousing operations. With such addition, warehousing customers who use the SMARTWay tool can more conveniently and completely quantify and optimize the energy performance of their supply chain logistics.

4   Conclusion and Remarks

Warehouses and their operations are expanding as they are asked to increasingly perform value-added services to help customers reduce costs and increase agility and responsiveness. Therefore, they play an increasingly significant role in improving the manufacturing and supply chain sustainability. Sustainability performance metrics, associated measurement guidelines, and sustainability improvement best practices should be developed in order to effectively improve sustainability. The warehouse industry has started such development that resulted in an initial set of metrics and a sustainability characterization tool. Further developments are necessary so that sustainability improvements can be realized in both large and small warehouses and deliver impact across the industry. To that end, this paper has outlined further directions in which the warehouse industry can pursue in conjunction with the SLI. . In addition, existing standards and approaches related to sustainability management, metrics, and guidelines that can form the basis for such further development directions have been provided. Although there are no specific metrics and guidelines for warehousing operations, these existing efforts have been found to be potentially useful resources.

Acknowledgement. The authors wish to thank Dr. Serm Kulvatunyou at the National Institute of Standards and Technology (NIST) who provided valuable new ideas and insights into a number of related activities and existing works in the supply chain sustainability.

References

1. Council of Supply Chain Management Profession: 2012 State of Logistics Report
2. Maltz, A., DeHoratius, N.: Warehousing: The Evolution Continues. Warehousing Education and Research Council (2005)
3. Unilever Sustainable Living,
   http://www.unilever.com/sustainable-living/greenhousegases/transport/
4. Ryder System, Inc.: Stonyfield Case Study (2012)
5. Hanes Carbon Footprint,
   http://www.hanesbrandscsr.com/carbon-footprint.html
6. Accenture: Outlook, Supply Chain Management: Why a Sustainable Supply Chain is Good Business (2012)

7. Forbes: If Sustainability Costs You More, You're Doing it Wrong (2012), http://www.forbes.com/sites/csr/2012/08/13/if-sustainability-costs-you-more-youre-doing-it-wrong/

8. American Society for Quality, Corporate Responsibility Officers Association, Institute for Supply Management, and Deloitte Consulting: Selected Sustainable Value Chain Research Findings (2012)

9. ISO 50001: Energy management systems – Requirements with guidance for use, Geneva, Switzerland (2011)

10. ISO 50006: Measuring Energy Performance using Energy Baselines & Energy Performance Indicators Committee Draft (2012)

11. ISO 50015: Measurement and Verification of Organizational Energy Performance – General Principles and Guidelines, Geneva, Switzerland (2011)

12. Regan, A.C., Song, J.: An Industry in Transition: 3PL in the Information Age. Transportation Research Board 80th Annual Meeting, Washington DC (2001)

13. Armstrong & Associates, Inc.: The Business of Warehousing in North America – 2012 Market Size, Major 3PLs, Benchmarking Costs, Prices and Practices Report

14. Armstrong & Associates, Inc.: U.S. Gains Carry 3PLs - 2011 3PL Market Analysis and 2012 Predictions

15. Cushman & Wakefield: New Age of Trade: The Americas (2009)

16. Lieb, R.C., Randall, H.L.: CEO Perspectives on the Current Status and Future Prospects of the US 3PL Industry. Transportation Journal 38(3), 28–41 (1997)

17. Sustainable Manufacturing Indicators Repository. National Institute of Standards and Technology, http://www.mel.-nist.gov/msid/SMIR/

18. The ENERGY STAR for Buildings & Manufacturing Plants, http://www.energystar.gov/index.cfm?c=business.bus_bldgs

19. Boyd, G.: Development of a Performance-based Industrial Energy Efficiency Indicator for Automobile Assembly Plants. Decision and Information Sciences Division, Argonne National Laboratory (2005)

20. Environmental Protection Agency (EPA): ENERGY STAR® Performance Ratings. Technical Methodology for Warehouse (2009)

21. Logistics Management: Sustainability: IWLA announces the Sustainable Logistics Initiative, http://www.logisticsmgmt.com/view/sustainability_iwla_announces_the_sustainable_logistics_initiative/sustainability

22. International Warehouse Logistics Association (IWLA) Sustainable Logistics Initiative, http://www.iwla.com/Events/CalDetails.aspx?Page=Home&id=355

23. Environmental Protection Agency SmartWay, http://www.epa.gov/smartway

24. Cullen, J.M., Carruth, M.A., Moynihan, M., Allwood, J.M., Epstein, D.: Reducing Embodied Carbon through Efficient Design. Learning Legacy Report, London (2012)

25. Galitsky, C., Worrell, E.: Energy Efficiency Improvement and Cost Saving Opportunities for the Vehicle Assembly Industry. An ENERGY STAR® Guide for Energy and Plant Managers (2008)

26. D'Andrea, R., Wurman, P.: Future Challenges of Coordinating Hundreds of Autonomous Vehicles in Distribution Facilities. In: IEEE International Conference on Technologies for Practical Robot Applications (2008)

27. Bonvillian, W.B.: Reinventing American Manufacturing: The Role of Innovation. Innovations: Technology, Governance, Globalization 7(3), 97–125 (2012)

28. Coletta, W., Battezzati, L.: Cooperative Logistic Postponement. In: 7th International Meeting for Research in Logistics (2008)

Energy Savings Opportunities and Energy Efficiency Performance Indicators for a Serial Production Line

Michael Brundage, Qing Chang*, Shiyao Wang, Shaw Feng, Guoxian Xiao, and Jorge Arinez

APMS 2013 International Conference Advances in Production Management Systems
Sustainable Production and Service Supply Chains
September 9-13, State College, PA
{Michael.Brundage,Qing.Chang,Shiyao.Wang}@stonybrook.edu,
Shaw.Feng@NIST.gov, {Guoxian.Xiao,Jorge.Arinez}@gm.com

Abstract. Modern manufacturing facilities waste various energy savings opportunities (ESO) and lack proper performance indicators to measure energy efficiency on the production line. The ESO is an opportunity window calculated from on-line production data, such as production count, machine downtime records, buffer levels, and machine idle status, allowing certain machines to be turned off for energy savings without negatively affecting throughput. New energy efficiency performance indicators are presented that use real time production data to identify the least energy efficiency machine on the line. The energy savings opportunity strategy utilizes the Energy Efficiency Performance Indicators (EEPI) to take the opportunity window for the least energy efficient machine at opportune times, allowing for improvements to be made to the machine, increasing the overall energy efficiency of the line.

Keywords: Energy Savings Opportunities, Energy Efficiency Performance Indicators.

1 Introduction

With escalating fuel prices and increasing global competition, manufacturing companies are seeking methods to cut costs in any way possible. There are many opportunities to reduce costs in the energy consumption of the facility. These companies are searching for a way to reduce energy cost without sacrificing quality or affecting the yield of their products. The energy consumption in the industrial sector has almost doubled in the past 60 years and accounts for about one-half of the world's total energy consumption [1,2]. In the US alone, the industrial sector spent over $100 billion in energy costs [3] and was responsible for approximately 34% of all energy consumed in 2006. In a typical manufacturing plant, the largest source of energy consumption is the production system

---

* Corresponding author.

V. Prabhu, M. Taisch, and D. Kiritsis (Eds.): APMS 2013, Part I, IFIP AICT 414, pp. 302–309, 2013.
© IFIP International Federation for Information Processing 2013

where 67% of the total energy cost is attributed to the production process [4]. Being the center of a manufacturing system, production operation directly impacts energy distribution within the manufacturing environment as a whole. The dynamics of the energy demand, largely determines the total energy cost, since the cost of energy (e.g., electricity) actually varies minute-by-minute depending on demand and peak power.

There are few studies that address factory floor planning while considering energy saving opportunities [5-8]. Previous work into this topic has been severely limited with most work focusing on maintaining the quality of the product and the desired productivity while neglecting the energy saving potential. These methods treat the energy consumption as an additional cost term for an optimization problem or the consumption is analyzed as a result of high level decision making and scheduling. The energy consumption is considered a byproduct of the production system and not a main driver in the decision process on the factory floor or the control scheme of the overall system.

Some existing methods, such as the energy treasure hunt developed at GE [9] focused on developing weekend and daily shutdown plans, and managing the leak tag program. Such program is mainly based on non-operation obvious waste, requires expert knowledge on the part of the inspector, and is a "trial and error" manual procedure. There is still a lack of integrated systematic control methodology to drive overall effective energy savings.

One main obstacle in providing an integrated systematic control scheme is the lack of appropriate performance indicators for the facility. While many companies are able to provide key performance indicators (KPI) for a plant, these indicators do not properly address the problem areas on the floor [10-11]. These indicators normally single out the machine with the most energy usage, however this machine may not necessarily be the key issue in terms of energy inefficiency. This is due to the nonlinearity of the production system, which makes it difficult to quantify the impact of individual downtime incidents on the entire operation. The machine center with the most energy usage may not be the least energy efficient machine because of the effects of downtime effects from other machines.

This paper develops and implements new Energy Efficient Performance Indicators (EEPI) that incorporate energy usage from all facets of the manufacturing floor and the facility, and provide energy saving opportunity in real-time production. The EEPI takes into account random downtime events on the manufacturing floor and will allocate the energy usage into two separate categories based on permanent production loss and the lack of synchronization on the floor. This allows the identification of the process that is the most energy inefficient. In addition, the ESO will be applied to save energy and reduce the peak energy consumption so as to reduce overall cost.

The rest of the paper is structured as follows. In section 2 we present background and assumptions. We discuss the energy efficiency performance indicators in Section 3. Section 4 provides simulation studies of the energy opportunities. We dissect the results and provide conclusions and future work in Section 5.

2   Assumptions and Background

This papers utilizes continuous flow models as seen in Figure (1) [12-14]. The continuous flow model will treat the quantity of jobs in the buffer as varying continuously from zero to the capacity of the buffer as opposed to integer steps. This is done for ease of analysis. The actual system dynamics are not affected by this assumption regardless if the system is continuous or discrete [15,16]. For the serial production line as seen above, we can make the following assumptions:

1. Each station S_i has a constant rated speed equal to $\frac{1}{T_m}$, where T_m is the cycle time of the station. A station will run at its rated speed if it is operational and is neither starved nor blocked.
2. A machine is starved if it is operational and its upstream buffer is empty.
3. A machine is blocked if it is operational and its downstream buffer is full.
4. The first machine, S_1, is never starved and the last machine, S_M, is never blocked.
5. Each Buffer $B_2, B_3, ..., B_M$ have a finite capacity. $B_2, B_3, ..., B_M$ denotes the maximum capacity of the buffer.
6. $S_{M*} = argmin_{m=1,...M} \frac{1}{T_m}$ is unique.
7. W is the actual energy consumption for the production system.
8. The total rated power consumption of the line is $P = P_1 + P_2+, ..., P_M$.
9. $d_i^* =$ The opportunity window of machine i [17-19].

Fig. 1. A Serial Production Line with M Machines and M-1 Buffers

3   Energy Efficiency Performance Indicators

For the development of the Energy Efficiency Performance Indicators, we must first introduce an energy baseline for the factory. The first step in this process if to define the overall production time of the manufacturing line. The entire production line is dictated by the slowest machine in the system, $S_m^* = 1/T_m^*$, where T_m^* is the cycle time of the slowest machine. If the production count of the line is M, then we can define the overall production time as:

$$t_p = \frac{M}{S_{m*}} = M \times T_{m*}. \tag{1}$$

Knowing that this is the baseline, this means that the actual time it takes to produce M parts will always be:

$$t_r \geq t_p, \tag{2}$$

where t_r is the actual production time to produce M parts. We can now quantify the energy consumption to a dynamic and static portion in the manufacturing process, and categorize the energy consumption in detail (production related and unrelated). The dynamic part is attributed to random disruptions on the line, while the static part is related to synchronization operation. The static part of the energy consumption can be defined as W_1, which can be seen in equation (3):

$$W_1 = W \times \frac{t_p}{t_r}. \tag{3}$$

The dynamic portion of the energy consumption due to random downtime events on the line is W_2 and can be defined as:

$$W_2 = W \times \frac{t_r - t_p}{t_r}. \tag{4}$$

As one can see the total energy consumption $W_1 + W_2 = W$. The next step in the process is to distribute the energy consumption at the machine level to aid in developing the Energy Performance Indicator (EPI) for the entire line. The portion of the energy consumption that is due to normal machine operation can be estimated using the power rating of the individual machines. It is defined as $W_{i,1}$:

$$W_{i,1} = W_1 \times \frac{P_i}{P}, \tag{5}$$

where P_i is the power consumption of machine i and P is the rated power consumption of the entire line. Next, we develop the portion of energy that is wasted during permanent production loss, which is $W_{i,2}$. Permanent production loss occurs when there is a downtime event, d_i, at machine i that is longer than the opportunity window d_i^*. This will cause the slowest machine to become blocked or starved depending on the location of the down machine. Using this knowledge, the formula for $W_{i,2}$ becomes:

$$W_{i,2} = W_2 \times \frac{(d_i - d_i^*)}{\Sigma(d_i - d_i^*)}. \tag{6}$$

We can then use $W_{i,1}$ and $W_{i,2}$ to find the energy consumption per part at each machine, $ECPP$:

$$ECPP = \frac{W_{i,1} + W_{i,2}}{M_i}, \tag{7}$$

where M_i is the production count of machine i. If we sum the $ECPP$ for every machine, this will give us the performance indicator for the production line, which we will delineate as the energy performance indicator (EPI_{Actual}).

$$EPI_{Actual} = \sum_{i=1}^{M} \frac{W_{i,1} + W_{i,2}}{M_i}. \tag{8}$$

When there is no energy waste the $W_{i,2}$ term goes to zero, which gives the energy baseline, defined as $EPI_{Baseline}$:

$$EPI_{Baseline} = \sum_{i=1}^{M} \frac{W_{i,1}}{M_i}. \qquad (9)$$

As one can see as the production becomes very inefficient and M_i becomes small, while $W_{i,1}$ and $W_{i,2}$ grow larger the EPI_{Actual} will grow larger than the baseline. The larger the gap between the baseline and the EPI_{Actual}, and the higher the EPI_{Actual} the less efficient the production line is performing.

However, the EPI_{Actual} cannot completely describe the energy efficiency of individual machines. For example, certain machines may have to consume larger energy than other machines, so it cannot be concluded that this machine is energy inefficient. The key is the proportion of the energy consumed in effectively producing products. Therefore, an additional performance indicator is defined as the Energy Efficiency Performance Indicator ($EEPI$). This performance indicator for an individual machine is equal to:

$$EEPI_i = \frac{W_{i,1}}{W_{i,1} + W_{i,2}}. \qquad (10)$$

4   Case Studies

The production system for the case study is a 5 Machine 4 Buffer system (5M4B) with maximum buffer contents of 18 parts for each buffer. The parameters of the line can be seen in Table 1. The simulation time for this study is 168 hours with an 8 hour warmup time

Table 1. Production Line Parameters

Parameter	m_1	m_2	m_3	m_4	m_5
CT (mins/part)	3	3	5	3	3
MTTR (mins)	37.5	37.5	0	37.5	37.5
MTBF (mins)	150	150	150	150	150
Efficiency (%)	80%	80%	100%	80%	80%
Power (kW)	500	500	100	500	500

4.1   Case 1: $d = 0$

The line is first run without any inserted opportunity windows. This will serve as our base scenario without any energy efficiency control strategy. The EPI_{Actual} for the entire line is calculated using the formula in equation (8) and can be seen in Figure (2).

The solid line indicates the $EPI_{Baseline}$, which is the energy consumption without any permanent production loss, calculated from equation (9). The dashed line represents the actual EPI for the entire manufacturing line. This case will allow us to compare the following cases when we insert downtime events into the

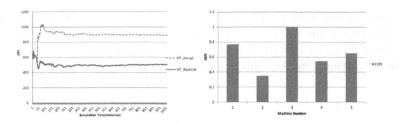

Fig. 2. EPI and EEPI with $d = 0$

production line. If the EPI_{Actual} is greater than this case then the production line is less energy efficient than without any energy opportunity windows. If the gap between the two is smaller than Case 1 then the line is more energy efficient.

To find the least energy efficient machine in the line, we utilize equation (10), and plot the results in Figure (2). This indicates the energy efficiency for individual machines since it takes into account the permanent production loss at each machine due to random downtime events. In this case, machine 2 is the least energy efficient machine as indicated by $EEPI$ since downtime events at machine 2 cause the slowest machine, machine 3, to become starved, therefore causing permanent production loss. Machine 3 has an $EEPI$ equal to 1.0 because it has no random downtime events, any time not producing parts is due to the other machines causing it to be blocked or starved.

4.2   Case 2: $d = d_i^*$

The next case takes into account inserted opportunity windows. There is permanent production loss for this case because the random downtime events due to machine inefficiencies cause the buffer levels to not reach their full capacity, therefore decreasing the opportunity window . The permanent production loss is 12.3% when compared to case 1.

The production count of machine 3 and machine 5 can be seen in Figure (3). Only two machines are shown since each machine except the slowest has the same parameters and would make it difficult to see the inserted opportunity windows in this figure if all were shown at once. Only a portion of the simulation is shown as well to better illustrate the production count of each machine.

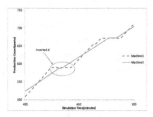

Fig. 3. Production Count of Machine 3 & 5 for $d = d_i^*$

The inserted opportunity window for machine 5 can be seen from approximately 425 mins - 450 mins where the machine has zero change in production count. The EPI_{Actual} and the $EPI_{Baseline}$ of the entire line with the inserted opportunity windows can be seen in Figure (4).

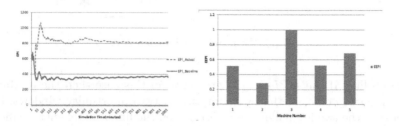

Fig. 4. EPI for the Entire Line with $d = d_i^*$

As one can see the EPI_{Actual} and the $EPI_{Baseline}$ decreases for the entire line with the insertion of energy savings opportunities, which is due to the small production loss. The $EEPI$ for each machine can be seen in Figure (4). The $EEPI$ once again illustrates that machine 2 is the least energy efficient. The $EEPI$ cannot be compared to other scenarios, as it is only an indicator of the machine efficiency for each given case. It enables us to identify the least energy efficient machine on the line. Theses results demonstrate that EPI_{Actual} and $EPI_{Baseline}$ decreases with inserted ESO. This is due to the fact that although the inserted downtime saves the overall energy consumption per part, too much ESO may have the risk to cause more energy consumed by the idling of the bottleneck machine. Therefore, an appropriate ESO strategy without sacrificing production is the key. Furthermore, $EEPI$ captured the portion of the energy used on actually producing parts for each machine rather than downtime and idling, therefore it is used to identify the least energy efficient machine of the production line and help to find the root cause of energy inefficiency.

5   Conclusions and Future Work

This paper investigates energy saving opportunities for a serial production line while developing new energy performance indicators for the production line and at the machine level. The performance indicators are tested using simulation studies using three different cases. These studies use different downtime events to prove the concept of the energy opportunity window as well as the energy performance indicators. The indicators are able to correctly identify the machine with the least energy efficiency for each case.

The next step in this research is to develop a control methodology to help alleviate the problem of the least energy efficient machine by utilizing the energy opportunity window or by performing preventative maintenance.

References

1. Nidumolu, R., Prahalad, C.K., Rangaswami, M.R.: Why Sustainability is Now the Key Driver of Innovation. Harvard Business Review (September 2009)
2. EIA, 2010, Annual Energy Review 2009 Report No. DOE/EIA-0384 (2009)
3. EIA, US Carbon Dioxide Emissions from Energy Sources 2009 Flash Estimate (2009b)
4. EIA, International Energy Outlook 2009 (2009a)
5. Chen, G., Zhang, L., Arinez, J., Biller, S.: Energy Consumption Reduction in Serial Production Lines via Optimal Startup Schedule. In: 6th Annual ASME International Manufacturing Science and Engineering Conference, Corvallis, OR (2011)
6. Guerrero, C.A., Wang, J., Li, J., Arinez, J., Biller, S., Huang, N., Xiao, G.: Production System Design to Achieve Energy Savings in an Automotive Paint Shop. International Journal of Production Research 49(22), 6679–6785 (2011)
7. Sun, Z., Biller, S., Gu, F., Li, L.: Energy Consumption Reduction for Sustainable Manufacturing Systems Considering Machines with Multiple Power States. In: 6th Annual ASME International Manufacturing Science and Engineering Conference, Corvallis, OR (2011)
8. Fan, K., Uhan, N., Zhao, F., Sutherland, J.W.: A New Approach to Scheduling in Manufacturing for Power Consumption and Carbon Footprint Reduction. In: Proceedings of NAMRI/SME, Corvallis, OR, vol. 39 (2011)
9. Data collection framework on energy consumption in manufacturing. In: IIE Annual Conference and Expo, Orlando, FL
10. Rockwell Software Enterprise Energy Management, Publication RSEEM-PP001A-En-P (November 2009)
11. Optimized energy system management with B. Data, Siemens.com/bdata
12. Sevast'yanov, B.A.: Influence of Storage Bin Capacity on the Average Standstill Time of a Production Line. Theory of Probability and its Applications 7(4), 429–438 (1962)
13. Wijngaard, J.: The Effect of Interstage Buffer Storage on Output of Two Unreliable Production Units in Series with Different Production Rates. AIIE Transactions 11(1), 42–47 (1979)
14. Gershwin, S., Schick, I.: Continuous Model of an Unreliable Two-Stage Material Flow System with a Finite Inter–stage Buffer. Technical Report 1039, Massachusetts Institute of Technology, MA (1980)
15. Gershwin, S.: Manufacturing Systems Engineering. Prentice-Hall, Englewood Cliffs (1994)
16. Li, J., Meerkov, S.: Production Systems Engineering, 3rd edn. Wing- Span Press, Livermore (2008)
17. Chang, Q., Xiao, G., Biller, S., Li, L.: Energy Saving Opportunity Analysis of Automotive Serial Production Systems. IEEE Transaction on Automation Science and Engineering (2012), doi:10.1109/TASE.2012.2210874
18. Chang, Q., Biller, S., Xiao, G., Liu, J.: Transient Analysis of Downtimes and Bottleneck Dynamics in Serial Manufacturing Systems. ASME Transaction, Journal of Manufacturing Science and Engineering 132(5), 051015 (2010)
19. Liu, J., Chang, Q., Xiao, G., Biller, S.: The Costs of Downtime Incidents in Serial Multi-Stage Manufacturing Systems. ASME Transaction, Journal of Manufacturing Science and Engineering 134(2), 02101 (2012)

Integration of Energy Information for Product Assembly and Logistics Processes

Shaw Feng[1], Senthilkumaran Kumaraguru[1], Kincho Law[2], and Kyeongrim Ahn[1]

[1] National Institute of Standards and Technology, Gaithersburg, MD, US
{shaw.feng,senthilkumaran.kumaraguru,kyeongrim.ahn}@nist.gov
[2] Civil and Environmental Engineering, Stanford University, Stanford, CA, US
law@stanford.edu

Abstract. This paper presents an on-going effort at NIST to model the energy information in assembly and logistics processes as a part of a larger sustainability improvement goal. Energy information comprises energy input, baseline energy consumption, and energy performance. An information model in this paper is developed for enabling integration of energy information in assembly and logistics processes. Based on this information model, industry will be able to share energy-related data on the overall plant level which is traceable to individual processes, equipment, and suppliers. This will enable manufacturers to identify energy saving opportunities in their assembly processes and supply chains.

Keywords: Assembly Equipment Characterization, Assembly Processes Characterization, Sustainable Manufacturing and Sustainability Measurement.

1 Introduction

The manufacturing industry has recognized that improvements in sustainability will depend on the industrial capacity to increase sustainability of individual components, including parts and subcomponents of final products [1]. A key factor to improve sustainability is energy efficiency. The energy embodied in a product is an aggregation of all of the energy embodied in the products' components, expended through its manufacturing processes and logistical activities. Yet, few standard measurement methods exist to measure energy, causing different companies to measure the use of energy differently. Additionally, the amount of energy used for product assembly processes is rarely traceable to individual processes and supply chains. The total energy and resource input into an assembled product is an aggregation of all of the energy and materials required in individual processes associated with the parts, components, and subsystems that are assembled into the final product. Even though, today's information technology is capable of providing traceable measurement and aggregation methods for resource efficiency assessment of product assembly and logistics operations across supply chains, however, there is a lack of standards on measuring energy input and performance [2]. Even a methodology for characterizing energy flow in assembly processes has not been fully developed to date. Manufacturing industries, therefore, use ad hoc methods to measure energy in their assembly processes which

V. Prabhu, M. Taisch, and D. Kiritsis (Eds.): APMS 2013, Part I, IFIP AICT 414, pp. 310–317, 2013.
© IFIP International Federation for Information Processing 2013

results in uncertain predictions. A methodology is needed to standardize the measurement of energy and material efficiencies in product assembly processes. Many energy management systems use energy performance indicators based on the past energy measurement data. However, science-based energy performance indicators [3, 4] need to be developed for characterizing sustainability performance of assembly and supply chain [5] processes. Romaniw has developed an activity based sustainability assessment model using SysML [6]. The scope of his model includes the manufacturing and assembly processes, and this information model can be further extended to define concrete energy performance indicators for sustainability characterization of individual assembly and supply chain processes. In view of the above, Section 2 defines the scope and requirements of information modeling necessary to develop the methodology. Section 3 proposes a new model of integrating energy, assembly process, equipment, and logistics. Section 4 concludes possible effects of the model and points to opportunities for future work.

2   Model Requirements

The scope of our modeling is energy information in assembly processes and equipment in a factory and the energy embedded in supplied parts from third-party providers. Figure 1 shows the chosen boundary and the energy flows in a typical assembly factory with energy consumed by supply chains. Assembly equipment provides the necessary energy for the assembly processes. Some assembly processes have to be supported by auxiliary processes. The auxiliary equipment provides the

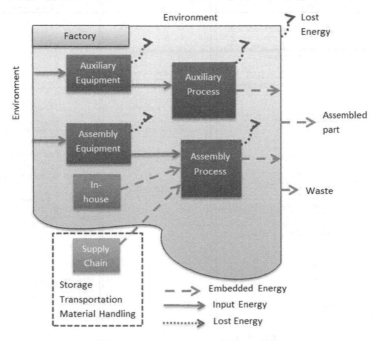

Fig. 1. Energy aggregation in product assembly and supply chain

necessary energy for the auxiliary processes. Some parts are manufactured in-house, and the other parts are provided from supplier through supply chains. The total energy embodied in a final product has to include energy used to make; store; transport; assembly all its parts and components, and embedded energy in those parts; components; and factory infrastructure overhead.

The National Institute of Standards and Technology (NIST) is proposing to develop information model for integrating energy information in product assembly processes and supply chain activities (figure 1). The major requirement is to model processes, activities, equipment, and their input, output and control based on a previously developed product assembly model [7]. Describing information requirements, Figure 2 shows an activity diagram of assembly, accounting for energy performance measurement from logistic and parts handling processes in supply chains. Product assembly starts with the Original Equipment Manufacturer (OEM) (manufacturer), executing a product assembly process plan. The OEM has to acquire those parts that are not manufactured in-house by sending orders to supplier(s). The suppliers prepare or make parts for delivery or move to warehouses, consuming energy. A third party logistics provider may be included for moving and storing parts and deliver them to the OEM by the due date. The OEM starts to assemble parts into products. Note that individual parts are either supplied by supplier or manufactured in-house. Parts and subassemblies are assembled in a predefined sequence in an assembly factory.   Energy use can be measured for each assembly process. The NIST proposed model is presented in the next section.

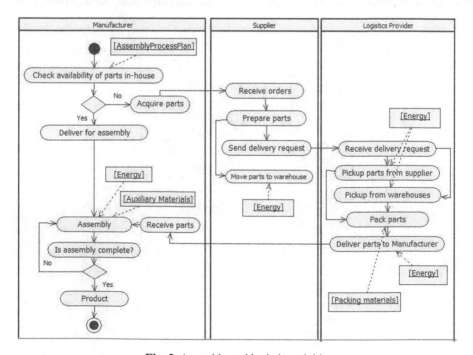

Fig. 2. Assembly and logistic activities

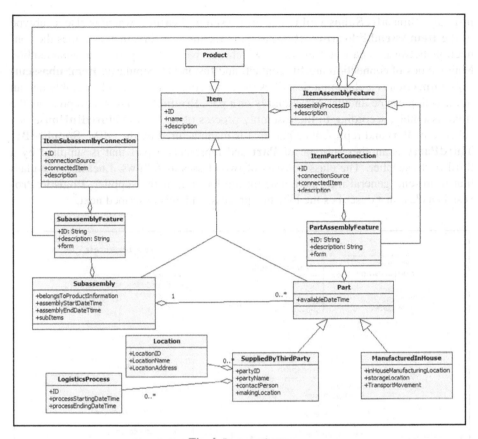

Fig. 3. Item package

3   Information Model Design

The proposed information model is in class diagrams using the Unified Modeling Language (UML) [8]. The four diagrams are Item package[1], AssemblyProcess package, LogisticsProcess package, and EnergyInProcess package. The Item package is the root package in the model. Figure 3 is the diagram of all the classes in the Item Package. The **Item**[2] class is the root of the Item package. An item is a workpiece in the assembly process. For assembly, an item has assembly feature(s) that is connected to assembly feature(s) of another item. **ItemAssemblyFeature** is a class that represents assembly feature. An item can be a single part, subassembly, or product; therefore, **Product, Subassembly**, and **Part** are subclasses of **Item**. **Part** has **PartAssemblyFeature**, which is a subtype of the **ItemAssemblyFeature**. Part is a single object that is either supplied by a supplier in the supply chain or manufactured

---

[1] Package is a construct to organize model elements into a group that depicts as a file folder and can be used by other UML diagrams.

[2] Class name is in bold.

in-house. Similarly, **Subassembly** has **SubAssemblyFeature**, which is also a subtype of the **ItemAssemblyFeature**. **ItemPartConnection** is a class that describes the connection between a part and an item, which can be another part or a subassembly. Major types of connection are fit, contact, and fusion [1]. Similarly, **ItemSubassemblyConnection** is a class that describes the connection between a subassembly and an item, which can be another subassembly or a part. **Product** is class that represents the final assembly, according to the assembly process plan. **ManufacturedInHouse** is a subtype of **Part** and represents a part that is manufactured by the OEM. **SuppliedByThirdParty** is another subtype of **Part** and represents a part that is supplied by a third-party supplier. The class consists of two classes as follows. **Location** is a class that represents general information about the location of the supplier. **LogisticsProcess** is a class that describes the logistics process, which is described next.

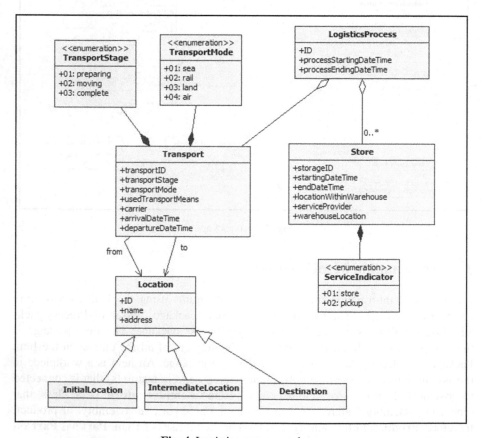

Fig. 4. Logistics process package

Figure 4 is the class diagram for the LogisticsProcess Package. **LogisticsProcess** class is the root class in the LogisticsProcess package. The class describes the logistics of parts transported from the supplier's location to the OEM location for assembly. The two major components of the class are the **Transport** class and the **Store** class. **Transport** represents the part transportation from one location to another from the supplier to the OEM. **Location** is used to indicate where a piece of equipment, a factory, a warehouse, or a supplier is. **InitialLocation**, a subclass of **Location**, describes the supplier's location. **Destination**, a subclass of **Location**, describes the OEM location. **IntermediateLocation**, a subclass of **Location**, describes an intermediate location of warehousing the parts between the initial location and destination. Transport class uses two enumeration types: **TransportStage** and **TransportMode** for representing the stage and the mode of transportation. Store is a class that represents warehousing the part. The class uses the enumeration type of **ServiceIndicator** for the type of services that the warehouse provides. Some information classes in this package and in the model, such as location and time and date, will be consistent with information entities defined by the United Nations (UN) Centre for Trade Facilitation and E-business (CEFACT) Core Component Library (CCL) [9, 10]. Energy in the logistics process will be described after the AssemblyProcess package.

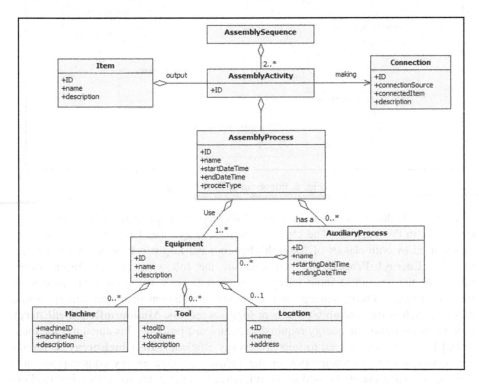

Fig. 5. Assembly process package

Figure 5 is the diagram of the classes in the AssemblyProcess Package. **Assembly-Process** is the root class in the package. The class represents the actual operation that connects two or more parts and/or subassemblies by fitting, making contact, or fusion. **AuxiliaryProcess** is a class that represents an auxiliary process that supports the completion of the assembly process but is not directly contributing to the assembly process.

Equipment is a class that represents equipment that is used in an assembly process or an auxiliary process. **Machine** and **Tool** are the classes representing machines and tools of the equipment. Both assembly process and logistics process requires energy. The energy-related classes for these two components are described next. The energy related classes for supplier (figure 2) are outside the scope of this paper.

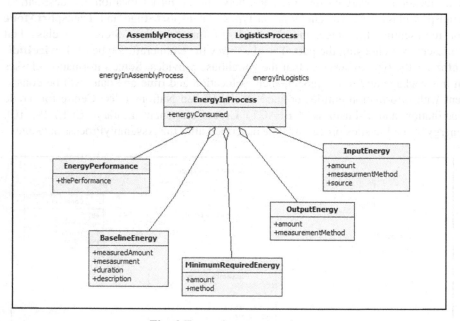

Fig. 6. Energy in process package

Figure 6 is the diagram of the EnergyInProcess Package. **EnergyInProcess** is the root class in this package. The class represents energy-related measures for a process and is used by both classes of **AssemblyProcess** and **LogisticsProcess**, described previously. **EnergyInProcess** has attributes of the following classes. **InputEnergy** represents the amount of input energy to a process, such as the assembly process or logistics process. **OutputEnergy** is a class that the amount of output energy from a process, such as the assembly process or logistics process. **MinimumRequiredEnergy** represents the minimum energy required to complete a process. This amount is the theoretical limit and can be used to improve energy efficiency. **BaselineEnergy** represents the historical energy consumption or the industry average energy consumption of a process. Baseline energy is used as the reference for energy improvement. **EnergyPerformance** class represents the energy performance, which is the ratio of the amount of production to a unit amount of energy, of a process. Classes in the EnergyInProcess package provide the capability of evaluating energy performance of a process.

The UML classes comprise the initial information model. The model enable manufacturing companies to share or exchange energy information in assembly processes and logistics activities. The model also provides software developers to develop new tools to evaluate energy performance in assembly and logistics processes.

4   Conclusion

This paper proposes a newly developed information model for representing energy consumption and performance for product assembly processes and logistics activities, including transportation and warehousing. This model provides a formalization of knowledge about the energy performance evaluation in product assembly and logistics. This model also enables integration of energy performance, assembly processes, equipment, and logistics processes. The use of model is expected for sharing information and new software tool development for enabling energy performance evaluation. Future work includes refining the model, and testing, validation, and implementation of the model.

Disclaimer: Certain commercial products may have been identified in this paper. These products were used only for demonstration purposes. This use does not imply approval or endorsement by NIST, nor does it imply that these products are necessarily the best for the purpose.

Acknowledgement. Work described in this paper was partially funded by an existing co-operating agreement 70NANB12H273 between NIST and Stanford University.

References

1. Kalpakjian, S., Schmid, S.: Manufacturing Engineering and Technology, 6th edn. Prentice Hall, New York (2010)
2. Lewandowska, A.: Environmental Life Cycle Assessment as a Tool for Identification and Assessment of Environmental Aspects in Environmental Management Systems (EMS) – Part 1: Methodology. International Journal of Life Cycle Assessment 16, 178–186 (2011)
3. Joung, C., Carrell, J., Sarkara, P., Feng, S.: Categorization of indicators for sustainable manufacturing. Ecological Indicators 24, 148–157 (2012)
4. Feng, S., Joung, C.: A measurement infrastructure for sustainable manufacturing. International Journal of Sustainable Manufacturing 2(2/3), 204–221 (2011)
5. Supply Chain Council, Supply Chain Operations Reference (SCOR®) model Overiew, Version 10.0, Cypress, TX (2010)
6. Romaniw, Y.A.: An Activity Based Method for Sustainable Manufacturing Modeling and Assessments in SYSML. Master's Thesis (2010)
7. Sudarsan, R., Han, Y., Foufou, S., Feng, S., Roy, U., Wang, F., Sriram, R., Lyons, K.: A Model for Capturing Product Assembly Information. Transactions of ASME, Journal of Computing and Information Science in Engineering 6, 11–21 (2006)
8. Rumbaugh, J., Jacobson, I., Booch, G.: The Unified Modeling Language Reference Manual, 2nd edn. Addison Wesley (2004)
9. UN/CEFACT, Business Requirements Specification, V.2.0, Rel. 1.0 (May 2012)
10. UN/CEFACT, Requirements Specification Mapping, V.2.0, Rel. 1.0 (May 2012)

Supply Chain Interoperability Efforts Missing Key Data

Christopher Peters

The Lucrum Group, Annapolis, MD, USA
cpeters@thelucrumgroup.com

Abstract. True manufacturing supply chain interoperability—where the assembly, reconfiguration and reconstitution of supply chains are done with minimal effort, time or cost—can dramatically alter the way that business is done today. Much of the existing research on supply chain interoperability focuses on established trading partners. However, we must consider both the sourcing and connecting processes in order to create true, dynamic supplier networks that can be easily assembled, reconfigured or reconstituted. This paper identifies why this is important, presents key challenges and proposes additional research that is needed to fill in the gaps.

Keywords: Supply chain, supplier networks, interoperability, manufacturing.

1   Introduction

Manufacturing supply chain interoperability efforts are missing key data that must be addressed if manufacturers are to achieve the vision of fluid, dynamic supplier networks. Much of the existing research focuses on supply chain interoperability between established supply chain participants. In many cases, the supply chain is considered to be "interoperable" if the participants are connected at the data, service, process and business levels. (Veronica Pazos Corella, 2013) (Ray & Jones)

What happens when new supplier networks need to be assembled, or when new participants must be added to existing supplier networks to increase capacity or replace a lost supplier? How does someone first locate a manufacturer with the right capabilities and capacity at the right time? How do they then know that the new participant's systems and processes will fit with those of the existing supplier network participants? Finally, what effort will be required to "onboard" the new supplier—that is, to connect the supplier's data, services, processes and businesses?

The missing data is how to efficiently source and seamlessly connect to new trading partners. It is this capability that helps manufacturers move from their reliance on static supply chains of existing partners to dynamic supplier networks, which can easily be assembled, reconfigured or reconstituted. The following definition, which is a variation on other commonly used definitions, is proposed to support that approach.

> "Supplier network interoperability is the property of an organization, whose capabilities and interfaces are completely understood, to work with other organizations, present or future, without any restricted access or additional implementation."

V. Prabhu, M. Taisch, and D. Kiritsis (Eds.): APMS 2013, Part I, IFIP AICT 414, pp. 318–324, 2013.

Unfortunately, there is little research to fully flesh out this challenge, particularly for the unique demands of complex manufacturing supply chains. This paper identifies the various issues and the work that is needed to advance efforts in this area.

2   Motivation

The benefits of addressing and solving these challenges can yield significant value to both buyers and suppliers of manufactured goods. Challenges ranging from increased personalization to demand fluctuation and sourcing closer to the point of consumption can't be met easily with today's inflexible supply chains. Supply chain risk mitigation strategies also are limited today and could change dramatically if the time and effort to add or substitute suppliers were slashed.

In short, achieving a "plug and play" supplier network—where new supplier networks can be assembled and new participants added or substituted at very little cost and with minimal time or effort—would change everything. Examples of specific benefits include:

- More quickly field new products;
- Readily secure capacity closer to the point of demand;
- Easily add capacity to meet demand fluctuations; and
- Recover immediately from supply chain disruptions.

3   Manufacturing Supply Chain Interoperability Challenges

The process of sourcing (locate, evaluate, query, qualify, negotiate and contract) and connecting (data, services, processes and businesses) new trading partners is costly and time-consuming. Many companies simply work with the same base of suppliers over and over again to avoid these issues. In addition to limiting supply chain flexibility, this approach also limits the ability to apply pricing pressure and stifles innovation. Following are some of the specific challenges for various steps in sourcing and connecting manufacturing supply chains.

3.1   Sourcing a Manufacturer (Locate, Evaluate)

This challenge is compounded by the fact that there are a number of considerations to even begin choosing a manufacturer. For instance, standard questions determine if potential suppliers have:

- The tools and experience to work with the specified materials;
- Equipment to handle the size and tolerances required; and
- Skill sets and certifications to help ensure quality and delivery.

Beyond the basic requirements, buyers today are looking for increasingly sophisticated information to help them make sound sourcing decisions:

- Are supplier facilities close to the desired point of manufacture, distribution or consumption?
- Does the supplier have sustainable practices?
- How well does the supplier collaborate and innovate?

Identifying and quantifying some of these considerations just to help locate and evaluate firms to be included in sourcing efforts can be very difficult. First, there is the mismatch between the description of a buyer's need and a manufacturer's capability. There then are the challenges of disparate formats and terminologies, often describing the exact same process or capability.

3.2   Sourcing a Manufacturer (Query)

Once a target list of manufacturers is identified, prospective suppliers must be queried to gather key information. This query is typically a sourcing event, such as a request for quote (RFQ) or request for proposal (RFP). In the past, the buyer was often focused on price, quality and delivery. However, buyers today increasingly are seeking information that has no standard definition and is not included in common electronic data interchange (EDI) or Extensible Markup Language (XML) schema. For example, specific technical capabilities, information on sustainable practices and innovation experience are becoming increasingly important when selecting manufacturers.

There are a number of challenges to effectively sourcing manufacturers. The first is just sending an RFQ that all recipients can open, interpret and respond to in a consistent manner. While that would seem simple with today's technology, there is still considerable effort involved. Each buyer's RFQ format is different and quite often requires clarification and augmentation before a supplier can provide a quote. (In fact, many manufacturers still send RFQs and technical data via fax, mail and email.) The second challenge is clearing the hurdles around technical data, which can include formatting, intellectual property control and translations.

3.3   Sourcing a Manufacturer (Qualifying)

A major hurdle in working with a new manufacturer is the qualification process. This challenge is particularly important to industries with complex products, such as aerospace, defense, automotive, medical equipment and others. One of the most typical, but least efficient, qualification means is to conduct an onsite visit to gather information about past performance and document processes, skill sets and equipment capabilities. While this qualification process often is crucial to help ensure the supply chain delivers quality goods on time, the process inhibits exploration of new partners.

Some work has been done to identify how an "interoperability potentiality measure" could help determine the level of effort required to work with a new partner. (Chen, Vallespir, & Daclin, 2008) However, this approach is still in the nascent stages and primarily focuses on the conventional aspects of interoperability for data, services, processes and business. Product interoperability standards (Will this supplier's product meet my requirements and be delivered on time for the right price?) have not been adequately addressed.

3.4   Connecting a Manufacturer

Once each manufacturer is chosen (remember that assembling a supply chain is often a serial process), the effort begins to connect each to enable the "Three C's" of successful supply chains: communication, coordination and collaboration. When you consider that complex supply chains can contain hundreds or thousands of suppliers, this is a daunting task.

Immediately, the supply chain has to begin exchanging data for technical requirements, demand and production to begin aligning processes, such as sales and operations planning or financial reporting. There then is the issue of coordinating task timeframes and responsibilities, and determining what metrics will be used and how they'll be reported.

All of this must be done with data that have different definitions and formats and come from disparate software programs. In fact, a recent study identified that "more than 50% of the information exchanged between business partners travels over fax, email and phone rather than flowing directly between business applications via B2B integration technologies such as EDI and XML." (Gillai & Yu, 2013) Even those companies that use EDI or XML typically require an effort to align definitions and formats.

4   Promising Efforts Currently Underway

There are very interesting pockets of innovation that are addressing some of the challenges in assembling and coordinating complex manufacturing supply chains.

4.1   OAG – Standard Manufacturing Service Capability Model

A new Open Applications Group (OAG) activity is being initiated to advance computer-interpretable communication of manufacturing information. For the purpose of initial analysis, manufacturing information necessary to enable contract manufacturing and custom parts ordering within the supply chain is investigated. The goal of the activity is to achieve greater automation in processing manufacturing information, which is typically (1) carried in the RFQ and other electronic documents and (2) exposed online by manufacturing suppliers. The manufacturing information may include manufacturing process capability information, manufacturing information processing capability information (software capability), product functions and product design features. (Ivezic, 2012)

4.2   NIST – Manufacturing Services Network Models Project

The National Institute of Standards and Technology (NIST) is conducting a project to enable small- to medium-sized enterprises (SMEs) to more readily participate in advanced production networks. Following their discovery and qualification, SMEs need to be able to receive and use digital manufacturing data and effectively respond to the requests to make the parts. The Manufacturing Services Network Models Project aims to provide cutting-edge semantic model development and an evolution methodology that allows for rigorous development of a semantic-rich standard for representing and communicating manufacturing service capabilities, including material processing and manufacturing information processing capabilities. Project deliverables include reference models, methods and tools to support the manufacturing service capabilities standard development. (Kulvatunyou, Ivezic, Lee, & & Jones, 2012)

4.3   KITECH – *i*-Manufacturing

South Korea's KITECH organization has developed a collaborative manufacturing platform that essentially allows its SMEs to plug in once and connect to many, regardless of disparate systems. Started in 2004, this system facilitates supply chain collaboration for more than 1,000 companies across multiple manufacturing supply chains. While its initial focus was on the molding industry, it is quickly expanding into other industries and delivering quantitative benefits that include a 33% reduction in time and a 16% reduction in costs.

5   Research That Is Needed

There is plenty of anecdotal evidence to support these challenges. However, there is very little in the way of quantitative evidence to identify just how bad the problem is and help provide direction and priorities for solving the challenges. This is particularly important to help manufacturing supply chains become more globally competitive.

5.1   Research Need #1 – Quantify the Process Inefficiencies

The first step should be to quantify the time and effort required to perform the sourcing and connecting tasks today. As the results will vary by industry, manufacturing complexity and other factors, a framework should be developed that would accommodate and capture those differences. This effort must look across all nodes of a supply chain, as there will be differences at the various tiers. Finally, manufacturers must understand the impacts of those inefficiencies, particularly on products and production, and identify how companies currently negate them.

5.2   Research Need #2 – Identify Information Flow Details

Streamlining the effort to source and connect new manufacturers requires understanding what information is needed for these tasks and how that information is exchanged today. This is particularly important for the volumes of unstructured data that are required to source and connect to new suppliers. Due to the complexities of manufacturing supply chains, there are numerous issues beyond what is normally contained in EDI or XML schema, such as the exchange and protection of technical data and the collaboration around it.

5.3   Research Need #3 – Build the Business Case

Once the "as-is" picture is understood, a case needs to be made for the "to-be" scenarios. Some of the easiest projections will be simple reductions in cost and time. However, the greatest business opportunities won't be as readily obvious or as easily quantified. Some examples of revised thinking include the following:

- Could the need for and trappings of long-term agreements be negated?
- Can pricing and volume be decoupled, making feasible a lot size of one?
- How does complete supply chain flexibility alter product customization?
- What risk mitigation strategies are best if adding new suppliers is frictionless?

6   Summary

True manufacturing supplier network interoperability—where the assembly, reconfiguration and reconstitution of supplier networks is done with minimal cost or effort—can dramatically alter the way that business is done today. However, achieving truly dynamic supplier networks requires a considerable amount of work. In fact, the National Coalition for Advanced Manufacturing (NACFAM) wrote about these very issues in "Exploiting E-Manufacturing" in 2001, yet little progress has been made to-date. (National Coalition for Advanced Manufacturing, 2001)

Despite all of today's advanced technology, the assembly and coordination of manufacturing supply chains is still very inefficient. While most people in the manufacturing industry can share many anecdotal tales that illustrate these inefficiencies, the industry does not have solid, quantitative evidence of the impact on products and production. Such evidence would be an eye-opener for many and can help identify where the needs are the greatest.

The really exciting opportunity is to identify how dynamic supplier networks could be assembled and coordinated in the future. If all information is interoperable, will modeling and simulation agents be able to analyze myriad permutations to design a supplier network that yields the best product for the consumer while optimizing production and profits for the suppliers? Will technology facilitate the design and assembly of unique supplier networks for each order? Will we reach a point where suppliers can be added or swapped out of supplier networks with little time, effort or cost?

Building a sound business case for a future vision of dynamic manufacturing supplier networks will provide the industry with a roadmap of what needs to be done to achieve that vision.

References

Chen, D., Vallespir, B., Daclin, N.: CEUR Workshop Proceedings, vol. 341 (June 16-17, 2008) from CEUR Workshop Proceedings, http://ceur-ws.org/Vol-341/paper1.pdf (retrieved March 23, 2013)

Gillai, B., Yu, T.: B2B Managed Services: Business Value and Adoption Trends. Stanford Global Supply Chain Management Forum, Stanford (2013)

Ivezic, N.: Advancing Computer-Interpretable Communication of Manufacturing Information (November 29, 2012) from Open Applications Group, http://www.oagi.org/oagi/downloads/meetings/2012_1128_SFO/Advancing%20Communication%20of%20Manufacturing%20Information-v1.0-formatted.pdf (retrieved March 23, 2013)

Kulvatunyou, B., Ivezic, N., Lee, Y., Jones, A.: Enhancing Communication of Manufacturing Service Capability Information. National Institute of Standards and Technology, Gaithersburg (2012)

National Coalition for Advanced Manufacturing, Exploiting E-Manufacturing: Interoperability of Software Systems Used by U.S. Manufacturers. NACFAM, Washington (2001)

Ray, S., Jones, A., (n.d.): Manufacturing Interoperability, from National Institute of Standards and Technology, http://www.mel.nist.gov/msidlibrary/doc/mirj.pdf (retrieved March 26, 2013)

Corella, V.P., Chalmeta, R.: SCIF-IRIS framework: a framework to facilitate interoperability in supply chains. International Journal of Computer Integrated Manufacturing 26(1-2), 67–68 (2013)

A Framework for Developing Manufacturing Service Capability Information Model

Yunsu Lee and Yun Peng

Department of Computer Science and Electrical Engineering,
University of Maryland, Baltimore County,
1000 Hilltop Circle, Baltimore, MD 21250
{yunsu.lee,ypeng}@umbc.edu

Abstract. Rapid formation and optimization of manufacturing production networks (MPN) requires manufacturing service capability (MSC) information of each party be accessible, understandable, and processible by all others in the network. However, at the present time, MSC information is typically encoded according to local proprietary models, and thus is not interoperable. Related existing works are primarily for integration in "isolated automation" of pair-wise or small size networks and thus are not adequate to deal with the high degree of diversity, dynamics, and scales typical for a MPN. In this paper, we propose a model development framework which enables to evolve a reference model for MSC information based on the inputs from proprietary models. The developed reference model can serve as a unified semantic basis supporting interoperability of MSC information across these local proprietary models. Methodology for resolving structural and other semantic conflicts between deferent models in model development is also presented.

Keywords: manufacturing service capability, ontology development, pattern-based ontology transformation, canonicalization.

1   Introduction

Today, service capability information of manufacturers is typically represented according to some models developed by individual enterprises or communities. These local proprietary MSC information models are not interoperable because of their differences in service category, capability structure and values. As a result, manufacturers often have difficulty in quickly discover suppliers with required capabilities without a significant level of human involvement. A MSC information reference model that is semantically rich can help reconcile semantic difference among local proprietary models and increase access and precision to capability information. However, related existing works [1, 2, 3] are primarily for integration in isolated automation of pair-wise or small size networks with less semantic diversity and thus are not adequate to deal with the high degree of diversity, dynamics, and scales typical for a manufacturing production networks (MPN).

V. Prabhu, M. Taisch, and D. Kiritsis (Eds.): APMS 2013, Part I, IFIP AICT 414, pp. 325–333, 2013.

In this paper, we propose a framework that helps to develop such a MSC information reference model. This framework takes a transformational approach and is centered on the ability to evolve a reference model based on the inputs from proprietary models. And that ability is provisioned by the abilities to perform the semantic gap analysis which identifies the semantic differences between the input models and the reference model. The differences are then used to drive the evolution of the reference model. A challenge for semantic gap analysis in this framework is to deal with the structural conflicts between the input from the local models and the reference model. This is addressed by aligning the structural representations of the input with the set of modeling conventions used in the reference models known as ontology design patterns (ODPs).

The rest of the paper is structured as follows. In the next section, we describe the proposed model development framework. In Section 3, we discuss the possibility of semantic loss after ontology transformation. And, finally we describe related works before giving conclusion and future plans.

2   Model Development Framework

The proposed reference model development framework is outlined in Fig. 1. We assume that each proprietary model uses its own syntax such as relational databases, XML and XML schemas. In the first step (*Transformation*), these heterogeneous syntaxes are transformed into a common syntax (OWL in our framework). The output of this step is an input into the following *Canonicalization* step. Another input to the canonicalization step is the patterns library which contains ontology design patterns (ODPs) from the reference model. The canonicalization step resolves the structural conflict by aligning the structural representations of a proprietary model with a set of modeling conventions used in the ODPs. The output of the canonicalization step is called canonicalized proprietary model. In the next step (*Semantic Gap Analysis*), the semantic differences between the canonicalized proprietary model and the reference model are identified. The differences are then used to evolve the reference model. The changes in the reference model are then verified for consistency in the *Verification/Reasoning* step. Details of each of these steps and ODP are given next.

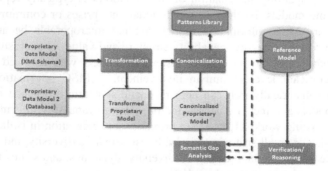

Fig. 1. The reference model evolution framework

2.1   Transformation

This step takes each proprietary model as input and converts them into common syntax of OWL. The output of this step is called a transformed proprietary model. Because the proprietary models take different conceptualization of the domain the result of the transformation still remains to be structurally and semantically different. This step can be largely automated when the proprietary model is well-structured (e.g., relational database and XML schema) as opposed to unstructured (e.g., text, HTML). In our work, we assume that the proprietary models are in relational databases. Currently, there are many tools to support RDB-to-OWL transformations. We have investigated D2RQ in particular and found that the D2RQ is capable of supporting the automatic transformation for the proposed framework [14, 15].

Fig. 2 below shows an example of the transformation from a relational database table into OWL. The *PartLength* table is converted into an *owl:Class* named *s:PartLength*. The *LengthValue* attribute is converted into *owl:DataProperty* named *s:PartLength_Value*. The record, which has the value 4 as its key, is converted into an *owl:NamedIndividual* named *s:PartLength_4*. Its *Value* attribute value *6cm – 48cm* is an *xsd:String* value of the *s:partLength_Value* data property.

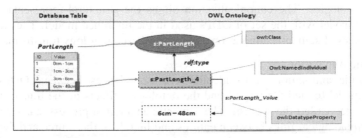

Fig. 2. RDB to OWL transformation example

2.2   Ontology Design Patterns

An ODP is a reusable successful solution to a recurrent semantic modeling problem, written in an ontology language such as OWL [8]. ODPs can be viewed as generic, small ontologies or ontology components with explicit documentation of design rationales and best reengineering practices. Pattern-based approach for ontology design has been gaining popularity recently because by reusing existing tested patterns as building blocks a domain ontology can be constructed quickly with high quality and less conceptualization divergence. A large amount of ODPs have been proposed in the ontology design community [9]. In this paper, we define a formal representation of ODPs as follows and show in Fig. 3 a simple exemplary ODP that captures the concept of *LengthCapability* with two *DatatypeProperty*, *hasMin* and *hasMax*.

- Definition 1: ODP is a 2-tuple {Sig, BE}
    - Sig is a non-empty set of Ontology Signature
    - BE is a non-empty set of binding expressions

- Definition 2: Ontology Signature is a 2-tuple {E, X}
  - E is a non-empty set of entity and literal parameters
  - X is a set of axioms
- Definition 3: Binding Expressions is a 2-tuple {P, C}
  - P is a non-empty set of parameters in the Signature
  - C is a non-empty set of concepts and values giving a specific meaning to the ODP signature

ODP	Signature	Binding Expression
PartLength	C1 (Class) — rdf:type → I1 (Instance); DP1, DP2 → L1 (Literal), L2 (Literal)	C1 = p:LengthCapability DP1 = p:hasMax DP2 = p:hasMin

Fig. 3. Exemplary ODP

2.3   Canonicalization

The canonicalization is a methodology to resolve structural differences between two different ontologies. The canonicalization aligns the structural representations of a proprietary model with the set of ODPs used in the reference model. The canonicalization consists of semantic annotation and pattern-based ontology transformation.

- Semantic Annotation

The semantic annotation is to identify correspondences between ODPs of the reference model (called the target) and the ontology artifacts of the transformed proprietary model (called the source). The semantic annotation process starts with establishing terminological links between entities and literals in the source and those in the ODPs of the target by matching their meaning or semantics. Many approaches have been proposed for determining semantic similarity between entities of two ontologies [7, 8]. The similarity can be measured purely based on lexical information in the labels of two ontology artifacts. And, the structural information can be considered as well. For instance, *s:PartLength* is linked to *p:LengthCapability*. With these terminological links and their binding expressions, the ODPs that are related to these terms are retrieved as shown in Fig. 4. The resulting correspondence indicates which ODP of the target should be applied to which set of the source artifacts.

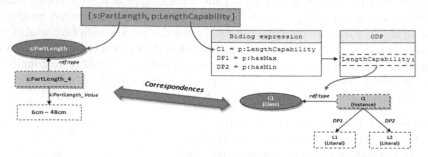

Fig. 4. Correspondence between the transformed proprietary model and ODP

• Pattern-based Ontology Transformation

The pattern-based ontology transformation first identifies sub-structures of the transformed proprietary model that is semantically close to a target ODP. Then, the patterns of the identified sub-structures are identified and they are called source ontology patterns and represented by the formal representation given in Section 2.2. In the next step, the pattern transformation rules are generated. A pattern transformation rule specifies relations between parameters in the source and target ODPs. These relations describe how the source ontology pattern should be transformed to the corresponding target ontology pattern. For instance, let's assume that the target ontology pattern has two data properties including *hasMin* and *hasMax* and the source ontology pattern has only one data property that represents the part length capability min and max values with a single literal value such like *6cm – 48cm*. To deal with this situation, a literal value pattern is defined with the string regular expression, *([0-9]+)cm - ([0-9]+)cm*. The first group in the regular expression corresponds to the minimum part length value and the second group corresponds to the maximum part length value. Fig. 5 below illustrates the pattern transformation rule for this situation.

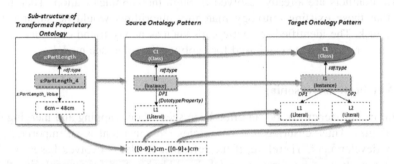

Fig. 5. Pattern transformation rule generation

Then, the transformation rules are executed on the transformed proprietary model and it is called pattern transformation. The pattern transformation is divided into two sub-processes, pattern instances detection and transformation rule application. The pattern instances detection process applies the source ontology pattern to find all pattern instances in the transformed proprietary model using the SPARQL. The SPARQL query generated from the source ontology pattern is shown in Fig. 6. It retrieves all the pattern instances which conforms the source ontology pattern. A pattern instance is a set of the transformed proprietary model's entities and literals that use the pattern.

```
PREFIX rdf:  http://www.w3.org/1999/02/22-rdf-syntax-ns#
PREFIX s:  <http://www.nist.gov/el/sid/msnm/PortalB.owl#>
SELECT distinct *
     WHERE {
         ?I1 rdf:type s:PartLength .
         ?I1 s:PartLength_value ?L1 .      }
```

Fig. 6. SPARQL query generated from the source ontology pattern

The transformation rule application process applies the transformation rule on the retrieved entities and literals in the transformed proprietary model. The output entities and literals provide all the necessary elements to establish the set of axioms in the target ontology pattern. The result of the pattern transformation is called canonicalized proprietary model which is the final output. The canonicalized proprietary model is expected to be structurally aligned with the structure of the reference model.

2.4   Semantic Gap Analysis

The semantic gaps between the canonicalized proprietary model and the reference model can be identified by mapping between those two different models. The mapping can be done manually and/or semi-automatically. Works in ontology matching in the past decade are summarized and analyzed in [7]. These works have been largely focused on achieving full ontology mapping or alignment, and, as indicated by the authors, left several open issues, particularly the issues of matching across entity types (i.e., to match across structural conflicts). However, in our framework, the structural conflicts are already resolved through the canonicalization. Therefore, we expect that those existing ontology matching algorithms would be suitable to this mapping task. The identified semantic gaps such as newly found concepts, relations, and axioms are documented and used for evolving the reference model.

2.5   Verification/Reasoning

Semantic inconsistency errors can often been seen when mapping and merging different ontologies. Thus, ensuring that ontologies are consistent is an important part of ontology development. Therefore, if the reference model is evolved based on the semantic gap analysis, the reference model should be verified for guaranteeing the consistency of the evolved model. The verification/reasoning step checks and verifies consistency across the proprietary model, proprietary data and the reference model. This includes translation checking, consistency checking, redundancy checking, etc. If inconsistency is found in this step, the semantic gap that causes this inconsistency should be re-analyzed and the changes should be reconsidered, and the verification/reasoning and semantic gap analysis steps shall be executed in iterations until there is no inconsistency.

3   Discussion

In this section, we discuss the possible semantic loss in canonicalization. The canonicalization is a type of ontology transformation. A key requirement for ontology transformation is that while syntactical changes are being made to data structures, the semantic meaning of that data should not be changed. Although all of the data transformed from original structure to canonical form is syntactically correct, it may be semantically incorrect and results in information loss. Thus, it is essential to consider the semantic effects of syntactic changes to correctly perform canonicalization.

In [4], the authors sketched a set of possible ontology change operations and discussed the effects of these changes with respect to the instance data preservation. The effects of the ontological changes can be classified as information-preserving, transformable, and information loss. The ontological changes with information loss should be very carefully handled while performing canonicalization. If one entity exists only in the proprietary model and does not exist in the reference model, we need to investigate whether the entity is meaningful and should be considered as a new concept or not. In the case of the former, the entity should be kept and additional information should be annotated so that it would be listed up in the gap analysis step. And, in the case of the latter, the entity should be excluded from the transformation rule and as a result it would be removed after canonicalization.

4   Related Work

In this section, we briefly review existing works that are relevant to ontology construction. The key ontology engineering activities in ontology construction are summarized in [10], which also stressed the need for guidance on ontology reuse. Guidance for building ontologies either from scratch or reusing other ontologies can be found in [11]. After establishing the ontology, an important issue is that ontology tends to change and evolve over time due to changes in the domain, changes in conceptualization, or changes in the explicit specification [12]. Works in managing ontology change and evolution are well-summarized in [13].

Canonicalization has been studied in several works. [5, 6] provide workable methods and tools including key enablers. They provide well defined XML schema for the pattern transformation definition (including pattern definitions and transformation rules). For pattern instances detection engine, PATOMAT provides the functionality to generate SPARQL query from the pattern transformation definitions and its pattern transformation engine uses OPPL application interface for pattern transformation. PATOMAT also has the TPEditor component which is an editor of source and target ontology patterns and associated transformation rules.

5   Conclusion and Future Works

Our work is motivated by the need to improve precision and interoperability of manufacturing services models to enable sharing precise information models of suppliers' manufacturing services in manufacturing production networks. In order to effectively develop such manufacturing services models, we propose a model development framework which enables a reference model to evolve based on the inputs from proprietary or other existing standard models. The differences between the input models and the reference model identified by the semantic gap analysis are used to evolve the reference model. The reference model is then verified for ensuring its consistency.

In this framework, we propose a canonicalization methodology to align the structural representations of a proprietary model with the set of modeling conventions (ODPs) used in the reference model. The benefit of canonicalization is the reduction of the mapping complexity by reducing the number of entities and structural complexity in the manufacturing service models and the number of mappings in semantic gap analysis.

As of our future work, we are working on analyzing requirements for manufacturing services capability to create a basic information model which will be a basis to derive representation patterns for manufacturing services capability. Based on the basic information model, we will create a library of representation patterns for the manufacturing services capability. We will also be conducting more in depth researches on core components of the model development framework. Finally, we will develop processes and tools to create a reference model using representation patterns for the manufacturing services capability.

References

1. W3C Semantic Web Activity, http://www.w3.org/2001/sw/
2. Kalfogloul, Y., Schorlemmer, M.: Ontology Mapping: The State of The Art. The Knowledge Engineering Review (2003)
3. Kim, J.: A Semantic Analysis of XML Schema Matching for B2B Systems Integration. PhD dissertation, Department of Computer Science and Electrical Engineering, University of Maryland, Baltimore County (2011)
4. Natalya, F.N., Michel, K.: Ontology Evolution: Not the same as Schema Evolution. Knowledge and Information Systems 6(4), 428–440 (2004)
5. Šváb-Zamazal, O., Svátek, V., Scharffe, F., David, J.: Detection and Transformation of Ontology Patterns. In: Fred, A., Dietz, J.L.G., Liu, K., Filipe, J. (eds.) IC3K 2009. CCIS, vol. 128, pp. 210–223. Springer, Heidelberg (2011)
6. Svab-Zamazal, O., Svatek, V.: OWL Matching Patterns Backed by Naming and Ontology Patterns. In: Znalosti (ed.) 10th Czecho-Slovak Knowledge Technology Conference, StaraLesna, Slovakia (2011)
7. Pavel, S., Jérôme, E.: Ontology matching: State of the art and future challenges. IEEE Transactions on Knowledge and Data Engneering X(X), 1–20 (2012)
8. Gangemi, A.: Ontology Design Patterns for Semantic Web Content. In: Gil, Y., Motta, E., Benjamins, V.R., Musen, M.A. (eds.) ISWC 2005. LNCS, vol. 3729, pp. 262–276. Springer, Heidelberg (2005)
9. Presutti, V., et al.: NeOn Project Delivery - D2.5.1. A Library of Ontology Design Patterns: reusable solutions for collaborative design of networked ontologies, http://www.neon-project.org/web-content/images/Publications/neon_2008_d2.5.1.pdf
10. Jones, D., Bench-Capon, T., Visser, P.: Methodologies for Ontology Development. In: Proc. of the IT&KNOWS Conference of the 15th IFIP World Computer Congress (1998)
11. Staab, S., Schnurr, H.P., Studer, R., Sure, Y.: Knowledge Processes and Ontologies. IEEE Intelligent Systems 16(1), 26–34 (2001)
12. Noy, N.F., Klein, M.: Ontology evolution: Not the same as schema evolution. Smi 2002-0926, University of Stanford, Stanford Medical Informatics, USA (2002)
13. Flouris, G., Manakanatas, D., Kondylakis, H., Plexousakis, D., Antoniou, G.: Ontology change: classification and survey. The Knowledge Engineering Review Journal 23(2), 117–152 (2008)

14. Bizer, C.: D2R MAP: A Database to RDF Mapping Language. In: Proceedings of the 12th International World Wide Web Conference, Budapest, Hungary (2003)
15. Bizer, C., Seaborne, A.: D2RQ–treating non-RDF databases as virtual RDF graphs. In: McIlraith, S.A., Plexousakis, D., van Harmelen, F. (eds.) Proceedings of 3rd International Semantic Web Conference, Hiroshima, Japan. LNCS, vol. 3298. Springer, Heidelberg (2004)

A Consilience-Based Approach to Engineering Services in Global Supply Chains

Eswaran Subrahmanian[1] and Albert Jones[2]

[1] Carnegie Mellon University, Pittsburgh, PA, 15213, USA
asub@cmu.edu
[2] Systems Integration Division, NIST, 100 Bureau Drive Gaithersubrg, MD, 20899 USA
albert.jones@nist.gov

Abstract. Technology life cycles are becoming shorter as is the time for those technologies to become ubiquitous in the society. The Industrial Revolution took about 150 years; but the computer revolution took only 50 years. Cell phones, which hit the market in the early 1980s took only 25 years to become a global phenomenon. Computers and cell phones are two examples of a growing number of products that marry hardware, software, communications, and physical components into what are called cyber physical systems. Even though humans are, for the most part, only users of these systems, they are already having a considerable impact on the evolution of society. In this paper, we focus on the next stage of that evolution, cyber-physical systems. We also focus on changes in how these systems are engineered. Formally designed only by OEMs, these systems are now engineered across the supply chain. A number of companies now provide engineering services. We discussed a number of existing approaches to systems engineering and concluded that they are inadequate. Finally, we propose a new, consilience-based approach that draws on the disciplines and practices that can inform and help resolve those inadequacies.

1   Introduction

Large, man-made systems have undergone a major transformation over the past 100 years. They have grown in both size and complexity making the integration of sensing and control significantly more difficult. They have incorporated substantial amounts of hardware and software and they have achieved unprecedented degrees of automation. All of which has led to emergent behaviors that are difficult to predict and often have disastrous consequences. As a result, the engineering of these systems has also undergone significant changes.

Starting about 50 years ago systems were designed by a small team of engineers at the Original Equipment manufacturer (OEM) – the supply chain only produced the components in that design. The design was created using the three-step reductionist approach developed more than 400 years ago by Rene Descartes. The first step is to decompose the system into a hierarchy of constituent components. You then compute their performance capabilities and material properties using well-known scientific theories. Finally, you infer the behavior of the entire system from the behavior of its components.

V. Prabhu, M. Taisch, and D. Kiritsis (Eds.): APMS 2013, Part I, IFIP AICT 414, pp. 334–343, 2013.

The reductionist approach is typically visualized using the classic V model used in systems engineering. The V model encompasses a series of processes beginning with requirements definition and hierarchical decomposition, through functional mapping, component design (down the left-hand-side of the V) and component performance testing, subsystem integration test, and, finally, system validation test (up the right-hand side). The thinking behind a reduction approach is ubiquitous - permeating nearly every facet of engineering practice. It has succeeded to the point where most engineers exclusively focus on a single component or technical discipline of the system - often ignoring the fact that it is, indeed, part of a system.

Until recently, this "components-first, interactions- later" V approach served engineering well. For a number of reasons, this approach has proven to be too costly, too time consuming, and too error prone. This paper focuses on two of those reasons. First, engineering is no longer provided solely by the OEMs. Engineering is now provided as a service by several members of the supply chain. This means that systems and their components are now engineered and produced across the globe. Second, those systems and components are no longer just physical; they are now inherently cyber and physical.

2   The Emergence of Cyber-Physical Systems

There has been a large-scale infusion of cyber technologies into these systems and components. We use the term cyber technologies broadly to include computers, micro-processors, software, sensors, and networks. The fusion of, and in some cases the replacement of, physical components with cyber components has been termed Cyber-Physical Systems (CPS) This is not about adding cyber technologies "on top of" conventional physical components where both sides maintain separate identities. This is about marrying cyber technologies with physical components, at multiple temporal and spatial scales, to create new kinds of systems. These new systems are, to a large extent, autonomous. Clearly, the technological advantages – particularly safety, efficiency, and reliability - brought about such a marriage can have broad benefits on the economy and the society.

We must stress cyber-physical systems are not simply the connection of different kinds of components. They are rather a new system category that is intrinsically a multi-layered network of interacting physical, computational, and human components. The resulting systems exhibit evolutionary behaviors that are (1) increasingly dynamic, unpredictable, and complex, (2) the results of the structural interactions among the various components, and, (3) whose cause and effects are often separated in time and space [19]. It is not possible, however, to determine whether these evolutionary behaviors are the result of components acting alone or combinations of components working together.

Effective methods and tools for designing and predicting the behaviors of physical components and physical system and have been in common use for years. These methods and tools work because compositionality and composability assumptions are valid for physical systems. There is a growing belief that these assumptions are not valid for cyber-physical systems. Consequently, new methods and tools are needed that allow us to engineer these cyber-physical systems [10].

In the following sections, we provide an historical perspective on OEM engineering practices and discuss the impacts of the change to supply-chain engineering services. We then propose a new consilience-based approach that addresses those changes.

3   Historical Approaches to Engineering

3.1   Systems Engineering

The classic model of systems engineering is embodied in the V shape. The V shape comprises a set of methods starting from requirements, hierarchical decomposition, component design (down the left-hand-side of the V) and component testing, subsystem composition test, and, finally, systems testing (up the right-hand side). This methodology focusses on the design of the system in very top down fashion. This process has worked extremely well for purely physical systems; it has had problems, however, since the emergence of cyber-physical systems. The fundamental reason is the added complexity introduced by the cyber components. The historical evolution and increase of complexity and the rise of new approaches and trans-disciplinary efforts to address that complexity illustrate this best.

Before the use of computing and software, most early systems were electro-mechanical systems with a clear definition of functional boundaries. This clarity was present even when there were numerous possible choices (say n) for the functional decompositions. Further, for each such decomposition there were many possible realizations (say m) of the physical artifact. This led to $n*m$ *(order n squared)* possibilities to realize a given system design; at of the each levels of system, subsystems and sub-subsystems. However, with the introduction of cyber components, the boundaries between mechanical and electrical components have become more ambiguous. Ambiguity arises because of the potential for computationally efficient choices (say r) for replacing some or all of the functions of, and the interfaces between, existing electrical and mechanical components.

Such choices add to the complexity of both the design process and the result products. They change the original functional-to-physical mapping into a functional-technology-realization mapping. The resulting complexity goes from $n*m$ (n squared) to n*r*m (order *n cubed*) for each subsystem in the system network [13]. In addition, the specification of interface requirements has become dramatically more difficult. This happens because of the constant change in the boundaries between the physical and cyber components. As the authors in [31] have observed most failures in systems design happen at the interfaces, which presents significant design challenges.

There has been a long tradition of studying and modeling socio-technical systems where the work requires deciphering and understanding the social interactions, social norms, and behavior in the design of these systems [35]. The focus of this effort was increasing participation of the employees in the design of the systems to humanize, the industrial aspects of a technical system. This view came of out of the ideas of learning organizations and the development of idea that practice is guided by "theory of use" [2]. The methods that arose out of this work are often termed soft systems methodology [9]. More recently, the rise of modeling social systems as computer models have opened up the possibility to model different forms of social in terms of agency and actor motives and goals [12, 36]. In line with these developments, more recently there have been calls for rethinking socio-technical perspective calling for co-design and analysis of both the physical and organizational systems using actor based models [11].

3.2   Software Engineering

One can observe that the field of software engineering has changed from the earlier approaches of waterfall model of software development to more flexible model represented by Spiral model of development [5]. Currently software engineering is moving away from Value-neutral approaches (requirements to product without any analysis of the intrinsic and explicit value of software products) to Value based approaches that advocate concurrent engineering, justification of choices, evaluation of real options in terms of strategy and evolution and issues of ethical production of software [6, 7]. These efforts not only address the issue of the tangible and intangible value of these systems but also the fact that to avoid failure, concurrent engineering must focus on the interfaces between different systems [16].

3.3   Concurrent Engineering

Concurrent engineering is another approach that originated in the 1980's in the design of complex engineered systems like cars, aircraft and other products [21]. The main focus of this approach has been to bring the variety of functional perspectives and disciplines in the context of design and manufacture of systems. These approaches focus on ensuring that identification potential mismatches between the different sub-system and the interfaces early in the process of design. It is well known that the cost of mismatch when caught early in the process is less than when the mismatch is identified at the later stages of product development and manufacturing process. To facilitate concurrent engineering, considerable effort was placed on developing collaborative engineering tools some of which have evolved over time and entered the main stream in engineering [15].

3.4   Cognitive Systems Engineering

Another discipline that has made an impact on the design of physical systems over the last 25 years is cognitive systems engineering. Cognitive systems engineering has focused on the match between the human cognitive ability and the interface to the physical system. Originally, started from the design of operator rooms for nuclear power plants, this effort has moved to the area of cockpit design for aircraft and other interfaces where the criticality of reaction of the human in the loop to respond to the state of system [17]. In this view of systems design, the combination of operators and machines constitutes the system. Operators here are not users in the sense of human-computer interaction but of humans, machines, and systems that constitute the workplace.

Cognitive systems engineering is distinguished from the study of human computer interaction (HCI). HCI has evolved into the new discipline of Interaction Design. The history of this evolution is recounted by Moggridge in his book "Designing Interactions" [20]. Here, the human is considered a user with a free range of operations – examples include the mouse and the smartphone. The underlying principles of interaction design still have limitations in the sense of treating the process of interaction as purely an information processing task [pg 17-19, 17]. As more of these devices become part of the work environment, the necessity to incorporate the lessons of cognitive systems engineering will become critical, since users will no longer have complete freedom. Instead, they will become operators in the work environment with specified functions to perform.

3.5   Model-Based Engineering

In systems engineering a new trend is to increase the use of computer-interpretable models especially in the specification and design stages, . This approach is generally known as model-based engineering. Model-based engineering is an attempt to codify the underlying information models that characterize the different aspects of designed product. The model-based effort has always existed in the form of modeling physical systems through differential equations and other mathematical and graphical formalisms in systems engineering. What is new in the recent effort is create models that represent software in languages such as UML. In the systems engineering domain, the extension and adaptation of UML to systems design has resulted in intuitive modeling tools such as SYSML.

3.6   Social Aspects of Engineering

For the most part, the social aspects of systems engineered using the aforementioned approaches are neglected. That is, the role that humans play in the operation and maintenance of such systems is rarely included in their design. The famous sociologist, Charles Perrow, in his analysis of the accidents at Three Mile Island and other complex engineered systems, points out that it is impossible to identify all the paths and dependencies in such a system. He concluded, therefore, that many of these catastrophic accidents are what he called "normal" [23]. What he meant by this term is that such accidents are a part of the systems design that often remain unknown to the designers. He and others recently refined this theory of "Normal Accidents" to make the case that as the complexity of the engineered system increases, the humans organizations that interact with and manage these systems often contribute to their failure [23]. He also argues that if the system is monolithic and tightly integrated the potential for dire consequences of such failures can be catastrophic as was the case in Fukushima, recent financial crisis and other disasters [24, 26]. In his essay on complexity, catastrophe and modularity [25], he argues such systems should be linearized

individual components, their behaviors, and their properties. New synergistic techniques are needed to integrate these component models together layer by layer until the system model is generated. At every step, the behaviors, and where relevant the material properties, of these models are checked against the requirements. The real-world system will be constructed, or modified if it exists already, only after meeting all of the requirements.

To ensure that such modeling efforts are carried out consistently to address the problem of integrating the different disciplines new metrics and measurement methods will be needed. Beyond measurements there would be an explicit need to develop standards for the different modeling paradigms that will be encountered in the design of these complex interlinked networks. We will also need standards for modeling and designing these network topologies of the socio-technical organizations that will ensure linearization properties that can minimize the scope consequences of failures. Scale-free networks provide such possibilities but they are also vulnerable to catastrophes under certain design conditions [28, 3]. The need for modeling and designing such networks is still a nascent field. In all of these domains of enquiry, the timely availability of models for testing conformance to specified behavior and standards will be critical.

5   Summary

Technology life cycles are becoming shorter as is the time for those technologies to become ubiquitous in the society. In [14], the authors estimate that the Industrial Revolution took about 150 years; but the computer revolution took only 50 years. Cell phones, which hit the market in the early 1980s took only 25 years to become a global phenomenon. Computers and cell phones are two examples of a growing number of products that marry hardware, software, communications, and physical components into what are called cyber physical systems. Even though humans are, for the most part, only users of these systems, they are already having a considerable impact on the evolution of society.

In this paper, we have focused on the next stage of that evolution, cyber-physical systems, and the change to supply-chain engineering services. We claimed that humans and other social organizations would play a much more active role in these systems – often contributing directly to their success or failure. Because of this, we have argued that the roles of the humans and organizations must be taken into account when engineering these systems. We discussed a number of approaches to systems engineering and concluded that they are inadequate for this purpose. Finally, we propose a new, consilience-based approach that draws on the disciplines and practices that can inform and help resolve those inadequacies in the design of CPS. This new approach would critically depend on the development of new measurements and standards for the design and performance of these systems at varied interfaces between these systems.

References

1. Amanna, A.: Overview of IntelliDrive / Vehicle Infrastructure Integration (VII), Virginia Tech. Transportation Institute (May 2009)
2. Argyris, C., Schon: Theory in Practice. Jossey-Bass, Sanfranciso (1974)
3. Barabasi, A.: Scale-Free Networks: A Decade and Beyond. Science 325(5939), 412–413 (2009)
4. Bashshur, R., Reardon, T., Shannon, G.: Telemedicine: A new Kind of Health Care System. Annual Reviews of Public Health 21, 613–637 (2000)
5. Boehm, B.: A Spiral Model of Software Development and Enhancement. ACM SIGSOFT Software Engineering Notes 11(4), 14–24 (1986)
6. Boehm, B., Huang, L.G.: Value based software engineering: A case study. IEEE Computer (March 2003)
7. Boehm, B.: Value based Software engineering: Seven Key elements and ethical considerations. In: USC-CSE 2005, University of Southern California (2006), http://csse.usc.edu/csse/TECHRPTS/2006/usccsse2006-640/usccsse2006-640.pdf
8. Booch, G., Rumbagh, J., Jacobson, I.: Unified Modeling language user guide. Addison Wesley, New York (2005)
9. Checkland, P.: Soft systems methodology: A thirty year retrospective. Systems and Behavioral Science (17), 11–58 (November 2000)
10. CPS Summit, Report from the Cyber-Physical Systems Summit, St. Louis (April 24-25, 2008)
11. de Bruijn, H., Herder, P.M.: System and actor perspctives on Sociotechnical systems. IEEE Transactions on Systems, Man and Cybernetics – Part A; Systems and Humans 39(5), 981–993 (2009)
12. Epstein, J.M.: Generative Social Science. Princeton University Press (2006)
13. Erens, F.J.: The synthesis of variety: developing product families. PhD thesis, Technical University of Eindhoven (1996)
14. Evans, P., Annunziata, M.: Industrial Internet: Pushing the Boundaries of Minds and Machines (2012), http://files.gereports.com/wp-content/uploads/2012/11/ge-industrial-internet-vision-paper.pdf
15. Fenves, S.J., et al.: Product information exchange: practices and standards. Transactions of the ASME-S-Computing and Information Science in Engineering 3, 238–246 (2005)
16. Finger, S., Konda, S.L., Subrahmanian, E.: Concurrent design happens at the interfaces. M 9(2), 89–99 (1995)
17. Hollnagel, E., Woods, D.D.: Joint Cognitive System: Foundations of Cognitive Systems Engineering. Taylor and Francis (2005)
18. Lee, E.: Cyber Physical Systems: Design Challenges. In: Proceedings of ISORC, Orlando (May 2008)
19. Meadows, D.: Thinking in Systems. Chelsea Green Publishing Company (2008)
20. Moggridge, B.: Designing Interactions. MIT Press (2007)
21. Nevins, J.L., Whitney, D.: Concurrent design of Products and Processes. McGraw Hill (1989)
22. NextGen, http://www.faa.gov/nextgen/ (December 6, 2012)
23. Perrow, C.: Normal Accidents: Living With High Risk Technologies, revised edn. Princeton University Press, Princeton (1999)
24. Perrow, C.: Fukushima, risk, and probability: Expect the unexpected. Bulletin of the Atomic Scientists (2011)

25. Perrow, C.: Complexity, Catastrophe, and Modularity. Sociological Inquiry 78(2), 162–173 (2008)
26. Perrow, C.: The meltdown was not an accident. In: Lounsbury, M., Hirsch, P.M. (eds.) Markets on Trial: The Economic Sociology of the U.S. Financial Crisis: Part A, Research in the Sociology of Organizations, vol. 30, pp. 309–330. Emerald Group Publishing Limited (2010)
27. Perrow, C.: The Next Catastrophe: Reducing Our Vulnerabilities to Natural, Industrial, and Terrorist Disasters. Princeton University Press, Princeton (2011)
28. Perrow, C.: Software Failures, Security, and Cyberattacks, Paper available at http://www.yale.edu/sociology/faculty/pages/perrow/ (December 6, 2012)
29. Rajkumar, R.: Cyber physical Future. Proceedings of the IEEE, 1309–1312 (March 2012), http://www.rockwellautomation.com/resources/downloads/rockwellautomation/pdf/about-us/company-overview/TIMEMagazineSPMcoverstory.pdf (December 6, 2012)
30. Subrahmanian, E., et al.: Boundary objects and prototypes at the interfaces of engineering design. Journal of CSCW (April 2003)
31. Subrahmanian, E., Reich, Y., Smulders, F., Meijer, S.M.: Design as synthesis of spaces. In: Proceedings of the International Association of Design Research Societies (November 2011)
32. SysML, http://www.sysml.org/ (December 6, 2012)
33. Tassey, G.: The Technology Imperative. Edward Elgar (2007)
34. Tripp, E.: The Evolution of Socio-technical systems, Occasional paper, no 2, Faculty of Environmental Studies, York University, Toronto (1981), http://www.sociotech.net/wiki/images/9/94/Evolution_of_socio_technical_systems.pd
35. Whitworth, B.: Socio-Technical systems. In: Handbook of Human Computer Interaction, pp. 531–541 (2006), http://brianwhitworth.com/hci-sts.pdf
36. Wilson, E.O.: Consilience: The Unity of Knowledge. Knopf (1998)

Manufacturing Capability Inference and Supplier Classification Based on a Formal Thesaurus

Farhad Ameri and Stan Thornhill

Department of Engineering Technology, Texas State University,
601 University Dr.
San Marcos, TX 78666, U.S.A
{ameri,sjthornhill}@txstate.edu

Abstract. Standard representation of manufacturing capability information is a necessity for efficient configuration of loosely-coupled supply chains. ManuTerms is a formal thesaurus that provides a set of standard vocabulary that can be used for description of manufacturing capabilities. In this paper, a method is proposed for supplier characterization and classification guided by ManuTerms. The tools developed in this work use the capability narrative of manufacturing suppliers as the input and extract key concepts that refer to certain aspects of manufacturing capabilities in order to characterize and classify manufacturing suppliers. Through an experimental study, the supplier classification method was validated with respect to the level of agreement with human judgment.

Keywords: supply chain interoperability, manufacturing capability, thesaurus, supplier characterization.

1 Introduction

Effective configuration and operation of distributed supply chains highly depends on the ability to meaningfully exchange engineering information among the supply chain members. The main body of research in supply chain information interoperability has been focused on information exchange among the supply chain participants *after* the supply chain is configured [1]. However, information interoperability in *pre-configuration stages* is equally important as it improves the quality of communication among suppliers when searching for appropriate manufacturing counterparts [2]. A significant portion of the information exchanged and consumed during the supply chain pre-configuration stages is related to the *manufacturing capabilities* that different suppliers can offer. Manufacturing capability of a supplier refers to the aggregate abilities, skills, and expertise a supplier can provide to the customers enabled by its internal and external resources. The existing models for manufacturing capability representation are often proprietary and unstructured or semi-structured without well-defined semantics. This has resulted in information loss and information ambiguity in supply chain communications. In order to streamline information exchange in the early stages of supply chain lifecycle, it is imperative to develop

V. Prabhu, M. Taisch, and D. Kiritsis (Eds.): APMS 2013, Part I, IFIP AICT 414, pp. 344–351, 2013.

standard models for manufacturing capability representation with uniform and explicit semantics agreeable among larger supplier communities. If the representation can be formalized, then it also enables active participation of machine agents in autonomous supply chain configuration process. One promising approach for addressing the interoperability issue is the use of formal ontologies that encode explicit capability knowledge. In fact, several research projects have used ontological approach for dealing with information interoperability in manufacturing supply chains [1, 3, 4]. One of the key challenges in developing ontologies is *knowledge acquisition* especially when dealing with a vast and complex domain such as manufacturing. There are multiple sources of knowledge that can be utilized for collecting manufacturing engineering knowledge including domain experts, engineering handbooks, and web portals. The online profiles of manufacturing suppliers, in particular, contain a wealth of information pertaining to the capabilities of suppliers. In their webpages, manufacturing companies typically provide different types of information such as their primary and secondary services, the materials they can process, the processes they are expert in, and the types of products or geometries they typically produce. The terms that suppliers use in their capability narratives are essentially the basic building blocks of the capability knowledge model. Therefore, by systematically analyzing supplier profiles and organizing the key terms, it is possible to arrive at a conceptual model that can be incrementally evolved into more complex and axiomatic ontologies.

In a previous research, a thesaurus was developed based on the terms collected from the online profiles of manufacturing suppliers [5] . This paper describes how the developed thesaurus can be used for inferring new knowledge about manufacturing capabilities of suppliers and also classifying and clustering suppliers based on the information patterns that appear in their online profiles. Through inferring new knowledge about the capabilities of manufacturing suppliers, the intelligence of autonomous supplier discovery solutions will be enhanced. Automated characterization and clustering of suppliers is particularly helpful in web-based scenarios in which the supply pool is fairly large and searching and screening process becomes a labor-intensive task.

2   Manufacturing Capability Thesaurus

ManuTerms, a formal thesaurus for manufacturing terms, was developed with the objective of collecting the key terms, or concepts, used in manufacturing capability representations [5]. The collected concepts constitute the conceptual model that serve as the steppingstone for more formal ontologies such as MSDL [6]. The online profiles of manufacturing suppliers, mainly in contract machining sector, were used as the main resources when developing ManuTerms. Simple Knowledge Organization System (SKOS)[1] is used for syntactic and semantic representation in ManuTerms. SKOS is a formal language for thesaurus representation and is built upon Resource Description Framework (RDF) and RDFS and enables publication of controlled vocabularies on the Semantic Web as an RDF graph. SKOS core vocabulary is a set

---

[1] http://www.w3.org/TR/skos-reference/

of RDF properties and RDFS classes. Each term in SKOS has a *preferred* label and one or more *alternative* labels. *Broader*, *narrower*, and *related* are the semantic relations used in any SKOS thesaurus. Also, each SKOS concept can have a definition provided in natural language. ManuTerms currently has more than 2100 concepts that are organized in eighteen categories such as processes, materials, and machinery. Approximately, 2800 alternative terms have been identified for those concepts.

3   Capability Inference

A formal SKOS thesaurus such as ManuTerms, together with its associated document indexing and concept extraction tools, can enable different types of statistical analysis and data mining that will lead to generation of new knowledge and insight about the population under study. In particular, since ManuTerms was initially developed to organize the vocabulary adopted by manufacturing suppliers for describing their capabilities, it can be used for discovering useful patterns and statistics in a sample of supplier profiles. For example, one can learn about the advertising behavior of suppliers in different domains such as precision machining or electrical discharge machining through analyzing the type and the frequency of concepts used in the supplier profiles. This in turn can lead to development of more intelligent supplier search algorithms that customize their search logics based on the search context. A sample of 50 suppliers from different service categories including machining, casting, and assembly was formed for the purpose of this study. The selected suppliers each had a website in which the core capabilities and services were described in natural language (English) with at least 200 words.

In order to rapidly analyze a large sample and improve the statistical significance of the results, a Java-based concept extraction program was developed for automatically extracting ManuTerms concepts from the imported text. Fig. 1 shows the user interface of the concept extraction program. The extractor tool exports the identified concepts for each supplier to an Excel worksheet for further analysis. Fig. 2 shows the ManuTerms concepts extracted from the profile of one of the suppliers of CNC milling services and sorted according to

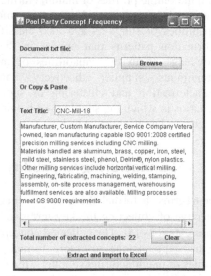

Fig. 1. The GUI of the concept extractor program

the concept score. The concept extractor tool indexes a profile by a concept if the preferred or alternative labels corresponding to the concept appear in the profile. Concept score is calculated based on *frequency* and *location* of its corresponding terms in the capability narrative. The location score assigns more weight to the terms that appear earlier in the text. Some of the high-score concepts extracted for the supplier narrative shown in Fig. 2 are Milling, Custom Manufacturing Service, Precision Machining, Steel, and Aluminum. Therefore, just by studying the ranked list of returned concepts, one can conclude that this supplier most likely provides precision machining services for steel and aluminum parts. It can also be inferred that this supplier provides assembly and stamping services as secondary services since these concepts are among the top twenty concepts returned by the extractor but not ranked high in the list.

Manufacturer, Custom Manufacturer, Service Company Veteran-owned, lean manufacturing capable ISO 9001:2008 certified precision milling services including CNC milling. Materials handled are aluminum, brass, copper, iron, steel, mild steel, stainless steel, phenol, Delrin®, nylon plastics. Other milling services include horizontal vertical milling. Engineering, fabricating, machining, welding, stamping, assembly, on-site process management, warehousing fulfillment services are also available. Milling processes meet QS 9000 requirements.

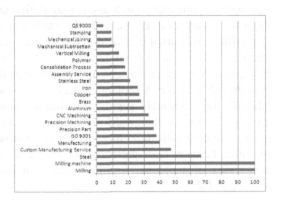

Fig. 2. The capability narrative of a sample supplier along with the listing of the concepts extracted from this profile

In the studied sample of 50 suppliers, 24 suppliers had Precision Machining in their top five lists. However, only two of twenty two suppliers provided stamping processes. Therefore, one can conclude that these two data points are outliers and do not provide a strong evidence for the hypothesis that "*providers of precision machining services usually provide stamping service as well*". Table 1 shows some of the discovered patterns of service provision based on the concepts extracted from the studied sample.

Table 1. The discovered patterns based on a sample of 50 suppliers

Pattern / finding	Occurrence percentage
Providers of Micromachining services serve Medical industry.	67%
Providers of Swiss Machining services are capable of High Volume production.	53%
Providers of CNC machining services provide CAD/CAM services as well.	71%
Providers of Casting services provide Heat Treating services as well.	75%

4   Supplier Classification

Concept extraction results in *semantic tagging* of supplier profiles by ManuTerms concepts. Semantic tagging and annotation is particularly helpful for automated search and retrieval of suppliers. Machine agents can use the extracted concept cloud in order to characterize and categorize manufacturing suppliers based on their asserted and inferred capabilities, thus generating more precise search results. Supplier characterization is the first step in forming specialized supplier families. As an example, a particular search agent may define an arbitrary family if suppliers called *high-tech suppliers* representing the suppliers that possess 5-axis micromachining capabilities supported by CMM and CAM services. An array of ManuTerms concepts such as 5-Axis Machining, CMM Service, CAM Service, and Micromachining Service can be defined as the concepts that qualify a supplier as a high-tech supplier. A semantic query over the annotated profiles can be executed to identify the "high-tech" suppliers within the search space depending on the presence of one or more of the *qualifying concepts* in each profile. Through employment of scoring and normalization measures, it is possible to quantify the strength by which a supplier belongs to a particular family. For the purpose of experimentation, six categories of suppliers, together with their qualifying concepts, were defined as shown in Table 2.

Table 2. Example supplier categories together with their description and qualifying concepts

Category Title	Description	Qualifier concepts
Small-part suppliers	Suppliers who are capable of producing small parts.	Swiss Machine, Screw Machine, Chucking Machine, Small Part, Precision Small Part, Swiss Machining, Screw Machine Part
Large-part suppliers	Suppliers who are capable of producing large parts.	Large Part, Medium-to-large Part, Large Machining Job, Vertical Boring, Vertical Boring Machine, Trunkey component, Trunkey Manufacturing
Aerospace suppliers	Supplier who serve aerospace industry.	Aerospace Industry, Aircraft, Spacecraft, Aircraft Manufacturing, Aerospace Alloy, Aerospace Part
Precision suppliers	Supplier who provide precision manufacturing services.	Precision Small Part, CNC Precision Turning, Precision Machining, Precision Measuring Instrument

Table 2. (*continued*)

Complex-parts suppliers	Supplier who provide manufacturing services for complex parts	Complex Part, Complex Geometry, 5-Axis Machining
High-tech suppliers	Supplier who provide high-end manufacturing services and possess modern manufacturing and inspection equipment.	5-Axis Machining, CMM Service, CAM Service, Micromachining

Twenty suppliers were selected for the classification experiment based on the 6 categories described in Table 2. The concepts extracted automatically for each supplier were analyzed to come up with a numeric value for the membership strength with respect to each category. The membership strength is calculated using the following equation:

$$MS_{ij} = \frac{SQC_{ij}}{QC_j} \qquad (1)$$

Where MS_{ij} is the membership strength of the supplier i with respect to the category j, SQC_{ij} is the sum of the number of qualifier concepts for j^{th} category extracted from the profile of the ith supplier, and QC_j is the number of qualifier concepts for the jth category. For example, there are seven qualifier concepts for the *small parts* supplier category. Then if three of these concepts appear directly or indirectly in the profile of particular supplier, the membership strength of this supplier to small parts supplier category is 3/7=0. 42.

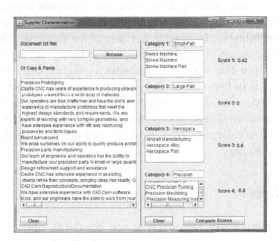

Fig. 3. The screenshot of the supplier characterization tool

A Java-based tool, called supplier characterization tool, was developed for calculation of membership strength based on the capability narrative of the supplier as shown in Fig. 3 . It should be noted that semantic equivalence (i.e., alternative label) is taken into account when calculating MSij.

The supplier classification tool receives the capability narrative of the supplier as the input and calculates the membership strength along different categories. To this end, the tool interacts with an API of a thesaurus builder software tool, Pool Party Extractor (PPX), to obtain a list of concepts extracted from the narrative of the suppliers. The particular supplier shown in this figure is mainly categorized as a "precision supplier" since about 80% of the qualifying concepts related to precision suppliers incurred in the profile of this supplier. This finding was compared against human expert's judgment that was asked to assign membership strength values for different categories after studying the narrative of the supplier. Validation based on expert's judgment was conducted for all sampled suppliers. One interesting observation in the supplier characterization experiment was that most of the suppliers that were strongly characterized as "small-part suppliers", ranked high with respect to precision and complexity measures as well. That is, an intelligent learning algorithm may be developed in the future to use such information to infer capability.

Another experiment was conducted to compare and contrast the capability descriptions collected from the e-sourcing portals and the capability descriptions available in the websites of suppliers. The null hypothesis was that suppliers describe the same capabilities in an e-sourcing portal and in the company's website. For this experiment, the same sample of suppliers used in the characterization experiment was studied. A particular e-sourcing portal widely used in the contract manufacturing industry was selected for this study. After quantitative analysis of the commonalities and differences of the returned sets, it was observed that, for the majority of the studied suppliers, the set of concepts extracted from the portal profile is considerably different from the concept set extracted from the supplier's website. This discrepancy is mainly attributed to the predefined template and keywords imposed by the portals for capability description that provide suppliers with a limited set of options for describing their capabilities. In general, because of the flexibility that suppliers have when describing their capabilities in the company website, the information content of the text extracted from the suppliers' websites is higher compared to e-sourcing portals. This finding is in favor of the distributed sourcing solutions that consume the capability data generated in a decentralized fashion. In a distributed sourcing scenario, ManuTerms can serve as a neutralizing middle agent that converts the contents of heterogeneous profiles collected from the Web into uniform capability models that share a common vocabulary.

5   Conclusions

This paper presented novel approaches for capability inference and supplier classification based on ManuTerms. Classification of suppliers is beneficial in the early stages of supply chain configuration as it narrows down a larger pool of suppliers to a smaller subset composed of suppliers that are relevant to particular search scenarios. The proposed classification technique was evaluated experimentally to verify its agreement with human judgment. More sophisticated search techniques based on axiomatic ontologies such as MSDL can be conducted on the returned subset in order to arrive at a more fine-tuned search results. The advantage of using a formal thesaurus is that it can be used for automatically converting heterogeneous capability narratives into homogenous conceptual models composed of standard capability terms. One of the future tasks in this research is to use ManuTerms as an intermediary model for Ontology-based Information Extraction (OBIE) from web-based profiles of manufacturing suppliers.

References

[1] Vujasinovic, M., Ivezic, N., Kulvatunyou, B., Barkmeyer, E., Missikoff, M., Taglino, F., Marjanovic, Z., Miletic, I.: A Semantic-Mediation Architecture for Interoperable Supply-Chain Applications. International Journal of Computer Integrated Manufacturing 22(6), 549–561 (2009)

[2] Janssen, M., Feenstra, R.: Service Portfolios for Supply Chain Composition: Creating Business Network Interoperability and Agility. International Journal of Computer Integrated Manufacturing 23(8-9), 747–757 (2010)

[3] Blomqvist, E., Levashova, T., Öhgren, A., Sandkuhl, K., Smirnov, A.V., Tarassov, V.: Configuration of Dynamic Sme Supply Chains Based on Ontologies. In: Mařík, V., William Brennan, R., Pěchouček, M. (eds.) HoloMAS 2005. LNCS (LNAI), vol. 3593, pp. 246–256. Springer, Heidelberg (2005)

[4] Ye, Y., Yang, D., Jiang, Z.B., Tong, L.X.: Ontology-Based Semantic Models for Supply Chain Management. International Journal of Advanced Manufacturing Technology 37(11-12), 1250–1260 (2008)

[5] Ameri, F., Mcarthur, C., Urbanovsk, C.: A Systematic Approach to Developing Ontologies for Manufacturing Service Modelin. In: Proc. 7th International Conference on Formal Ontology in Information Systems (FOIS 2012), Graz, Austria (2012)

[6] Ameri, F., Dutta, D.: An Upper Ontology for Manufacturing Service Description. In: Proc. ASME IDETC/CIE Conference Proceedings, pp. 651–661 (2006)

Excellent Manufacturer Scouting System (EMSS) for Korean Molding Industry

Moonsoo Shin[1], Sangil Lee[2], Kwangyeol Ryu[2,*], and Hyunbo Cho[3]

[1] Hanbat National University, Daejeon, Korea
shinms@hanbat.ac.kr
[2] Pusan National University, Pusan, Korea
{lscall,kyryu}@pusan.ac.kr
[3] Pohang University of Science and Technology, Pohang, Gyeongbuk, Korea
hcho@postech.ac.kr

Abstract. As up-to-date competitive environment of manufacturing business has accelerated global outsourcing, the selection of the right partners becomes more important than ever in securing competitiveness. To have the best partner selections, it is necessary to discover potential partners (either suppliers or buyers) located in all over the world and to evaluate their capability to produce eventual profits. e-marketplaces of manufacturing services are collaboration systems that support cooperation between suppliers and buyers. The objective of this paper is to present a web-based collaboration system, referred to as excellent manufacturer scouting system (EMSS). EMSS provides collaboration services for discovering, evaluating, negotiating and cooperating to ensure interoperability amongst manufacturing companies. EMSS employs an ontology-based mechanism for semantic interpretation, and it is equipped with an assessment model of core manufacturability. In this paper, a supply chain collaboration model using EMSS for molding industry is also proposed.

Keywords: Interoperability, Supplier scouting, e-Marketplace, Manufacturability assessment, Manufacturing service.

1   Introduction

Nowadays, owing to the competitive environment of manufacturing business, the manufacturing paradigm has been changed toward global collaboration. Especially, construction of collaboration network via global outsourcing is a representative strategy for manufacturing companies to survive. Thus, discovery and selection of the right partners becomes more important in securing competitiveness. In such a line of thought, manufacturing companies should efficiently find out competitive outsourcing partners located anywhere in the world, and the potential outsourcing partners should effectively inform their core capabilities to the global customers. Actually, it has been shown that the ability to establish partnership with global customers provides

---

* Corresponding author.

V. Prabhu, M. Taisch, and D. Kiritsis (Eds.): APMS 2013, Part I, IFIP AICT 414, pp. 352–360, 2013.
© IFIP International Federation for Information Processing 2013

competitive advantage to SMEs in Korea over those in other developing countries such as China, Vietnam, and so on [1].

Recently, a target of global outsourcing has been changed from non-core services such as human force for back-end business operations to a higher value-added business such as knowledge outsourcing. Thus, collaboration style for global outsourcing has been changed from ad hoc buyer-supplier relationship to a strategic partnership (i.e., long term exclusive relationship) as illustrated in Fig. 1.

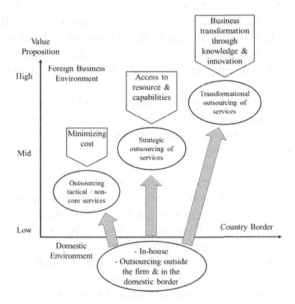

Fig. 1. Change of the collaborative approaches [2]

In this paper, a web-based collaboration system that provides collaboration services for discovering, evaluating, negotiating and cooperating is presented to ensure interoperability amongst manufacturing companies. The system is referred to as excellent manufacturer scouting system (EMSS). EMSS is a sort of e-marketplaces for manufacturing services that support strategic cooperation between suppliers and buyers. EMSS is equipped with ontology-based semantic interpretation mechanism to secure interoperability, and it employs an assessment model of manufacturability.

In Section 2, existing e-marketplaces are briefly introduced. In Section 3, EMSS is presented. Then a supply chain collaboration model using EMSS for molding industry is presented in Section 4. Finally, Section 5 is devoted to concluding remarks and further research topics.

2   Manufacturing e-Marketplaces

In general, manufacturing companies exhaust their resources and time to find a new collaboration partner by means of participating in various industrial expositions or conferences. They have recently used various websites or e-marketplaces (e.g., alibaba.com, EC21.com, mfg.com) for searching and scouting their buyers or suppliers in order to reduce costs. Conventional websites that support supplier discovery services just provide general or brief information of manufacturing companies in a list format; or they restrictedly assist in establishing business contracts between buyers and suppliers mainly by human. However, the basic information is insufficient for evaluating company's manufacturability.

Alibaba.com [3] is a well-known e-marketplace specialized in manufacturing industry. It focuses on the service on commercial transactions such as product lists, product search, supplier search, buyer search, intermediary services, and so on. However, it does not provide matching services and evaluation services for buyers and it only provide a simple searching service by using keywords. Therefore, buyers have to evaluate suppliers by themselves. Furthermore, the quality of searching service is not good enough to find right suppliers effectively because of its limitation of keyword searching.

EC21.com [4] focuses on not only manufacturing industry but also other industries such as agriculture and service industry. Its services are similar with those of alibaba.com but EC21.com provides company's homepage and catalog services. However, such additional services are insufficient for practical support for matching buyers and suppliers.

Mfg.com [5] provides not only searching services but also matching services and negotiation service between buyers and suppliers in manufacturing industry such as molding, forge welding, assembly, and so on. Buyers can find a suitable supplier easily and conveniently by using it. However, the level of services provided depends on the membership fee monthly paid. Furthermore, because the discovery process is performed by human, it is inefficient in terms of cost and time. We also cannot get accurate evaluation results, reflected by human's subjectivity.

In sum, legacy e-marketplaces provide limited searching services based on keyword search methods, and they do not provide matching and evaluation services except for mfg.com. Even mfg.com employs a manual evaluation mechanism. Thus, it is required to build more effective searching mechanism based on a semantic search rather than simple keyword search. In addition, an automated evaluation method of core capabilities of manufacturing companies should be developed. Furthermore, the discovering services are required to be incorporated with post-discovering services devoted to negotiation and collaboration. EMSS proposed in this paper meets these requirements.

3   Excellent Manufacturer Scouting System(EMSS)

3.1   Supply Chain Formation

EMSS serves manufacturing services that plays a role of a matchmaker between buyers and suppliers. EMSS helps globally located buyers to discover and evaluate outsourcing partners, and provides potential suppliers with business opportunities. Fig. 2 shows overall procedure for supply chain formation via partner selection using EMSS, that consists of three stages including 1) discovery, 2) negotiation, and 3) collaboration. In the stage of discovery, which is the scope of this paper, EMSS provides a buyer with candidate suppliers that conform to its requirements of manufacturing capabilities, quality level, etc. The buyer makes the final selection of its supplier in the stage of negotiation, and then orders are placed to the selected supplier for making products or services in the stage of collaboration. It is assumed that a web-based collaboration system, referred to *i*-MFG, is employed in the collaboration stage. *i*-MFG was developed by a government-led project in Korea, and it serves various functions for collaboration[6-9].

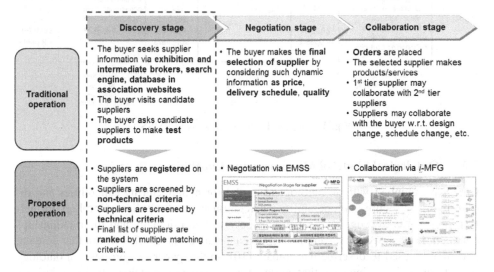

Fig. 2. Overall procedure for supply chain formation

3.2   Supplier Discovery Process

Supplier discovery process of EMSS includes 1) filtering, 2) matching, and 3) ranking, as illustrated in Fig. 3. At the filtering phase, EMSS filters out inappropriate suppliers from registered suppliers, based on non-technical criteria such as general information, exportation experience, customer portfolio, etc. Non-technical information is usually expressed as a string type of text. Therefore, a text-based keyword matching method incorporated with a binary search is applied to find out suppliers that meet the non-technical requirements of a buyer. For example, if a buyer wants to find a supplier located near a harbor, EMSS finds out suppliers of which profile shows some related keywords such as 'near harbor' or the names of principal harbor cities. Other suppliers are eliminated from the search space. At the matching phase, EMSS selects some suppliers that meet the technical requirements of a buyer. Because technical requirements are usually described by various terminologies in isolation, their true meanings may not be uniformly interpreted. Thus, EMSS employs an ontology-based method for semantic interpretation of technical requirements. In the final step, i.e., ranking phase, EMSS evaluates capabilities of selected suppliers, based on additional non-technical criteria. Their ranked list is reported to the buyer, and the buyer goes through a negotiation process with the recommended suppliers.

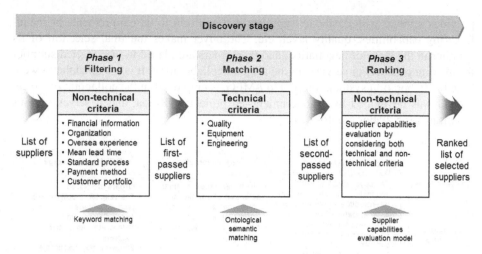

Fig. 3. Supplier discovery process in EMSS

3.3   Ontological Model of Manufacturing Capability

EMSS is equipped with an ontological model for manufacturing capabilities and re-quirements to secure interoperability between buyers and suppliers. Ontology formal-ly represents knowledge as a set of concepts within a domain, and the relationships between those concepts. It can be used to reason about the entities within that domain, and may be used to describe the domain [10]. In this paper, we propose an ontology model for molding industry that is devoted to semantic matching between buyer's technical requirements and supplier's manufacturing capabilities.

Fig. 4 shows the first layer of ontology for molding industry. Hexagon means an association that expresses relationship between topics or subordinates and superiors. Decagon indicates a target like a class or an object in the object-oriented modeling notations. Square means occurrence that contains knowledge or data such as the name of tools, process data, and information of quality certification, and so on.

The proposed ontology model contains technical criteria such as product quality in-formation, equipment names, model numbers, and the type of a mold. It also contains non-technical criteria such as company names, financial information, overseas expe-rience, etc. Currently, we are still under development of ontology for EMSS by using protégé software [11], Manufacturing Service Description Language (MSDL) [12], and web ontology language (OWL) [13] are used for designing and developing ontol-ogy as well as database.

For semantic interpretation of buyers' requirements, we use an inference method based on the proposed ontology model to calculate similarity of suppliers' features (such as capable manufacturing processes, feasible equipment and tools, etc.) with the requirements. For example, a buyer wants to find a supplier who has manufacturing capabilities of milling, drilling and 3D design, and principal features of potential sup-pliers are shown in Fig. 5. In this case, the profile of supplier 2 does not explicitly have the capability of 3D design. However, the capability of supplier 2 can be implicitly inferred because 'mold 2' requires the capability of 3D design. Consequently, supplier 2 is preferred in terms of the buyers' requirements than supplier 1 who does not have milling capability but has limited drilling capability by tool 2.

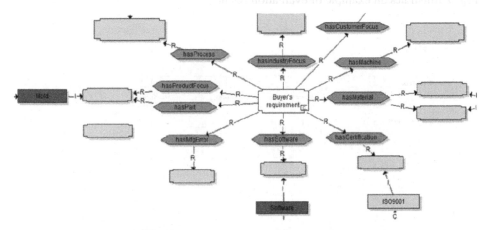

Fig. 4. An ontology for molding industry

Finding suppliers who have {Milling, Drilling, 3D design}

Inference Features	Supplier 1	Supplier 2
Process described in supplier profile	3D	-
Tool described in profile related to such process	Tool2	Tool1
Mold described in profile related to such process	-	Mold2
Total set of capable process	{'3D', half of 'D' by Tool2} = {'3D', $\frac{1}{2}$'D' }	{'M' + 'D' by Tool1, 'D' + '3D' for Mold2} = {'M', 'D', '3D'}
Similarity	50% (=1.5/3)	100%(=3/3)

Supplier 2 is more similar to the company which buyer wants to find

Fig. 5. An exemplary scenario of manufacturability inference

3.4   Manufacturability Assessment

EMSS is equipped with an assessment model of manufacturability to evaluate capabilities of suppliers, selected in the matching phase of supplier discovery process, and make a ranked list of them. In the ranking phase, the selected suppliers are evaluated based on a non-technical criterion that is hierarchically decomposed into following performance criteria; 1) general information, 2) finance, 3) quality, 4) management, 5) product, and 6) strategy and innovation, as shown in Fig. 6. Each performance criterion has various sub-criteria to rate the candidates quantitatively. The sub-criteria are also decomposed into next-tier sub-criteria, if necessary. Even though qualitative criteria such as strategic policies and mission statements are excluded from automatic calculation while rating them, they are evaluated in the measure of "yes" or "no". Fig. 7 illustrates an example of evaluation result.

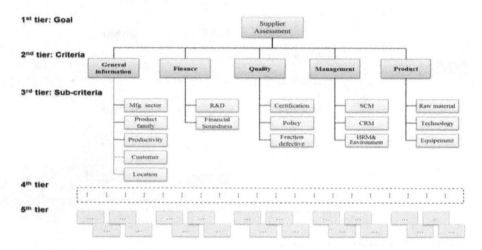

Fig. 6. Hierarchy of assessment criteria

Search Result

Evaluation Result (G:0.2, F:0.2, Q:0.2, M:0.2, P:0.2)

Group	Number of companies	Company name	Location
1st Group	3	BuminMold	Ulsan
		Daeil Mold	Busan
		Daesung Mold Co.	Busan
2nd Group	3	Gangil Mold	Busan
		Hankuk Mold	Ulsan
		Kukyoung Mold	Ansan

Number of Found Suppliers : 24

	Adjust weights if necessary					
	Service & Customers	Facilities & Human Resource	Quality Assurance	Contact & Delivery	Financial Status	Total Score
Weight	0.2	0.2	0.2	0.2	0.2	1.0

* Change Weight Value before RUN

Run

Fig. 7. Supplier evaluation module in EMSS

4   Collaborative Business Model

Fig. 8 shows an overall collaborative business model for EMSS-based supply chain. EMSS provides buyers with collaboration services to discover and evaluate outsourcing partners. In addition, some customized services are also provided for buyers and suppliers. EMSS amasses profiles of suppliers and buyers in order to evaluate suppliers' manufacturability to meet buyer's requirements. Based on the profiles, EMSS provides customized services such as introducing of a language translator, a shipping agency, or a banking agency, etc.

EMSS is required to provide an interface service to *i*-MFG for both buyers and suppliers. The buyers cooperate with selected suppliers via *i*-MFG. In addition, EMSS is required to cooperate with trade agencies (either public or private) in order to offer extensive information on various business opportunities.

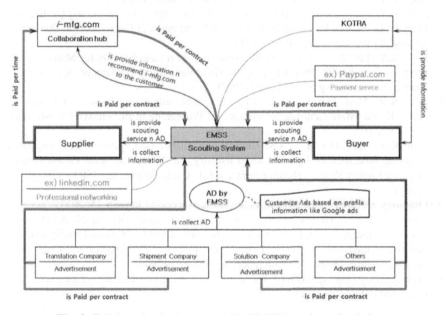

Fig. 8. Collaborative business model in EMSS-based supply chain

5   Conclusion

EMSS is a web-based collaboration system that implements an e-marketplace for manufacturing capabilities and provides discovery and evaluation services of outsourcing partners. Eventually, EMSS supports systematic construction of supply chains in collaboration with *i*-MFG system. In this paper, overall framework for supply chain formation based on EMSS has been presented. EMSS secures interoperability by means of an ontological model for technical descriptions, and it provides an evaluation mechanism for manufacturing capabilities based on non-technical criteria. Currently, EMSS is under development for Korean molding industry.

Acknowledgements. This research is supported by the *i*-Manufacturing projects funded by the Ministry of Knowledge Economy (MKE) of Korea. The authors would like to thank for their support.

References

1. Korea Trade Commission: Survey of the competitiveness of mold industry, annual report (2008)
2. Javalgi, R.R., Dixit, A., Scherer, R.F.: Outsourcing to emerging markets: theoretical perspectives and policy implications. Journal of International Management 15(2), 156–168 (2009)
3. Alibaba.com, http://www.alibaba.com/ (accessed March 30, 2013)
4. EC21, http://kr.ec21.com/ (accessed March 30, 2013)
5. Mfg.com, http://www.mfg.com/ (accessed March 30, 2013)
6. Ryu, K.Y., Lee, S.S., Choi, H.J.: Toward e-Manufacturing by Integrating On-line and Offline Collaboration. In: Proceeding of the 36th International Conference on Computers and Industrial Engineering, pp. 4567–4577 (2006)
7. Ryu, K.Y., Lee, S.S., Choi, H.J.: Strategies based on Collaboration for Manufacturing Innovation in Korea. In: Proceeding of the 37th International Conference on Computers and Industrial Engineering, pp. 954–960 (2007)
8. Ryu, K.Y., Shin, J.H., Lee, S.S., Choi, H.J.: i-Manufacturing Project for Collaboration-based Korean Manufacturing Innovation. In: Proceeding of the PICMET Conference, pp. 253–258 (2008)
9. Ryu, K.Y., Mok, H.S., Lee, S.S., Choi, H.J.: Collaboration Systems facilitating Remanufacturing Processes for Injection Mold Industry. In: Proceeding of the Global Conference on Sustainability Product Development and Life Cycle Engineering (SRM VI), pp. 59–163 (2008)
10. Ontology, http://www.wikipedia.com/ (accessed January 15, 2013)
11. Protégé, http://protege.stanford.edu/ (accessed October 24, 2011)
12. Ameri, F., Dutta, D.: An Upper Ontology for Manufacturing Service Description. In: Proceeding of International Design Engineering Technical Conferences and Computers and Information in Engineering Conference, pp. 651–661 (2006)
13. Web ontology language (OWL), http://www.w3.org/TR/owl-features/ (accessed October 24, 2011)

Use Case Analysis for Standard Manufacturing Service Capability Model

Yunsu Lee, Boonserm (Serm) Kulvatunyou, Marko Vujasinovic, and Nenad Ivezic

Systems Integration Division, NIST, Gaithersburg, USA
{yun-su.lee,serm,marko.vujasinovic,nivezic}@nist.gov

Abstract. Manufacturing enterprises are becoming globally distributed production systems. Rigid supply chains are giving way to dynamic supply networks that are cost-efficient and can respond to change quickly. A key factor in the formation of dynamic supply networks is the communication of manufacturing capabilities – both production capabilities and information processing capabilities. These are collectively referred to as manufacturing service capability (MSC) information. Presently, MSC information is provided using many different, proprietary terminologies and representations. The lack of a standard model impedes communications of MSC information. We propose the development of a standard MSC model to enhance the MSC information communications. This paper motives such development by presenting a use case analysis that illustrates the current and a desirable future state of MSC information communication. The future state, which relies on a standard MSC model can advance the current practice and allow precise and computer-interpretable representation of MSC information.

Keywords: manufacturing service, manufacturing service capability, dynamic supply chain.

1   Introduction

Accurate information about manufacturing capabilities is essential when forming a manufacturing supply network. Key supplier capability factors are production processes, quality, capacity, cost, and digital information processing ability. These are collectively referred to as manufacturing service capability (MSC) information. Manufacturing service capability (MSC) information must be accurate and easily accessible to the supply chain. Multiple manufacturing communities and enterprises have developed proprietary MSC models. These models differ semantically, structurally, and representationally – they have different taxonomies for categorizing manufacturing services, different representations for expressing production requirements. In addition, the models still rely largely on unstructured data. Therefore, there are challenges in today's industry practices to assemble a manufacturing supply chain. For instance, the current means of matching a customer's requirements to a supplier's capabilities is largely manual and inefficient. Supply chain data are transformed manually throughout the supply chain. In many cases the manufacturing software

V. Prabhu, M. Taisch, and D. Kiritsis (Eds.): APMS 2013, Part I, IFIP AICT 414, pp. 361–369, 2013.
© IFIP International Federation for Information Processing 2013

applications are incompatible between the sender and receiver. This can cause data errors and data quality to deteriorate as data are being passed to lower tier suppliers. These situations ultimately impede effective sourcing and can lead to production issues.

The focus of our work is to enhance communication of MSC information carried in the form of MSC description instantiated from a standard MSC model. MSC descriptions may be carried in electronic documents as manufacturing requirements (e.g., RFQ - Request for Quotation) or may be exposed on suppliers' web sites and web-based information-sharing portals as supplier's manufacturing capabilities.

This paper proposes the development of a standard MSC model by presenting a use case analysis that illustrates the current and a desirable, standard-based future state of MSC information communication. The use case scenario provides context for the standard MSC model information requirements. The rest of the paper is structured as follows. In section 2, we provide a RFQ use-case scenario illustrating MSC information that needs to be communicated between a manufacturing customer (customer, for short) and suppliers. In section 3, we analyze the current state where MSC information is communicated using proprietary MSC models and descriptions; and illustrate the desirable future state. Due to space limitation and for simplicity, these proprietary and standard models are illustrated as data elements in tabular form, while the actual standard model is expected to be represented in a formal representation language. We then describe related work in section 4. Finally we provide conclusions and future plans which include developing an MSC model evolution framework and tools as well as working with industry to develop a standard model.

2   Request for Quote Use Case Scenario

In this scenario, a customer needs a supplier to produce a custom bearing with specific requirements. Below, two ways in which MSC information (in this case, the manufacturing requirements) can be communicated are shown using *product-centric* or *process-centric* MSC descriptions for a custom bearings manufacturing RFQ.

Product-Centric MSC description

- Bearing Type: Spherical
- Order quantity: 1,000
- Delivery date: Dec 31, 2012
- Application: Military
- Metric: Inch
- Lubrication port: Required
- Sealed: No
- Bore diameter: 15 cm
- Outer diameter: 21.875 cm
- Width: 11.875 cm
- Housing width: 10.3125 cm
- Basic dynamic load rating: 17630 kg
- Basic static load rating: 530612 kg
- Ball material - Alloy steel, heat treated, hard chrome plated.
- Race material - Stainless steel, heat treated

Process-Centric MSC description

- Order quantity: 1,000
- Stock shape: Tubes or Round stock
- Material: Alloy steel
- Industry: Military
- Required manufacturing processes
  - o Turning
    - − Outside Diameter: 21.875 cm
    - − Diametric tolerance: 0.125 mm
    - − Concentricity: 0.025 mm
  - o Process annealing to 260 °C
  - o Grinding
    - − Surface finish: 12 RA
    - − Outside diameter: 21.875 cm
    - − Inside diameter: 15 cm
  - o File format: CATIA version 4

A product-centric MSC description conveys manufacturing requirements via required product design features and functional properties such as *Bearing Type*, *Lubrication port*, and *Sealed*. On the other hand, the process-centric MSC description conveys manufacturing requirements in terms of process capabilities required to produce a product. Process-centric MSC descriptions may be expressed with process-oriented information, resource-oriented information, or combination of the two. The process capabilities include manufacturing process capabilities and information processing capabilities. The process-centric description using process-oriented information describes information in terms of particular manufacturing processes, such as CNC (Computer Numerical Control) machining, EDM (Electric discharge machining); and software functions, such as support for CAD (Computer-Aided Design) file formats or mechanical or design analysis. The process-centric description using resource-oriented information, on the other hand, describes information in terms of available resources including machines, tools, and software (e.g., 3-axis Vertical CNC machining center, specific CAD System).

3 Current and Future State Analyses of Communication via MSC Descriptions

This section illustrates the current and desired state of communicating MSC descriptions using the custom bearings example.

3.1 Product-Centric MSC Models

The proprietary MSC models, *m1*, *m2*, and *m3*, shown below illustrate current product-centric MSC models that are used by suppliers to create their MSC descriptions. The custom bearing customer uses these models and descriptions to communicate MSC information – in this case matching manufacturing requirements (from the customer) with capabilities (from suppliers). Below, three proprietary product-centric MSC models for custom bearing and respective properties from the custom bearing manufacturers are analyzed. These three models are respectively based on a proprietary RFQ form on a supplier web site, a proprietary product catalog, and a search form from a supplier search portal.

The *m1* proprietary MSC model uses a natural language description of the required functions (a lot of data fields have string data types) and proprietary characterization of desired performances and data based on proprietary representation of geometric schematics (of product model).

The *m2* proprietary MSC model uses proprietary material and part classifications (i.e., proprietary code lists) and proprietary characterization of desired performances. The model *m2* is more limited than the model *m1*. A number of design features and functionalities in the manufacturing requirements cannot be captured using this *m2* model. However, some requirements, such as the *Sealed* and *Application* properties, which could not be represented with the model *m1*, are representable with the model *m2*. These properties are used as part of the customer requirements.

The last proprietary MSC model, *m3*, uses proprietary part classification, proprietary characterization of desired performances, and ad hoc classification of material and functional features using proprietary code lists. This model has also a number of issues: it cannot capture all the manufacturing requirements from our example; properties are semantically ambiguous e.g., *Load Capacity* property does not differentiate between *Basic **Dynamic** Load Rating* and *Basic **Static** Load Rating*; dimensional properties such as *Bore Diameter* and *Outside Diameter* are specified in data value ranges (conveyed via code lists) rather than as precise numeric values; there may be differences in concepts based on the terminology such as *Length through Bore* vs. *Width*.

Product-centric MSC model derived from RFQ Form (*m1*)	Product-centric MSC model derived from Product Catalog (*m2*)	Product-centric MSC model derived from Search Form (*m3*)
· Application: code list	· Inner Ring Material: code list	· Design units: code list
· Quantities to quote: number	· Outer Ring Material: code list	· Bore diameter: code list
· Usage: string	· Maintenance Free: boolean	· Length through Bore: code list
· Grooved for lubrication / Plain: code	· Sealed: boolean	· Outside diameter: code list
· B (Bore diameter): number	· Angle of misalignment: number	· Maximum Angular Misalignment: code list
· D (Outside diameter): number	· Applications: code list	· Load capacity: code list
· W (Width): number	· Quantity: number	· Material: code list
· H (Housing width): number		· Self-lubricating: boolean
· a (Misalignment angle): number		· Lubrication Port: boolean
· Material for Ball: string		· Corrosion Resistant: boolean
· Material for Race: string		· Suitable for Rotating Shaft: boolean
· Material for Liner: string		
· Type of Bearing Loads: string		
· Radial Bearing Load: number		
· Axial Bearing Load: number		
· Operating Temperature: number		
· Corrosion: string		
· Washdown: string		

The properties captured in those three presented proprietary product-centric MSC models illustrate the heterogeneities and limitations of how bearing features and functions are communicated. A customer having MSC description of the custom bearing described in section 2 would need to convert his/her MSC description to these various manufacturer MSC information models, if at all possible, to engage in an RFQ transaction and supply chain assembly with potential suppliers. Such communication limitation prevents customers from getting to suppliers with the right capability at the right time with the right effort.

A future state of enhanced MSC information communication for custom bearings can be enabled by a standard product-centric MSC model. Table 1 shows a possible standard MSC model constructed by harmonizing properties from the three analyzed proprietary product-centric MSC models. In this case, free-form text field and proprietary code lists are replaced with standard code lists that may be supplemented by respective ontologies. The proposed model is semantically rich and can cover more bearing characteristics than those necessary to describe the example manufacturing requirements. That is, *<no requirement>* in Table 1 denotes properties, identified in the analyzed proprietary product-centric MSC models, but not required in the example manufacturing requirements. This means the possible standard model is richer in semantics and can support more variations of bearing specifications. Only with a standard MSC model, the customer can effectively communicate with a large pool of suppliers using shared concepts and semantics and be able to get to the right supplier with the right capability at the right time and effort.

Table 1. Possible data elements for standard product-centric MSC model

Property Group	Property: Data Type	Customer Requirement Map (from the Product-Centric MSC description)
Production	Quantity: number	Order quantity
	Expected delivery date: date	Delivery date
Dimension	Design units: standard code list	Metric
	Bore diameter: number	Bore diameter
	Length through Bore: number	Width
	Outside diameter: number	Outer diameter
	Housing diameter: number	Housing width
Performance specification	Type of Bearing Loads: standard code list	Dynamic load or Static load
	Radial Bearing Load: number	Dynamic load or Static load value
	Axial Bearing Load: number	*<no requirement>*
	Maximum Angular Misalignment: number	*<no requirement>*
Material	Ball: standard code list	Ball material
	Race: standard code list	Race material
	Liner: standard code list	*<no requirement>*
Application	Type: standard code list	*<no requirement>*
	Application area: standard code list	Application
	Usage: string	Usage
	Operating temperature: number	*<no requirement>*
Features	Self-lubricating: boolean	*<no requirement>*
	Lubrication Port: boolean	Lubrication port
	Corrosion Resistant: boolean	*<no requirement>*
	Suitable for Rotating Shaft: boolean	*<no requirement>*
	Suitable for Washdown: boolean	*<no requirement>*
	Maintenance-free: boolean	*<no requirement>*
	Sealed: boolean	Sealed

3.2   Process-Centric MSC Models

Below, three current proprietary process-centric MSC models, *m4*, *m5*, and *m6*, from three custom bearing manufacturers are shown. The first two are based on proprietary MSC descriptions from web sites of two suppliers. The other is based on a search form of a supplier information sharing portal. The first two use combination of process-oriented and resource-oriented information while the other uses only process-oriented information.

In *m4*, a number of manufacturing requirements cannot be specified, including *Order quantity*, *Stock shape*, *Concentricity tolerance*, and *Process annealing temperature*.

As with *m4*, the second proprietary MSC model, *m5*, cannot support a number of manufacturing requirements including *Order quantity*, *Stock shape*, *Surface grinding finish tolerance*, and *Process annealing temperature requirement*. Furthermore, the *annealing process* requirement can only be specified using a more generic concept, the *heat treatment* process.

The last proprietary MSC model, m6, also cannot support a number of manufacturing requirements, including *Order quantity*, *Stock shape*, *Surface grinding finish tolerance*, *Process annealing temperature* and *File format*.

Process-centric MSC model derived from Supplier profile 1 (m4)	Process-centric MSC model derived from Supplier profile 2 (m5)	Process-centric MSC data-set model derived from Search form (m6)
· Machining Processes: proprietary code list	· Machining Processes: proprietary code list	· Capabilities: proprietary code list
· Equipment: proprietary code list	· Equipment: proprietary code list	· Number of Axes: proprietary code list
· Machinery Axis: number	· Equipment Capabilities: proprietary code list	· Specialty Machining: proprietary code list
· Fixturing: proprietary code list	· Machinery Axis: number	· Diameter Capacity: proprietary code list
· Maximum Part Diameter (Turning): number with constraint	· Fixturing: proprietary code list	· Length Capacity: proprietary code list
· Maximum Part Length (Turning): number with constraint	· CNC Turned Part Diameter: number	· Micro Machining: boolean
· Maximum Bar Feed Diameter Capacity (Turning): number	· CNC Turned Part Length: number	· Materials: proprietary code list
· Maximum Swing (Turning): number with constraint	· CNC Milled Part Length: number	· Secondary Services Offered: proprietary code list
· Maximum Part Size (CNC Milling, Vertical): formatted string	· CNC Milled Part Width: number	· Additional Services: proprietary code list
· Industries: proprietary code list	· CNC Milled Part Height: number	· Location: proprietary code list
· Industry Standards: proprietary code list	· Straightness : number	
· Efficiency: proprietary code list	· Diameter Tolerances (out/in) : number	
· File Formats: proprietary code list	· Concentricity : number	
· Maximum Part Size (CNC Milling, Horizontal): formatted string	· Length Tolerances: number	
· Production Tolerances (+/-): number with constraint	· Intended applications: proprietary code list	
· CNC Products Type: proprietary code list	· Materials (Metals) : proprietary code list	
· Materials: proprietary code list	· Materials (Plastic Polymers) : proprietary code list	
· In House Additional Services: proprietary code list	· Secondary Services: proprietary code list	
· Additional Services: proprietary code list	· Production Volume: proprietary code list	
· Inspection: proprietary code list	· Industries Served: proprietary code list	
· Quality: proprietary code list	· Industry Standards: proprietary code list	
· Inventory Control: proprietary code list	· Lead Times Available: proprietary code list	
· Production Volume: proprietary code list		

A future state of enhanced MSC information communication for custom bearing manufacturing can be enabled by a standard process-centric MSC model. Table 2 shows a possible standard MSC model, which extends a merge of a subset of the properties defined in the three proprietary process-centric MSC models. The standard MSC model would be formal and structured specifications of required manufacturing capabilities and process requirements using shared concepts and semantics. The model is semantically rich and can cover more manufacturing characteristics than those necessary to describe the manufacturing requirements for our custom bearings example. Proprietary code lists are replaced with standard code lists that may be supplemented by respective ontologies. It should be noted <no requirement> signifies the same meaning as that in Table 1.

Table 2. Possible data elements for standard process-centric MSC model

Property: Data Type	Customer Requirement Map (from the Process-Centric MSC description)
Machining process: standard code list	Turning , Grinding
Specialty machining process: standard code list	<no requirement>
Equipment: standard code list	<no requirement>
Machinery axis: number (2 – 9)	<no requirement>
Fixturing: standard code list	<no requirement>
Turning max part diameter: number	21.875 cm
Turning max part length: number	<no requirement>
Turning max bar feed diameter: number	<no requirement>
Turning Swing: number	<no requirement>
Milling max part length: number	<no requirement>
Milling max part width: number	<no requirement>
Milling part height: number	<no requirement>
Micro machining: number	<no requirement>
Straightness: number	<no requirement>
Diameter tolerances: number	0.125 mm
Concentricity: number	0.025 mm
Length tolerances: number	<no requirement>
Materials: standard code list	Alloy Steel, Stainless Steel
Secondary services: complex structure	Heat treating to 260 °C
Quality control capabilities: standard code list	<no requirement>
Inventory control capabilities: standard code list	<no requirement>
Lead time capabilities: standard code list	<no requirement>
Inspection capabilities: standard code list	<no requirement>
Production volume: standard code list	Medium
Industries served: standard code list	Military
Product focus: standard code list	Bearing
Industry standards: standard code list	<no requirement>
File formats accepted: standard code list	Catia version 4
Location: standard code list	<no requirement>

4   Related Work

There are efforts towards standardization of MSC model and its semantic-enhancement. Ameri and Dutta [1] have built Manufacturing Service OWL (Web Ontology Language) ontology to provide for shared semantics of the process-centric MSC information. Jang et al. [7] developed similar OWL-based manufacturing service ontology, however, in product-centric way using machining features. A resource model developed by Vichare et al. [8] can be a basis for shared semantics of the resource-oriented process-centric MSC information. Ontology for representing fixture design knowledge in Ameri and Summers [2] can also provide a basis for resource-oriented MSC information of fixtures. In addition to these ontology-based efforts, other related standardization efforts include ISO 14649 (STEP-NC) [5] standard for machining features, ISO 15331 [6] standard for representing machining resources, ISO 13399 [4] standard for representing cutting tool information, and ASME B5.59-2 [3] standard for describing the performance and capabilities of milling and turning machines.

5   Conclusion and Future Work

This paper highlights the inefficiency in communication of MSC information via MSC descriptions between suppliers and manufacturers. Communicating MSC information is important for enabling supply chain agility. The lack of effective standards is a barrier to improving MSC information communication. As the first stage in developing a standard, this paper provided an illustrative use case analysis of the current and future communications of MSC information via respective MSC models. MSC descriptions are characterized into product- and process-centric MSC descriptions, and the process-centric MSC descriptions may be specified with resource- and/or process-oriented information. The MSC descriptions conforming to an advanced and standardized MSC model should significantly enhance current practice in communicating requirements and capabilities for manufacturing services. Our immediate future work will include more comprehensive MSC information requirements analysis, followed by creating and validating the target standard MSC model that enables semantically precise representation of product- and process-centric MSC descriptions.

6   Disclaimer

Certain commercial software products are identified in this paper. These products were used only for demonstration purposes. This use does not imply approval or endorsement by NIST, nor does it imply these products are necessarily the best available for the purpose.

References

1. Ameri, F., Dutta, D.: An Upper Ontology for Manufacturing Service Description. In: ASME Conference Proceeding 2006, p. 651 (2006), doi:10.1115/DETC2006-99600
2. Ameri, F., Summers, J.D.: An ontology for representation of fixture design knowledge. Computer Aided Design and Applications 5, 601–611 (2008)
3. ASME B5.59-2. Information technology for machine tools - part 2: Data specification for properties of machine tools for milling and turning, draft (2005)
4. ISO 13399-1 Cutting tool data representation and exchange - part 1: Overview, fundamental principles and general information model (2006)
5. ISO 14649-1 Industrial automation systems and integration - physical device con-trol - data model for computerized numerical controllers, part 1: Overview and fundamental principles (2002)
6. ISO 15531-1 Industrial automation systems and integration - industrial manufac-turing management data – part 1: General overview (2003)
7. Jang, J., Jeong, B., Kulvatunyou, B.S., Chang, J., Cho, H.: Discovering and Integrating Distributed Manufacturing Services with Semantic Manufacturing Capability Profiles. International Journal of Computer-Integrated Manufacturing 21(6), 631–646 (2008)
8. Vichare, P., Nassehi, A., Kumar, S., Newman, S.: A Unified Manufacturing Resource Model for Representation of CNC Machining Systems. In: 18th International Conference on Flexible Automation and Intelligent Manufacturing (FAIM), Skövde, June 06-July 02 (2008)

Governing and Managing Customer-Initiated Engineering Change: An In-Depth Case Study of a Global Industrial Supplier

Anita Friis Sommer, Simon Haahr Storbjerg,
Iskra Dukovska-Popovska, and Kenn Steger-Jensen

Institute for Mechanical Engineering and Production, Aalborg University, Denmark
(sommer,shs,iskra,kenn)@m-tech.aau.dk

Abstract. Engineering change management is managing an alteration made to the technical system and/or its related value chain processes and documentation that have already been released during the product and process design process. The change can either emerge during the process or be initiated internally or externally by for instance customers. Managing initiated engineering changes is a vital source for improving product performance and radically reducing change costs. Customer-initiated engineering change is an area growing in importance decreasing product life cycles and increasing demand for customisation. Through an in-depth case study, this paper investigates which process and what governance setup is appropriate to manage customer initiated engineering changes, referred to as request management. The paper includes a proposal for a request management framework and a task-based iterative process model based on existing engineering change management theory and case study findings.

Keywords: Engineering change management, customer-initiated change management, request management, case study.

1 Introduction

Shortening product life cycles and increasing customer demands are inevitable parts of the on-going change in today's industrial markets [1]. Changes in customer products creates in many cases a need for change in supplier products due to product interdependencies [2]. Consequently suppliers now face an increasing need to develop a request management process to handle the increasing amount of external requests for product changes [2]. Changes to existing products may encompass all levels of innovation from incremental changes to radical innovation [3, 4]. Engineering Change Management (ECM) is a research area that has gained increased attention during recent years [4]. In its initial scope, ECM was mainly viewed as a process for managing design oscillations in interdependent product parts during new product development [5]. Now the scope has been broadened, and ECM is considered relevant in all stages of the product life cycle [6, 7]. Research topics of increasing interest within ECM include among others, managing customer-initiated engineering change

V. Prabhu, M. Taisch, and D. Kiritsis (Eds.): APMS 2013, Part I, IFIP AICT 414, pp. 370–382, 2013.

[8]. Researchers are still to unfold and understand the customer-initiated ECM process and enabling processes including governance mechanisms, and how this ECM process diverts from internally initiated ECM [2]. For instance, customer-initiated ECM is expected to include other challenges than internally initiated ECM related to for instance customer-supplier interaction, customer relationship management, impact analysis, portfolio management, and cross-organizational knowledge management. In this paper, we have chosen to use the term request management for customer-initiated ECM. The aim of this research is to investigate which ECM process and process governance approach is appropriate for request management. The paper is structured as follows: Firstly, the theoretical background is introduced including ECM, ECM governance, and customer-initiated ECM. Secondly, the research method is presented including description of the case company, which is used for an in-depth investigation. Finally, the results are presented and analyzed, providing a proposal for a request management framework, followed by a brief discussion and a conclusion.

2   Theoretical Background

This section will provide the theoretical background. First the research area of ECM is introduced followed by a presentation of existing research on customer-initiated change management. Based on the literature we propose a framework for request management, which is used in the following method and analysis.

2.1   Engineering Changes

The phenomenon of engineering change has been a topic for research in several years. One of the earliest contributions having engineering change as the primary topic is noted to be Dale in 1982 [9] [10]. Since his study, several other contributions have been given and the research on engineering change has expanded into several different focus areas. Making all design decisions right the first time is clearly an illusion; designing is an iterative process meaning that changes to existing design decisions are inevitable [5]. Furthermore, for the majority of manufacturing companies, design is not a single event for a single technical system, but a repetitive activity for portfolios or families of products and services introducing both simultaneous variants and generational variants. In many cases design does not begin with a blank sheet, but originates from already existing design. As a collective name, these changes have been termed "engineering changes" [4]. Based on case studies several definitions have been given in literature, the definition in closest to the authors experience is brought by Jarratt, Eckert, Caldwell and Clarkson [4]: "An engineering change is an alteration made to parts, drawings or software that has already been released during the product design process, regardless of the scale of the change." This paper takes an even broader perspective, engineering change is thus defined as; 'an alteration made to the technical system and/or its related value chain processes and documentation that has already been released during the product and process design process'.

One of the fundamental characteristics of a system is that the parts that make up the system are interrelated [11]. In products these relations can take on many forms, e.g. mechanical, electrical, thermal etc. and are most often difficult to foresee, especially in complex systems [5]. Given these relations, making changes to existing design i.e. technical systems is very seldom having isolated effects. As a consequence introducing an engineering change most often cause several other changes. This nature of change is highlighted by several, and framed in the term change propagation, which refers to the process by which an engineering change to parts of a product results in one or more additional engineering changes to other parts of the products [12]. In addition to the complex cause-effect patterns of introducing engineering changes to technical systems, the management of engineering changes involves a complex web of stakeholders. The importance of doing thorough ECM is thus only further underlined when the organizational perspective is considered. Fricke, Gebhard, Negele and Igenbergs [6] also states straight-forwardly that ultimately two alternatives exist without an adequate ECM: to die of changes, or to miss the chance of successful products.

Concerning the source of the engineering change, two fundamental types of changes exists; changes that have to be avoided, e.g. changes which are consequences of bad design decisions or propagation effects, and changes which are an opportunity for the company e.g. changes that facilitate the continuous innovation [6]. These two types of changes are in literature most often referred to as emergent changes and initiated changes. Eckert, Clarkson and Zanker [8] define these two types as: *Emergent changes* - changes that are caused by the state of the design, where problems occurring across the whole design and throughout the product life cycle can lead to changes. *Initiated changes* - changes arising from an outside source, typically a new requirement from customers, certification bodies, or initiated by the manufacturer. This paper supports the perspective that engineering changes occur throughout the entire product life cycle [7], and that engineering changes can range from minor changes to more complex changes affecting several modules and systems [4]. Concerning the object of change, the types of engineering changes depends on the contextual scope and setup of ECM, and thus several different types of ECM exist. It is the authors' experience that most often the scope of ECM covers changes to primary design documentation, e.g. drawings, 3D-models, Bill of Materials (BOMs) and system changes, e.g. ERP or MRP master data. In some firms engineering changes also encompass changes in process documentation, e.g. work instructions, and routings, and secondary design documentation, as e.g. design failure mode analysis and design verification plans.

2.2   Managing Engineering Change Processes

As highlighted by Jarratt, Eckert, Caldwell and Clarkson [4] different authors have proposed distinct engineering change processes. They divide the process into different numbers of phases. For example, Dale [9] proposes a formal process split into two phases, whereas Maull, Hughes and Bennett [13] suggests a process made up of five parts. Despite the different types of engineering changes, the literature has so far only briefly addressed different types of ECM processes. Generally speaking, two fundamental types of ECM processes are described in literature, a formal and linear process and an informal and more ad-hoc approach. A highly central element of the ECM process is ensuring a proper evaluation of the proposed change based on impact analysis., e.g. Huang and Mak [10] propose that evaluating changes quickly as one of 13 guidelines for efficient ECM, similarly Eckert, Clarkson and Zanker [8] conclude that successful ECM requires knowledge on the consequences of a change on product quality, cost, and time to market. Change evaluation and impact analysis is also addressed as a separate theme in several other publications [12, 14, 15]. A topic not addressed in literature is how to ensure that proper impact assessment is being done when a more iterative change process is needed as in the change process described in the case study of this paper. In existing literature several governance mechanisms are described including governance structures and enabling processes. The term business process governance refers to the direction, coordination, and control of individuals, groups, or organizations that are at least to some extent autonomous: that is, not directly subject to the same hierarchical authority [16]. Business process governance encompasses a variety of mechanisms including laws, rules and personal mechanisms administered by individuals [16]. These mechanisms are considered to be at least as important as managing the ECM process itself, since the ECM process spans both functional and organizational boundaries. The identified ECM governance mechanisms are divided according to the four management aspects technology, organization, people and strategy, introduced by [17], and enabling management processes:

- *Technological aspects* - ECM systems, Product Data Management (PDM) systems, and CAD/CAM systems [2, 10, 18]
- *Organizational aspects* - Decision making structure and processes, ECM roles and responsibilities [8, 10, 19]
- *People aspects* - Skills and competencies, team working, training, learning [2, 8, 20]
- *Strategic aspects* - ECM strategy [4, 6]
- *Enabling management processes* - Portfolio management, resource management, knowledge management, visual management, performance management [4, 20, 21]

2.3   Customer-Initiated Engineering Change

Customer-initiated engineering changes are regarded to be a value adding activity [2]. Based on multiple case studies Wasmer, Staub and Vroom [2] develop an information system solution for customer-initiated ECM, with the purpose of enabling companies to accept more customer requests within the same financial limitations. The goal of an ECM information system is to make the process more dynamic by facilitating cross-organizational interaction [2]. The information system functions as a governance structure increasing transparency of the process and facilitating communication and knowledge sharing. To the authors' knowledge, this is the first research study on governance mechanisms of customer-initiated engineering change, and so far no overview of governance aspects within this area exists.

The information system developed by Wasmer, Staub and Vroom [2] is successfully implemented and tested, and they report positive results including process lead-time improvements by 20-40%. In this paper, customer-initiated ECM is termed request management, since this type of ECM revolves around management of a customer request for engineering change. Based on the review of existing literature, a systemic process framework for request management is proposed, which is presented in figure 1. The framework includes the ECM process, process governance, and specifies process characteristics of request management.

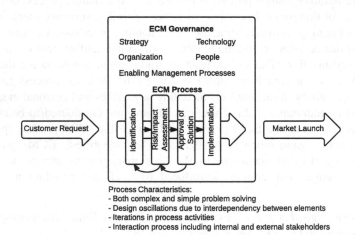

Fig. 1. Systemic Process Framework for Request Management inspired by existing ECM research

3   Method

This research includes an in-depth case study, which is conducted using design science research [22]. Design science research is a design-oriented, prescriptive research approach [23]. The purpose of design science is to: *"... develop knowledge that the professionals of the discipline in question can use to design solution for their field problems"*[24]. At its core, design science is directed toward understanding and improving the search among potential components in order to construct an artifact that is intended to solve a problem [25, 26]. Design science research is sometimes called "Improvement Research" and this designation emphasizes the problem-solving/performance-improving nature of the activity [27]. *Suggestions* for a problem solution are abductively drawn from the existing knowledge/theory base for the problem area [27, 28]. Design science can be viewed as a research paradigm, revolving around development and implementation of artefacts [29, 30]. The method includes elements of abductive reasoning and deductive reasoning, and consists of five iterative phases; awareness of problem, suggestion, development, evaluation, conclusion [31]. During the first two phases the problem is realized and a suggestion for solution is made through abduction. Operations management is essentially a practical field dealing with practical problems [23, 32], and like a large number of researchers we assume the role of problem solver, actively seeking to develop solutions, not merely explanations. The case includes a three-year collaboration project from 2010 to 2012 (both years included) between the research team and a large industrial manufacturer, here referred to as Alpha. Both parties agree on joint problem solving for the company and it's customers, and it is agreed that all data can be used for scientific purposes, but without publication of the company's name. The objective for the case company is to develop and implement a solution for request management, which can be used in the existing manufacture-to-stock setup.

During the collaboration period, cross-organizational interview studies were made before and after implementation of the solution. In total, 20 formal and more than 30 informal interviews was conducted internally, and additionally formal interviews was conducted with four manufacturing customers. The formal interviews included a semi-structured interview guide. The interviews aimed at identifying the activity flow of the request process, the governance aspects, and understand how coordination and collaboration is conducted in practice. Furthermore, the study aimed at identifying current challenges in the process, and how a future ideal solution could be for the interviewee. Finally, a set of questions was aimed at identifying the current strengths of the process, to develop a nuanced understanding of the process, not simply focusing on problem solving, but also considering the strengths of the existing process. Interviews were analysed using open coding and pattern matching in relation to the request management framework [33, 34]. Information on data handling and documentation was collected through available information in the IT system, which included spread sheets, email threads and data in the customer relationship management system, and analysed in relation to the identified needs of a request management process. Researchers have influenced development and implementation of the solution by communicating results of interview studies and data analysis to involved managers, both recurring to local management and at monthly management board meetings. Relevant research findings were presented, including possible solutions for inspiration. Researchers were active partners in discussions of possible solutions, and advisers on 'state-of-the art' from an academic perspective.

4   Case Description

The case company is a large global supplier within the automation and control industry, and employs more than 30.000 people worldwide. The case study takes place at a business unit specialized in mass-production for industrial manufacturers, which employs around 600 employees and has a turnover on more than 2 mill standard products each year. The business unit has production facilities in China,

Denmark (headquarters), Poland, and the United Kingdom, and more than 230 sales companies, agents and distributors worldwide. The business unit has four main product types: Fluid controls, pressure monitors & controls, temperature monitors & controls, and contactors and motor starters. Each year, the business unit receives around 150-300 customer requests for new products or customer change requests to existing products from their sales offices worldwide. The requests include varying degree of complexity, but in general there are about 60-70% simple change requests, 20-30% large changes to existing products, and 5-10% classified as new products involving both new technology and radical innovation. Previously, the company has managed customer requests ad hoc in the technical service department, which is responsible for process management, including coordination and collaboration across involved functions. Technical service developed a request specification sheet and a stage-gate process model as a first take to manage the request process. Sales employees are advised to fill out the specification sheet, called the Customer Request Sheet (CRS), in the enquiry phase for request evaluation by technical service. Based on the specifications technical service evaluates the business potential, based on their knowledge on expected production costs. If they accept the request, the product is developed by the engineering department and sent to production for pre-production and quality test. Afterwards, the product is set up as a standard product in the system, and awaits the first customer orders before production is initiated.

During the collaboration period, the company sought to improve the success-rate of the process. Their aim of measure is a so-called 'hit-rate', which indicated 'how many of the products developed for market launch are ever sold'. In the beginning of 2010 the hit-rate was a staggering 40%, meaning that customers never ordered 60% of the developed products. During the collaboration period, the company develops an increased understanding of their process, and due to implementation of improvement initiatives both to the process and governance of the process, the hit-rate in the end of 2012 was up to around 75-80%, which was viewed as a grand success. As explained by the production facility manager in Denmark, the goal is not to reach 100% hit-rate, since this might indicate that they do not take enough chances.

5 Results

From an open-systems perspective request management is dependent on a strong governance structure to among others support the process across the internal and external barriers. Here we focus on deducing which governance aspects of request management are additional to governance of internally initiated ECM.

Strategic Governance Aspects - Product and market strategy of the company are identified to be affecting request management, thereby functioning as governance mechanisms. For instance, Alpha's newest market strategy devotes special focus to the water control markets, but excludes locomotive turbines. The direct effect on request management is that customers from the locomotive industries are now categorically rejected, while the amount of requests from water control customers is increasing at a global scale. Similarly the product strategy includes reduction of product variant generation in all areas and especially within the solenoid valve series, which is challenging the request management process that generates variants to the extent that older products are allowed to endure. The different strategies are in the case company found to develop deliberate tensions between strategic management boards. Compared to internally initiated ECM, an important finding from the case is that both product and market strategies not only affects the ECM process, but also has a direct effect on the customer relationship through the request management process. Every time a request is rejected or accepted, following the strategic guidelines, the customer relationship is either enhanced towards a strategic relationship or the Alpha is degraded/maintained as a standard product supplier.

Technological Governance Aspects - The information system functions as the platform of the request management process. The system includes PDM system, CAD/CAM programs, and a process management information system, which in Alpha is a SharePoint solution with shared documents. Compared to internally initiated ECM, request management includes the customer in process iterations. From a knowledge management perspective, the information system should enable knowledge sharing externally and internally. The case shows that in practice, the challenge is to open access to information systems without sharing too much internal information. The company is seeking to implement an information system for controlled external information sharing, but has not yet found a suitable solution. Today, they share product information by sending physical prototypes and drawings back and forth. The initial part of the process, which is part of the sales process, is managed through a SAP Customer Relationship Management (CRM)-system. The ideal solution according to the company, is one information platform to share the entire process, both internally and externally, that includes functionality to share both process and governance related information, while including the ability to manage information access and information sharing across the process.

Organizational Governance Aspects - The organization of Alpha is, like most industrial manufacturers, a functional machine bureaucracy. The request process is managed across functions with shifting and/or shared process ownership through the process activities. The functional setup includes a departmental segregation of competences relevant for the process. Compared to ECM-processes that often have one process owner and a dedicated team, the nature of the request management process generates a need for multiple iterations. The customers have unique domain knowledge about their needs and dependencies to customer products, which makes the iterations both intra- and inter-organizational adding to the complexity compared to internally initiated ECM. Roles and responsibilities include considerations in relation to the customer. The study shows that sales managers are responsible for financial negotiations and relationship management, while engineers and technical employees are in direct contact with customers for joint prototyping and product knowledge sharing. Hence, roles and responsibilities towards the customer differ according to the functions' responsibility area.

People Governance Aspects - Skills and competencies, both concerning domain knowledge and in relation to managing the process, are vital for process performance. Having to do with request management, which most often increases the cultural differences of the involved, enhances the challenge of the people governance aspect. Globally distributed sales offices and customers make culture management an important management skill. For instance, process managers found that they have to be more formal and polite when communicating to Chinese and American sales employees, whereas a more informal tone is used to employees and customers in Scandinavian countries. Additionally to internally initiated ECM is the knowledge transfer from customers to the company, and the company's absorptive capacity in this regard. During process improvement initiatives, the company has increased ECM training on customer related aspects, including customer relationship management, value selling, and collaboration between local sales departments and headquarters.

Enabling Management Processes - Two management processes are identified as enablers, which are customer relationship management and demand chain management. These are an addition to the known ECM enabling processes including knowledge management, ECM portfolio management, resource management and visual management. Knowledge management as an enabling governance mechanism includes buyer-supplier knowledge sharing during the request management process. Request portfolio management includes overview of all requests and analysis of request management at the aggregated level including analysis of customer responses to rejected requests, requested products market performance, and knowledge transfer management. During the improvement period in Alpha, the incoming requests are pooled into similar technology and product type, using project portfolio management methods. Risk and impact assessment benefitted from pooling similar requests in calculating future production costs. For instance, Alpha continuously rejected requests for plastic valves due to a high investment in new production equipment. However, when the requests were pooled, they realized that in total the investment would be reasonable compared with future profitability, and based on the pooled impact analysis, Alpha invested in new production equipment for plastic valves. At the end of 2012, the turnover on plastic vales was still increasing, and the investment proved to be profitable. To manage the portfolio of potential requests, Alpha now uses an opportunity management application in their SAP-CRM system. Thereby, Alpha headquarters gains a global overview of potential requests, which is kept up to date through their local sales offices.

Request Management Processes - The request management process in Alpha includes complex problem solving with a large degree of iterations depending on the complexity of the customer request. In practice, process managers spend a large amount if time bypassing the linear process management model. Iterations to previous phases are part of complex change requests, however the iterations are not documented since the process model does not support back-loops. Thereby the process becomes clouded and it is unclear at what stage the request exactly is, because the model does not provide a visual representation of the iterations. Alphas senior process improvement manager proposes that an iterative process model with a circular design would support process management, however such a model has not yet been implemented in Alpha. Request management processes differs from internally initiated ECM processes by including the customer actively during the process. This study shows that customers in request management interact with employees at every process stage, generating iterations across the process' functional flow. Therefore, request management includes an interaction process revolving around a solution design, most often starting with a CAD/CAM drawing of a prototype and later a physical prototype. Based on the case study findings, a framework for request management has been developed (figure 2), adding the additional aspects to the findings on customer-initiated ECM from existing literature.

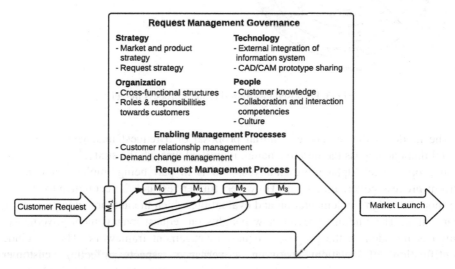

Fig. 2. Request management framework of additional governance and process aspects to internally initiated ECM

6   Discussion and Conclusion

This study initiates with an investigation of which process model and governance structure is appropriate for request management. The findings of a literature review show that an iterative process model should be applied to manage the intra-organizational and inter-organizational iterations. Inspired by ambitions of the case company and the latest research on ECM, an iterative task-based process model is proposed to Alpha. In essence, this model contains both the iterative and linear aspects of request management, while encompassing the process activities or tasks. The model is called 'Develop A Request Task Status (DARTS)', which fits the visual management principles [4, 8] having a logical structure and the goal of being a visual process management support artefact. The DARTS-model is presented in figure 3.

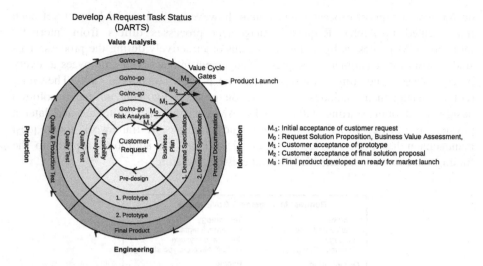

Fig. 3. Proposed task-based request process model

The model is the researchers' initial proposal of a request management process model that encompass the iterative nature identified through the study. The model has been proposed to Alpha representatives, and is in part being implemented in the current process governance setup. However, further research is recommended to test the model through implementation and evaluation, which the authors attempt to do in near future. The findings provide new insights on request management governance, which is included in the proposed request management framework. These include identification of relations between governance aspects affecting customer relationships, yet we still lack a complete overview of the interdependencies between governance and product performance, and further research on this subject is recommended. As for now, we have established the importance of additional customer-related governance aspects for request management compared to internally initiated ECM.

In this study, request management is framed in the context of ECM. However, customers may also request for new product development, thereby being the driver and active participant in the new product development process. This aspect of request management is relevant to consider conjointly with the ECM-process, and research is recommended uniting request management with customer-driven product development. Finally, this research points at information systems as an essential governance structure for request management, and proposed information systems solutions do exist that report of lead time reductions of up to 40% [2]. Hence, further research within information systems for request management is recommended.

References

1. Büyüközkan, G., Arsenyan, J.: Collaborative product development: a literature overview. Production Planning & Control 23, 47–66 (2011)
2. Wasmer, A., Staub, G., Vroom, R.W.: An industry approach to shared, cross-organisational engineering change handling-The road towards standards for product data processing. Computer-Aided Design 43, 533–545 (2011)
3. Tavčar, J., Duhovnik, J.: Engineering change management in individual and mass production. Robotics and Computer-Integrated Manufacturing 21, 205–215 (2005)
4. Jarratt, T.A.W., Eckert, C.M., Caldwell, N.H.M., Clarkson, P.J.: Engineering change: an overview and perspective on the literature. Research in Engineering Design 22, 103–124 (2011)
5. Hubka, V., Eder, W.E.: Theory of technical systems: a total concept theory for engineering design. Springer, Berlin (1988)
6. Fricke, E., Gebhard, B., Negele, H., Igenbergs, E.: Coping with changes: causes, findings, and strategies. Systems Engineering 3, 169–179 (2000)
7. Shankar, P., Morkos, B., Summers, J.D.: Reasons for change propagation: a case study in an automotive OEM. Research in Engineering Design, 1–13 (2012)
8. Eckert, C., Clarkson, P.J., Zanker, W.: Change and customisation in complex engineering domains. Research in Engineering Design 15, 1–21 (2004)
9. Dale, B.G.: The management of engineering change procedure. Engineering Management International 1, 201–208 (1982)
10. Huang, G.Q., Mak, K.L.: Current practices of engineering change management in UK manufacturing industries. International Journal of Operations & Production Management 19, 21–37 (1999)
11. Von Bertalanffy, L.: General system theory: Foundations, development, applications. George Braziller, New York (1968)
12. Koh, E.C.Y., Caldwell, N.H.M., Clarkson, P.J.: A method to assess the effects of engineering change propagation. Research in Engineering Design, 1–23 (2012)
13. Maull, R., Hughes, D., Bennett, J.: The role of the bill-of-materials as a CAD/CAPM interface and the key importance of engineering change control. Computing & Control Engineering Journal 3, 63–70 (1992)
14. Aurich, J., Rößing, M.: Engineering change impact analysis in production using VR. Digital Enterprise Technology, 75–82 (2007)
15. Ahmad, N., Wynn, D.C., Clarkson, P.J.: Change impact on a product and its redesign process: a tool for knowledge capture and reuse. Research in Engineering Design, 1–26 (2012)
16. Markus, M.L., Jacobson, D.D.: Business process governance. In: Handbook on Business Process Management 2, pp. 201–222. Springer (2010)
17. Leavitt, H.J.: Applied organizational change in industry: Structural, technological and humanistic approaches. In: March, J.G. (ed.) Handbook of Organizations, Rand McNally, Chicago (1965)
18. Jarratt, T., Eckert, C., Clarkson, P.J.: Development of a product model to support engineering change management. In: Proceedings of the TCME, pp. 331–344 (2004)
19. Pikosz, P., Malmqvist, J.: A comparative study of engineering change management in three Swedish engineering companies. In: Proceedings of Design Engineering Technical Conference, Atlanta, vol. 1 (1998)

20. Hölttä, V., Mahlamäki, K., Eisto, T., Ström, M.: Lean Information Management Model for Engineering Changes. World Academy of Science, Engineering and Technology 42, 1459–1466 (2010)
21. Alblas, A., Wortmann, H.: Impact of product platforms on lean production systems: evidence from industrial machinery manufacturing. International Journal of Technology Management 57, 110–131 (2012)
22. Vaishnavi, V., Kuechler Jr., W.: Design science research methods and patterns: innovating information and communication technology (2008)
23. Holmström, J., Ketokivi, M., Hameri, A.-P.: Bridging Practice and Theory: A Design Science Approach. Decision Sciences 40, 65–87 (2009)
24. van Aken, J.E.: Management Research as a Design Science: Articulating the Research Products of Mode 2 Knowledge Production in Management. British Journal of Management 16, 19–36 (2005)
25. Baskerville, R.L., Myers, M.D.: Fashion Waves in Information Systems Research and Practice. MIS Quarterly 33, 647–662 (2009)
26. Van de Ven, A.H.: Engaged scholarship: A guide for organizational and social research, OUP Oxford (2007)
27. Järvinen, P.: Action Research is Similar to Design Science. Quality & Quantity 41, 37–54 (2007)
28. C.S. Pierce, C. Harshorne, W. P.: Collected Papers. Harvard University Press (1931)
29. Iivari, J.: A Paradigmatic Analysis of Information Systems As a Design Science. Scandinavian Journal of Information Systems, 39–64 (2007)
30. Hevner, A.R., March, S.T., Park, J., Ram, S.: Design science in information systems research. Mis Quarterly 28, 75–105 (2004)
31. Kuechler, B., Vaishnavi, V.: On theory development in design science research: anatomy of a research project. European Journal of Information Systems 17, 489–504 (2008)
32. Meredith, J.R.: Hopes for the future of operations management. Journal of Operations Management 19, 397–402 (2001)
33. Auerbach, C.F., Silverstein, L.B.: Qualitative data: An introduction to coding and analysis. New York University Press, New York (2003)
34. Yin, R.: Case Study Research: Design and Methods. Sage, CA (1994)

Supplier Value of Customer-Initiated Product Development: An In-Depth Case Study of a European Industrial Mass-Producer

Anita Friis Sommer, Iskra Dukovska-Popovska, and Kenn Steger-Jensen

Institute for Mechanical Engineering and Production, Aalborg University, Denmark
{sommer,shs,iskra,kenn}@m-tech.aau.dk

Abstract. Increased market demand and shortened product life cycles generate industrial customer requests for collaborative product development. Manufacture-to-stock suppliers struggle to manage the request process to obtain profitability. The purpose of this paper is to investigate if request management is profitable for mass-producing suppliers, and to examine possible relations between profitability of requests and the requesting customer. Through a case study, request management is identified as a profitable process due to long-term accumulated profit from developed products. Request profitability is not identified as related to profitability or turnover of existing customers, and thus profitability of requests cannot be predicted based on these customer data. Results from a coupled interview study indicate that request management has a large potential for future exploitation, and an outline of the supplier value potential of collaborative product development is proposed.

Keywords: profitability, supplier value, collaborative product development, supply chain integration.

1   Introduction

Increased market demand and shortened product life cycles are generating an increased amount of customer requests for new products [1, 2]. Suppliers struggle to meet these demands and manage collaborative product development. Suppliers must change their innovation strategies from 'innovating for customers' to 'innovating with customers' involving customers in a co-development process [3]. However, the challenge is to combine integration and innovation, responsiveness and flexibility [4]. Some argue that customer co-development cannot reveal innovative customer needs and only generates incremental products [5-7], while others state the opposite that and customer co-creation increases innovation [8, 9]. Regardless of the innovation level, the topic of crucial importance is whether or not co-development generates long-term supplier value. The most important supplier value in this regard is long-term profitability [10]. Additionally, supplier value in collaborative product development includes reduction in development costs, risks, and development time, and more tacit

V. Prabhu, M. Taisch, and D. Kiritsis (Eds.): APMS 2013, Part I, IFIP AICT 414, pp. 383–394, 2013.

values like achieving a wider range of skills and competencies [11]. Buyer-supplier relationships can also be strengthened through the co-development process [12].

Customer requests for new products must be managed in a go/no-go decision process before co-development can be initiated [13]. Request management includes an assessment of the potential supplier value, however a high level of uncertainty in complex product development complicates value assessment. Therefore, it is questioned if accepting a broader range of requests will increase total supplier value, especially long-term profitability.

Sherden [14] argues that in industrial companies the top 20% of the buyers generate as much as 80% of the profits, but that half of these profits are lost because of the bottom 30% of the buyers who are unprofitable. So far there is only limited research indicating if the same relation is present for co-development processes. Therefore, the aim of this study is to investigate long-term supplier profitability of request management, and how request profitability is related to customer profitability.

The paper is structured as follows: Firstly, the theoretical background is presented, which includes reviews of relevant literature within supply chain integration and collaborative product development. Secondly, the method is described including case presentation, and finally the results are presented and analyzed in a separate section followed by a section containing discussion and conclusion.

2   Theoretical Background

Supply chain integration is defined by Bagchi et al [15] as 'the comprehensive collaboration among supply chain network members in strategic, tactical and operational decision-making. Tan and Tracey [16] defines integration in the context of supply chain management as 'interaction and collaboration between departments and organizations to achieve shared supply chain goals'. The purpose of supply chain integration is to improve performance, where the dominant performance measures are supply chain performance and financial performance [17]. Until recently, the dominant view on supply chain integration has been 'the more, the better'[15]. However, this approach has been criticized and differentiated supply chain integration strategies have been proposed [4, 18]. They include a change from holistic integration towards selectively integrated, horizontally specialized supply chain processes and capabilities [4]. Hence, integration should be in relation to the context of the supply chain relationship. For suppliers, this entails segmentation according to e.g. customer behavior, product characteristics and lead times [19]. Customers can be segmented according to the ABC segmentation method [2, 3]. Segmentation can be done according to customer size, profitability, and/or business potential among others. The A-segment is the strategically important segment, which is why we consider supply chain integration as relevant mainly for this segment.

2.1   Collaborative Product Development

Supply chain integration entails collaboration within different areas [20]. These areas include R&D, procurement, inventory management, manufacturing, distribution, supply chain design, and/or supply chain software [15]. Also, collaborative product development is an area within supply chain integration [21, 22]. Collaborative product development is defined as 'any activity where two (or more) partners contribute differential resources and know how to agree complimentary aims in order to design and develop a new or improved product'[23, 24]. According to Büyüközkan and Arsenyan [23] collaborative product development consists of three elements: partnership process, collaboration process and product development process. The challenge in collaborative product development is to manage these three processes and the interrelation between them [23]. Suppliers must develop routines and practices to collaborate with customers and internal cross-functional employee teams [25]. However, relationships between companies are subtle and complex and no one recipe exists on how supply chains achieve best performance [4]. Collaborative product development is initiated through a request from one of the supply chain members. In this paper, we look at the situation where the customer is the requestor of a new supplier product or changes to an existing supplier product. From the supplier perspective, collaborative product development then initiates with the customer request, and depending on the potential business value, the supplier accepts or rejects the request. Accepted requests will be developed in collaboration with the customer. The request process for customer-initiated collaborative product development is presented in figure 1:

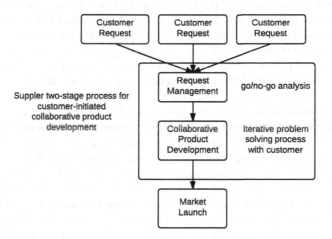

Fig. 1. Customer-initiated collaborative product development

2.2   Supplier Value in Collaborative Product Development

The potential benefits of collaborative product development are the acquisition of a wider range of skills and competencies and a reduction in the costs, risks, and time taken to develop products [11]. Naveh [7] suggests that buyer-supplier collaboration is positively related to efficiency but negatively related to innovation, whereas Un et al. [26] finds that collaboration with customers do not appear to facilitate product innovation. This is contradicted by other research findings indicating that efficiency and innovation can co-exist in collaborative product development [27, 28], and that customers are key sources of innovation [8].

Hilletofth and Eriksson [2] studies coordination of new product development and supply chain management. They identify four success factors for new product development within four characteristics including market characteristics, product characteristics, strategy characteristics, and process characteristics. The essence is to balance value creation with value delivery [2].

According to Büyüközkan and Arsenyan [23], the motivations for engaging in collaborative product development are:

- Sharing risks, reducing costs
- Technology, knowledge, experience
- Reducing time to market
- Market opportunities, competition
- Expending product family, innovation
- Administrative initiative, corporate culture

As opposed to these findings, the reasons for suppliers engaging in collaboration has been examined by Littler et al. [11]. They find that the main reason for suppliers engaging in customer collaboration is a direct response to customer requests. Hence, whereas a range of motivations for engaging in collaborative product development might be true for customers, suppliers are found to engage in collaborative product development through customer requests, and therefore supplier value of collaborative product development is dependent on request management performance.

Research indicates that top 20% of customers generate as much as 80% of the profit, but that half of these profits are lost because of the bottom 30% of the buyers who are unprofitable [14]. Therefore, suppliers must manage the go/no-go decision process for customer requests, including risk management, impact assessment and business value evaluation. The go/no-go criteria for product development include, among others, project total cost, availability of resources, alignment with strategy, window of opportunity, market acceptance, payback time, and long-term sales growth [29]. Suppliers should carefully choose the right requests for collaborative product development. This is no easy task, since collaborative product development is based on complex problem solving, where the results are hard to predict [30, 31]. To increase the chances of market success of co-developed products due to radically new innovation, suppliers must be ready to accept innovation failure [32]. Therefore, suppliers have to accept requests with a wide range of innovative ideas to increase the chances of market success. Yet, this approach includes acceptance of risky requests, which contradicts traditional cost-based approaches [33]. Furthermore, it is not certain, that such an approach will generate long-term supplier profit. To our knowledge, no existing research investigates long-term supplier profitability of collaborative product development. Based on the literature review, we suggest that: *A broad approach to acceptance of customer requests for collaborative product development is positively related to total supplier profitability.*

To the authors, several large industrial suppliers have proposed that collaborative product development should only be for a selected few strategic customers. Strategic customers are often chosen from direct value functions including profit, volume and safeguard (the possibility of 'guaranteeing' a level of business and revenue) [34]. Within lead-user innovation research, it has been found that collaborative innovation should be conducted with customers who are front runners of innovation in their respective markets [35, 36]. We deduced from this body of literature that there might be a relation between the direct value functions of existing customers and the changes of success from collaborative product development with the given customer. This leads us to suggest that: *Customer profitability is positively related to the corresponding single request profitability.*

The propositions have direct impact on supplier practice and the results will provide basis for guidelines to handle request management for collaborative product development. The theoretical contribution to supply chain integration research is an increased understanding of financial supplier value in collaborative product development.

3   Method

The method includes an in-depth case study of a large European industrial mass-producer here named Termodyna. The in-depth case study was chosen to develop a rich contextual understanding of collaborative product development based on customer requests, to frame a financial data analysis. Termodyna was chosen as case company because they implemented a request management and collaborative product development process in 2007, and has documented financial performance data of the process and involved customers since that time allowing for a long-term financial analysis. Furthermore, the company has during the entire period chosen a broad acceptance approach in their go/no-decision process, which is one of the main subjects of relational analysis in this paper.

Termodyna allowed for the research team to gain an open access to financial data stored in their ERP-system. The data included turnover and profit for all products and customers, handled through a collaborative product development process, in the 5-year period since the process was implemented (2008-2012 both years included). This enabled a long-term financial data analysis including both product and customer specific data. Data on product and customer profitability was extracted for the entire time-span to investigate the financial potential of collaborative product development for a mass-producing supplier. Mapping of the Group Gross Profit (GGP) according to year of request and year of income, generated an accumulated profit overview. In GGP, the cost subtracted from income includes both variable costs and overhead costs. Development costs are not included in the GGP and are currently not measured in Termodyna at the single request level. We estimate, in coherence with Termodyna's process management group, that the main development costs are human resources. In total, the request process employs about 8 full-time employees a year, which is about € 650.000. These development costs have to be contracted the total request profitability measured from GGP to evaluate the total long-term profitability. The second aim is to investigate the proposed relation between customer profitability and request profitability. This was done through a qualitative data analysis comparing five years of profitability statistics for customers and products [37]. The financial data includes all data on products developed through the collaborative product development process and the corresponding customer profitability on additional sales.

To support the financial data, an interview study has been conducted as part of a larger research study on request management in Termodyna, which provides contextual grounding in analysis of the financial data. The interview study included employees from three internal functions, operations managers, and the process manager. Furthermore, four customers were interviewed, which provided an understanding of the process, customer value and incentives for customers engaging in collaborative product development with the supplier. An overview of the interviews is presented in table 1.

Table 1. Overview of interviews in each internal function and at the customer.

Functions / Interviews	Operations and process manager	Engine ering	Technical Service	Sales	Customers
Number of interviews (1 hour)	4	2	4	4	4
Participants in group interviews (2 X 2 hours)	2	-	2	2	-

The interview study is based on semi-structured interview guide, including open-ended questions aiming at a detailed description of the process from a holistic viewpoint. Single interviews lasted approximately one hour and group interviews about two hours. All interviews were recorded and notes were made during each session. Afterwards, recordings were transcribed and compared to the notes, and then analyzed using open coding and pattern matching to a theoretical framework on request management [38, 39]. Here, the interview study provides increased understanding of supplier and customer value of collaborative product development, as well as providing the mentioned contextual grounding of the financial analysis.

Termodyna is a large European industrial mass-producer within the automation and control industry, which is globally distributed with manufacturing and/or sales offices on all continents. The company employs more than 30.000 worldwide. The company is traditionally a manufacture-to-stock supplier, offering standard high quality products to manufacturing customers and retailers. About five years ago, the company experienced an increasing amount of requests for new products, varying between 150-300 requests pr. year. A request management process was set up in 2007 to consciously manage the requests including collaborative product development, and sales managers were from then on encouraged to send in customer requests for evaluation. Since initiation the company has accepted around 30% of the incoming requests each year. Evaluation has been conducted ad hoc by a technical service function in company headquarters with a focus on potential profit of each request, considering production costs in relation to sales price and volume. Accepted products are developed in collaboration with customers, typically Original Equipment Manufacturers (OEM)'s, from various industries. Customer interaction varies according to the degree of complexity and uncertainty in the request. Finalized products are registered in the company's SAP system including detailed product and customer data. The requests include about 60-70% simple change requests, 20-30% large changes to existing products, and 5-10% classified as new products involving new technology and radical innovation. Collaborative product development is less dominant for simple change requests, however customers may be actively involved through all requests depending on relevance and necessity. The request process is managed by the company through use of a stage-gate process model, presented in figure 2.

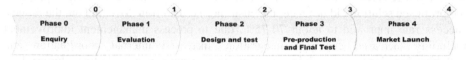

Fig. 2. Stage-gate request process

4   Results and Analysis

4.1   Supplier Profitability of Collaborative Product Development

The accumulated profit from the five years, show an increasing total profit over the years, which is created by continuous sales from the developed product. The analysis reveals that profitability of requested products is spread over the entire time period, and for most products is still increasing during the first 3-4 years. This indicates that product life in this case has a maturation phase exceeding three years and thus profitability should be considered according to the product life cycle. This corresponds to interview findings that Termodyna's products generally have a product life cycle above 10 years. As mentioned, the GGP used for this analysis does not include development costs. The development costs have been estimated, in collaboration with company management, to be approximately € 650.000 per year. The accumulated GGP for each year are presented in Figure 3.

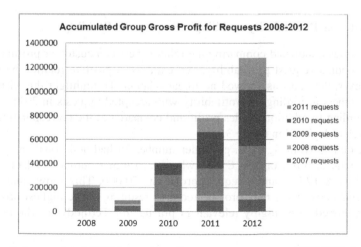

Fig. 3. Accumulated GGP for products from customer requests 2008-2012 (in €)

As presented in figure 3, profit from requested products has a potential increase over the years from implementation and exceeded the development costs in the third quarter of 2011. This indicates that implementation of request management will start to be profitable four years after process implementation. This includes total development costs, which contains time spent on *all* development projects, including those that have either been rejected by customer or supplier. Here it must be noted that about 50% of the accepted requests in 2007-2009 were never sold. They were at some point rejected by the customer either because they chose a different supplier or the proposed solution did not meet the customer needs. From 2010 and on, the request success rate improved to about 70-75%, due to process management improvement including increased customer integration, increased internal coordination and collaboration, increased efficiency in request management including shorter lead times and decreased redundancy of activities. The improvement results are not necessarily directly related to the increased profitability from 2010-2012, yet it is expected that the initiatives at least have had an indirect effect on profitability through increased request acceptance rates due to increased process efficiency. Through the financial analysis we have found that a mass-producing industrial supplier with a wide acceptance approach to request management can obtain long-term profitability.

Additionally, the case indicates that developing products for existing customers can be a crucial maintenance factor. In the case both sales employees and customers stated that acceptance of requests was a prerequisite for retaining additional sales. Customers require reduction of their amount of suppliers, so suppliers must supply 'the entire package' of products to be competitive. Thus, if the supplier rejects to develop the needed product, the customer will move to another supplier with their co-development request and take their orders on standard products with them. One of the interviewed customers had recently had an unsuccessful request, and chose to move to a competing supplier, with their yearly turnover on standard products with a turnover on more than € 70.000. This example highlights the importance of the considerations that must go into rejections in the go/no-go decision process.

4.2   Customer Profitability and Single Request Profitability

An analysis was conducted comparing the relation between customer profitability and the corresponding request profitability. We expected a positive relation between the two. However, the analysis showed no linear relation. To highlight this visually, the top 25 customers according to profitability with accepted requests in 2011 have been sorted according to additional sales profit and compared to the corresponding request profit, which is depicted in figure 3.

As an example from figure 4, customer number 25 had additional sales on € 1,6 mill and a request profit on just € 970, whereas customer number 11 had additional sales on about € 17.000 and a request profit on €70.000. This shows that currently low-segmented customers may provide requests resulting in the highest profitability. This result proved to be highly relevant in practice for Termodyna, who at the time

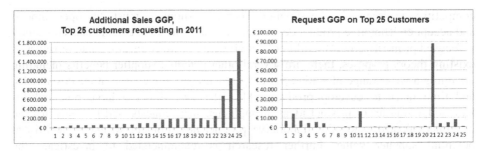

Fig. 4. Top 25 customers; additional sales- and corresponding request-profit

considered rejecting all low segment customers from product development. The analysis suggests that profitable request outcomes cannot be predicted from financial customer data, and thus this relation has been contradicted. Instead, the analysis leads us to suggest that suppliers may benefit from a wide acceptance approach to customer requests.

5   Discussion and Conclusion

The case study findings show that a broad acceptance approach to request management can be a central part of a long-term profitable collaborative product development process. Suppliers can use this case study as inspiration in handling the increasing amount of customer requests for new products and product changes. The case indicates that implementation of request management for collaborative product development in a mass-producing context can be profitable within four years from implementation, even without considering the potential supplier value gained from knowledge transfer of ideas and domain knowledge from customers. However, a single case study does not have the necessary empirical grounding for generalizability, and therefore more research is necessary to examine if this case study findings have general applicability. A consideration in relation to generalizability is the context and type of case company. This case company is an industrial mass-producer and a manufacturer-to-stock company. These suppliers are typically not engaged in collaborative product development compared to engineer-to-order suppliers surviving on customer requests. Furthermore, the involved customers are industrial Original Equipment Manufacturers (OEM)s. This context is important to consider, since both supply chain members have technical product understanding and employed engineers that engage in collaborative product development on similar terms. Therefore, the case study findings are not comparable to either the engineer-to-order supplier context or the context of consumer- or user-integration in product development. Instead, the case provides new findings from the context of mass-producing industrial suppliers and their OEM customers.

The case study contributes to supplier practice suggesting a wide acceptance approach to request management. By accepting innovation failure to some extent, suppliers increase the possibility of innovation success. In other words, it might be the smallest of customers that suddenly proposes the one brilliant idea, which changes the competitive landscape for the supplier. Therefore, suppliers must stay open-minded and accept collaborative product development failures to some extent. This case study is focused primarily on profitability of collaborative product development, however as existing theory proposes, there are several other potential supplier benefits including obtaining a wider range of skills and competencies and a reduction in the costs, risks, and time taken to develop products [11]. The case shows a large potential for knowledge transfer of product ideas through customer requests, and it seems that the customer-initiated type of collaborative product development withholds additional potential supplier value. Further research is recommended to investigate the difference between types of collaborative product development and the corresponding customer and supplier value.

It was found that request rejection might result in customers changing supplier, including purchase of standard products, whereas request acceptance generates a strategic partnership. Either way, the future buyer-supplier relationship is likely to change based on the outcome. In this way, the request for collaborative product development can be seen as a 'make it or brake it' point for the relationship. If this proves to be a generalizable relation, collaborative product development has a much larger impact on the supply chain than previously considered. Based on this, we question if collaborative product development could be a key driver in supply chain formation and disintegration, and recommend further research to examine this proposal. Based on the discussion of case findings and existing literature, a list of potential supplier value from collaborative product development has been derived. Customer-initiated collaborative product development includes the following potential supplier values:

- Increased profitability
- Strategic relationships
- Transfer of innovative ideas
- Transfer of domain knowledge
- Decreased lead-times
- Increased innovation
- Maintenance of existing customers

The list of supplier values is based on the case study in relation to existing literature, and has not been tested for generalizability. Therefore, future research studies are recommended to test the generalizability of the findings both at a larger scale and within different contexts. Finally, we have a concluding remark on the practical impact of our research, which shows that academic research can make a valuable difference for industrial collaboration partners. During our case study, top management in Termodyna considered termination of collaborative product development and to base new product development solely on the work in the R&D department, which was decoupled from customer requests. 'We are after all a mass-producing supplier' was the leading argument, while they were convinced that collaborative product development was expendable. Our case study changed their minds. Now, top management has authorized a major organizational change including process integration between R&D and request management for increased collaborative product development.

References

1. Butner, K.: The smarter supply chain of the future. Strategy & Leadership 38, 22–31 (2010)
2. Hilletofth, P., Eriksson, M.D.: Coordinating new product development with supply chain management. Industrial Management & Data Systems 111, 6 (2011)
3. Desouza, K.C., Awazu, Y., Jha, S., Dombrowski, C., Papagari, S., Baloh, P., Kim, J.Y.: Customer-driven innovation. Research-Technology Management 51, 35–44 (2008)
4. Bask, A.H., Juga, J.: Semi-integrated supply chains: towards the new era of supply chain management. International Journal of Logistics 4, 137–152 (2001)
5. Christensen, C.M., Bower, J.L.: Customer power, strategic investment, and the failure of leading firms. Strategic Management Journal 17, 197–218 (1996)
6. Berthon, P., Hulbert, J.M.: To serve or create? California Management Review 42, 37–58 (1999)
7. Naveh, E.: The effect of integrated product development on efficiency and innovation. International Journal of Production Research 43, 2789–2808 (2005)
8. Bonner, J.M.: Customer interactivity and new product performance: Moderating effects of product newness and product embeddedness. Industrial Marketing Management 39, 485–492 (2010)
9. Atuahene-Gima, K.: An exploratory analysis of the impact of market orientation on new product performance. Journal of Product Innovation Management 12, 275–293 (1995)
10. Lindgreen, A., Wynstra, F.: Value in business markets: What do we know? Where are we going? Industrial Marketing Management 34, 732–748 (2005)
11. Littler, D., Leverick, F., Bruce, M.: Factors Affecting the Process of Collaborative Product Development. Journal of Product Innovation Management, 16–32 (1995)
12. Johnsen, T., Ford, D.: Customer approaches to product development with suppliers. Industrial Marketing Management 36, 300–308 (2007)
13. Sommer, A.F., Steger-Jensen, K.: What and how about customer-driven product development. In: De Koster, R., Van Donk, P.D., De Leeuw, S., Fransoo, J., Van der Veen, J. (eds.) 19th International Annual EurOMA Conference: Serving the World, University of Amsterdam, Amsterdam (2012)
14. Sherden, W.A.: Market ownership: the art & science of becoming# 1. American Management Association (1994)
15. Bagchi, P.K., Ha, B.C., Skjoett-Larsen, T., Soerensen, L.B.: Supply chain integration: a European survey. The International Journal of Logistics Management 16, 275–294 (2005)
16. Tan, C.L., Tracey, M.: Collaborative New Product Development Environments: Implications for Supply Chain Management. Journal of Supply Chain Management 43, 2–15 (2007)
17. Fabbe-Costes, N., Jahre, M.: Supply chain integration and performance: a review of the evidence. The International Journal of Logistics Management 19, 130–154 (2008)
18. Jahre, M., Fabbe-Costes, N.: Adaptation and adaptability in logistics networks. International Journal of Logistics: Research and Applications 8, 143–157 (2005)

19. Godsell, J., Diefenbach, T., Clemmow, C., Towill, D., Christopher, M.: Enabling supply chain segmentation through demand profiling. International Journal of Physical Distribution & Logistics Management 41, 296–314 (2011)
20. Stonebraker, P.W., Liao, J.: Supply chain integration: exploring product and environmental contingencies. Supply Chain Management: An International Journal 11, 34–43 (2006)
21. Jüttner, U., Christopher, M., Godsell, J.: A strategic framework for integrating marketing and supply chain strategies. The International Journal of Logistics Management 21, 104–126 (2010)
22. Fliess, S., Becker, U.: Supplier integration—Controlling of co-development processes. Industrial Marketing Management 35, 28–44 (2005)
23. Büyüközkan, G., Arsenyan, J.: Collaborative product development: a literature overview. Production Planning & Control 23, 47–66 (2011)
24. Dodgson, M.: Organizational learning: a review of some literatures. Organization Studies 14, 375–394 (1993)
25. Mishra, A.A., Shah, R.: In union lies strength: Collaborative competence in new product development and its performance effects. Journal of Operations Management 27, 324–338 (2009)
26. Un, C.A., Cuervo-Cazurra, A., Asakawa, K.: R&D Collaborations and Product Innovatio. Journal of Product Innovation Management 27, 673–689 (2010)
27. Lee, A.H.I., Chen, H.H., Tong, Y.: Developing new products in a network with efficiency and innovation. International Journal of Production Research 46, 4687–4707 (2008)
28. Miron, E., Erez, M., Naveh, E.: Do personal characteristics and cultural values that promote innovation, quality, and efficiency compete or complement each other? Journal of Organizational Behavior 25, 175–199 (2004)
29. Carbonellfoulquie, P.: Criteria employed for go/no-go decisions when developing successful highly innovative products. Industrial Marketing Management 33, 307–316 (2004)
30. Stabell, C.B., Fjeldstad, Ø.D.: Configuring value for competitive advantage: on chains, shops, and networks. Strategic Management Journal 19, 413–437 (1998)
31. Pina e Cunha, M., Gomes, J.F.S.: Order and disorder in product innovation models. Creativity and Innovation Management 12, 174–187 (2003)
32. Hamel, G., Breen, B.: The future of management. Harvard Business Press (2007)
33. Tracey, M.: A Holistic Approach to New Product Development: New Insights. Journal of Supply Chain Management 40, 37–55 (2004)
34. Möller, K.E.K., Törrönen, P.: Business suppliers' value creation potential: A capability-based analysis. Industrial Marketing Management 32, 109–118 (2003)
35. von Hippel, E.: Lead users: A source of novel product concepts. Management Science 32, 791–805 (1986)
36. Von Hippel, E.: "Sticky information" and the locus of problem solving: Implications for innovation. Management Science, 429–439 (1994)
37. Arbnor, I., Bjerke, B.: Methodology for creating business knowledge. SAGE Publications Ltd., London (2008)
38. Yin, R.: Case Study Research: Design and Methods. Sage, CA (1994)
39. Auerbach, C.F., Silverstein, L.B.: Qualitative data: An introduction to coding and analysis. New York University Press, New York (2003)

Long Term Analysis of Energy Payback Time
for PV Systems

Simone Zanoni and Laura Mazzoldi

Department of Mechanical and Industrial Engineering,
Università degli Studi di Brescia, Via Branze, 38, I-25123, Brescia, Italy
{zanoni,laura.mazzoldi}@ing.unibs.it

Abstract. The energy payback performance of an energy generating technology such as PV, is usually based on a single system considering static parameters for its evaluation. However it is recognized that performances of an installed systems decrease over time, while, on the other hand, the performances of new systems is expected to slightly increase over time. Additionally the energy required for manufacturing a new system has decreased significantly in the last years and additional decrease is expected in the near future; moreover the opportunity to recycle materials from dismantled PV installations is becoming massively investigated and some technologies are already on industrial scale. These dynamic aspects inspired the present work that firstly consider the calculation of the energy payback of PV systems that should drive the most sustainable decision regarding the optimal timing for dismissing of an old PV system and replacement with a new one.

Keywords: Energy payback, energy breakeven, PV systems.

1 Introduction

Photovoltaic is a fast growing market: it has boomed over the last decade, and its expansion is expected to continue worldwide in 2011 about half of the previously cumulated PV module capacity entered the market.

Energy Payback Time is defined as the period required for a (renewable) energy system to generate the same amount of energy (in terms of primary energy equivalent) that was consumed by the system itself during its life. New energy technologies are evaluated by this criteria in order to estimate their ability to contribute to our growing energy needs and to deal with carbon emissions problems [1]. However it should be noted that the Energy Payback Time of PV systems is dependent on the geographical location: PV systems in Northern Europe need around 4 years to balance the inherent energy, while PV systems in the South equal their energy input after 2 years and less.

The environmental performance of PV systems was characterized in life cycle studies [2]-[3].

The energy performance of new technologies can and often does improve as the technology evolves.

V. Prabhu, M. Taisch, and D. Kiritsis (Eds.): APMS 2013, Part I, IFIP AICT 414, pp. 395–401, 2013.
© IFIP International Federation for Information Processing 2013

In the last 10 years, the efficiency of average commercial wafer-based silicon modules increased from about 12% to 15%; moreover usage for silicon cells has been reduced significantly during the last 5 years from around 16 g/Wp to 6 g/Wp due to increased efficiencies and thinner wafers.

Gutowski et al. [1] studied performance of growing energy systems ensembles, identifying an optimum growth rate (largest value of net energy production) and critical growth rate (rate at which the ensemble generates no new energy). A case study on PV ensembles is presented and discussed.

Another important aspect for the long-term sustainability of the PV industry is the end-of-life photovoltaic (PV) module recycling, considering the large future expected waste volumes.

As indicated by the inclusion of photovoltaic (PV) in the European Union Directive on Waste Electrical and Electronic Equipment (WEEE), end-of-life module recycling is important to the long-term sustainability of the PV industry. In addition, in order to help the management of large future expected waste volumes [4], PV recycling can contribute to resource efficiency by preserving valuable raw materials (glass, copper, aluminium, semiconductor materials, etc.) for future use in PV modules or other new products.

Recycling activity extract from PV modules three primary recyclable materials: aluminium, glass and unrefined semiconductor material. The life cycle assessment of CdTe PV module recycling has been described in [5]-[6].

Many of these effects could affect the energy performance parameters. Therefore we will show that Energy Payback Time should be properly adjusted when considering an already installed system and the decision on dismantling and replace it with a new system.

2   Model

In the following, we develop a model that is the starting point for the development of a further analysis, which is aimed to determine when a PV system should be dismantled and/or substituted by a new one.

Figure 1 presents a typical Energy Balance for a PV system, where the Energy Payback Time (EnPBT^1) and the Embodied Energy (E^1_E) required to manufacture all the components included into the system are considered.

At t=0 the PV system is installed, and the Embodied Energy (E^1_E) required to manufacture all the components is taken into consideration. After installation, the system produces a certain amount of energy (namely the annual produced energy, E$_{P,t}$), which is a function of the total power installed (P), the efficiency (η_t, for the t-th year after installation), and the annual number of equivalent hours of production, which is usually considered as a constant over time and it depends on the geographical location of the plant.

After n years (t = EnPBT^1) the PV system starts to be energetically profitable, i.e. the cumulative energy assumes positive values after n years. Usually a PV system is

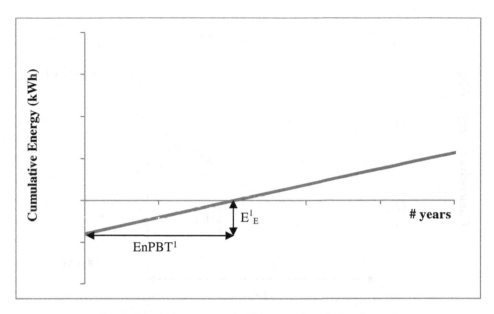

Fig. 1. Cumulative energy of a PV system installed at time t=0

considered operative until the end of its lifetime (LT), which is usually assumed to be 25 years. However the introduction of new technologies can lead to the decision of replacing the installed modules with new modules, on the same available space.

Thus after t_1 years from its installation, plant #1 can be replaced by plant #2: the cumulative energy (CE_{t1}) decreases dramatically, as the Embodied Energy for the production of the modules included in plant #2 (E^2_E) must be summed up to the cumulative energy produced by #1 until t_1. In Figure 2 it is assumed that $E^2_E \leq CE_{t1}$, so that the total cumulative energy ($CE_{t1} - E^2_E) \geq 0$.

After t' ($t_1 \leq t' \leq t_2$) from the first installation of #1, the expected cumulative energy related to plant #1, would be $CE^1_{t'}$ while the effective cumulative energy related to plant #2 is $CE^2_{t'}$, with $CE^1_{t'} \geq CE^2_{t'}$; only after t_2 years from the first installation (plant #1) the effective cumulative energy assumes the same value of the expected one, i.e. $CE^1_{t'} = CE^2_{t'}$, and the Time To Energy Equivalence is $TTEE^{1-2}$.

Starting from the considerations introduced in the first paragraphs, the Embodied Energy E^2_E required to manufacture the system #2 is lower than the energy required to produce system #1. The reason is that with the introduction of new technologies, the required production energy is lower, i.e. developing new processes that requires less semiconductor material. Thus the relationship of embodied energy of modules related to plant #1 and #2, is $E^2_E \leq E^1_E$.

Moreover Figure 2 shows that the curve representing the cumulative energy related to plant #2 has a greater slope the one related to plant #1: this is a consequence of the increased performances of system #2, that allow to install a greater power on the same area of plant #1.

Therefore the respective relationship on Energy Payback Time for the new systems ($EnPBT^2$), with respect to the old one ($EnPBT^1$) becomes $EnPBT^2 \leq EnPBT^1$. It should

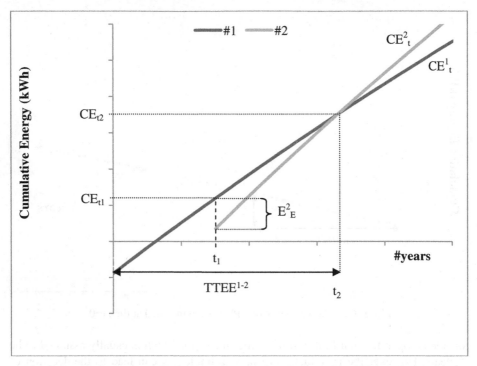

Fig. 2. Cumulative energy of two PV systems (#1 installed at t=0 and #2 installed ad t=t$_1$)

be noted that those two Energy Payback Time are calculated with respect to the base case scenario of no previous system installed.

In order to answer the first question "should the system installed at time t=0 be replaced by a new system after some years from its installation, from an energy point of view?"

For $0 \le t \le TTEE^{1-2}$ (where TTEE indicates the time to equivalent energy of system #1 and system #2) the cumulative energy produced by system #1 (effectively for t < t', theoretically for $t' \le t < TTEE^{1-2}$), represented by the black continuous line in Figure 3, is higher than the cumulative energy produced when substitution t = t' is implemented (grey dashed line in Figure 3), while for $t \ge TTEE^{1-2}$ the opposite situation arises.

In Figure 3 it is also highlighted the value of $ReEnPBT^{t',(1-2)}$, which represents the *Replacement* Energy Payback Time of the plant #1 with plant #2, at time t': the next paragraph focuses the discussion on such a value, in order to determine whether or not it is convenient (from the energy point of view) to replace an existing system, or to install another one next to it.

Recalling the main considerations presented in the previous paragraph, such as the reduction in energy required for manufacturing a module, lead to a decrease in Energy Payback Time for the single plant. Thus, as reported in Figure 4, the *Replacement* Energy Payback Time is a decreasing function of the substitution time t'. Typically for three different substitution times, t'_A, t'_B and t'_B, with $t'_A \le t'_B \le t'_B$:

$$ReEnPBT^{t'A} \ge ReEnPBT^{t'B} \ge ReEnPBT^{t'B}$$

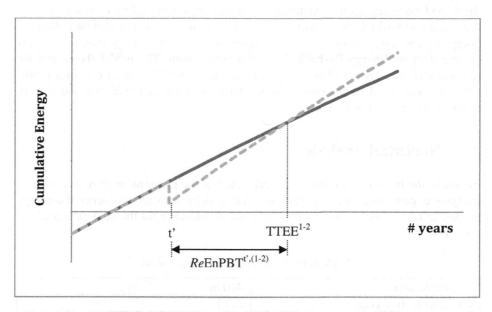

Fig. 3. *Replacement* Energy Payback Time of PV system #2

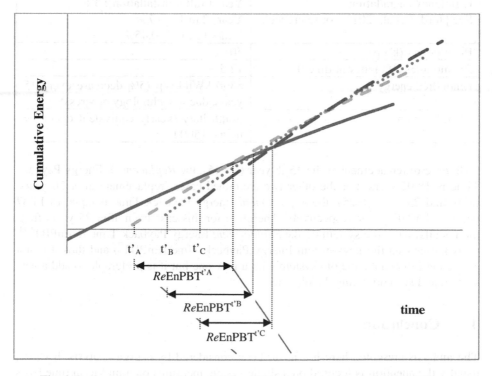

Fig. 4. *Replacement* Energy Payback Time of PV systems replaced at different times

Such evidence suggests the existence of a replacement time value, t^*, that represents the value under which the substitution of the plant modules is not profitable from an energy production point of view: the associated *Replacement* Energy Payback Time is greater than the Energy Payback Time of a new system. The model shows that for replacement time greater than t^* the replacement of the PV system becomes profitable: the associated *Replacement* Energy Payback Time is lower than the Energy Payback Time of a new system.

3   Numerical Analysis

To study the behaviour of the model presented in the previous section, a numerical analysis is performed to investigate how the model parameters influence the energy model. In table 1 main parameters considered as reference for the numerical analysis are reported.

Table 1. PV System parameters considered

Available area	400 m^2
First installation year	2012
PV modules technology	Si poly-crystalline
Efficiency degradation See [Jordan et al., 2011] for reference	Year 1 (after installation): 3% Years 2 to 10: 0.7% Years 11 to 25: 0.45%
Plant power (kWp)	50
PV modules efficiency at time 0	12.5%
Embodied energy	8890 kWh/kWp (5% decrease every 15 years, due to technology progress)
Plant location	South Italy (yearly equivalent operating hours: 1500 h)

In case of replacement at the 15-th year ($t = 15$), the *Replacement* Energy Payback Time is 18.02 years. For the other two examined cases (replacement after 20 years, t=20, and 25 years, t=25), the *Replacement* Energy Payback Time is equal to 14.37 years and 12.02 years, respectively. Therefore for this case even after 25 years from the installation of the system #1 the *Replacement* Energy Payback Time $ReEnPBT^{t,(1\text{-}2)}$ is larger than the new system Energy Payback Time ($EnPBT^2$) and thus it is not convenient to replace the old system with a new one but it is preferable to add a new system and keep operating the old one.

4   Conclusion

The analysis presented here has never been considered by energy analysts, because, usually the attention is focused on a single system measures on a mid-term time basis and main energy basis considered parameters, such as, mainly, the energy payback time of a new installation. Due to the described growth in the number of PV installations in recent years we are convinced that also a long term analysis should be valuable, considering the option of replacing an old system after several years of production in favour of a new and most performing system. This work is the first attempt to depict the problem of the replacement decision on an energy basis considering most of the parameters that influence the problem. Next step of the work is the development of an analytical model so as to perform an analytical sensitivity analysis of the break even time from which it is convenient to replace the old installation. Moreover an economic analysis of the problem presented could be valuable, even if from this point of view the analysis is strongly affected by the country and year of the considered PV installation (due to differences in the incentive scheme and changes of that over time). Finally it should be noted that the analysis included here, if properly adjusted, could be applied to any kind of energy system from wind power to biomass or biogas systems.

References

1. Gutowski, T.G., Gershwin, S.B., Bounassis, T.: Energy payback for energy systems ensembles during growth. In: Proceedings of the 2010 IEEE International Symposium on Sustainable Systems and Technology, ISSST 2010, art. no. 5507729 (2010)
2. Raugei, M., Bargigli, S., Ulgiati, S.: Life cycle assessment and energy pay-back time of advanced photovoltaic modules: CdTe and CIS compared to poly-Si. Energy 32(8), 1310–1318 (2007)
3. Fthenakis, V.M., Kim, H.C., Alsema, E.: Emissions from photovoltaic life cycles. Environmental Science & Technology 42(6), 2168–2174 (2008)
4. Sander, K., Schilling, S., Reinschmidt, J., Wambach, K., Schlenker, S., Müller, A., Springer, J., Fouquet, D., Jelitte, A., Stryi-Hipp, G., Chrometzka, T.: Study on the Development of a Take Back and Recovery System for Photovoltaic Products. Ökopol GmbH, Hamburg (2007)
5. Held, M.: Life Cycle Assessment of CdTe Module Recycling. In: 24th EU PVSEC Conference, Hamburg, Germany (2009)
6. Sinha, P., Cossette, M., Ménard, J.-F.: End-of-life cdtepv recycling with semiconductor refining. In: 27th European Photovoltaic Solar Energy Conference and Exhibition, pp. 4653–4656 (2012)

An Optimization Model for Advanced Biofuel Production Based on Bio-oil Gasification

Qi Li and Guiping Hu[*]

Industrial and Manufacturing Systems Engineering, Iowa State University,
Ames, IA, 50011, United States
gphu@iastate.edu

Abstract. Biomass can be converted to transportation fuels through gasification. However, commercialization of biomass gasification has been hampered by its high capital and operating costs, in addition to the difficulties of transporting bulky solid biomass over a long distance. A novel approach is to convert biomass to bio-oil at widely distributed small-scale fast pyrolysis plants, transport the bio-oil to a centralized location, gasify the bio-oil to syngas, and upgrade the syngas to transportation fuels. In this paper, a two-stage stochastic programming is formulated. The first-stage makes the capital investment decisions including the locations and capacities of the bio-facilities (fast pyrolysis and refining facility) while the second-stage determines the biomass and biofuels flows. This paper aims to find the optimal design of the supply chain for this certain path considering uncertainties in biomass yield, biofuel price and transportation costs.

Keywords: stochastic programming, bio-oil gasification, supply chain.

1   Introduction

Second generation biofuel is a potential substitute for petroleum-based fuel in the perspectives of environmental, economic, and social benefits. [1]. According to the revised Renewable Fuel Standard (RFS2), at least 36 billion gallons per year of renewable fuels will be produced by 2022, of which at least 16 billion gallons per year will be from cellulosic biofuels [2]. However, the cellulosic biofuel volume standard for 2012 is only 10.45 million gallons per year according U.S. Environmental Protection Agency (EPA) in 2011 [3].

Biomass can be converted to transportation fuels by various methods. Fast pyrolysis and gasification are two of the most prominent technologies for thermochemical conversion of biomass. Fast pyrolysis produces bio-oil, bio-char and non-condensable gases [4]. However, commercialization of the biomass gasification has been hampered by its high capital and operating costs due to the challenge of transporting bulky solid biomass over a long distance, processing the solid feedstock at high pressure, and removing contaminants from gas stream. Feedstock production and logistics constitute 35% or more of the total production costs of advanced biofuel [5]. And

---

[*] Corresponding author.

V. Prabhu, M. Taisch, and D. Kiritsis (Eds.): APMS 2013, Part I, IFIP AICT 414, pp. 402–408, 2013.

logistics associated with moving biomass from land to bio-refinery can make up 50–75% of the feedstock costs [6]. A novel approach for reducing these costs is to convert biomass to bio-oil at distributed small-scale fast pyrolysis processing plants, transport the bio-oil to a centralized location, gasify the bio-oil to syngas, and upgrade the syngas to transportation fuels. There is a rich literature on supply chain network design. Shah [7] reviewed the precious studies in modeling, planning, and scheduling with some real world examples. An et al. [8] compared the supply chain research on petroleum based fuel and biofuel. However, only a few literature concerns the uncertainty. Kim et al. [9] considered a two-stage stochastic model to determine the capacities and location of the bio-refineries. Marvin et al. [10] gave a mixed integer linear programming to determine optimal locations and capacities of bio-refineries. As a result, it is of importance to build an optimization model to deal with the uncertainties such as biomass supply, shipping cost and biofuel demands.

The rest of the paper is organized as follows: in Section 2, the problem statement and assumptions is presented. Then, we discuss the deterministic linear programming model and the two-stage stochastic programming models for this problem in Section 3. Section 4 gives a brief discussion of settings and result of a toy case study. Finally, we conclude the paper in Section 5 with summary and future research directions.

2   Problem Statement and Assumptions

The biofuel industry is highly affected by the uncertainties among the supply chain such as biomass supply, shipping cost and biofuel demands. Stochastic programming is one of the most widely used methods to consider the impacts of decision making under uncertainties. This paper aims to provide a mathematical programming framework with a two-stage stochastic programming approach to deal with the uncertainties among the biofuel industry. The optimality model provides suggestions about the capital investment decisions and logistic decisions of this pathway.

In this model, several assumptions are made. Biomass supply is assumed from the county level. Candidate fast pyrolysis and the refining facilities are assumed at the county centroid. Only one centralized refining facility is being planned and the decentralized fast pyrolysis facilities can be of several capacity levels (low, medium and high levels). It is assumed that the unit collection cost of biomass includes the feedstock inventory cost.

3   Model Formulation

In this section, we introduce both the deterministic and stochastic model for this biofuel supply chain design problem. The deterministic mixed integer linear programming model is first introduced as a baseline model and then a two-stage stochastic model is discussed to address the uncertainties in the supply chain design problem.

3.1   Deterministic Mixed Integer Linear Programming Model

In the deterministic mixed integer linear programming model, all the data and modeling parameters are assumed to known with certainty. The notations used in this model are listed in Table 1.

Table 1. Notations for Deterministic Linear Programming Model

Subscripts		
i	$1, 2, \ldots, I$	Biomass supply locations
j	$1, 2, \ldots, J$	Candidate fast pyrolysis facility locations
k	$1, 2, \ldots, K$	Gasoline and diesel fuel demand locations
l	$1, 2, \ldots, L$	Allowed fast pyrolysis capacity levels
m	$1, 2, \ldots, M$	Candidate refining facility locations
Decision Variables		
x_{ij}	Amount of biomass transported from supply location i to candidate fast pyrolysis facility location j	
y_{jm}	Amount of bio-oil transported from candidate fast pyrolysis facility location j to candidate refining facility location m	
z_{mk}	Amount of gasoline and diesel fuels transported from refining facility location m to demand location k	
a_{jl}	Whether a fast pyrolysis facility of capacity level l is planned at the candidate facility location j (binary variable)	
g_m	Whether a refining facility exists in candidate refining facility location m (binary variable)	
Parameters		
B	Total budget	
C^{UP}	Capital cost of the centralized refining facility	
C_l^{Cap}	Capital cost of the decentralized fast pyrolysis facility at level l	
P_k	Gasoline and diesel fuels price at demand location k	
D_k	Gasoline and diesel fuels demand at demand location k	
Pe_k	Penalty for not meeting the demand at demand location k	
$Pe_k{}'$	Penalty for exceeding the demand at demand location k	
C_i^{Col}	Unit biomass collecting cost at supply location i	
C^{MO}	Unit conversion cost from dry biomass to bio-oil	
C^{OF}	Unit conversion cost from bio-oil to biofuels	
C_{ij}^{BM}	Unit biomass shipping cost from supply location i to candidate fast pyrolysis facility location j	
C_{jm}^{BO}	Unit bio-oil shipping cost from candidate fast pyrolysis facility location j to candidate refining facility location m	
C_{mk}^{BF}	Unit biofuel shipping cost from candidate refining facility location m to demand location k	
U_l	Capacity of fast pyrolysis facility at level l	
V	Capacity of refining facility	
S_i	Available biomass feedstock at location i	
α	Sustainability factor	
β	Conversion factor from wet biomass to dry biomass	
γ	The loss factor of biomass during collection and transportation	
θ_1	Conversion ratio, ton of bio-oil per ton of dry biomass	
θ_2	Conversion ratio, ton of gasoline per ton of bio-oil	

3.1.1 Objective Function

The objective of this model is to maximize the total profit, which can be defined as the income from selling the biofuel subtracted by the penalty and the total cost. There is a penalty on not meeting the demand and an additional storage penalty for any surplus production. Different types of costs are considered in this model including the capital investment, collection cost, conversion cost, and shipping cost [11]. The shipping cost includes the transportation costs for biomass feedstock, intermediate bio-oil, and upgrading transportation fuels.

3.1.2 Constraints in the Model

The following constraint is used to ensure that the total capital cost does not exceed the budget.

$$B - C^{UP} - \sum_{j=1}^{J} \sum_{l=1}^{L} C_l^{Cap} a_{jl} \geq 0 \tag{1}$$

The total amount of biomass transported from supply location i to candidate fast pyrolysis facility locations should not exceed the available feedstock at each supply location where α is the sustainability factor.

$$\sum_{j=1}^{J} x_{ij} \leq (1 - \alpha) S_i, \forall i \tag{2}$$

The capacity constraints are used in the model. The loss factor $\gamma \in [0,1)$ is the fraction weight loss of biomass during the collection and transportation and β is the conversion factor from wet biomass to dry biomass.

$$\sum_{l=1}^{L} U_l a_{jl} - (1 - \gamma)\beta \sum_{i=1}^{I} x_{ij} > 0, \forall j \tag{3}$$

$$V g_m - \sum_{j=1}^{J} y_{jm} \geq 0, \forall m \tag{4}$$

There should be no more than one fast pyrolysis facility exists in each candidate facility location. And only one centralized refining facility is built.

$$\sum_{l=1}^{L} a_{jl} \leq 1, \forall j \tag{5}$$

$$\sum_{m=1}^{M} g_m = 1 \tag{6}$$

We assume that biomass is converted to bio-oil with a conversion ratio θ_1 and bio-oil is converted to biofuel with a conversion ratio θ_2. Thus, we have the following conversion balance constraints:

$$(1 - \gamma)\beta \theta_1 \sum_{i=1}^{I} x_{ij} - \sum_{m=1}^{M} y_{jm} = 0, \forall j \tag{7}$$

$$\theta_2 \sum_{j=1}^{J} \sum_{m=1}^{M} y_{jm} - \sum_{m=1}^{M} \sum_{k=1}^{K} z_{mk} = 0 \tag{8}$$

3.1.3   Summary of the Deterministic Model

The deterministic linear programming model is formulated as follows:

$$max\ \zeta = income - penalty - cost = \sum_{k=1}^{K}(P_k \sum_{m=1}^{M} z_{mk}) - \{(D_k - \sum_{m=1}^{M} z_{mk})_+ *$$
$$Pe_k + (\sum_{m=1}^{M} z_{mk} - D_k)_+ * Pe'_k\} - \{\sum_{j=1}^{J} \sum_{l=1}^{L} C_l^{Cap} a_{jl} + \sum_{i=1}^{I} \sum_{j=1}^{J} C_i^{Col} x_{ij} +$$
$$C^{MO}(1-\gamma)\beta \sum_{i=1}^{I} x_{ij} + C^{OF} \sum_{j=1}^{J} \sum_{m=1}^{M} y_{jm} + \sum_{i=1}^{I} \sum_{j=1}^{J} C_{ij}^{BM} x_{ij} +$$
$$\sum_{j=1}^{J} \sum_{m=1}^{M} C_{jm}^{BO} y_{jm} + \sum_{m=1}^{M} \sum_{k=1}^{K} C_{mk}^{BF} z_{mk}$$

$$s.t.\ Constraints\ (1) - (8),\ x_{ij}, y_{jm}, z_{mk} \geq 0, a_{jl}, g_m \in \{0,1\}, \forall i, j, l, m, k$$

This mixed integer linear programming model maximizes the total profit by giving capital investment and logistics decisions at the same time in deterministic case. It's the baseline model for next step.

3.2   Two-Stage Stochastic Programming Model

In this paper, we consider the uncertainties of the shipping cost, available biomass feedstock and gasoline and diesel fuels prices. The stochastic parameters in this study are assumed to be discretely distributed. We use subscript s to represent scenario with probability Pr_s and add this subscript to some decision variables and parameters. λ_s is percentage change of the shipping cost in scenario s comparing to the base scenario. The two-stage stochastic programming model is formulated as follows:

$$max\ \zeta = -\sum_{j=1}^{J} \sum_{l=1}^{L} C_l^{Cap} a_{jl} + \sum_{s=1}^{S} Pr_s \{\sum_{k=1}^{K} \sum_{m=1}^{M} (P_{ks} z_{mks}) - ((D_k -$$
$$\sum_{m=1}^{M} z_{mks})_+ * Pe_k + (\sum_{m=1}^{M} z_{mks} - D_k)_+ * Pe'_k) - (\sum_{i=1}^{I} \sum_{j=1}^{J} C_i^{Col} x_{ijs} +$$
$$C^{MO}(1-\gamma)\beta \sum_{i=1}^{I} x_{ijs} + C^{OF} \sum_{j=1}^{J} \sum_{m=1}^{M} y_{jms} + (\lambda_s (\sum_{i=1}^{I} \sum_{j=1}^{J} C_{ij}^{BM} x_{ijs} +$$
$$\sum_{j=1}^{J} \sum_{m=1}^{M} C_{jm}^{BO} y_{jms} \sum_{m=1}^{M} \sum_{k=1}^{K} C_{mk}^{BF} z_{mks})))\}$$

$$s.t.\ \ Constraints\ (1), (5), (6).$$

$$\sum_{j=1}^{J} x_{ijs} \leq (1-\alpha) S_{is}, \forall i, \forall s \tag{9}$$

$$\sum_{l=1}^{L} U_l a_{jl} - (1-\gamma)\beta \sum_{i=1}^{I} x_{ijs} \geq 0, \forall j, \forall s \tag{10}$$

$$V g_m - \sum_{j=1}^{J} y_{jms} \geq 0, \forall m, \forall s \tag{11}$$

$$(1-\gamma)\beta \theta_1 \sum_{i=1}^{I} x_{ijs} - \sum_{m=1}^{M} y_{jms} = 0, \forall j, \forall s \tag{12}$$

$$\theta_2 \sum_{j=1}^{J} \sum_{m=1}^{M} y_{jms} - \sum_{m=1}^{M} z_{mks} = 0, \forall s \tag{13}$$

$$x_{ijs}, y_{jms}, z_{mks} \geq 0, a_{jl}, g_m \in \{0,1\}, \forall i, j, k, m, l, s$$

In this model, the first-stage decision variables are a_{jl} and g_m, which make the capital investment decisions including the locations and capacities for the conversion facilities. While the second-stage decision variables x_{ijs}, y_{jms}, and z_{mks} determine the biomass and biofuels flows. Constraints (1), (5), and (6) are the first-stage constraints, these constraints remain the same. The rest of the constraints will change accordingly to the set of scenarios.

4   Case Study

A case study based on state of Iowa has been carried out to illustrate the modeling framework. Historical data from EIA, USDA, and Census Bureau supplemented by the literatures have been employed in the case study. Three levels of uncertainties for each parameter have been considered. The 27 scenarios are assumed to have equal probability. The results show that in the deterministic case, we should build 51 distributed fast pyrolysis plants (one low-capacity facility, no medium-capacity facility and 50 high-capacity facilities). The yearly profit is about 886 million dollars. The capital investment could be recovered in 6 years with the interest rate of 10%. While in the stochastic case, 63 distributed fast pyrolysis plants (one low-capacity facility, 14 medium-capacity facilities and 48 high-capacity facilities). It is observed that the stochastic programming modeling framework demonstrates superior economic outcome than the deterministic case and the value of the stochastic solution (VSS) is about 65 million dollars per year.

5   Conclusion

This paper provides a mathematical programming framework with a two-stage stochastic programming approach to deal with the uncertainties in the supply chain design among the biofuel industry. The optimality model provides suggestions for the decision makers on the capital investment decisions and logistic decisions of the thermochemical conversion pathway based on bio-oil gasification. A case study has been carried out to illustrate and validate the modeling framework. This paper provides a preliminary framework and initiates a future research direction for uncertainty analysis in biofuel supply chain design. Additional constraints on the detailed process design can be incorporated to the modeling framework. It should also be noted that additional uncertainties can be considered and more realistic criterion to generate scenarios for the stochastic programming can be investigated.

References

1. Carriquiry, M.A., Du, X., Timilsina, G.R.: Second generation biofuels: Economics and policies. Energy Policy 39(7), 4222–4234 (2011)
2. Schnepf, R.: Renewable fuel standard (RFS): overview and issues. Diane Publishing (2011)
3. EPA, EPA finalizes 2012 renewable fuel standards (2011)
4. Brown, R.C.: Biorenewable resources. Iowa State Press (2003)
5. Wooley, R., Ruth, M., Sheehan, J., Ibsen, K., Majdeski, H., Galvez, A.: Lignocellulosic biomass to ethanol process design and economics utilizing co-current dilute acid prehydrolysis and enzymatic hydrolysis current and futuristic scenarios (No. NREL/TP-580-26157). National Renewable Energy Lab Golden Co. (1999)

6. Grant, D., Hess, J.R., Kenney, K., Laney, P., Muth, D., Pryfogle, P., Radtke, C., Wright, C.: Feasibility of a producer-owned ground-straw feedstock supply system for bioethanol and other products, p. 115. INL, Idaho (2006)
7. Shah, N.: Process industry supply chains: Advances and challenges. Computers & Chemical Engineering 29(6), 1225–1236 (2005)
8. An, H., Wilhelm, W.E., Searcy, S.W.: Biofuel and petroleum-based fuel supply chain research: a literature review. Biomass and Bioenergy 35(9), 3763–3774 (2011)
9. Kim, J., Realff, M.J., Lee, J.H.: Optimal design and global sensitivity analysis of biomass supply chain networks for biofuels under uncertainty. Computers & Chemical Engineering 35(9), 1738–1751 (2011)
10. Alex Marvin, W., Schmidt, L.D., Benjaafar, S., Tiffany, D.G., Daoutidis, P.: Economic optimization of a lignocellulosic biomass-to-ethanol supply chain. Chemical Engineering Science 67(1), 68–79 (2012)
11. Li, Y., Brown, T., Hu, G.: An optimization model to determine the capacities and locations for a thermochemical biorefinery supply network. Iowa State University. Technical report

A Sequential Fast Pyrolysis Facility Location-Allocation Model

Yihua Li and Guiping Hu[*]

Industrial and Manufacturing Systems Engineering, Iowa State University
Ames, IA, 50011, USA
gphu@iastate.edu

Abstract. The revised Renewable Fuel Standard (RFS2) mandates the U.S. consume16 billion gallons per year (BGY) of biofuels from cellulosic sources by the year 2022. Fast Pyrolysis of biomass is a renewable conversion process developed for producing liquid transportation fuels, such as gasoline and diesel.

The pathway investigated in this study is fast pyrolysis and hydroprocessing to produce transportation fuels from corn stover. A mathematical model is formulated to study the supply chain design problem. The objective is to optimize an orderly fast pyrolysis facility locations and capacities that maximize the net present value (NPV) of the total profit for the next 10 years (2013-2022). Numerical examples for Iowa are also presented.

Keywords: cellulosic biofuels, fast pyrolysis, sequential location.

1 Introduction

Biofuels has been recognized as important sources of renewable energy for their potential benefit on the environment, rural development, and reducing dependency on petroleum import. With the stimulation of enactment of Renewable Fuel Standard (RFS2) (1) in 2007, cellulosic based biofuels are gaining more attention. Biofuel industry can help improve the rural economics and job creation. Cellulosic biofuel production technologies are still mainly on the experimenting stage (2, 3). Studies on biomass logistics and biofuel supply chain management are also emerging. Stephen et al. show technology selection strategy based on biomass moisture content, energy density and load capacity of different transportation mode (4). Kocoloski et al. develop a mathematical model to optimize facility placement, and examine the impact of location and sizing selection (5). Ekşioğlu et al. propose a mixed integer programming model to design supply chain and manage logistics considering biomass transportation, inventory and process ability (6). And intermodal transportation is taken into consideration in the following work (7). In this paper, a sequential location allocation model for the fast pyrolysis facilities is investigated. Formulations are

---

[*] Corresponding author.

V. Prabhu, M. Taisch, and D. Kiritsis (Eds.): APMS 2013, Part I, IFIP AICT 414, pp. 409–415, 2013.
© IFIP International Federation for Information Processing 2013

presented in Section 2, and case study based on Iowa is included in Section 3. Paper concludes in Section 4 with major findings and future research directions.

2   Methodology

2.1   Problem Description

This study considers lignocellulosic biomass as the feedstock for fast pyrolysis facility to produce bio-oil, and the bio-oil will be used as feedstock of biorefinery, where it is converted to liquid transportation fuels. Fig. 1 illustrates the supply network setting.

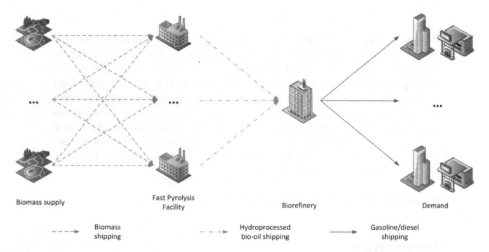

Fig. 1. Supply chain structure for cellulosic biomass pyrolysis – hydroprocessing –refining process

Major assumptions used in modeling are listed as follows:

1. Facility construction time is one-year and the facility life is 20-year.
2. A biorefinery with enough capacity exists in Iowa, and the location of the biorefinery is the county centroid that minimizes the total annual cost if all facilities are at optimal locations and capacities.
3. The facility location and material (feed and products) allocation decisions are made to maximize total profit of all facilities as a system.
4. The requirement for Iowa biofuel consumption in transportation increase linearly from 2013 to 2022, with demand in 2013 set at 0, and in 2022 set as the total gasoline demand within Iowa.
5. Fast pyrolysis and hydroprocessing for the cellulosic biomass are performed at distributed fast pyrolysis facility, while the hydroprocessed bio-oil are refining to gasoline/diesel range fuels in a centralized biorefinery.
6. Annual budget is set for construction of the distributed fast pyrolysis facilities.

2.2   Model Formulation

Notations:

i	Index for biomass supply locations
j	Index for candidate fast pyrolysis facility locations
k	Index for gasoline demand locations
l	Index for fast pyrolysis facility capacity level
t	Index for time period (decision making time)
GP_t	Projected gasoline price (8)
BCC_i	Unit biomass collecting cost (9)
BSC_{ij}	Unit biomass shipping cost (10, 11), $BSC_{ij} = FSC + VSC \times D_{ij}$, which is a combination of fixed shipping cost and variable shipping cost (related to shipping distance)
HSC_j	Unit hydroprocessed bio-oil shipping cost (11, 12)
GSC_k	Unit gasoline shipping cost (12)
FOC_l	Fixed facility operating cost (3)
GCC	Gasoline conversion cost, derived from variable facility operating cost, related to facility operating level (proportional to gasoline production amount) (3)
FFC_l	Fast pyrolysis facility capital cost, using scaling factor of 0.6 (3)
AFC_l	Amortized fast pyrolysis facility capital cost, derived from facility capital cost, with facility life of 20-year (3)
SPP_{it}	Maximum biomass supply amount, total corn stover available amount (13, 14) times maximum removal proportion (15)
$loss$	Biomass loss during transportation, assumed to be 5 wt%
θ_1	Conversion ratio from cellulosic biomass to hydroprocessed bio-oil (3)
θ_2	Conversion ratio from hydroprocessed bio-oil to gasoline diesel fuel (3)
$\overline{Dmn}_k$	Total gasoline demand level (16)
Dmn_t	Gasoline demand, $Dmn_{kt} = \sum_k \overline{Dmn}_k \times pr_t$, pr_t is the mandate proportion of total demand to be satisfied during the tth year
F_t	Fund raised from government or company
r	Annual interest rate, assumed to be 10%
x_{ijt}	Cellulosic biomass shipping amount (decision variable)
y_{jt}	Hydroprocessed bio-oil shipping amount (decision variable)
z_{kt}	Gasoline shipping amount (decision variable)
A_t	Total available fund (decision variable)
δ_{jlt}	Indicator of fast pyrolysis facility construction state (decision variable)

Mixed integer linear programming method is used to formulate the sequential location and allocation problem. The objective is to maximize the net present value (NPV) of the total profit of the next 10 years (2013-2022). Total profit calculation considers revenue from selling products, feedstock costs (collecting and shipping costs), intermediate product (hydroprocessed bio-oil) shipping costs, final products shipping costs, facility capital cost, and operating costs (reflected by fixed operating costs and conversion cost).

Objective function is presented below:

$$\max \sum_{t=1}^{T}(1+r)^{-t}\left(\sum_{k=1}^{K} z_{kt}(GP_t - GCC) - \sum_{i=1}^{N}\sum_{j=1}^{M}(BSC_{ij} + BCC_i)x_{ijt} - \sum_{j=1}^{M} HSC_j y_{jt} - \sum_{k=1}^{K} GSC_k z_{kt} - \sum_{j=1}^{M}\sum_{l=1}^{L} FOC_l \delta_{jlt}\right) - \sum_{t=1}^{T}(1+r)^{-t}\sum_{j=1}^{M}\sum_{l=1}^{L} AFC_l \delta_{jlt} \tag{1}$$

Major constraints include: biomass supply availability due to total grown amount and sustainability factor (2), biofuel conversion balance with conversion ratios from pathway techno-economic analysis (3,6), fast pyrolysis facility existence and capacity limit (4), a maximum of one facility per candidate facility construction location (5), no destruction of facility (9), minimum demand requirement and demand upper bound with linearly increase demand each year (7,8), limited available construction budget (10-12), and initialization of current situation of fast pyrolysis facility, which is none of such facilities exist at current stage (13).

$$\sum_{j=1}^{M} x_{ijt} \leq Spp_{it}, \quad \forall i, t \tag{2}$$

$$y_{jt} = (1 - loss)\theta_1 \sum_{i=1}^{N} x_{ijt}, \quad \forall j, t \tag{3}$$

$$(1 - loss)\sum_{i=1}^{N} x_{ijt} \leq \sum_{l=1}^{L} \delta_{jlt} C_l, \quad \forall j, t \tag{4}$$

$$\sum_{l=1}^{L} \delta_{jlt} \leq 1, \quad \forall j, t \tag{5}$$

$$\theta_2 \sum_{j=1}^{M} y_{jt} = \sum_{k=1}^{K} z_{kt}, \quad \forall t \tag{6}$$

$$\sum_{k=1}^{K} z_{kt} \geq \sum_{k=1}^{K} Dmn_{kt}, \quad \forall t \tag{7}$$

$$\overline{Dmn_{kt}} \geq z_{kt}, \quad \forall k, t \tag{8}$$

$$\delta_{j,l,t} \geq \delta_{j,l,t-1}, \quad \forall j, l, t \geq 2 \tag{9}$$

$$\sum_{j=1}^{M}\sum_{l=1}^{L} FFC_l \delta_{j,l,2} \leq F_1 \tag{10}$$

$$\sum_{j=1}^{M}\sum_{l=1}^{L} FFC_l\left(\delta_{j,l,t+1} - \delta_{j,l,t}\right) \leq A_{t-1}(1+r) + F_t, \tag{11}$$

$$\forall T - 1 \geq t \geq 2$$

$$A_t = A_{t-1}(1+r) + F_t - \sum_{j=1}^{M}\sum_{l=1}^{L} FFC_l\left(\delta_{j,l,t+1} - \delta_{j,l,t}\right), \tag{12}$$

$$\forall T - 1 \geq t \geq 2$$

$$\delta_{j,l,1} = 0, \quad \forall j, l \tag{13}$$

$$x_{ijt}, y_{jt}, z_{kt} \geq 0, \delta_{jlt} \in \{0,1\}, \quad \forall i, j, k, l, t \tag{14}$$

3   Results and Discussion

In this section, the results of a case study in Iowa are illustrated. Candidate fast pyrolysis facility locations are the county centroids in Iowa, and four facility capacities are allowed: 400, 1000, 1500, and 2000 metric ton of dry basis biomass per day, respectively.

To satisfy the minimum demand requirement, available fund per year needs to be at least enough to construct two 2000 metric ton/day facilities. The results under this minimum budget scenario are shown in Fig. 2. The county that is assumed to locate the existing biorefinery is represented using cross-shaded lines. Stars represent the fuel demand locations (centroids of MSAs), and star sizes illustrate the magnitude of fuel demand from the MSAs. From the results, all facilities built are of the highest allowed capacity, and in the figure, different color circles are used to represent the difference in construction order. The labeled year is the first year the corresponding facility starts to operate (construction finished). Facility locations are listed in legend, using FIPS codes of facility-located counties. The optimal NPV in the scenario is $5.28 billion.

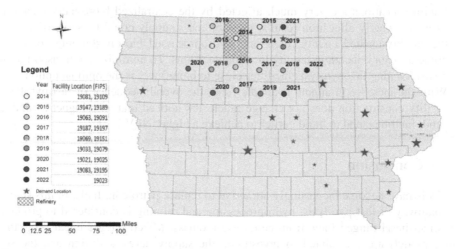

Fig. 2. Sequential facility construction under annual fund of twice the capital cost of 2000 metric ton/day facility

If annual available fund increases to 2.5 times capital cost of 2000 metric ton/day facility, the results are shown in Fig. 3. It could be seen in the figure, that with more available fund, it takes fewer years to finish constructing all facilities needed for the demand goal in 2022. The optimal NPV in the scenario is $6.03 billion.

Comparing the results under different budget limitations, several observations are summarized as follows:

- All facilities are built with the highest allowed capacity level. This is due to the scaling factor in capital cost estimation, which makes larger capacity facilities more cost-effective.

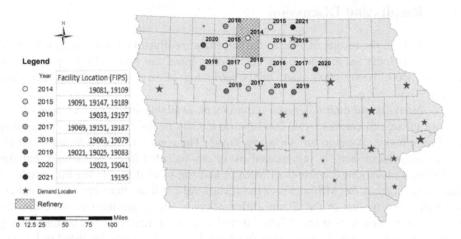

Fig. 3. Sequential facility construction under annual fund of 2.5 times capital cost of 2000 metric ton/day facility

- Facility locations are very much affected by the centralized biorefinery location. From the yearly allocation results, most biomass supply could be satisfied within the facility-located county; therefore, hydroprocessed bio-oil shipping costs become a major concern in facility location decisions. To minimize the transportation costs, locating fast pyrolysis facilities close to biorefinery is the optimal option.
- With the increase in annual available fund, the overall sequence of fast pyrolysis facility construction does not change much. It's noticed that with higher available fund, facilities tend to build earlier to achieve a higher NPV.

4   Conclusion

Biofuels have become increasingly attractive to replace petroleum fuels. In this study, the pathway of fast pyrolysis, hydroprocessing and refining is considered to produce gasoline-diesel ranged fuels from cellulosic biomass. Mixed integer linear programming models are formulated to investigate the supply network design and the sequence of the facility construction. The objective is to maximize the NPV of the total profit till 2022, which is the target year of RFS2. A case study in Iowa is conducted to illustrate the modeling approach. Numerical results show the preference for high capacity facilities, facility locations that are close to existing biorefinery, and earlier construction time as long as the budget allows. It is also concluded that the increase in annual available fund level does not have much impact on the construction sequence.

It should be noted that this sequential facility location problem is an ongoing research work that can be further investigated. Better data or modeling information, including the annual requirement of bio-based fuels, annual budget, and uncertainties in the feedstock availability and logistic cost, are to be investigated for more realistic decision making. In addition, facility capacity expansion could also be taken into consideration in the modeling framework.

References

1. Coyle, W.T.: Next-Generation Biofuels: Near-Term Challenges and Implications for Agriculture. Diane Publishing Company (2010)
2. Brown, T.R., Zhang, Y., Hu, G., Brown, R.C.: Techno-economic analysis of biobased chemicals production via integrated catalytic processing. Biofuels, Bioproducts and Biorefining 6(1), 73–87 (2012)
3. Wright, M.M., Daugaard, D.E., Satrio, J.A., Brown, R.C.: Techno-economic analysis of biomass fast pyrolysis to transportation fuels. Fuel 89(suppl. 1), S2–S10 (2010)
4. Stephen, J.D., Mabee, W.E., Saddler, J.N.: Biomass logistics as a determinant of second-generation biofuel facility scale, location and technology selection. Biofuels, Bioproducts and Biorefining 4(5), 503–518 (2010)
5. Kocoloski, M., Michael Griffin, W., Scott Matthews, H.: Impacts of facility size and location decisions on ethanol production cost. Energy Policy 39(1), 47–56 (2011)
6. Ekşioğlu, S.D., Acharya, A., Leightley, L.E., Arora, S.: Analyzing the design and management of biomass-to-biorefinery supply chain. Computers & Industrial Engineering 57(4), 1342–1352 (2009)
7. Ekşioğlu, S., Li, S., Zhang, S., Sokhansanj, S., Petrolia, D.: Analyzing Impact of Intermodal Facilities on Design and Management of Biofuel Supply Chain. Transportation Research Record: Journal of the Transportation Research Board 2191(-1), 144–151 (2010)
8. Petroleum product prices, U.S. Energy Information Administration
9. Graham, R.L., Nelson, R., Sheehan, J., Perlack, R.D., Wright, L.L.: Current And Potential U.s. Corn Stover Supplies. Agron. J. 99(1), 1–11 (2007)
10. Searcy, E., Flynn, P., Ghafoori, E., Kumar, A.: The relative cost of biomass energy transport. Applied Biochemistry and Biotechnology 140(1), 639–652 (2007)
11. CBO. Energy use in freight transportation. Congressional Budget Office (CBO) (1982)
12. BTS. Average Freight Revenue per Ton-mile. Bureau of Transportation Statistics, http://www.bts.gov/publications/national_transportation_statistics/html/table_03_21.html (accessed November 2012)
13. USDA/NASS Quickstats
14. Heid Jr., W.G.: Turning Great Plains crop residues and other products into energy. U.S. Dept. of Agriculture, Economic Research Service, Washington, D.C. (1984)
15. Papendick, R.I., Moldenhauer, W.C.: Crop Residue Management to Reduce Erosion and Improve Soil Quality: Northwest. U.S. Department of Agriculture Conservation Research Report; 1995:10-6
16. DOE/EIA. Annual Energy Review 2010 (2011)

Potential Woody Biomass Supply Chain Scenarios: A Conceptual Study

Evelyn A. Thomchick[1] and Kusumal Ruamsook[2]

[1] Department of Supply Chain & Information Systems,
The Pennsylvania State University, USA
Ethomcick@psu.edu
[2] Center for Supply Chain Research, The Pennsylvania State University, USA
Kusumal@psu.edu

Abstract. The interconnectivity among various business entities and physical functions of woody biomass supply chains requires a system-wide perspective. Extant studies largely focus on individual business units or sets of activities. This paper takes a supply chain perspective to gain an understanding of potential woody biomass supply chains. The study draws insights from an extensive review of literature to conceptualize potential woody biomass supply chain scenarios. Three woody biomass supply chain scenarios and associated logistics activities were defined from the analysis of literature content. They are woody biomass sourcing from forest product manufacturers, forest landowners, and biomass pre-processers. Findings suggest that woody biomass as a marketable commodity creates business opportunities for loggers and forest product manufacturers. In moving forward, infrastructure and technological development is vital, encompassing logging capability and transportation and industrial infrastructure.

Keywords: Woody biomass, logistics strategies, supply chain scenarios.

1 Introduction

Diminishing fossil fuel resources, increased competition for those fuels, and a growing realization of the economic and environmental impacts of the dependence on fossil fuels have led to a need to develop renewable energy resources. Bio-energy is one potential component of a renewable energy scenario for the future, accounting for approximately half (49%) of total renewable energy produced and consumed in the United States in 2012. A wide variety of biomass feedstock is currently used to produce bio-energy, ranging from woody biomass, agricultural wastes, to urban wastes. Of these feedstock varieties, woody biomass accounted for nearly half (45%) of the total biomass-based renewable energy consumed in 2012 (US Energy Information Administration, 2013). These figures demonstrate the considerable contribution of bio-energy, notably woody biomass-based energy, for national renewable energy effort.

V. Prabhu, M. Taisch, and D. Kiritsis (Eds.): APMS 2013, Part I, IFIP AICT 414, pp. 416–424, 2013.

However, managing biomass feedstock supply and its associated logistics activities are persistent issues. Intrinsically low in bulk densities, biomass feedstock creates logistics challenges in terms of its volume that has to be handled, stored, and transported (Benjamin et al., 2009; Damery and Benjamin, 2007; Sokhansanj and Fenton, 2006; Weiner, 2010). Given the low value of biomass materials and logistics challenges involved, the costs of moving biomass feedstock from supply sources to a bio-refinery plant can be prohibitive and often exceed market values for the biomass itself (Kram, 2008; Nicholls et al., 2008).

Managerial predicaments also arise due to the many business entities that make up a woody biomass supply chain. These entities perform two important physical functions of a supply chain. The first function involves *production,* encompassing forest landowners who produce forest materials; loggers who harvest and convert trees into logs or wood chips; forest product manufacturers whose process residues produce woody biomass; pre-processors who turn forest materials into processed woody biomass such as wood chips and pellets; and bio-refineries who convert woody biomass into heat, electricity, chemicals, and transportation fuels to serve different customers (Allen et al., 1998; D'Amours et al., 2008; Frisk et al., 2010; Sokhansanj and Fenton, 2006). The second function involves *logistics* of moving the various stages of products from one point in the supply chain to the next, encompassing key activities such as transportation, materials handling, warehousing and storage, and inventory control (Coyle et al., 2008; Fisher, 1997).

The interconnectivity among various entities, the associated physical functions, and supply sourcing challenges require a total supply chain perspective. Yet, extant studies on woody biomass largely focus on individual entities or sets of activities. The gap in research, coupled with the still evolving nature of the industry, lead to woody biomass supply chains that are currently not well perceived. The primary objective of this paper is to conceptualize potential supply chain scenarios associated with woody biomass. Insights gained are imperative as a basis for further research to promote economically feasible bio-energy as a component of renewable energy scenario for the future.

2   Methodology

To conceptualize and evaluate potential woody biomass supply chain scenarios, the study draws insights from extensive review of literature. Journal articles in the areas of supply chain and logistics, forest products, biomass feedstock, and bio-energy were selected from archival material available electronically at ProQuest and Academic Search Complete. Other principal data sources are the government and organization websites such as the US Energy Information Administration, the US Forest Service, and the International Energy Agency. Along with these data sources, informal interviews with five researchers in the fields of forest resources, agricultural sciences, and biomass energy were conducted to clarify and verify insights drawn from the literature.

Over 800 pages of documents were examined and coded on three levels according to Glaser and Strauss (1967) and Strauss and Corbin (1998). In the first level, key activities pertinent to the production and logistics functions of supplying woody biomass to a bio-refinery are identified, and the properties that characterize each activity are examined. Then, in the second level, we made connections between categories (in this case, the key activities identified above) by exploring the conditions and interactions that influence the processes of supplying woody biomass. This coding allowed us to integrate data into core categories or potential woody biomass supply chain scenarios. Then, using the core supply chain scenarios as a guide, we selectively coded the existing data obtained from literature survey and additional data gathered from the informal interviews to describe each scenario. At the end of this third-level coding, we have established the descriptions of potential supply chain scenarios.

3   Conceptualizing Woody Biomass Supply Chain Scenarios

Three potential woody biomass supply chain scenarios are identified and depicted in Figures 1–3. They are: (1) woody biomass sourcing from forest product manufacturers, (2) woody biomass sourcing from forest landowners, and (3) woody biomass sourcing from biomass pre-processors. We briefly describe each scenario in turn as follows.

3.1   Woody Biomass Sourcing from Forest Product Manufacturers

The first scenario, depicted in Figure 1, is currently preferred by most bio-refineries (Morgan, 2009).

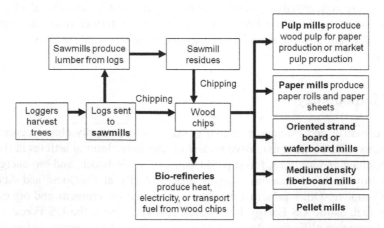

Fig. 1. Woody Biomass Sourcing from Forest Product Manufacturers

In this scenario, residues produced by primary wood processors, such as sawmills and their lumber customers, are the primary feedstock for both the bio-refineries and secondary forest product manufacturers such as pulp mills, paper mills, and pellet mills (Ray, 2010). Classified as industrial private landowners, these forest product manufacturers possess large forest assets for uses in their manufacturing requirements (Benjamin et al., 2009; Frisk et al., 2010; IBISWorld, 2009; McDill, 2011). They contract independent loggers for harvesting timber and delivering logs from their forestland to their production facilities (Myers and Richards, 2003). In general, approximately 80 percent of the output loggers generated—typically the lower part of the tree that has a larger diameter, and thus a higher value—is transported directly to a nearby sawmill for processing. The upper, thinner parts of the tree that have lower value are commonly delivered to pulp mills and paper mills (Crooks, 2005; D'Amours et al., 2008; Frisk et al., 2010; IBISWorld, 2009, 2010). These loggers typically use trucks and equipment they owned or leased to make the deliveries to the mills (IBISWorld, 2010), although in some cases transport service providers or contract haulers (e.g. trucking companies and rail carriers) may also be involved (Bolding et al., 2009). In turn, the mills deliver mill chips to the bio-refineries according to the arrangement between the parties, which vary in terms of transportation mode used, and size and frequency of deliveries (Liu, 2010; McDill, 2011; Roth, 2010).

3.2   Woody Biomass Sourcing from Forest Landowners

The second scenario, depicted in Figure 2, makes use of forest materials that contribute the potentially most abundant sources of woody biomass in the United States (Nicholls et al., 2008).

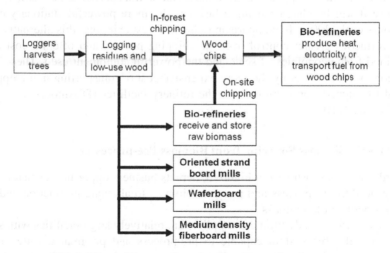

Fig. 2. Woody Biomass Sourcing from Forest Landowners

In this scenario, forest biomass is sourced from landowners that can be public entities (e.g. federal, state, and local and municipal land and forests), private industrial entities (e.g. saw mills, and pulp and paper mills), or non-industrial private entities (e.g. individuals or corporations other than forest product industry) (Biomass Research and Development Board, 2008b; D'Amours et al., 2008). As in the first scenario, forest landowners contract loggers for felling standing timber, delivering the outputs, and disposing logging residues. Decisions on the methods of residue disposal (e.g. piling and burning, scattering throughout a site to decompose, and processing as biomass) may be left to the loggers, or set forth by landowners and third-party environmental certification standards for sustainable forest management practices (Benjamin et al., 2009; Elmore, 2009; Yepsen, 2008).

In turn, bio-refineries transact with the loggers for the forest biomass. Biomass can be delivered in either chipped or non-chipped forms. The former involves in-forest chipping, which is well integrated into existing timber harvesting systems (D'Amours et al., 2008; Gunnarsson et al., 2004). In this case, loggers with portable wood-chipping equipment produce wood chips from logging residues and from whole trees of non-merchantable quality for direct sale to bio-refineries and other buyers such as pulp and paper mills (D'Amours et al., 2008). Unlike clean chip by-products from forest product manufacturers, these logging chips (also called dirty chips and hog fuel) are characterized by high moisture and varied physical quality in terms of size, shape, and chemical makeup (Benjamin et al., 2009; Kimbell et al., 2009; Kram, 2008; Weiner, 2010; Yepsen, 2008). These characteristics render biomass that has low net energy density by mass, is unsuitable for long-term storage, and is uneconomical for long distance transportation (Crooks, 2005; Goldstein, 2006; Jackson et al., 2010; Liu, 2010; McDill, 2011; Wallace, 2011; Richard, 2011). Coupled with the often geographically dispersed forest lands, transportation cost could easily exceed the costs of biomass itself (Bolding et al., 2009).

Alternatively, non-chipped forest biomass can be transported to bio-refinery facilities where it will be chipped using a larger-scale, more powerful stationary chipper (D'Amours et al., 2008). In comparison to the in-forest chipping, this alternative gives the bio-refineries greater control over the chipping process and offers a cost advantage gained from economies of scale and the powerful equipment used. These advantages, however, are offset by the more expensive cost of transporting non-chipped, as opposed to chipped, forest biomass to the refinery facilities (D'Amours et al., 2008; Jackson et al., 2010).

3.3   Woody Biomass Sourcing from Biomass Pre-processers

The third scenario, illustrated in Figure 3, depicts business opportunities that emerged from the need to pre-process and pre-treat biomass to alleviate production and logistics issues pertinent to biomass.

In this scenario, woody biomass suppliers are relatively large facilities with storage capacity and flexible system capable to pre-process and pre-treat a wide range of biomass materials. The biomass supply chain in this scenario resembles that of a hub-and-spoke system of biomass processing and distribution (Carolan et al., 2007; Roth, 2010; Yepsen, 2008, 2009). A typical biomass pre-processer assumes a role of an *intermediary* who engages in securing and establishing contracts for various types of biomass from various sources. It also manages the collection, storage, pre-process, and delivery of biomass to the bio-refinery and other biomass users (Carolan et al., 2007; Sokhansanj and Fenton, 2006).

A pre-processor's large-scale, flexible system permits physical transformation (e.g. pre-processed briquettes, pellets, and torrefied biomass) and chemical transformation (e.g. pre-treated to alter chemical component) of a wide range of biomass feedstock to satisfy the quality and quantity requirements of biomass users before making delivery (Roth, 2010; Yepsen, 2008). Hence, aside from improving the quality of biomass as feedstock, these processing technologies are also logistically advantageous, making it possible to economically transport biomass over greater distances and to store large quantities of biomass for longer periods of time. Production cost advantage is also achieved because of economies of scope gained from the variety of feedstock used and flexible product mix, and economies of production scale and powerful equipment used (Carolan et al., 2007; Jackson et al., 2010; Sokhansanj and Fenton, 2006; Taylor et al., 2010).

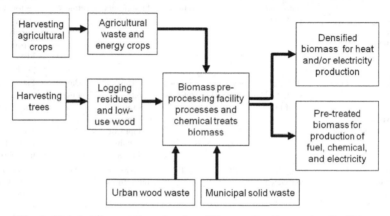

Fig. 3. Woody Biomass Sourcing from Biomass Pre-Processing Facilities

4   Conclusion

This conceptual study identifies three potential woody biomass supply chains and reveals the roles and interactions between different members in performing the production and logistics functions of the supply chains. Three important implications in moving woody biomass-based bio-energy forward arise from the findings summarized in Table 1.

First, loggers play an important production role in all three scenarios. To take advantage of the new biomass market opportunities, logging capacities must be developed and new managerial and operational practices must be devised to integrate the existing operations and emerging biomass business (Benjamin et al., 2009; Biomass Research and Development Board, 2008b; Damery and Benjamin, 2007; Elmore, 2009; Kram, 2008; Yepsen, 2008, 2009).

Second, forest product manufacturers possess technological and infrastructural advantages that render them competitive as biomass suppliers. They have access to their abundant industrial forestlands, well-established transportation systems, and the on-site infrastructure for pre-processing, storage, and handling of woody biomass. The new markets of biomass as feedstock for bio-energy present great opportunities for business expansion that leverage these existing capital investment and resources (Benjamin et al., 2009; Frisk et al., 2010 Jackson et al., 2010; Sklar, 2008). A more vertically integrated avenue is to expand into the bio-refinery business and become an "integrated forest product bio-refinery" enterprise that produces bio-products (e.g. heat, transport fuel, and bio-chemical) in addition to conventional forest products (Damery and Benjamin, 2007; Feng et al., 2010; Kimbell et al., 2009).

Table 1. Woody Biomass Supply Chain Scenarios: Key Parties, Roles, and Advantages/ Disadvatages

Scenarios	Forest material production	Harvesting	Physical pre-processing	Chemical pre-treating	Biomass delivery	Biomass storage	Advantage/ Disadvantage to Biomass Buyers
Sourcing from Forest Product Mfr. (FPM)	FPM	Logger contracted by FPM	FPM	Bio-refinery	Between bio-refinery and FPM	Bio-refinery	• Established sector; Clean chips • Supply depending on FPM production
Sourcing from Forest Landowner (FLO)	FLO	Logger contracted by FLO	Logger or bio-refinery	Bio-refinery	Bio-refinery arranges own shipment with loggers	Bio-refinery	• Established sector, potentially most abundant sources • Dirty chip; high transport cost
Sourcing from Pre-processer (PP)	FLO	Logger contracted by PP	PP	PP	Between bio-refinery and PP	PP	• Economy of scale and scope; feedstock to specification • Not yet established sector

Finally, infrastructure development is vital to enhance reliability and efficiency of the production and logistics functions of woody biomass supply chains. Transportation infrastructure, in particular, is much needed to tap into the abundant, yet highly dispersed forest biomass resources. Additionally, an extensive industrial infrastructure is required to advance the current experimental operations to commercial stages. Industrial infrastructure encompasses not only the bio-refinery facility itself, but also pre-processing and treatment facilities, and communication technology needed to improve logging and biomass harvest efficiencies (Benjamin et al., 2009; Jackson et al., 2010; Kimbell et al., 2009).

Acknowledgments. This work was funded by a Pennsylvania State Sustainability Seed Grant awarded by the Pennsylvania State Institutes of Energy and the Environment (PSIEE). We thank Dr. Jude Liu, Dr. Marc E. McDill, Dr. Tom Richard, Dr. Gregory W. Roth, and Mr. Bob Wallace for their valuable insights on the woody biomass, forest management, and renewable energy industries.

References

1. Allen, J., Browne, M., Hunter, A., Boyd, J., Palmer, H.: Logistics Management and Costs of Biomass Fuel Supply. International Journal of Physical Distribution and Logistics Management 28(6), 463–477 (1998)
2. Benjamin, J., Lilieholm, R.J., Damery, D.: Challenges and Opportunities for the Northeastern Forest Bioindustry. Journal of Forestry 107(3), 125–131 (2009)
3. Bolding, M.C., Kellogg, L.D., Davis, C.T.: Productivity and Costs of an Integrated Mechanical Forest Fuel Reduction Operation in Southwest Oregon. Forest Products Journal 59(3), 35–47 (2009)
4. Carolan, J.E., Joshi, S.V., Dale, B.E.: Technical and Financial Feasibility Analysis of Distributed Bioprocessing Using Regional Biomass Pre-Processing Enterprises. Journal of Agricultural & Food Industrial Organization, Special Issue: Explorations in Biofuels Economics, Policy, and History 5(2), 1–29 (2007)
5. Coyle, J.J., Langley Jr., C.J., Gibson, B.J., Novack, R.A., Bardi, E.: Supply Chain Management: A Logistics Perspective. South-Western Cengage Learning, Mason (2008)
6. Crooks, A.M.: Protecting Forests and Supporting Renewable Energy. BioCycle 46(4), 68–71 (2005)
7. D'Amours, S., Rönnqvist, M., Weintraub, A.: Using Operational Research for Supply Chain Planning in the Forest Products Industry. INFOR 46(4), 265–281 (2008)
8. Damery, D.T., Benjamin, J.: The Northeast Forest Bio-products Puzzle. Forest Products Journal 57(11), 14–15 (2007)
9. Elmore, C.: No Chip Left Behind. OEM Off-Highway 27(3), 24–26 (2009)
10. Feng, Y., D' Amours, S., LeBel, L., Nourelfath, M.: Integrated Bio-Refinery and Forest Products Supply Chain Network Design Using Mathematical Programming Approach. Report CIRRELT-2010-50 (November 2010)
11. Fisher, M.L.: What is the Right Supply Chain for Your Product? Harvard Business Review, 105–116 (March-April 1997)
12. Frisk, M., Gothe-Lundgren, M., Jörnsten, K., Rönnqvist, M.: Cost Allocation in Collaborative Forest Transportation. European Journal of Operational Research 205(2), 448–458 (2010)
13. Glaser, B.G., Strauss, A.: The Discovery of Grounded Theory: Strategies for Qualitative Research, Aldine, Chicago, IL (1967)
14. Goldstein, N.: Woody Biomass as Renewable Energy Source. BioCycle 47(11), 29–31 (2006)
15. Gunnarsson, H., Mikael, R., Lundgren, J.T.: Supply Chain Modeling of Forest Fuel. European Journal of Operational Research 158(1), 103–123 (2004)
16. IBISWorld: Timber Services in the US Industry Report [11311] (December 2009)
17. IBISWorld: Logging in the US Industry Report [11331] (June 2010)
18. Jackson, S.W., Rials, T.G., Taylor, A.M., Bozell, J.G., Norris, K.M.: Wood2Energy: A State of the Science and Technology Report. The University of Tennessee (May 2010)
19. Kimbell, A.R., Thomas, M., Hutch, B., Bowyer, J.L., Argow, K.A.: More Energy from Wood: What Are the Prospects? Journal of Forestry 107(5), 267–272 (2009)
20. Kram, J.W.: Is Biomass Harvesting Sustainable? Biomass Magazine (September 2008)
21. Liu, J.: Assistant Professor of Agricultural and Biological Engineers, Department of Agricultural and Biological Engineering, Agricultural Sciences, Pennsylvania State University. Personal conversation with authors (October 21, 2010)

22. McDill, M.E.: Associate Professor of Forest Management and Program Chair for Forest Science, School of Forest Resources, Agricultural Sciences, Pennsylvania State University. Personal conversation with authors (January 25 and September 16, 2011)
23. Morgan, T.A.: Woody Biomass: Can Forests Fuel Our Future? Montana Business Quarterly 47(4), 2–6 (2009)
24. Myers, J., Richards, E.W.: Supporting Wood Supply Chain Decisions with Simulation for a Mill in Northwestern BC. INFOR 41(3), 213 (2003)
25. Nicholls, D.L., Monserud, R.A., Dykstra, D.P.: Biomass Utilization for Bioenergy in the Western United States. Forest Products Journal 58(1/2), 6–16 (2008)
26. Ray, C.D.: Project-Based Overview of Woody Biomass Initiatives in the Generation of Thermal Energy, Electricity, and Transportation Fuels in the Eastern Hardwood Region of the United States. Report submitted to USDA Forest Service (March 2010)
27. Richard, T.: Director of Penn State Institutes of Energy and the Environment, Professor of Biological Engineering, Penn State University. Personal conversation with authors (August 31, 2011)
28. Roth, G.W.: Professor of Agronomy, Department of Crop and Soil Sciences, Agricultural Sciences, Pennsylvania State University. Personal conversation with authors (October 20, 2010)
29. Sklar, T.: Ethanol from Wood Waste an Opportunity for Refiners. Oil & Gas Journal 106(21), 54–59 (2008)
30. Sokhansanj, S., Fenton, J.: Cost Benefit of Biomass Supply and Pre-Processing. Synthesis Paper, A BIOCAP Research Integration Program (March 2006)
31. Strauss, A., Corbin, J.: Basics of Qualitative Research: Grounded Theory Procedures and Techniques. Sage, Newbury Park (1998)
32. Taylor, E.L., Holley, A.G., Blazier, M.: Comparisons of In-Woods Densification Options in the Western Gulf. Rutgers eXtension (last modified March 12, 2010)
33. US Energy Information Administration: Monthly Energy Review. Table 10.1 Renewable Energy Production and Consumption by Source (April 2013)
34. Wallace, R.: Associate, BooziAlleniHamilton. Email sent to authors, August 12, and conference call with authors August 17 (2011)
35. Weiner, L.: The Ripple Effect. Minority Business Entrepreneur 27(2), 30–32 (2010)
36. Yepsen, R.: Forest Thinning Strategies for Biomass Utilization. BioCycle 49(12), 32–36 (2008)
37. Yepsen, R.: Wood Processing Innovations. BioCycle 50(2), 25–26 (2009)

Closed Loop Supply Chains for Sustainable Mass Customization

Kjeld Nielsen and Thomas Ditlev Brunø

Department of Mechanical and Manufacturing Engineering, Aalborg University, Denmark
kni@m-tech.aau.dk

Abstract. Closed loop supply chains reducing waste, energy consumption and natural resource depletion which all contribute to more sustainable production and products. For mass customization however, the challenges of closed loop supply chains are emphasized by the large variety of inbound end-of-life products from customers which complicates handling and forecasting. This paper analyses these challenges in the specific context mass customization using theoretical considerations and three case studies.

Keywords: mass customization, sustainability, remanufacturing, reuse, recycling.

1 Introduction

Mass Customization (MC) popularized by Pine [6] has proven a successful business strategy in various industries and markets and for several different product types. Mass customization is fundamentally different from mass production in several different ways, spanning from product design and production to sales and marketing and fit with customer needs. Sustainability is a concept that is gaining more and more attention, and companies are experiencing a greater demand for sustainable products as well as legislation requiring lower environmental impacts [3]. Several concepts are commonly applied to achieve greater sustainability in product design and manufacturing. Among these is Eco-design, which is a concept that attempts to integrate environmental aspects into the product development process thereby creating products with lower negative environmental impacts and thus more environmentally sustainable products [3]. Generally, what happens to a product at its end of life (EOL) is very important in relation to sustainability. This is the case for two reasons: 1) if a product is disposed by land filling or incineration, the materials in the product may harm the environment. 2) The amount of materials available in the world is finite, and if raw materials are extracted at the same pace in the future as they are today, certain materials will become scarce. If an EOL product is simply disposed by land filling or incineration, the materials used in the product are lost, and thus more new material must be extracted for manufacturing new products. Reusing or recycling a product addresses both the issues regarding land filling or incineration as well as resource consumption, since EOL products are either recycled and the materials are transformed

V. Prabhu, M. Taisch, and D. Kiritsis (Eds.): APMS 2013, Part I, IFIP AICT 414, pp. 425–432, 2013.

into other products or the products are used in their original form. However, even though reverse logistics may help to safely dispose of EOL products, extending the concept to closed loop supply chains has proven to reduce the environmental impact even more [7]. A closed loop supply chain is a combination of a reverse supply chain and a traditional forward supply chain where the components or materials retrieved from products in the reverse supply chain are used to manufacture products for the forward supply chain, thus closing the materials loop.

Rose [7] performed a quantitative Analysis of the environmental impact from a variety of different consumer electronics for the different recycling loops also referred to as EOL strategies. She found that with no exceptions, the environmental impact of a product would increase each time a larger loop was applied. Based on this, she introduced the hierarchy of EOL strategies illustrated in figure 1 [7] and concluded that a product should be designed to apply EOL strategies as high in the hierarchy as possible, corresponding to shorter closed loop supply chains [7].

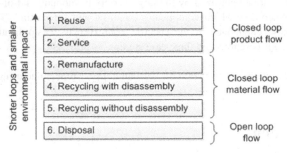

Fig. 1. Hierarchy of product EOL strategies [7]

Apart from the environmental perspective, applying short closed loop supply chains are also usually favorable from an economic perspective. The reason for this is that materials used in products higher in the EOL hierarchy have more value added than lower in the hierarchy. As examples, product reuse requires no or very little additional value added before the product can be used by a new (second hand) customer, whereas a disposed product represents zero or very little value if it is incinerated for energy production.

2   Research Method

The research objective of this paper is to identify how well mass customized products can become more sustainable by utilizing closed loop supply chains. The research question is: "How can end-of-life strategies with closed loop supply chains be applied to mass customized products?" To answer this question, it is first clarified how well the EOL hierarchy and mass customized products combine. Secondly the concepts of closed loop supply chains with different EOL strategies are analyzed for various mass customized products. Finally the findings from the analysis and the case studies are identified and presented. The analysis is performed as an empiric research based on

Rose's product EOL strategy hierarchy as presented in figure 1. It is analyzed which issues typically arise for mass customized products in end-of-life. This is done for each of the 6 levels in the EOL hierarchy (fig. 1). The concepts of closed loop supply chains are further analyzed in three mass customization cases all with EOL strategies and different levels in the hierarchy. The case studies present and analyze how the EOL strategies have been implemented in consumer electronics, automobile and furniture industry. The findings from the analysis and case studies are presented as a general overview of advantages and disadvantages of mass customized products combined with EOL strategies and a comparison of EOL strategies of the case studies.

3   Closed Loop Supply Chain and Mass Customization

Much research has been done in the areas reverse logistics and closed loop supply chains, however, no studies have been identified focusing on these issues related specifically to mass customized products. Mass customized products are distinguished from non-mass customized products, primarily by their vast variety, as each product is uniquely produced for a specific customer. This is expected to bring up new challenges in relation to reusing and recycling products. In the following sections, the challenges specific to mass customized products will be discussed. The analysis will be structured by the levels in the product EOL strategy hierarchy shown in figure 1.

3.1   Reuse

Reuse (1) is the EOL strategy which will use least resources compared to   other EOL strategies, simply because following the definition expressed by Rose [7] as "... the second hand trading of a product for use as originally designed", the products involved in a reuse process change owners without any involvement of the original manufacture and other further resources involved. Implementing reuse as an EOL strategy should be easy for standard products but for MC products there are several difficulties which have to be addressed.

  One issue related to MC products is that the customized product specifically made for a specific customers requirements, can be difficult to reuse. Difficult to reuse, because the products will not fit the new customers' requirements; as examples, it could be tailor fitted products, as suits, shoes, furniture etc.

  Implementing an EOL strategy should on the other hand lead to MC products which should be easy to reuse and even in the reuse process are able to customize further for the second hand owner.

3.2   Service

If a product is to be replaced due to "wear and tear", i.e. the product is somehow worn or defective and thus cannot be reused, which is the preferred EOL strategy according to the hierarchy, the strategy "service" should be considered [7]. In this strategy, the life of a product is extended by repairing or servicing the product thus pushing the time where a new product will have to be manufactured to fulfill a user's needs. There is no apparent and strong relation between this strategy and mass customization, however the variety of parts included in the product may cause some issues if spare parts are necessary. This would be the case if the parts, which are to be replaced to repair the product, are custom fabricated, as opposed to a customized product assembled from standard components. If a custom fabricated component is required for repairing or servicing the product, this would likely be more expensive than repairing a product using standard components, since the spare part would need to be manufactured specifically for that product which would likely introduce higher logistical costs as well as a problem regarding the identification of specifications for manufacturing that specific part.

An example of mass customized products which have a modular architecture that supports upgrading is personal computers. If a user finds that a computer is lacking certain functionality or performance, in many cases this will be possible to address by adding or replacing modules in the computer such as CPU, processor or other expansion cards. This is obviously more appropriate from an environmental perspective since a new computer will not have to be produced to fulfill the user's new needs.

3.3 Remanufacture

The EOL strategy remanufacturing implies according to Rose [7] that EOL products are returned from the customer to a remanufacturing plant where they are disassembled; the parts are reconditioned and used in the manufacturing of new products using newly manufactured parts as well. In contrast to the service EOL strategy, the product is here completely disassembled and components are collected and kept in stock until needed. By choosing the remanufacturing strategy, the material and energy used for originally manufacturing the products is not lost which apart from reducing negative environmental impact can be economically beneficial as well [9].

The degree to which an MC product is suitable for remanufacturing will be very dependent on how the product architecture is defined. One way to mitigate the challenges derived from component variety described above by means of product architecture would be to enable remanufacturing of the components common to all products in a product family, commonly referred to as the product platform, which is commonly used in MC products [1], whereas the modules providing customization could be recycled for materials. This however would require the components in the platform to be sufficiently durable for multiple life cycles.

3.4 Recycling with Disassembly

When applying the recycling with disassembly EOL strategy, EOL products are taken to recycling facilities where they are disassembled and recycled. In contrast to recycling without disassembly, this strategy implies that the value and energy accumulated in the products is to some extent retained. Recycling with disassembly also allows removing components or substances which would otherwise contaminate the recyclable materials, as well as valuable components can be removed and reused or remanufactured [7].

When considering recycling with disassembly in relation to MC products, several different factors influence the possibilities for recycling. As the products need to be disassembled, which is usually a manual process, the disassembly process is likely to account for much of the total costs associated with recycling. As MC products will often have varying product structures compared to non MC products, the disassembly process will also vary more than for non MC products. As a consequence, it will be more difficult to optimize the disassembly process as well as applying automation.

3.5   Recycling without Disassembly and Disposal

Recycling without disassembly is the EOL strategy with the longest materials loop and thus the least desirable of the closed loop supply chain strategies, however still preferable over disposal. Recycling without disassembly is usually performed by shredding; by doing this the shredded products can be sorted into material fractions which can be recycled. Since all products are treated alike when recycled without disassembly, no specific challenges regarding MC products are identified for this EOL strategy. The EOL strategy disposal is the least desirable in the hierarchy, since the value and energy accumulated in the products is not recovered. As for the recycle without disassembly strategy, all products are treated alike when disposed, and no specific challenges regarding MC products are identified for this EOL strategy.

4   Case Analyses

To address how different types of companies have been using reverse logistics in practice, a number of case studies have been identified in literature.

Dell Inc. sells and produces personal computers which are all customized according to the customer specific configuration. Dell has implemented a closed loop supply chain to make use of EOL computers which are traded in by Dell's customers. This case is thoroughly described by Kumar & Craig [5]. When comparing the paths of EOL computers at Dell to the classification of EOL strategies shown in figure 1, Dell makes use of several of these strategies:

- Reuse: EOL computers which do not require any parts changed are reinstalled with an operating system and resold, physically unchanged.
- Service or Remanufacture: computers which require replacement of components are changed physically and are, depending on how many components are changed, either serviced or remanufactured.
- Recycle with disassembly: computers which are not reused, serviced or remanufactured are disassembled and shipped to appropriate recycling facilities.

This multilevel approach to handling EOL computers allows Dell to utilize the shortest closed loop supply chain as possible. What enables this is that the modularity of Dell computers allows components to be easily replaced and allows reuse of components from EOL computers. Furthermore, Dell's volume makes it profitable to run remanufacturing facilities.

Numerous car manufacturers are mass customizing their cars. This is enabled by a modular product platform which allows customization by assembling the car from a common platform and a number of different modules creating the variety. Contrary to the Dell case, car manufacturers do not take back whole cars for remanufacturing, which can be due to a number of reasons. Cars usually have a much longer life than personal computers and are thus regularly serviced for extending their life. Relating the automobile industry to the classification of EOL strategies in figure 1, it shows that the car industry also utilizes multiple levels.

- Service: When a used car is traded in by a dealership, it is serviced and resold, typically in an unchanged configuration; however, the car manufacturer is not involved in this.
- Remanufacturing: Worn components are traded in for a discount on a remanufactured component and remanufactured to as new condition by specialized companies
- Recycling with disassembly: EOL vehicles are returned to third party car recycling facilities and disassembled for spare parts and material recycling.

The automobile industry is similar to the Dell case since mass customized products are resold in a fixed configuration which cannot be reconfigured.

Ahrend is a Dutch manufacturer of office furniture, which has done a significant effort on reducing the negative environmental impact from production and product life cycles. Ahrend produces office chairs and desks for the professional market and their furniture are individually customized and can thus be considered mass customized products. Ahrend has as one of the means to control supply of EOL products, introduced a residual value on repurchase program for its customers allowing them to return their product to Ahrend after ended use and receive a partial refund. After receiving the used products Ahrend is to refurbish certain components and renew others and sell new products which contain refurbished as well as new components. These new products are again customized. Comparing the Ahrend case to the EOL hierarchy of figure 1 shows that Ahrend contrary to the two other cases makes use of remanufacturing used products to create new mass customized products by reusing on module level.

5   Findings

In figure 2, an overview of the different EOL strategies and their implications for MC products is presented. For the upper 4 levels a number of challenges exist which are specific to MC products, however a number of characteristics of MC products also provide benefits for the different closed loop supply chain EOL strategies compared to non MC products. Finally, no differences were found for the lower two EOL strategies between MC and non MC products.

Figure 3 shows a comparison of EOL strategies chosen in the three different cases presented in this paper as well as the EOL options for a generic MC product. For a generic MC product, i.e. any MC product, for which the manufacturer has not actively chosen an EOL strategy, the options for the customer when disposing the product will be either to sell it as second hand, given the second hand purchaser can accept the product configuration or bring it to recycling facilities or disposal. What can also be concluded from the comparison is that in only the Ahrend case, the products are remanufactured and offered as individually mass customized products again, whereas the other two cases offer used products in an as-is configuration. It is furthermore common to use mixed EOL strategies, since the difference in wear and obsolescence makes different EOL strategies suitable for different products in the supply of used products.

	Advantages	Disadvantages
Reuse	Reconfigurability allows customization to new user	Poor fit to diverse customer demands
Service	Modularity enables replacement of defective modules	Product variety increases variety of spare parts
Remanufacturing	Modular products enable component replacement Product platform architecture enables remanufacturing of modules common to one product family	Product variety in EOL product supply complicates demand planning Custom manufactured components are unsuitable for remanufacturing
Recycle with disassembly	Easier disassembly due to modular product architecture	Difficult to optimize or automate disassembly process due to product structure variety
Recycle without disassembly	None	None
Disposal	None	None

Fig. 2. Overview of product EOL strategies and implications for mass customization products compared to mass produced products

As mentioned above, many MC products can be reused in an as-is configuration. While this would likely be beneficial in terms of environmental impact, the business potential is negligible unless the manufacturer is involved in the second hand trading of the product as in the Dell case.

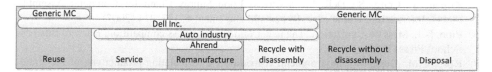

Fig. 3. Comparison of EOL strategies for case products

Finally the case comparison revealed that there are differences in whether the manufacturer manages the closed loop supply chains or a specialized third party company is involved. General for all cases is that the product families apply modular product architectures, which is not surprising since modular architecture enables mass customization and remanufacturing [2], [4].

6   Conclusion

From the analysis of EOL strategies and cases it can be concluded that it is indeed possible to utilize closed loop supply chains in mass customization settings. However, utilizing closed loop supply chains requires certain aspects to be considered regarding product design as well as manufacturing and supply chain design.

Utilizing closed loop supply chains has a great potential in achieving a higher degree of product sustainability, since this will reduce the amount of waste produced as well as reducing the demand for raw material production and energy consumption. Although only a minor part of mass customizers are utilizing closed loop supply chains, the case studies have shown that it can be an attractive business proposition to e.g. remanufacture products and resell them.

However, to provide the customer with the highest value, and thereby charge a price premium, the remanufactured product should be re-customized to specific customer requirements as done in the case study of Ahrend instead of reselling products as second hand in as-is configurations. This however presents a number of logistical challenges as well as challenges in developing the solution space for configuring remanufactured products. Furthermore, this research addresses only mass customization of physical products. Mass customization of services and software is also relevant but will require entirely different considerations regarding sustainable supply chains.

References

1. Huang, G.Q., Simpson, T.W., Pine II, B.J.: The Power of Product Platforms in Mass Customisation. International Journal of Mass Customisation 1, 1–13 (2005)
2. Ishii, K.: Modularity: A Key Concept in Product Life-Cycle Engineering. In: Handbook of Life-cycle Engineering (1998)
3. Karlsson, R., Luttropp, C.: EcoDesign: What's Happening? an Overview of the Subject Area of EcoDesign and of the Papers in this Special Issue. J. Clean. Prod. 14, 1291–1298 (2006)
4. Krikke, H., le Blanc, I., van de Velde, S.: Product Modularity and the Design of Closed-Loop Supply Chains. Calif. Manage. Rev. 46, 23–39 (2004)
5. Kumar, S., Craig, S.: Dell, Inc.'s Closed Loop Supply Chain for Computer Assembly Plants. Information, Knowledge, Systems Management 6, 197–214 (2007)
6. Pine, B.J.: Mass customization: The new frontier in business competition. Harvard Business School Press (1993)
7. Rose, C.M.: Design for environment: A method for formulating product end-of-life strategies. In: Design for Environment: A Method for Formulating Product End-of-Life Strategies. Stanford University (2000)
8. Subramoniam, R., Huisingh, D., Chinnam, R.B.: Remanufacturing for the Automotive Aftermarket-Strategic Factors: Literature Review and Future Research Needs. J. Clean. Prod. 17, 1163–1174 (2009)

Determination of the Spare Parts Demand for Maintenance, Repair and Overhaul Service Providers

Uwe Dombrowski and Sebastian Weckenborg

Technische Universität Braunschweig,
Institute for Advanced Industrial Management,
Langer Kamp 19, 38106 Braunschweig, Germany

Abstract. Service providers for maintenance, repair and overhaul (MRO) of aircrafts and components face major challenges. The calculation of an optimal stock level for components is one of these. The optimal stock level is highly influenced by the customers demand. Furthermore the stock level influences the profitability of the processes. The challenge for MRO service provider is to respond to the changing customer base and to adapt the stock level for components dynamically. For this purpose, an approach for the determination of the spare parts demand is described in this paper. The approach consists of a hierarchical derivation of reliability parameters in the first step and finally an assessment of the derived reliability parameters. By this assessment the relevance of different impact factors can be determined. The determination of the spare parts demand and the optimal stock level can thereby be determined much more accurately.

Keywords: Spare parts management, MRO, Maintenance, Repair, Overhaul

1   Introduction

The efficient spare parts supply during the entire life cycle of the primary product is a differentiating quality characteristic in competition. It can lead to an improved customer satisfaction and strengthens the company in the market. [1], [2], [3]

For the realization of an effective spare parts management, it is important to understand the correlations between different impact factors regarding the spare parts demand. Both the life cycle of the primary product and the life cycle of the component have to be considered. There are different strategies for the spare parts supply during and after the serial production of the primary product. These result from the number of primary products on the market and especially from the technological characteristics of the individual components as well as the reliability parameters. This results in different demand patterns, not only in volume, but also in demand continuity and the demand predictability. [4], [5], [6], [7]

The life-cycle-oriented spare parts management focuses on this specific problem and contains several supply strategies to realize an efficient post-series supply. These supply strategies are the development of a compatible successive product generation,

V. Prabhu, M. Taisch, and D. Kiritsis (Eds.): APMS 2013, Part I, IFIP AICT 414, pp. 433–440, 2013.

the storing of a final lot, the periodical internal or external production, the reuse of used components and the repair of used components. [8], [9], [10]

The aviation industry is characterized by extremely long life-cycles of the primary products with a high degree of efficiency, small lot sizes, a strict regulation and a high degree of individualization. The share of the services business in the aviation industry is very high. [11] Airlines often buy the maintenance services, in order to concentrate on their core business. Compared with other industries, the repair of components in the aviation industry is highly profitable and is therefore common practice [12]. [13]

2   Tasks and Challenges of Maintenance, Repair and Overhaul Service Providers

The range of tasks of a service provider in the aviation field is very large. A classification of the tasks is possible by the distinction between the value adding organizational units of a service provider. These organizational units are the spare parts supply, the spare parts maintenance, the logistics and the aircraft maintenance. The supply of spare parts and spare parts maintenance form the spare parts management which is in the focus of this paper. [14], [15]

The spare parts supply has the inventory and planning responsibility for the spare parts. The spare parts maintenance can be seen as a service for the spare parts supply. The spare parts maintenance is responsible for the repair of spare parts. For this purpose, the spare parts maintenance has its own manufacturing and workshop areas. By the logistics the spare parts are transported from/to the customer. The aircraft maintenance takes place on the basis of strict regulations within different maintenance events. [14]

To avoid long-term ground time of an aircraft, so-called Line Replaceable Units (LRU) are used in aircrafts when possible. A change of these LRUs is carried out quickly and the aircraft is therefore immediately ready for use again. Meanwhile, the exchanged part is repaired or overhauled and preserved for the next installation. [16] Furthermore large service providers sometimes offer a component pooling service for aircraft operators. If a defect of a component occurs a new component is provided by the pool provider. The removed part will be analyzed by the service provider afterwards and depending on technical and economic aspects the decision is made whether the component will be repaired or replaced. [11], [15]

In the context of the spare parts supply the determination of the spare parts demand is a major challenge, especially for service providers. [14], [17] This is caused by a variety of different aspects. The primary products in the aviation industry have very long life cycles. On average, aircrafts fly over 20 years. This leads to many different generations of aircraft and many different generations of components which should be supplied by a service provider. Electronic components in today's aircrafts are from the period in which the aircraft were developed. Furthermore the costs of the components in the aviation industry are very high. Because of these high costs, the very long life-cycles, the small amounts of components the repair of components in the aviation industry is highly economical. [11] The failure behavior of many components is not known, the absolute number of failures of a specific component is usually very low. It can be assumed that the different generations of components installed have different failure rates. In many cases, the information about the components installed is missing. This is because the cost of the identification would be very high and also the operator of an aircraft does not have this information. This may be because the operator has leased the aircraft. In this case the probabilities of installation for different components have to be determined.

3   Approach for Determination of Spare Parts Demands

3.1   Impact Factors Regarding the Spare Parts Demand

A basic approach for the determination of the spare parts demand (D) is by using the correlation of the intensity of use for a future period and the failure rate of a component [18]. This and other approaches, however, are only partially applicable for MRO service providers. Other approaches can exemplary be found in [19], [20], [21], [22], [23]. While the intensity of use of the primary product (the aircraft) can be determined well, there are difficulties in determining the intensity of use of a component of the aircraft. This is due to the fact that the components used are often not known. This complicates the determination of a reliable failure rate for different components. However, the knowledge about the impact factors regarding the failure rate and thus the spare parts demand is essential for a MRO service provider.

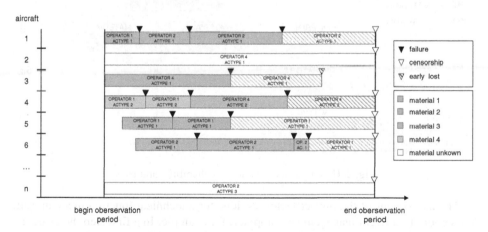

Fig. 1. Data base in a certain observation period

In figure 1 the existing data base and the uncertainties are shown exemplarily. The failures of materials are recorded in a certain observation period for different aircrafts. By the definition of the observation period the data is censored at the beginning and at the end of this period. Furthermore, the data of aircrafts, in which the components are not known, is recorded to. All censored data is considered in the analysis.

Different impact factors regarding spare parts demand are mentioned in literature. These impact factors can be assigned to the primary product, the spare part itself, the maintenance strategy or to the market situation and other surroundings [13], [17]. For simplicity, in the following part the focus will be on a limited number of impact factors. The approach allows the integration of further and other impact factors.

It is assumed that the demand (failure rate) is proportional either to the flight hours (FH), the flight cycles (FC) or the calendar time (CT). In the following these impact factors are described as measurable impact factors. Furthermore categorical impact factors are assumed. These can be the aircraft type, the operator of the aircraft and the material which is used, for example. The influence of these factors has been shown in different studies [16] but in general the relationship between the mean demand and flying hours or flight cycles is not well understood [24].

3.2   Hierarchical Derivation of Reliability Parameters

The assessment of impact factors regarding the spare parts demand of MRO service providers is a main objective of this approach. In the context of the assessment of the impact factors the handling of the uncertainties is an important aspect, which is not in the focus of this paper. It is important to know that the uncertainties about the components used are closely linked to the assessment of the impact factors.

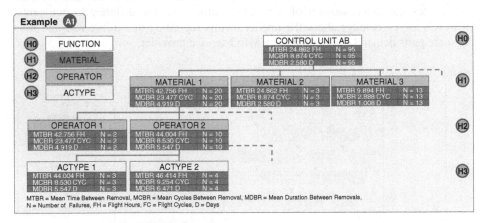

Fig. 2. Hierarchical derivation of reliability parameters

The assessment of the impact factors is done for a technical function in an aircraft. This could be a flight management computer, for example. In a first step the categorical impact factors are combined according to their potential relevance in any combination. For three different impact factors six different combinations can be created. Each combination represents a hierarchical alternative for the impact factors.

In figure 2 a hierarchical alternative is shown as an example. The first level is always represented by the technical function (H0). In this example the second level is defined by the material (H1), underlying the operator (H2) and finally the aircraft type (A3). A technical function is always defined by all impact factors. This means it is defined by a certain material, an operator and an aircraft type. However, it is not useful to determine an individual reliability parameter for each possible combination.

One reason for this is the large variance of possible failure intervals. Because of this the significance of each combination is analyzed. With the three measurable impact factors (FH, FC, CT) three different reliability parameters can be derived. The mean time between removal (MTBR), the mean cycles between removal (MCBR) and the mean duration between removal (MDBR). These are calculated by the sum of all flight hours (or all flight cycles or the calendar time) of the whole aircraft population (m), multiplied with the quantity per aircraft of the component (QPA) in a certain observation period divided by the number of failures (see equation 1). [12]

$$MTBR = \frac{\sum_{i=1}^{m} QPA_i * FH_i}{n} \ [FH], \quad MCBR = \frac{\sum_{i=1}^{m} QPA_i * FC_i}{n} \ [FC], \quad MDBR = \frac{\sum_{i=1}^{m} QPA_i * CT_i}{n} \ [D] \qquad (1)$$

At each step from one to the next hierarchical level, it is checked whether a separation of the failure rate regarding the overlying hierarchical level is significant. If the reliability parameter is significantly different this value is separated and the underlying hierarchical level receives an individual reliability parameter. In figure 2 material 1 and material 3 are determined to be significant. Material 2 is not significantly different from the technical function and the reliability parameter is set the same as the reliability parameter of technical function. The significance is analyzed in each hierarchical level.

3.3 Assessment of the Derived Reliability Parameters

The derived reliability parameters are assessed in the next step. For this purpose the complete data set has been separated into two random data sets. The determination of the reliability parameters is done on the trainings set and the quality of these is reviewed on the basis of the test set. With the values determined in the training set, the resulting changes in the test set are calculated. [17]

Table 1. Assessment of the derived reliability parameters

				reliability parameter			actual changes				calculated changes			measure		
				[FH]	[CYC]	[D]		[FH]	[CYC]	[D]	[FH]	[CYC]	[D]			
FUNCTION	MATERIAL	OPERATOR	ACTYPE	MTBR	MCBR	MDBR	N	FH	CYC	D	MTBR	MCBR	MDBR	MTBR	MCBR	MDBR
A1 CONTROL UNIT AB	MATERIAL 1	OPERATOR 1	ACTYPE 1	41.245	7.536	4.765	4	214.474	38.282	17.344	5,20	5,08	3,64	1,44	1,17	0,13
A1 CONTROL UNIT AB	MATERIAL 1	OPERATOR 1	ACTYPE 2	40.293	7.430	8.374	3	139.010	26.079	25.373	3,45	3,51	3,03	0,20	0,26	0,00
A1 CONTROL UNIT AB	MATERIAL 1	OPERATOR 2	ACTYPE 1	44.004	8.530	5.547	4	197.137	40.261	10.428	4,48	4,72	1,88	0,23	0,52	4,49
A1 CONTROL UNIT AB	MATERIAL 1	OPERATOR 2	ACTYPE 2	44.004	8.530	5.547	2	93.288	13.989	9.873	2,12	1,64	1,78	0,01	0,13	0,05
A1 CONTROL UNIT AB	MATERIAL 2	OPERATOR 1	ACTYPE 1	24.862	8.874	2.580	1	23.370	9.850	2.167	0,94	1,11	0,84	0,00	0,01	0,03
A1 CONTROL UNIT AB	MATERIAL 2	OPERATOR 2	ACTYPE 1	19.872	5.472	2.092	2	47.295	10.725	4.727	2,38	1,96	2,26	0,14	0,00	0,07
A1 CONTROL UNIT AB	MATERIAL 3	OPERATOR 1	ACTYPE 1	7.832	2.834	1.402	3	22.321	6.886	6.981	2,85	2,43	4,98	0,02	0,33	3,92
A1 CONTROL UNIT AB	MATERIAL 3	OPERATOR 1	ACTYPE 2	9.894	2.888	1.008	4	33.243	13.862	6.289	3,36	4,80	6,24	0,41	0,64	5,01
A1 CONTROL UNIT AB	MATERIAL 3	OPERATOR 2	ACTYPE 1	7.832	2.834	1.402	5	41.118	15.587	3.505	5,25	5,50	2,50	0,06	0,25	6,25

Root-mean-square error 0,5302 0,6058 1,4888

				reliability parameter			actual changes				calculated changes			measure		
A5 CONTROL UNIT AB	MATERIAL 1	OPERATOR 1	ACTYPE 1	38.273	7.432	2.876	4	214.474	38.282	17.344	5,60	5,15	6,03	2,57	1,32	4,12
A5 CONTROL UNIT AB	MATERIAL 1	OPERATOR 1	ACTYPE 2	32.754	4.732	4.873	3	139.010	26.079	25.373	4,24	5,51	5,21	1,55	6,31	4,87
A5 CONTROL UNIT AB	MATERIAL 1	OPERATOR 2	ACTYPE 1	38.273	7.432	2.876	4	197.137	40.261	10.428	5,15	5,42	3,63	1,32	2,01	0,14
A5 CONTROL UNIT AB	MATERIAL 1	OPERATOR 2	ACTYPE 2	39.283	7.463	2.743	2	93.288	13.989	9.873	2,37	1,87	3,60	0,14	0,02	2,56
A5 CONTROL UNIT AB	MATERIAL 2	OPERATOR 1	ACTYPE 1	22.735	4.736	1.734	1	23.370	9.850	2.167	1,03	2,08	1,25	0,00	1,17	0,06
A5 CONTROL UNIT AB	MATERIAL 2	OPERATOR 2	ACTYPE 1	38.273	7.432	2.876	2	47.295	10.725	4.727	1,24	1,44	1,64	0,58	0,31	0,13
A5 CONTROL UNIT AB	MATERIAL 3	OPERATOR 1	ACTYPE 1	4.872	1.648	1.220	3	22.321	6.886	6.981	4,58	4,18	5,72	2,50	1,39	7,41
A5 CONTROL UNIT AB	MATERIAL 3	OPERATOR 1	ACTYPE 2	14.230	1.972	1.543	4	33.243	13.862	6.289	2,34	7,03	4,08	2,77	9,18	0,01
A5 CONTROL UNIT AB	MATERIAL 3	OPERATOR 2	ACTYPE 1	5.364	2.463	1.102	5	41.118	15.587	3.505	7,67	6,33	3,18	7,11	1,76	3,31

Root-mean-square error 1,4354 1,6146 1,5849

| basis: training set | basis: test set |

The deviation between the actual changes and the calculated changes is used as a measure for the quality of forecast. This is done for each hierarchical alternative and each reliability parameter. By repeating this random separation of the data set into two data sets the best hierarchical alternative as well as a best reliability parameter (MTBR, MCBR and MDBR) can be determined. An example of this assessment is shown in table 1. This example shows two different hierarchical alternatives (A1 and A5) and the reliability parameter for the different combinations. In this example the MTBR is the best reliability parameter and the relevance of the impact factors is set by the hierarchical alternative A1. In the next step it should be analyzed whether it is possible to determine the relative influence of the different reliability parameters.

3.4   Customer Projects of MRO Service Providers

The integration of new customers, new components or new aircraft types, for example, is a recurring and challenging task for MRO service providers. These integrations are called customer projects in general and are a special characteristic of MRO service providers. [14] Due to missing information regarding material, aircraft type or customer it is difficult to assign a reliability parameter.

	OPERATOR	ACTYPE	MATERIAL
C1	known	known	known
C2	known	known	new
C3	known	new	known
C4	known	new	new
C5	new	known	known
C6	new	known	new
C7	new	new	known
C8	new	new	new

	A1	A2	A3	A4	A5	A6
C1	H3	H3	H3	H3	H3	H3
C2	H0	H0	H2	H1	H1	H2
C3	H2	H1	H1	H2	H0	H0
C4	H0	H0	H1	H1	H0	H0
C5	H1	H2	H0	H0	H2	H1
C6	H0	H0	H0	H0	H1	H1
C7	H1	H1	H0	H0	H0	H0
C8	H0	H0	H0	H0	H0	H0

	A1	A2	A3	A4	A5	A6
H0	FUNCTION	FUNCTION	FUNCTION	FUNCTION	FUNCTION	FUNCTION
H1	MATERIAL	MATERIAL	OPERATOR	OPERATOR	ACTYPE	ACTYPE
H2	OPERATOR	ACTYPE	ACTYPE	MATERIAL	MATERIAL	OPERATOR
H3	ACTYPE	OPERATOR	MATERIAL	ACTYPE	OPERATOR	MATERIAL

Fig. 3. Application of hierarchical derivation on customer projects

Different forms of customer projects can be distinguished. In figure 3 different customer projects are shown. Out of three different impact factors eight customer projects can be derived. The customer projects can be differentiated whether an impact factor is known or new. The complexity increases significantly by adding additional impact factors. In customer project C3, for example, a known customer wants to be supplied with a known material, which is installed in a new aircraft type. For this technical function the hierarchical alternative A4 has been determined methodically. In combination, in this customer project the reliability parameter of the hierarchical level H2 should be used. By the hierarchical assessment of the impact factors it is possible to react to missing information accordingly.

4   Summary

The efficient spare parts supply during the entire life cycle of the primary product is a differentiating quality characteristic in competition. For the realization of an effective spare parts management, it is important to understand the correlations between different impact factors regarding the spare parts demand. The aviation industry is characterized by extremely long life-cycles of the primary products with a high degree of efficiency, small lot sizes, a strict regulation and a high degree of individualization. In the context of the spare parts supply the determination of the spare parts demand is a major challenge, especially for service providers. Existing approaches for the determination of the spare parts demand are only partially applicable for MRO service providers. These challenges are faced in a new approach. Within this approach the relevance of different impact factors can be determined and the stock can thereby be analyzed much more accurately. Therefore the cost effectiveness of the services and the customer satisfaction can be increased.

Acknowledgements. The results presented in this paper were developed in the research project "Demand control loops for a global component spare parts management". This research project is part of the regional aviation research program LUFO II-2 funded by the German Federal State of Hamburg (Behörde für Wirtschaft, Verkehr und Innovation).

References

1. Dombrowski, U., Schulze, S., Wrehde, J.: Efficient Spare Part Management to Satisfy Customers Need. In: Proceedings of the International Conference on Service Operations and Logistics and Informatics, Philadelphia, pp. 304–309 (2007)
2. Leichnitz, H.: Bewertungsverfahren von Produktportfolios im Rahmen des Obsolescence Management. Dissertation. Shaker, Aachen (2010)
3. Quantschnig, M.: Planungsmodell kostenoptimaler Versorgungsstrategien im OEM-Ersatzteilmanagement. Dissertation. Shaker, Aachen (2010)
4. Dombrowski, U., Schulze, S., Weckenborg, S.: Life Cycle Costing as a Tool for effective Spare Parts Management. In: Proceedings of the 16th CIRP International Conference on Life Cycle Engineering, Cairo, Egypt, pp. 478–483 (2009)
5. Loukmidis, G., Luczak, H.: Lebenszyklusorientierte Planungsstrategien für den Ersatzteilbedarf. In: Barkawi, K., Baader, A., Montanus, S. (eds.) Erfolgreich mit After Sales Service: Geschäftsstrategien für Servicemanagement und Ersatzteillogistik, pp. 250–270. Springer, Heidelberg (2006)
6. Wrehde, J.: Planung und Umsetzung der Nachserienversorgung in der Nachserienversorgung. Dissertation. Shaker, Aachen (2011)
7. Bothe, T.: Planung und Steuerung der Ersatzteilversorgung nach Ende der Serienfertigung. Dissertation. Shaker, Aachen (2003)
8. Hesselbach, J., Dombrowski, U., Bothe, T., Graf, R., Wrehde, J., Mansour, M.: Planning Process for the Spare Part Management of Automotive Electronics. WGP Production Engineering XI(1), 113–118 (2004)

9. Dombrowski, U., Weckenborg, S., Schulze, S.: Method-supported Product Development for Post-series Supply. In: Bernard, A. (ed.) Global Product Development. Proceedings of the 20th CIRP Design Conference, Ecole Centrale de Nantes, Nantes, France, April 19-21, pp. 339–345. Springer, Heidelberg (2011)

10. Dombrowski, U., Weckenborg, S., Engel, C.: Consideration of Changing Impact Factors for Optimization of Post-series Supply. In: Frick, J., Laugen, B.T. (eds.) APMS 2011. IFIP AICT, vol. 384, pp. 140–147. Springer, Heidelberg (2012)

11. Schmidt, T., Laucht, O., Bauer, A.: Mehrwert schaffen durch Fokussierung auf das Servicegeschäft. In: Barkawi, K., Baader, A., Montanus, S. (eds.) Erfolgreich mit After Sales Service: Geschäftsstrategien für Servicemanagement und Ersatzteillogistik, pp. 95–111. Springer, Heidelberg (2006)

12. Meifarth, K., Weber, B., Bauer, A.: Ersatzteilmanagement elektronischer Bauteile – Randbedingungen und Anforderungen in der Zivilluftfahrt. Lufthansa Technik AG, VDI Tagung Lebenszyklusorientiertes Ersatzteilmanagement, Stuttgart (2004)

13. Dombrowski, U., Schulze, S.: Lebenszyklusorientiertes Ersatzteilmanagement – Neue Herausforderungen durch innnovationsstarke Bauteile in langlebigen Primärprodukten. In: Nyhuis, P. (ed.) Beiträge zu einer Theorie der Logistik, pp. 439–462. Springer, Heidelberg (2008)

14. Bauer, A.: Lebenszyklusorientierte Optimierung von Instandhaltungssystemen für hochwertige Investitionsgüter. Dissertation. Shaker, Aachen (2002)

15. Hinsch, M.: Industrielles Luftfahrtmanagement: Technik und Organisation luftfahrttechnischer Betriebe. Springer, Berlin (2010)

16. Wagner, M., Fricke, M.: Estimation of daily unscheduled line maintenance events in civil aviation. In: 25th International Congress of Aeronautical Science, Hamburg (2006)

17. Dombrowski, U., Weckenborg, S., Mederer, M.: Demand control loops for a global spare parts management. In: Emmanouilidis, C., Taisch, M., Kiritsis, D. (eds.) APMS 2012, Part II. IFIP AICT, vol. 398, pp. 407–414. Springer, Heidelberg (2013)

18. Linser, A.: Performance Measurement in der Flugzeuginstandhaltung. Dissertation. Universität, Hochschule für Wirtschafts-, Rechts- und Sozialwissenschaften (HSG), St. Gallen (2005)

19. Regattieri, A., Gamberi, M., Gamberini, R., Manzini, R.: Managing lumpy demand for aircraft spare parts. Journal of Air Transport Management 11, 426–431 (2005)

20. Bevilacqua, M., Braglia, M., Frosolini, M., Montanari, R.: Failure rate prediction with artificial neural networks. Journal of Quality in Maintenance Engineering 3, 279–294 (2005)

21. Ghobbar, A.A., Friend, C.H.: Evaluation of forecasting methods for intermittent parts demand in the field of aviation: a predictive model. Computers & Operations Research 30, 2097–2114 (2003)

22. Louit, D.M., Pascual, R., Jardine, A.K.S.: A practical procedure for the selection of time-to-failure models based on the assessment of trends in maintenance data. Reliability Engineering and System Safety 94, 1618–1628 (2009)

23. Luxhøj, J.T., Trefor, P.W., Shyur, H.-J.: Comparison of regression and neural network models for prediction of inspection profiles for aging aircraft. IIE Transactions 29, 91–101 (1997)

24. Ghobbar, A.A., Friend, C.H.: Sources of intermittent demand for aircraft spare parts within airline operations. Journal of Air Transport Management 8, 221–231 (2002)

Using Cloud, Modularity, and Make-to-Upgrade Strategy for Integrating Customized-Oriented Supply Networks

Afshin Mehrsai[1,*], Hamid-Reza Karimi[2], and Klaus-Dieter Thoben[1]

[1] BIBA – Bremer Institut für Produktion und Logistik GmbH
Hochschulring 20,28359 Bremen, Germany
meh@biba.uni-bremen.de
[2] Department of Engineering, University of Agder, Grimstad, Norway

Abstract. In the current global business individual demand play crucial roles. Customized-oriented supply networks are being proliferated in manufacturing industries, yet integration of their members is still quite challenging. As a practical solution, in this paper a new collaborative approach out of modularity structure, cloud computing, and a novel production strategy, called Make-to-Upgrade (MTU), is suggested. The complementary aspects of these techniques are highlighted and briefly explained here. MTU is as a strategy for future products with new characteristics, e.g., upgradability.

Keywords: Supply Network Integration, Cloud Computing, Modularity, Make-to-Upgrade Production Strategy.

1 Introduction

The phenomenon of globalization has been influencing all kind of businesses, in particular, manufacturing industries. Thereby, a wide range of opportunities as well as threats has been introduced to enterprises, which cause their businesses to survive or collapse. In such an environment, customized orders by individual customers are no more dispensable but advantageous to pioneer enterprises. Employment of new business strategies, models, and technologies can assist enterprises and their supply networks (SNs) to be successful in the dynamic environment, i.e., volatile market, expansion of scale and scope, mass-customized demands, scarce resources, growing complexity, shifting authority from final producers to their suppliers and customers, etc., [1] [2]. On top of these challenges, paying attention to alternative customer demands with individual requirements – mentioned or not – while being integrated with other production and product stakeholders have got a high priority from enterprises. This concern has been interpreted by industries as the mass-customization (MC) strategy as well as individualization of products and operations. Initially, Davis [3] in 1987 coined the term of MC to reflect the large scope of providing personalized products and services [4]. Nevertheless, in dealing with the challenge of customization, isolated enterprises was no longer successfully functioning in the market. But they

---

* Corresponding author.

V. Prabhu, M. Taisch, and D. Kiritsis (Eds.): APMS 2013, Part I, IFIP AICT 414, pp. 441–449, 2013.

rather needed to collaboratively perform in harmony with the other players in the context of SNs [5]. Therefore, coordinating, administrating, and orchestrating the operations of such enterprises have become the biggest organizational challenges, to be dealt with by their respective SNs. On the contrary, while cooperating with other supply members, individual enterprises, as independent entities, like to keep their own interests and concerns. This fact originates several contradictions between the members who have to competently cooperate and collaborate with each other to achieve the overall goal of the network. In that regard, exploitation of modularity approach as a new business structure, cloud computing as the state-of-the-art technology, and development of a new compatible production/delivery strategy, called Make-to-Upgrade (MTU), together are seen as a novel solution for such customized-oriented SNs. Here, fulfillment of individual demands is sought, whilst harmonizing the entire production operations through a wide-range of virtual integrations. Indeed, the inherent structure of cloud computing and modularity, as distributed entities, but in a holistic body, make them quite adjustable techniques for being implemented on MC-oriented SNs. Moreover, MTU assists new performing SNs to exploit modularity in (product, process, and resource) for postponing the configuration of their final-products and enriching the scope via upgradability specification of modules.

In exploring this claim, first a brief literature review on customization, modularity and supply network integration (SNI) is given. Then modularity and MTU are shortly discussed. Compatibility of cloud for SNI is highlighted too. To verify the recommended strategy a discrete-event simulation model is experimented at the final section. The conclusion and prospective works are explained at the end of the paper.

2   Review of Customization, Modularity, and SN Integration

A Literature review unfolds the key role of MC in enabling industries to become competitive on the current and prospective market. Generally, MC aims at satisfying customers by means of considering their personality and subjective needs. This objective has been interpreted by producers as shifting from traditional mass-production (MP) to individualized products, while keeping the cost, volume, and efficiency of MP. Salvador et al. [9] say MC "is a mechanism that is applicable to most businesses, provided that it is appropriately understood and deployed". Thus, MC is about aligning an organization with its customers' needs including reasonable costs.To fulfill these requirements, several enablers of MC can be listed as methodologies and techniques [4], e.g., lean and agility, order elicitation, design postponement, design product platforms, supply chain (SC) coordination, decoupling point, manufacturing technologies like flexible manufacturing systems, and information technologies like cloud computing. On this basis, among several enablers of MC modularity and postponement strategy are seen as two main approaches of companies to producing large product diversity [10]. As Mikkola [11] explains MC "is enabled through modular product architectures, from which a wide variety of products can be configured and assembled". Kumar [12] says "… given that product modularity is a key element of a mass customization strategy". Modularity in design of products enables companies to employ assemble-to-order (ATO) production strategy throughout their SCs. However, other strategies like deliver-on-demand (DOD), make-to-order (MTO), or design-to-order (DTO), can also be adopted by customized-oriented companies. The purpose of these strategies is to integrate customers with various configurations into the several phases of product development and into production stakeholders, by means of devising a decoupling point (DP). Reijers et al. [14] explain the modularity as "the design principle of having a complex system composed from smaller subsystems that can be managed independently yet function together as a whole". Initially, modularity looks for the favorable goal of plug and play, which for SNs can be realized through cloud advantages. In this regard, Schön [2] defines a module as "a unit with strong connections between its components which can be removed non-destructively from a system as a whole".Generally, modularity approach can be applied to different aspects of an industrial system, i.e., products, processes, and resources [15], see figure 1. Modularity in product design plays a crucial role in customizing final products (goods) and in easing production procedure, whereas modularity in process [14] can assist companies to deliver sustainable, adaptable, flexible, and customizable services either as final products or manufacturing/logistics operations. Moreover, as Pereira [5] mentions, a managed integration of SCs is required to achieve competitiveness, revenue, innovation, value, and cost reduction. However, he believes it is necessary to reevaluate the traditional and vertically integrated model of supply chains, by means of increased information sharing and cooperation, in order to achieve a global reach and local responsiveness. Bosona et al. [7] for SNI suggest close information sharing among several clusters and emphasize this importance in facing complex SNs. Winkler in [25] see the role of communication and information system throughout SNs as an important prerequisite for realizing flexibility as well as integration in SNs.Ye et al. [26] interpret SCI as integration of information. Some arguments about web-based information integrators are given that include the pros and cons of XML, extensible markup language (OWL), and extensible markup language (SWRL).

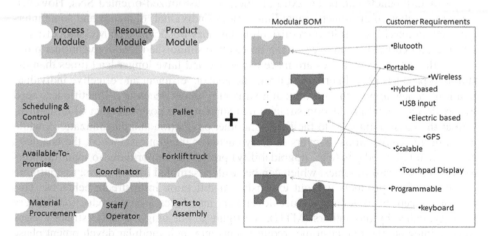

Fig. 1. Modular structure and customer integration in fulfilling MTU by using cloud privileges

All in all, regarding the characteristics of modularity and the mentioned requirements of SNI they seem quite compatible with each other. A common approach of the most studies on SNI refers to flexible, simple, and effective data integration. Thanks to new achievements in ICT and the proliferation of the cloud computing concept, these desires are getting closer to practice. Cloud with its novel distributed as well as integrated structure can complementarily contribute to this superior combination.

3   Product Modularity and Make-To-Upgrade (MTU) Strategy

In general, modularity in design of products brings about a large scale of product variety, while applying similar modules for alternative products (family). For instance, Porsche at a time period used a door module for three different car models. Or Nike, Adidas, and Dell follow the same concept of modularity to customize their products, yet by means of customer integration [20]. In the near future, thanks to modular body of products with new characteristics as upgradability and traceability (e.g., via product Avatar [17]), product obsolescence, waste, and scrap will drastically drop as great contributions to sustainability issue. By considering the specifications of such future products (called "meta-product" by FP7 EU), some advantages of modular vs. integrated design can be significantly highlighted as: scalability vs. non-scalability, simplicity vs. complexity, flexibility vs. rigidity, re-configurability vs. strictness, exchangeability vs. irreplaceability, upgradability vs. constancy or even downgradability, sustainability vs. non-sustainability (shorter lifecycle of modules by longer lifecycle of the entire product). These are some privileges of modular design, which directly contribute to the requirements of MC and MTU. A well-known example of such modular design is LEGO. Each of these accompanied characteristics with modular approach can be seen as a driver for developing a framework of future products in beyond the state of the art. Employment of Webpages for directly integrating customers to design their products is an outstanding advantage, which reflects demand penetration and ATO production strategies. Incorporation of customers towards the ramp-up phase of developing meta-products can be an extra privilege of customized-oriented SNs. However, early integration of customers, regarding various (individual) demands and some internal preparations [21], has its own difficulties and may not achieve an MC with efficient volume and cost [8]. Moreover, it can be easily distinguished that conventional products with customized features are more expensive and have longer lead times than the standard products [22]. In order to pursue the goal of "efficient and effective individualization" a new approach to production strategies seems necessary. Practitioners need to develop a special production strategy that supports the postponement of customization at the latest point (i.e., to facilitate smoother production and customization), while avoiding the conventional barriers of early customer integration. Indeed, the characteristics of future products (e.g., upgradability) provide an opportunity to manufacturers to develop standard modules, which can be easily assembled by end-users; to configure alternative final products without expensive modification in upstream echelons. This sought concept by modular product developers introduces a new production/delivery strategy, called by the authors (MTU), see figure 2. Pursuing the MTU strategy urges SNs to integrate the real customer requirements into their modular development phase as early as possible, whilst postponing the assembly of the modules and configuration of final products to the customer side. Member companies with the modularity approach set standard operations for producing their products (i.e., split in modules), while deriving modular processes at the very downstream of their SCs. Whereas MTU smoothes the production operations with a very adequate speed, customization is

realized at its most competent level too. The MTU strategy may be more understandable once combining the performance of IKEA [16] and the concept of LEGO in postponement and modularity. Producers are virtually connected to consumers and get
feedbacks to produce and upgrade their products in the form of compatible modules.
However, the further step beyond the state of the art is to provide an environment to
make possible the assembly phase of modules at the customer location. This draws a
virtually integrated social network that all stakeholders of products are connected and
engaged like the concept of product Avatar [17] existing on social networks like
facebook [23] [24].

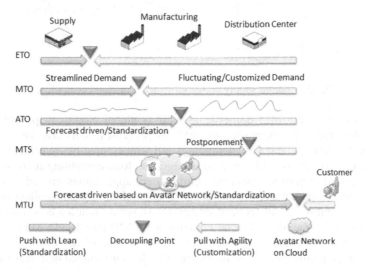

Fig. 2. Production strategies for developing MC product from state of the art to beyond

4   Cloud and Integration

In order to realize the modern approach to SNI and the recommended modularity's
concept for the building-blocks of enterprises and the structure of SNs, cloud computing seems quite practical. Alternative forms of cloud services and the progressive
development of each form, can positively comply with the integration of disturbed
and heterogeneous entities. Once the cloud configures a virtual network, the entities
of an industry from micro-scale (e.g., logistics objects) to macro-scale (network partners) can used the nature of cloud and even move beyond passive modules in a collaborative environment, i.e., towards autonomous units with collaborative capabilities
on a common platform. Generally, cloud computing has several service and deployment models which can be employed for modular and autonomous systems. Some
regular services are following [18], but not limited to: Infrastructure-as-a-Service
(IaaS), Platform-as-a-Service (PaaS), Software-as-a-Service (SaaS). These main
(XaaS) can positively cooperate to bring the concept of modular and autonomous
entities in an SN closer to practice. Moreover, several deployment models of cloud
can be imagined for logistics and production environments, employing recognized
models as [19]: Private cloud, Community cloud, Public cloud, Hybrid cloud. However, their detailed contributions and compatibilities are not explained in this paper.

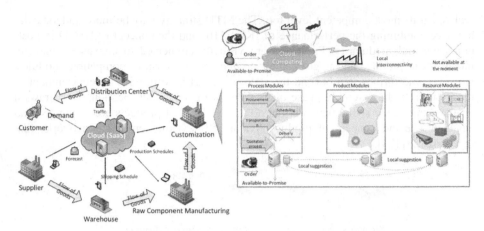

Fig. 3. Modular supply network by means of cloud computing

Indeed, development of a domestic as well as global cloud can provide a large common platform with alternative modules of processes, software, virtual product parts, virtual resources, and virtual suppliers; all with compatible interfaces for being joined together. In this regard, some advantages of cloud computing used by partners and SNs are [18]: improved business agility to get applications up and run quicker, reduced capital expenditure, increased end-user productivity and collaboration that improve manageability, and reduced energy consumption that leads to less maintenance. Accordingly, the idea of cloud computing for SNI (see figure 3) is inspired by several advantages. These issues can mainly be summaries as follows: 1) Narrow international competitions and the necessity of highly customized demands of international customers. 2) Deep interest for innovative products and production systems at superior flexible and agile enterprises/networks. 3) High complexity of organizing and coordinating endeavors in SNs with modular systems. 4) New developments in state-of-the-art ICT (e.g. autonomous entities, cloud computing) and their competent provided infrastructure. 5) Facilitation of employing best practices from domestic and global experiences through connectivity and learning, realizable by new structured cloud. 6) Profound desire for increasing productivity and efficiency in enterprises and SNs by new cooperative and collaborative networks to be facilitated by cloud and smart modules. 7) Great academic encouragement for recognizing real-time material flow control and prompt changeability of processes in practice.

5   Exemplary SN Simulation

In order to experiment the performance of prospective SNs by means of cloud computing for virtually integrating and optimizing the processes of network partners, a discrete-event simulation model is set up. The developed scenario out of a very simple SN reflects the applicability of cloud in organizing the flow of standard modules throughout the network from the source suppliers towards the customer side. Here, the mission of planning and control of flows is accomplished through cloud as SaaS, which is totally extendable to PaaS and IaaS in future works. The considered network is built out of four plants, i.e., a source plant, two parallel manufacturing plants, and an assembly plant (OEM), see figure 4. There are three modules (A, B, C) of a final product, which each two module can configure a product to end up with three alternatives. The results of the simulation (table 1) are grouped in three experiments as planning via cloud: 1. for just OEM, 2. for just source plant, 3. for source and OEM simultaneously. The performance criteria for evaluating the network are average throughput time (Avg. TPT), standard deviation of TPT, and throughput per hour (TP/h). The results show that the best performance is for the experiment 3.

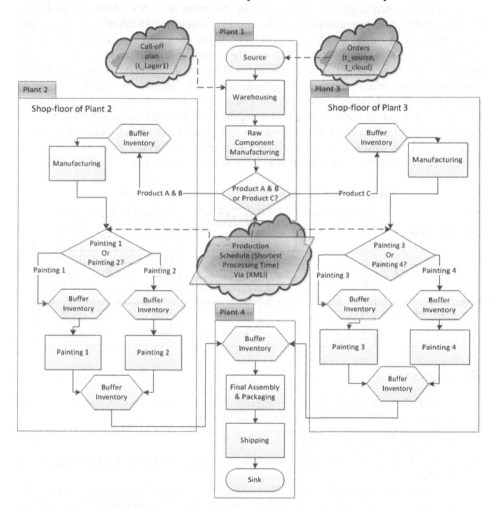

Fig. 4. Material and information flow of the network scenario

6   Conclusion and Discussion

In summary, the contribution of this paper to the ongoing challenges of current and prospective SNs included four major aspects as: integration of SNs, modularity structure (product, process, resource), MC and MTU production strategy, and cloud computing as web-based services. Among some potential alternatives (e.g., fully connected and coordinated SNs), this paper introduced a framework for complying with the production of individualized products. This suits to the turbulent global market using flexible and distributed, but integrated SNs. This novelty gives the opportunity to autonomous and distributed members of an SN to properly cooperate and collaborate with each other, whilst being coordinated at the cloud level. The advantage of the introduce framework encompasses: capability of promptly meeting market changes and quickly reconfiguring the structure of an enterprise or an SN (thanks to modularity, traceability, and upgradability), reducing investment in information systems, and competent coordination of all data exchange, using the common platform of cloud. Moreover, the simulation results proved the compatibility of modular design (for product, process, resource) with the common platform of cloud computing, employing distributed and virtual planning and coordination. The results showed that the more connected to the cloud the better performance of the network. As further works, exploration of different aspects of cloud computing in assisting the competitiveness of SNs is due. Alternative control approaches for coordinating heterogeneous modules of a network as well as the compatibility of alternative MTU has to be elaborated. Modularity in all aspects of industries is to be studied in later papers.

Table 1. Result of simulation in three experiment alternatives

	Module type	Avg. TPT (h)	stddev. TPT (h)	TP/h
Experiment 1	A	244	78	3.75
	B	244	152	4.36
	C	249	146	2.96
Experiment 2	A	245	157	1.12
	B	277	198	1.00
	C	118	67	1.00
Experiment 3	A	252	147	5.00
	B	109	42	4.33
	C	191	109	3.31

References

[1] Abdelkafi, N.: Variety Induced Complexity in Mass Customization: Concepts and Management, vol. 7. Erich Schmidt Verlag & GmbH (2008)
[2] Schön, O.: Business Model Modularity–A Way to Gain Strategic Flexibility? Controlling & Management 56, 73–78 (2012)
[3] Davis, S.M.: From future perfect: mass customizing. Planning Review 17(2), 16–21 (1989)
[4] Fogliatto, F.S., da Silveira, G.J.C., Borenstein, D.: The mass customization decade: An updated review of the literature. International Journal of Production Economics 138(1), 14–25 (2012)
[5] Pereira, J.V.: The new supply chain's frontier: Information management. International Journal of Information Management 29(5), 372–379 (2009)
[6] Danese, P., Romano, P., Formentini, M.: The impact of supply chain integration on responsiveness: The moderating effect of using an international supplier network. Transportation Research Part E: Logistics and Transportation Review 49(1), 125–140 (2013)

[7] Bosona, T.G., Gebresenbet, G.: Cluster building and logistics network integration of local food supply chain. Biosystems Engineering 108(4), 293–302 (2011)

[8] Smith, S., Gregory, C., Jiao, R., Chu, C.-H.: Mass customization in the product life cycle. Journal of Intelligent Manufacturing, 1–9 (2012)

[9] Salvador, F., De Holan, P.M., Piller, F.: Cracking the code of mass customization. MIT Sloan Management Review 50(3), 71–78 (2009)

[10] Da Cunha, C., Agard, B., Kusiak, A.: Design for cost: module-based mass customization. IEEE Transactions on Automation Science and Engineering 4(3), 350–359 (2007)

[11] Mikkola, J.H.: Management of product architecture modularity for mass customization: modeling and theoretical considerations. IEEE Transactions on Engineering Management 54(1), 57–69 (2007)

[12] Kumar, A.: Mass customization: metrics and modularity. International Journal of Flexible Manufacturing Systems 16(4), 287–311 (2004)

[13] Jacobs, M., et al.: Product and process modularity's effects on manufacturing agility and firm growth performance. Journal of Product Innovation Management 28(1), 123–137 (2011)

[14] Reijers, H.A., Mendling, J.: Modularity in process models: Review and effects. In: Dumas, M., Reichert, M., Shan, M.-C. (eds.) BPM 2008. LNCS, vol. 5240, pp. 20–35. Springer, Heidelberg (2008)

[15] Bask, A., et al.: The concept of modularity: diffusion from manufacturing to service production. Journal of Manufacturing Technology Management 21(3), 355–375 (2010)

[16] Bocconcelli, R., Tunisini, A.: Value Creation through Product Modularity: the User's Perspective. Use of Science and Technology in Business: Exploring the Impact of Using Activity for Systems, Organizations, and People 25, 165 (2009)

[17] Hribernik, K.A., Rabe, L., Thoben, K.-D., Schumacher, J.: The product avatar as a product-instance-centric information management concept. International Journal of Product Lifecycle Management 1(4), 367–379 (2006)

[18] Van der Molen, F.: Get Ready for Cloud Computing. Van Haren Pub. (2010)

[19] Chandrasekaran, M., Muralidhar, M., Dixit, U.: Online optimization of multipass machining based on cloud computing. The International Journal of Advanced Manufacturing Technology, 1–12 (2012)

[20] Wong, H., Lesmono, D.: On the evaluation of product customization strategies in a vertically differentiated market. International Journal of Production Economics (2013), http://dx.doi.org/10.1016/j.ijpe.2013.01.023

[21] Koufteros, X., Vonderembse, M., Jayaram, J.: Internal and External Integration for Product Development: The Contingency Effects of Uncertainty, Equivocality, and Platform Strategy. Decision Sciences 36(1) (2005)

[22] Xia, N., Rajagopalan, S.: Standard vs. custom products: Variety, lead time, and price competition. Marketing Science 28(5), 887–900 (2009)

[23] Wuest, T., Hribernik, K., Thoben, K.-D.: Can a Product Have a Facebook? A New Perspective on Product Avatars in Product Lifecycle Management. In: Rivest, L., Bouras, A., Louhichi, B. (eds.) PLM 2012. IFIP AICT, vol. 388, pp. 400–410. Springer, Heidelberg (2012)

[24] Wuest, T., Hribernik, K., Thoben, K.-D.: Digital Representations of Intelligent Products: Product Avatar 2.0. In: Smart Product Engineering, pp. 675–684. Springer (2012)

[25] Winkler, H.: How to improve supply chain flexibility using strategic supply chain networks. Logistics Research 1(1), 15–25 (2009)

[26] Ye, Y., Yang, D., Jiang, Z., Tong, L.: An ontology-based architecture for implementing semantic integration of supply chain management. International Journal of Computer Integrated Manufacturing 21(1), 1–18 (2008)

Reverse Logistics: Network Design Based on Life Cycle Assessment

Joanna Daaboul[*], Julien Le Duigou, Diana Penciuc, and Benoît Eynard

Université de Technologie de Compiègne
Rue du Dr Schweitzer, Compiègne, 60200 Cedex, France
{joanna.daaboul,julien.le-duigou,diana.penciuc,
benoit.eynard}@utc.fr

Abstract. When aiming to a more sustainable world, enterprises such as aircraft and automobile industries are highly interested in light weight components and solutions. Of these solutions are aluminum wrought alloys that offer high potentials for dramatic weight reduction of structural parts. Nevertheless, the production of virgin aluminum is, however, highly energy consuming. Hence, and in SuPLight project, we are interested in recycled aluminum. The aim of this project is to address new industrial models for sustainable light weight solutions – with recycling in high-end structural components based on wrought alloys. In this article we address the issue of designing the reverse logistics chain assuring the needed volume of recycled aluminum for the production of L-shaped Front Lower Control Arms for personal cars.

Keywords: Reversed logistics design, LCA, wrought aluminum.

1 Introduction

Until recently, Reverse Logistics (RL) was not given a great deal of attention in organizations. Actually, implementing RL programs to reduce, reuse, and recycle wastes from distribution and other processes generates tangible and intangible value and can lead to better corporate image [1]. Its main drivers are legislations and directives, consumer awareness and social responsibilities towards environment [2-4]. Another motivating driver of RL is economic factors. RL can generate profits by re-selling valuable components or products [5]. Reverse logistics is of high importance for aluminum based products, since the production of virgin aluminum is highly energy consuming.

RL operations and chains they support are significantly more complex than traditional manufacturing supply chains [6-8]. Therefore, and similarly to how companies develop efficient logistics processes for new goods, it is necessary to plan operations for returned goods, taking into consideration that the processes are most probably quite different from those defined for forward distribution [9]. RL is not a symmetric

---

[*] Corresponding author.

V. Prabhu, M. Taisch, and D. Kiritsis (Eds.): APMS 2013, Part I, IFIP AICT 414, pp. 450–460, 2013.
© IFIP International Federation for Information Processing 2013

picture of forward distribution [10] and requires different management and planning approaches. For example, it is difficult, in the case of RL, to estimate supply-related parameters such as the unit operational costs directly from reported statistical data.

In this article we are interested in designing an effective reverse logistics network for the L-shaped Front Lower Control Arms (FLCA) (Figure 1) for personal cars [11] within the SuPLight[1] project which is a multidisciplinary research project, combining physics at the atomic scale level, metallurgy, continuum mechanics, structural mechanics, optimization algorithms, tolerance analysis, life cycle analysis, manufacturing and business modeling. The project addresses new industrial models for sustainable light weight solutions – with 75% recycling in high-end structural components based on aluminum wrought alloys.

Fig. 1. Front Lower Control Arm (FLCA) [6]

In our case study we are interested in designing the reverse logistics with the following characteristics:

1. The RL network should be environmental friendly as much as possible
2. The different facilities (collection locations, remanufacturing facilities, etc) are not necessarily owned by one company
3. The reverse flow has different sources and might have depending on these sources different disposal routes (reselling, remanufacturing, recycling, etc).

2   Related Works

Designing a reverse logistics network is usually achieved via mathematical programming. Generally a mixed-integer linear programming model is generated in order to define the optimum collection locations and recycling factories [12]. After analyzing the literature we concluded the following:

The literature presents three main types of networks: Forward logistics, reverse logistics, and forward/reverse logistics [12]. We are only considering the reverse logistics network.

The most considered decision criterion is the total cost of the network [13-17], followed by the service level [18], and the generated profit [12]. In the recent literature review in [12], the only objectives considered in RL or forward/reverse chain design are: cost, profit, responsiveness (Service level), source balance, and quality. [19]

---

[1] http://www.suplight-eu.org/

propose a generic model for reverse logistics design considering only costs as decision criteria. [20] propose a two-stage stochastic programming model for multiperiod reverse logistics network design with as main decision criteria the different investment and operational costs. [21] consider the environmental regulations as a constraint to their decision model but not as decision criteria. [22] also proposed a mixed integer linear programming model for supply chain planning including reverse logistics activities. Yet they consider the expected net present value (ENPV), as the decision criterion. In our case, we are interested not only in the total cost of the network, but also in the environmental impact of the network as a main decision criterion. Therefore, the remanufacturing and recycling processes impacts on environmental performance of the network need to be considered.

The main decisions of the models are: location/allocation of facilities and transportation values [13-18]. Moreover, most of the works found in the literature consider the network design problem with collection, sorting, and disposal facilities owned by one company which is collecting the reverse flow and reusing it. But in many cases, reverse logistics do not only include facilities owned by the company itself, but facilities owned by other partners in the chain. In this case, designing the best RL network consists of 2 main problems: choosing the partner and optimizing the whole network formed of facilities owned by different partners. Since reverse logistics are a part of green supply chains and since we are interested in the environmental performance of the network, the choice of the partners is to be made based on their impact not only on the total cost of the network, but also on the environmental performance of the network.

Most of the works found in the literature consider mainly the remanufacturing option of the disposal step [13], [14], [16-18] and only few consider the recycling option of the disposal step such as [15], [23]. But in our case, we are interested in recycling the reverse flow as well as remanufacturing it. In other words, we are interested in different sources of reverse flows which have each different disposal route.

3   A Framework for the Design of Reverse Logistics

3.1   Network Design Method

Considering our analysis of the literature and based on our specific needs, a life cycle approach seems adequate to analyze the performance of the chosen network. It permits assessing the environmental performance of the RL network alone and also its impact on the whole life cycle assessment of the product. Thus, we propose a comparison based method formed of 5 main steps described in Figure 2.

Step 1: Context definition
In this step, the company and the product (s) are described.

Step 2: Parameters definition
Since we are interested in defining the different partners in the RL network as well as the environmental performance of the different processes in the network, a framework linking the processes to the partners was developed.

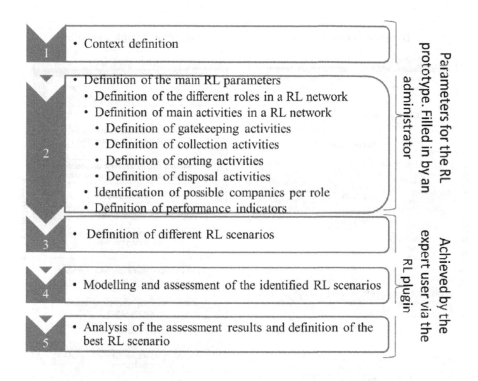

Fig. 2. Proposed method for reverse logistics network design

According to the literature, reverse logistics is formed of 4 main phases: gatekeeping, collection, sorting, and disposal [23-26]. The disposal step includes landfilling, remanufacturing, recycling and reselling. For each phase the set of activities to be achieved was identified based on literature analysis. Nevertheless, these activities differ between the design stage and the implementation (execution) stage. Thus, the differentiation between these activities was made and a framework based on design and implementation stages is proposed and presented in Figure 3.

The parameters definition consists of identifying the different roles in an RL chain, the responsibilities and activities per role, the requirements for these activities, and the performance indicators per requirement per activity. Four roles were identified: collector, sorter, disposer and the end collector of the reversed flow. A same partner may have more than one role. For each of these roles, the responsibilities and activities were identified for design and implementation stages based on the previously presented framework. These activities are at a macro level and need to be detailed at a micro level but for specific cases or products.

The requirements per activity are case dependent. Most of it depends on the type of the product. The recycling processes for example differ based on the product type. Whereas the general performance indicators are: Total cost of the network including cost of transportation, facilities, purchasing, activities, and stock, Total emission of

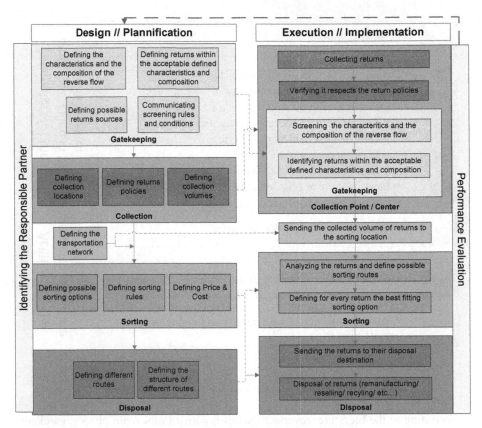

Fig. 3. Reverse Logistics Framework

CO_2, an aggregation of main used life cycle assessment indicators such as carbon footprint of product, energy related indicators, chemicals used, PFC/GHG emissions, fresh water consumption, use of renewable/nonrenewable energy, and recycling related indicators such as the amount of recycled material (in our case it is aluminum), the collection quota CQ (the quantity of secondary material, which is recovered by collection systems, related to the total quantity of used products), and the technical recycling quota RQ (it is the relation between the remelted and the collected quantity and describes the yield of technical processes) [27].

Moreover, in step 2, case dependent parameters are identified. These are the candidate companies for playing one or more roles in the RL network. For each company a description sheet is filled contating information on the company, some performance indicators, and constraints such as minimum quantity of reverse flow, replenishement lead time, etc.

Step 3: Scenarios definition

The scenario definition is achieved by the expert user in one of 3 ways:

1. Defining any RL network scenario, by choosing for each role one or more companies as well as the quantity of reverse flow and then by choosing the routes between these companies.

2. Defining the RL network step by step, using decision criteria per role. In this case, and for every role, the user may ask to identify the best company based on many decision criteria, such as distance, cost, processes used, labels, reverse flow quality, etc. This option is based on the Analytical Hierarchy Process (AHP). The steps that need to be followed in this option are described in figure 4. AHP is the most used decision support system for supplier selection [28]. This technique which was developed by Thomas L. Saaty [29] relies on the expertise of the user in order to generate the weights of attributes. It is based on the comparison of pairs of options and criteria. It has found widespread application in decision-making problems, involving multiple criteria in systems of many levels [30]. Its main advantages are:

   o consideration of non-tangible subjective attributes,
   o ability to structure a complex problem, multi-criteria, multi-person and multi-period hierarchically,
   o capability to investigate each level of the hierarchy separately, and to combine the results as the analysis progresses.
   o binary comparison of elements (alternatives, criteria and sub-criteria),
   o ease of its IT support.

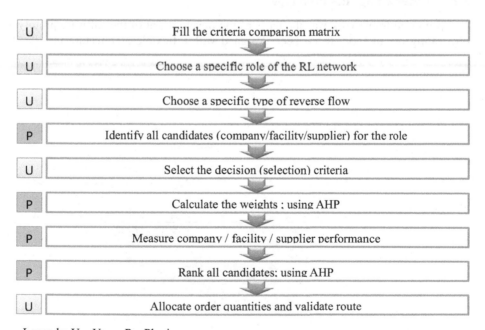

Legende: U = User ; P = Plugin

Fig. 4. Steps to use the multi-criteria decision aid option

3. Defining the optimal network based on the most used objective: the total cost using the optimisation option of the prototype. This option is a work-in-progress.

The user may choose many scenarios as desired and compare their performance in steps 4 & 5. In other words, the user may compare on the basis of all environmental and economic criterias the optimal scenario (based on cost only) with scenarios built with the decision aid option and with any other scenario built by the user alone without any aid of the system.

Steps 4 and 5: Assessment of RL scenarios and results analysis

After one or more scenarios are chosen, the different performance indicators are calculated. A comparision between the scenario is provided.

The evaluation of the RL network is achieved via a life cycle assessment software (SimaPro) [31]. This is possible within the Suplight project which aims at providing collaborative platform [32] allowing the communication and exchange of information between different software of which the Life Cycle Assessment software (LCA) and the RL demonstrator.

After the life cycle assesment of the different RL scenarios is received from the LCA software, a full analysis combing this assessment and the one achieved via the RL prototype (total cost of the network, quantity of recycled material, etc.) is provided to the user. A comparison of all created RL scenarios is then delivered to the user.

3.2   Reverse Logistics Prototype

The proposed framework was the basis of the development of the software prototype illustrating our method. It has been designed with a flexible architecture in order to

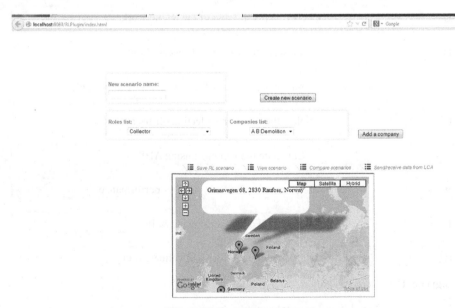

Fig. 5. RL Prototype main page

allow portability and interoperability with any external application. The software prototype implementation is based on the MVC software architecture pattern, using HTML5 and CSS to create the view and for the application logic the JAX-RS Java API for RESTful web services which are controlled by JavaScript (JQuery).

The RL prototype is focused on RL scenario definition allowing the user to: choose the partners of the RL chain and their roles and visualize them on a map; define RL routes -a single route is characterized by flow and transportation data (a flow type and quantity exchanged between two partners, transportation mean and distance)-; visualize the summary of the created scenario and display LCA indicators for the current scenario. The total cost is computed for each route. Google services are used for automatic distance calculation and map display based on data provided by the user. The prototype main page and the route definition interface are presented in Figures 5 and 6 respectively. On the main page the prototype shows the RL scenario on a map with a description of the different routes including the nodes names (companies' names) with the type of reverse flow, quantity of flow, transportation mode and distance between the two nodes. The different enterprises or facilities chosen for the RL chain are presented on the map. This map is dynamic and shows the chosen facility locations or the chosen suppliers as well as all related costs. This map serves only as a visualization tool for the chosen scenario.

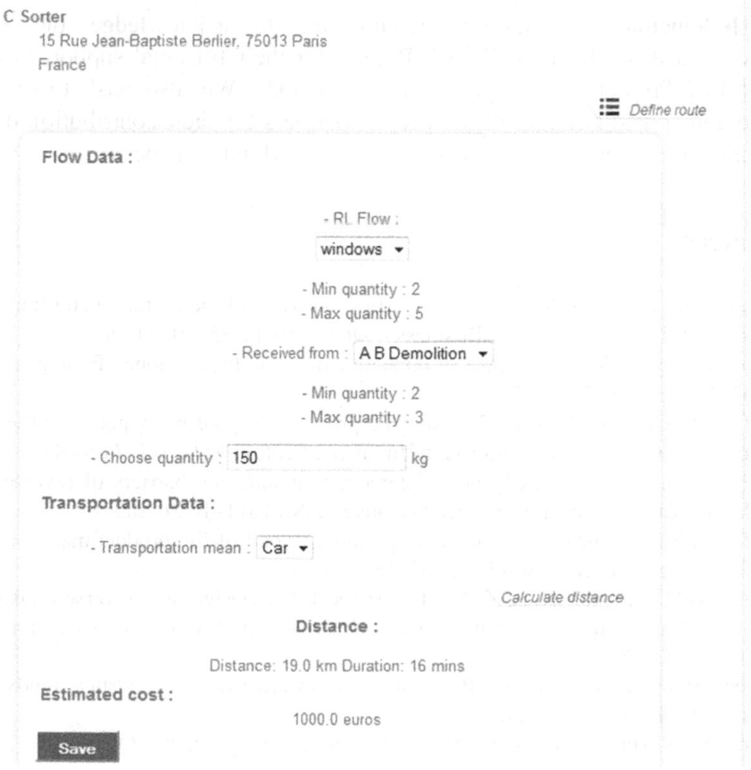

Fig. 6. Route definition interface of the RL prototype

This prototype is not intended for advanced planning of a supply chain such as APS software (Advanced Planning and Scheduling). But its main function is to provide a support for decision making in designing a reverse logistics chain. Even though APS software may provide "What if" analysis, it doesn't offer a decision aid method such as AHP, nor does it provide the optimal RL chain among all possible scenarios; it permits only to compare between manually created scenarios. The use of the proposed demonstrator doesn't eliminate the need to use APS software which is necessary to manage a RL network. The demonstrator may be considered as a plug-in for APS software.

4   Conclusion and Perspectives

In this article we presented a framework for designing an RL network based on life cycle assessment. We are interested in identifying the partners of the network and the routes connecting them based on the total cost of the network and its environmental performance as well. In the perspectives of the presented work is the achievement of the optimization option of the prototype as well as applying the method and testing the prototype in the LFCA case study in the Suplight project.

Acknowledgments. The authors would like to acknowledge the European Commission and the Picardie French Region for their financial support through the SuPlight FP7 Project (grant agreement n° 263302). We also wish to express our gratitude and appreciation to all the project partners for their contribution during the development of various ideas and concepts presented in this paper.

References

1. Carter, C.R., Ellram, L.M.: Reverse logistics: a review of the literature and framework for future investigation. Journal of Business Logistics 19(1), 85–102 (1998)
2. Ferrer, G., Ayres, R.: The impact of remanufacturing in the economy. Ecological Economics 32(3), 413–429 (2000)
3. Castell, A., Clift, R., France, C.: Extended producer responsibility policy in the European Union—a horse or a camel? Journal of Industrial Ecology 8(1-2), 4–7 (2004)
4. Ravi, V., Shankar, R.: Analysis of interactions among the barriers of reverse logistics. Technological Forecasting and Social Change 72(8), 1011–1029 (2005)
5. Toffel, M.W.: The growing strategic importance of end-of-life product management. California Management Review 45(3), 102–129 (2003)
6. Amini, M.M., Retzlaff-Roberts, D., Bienstock, C.C.: Designing a reverse logistics operation for short cycle time repair services. International Journal of Production Economics 96(3), 367–380 (2005)
7. Rogers, D.S., Tibben-Lembke, R.S.: Going backwards: reverse logistics trends and practices. RLEC Press, Pittsburgh (1999)
8. Mitra, S.: Revenue management for remanufactured products. Omega 35(5), 553–562 (2007)

9. Stock, J., Speh, T., Shear, H.: Many happy (product) returns. Harvard Business Review 80(7), 16–18 (2002)
10. Fleischmann, M., van Wassenhove, L.N., van Nunen, J.A.E.E., van der Laan, E., Dekker, R., Bloemhof-Ruwaard, J.M.: Quantitative models for reverse logistics: a review. European Journal of Operational Research 103(1), 1–17 (1997)
11. SuPLight. Document Deliverable 1.5: SuPLight application scenarios. SuPLight, EU FP7 Project, No. 263302 (2012a)
12. Ramezani, R., Bashiri, M., Tavakkoli-Moghaddam, R.: A new multi-objective stochastic model for a forward/reverse logistic network design with responsiveness and quality level. Applied Mathematical Modelling 37, 328–344 (2013)
13. Min, H., Ko, C.S., Ko, H.J.: The spatial and temporal consolidation of returned products in a closed-loop supply chain network. Comput. Indus. Eng. 51, 309–320 (2006)
14. Üster, H., Easwaran, G., Akçali, E., Çetinkaya, S.: Benders decomposition with alternative multiple cuts for a multi-product closed-loop supply chain network design model. Naval Res. Logist. 54, 890–907 (2007)
15. Listes, O., Dekker, R.: A stochastic approach to a case study for product recovery network design. Eur. J. Oper. Res. 160, 268–287 (2005)
16. Demirel, O.N., Gökçen, H.: A mixed-integer programming model for remanufacturing in reverse logistics environment. Int. J. Adv. Manuf. Technol. 39(11–12), 1197–1206 (2008)
17. Pishvaee, M.R., Kianfar, K., Karimi, B.: Reverse logistics network design using simulated annealing. Int. J. Adv. Manuf. Technol. 47, 269–281 (2010)
18. Du, F., Evans, G.W.: A bi-objective reverse logistics network analysis for post-sale service. Comput. Oper. Res. 35, 2617–2634 (2008)
19. Zhou, Y., Wang, S.: Generic Model of Reverse Logistics Network Design. Journal of Transportation Systems Engineering and Information Technology 8(3), 71–78 (2008)
20. Lee, D.-H., Dong, M.: Dynamic network design for reverse logistics operations under uncertainty. Transportation Research Part E: Logistics and Transportation Review 45(1), 61–71 (2009)
21. Lambert, S., Riopel, D., Abdul-Kader, W.: A reverse logistics decisions conceptual framework. Computers & Industrial Engineering 61(3), 561–581 (2011)
22. Cardoso, S.R., Barbosa-Póvoa, A.P.F.D., Relvas, S.: Design and planning of supply chains with integration of reverse logistics activities under demand uncertainty. European Journal of Operational Research 226(3), 436–451 (2013)
23. Wang, H.F., Hsu, H.W.: A closed-loop logistic model with a spanning-tree based genetic algorithm. Comput. Oper. Res. 37, 376–389 (2010)
24. Rogers, D.S., Tibben-Lembke, R.S.: Going backwards: Reverse logistics trends and practices. Reverse logistics executive council, Reno (1998)
25. Schwartz, B.: Reverse logistics strengthens supply chains. Transportation and Distribution 41(5), 95–100 (2000)
26. Stock, J.: Product returns/reverse logistics on Warehousing. WERC, Oak Brook (2004)
27. Quinkertz, R., Rombach, G., Liebig, D.: A scenario to optimise the energy demand of aluminium production depending on the recycling quota. Resources, Conservation and Recycling 33, 217–234 (2001)
28. Van der Rhee, B., Verma, R., Plaschka, G.: Understanding trade-offs in the supplier selection process: The role of flexibility, delivery, and value-added services/support. International Journal of Production Economics 120(1), 30–41 (2009)
29. Saaty, T.L.: The Analytic Hierarchy Process. McGraw-Hill, New York (1980)

30. Liu, F.-H.F., Hai, H.L.: The voting analytic hierarchy process method for selecting supplier. International Journal of Production Economics 97, 308–317 (2005)
31. SuPlight, Deliverable 4.3: LCA/LCC tools for lightweight solutions. SuPLight, EU FP7 Project, No. 263302 (2013)
32. SuPLight, Deliverable 3.2: Generic framework for simulation-based optimization. SuPLight, EU FP7 Project, No. 263302 (2012)

Modeling and Simulation of Closed-Loop Supply Chains Considering Economic Efficiency

Yoshitaka Tanimizu, Yusuke Shimizu, Koji Iwamura, and Nobuhiro Sugimura

Graduate School of Engineering, Osaka Prefecture University, Japan
tanimizu@me.osakafu-u.ac.jp

Abstract. This study proposes a basic model of closed-loop supply chains which includes not only traditional forward supply chains for the generation of products but also reverse supply chains for the reuse of products in consideration of economic efficiency for MTO (Make to Order) companies. The model consists of four model components, i.e., clients, manufacturers, suppliers, and remanufacturers. A remanufacturer is added to the previous model of forward supply chains as a new model component which collects used products from clients and provides reusable parts to manufacturers. Remanufacturers as well as manufacturers and suppliers modify their schedules and negotiate with each other in order to determine suitable prices and delivery times of products. Remanufacturers stimulate clients to discard used products to meet the demand of reusable parts. They can increase the amount of reused products and reduce wastes by creating a balance between supply and demand of reusable parts.

Keywords: Closed-loop supply chain, Reverse supply chain, Scheduling, Genetic algorithm, Negotiation.

1 Introduction

In recent years, many companies focus on incorporating environmental concerns into their strategic decisions [1]. Green supply chain management (GSCM) has gained increasing attention within both academia and industry [2]. The green supply chain is an approach which seeks to minimize a product or service's ecological footprint. The concept of the GSCM covers all the phases of a product's life cycle, from the extraction of raw materials through the design, production and distribution phases, to the use of products by consumers and their disposal at the end of the product's life cycle including reconditioning, reuse, and recycling of products [1]. Products and materials are returned from customers to suppliers or manufacturers through reverse supply chains in order to be recycled, reused or reconditioned. Gungor and Gupta [3] indicate that effort must be made for environmentally conscious manufacturing and product recovery systems to be profitable so that the incentive for development and planning of these systems continues.

This study proposes a closed-loop supply chain model for parts reuse in consideration of economic efficiency. A closed-loop supply chain includes not only traditional forward supply chains for the generation of products but also reverse supply chains

V. Prabhu, M. Taisch, and D. Kiritsis (Eds.): APMS 2013, Part I, IFIP AICT 414, pp. 461–468, 2013.

for the reuse of products. Figure 1 shows a basic configuration of a closed-loop supply chain. Model components in the reverse supply chain collect used products from customers and provide usable parts to assembly manufacturers or parts suppliers. The components are referred to as remanufacturers in this study. This study also proposes a negotiation protocol which synchronizes the demand of reusable parts and the supply of used products among the model components in the closed-loop supply chain. A lot of used products become waste products in traditional recovery approaches, since the customers may discard products without consideration for reuse of products whenever they want. In the proposed new protocol, remanufacturers create a balance between supply of used products from customers and demand of reusable parts to remanufacturers. When manufacturers require usable parts for generating new products, remanufacturers stimulate customers to discard products for reuse by indicating high required prices for used products to customers. On the other hand, when manufacturers require few parts, remanufacturers indicate low required prices to customers in order to discourage customers from discarding products. Remanufacturers can increase the amount of reused products and reduce waste products.

The reminder of this paper is organized as follows. Section 2 reviews the previous supply chain models for forward supply chains. Section 3 describes a new model and a negotiation protocol for closed-loop supply chains. Finally, Section 4 demonstrates experimental results.

2   Previous Supply Chain Model

There are a large number of literatures on a closed-loop supply chain which involves studies on network design problems, product acquisition management, marketing-related issues, etc. [4]. Design problems of closed-loop supply chain networks involve a high degree of uncertainty associated with quality and quantity of used products. Robust optimization, such as stochastic programming, is commonly used to deal with the uncertainty. However uncontrolled acquisition of used products results in excessive inventory levels or stock-outs due to insufficient used products. Marketing-related issues include the pricing of remanufactured products. Some researches develop game theory-based models to determine prices of remanufactured products.

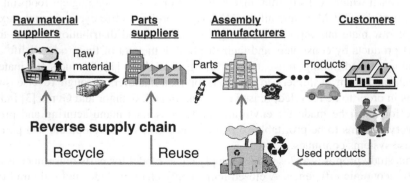

Fig. 1. Closed-loop supply chain

Our previous studies have represented a framework for dynamically forming and reconfiguring a supply chain as a dynamic supply chain [5]. Each organization in the supply chains can change business partners for every order to find suitable business partners and enter into profitable contracts. A three-layered dynamic supply chain model consisting of clients, manufacturers, and suppliers has been proposed as a minimum model for the multi-layered dynamic supply chains which involve MTO (Make to Order) companies with no inventories [6]. The model provided a negotiation protocol to determine suitable prices and delivery times for ordered products through the iteration of the negotiation process between the organizations, as well as through the modification processes of production schedules.

3   Closed-Loop Supply Chain Model

3.1   Modeling of Remanufacturer

In this study, a new model component, a remanufacturer, is added to the three-layered model in order to represent the negotiation protocol among organizations in closed-loop supply chains. A minimum model for the closed-loop supply chains consists of four components: clients, manufacturers, suppliers, and remanufacturers, as shown in Fig. 2. Remanufacturers have neither stock of usable parts nor used products.

Remanufacturer R_s generates an order and sends it to clients in order to collect a used product. The order includes information about the required price $pcr^O_{s,n}$ of a used product. The required price is estimated on the required price $pcc^O_{p,n}$ of a new product by using the following equation.

$$pcr^O_{s,n} = pcc^O_{p,n} \times pr_{s,n} \qquad (1)$$

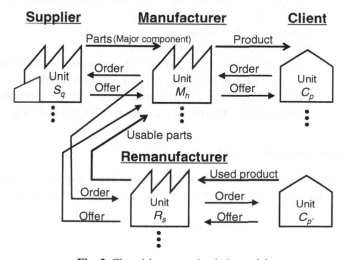

Fig. 2. Closed-loop supply chain model

where

— $prs_{s,n}$ A factor related to a required price of a used product

The remanufacturer also generates an offer of a usable part. The offer includes the possible delivery time and the bid price of the usable part. The possible delivery time $dtr^F{}_{s,h,n}$ and the bid price $pcr^F{}_{s,h,n}$ are determined as shown in the following equations based on the modified schedule of the remanufacturer.

$$dtr^F_{s,h,n} = ctr_{s,h,n} \tag{2}$$

$$pcr^F_{s,h,n} = tcr_{s,h,n} + rwr_{s,h,n} - pnr_{s,h,n} + \sum_{g=1}^{G} \Delta pnr^{Rv(s,n,r)}_{s,g} \tag{3}$$

$$tcr_{s,h,n} = dcr_{s,h,n} + rcr_{s,h,n} + ppr_{s,h,n} \tag{4}$$

$$rcr_{s,h,n} = pcc^O_{p,n} \times F(t) \times cr_{s,h,n} \tag{5}$$

$$ppr_{s,h,n} = pcr^O_{s,n} \tag{6}$$

$$pnr_{s,h,n} = km_{h,n} \times \max\{dtr^F_{s,h,n} - dtm^O_{h,n}, 0\} \tag{7}$$

where

— $ctr_{s,h,n}$ Completion time of a usable part generated by remanufacturer R_s
— $tcr_{s,h,n}$ Total cost of a usable part
— $rwr_{s,h,n}$ Reward for a usable part required by remanufacturer R_s
— $pnr_{s,h,n}$ Penalty charge due to delay of a usable part
— $\Delta pnr^{Rv}{}_{s,g}$ Penalty charge due to delay in delivery time of contracted orders
— $dcr_{s,h,n}$ Disassembly cost of a usable part
— $rcr_{s,h,n}$ Repair cost of a usable part
— $ppr_{s,h,n}$ Purchase price of an used product
— $F(t)$ Cumulative failure rate estimated based on the Weibull distribution
— $cr_{s,h,n}$ A factor related to a repair cost of a usable part
— $km_{h,n}$ Penalty charge factor representing penalty charge per unit time
— $dtm^O{}_{h,n}$ Required delivery time of a usable part for product $NC_{p,n}$.

3.2   Extension of Client Model

A client provides a new function to determine discarding a used product in this study. The client decides when to discard a used product by using the following equation.

$$utc_{p',n'} \geq plc_{p',n'} \tag{8}$$

where

— $utc_{p',n'}$ A period of time when a product has been used by client C_p.
— $plc_{p',n'}$ Product's life cycle estimated based on the Weibull distribution

In general, a client independently discards a product which has been used beyond its life cycle. The product is dealt with as a waste, if it is not required to be reused.

In the proposed model, a client firstly receives a requirement for reuse of a product from a remanufacturer as an order. The client receiving the order evaluates a motivation for discarding a product by using the following equations and determines which product is discarded. If some products satisfy the condition determined by Eq. (9), the client determines discarding a product which has the highest value of the motivation in Eq. (10).

$$mv_{p',n'} \geq rn \tag{9}$$

$$mv_{p',n'} = \frac{pcr^O_{s,n} - \left(pv_{p',n'} - dcc_{p',n'}\right)}{pcr^O_{s,n}} \tag{10}$$

where

— $mv_{p',n'}$ Motivation for providing a product to remanufacturers for reuse
— rn Random numbers
— $pv_{p',n'}$ Product's value which decreases with time of use of a product from the initial price. It is estimated based on the Weibull distribution.
— $dcc_{p',n'}$ Cost for discarding a product by client C_p.

3.3   Negotiation Protocol

In a conventional model, a client firstly determines which products should be discarded by using Eq. (8), regardless of the requirements from remanufacturers. Remanufacturers can only reuse the products discarded by the client. When no remanufacturers require the discarded products during a certain period of time, they must be waste products.

The proposed closed-loop supply chain model creates a balance between supply of used products from customers and demand of reusable parts for manufacturers. A remanufacture stimulates the intention of the client to discard a used product by providing the higher required price $pcr^O_{s,n}$, when the product is required for reuse. The client throws out the product easily, even if the product is not yet up to its life cycle described in Eq. (8). The remanufacturer deals with a client as a virtual warehouse. The amount of waste products decreases and a lot of used products are reused in the reverse supply chains.

Steps in the negotiation process in the closed-loop supply chains are as follows:

1. Manufacturer M_h sends a new order for a part to all suppliers and remanufacturers.
2. Remanufacturer R_s creates a new order for a used product and sends it to all clients.

3. Client $C_{p'}$ specifies candidates for discarding products by using Eq. (8), and generates an offer of the used product which is selected by Eqs. (9) and (10).
4. Remanufacturer R_s improves a schedule by using a genetic algorithm (GA) after
   adding disassembly processes and repair processes of the used product. Then, the
   remanufacturer creates an offer for a usable part and sends it to manufacturer M_h.
5. Manufacturer M_h selects one offer which has the lowest bid price. Then, the manufacturer improves a production schedule by using a GA after adding manufacturing
   processes of the selected part and generates an offer for client C_p.

This negotiation process is repeated among the organizations in the closed-loop supply
chains until the client accepts an offer from a manufacturer or cancels the order.

4   Computational Experiments

4.1   Experiments for Comparing Proposed Model with Conventional Model

A prototype of a simulation system for closed-loop supply chains has been developed
using Windows-based networked computers (Intel Core 2 Duo E8500 3.16 GHz CPU
with 1.99 GB of RAM). Two suppliers, two manufacturers, a remanufacturer, and a
client were implemented as agents on different six computers, as shown in Fig. 3.

In the initial conditions, the suppliers and the manufacturers had same job-shop
type production schedules consisting of 5 resources and 20 contracted parts, and 10
resources and 20 contracted products, respectively [6]. The client continuously generated 100 new orders and negotiated with two manufacturers during the experiments

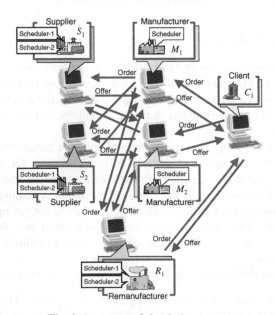

Fig. 3. Prototype of simulation system

for about 6 hours. The manufacturers generated orders and negotiated among the two suppliers and one remanufacturer every 30 seconds of bidding time in order to generate offers for the client. Population size, crossover rate, and mutation rate of the GA were 30, 0.8, and 0.2, respectively.

Ten experiments were carried out with the proposed model. The values of parameters $pr_{s,n}$ and $cr_{s,n}$ used in Eqs. (1) and (5) was set to 0.15 and 0.01, respectively. The experimental results are summarized in Table 1.

The experimental results were compared with the ones of a conventional model in which the client independently determines when to discard products. Ten experiments of the conventional model were also carried out on the same experimental conditions of the proposed method. The experimental results of the conventional model are summarized in Table 1. The remanufacturer of the proposed model can increase the rate of reused parts about 47 % more than the one of the conventional model.

Table 1. Comparison of experimental results

[average]	Num. of Reused products	Num. of Waste products	Rate of reuse to waste	Rate of reused parts to new parts	Profit of remanufacturer (*10^3 $)
Proposed model	43.2	37.7	53.4 %	54.6 %	89.7
Conventional model	5.7	50.2	10.2 %	7.8 %	40.7

4.2   Simulation for Performance Measurement

This prototype of a simulation system can be used for the organizations in the closed-loop supply chains to make effective plans for reuse of products in consideration of economic efficiency. In this paper, about 100 experiments were carried out on

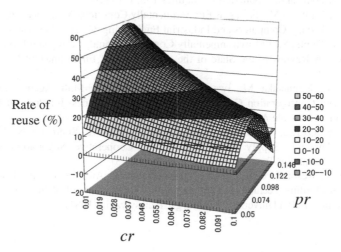

Fig. 4. Performance measurement of closed-loop supply chains

25 experimental conditions by changing the values of parameters $cr_{s,n}$ and $pr_{s,n}$ which was used to determine a repair cost of a usable part and a required price of a used product, respectively. Figure 4 describes the least squares approximation of the rate of reuse which has been derived from the experimental results. As shown in this figure, the parts with higher repair costs decrease the rate of reuse. Not only the used products purchased at low prices but also the ones purchased at high prices decrease the rate of reuse, since the client cannot provide the used products at lower prices than the product's value and the manufacturers cannot enter into a contract with the remanufacturer at higher price than the price which the manufacturer requires.

5   Conclusion

This study proposes a closed-loop supply chain model consisting of suppliers, manufacturers, remanufacturers, and clients, as a minimum model for the closed-loop supply chains. It also proposes a negotiation protocol among the organizations in the closed-loop supply chains. A prototype of a simulation system was developed to evaluate the effectiveness of the model and protocol. The proposed model was compared with a conventional model which discarded the used products without negotiation processes between remanufacturers and clients. The experimental results show that the proposed model can reuse products more than the conventional model. The prototype system can be used for performance measurement of closed-loop supply chains.

References

1. BearingPoint: 2008 Supply Chain Monitor "How Mature is the Green Supply Chain?". Survey report (2008)
2. Sarkis, J., Zhu, Q., Lai, K.: An Organizational Theoretic Review of Green Supply Chain. International Journal of Production Economics 130, 1–15 (2011)
3. Gungor, A., Gupta, S.M.: Issues in Environmentally Conscious Manufacturing and Product Recovery: a Survey. Computers and Industrial Engineering 36, 811–853 (1999)
4. Llgin, M.A., Gupta, S.M.: Environmentally Conscious Manufacturing and Product Recovery (ECMPRO): A Review of the State of the Art. Journal of Environmental Management 91, 563–591 (2010)
5. Tanimizu, Y., Yamanaka, M., Iwamura, K., Sugimura, N.: Multi-Agent Based Dynamic Supply Chain Configuration Considering Production Schedules. In: Proc. of International Symposium on Flexible Automation, pp. 572–578 (2006)
6. Tanimizu, Y., Ozawa, C., Shimizu, Y., Orita, B., Iwamura, K., Sugimura, N.: Flexible Multi-Layered Dynamic Supply Chain Models with Cooperative Negotiation. International Journal of Automation Technology 7(1), 128–135 (2013)
7. Lawrence, S.: Resource Constrained Project Scheduling: An Experimental Investigation of Heuristic Scheduling Techniques (Supplement), Graduate School of Industrial Administration, Carnegie-Mellon University, Pittsburgh, Pennsylvania (1984)

Development of a Strategic Model for Freight Transportation with a Case Study of the Far East

Louis Coulet[1], Sungbum Jun[2], and Jinwoo Park[2,*]

[1] Thales Services, Sophia-Antipolis, France
ldc200@gmail.com
[2] Dept. of Industrial Engineering at Seoul National University, Seoul, Republic of Korea
junsb87@mailab.snu.ac.kr, autofact@snu.ac.kr

Abstract. Developing a strategic model has become a major concern for decision-makers owing to free trade agreements (FTAs), environmental pollution and the risk of changing route conditions. The main purpose of this study is to evaluate the effect of these factors by measuring the performance of a complete transportation solution in terms of cost, delivery time and environmental impact. To solve the problem within reasonable time, the proposed model was linearized and solved by using the software ILOG OPL. This study also compared the optimal solutions under four different configurations. The proposed model may be useful for both exporting companies and government agencies as a tool for evaluating the benefits of new alternative routes.

Keywords: Freight transportation, Strategic Transportation model, Linear optimization, Korea-Europe trade.

1 Introduction

Freight transportation has become a major international concern owing to free trade agreements (FTAs), potential environmental pollution, and changing route conditions. FTAs are ratified to remove all tariff and non-tariff barriers on imports and exports. With the advent of FTAs, yearly commercial traffic across borders has increased considerably. Modern societies have experienced an increase in public awareness of the environmental impact that human polluting activities may have on the environment. The risk of attacks by Somali pirates and the frozen Artic Ocean also have a strong influence on transportation route selection.

Thus, anticipating environmental changes and evaluating different solutions is crucial to successfully adapting to the changes. This paper describes a strategic model for freight transportation that was developed to assist decision-makers like government planners, regulators, and shipping managers. The proposed model considers the effects of changes in the situation and route optimization to fulfill the demand of each

---

* Corresponding author.

V. Prabhu, M. Taisch, and D. Kiritsis (Eds.): APMS 2013, Part I, IFIP AICT 414, pp. 469–476, 2013.

market. Four experiments are presented; an aggregated objective function (AOF) was used to obtain more realistic solutions.

2   Literature Review

Transportation models have been studied thoroughly since the advent of computers, which enabled researchers and companies to develop detailed models (Vidal, 1995).

Albino et al. (2002) proposed a model that analyzes the flows and performances of a supply chain comprising transformation processes. To consider the environmental impact of a multistep chemical supply chain, Bojarski et al. (2009) proposed a holistic model. They applied their model to a maleic anhydride production supply chain spanning Western Europe. These two analytical models are relevant to a supply chain as a series of decisions (load balancing, paths, processes, distribution centers and suppliers locations, etc.), each with different performances and capacities, that lead to a particular supply chain network.

Lainez (2009) proposed an interesting transportation model that includes the dimen-sion of flexibility and presented the detailed performance of a complex supply chain consisting of several processes. He introduced capacity limitation in supply chain channels.

Onuoha (2009) researched piracy around the Gulf of Aden. He provided figures and tried to explain the causes of the recent rise in piracy. Gilpin (2009) proposed a busi-ness model to estimate the overall cost of piracy and proposed some solutions to lessen its cost. His model has proven useful in estimating the cost suffered by shipping companies—mainly insurance fees—but the solutions cannot be evaluated.

The following sections introduce a strategic transportation model that integrates rele-vant parts of previous approaches to select routes that minimize the cost, time, and environmental effects. This paper presents the design of an optimal supply chain in terms of several performance criteria (i.e., net present value, environmental impact, and delivery time) under different conditions.

3   Transportation Model

The proposed transportation model considers three performance criteria: delivery time, cost, and environmental impact. These criteria are expressed for each of the three parts of the transportation network. The first part is one of the four approach routes from Korea to Europe: through the Suez Canal, around the Cape of Good Hope, through the Arctic Ocean, and through Siberia via the Trans-Siberian-Railroad (TSR). The second part links the four approach points to the seaports. The third part links the seaports to the markets over the entire EU27.

The equations linking the performance criteria to the quantity transported along a certain path can be simplified into a linear model with an aggregated objective function (AOF).

3.1 Model Definition

Variables. The decision variables of the model are as follows:

Quantity from route a to seaport s (TEU): $(y_{as})_{a \in A, s \in S}$

Quantity from seaport s to market m (TEU): $(z_{sm})_{s \in S, m \in M}$

The quantity on route a: $(X_a)_{a \in A}$, is completely determined by (C2).

Constraints. The demand of each market at time t ($Dem_m(t)$) is given by the forecast of the GDP of m:

$$Dem_m(t) = Exports~(t) * \frac{GDP_m(t)}{\sum_{m \in M} GDP_m(t)}.$$

For a permanent state with no stocks held anywhere in the network,

The demand of each market is fulfilled (C1): $\sum_{s \in S} z_{sm} = Dem_m(t), \forall~m \in M$

Steady state on the visiting path (C2): $\sum_{s \in S} y_{as} = X_a, \forall~a \in A$

Steady state on the distribution (C3): $\sum_{a \in A} y_{as} = \sum_{m \in M} z_{sm}, \forall~s \in S$

Measures. The average delivery cost for market m (USD/TEU) is

$$Cost_m = \frac{1}{Dem_m} \sum_{s \in S/Y_s > 0} \left[c^z(z_{sm}) + \frac{z_{sm}}{Y_s} \sum_{a \in A/X_a > 0} \frac{y_{as}}{X_a} (c^X(X_a) + c^Y(y_{as})) \right], \quad (1)$$

where the total quantity in seaport s is $Y_s = a \in A~y_{as}$

The overall average environmental impact (ton eq. CO_2/TEU) is

$$Impact = \frac{1}{Exports} (\sum_{a \in A} p^X(X_a) + \sum_{a \in A} \sum_{s \in S} p^y(y_{as}) + \sum_{m \in M} \sum_{s \in S} p^z(z_{sm})). \quad (2)$$

The average delivery time for market m is

$$Time_m = \frac{1}{Dem_m} \sum_{s \in S/Y_s > 0} \left[t^z(z_{sm}) + \frac{z_{sm}}{Y_s} \sum_{a \in A/X_a > 0} \frac{y_{as}}{X_a} (t^X(X_a) + t^Y(y_{as})) \right]. \quad (3)$$

3.2 Objective Function

Route allocation is a multi-objective optimization problem since three self-competing criteria are being optimized. A mix of the different routes with the lowest cost, lightest environment impact, and quickest delivery of the goods is desired.

Aggregated Objective Function (AOF):

$$AOF \begin{pmatrix} (y_{as})_{a \in A, s \in S} \\ (z_{sm})_{s \in S, m \in M} \\ (\kappa, \varphi, \theta) \end{pmatrix} = \kappa * Cost + \varphi * Impact + \theta * Time \quad (4)$$

The coefficient φ translates the environmental impact in terms of cost, so the dimension of φ is [(USD/USDtransported)/unit of impact/USD] = [USD/unit of impact]. The amount φ ∗ Impact can be considered a tax on the impact on the environment that has been progressively appearing in reality. The coefficient θ translates the delivery time in terms of cost, so the dimension of θ is [(USD/USDtransported)/days] = [USD/(days × USDt)]. Goods that are on their way to their final markets constitute idle stocks, so they generate an opportunity cost to their owner (should it be the producer or final consumer) that can be represented by θ ∗ Time. Then, θ = E × ONIA can be used, where E is the amount of exports (USD) and ONIA is the overnight index average, or the cost incurred by keeping 1 USD of inventory for 1 day.

4   Experiment and Results

This section presents solutions to optimize transportation problems between Europe and Korea using the proposed model with four different configurations. The increase in piracy in the Gulf of Aden, length of the route to circumvent the Cape of Good Hope, melting of the Arctic Ocean, and limited capacity of the TSR as well as the distribution of demand were considered to solve the transportation model at the strategic level.

4.1   Experimental Description

The South Korean economy relies massively on its industrial sector, which exports high value added goods worldwide. Exports are growing rapidly as Korean companies have become serious global competitors in all industrial fields. Thus, the challenge of transportation between Korea and Europe is optimizing the time, cost, and environmental impact of long and dangerous routes between Korea and Europe. Moreover, as the planet and political concerns over it are heating up, Somali pirates have increased their attacks on more and bigger ships and the Arctic is melting, worsening the situation considerably.

In the experiment, the decision variables were the amount on each part of the route, and constraints were determined earlier. The objective function was the AOF. 37 seaports (including the TSR terminal) and 50 markets were considered for 1,850 decision variables minus 50 because of the demand constraint.

As shown above, the approach and harbor selection steps can be merged into a single set of decision variables. There are 10 seaport selection paths supplying 37 seaports, so there are 370 decision variables; however, because of the path themselves, only 153 are non-zeros. Because of the steady-state constraint, the amount unloaded in a seaport is equal to the amount sent from it to the markets, which translates into 37 constraints. Overall, the model consisted of 1,916 independent variables and a linear objective function.

The linear model was solved using the software ILOG OPL. The solution was the absolute optimal solution and was reached in less than a second. ILOG's engine contains the code of the optimization algorithm; the user can tweak its parameters and has to define the model.

Constraint C1 denotes the demand of each market that has to be fully fulfilled. C2 represents the steady state so that the three parts of the transportation course are the same. The linear model is simple and can be expressed quickly in ILOG because the objective function is simply a linear combination of the decision variables weighted by the cost, time, and pollution performances.

The model was optimized along the AOF to include the cost, weighted function of the total delivery time, and environmental impact. This section describes the optimal solutions in three configurations. In the first configuration, all four routes were available (Arctic, TSR, Suez Canal, and the Cape of Good Hope routes). In the second configuration, the Arctic route was considered unavailable; in the third configuration, only the Suez Canal and the Cape of Good Hope routes were available. The influence of increased piracy was evaluated and represented in configuration 4.

4.2   Results

Configuration 1. Figure 1 shows the transportation course when all routes were available. Europe was mostly supplied through the Arctic route. However, the Suez route performed better when delivering to the Italian, Greek, Turkish, and Balkan markets. The TSR only supplied Moscow and Kastornoye.

In this configuration, the delivery time ranged from 18.4 days for Norway to 23.8 days for Seville in Spain. The cost and pollution level were at their lowest in Norway (1,255 USD and 3.42) and highest in Romania and Bulgaria (1,806 USD and 8.17) as long land transportation was required. The importance (around 36% of goods) of the Bremerhaven and Rotterdam seaports should be noted.

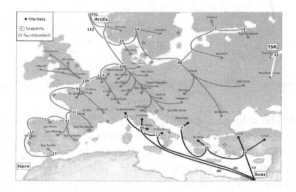

Fig. 1. Optimal transportation course of configuration 1: all routes available

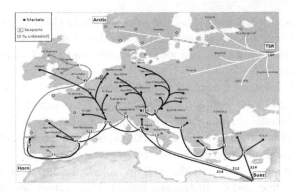

Fig. 2. Optimal transportation course of configuration 2: Artic Ocean frozen

Configuration 2. As the Arctic route, through which most of Europe was supplied in configuration 1, was no longer available, the area supplied through the Suez route expanded to most of Europe except for the northeastern area supplied through the TSR. In configuration 2, the performances sharply declined. The delivery time ranges from 20.3 days for Moscow, which was the terminal of the TSR, to 29.3 days for northern UK. The cost ranged from 1,456 USD for Moscow to 2,308 USD for Ireland; pollution ranges from 4.01 for southern Italy to 11.51 for Norway. More than 45% of goods were unloaded in the harbors of Marseille, Venetia, and Rijeka.

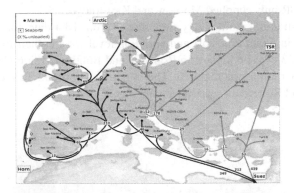

Fig. 3. Optimal transportation course of configuration 3: only Suez available

Configuration 3. The solution for configuration 3, where only the Suez Canal and the Cape of Good Hope routes were available, is presented in Fig. 3. Most of the markets were supplied through Mediterranean and Adriatic harbors, so a large volume of south-to-north land transportation was required. This considerably reduced the performances, especially the environmental impact. Of the goods, 54% were unloaded in the harbors of Marseille, Venetia, and Rijeka and then transported as far as Ireland, Sweden, and Novgorod.

The delivery time ranged from 21.2 days for Turkey to 31.9 days for Finland. The cost was from 1,609 USD for southern Italy to 2,391 USD for Finland, and the pollution level was from 4.01 for southern Italy to 11.49 for northern Russia.

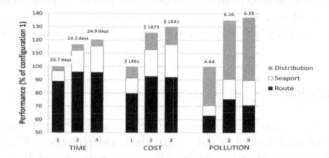

Fig. 4. Comparison of performances in three configurations

The overall weighted average performances in the three configurations were compared. Figure 4 shows the cost, time, and pollution of the optimal solutions in the three configurations.

The first configuration with the four routes available was taken as the reference (100%) as it was the best in terms of cost, time, and pollution. Suppressing the Arctic line led to an 18% increase in time, 25% increase in cost, and a staggering 35% hike in environmental impact. Suppression of the TSR route affected the performance to a lesser extent with increases of 3%–5%. The distribution part from seaport to market was rather fast compared to the route part but was costly and generated a lot of pollution.

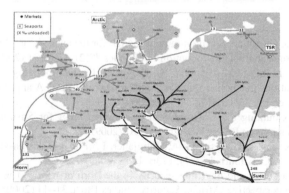

Fig. 5. Optimal transportation course of configuration 4: under increased piracy

Configuration 4. As Gilpin (2009) proposed, rerouting ships around Africa mitigates the cost of piracy. For every level of piracy and Suez Canal fee, there is a tradeoff between a longer route or a more expensive and risky one. Configuration 4 represents the transportation solution where a hypothetical increase in piracy has forced 60% of the shipments to go around the Cape of Good Hope.

Ships going around Africa were preferred for all seaports from Barcelona around the northern coast of Europe to St. Petersburg as the relative benefit of the Suez route decreased when the distance between the Suez Canal and a seaport increased.

These results can be used to find the optimal transportation course in different situations. They can also be used to evaluate the opportunity of further developing the TSR and Arctic routes which may greatly improve the performance of the transportation network.

5   Conclusion

In this study, the overall transportation course at a strategic level was modeled by expressing three performance criteria (cost, time, and pollution). The performance was mainly linear with regard to the transported quantity on a particular route. The relative importance of the nonlinear performance was neglected as an approximation. The linear model was implemented and optimized with the software ILOG. Although the proposed model was based on linear assumptions, it was relatively easy to obtain good solutions within a reasonable timeframe, and the model offers a significant amount of flexibility to decision-makers who can experiment with different configurations.

The optimal solution with all four routes available showed that the Arctic and TSR are very efficient and that the Suez route proved to be best only when delivering goods to Turkey, Greece, and Italy. The developed model may be useful for both exporting companies and government agencies as a tool to evaluate the benefits of developing new alternative routes.

References

1. Albino, V., Izzo, C., Kühtz, S.: Input–output models for the analysis of a local/global supply chain. International Journal of Production Economics 78(2), 119–131 (2002)
2. Bojarski, A.D., Laínez, J.M., Espuña, A., Puigjaner, L.: Incorporating environmental impacts and regulations in a holistic supply chains modeling: An LCA approach. Computers & Chemical Engineering 33(10), 1747–1759 (2009)
3. Raymond, G.: Counting the Costs of Somali Piracy. Center for Sustainable Economies. United States Institute of Peace, Washington DC (2009)
4. Laínez, J.M., Kopanos, G., Espuña, A., Puigjaner, L.: Flexible design-planning of supply chain networks. AIChE Journal 55(7), 1736–1753 (2009)
5. Onuoha, F.: Sea piracy and maritime security in the Horn of Africa: The Somali coast and Gulf of Aden in perspective. African Security Studies 18(3), 31–44 (2009)
6. Gilpin, R.: Counting the Costs of Somali Piracy, Center for Sustainable Economies, United States Institute of Peace Working Paper (2009)
7. Vidal, C.J., Goetschalckx, M.: Strategic production-distribution models: A critical review with emphasis on global supply chain models. European Journal of Operational Research 98(1), 1–18 (1997)

Semantic Web-Based Supplier Discovery Framework

Jaehun Lee[1], Kiwook Jung[1], Bo Hyun Kim[2], and Hyunbo Cho[1]

[1] Pohang University of Science & Technology, Pohang, Gyeongbuk, South Korea
{jaehun_lee,kiwook,hcho}@postech.ac.kr
[2] Korea Institute of Industrial Technology, Ansan, Gyeonggi, South Korea
bhkim@kitech.re.kr

Abstract. As companies move forward to source globally, supply chain management has gained attention more than ever before. In particular, the discovery and selection of capable suppliers has become a prerequisite for a global supply chain operation. Manufacturing e-marketplaces have helped companies discover new suppliers and/or buyers fast and effective for their products and services. Due to the description of requirements and capabilities in isolation, their true meanings may not be uniformly interpreted from each other. The issue of semantics between suppliers and buyers, then, remains an obstacle.

The main objective is to propose a semantic web-based supplier discovery framework for building a long-term strategic supply chain. Specifically, 1) a collaboration ontology is developed to represent the supplier's capability information and the buyer's requirements. 2) Supplier's potential capability is reasoned. 3) Buyer's requirements are semantically matched with supplier's capability information. In addition, a prototype demonstrates the practicality of the framework.

Keywords: Supplier Discovery, Supply Chain Building, Semantic Web.

1   Introduction

Rapid globalization of business across emerging markets has changed business competition from a 'company versus company' model into a 'supply chain versus supply chain' model. A supply chain is defined as a network of participants who procure materials, develop products, and deliver them to customers according to coordinated plans [1]. As companies move forward to source globally, supply chain management has gained attention more than ever before. In particular, the discovery and selection of capable suppliers has become a prerequisite for a global supply chain operation. Conventional supplier discovery practices, such as visiting expos, making phone calls, may not contribute to search for new suppliers located overseas.

Manufacturing e-marketplaces have helped companies discover new suppliers and/or buyers fast and effective for their products and services of interest. A few examples include Alibaba.com, mfg.com, and ec21.com. Fig. 1 shows a supplier discovery scenario in e-marketplace, where a buyer attempts to find global suppliers capable of manufacturing a car front bumper mold. Due to the description

V. Prabhu, M. Taisch, and D. Kiritsis (Eds.): APMS 2013, Part I, IFIP AICT 414, pp. 477–484, 2013.
© IFIP International Federation for Information Processing 2013

of requirements and capabilities in isolation, their true meanings may not be uniformly interpreted from each other. The issue of semantics between suppliers and buyers, then, remains an obstacle.

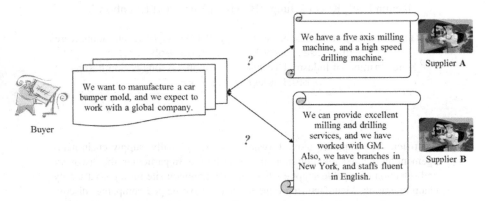

Fig. 1. Supplier discovery scenario

In response to this problem, the main objective of this paper is to propose a semantic web-based supplier discovery framework for building a long-term strategic supply chain.

2   Semantic-Web Based Supplier Discovery Framework

2.1   Dimensions of Buyer's Requirements and Supplier's Capability Information

Buyer's requirements consist of product requirements (that is, *'what to manufacture?'*), and supplier requirements (that is, *'whom to manufacture with?'*). On the other hand, supplier's capability comprises manufacturing capability and non-manufacturing capability. The sub-requirements will be matched with the sub-capabilities, when a buyer searches for suppliers of interest.

Matching buyer's requirements with supplier's capability requires semantic searches, because (1) buyer's requirements are not explicitly described, (2) suppliers use heterogeneous formats and terminologies in their capability description, and (3) buyers and suppliers use different level of details in describing their wishes. Therefore, the buyers may not well interpret suppliers' capabilities, and the suppliers may not recognize what the buyers want, either.

A literature survey shows that most discovery methods use product requirements only to match with the supplier's manufacturing capability at a semantic level [2-5]. These methods are not appropriate for building a long-term strategic supply chain, but for a single trading of specific products [6].

2.2   Overall Supplier Discovery Framework

A key ontology is developed to represent the supplier's capability information and the buyer's requirements. The framework includes ontology building, reasoning and semantic matching. Its brief diagram is shown in Fig. 2.

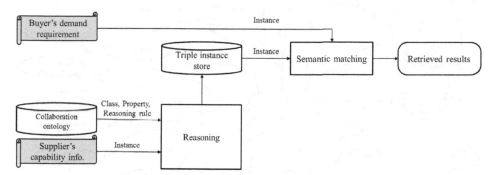

Fig. 2. Semantic-web based supplier discovery framework

1. A collaboration ontology is pre-built in order to be used for reasoning. This ontology is built in the form of Web Ontology Language (OWL), and OWL Rules Language (ORL).
2. Supplier's potential capability is reasoned from classes, properties, reasoning rules, and instances. OWL includes classes and properties, ORL is used for rules, and Resource Description Framework (RDF) for instances. Reasoning tool automates the reasoning process, and it stores the ontology model and its reasoned instances in the 'triple instance store'.
3. Finally, the buyer's requirement is semantically matched with supplier's capability information using query language.

3   Building a Collaboration Ontology

3.1   An Ontology for Supplier's Capability Information

Since the quality of the semantic search is directly determined by the richness of the representation, an ontology plays an essential part in this framework. The collaboration ontology is built using the formal representation language OWL, the most expressive semantic markup language [7]. Each ontology concept is represented as a class, using owl:Class. An OWL class is characterized by relationship-type properties using owl:ObjectProperty, or by data-type properties using owl:DatatypeProperty.

Fig. 3 shows a supplier ontology in which classes represent supplier's capability information consisting of manufacturing capability and non-manufacturing capability. For example, *tool*, *process*, *part* and *product* classes are used for reasoning regarding manufacturing capability, while *patent*, *location*, and *customer* classes are used for reasoning regarding non-manufacturing capability [8-9].

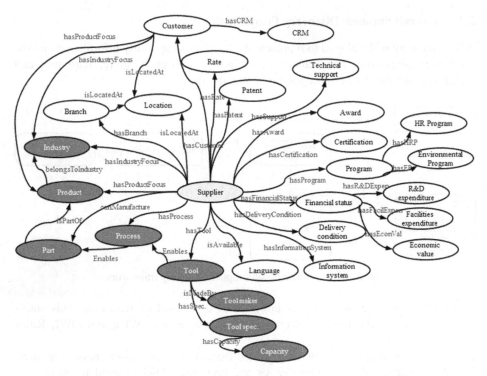

Fig. 3. Concept diagram of supplier ontology in a collaboration ontology

3.2   An Ontology for Buyer's Requirement

Fig. 4 shows a buyer ontology in which classes represent buyer's requirements consisting of product requirement and supplier requirement. For example, *process*, *part*, and *product* classes are used for reasoning regarding product requirements, while *supplier requirement* classes are used for reasoning regarding supplier requirements.

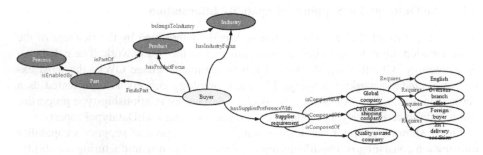

Fig. 4. Concept diagram of buyer ontology in a collaboration ontology

Table 1 describes explicit meanings for exemplary supplier requirements.

Table 1. Explicit meanings of supplier requirements

Supplier requirements	Explicit meanings
A global company	A supplier can be interacted in English, has overseas branch offices, has transaction experiences with foreign buyers, and can deliver products abroad
A company with delivery competitiveness	A supplier is located close to airport/port, has various delivery conditions, and has achieved high delivery performance
A company that provides assured quality	A supplier has high market share, has transaction experiences with principal customers, has received certifications by principal customers, has received quality awards

4   Reasoning Supplier's Potential Capability

Suppliers may not be fully aware of the buyer's requirements that they can potentially satisfy. Therefore, reasoning supplier's potential capability based on the input data is essential. In this framework, the 'triple instance store' is used to retain reasoned supplier's potential capability and input data.

Fig. 5 presents an exemplary concept diagram about how to reason manufacturing capabilities with the supplier ontology. A car bumper mold is manufactured by milling and drilling. In addition, milling is made possible if a supplier has a milling machine, and drilling is made possible if a supplier has a high speed drilling machine and a high pressure coolant system. Thus, we can reason a supplier can manufacture a bumper mold and also provide milling and drilling process, if a supplier has a milling machine, a high speed drilling machine, and a high pressure coolant system.

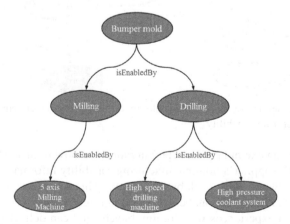

Fig. 5. Concept diagram for reasoning manufacturing capability

In addition, the following code presents an exemplary rule about how to reason non-manufacturing capabilities with the supplier ontology. If the location of supplier is different from that of supplier's customer, supplier's customer is verified to be a foreign buyer.

```
( ?c isa Supplier ) ( ?c hasCustomer ?r ) (c?isLocatedAt
?p1) ( ?r isLocatedAt ?p2)(?p1 isSame ?p2) -> (?r
isForeignBuyer true^^boolean)
```

5   Semantic Matching of Buyer's Requirements with Supplier's Capability Information

Semantic matching of buyer's requirements with supplier's capability information is required to solve the issue of buyers and suppliers using different level of details in their descriptions. In this framework, (1) the buyer's product requirements and the supplier's manufacturing capability, and (2) the buyer's supplier requirement and the supplier's non-manufacturing capability are semantically matched.

Fig. 6 presents an exemplary concept diagram about how to match buyer's product requirements with supplier's manufacturing capability information. First, all the manufacturing capabilities of the supplier, such as bumper mold, are reasoned via the described processes. Subsequently, buyer's product requirements are matched with the supplier's manufacturing capability. In this framework, the bumper mold instance in the buyer ontology is matched with the front bumper mold instance in the supplier ontology, because they have the identical instances.

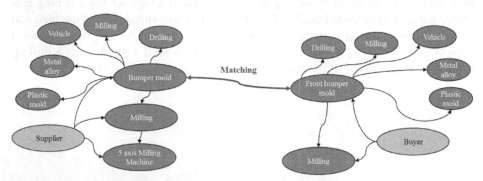

Fig. 6. Concept diagram for semantic matching: the buyer's product requirements and the supplier's manufacturing capability

Fig. 7 presents an exemplary concept diagram about how to match buyer's supplier requirements with supplier's non-manufacturing capability information. For example, a buyer wants to work with a 'global company.' This requirement is explicated as shown in Table 1: A supplier can be interacted in English, has overseas branch offices, has transaction experiences with foreign buyers, and can deliver products abroad.

Subsequently, buyer's supplier requirements are matched with the supplier's non-manufacturing capability. In this framework, the supplier instance is matched with the global company instance in the buyer ontology, because they have instances which have identical properties.

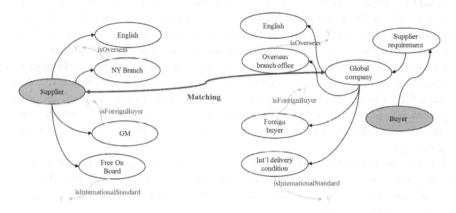

Fig. 7. Concept diagram for sematic matching: the buyer's supplier requirement and the supplier's non-manufacturing capability

6   Prototype

Most existing ontology-based systems have often been hindered by the slow reasoning speed of reasoning engines. Therefore, we have implemented a prototype to test feasibility. Ontology is built with *Protégé*, reasoning is automated with *Pro-Reasoner*, and semantic matching is performed with *SPARQL*.

Experiment is carefully conducted to measure the computational time of reasoning and matching by changing the number of suppliers. The results are shown in Table 2. Since suppliers are usually registered in the framework, the framework always has adequate time to execute reasoning on supplier's potential capability. Therefore, the reasoning time may be regarded as sufficiently fast. On the other hand, semantic matching of buyer's requirements with supplier's capability information is executed within a second. It proves the framework can be widely used in practice.

Table 2. Computational time of reasoning and matching

# of suppliers	Reasoning time (sec)	Matching time (sec)
100	38.39	<0.1
200	51.82	<0.1
600	84.12	<0.1
1,000	101.12	<0.1

7 Conclusion

The proposed semantic-web based supplier discovery framework includes ontology building, reasoning and semantic matching. 1) A key ontology is developed to represent the buyer's requirements and the supplier's capability information. 2) Supplier's potential capability based on the input data is reasoned, since suppliers may not be fully aware of the buyer's requirements that they can potentially satisfy. 3) Buyer's requirements are semantically matched with supplier's capability information.

Up until now, supplier discovery methods have only focused on matching product requirements with the supplier's manufacturing capability at a semantic level. As the proposed framework extends to consider supplier requirements as well as product requirements, the framework facilitates the building of a long-term strategic supply chain. Also, sustainable supply chain can be built since qualified suppliers are discovered strategically.

Finally, we have implemented a prototype of the framework to test feasibility. It proves the framework can be widely used in practice. In future work, to reflect industry realities, we will extend the ontology by capturing the supplier's capability information systematically.

References

1. Goffin, K., Szwejczewski, M., New, C.: Managing suppliers: when fewer can mean more. International Journal of Physical Distribution & Logistics Management 27(7), 422–436 (1997)
2. Ameri, F., Dutta, D.: A Matchmaking Methodology for Supply Chain Deployment in Distributed Manufacturing Environments. Journal of Computing and Information Science in Engineering 8(1), 1–9 (2008)
3. Cai, M., Zhang, W.Y., Chen, G., Zhang, K., Li, S.T.: SWMRD: a Semantic Web-based manufacturing resource discovery system for cross-enterprise collaboration. International Journal of Production Research 48(12), 3445–3460 (2010)
4. Jang, J., Jeong, B., Kulvatunyou, B., Chang, J., Cho, H.: Discovering and integrating distributed manufacturing services with semantic manufacturing capability profiles. International Journal of Computer Integrated Manufacturing 21(6), 631–646 (2008)
5. Kulvatunyou, B.S., Cho, H., Son, Y.J.: A semantic web service framework to support intelligent distributed manufacturing. International Journal of Knowledge-based and Intelligent Engineering Systems 9(2), 107–127 (2005)
6. Virolainen, V.: A survey of procurement strategy development in industrial companies. International Journal of Production Economics 56-57(1), 677–688 (1998)
7. McGuinness, D., Van Harmelen, F.: OWL web ontology language overview. W3C Recommendation, 1–22 (2004)
8. Dickson, G.W.: An analysis of vendor selection systems and decisions. Journal of Purchasing 2(1), 5–17 (1966)
9. Thanaraksakul, W., Phruksaphanrat, B.: Supplier evaluation framework based on balanced scorecard with integrated corporate social responsibility perspective. In: Proceedings of the International MultiConference of Engineers and Computer Scientists, vol. 2, pp. 5–10 (2009)

Simulating the Dominant Effect of a Few Critical Sites on Supply Chains Using the Inter-industry Relations Table

Sadao Suganuma and Masaru Nakano

The Graduate School of System Design and Management, Keio University
Kyosei Building, 4-1-1 Hiyoshi, Kohoku-ku, Yokohama
Kanagawa 223-8526, Japan
suganuma235@a6.keio.jp, nakano@sdm.keio.ac.jp

Abstract. We study supply chain disruptions, particularly in the passenger vehicles sector, caused by the mass industrial shutdowns due to the Great East Japan Earthquake in March, 2011, along with the restoration process to assess supply chain resiliency. We first investigate the extent of damage using the inter-industry relations table and then analyze from the viewpoints of geography, time, and economy. Following this, the layered structure was derived and the rate-determining factors of the restoration process were identified. Using these factors, we simulate the disruptions in and restoration of the passenger vehicles sector. This method using the I-O table is effective for assessment of supply chain resiliency.

Keywords: Supply chain disruptions, Sustainable manufacturing, Supply chain, Risk management, Inter-industry relations, I-O table, Automotive industry, Great East Japan Earthquake.

1   Introduction

Supply chains have recently emerged as complex global networks. As such, large natural disasters—such as the 2010 Icelandic volcano eruption, the 2011 Thailand floods, and the Great East Japan Earthquake of 2011—often cause global supply chain disruptions. Accordingly, supply chains need to be assessed to ensure resiliency and the ability to recover quickly. However, few such studies exist (1–2). The goal of this study is to establish a way of assessing supply chain resiliency.

In this paper, we study the supply chain disruptions caused by the Great East Japan Earthquake of 2011, particularly focusing on the passenger vehicles sector, which we take as a representative example of complex global supply chains. The automotive industry suffered considerably due to that disaster. Plants located in the affected regions comprised 30% of the supply chain; these were taken offline suddenly, disrupting automotive production in the world for several months. Efforts were made to resume production in other areas but initiating operations took much time. Damage assessment was made using various reports, newspapers, etc. (3–8). The main factors

V. Prabhu, M. Taisch, and D. Kiritsis (Eds.): APMS 2013, Part I, IFIP AICT 414, pp. 485–492, 2013.

were analyzed from the viewpoints of geography, time, and economy. We focus on the passenger vehicles sector owing to the complex nature and large size of its supply chain.

The input-output (I-O) table is a statistical table developed by American economist Wassily Leontief. This table has been used in various business fields, for example, in measuring the effectiveness of a policy, ascertaining the industrial structure, analyzing employment patterns, studying the globalization of industrial linkages, analyzing the environmental effect, and so on (10-11). There exist works investigating the economic influence of natural disasters (12-14) using the I-O table: these works study the impact of disasters on a region and industries from multiple viewpoints. We have noted that the regional inter-industry relations table provided by the Japanese government after surveying industries across the country gives quantitative details of the trade between industrial sectors across several districts. Using the inter-industry relations table (henceforth, the I-O table; 9), the layered structure of the vast and complex automotive supply chain was derived. The process was simulated to assess the disruption in and restoration of the supply chain due to a specific sector in a specific area that is deemed a critical sector, going offline.

2   Methodology

We focus on the recovery process of the supply chain in the passenger vehicles sector following the disruption caused by the Great East Japan Earthquake, and perform a simulation using the I-O table. Damage assessment was made using various reports by automotive manufacturers and by the Japan Automobile Manufacturers Association, general newspapers and industrial newspapers, etc.

2.1   Damage to and Recovery of the Passenger Vehicles Sector in 2011

Fig. 1 shows the monthly car production in Japan. In the figure, the drastic production declines following the Lehman Brothers' bankruptcy and the Great East Japan Earthquake can be easily seen. Comparing the two, the former had a long recovery time as it was a "demand shock," while the latter saw faster recovery as it was a "supply disruption."

2.2   Interregional I-O Table

Using the interregional I-O table published by the Ministry of Economy, Trade, and Industry every five years, we analyze the effect of the supply disruptions in East Japan on the firms in other areas.

Table 1 details the interregional I-O table in terms of areas and sectors. We use the latest edition (year 2005) and show the data for nine areas and 53 industrial sectors. The areas were integrated into disaster (Tohoku and Kanto) and non-disaster areas (Others). Fig. 2 (a) gives the earthquake-intensity and devastation maps for the Great East Japan Earthquake, and Fig. 2 (b) provides a map detailing the interregional I-O table.

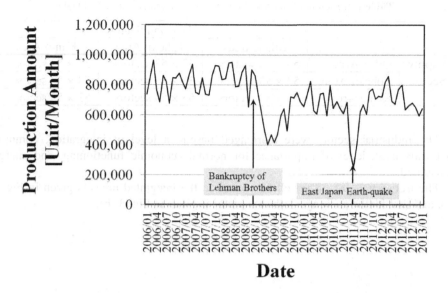

Fig. 1. Impact of the Great East Japan Earthquake on Monthly Passenger Vehicles Production

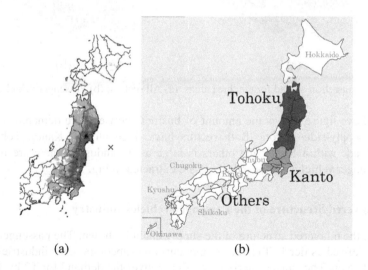

(a)   (b)

Fig. 2. Devastation map: (a) Earthquake-intensity map; (b) Map detailing the Interregional I-O Table

Table 1. Structure of intermediate sectors in the interregional I-O table

		Demand Sector		
		Other Areas	Tohoku Area	Kanto Area
Supply Sector	Other Areas	53 × 53 sectors	53 × 53 sectors	53 × 53 sectors
	Tohoku Area	53 × 53 sectors	53 × 53 sectors	53 × 53 sectors
	Kanto Area	53 × 53 sectors	53 × 53 sectors	53 × 53 sectors

The industrial sectors were rearranged based on level of integration, common materials used, level of importance for normal economic functioning, and energy consumed.

The transaction spread for all 53 sectors in the integrated areas is given in Fig. 3 (a), and that for the passenger vehicles sector is given in Fig. 3 (b).

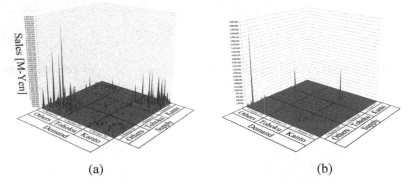

(a)   (b)

Fig. 3. Transaction spread for the three areas: (a) All sectors; (b) Passenger vehicles sector

The above figure shows the amount of business between the demand-side sectors and the supply-side sectors. Both sectors have three blocks: Kanto, Tohoku, and others. Trade within Kanto and others is large as the industries here are integrated. The passenger vehicles sector industries are extracted in Fig. 3 (b).

2.3   Layered Structure of the Passenger vehicles Industry

In Fig. 4, the 6-layered structure of the supply chain is shown. The passenger vehicles sector is defined as tier 1 (T1), the components and subcomponents industries as tier 2 (T2), and so on. The square matrix in the figure gives the demand for T2 by T1, and is called the L1 trade matrix. We call it as layer 1 (L1). The linear matrix of the sum of demand from each L1 supply-side sector is called the L1 output matrix, and is the L2 demand matrix. The L2 trade matrix is calculated using the L2 demand matrix and the input coefficients matrix.

We thus obtain the 6-layered structure of the supply chain. Fig. 4 shows the trade matrix for each layer of the supply chain at equilibrium, and is also referred to as the 3-D trade amount table.

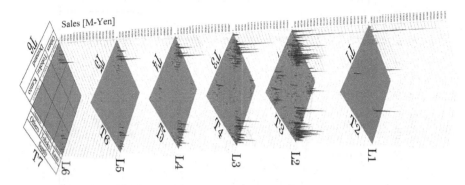

Fig. 4. Layered structure of the supply chain (3-D trade amount table)

In this way, the layered structure of the supply chain is completed and illustrated in Fig. 4. T1 on L1 covers the passenger vehicles manufacturers. T2 on L1 covers the suppliers who provide manufacturers with the parts; these same suppliers form the demand-side sectors that are supplied with parts by T3 industries in L2. As we move from L1 to L6, dominant trades shift to sectors of small parts and raw materials.

3   Results

As each supplier prepares its production capacity for the assigned amount, the 3-D trade amount table can be regarded as a 3-D structured capacity table. Although capacity varies with the amount of trade and vice versa, the 3-D structured capacity value is the value when the demand for the final product equals its production. The 3-D structured capacity table is converted to a normalized table named the 3-D utilization table. In the normalized table, in case of a trade at the cross-point of a supply-side sector and a demand-side sector, the value assigned is 1. Otherwise, no value is assigned. This table thus gives all cross-points at which trades were made.

In this table, the values of all trading sites are 1 under equilibrium, and decrease to 0 if total disruption is observed. The data were collected using various reports, newspapers, etc., and the operation status of each sector in each tier was determined and marked. We thus created a 3-D recurrence equation matrix to express the disruption ripple effect from the lower to upper tiers. The final industrial production level was given by the completion of that matrix.

Each demand sector's procurement rate is given by the lowest availability factor of its supply sectors. The dominant procurement rate of a T1 manufacturer is thus obtained using this sequence, and its total production in that period is then obtained by multiplying procurement rate and gross equilibrium output. Similarly, the production recovery profile is obtained. The simulation results for the disruption in and recovery of the passenger vehicles sector are given in Fig. 5.

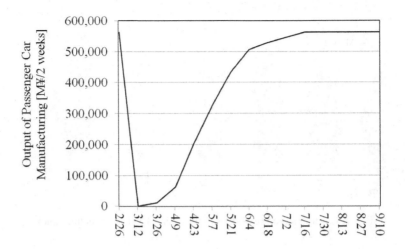

Fig. 5. Disruption in and recovery of the passenger vehicles sector

The Great East Japan Earthquake occurred on March 11, 2011. Fig. 5 shows that the output of passenger vehicles became zero on March 12, reached 100,000 after a month, 300,000 after two months, and 500,000 in June. Actually, the output fell to about 250,000 but did not become zero when the earthquake hit. This was caused by the buffer effect of stocking components and spare parts. Except this buffer, the disruption in and recovery of the passenger vehicles sector by disaster are simulated fairly well in Fig. 5.

4   Discussion

We found that the disruption in the supply of semiconductor parts and rechargeable batteries in Kanto area primarily affected the restoration rate. These days, semiconductor parts perform major functions in cars such as in transmissions and brakes, engines, fuel distribution systems, in-care entertainment systems, etc. Semiconductors are important for fuel regulation systems, acting in the anti-pollution and fuel efficiency roles. Given the close relationships between the various industries, a total disruption in a low-tier industry can cause the same in a higher-tier one.

Immediately after the disaster, the power and communications blackout shut all business operations even if no actual damage was experienced. We can simulate this by setting the transaction values for the transport sector as zero. Further, though excess capacity in other regions ensured adequate replacements for some other items, transportation remained an issue.

The affected plants took six months to reach pre-disaster production levels, primarily because both restoring production in the semiconductor plants and ensuring replacements in these sectors turned out to be cumbersome affairs.

While our simulation reproduced fairly well the disruption in and restoration of the automotive industry, our model did not consider real buffer effects thereby deeming the immediate post-disaster production values to be nil. We plan to investigate the buffer effects in the future and thus do not discuss these here.

5   Conclusion

From a review of the reports and news on the disruption and restoration process, we get that the restoration time of each supplier-sector in the supply chain varied with industrial characteristics. We also get that the limited/non-availability of sectors with long restoration time created ripples over the entire supply chain. We have simulated this ripple effect using the regional I-O table.

We also note that the intermediate table of the I-O table is a matrix showing the trade between demand-sectors and supply-sectors, and thus develop the supply-chain tier structure. Using the tier structure of the regional I-O table, we were able to specify the disaster attack point and vary the availability profile for each bottleneck sector. Using this 3-D matrix and the recurrence equation, we quantitatively estimate the indirect loss of production in the entire supply chain as a function of time.

Thus, this method can ascertain the indirect loss of production in a supply chain due to bottle-neck sectors. Our method can be utilized for priority decision making during/post disasters and for the economic evaluation of the effectiveness of preventive action for improving supply-chain resiliency.

The I-O table is often used in various business fields. We found that it can also be used to easily ascertain the industrial structure and the key processes from the view point of supply chain resiliency. Governments and industries can put this method to formulate a policy that prioritizes disaster management.

Acknowledgments. This work was supported in part by a Grant in Aid from the Global Center of Excellence Program for "Center for Education and Research of Symbiotic, Safe and Secure System Design" from the ministry of Education, Culture, Sport, and Technology in Japan.

References

1. Kouvelis, P., Chambers, C., Wang, H.: Supply Chain Management Research and Production and Operations Management: Review, Trends, and Opportunities. Production and Operations Management 15(3), 449–469 (2006)
2. Inoue, Y.: A Comprehensive Study on Research Approaches to Supply Chain Risk Identification. Shogaku Shushi 82(1), 45–60 (2012)
3. The Nikkei, The Asahi, The MID Japan Economist, and Nikkan Jidosha Newspaper
4. Asset securities reports of automotive manufacturers and reports by Japan Automobile Manufacturers Association
5. Trends in the automotive industry (manufacturer financial reports)

6. Tokui, et al.: Effects of the Great East Japan Earthquake on Economics, RIETI Policy Discussion Paper Series 12-P-004 (March 2012)
7. Dick, et al.: Japan's 2011 Earthquake and Tsunami: Economic Effects and Implications for the United States, CSR Report for Congress (April 20, 2011)
8. Walid, K.: Modeling Approaches for the Design of Resilient Supply Networks under Disruption. International Journal Production Economics 135(2), 882–898 (2012)
9. 2005 Inter-Regional Input-Output Tables (sectors 12, 29, and 53), Ministry of Economy, Trade and Industry (March 26, 2010)
10. Stewart, R., Stone, J.B., Streitwieser, M.L.: U.S. Benchmark Input-Output Accounts, 2002. Survey of Current Business, 19–48 (2007)
11. Andrew, R., Glen, P.: A Multi-Region Input–Output Table Based on the Global Trade Analysis Project Database (GTAP-MRIO). Economic Systems Research 25(1), 99–121 (2013)
12. Hallegatte, S.: An Adaptive Regional Input-Output Model and its Application to the Assessment of the Economic Cost of Katrina. Risk Analysis: An International Journal 28(3), 779–799 (2008)
13. Yamano, N., Kajitani, Y., Shumuta, Y.: Modeling the Regional Economic Loss of Natural Disasters: The Search for Economic Hotspots. Economic Systems Research 19(2), 163–181 (2007)
14. Anderson, C.W., Santos, J.R., Haimes, Y.Y.: A Risk-based Input-Output Methodology for Measuring the Effects of the Northeast Blackout. Economic Systems Research 19(2), 183–204 (2007)

Dependability a Key Element for Achieving Competitive Advantage: A Study of Information Service Firms

Vikas Kumar[1,*], Archana Kumari[2], Jose Arturo Garza-Reyes[3], and Ming Lim[3]

[1] Dublin City University Business School, Dublin City University, Dublin, ROI
vikas.kumar@dcu.ie
[2] Department of Business Economics, University of Delhi, New Delhi, India
archana_mbe2008@yahoo.com
[3] Centre for Supply Chain Improvement, The University of Derby, Derby, UK
{J.Reyes,M.Lim}@derby.ac.uk

Abstract. In the current economic climate and intense competitive environment achieving sustainable competitive advantage has become vital for any organisation's survival. Organisations around the globe are seeking ways to distinguish themselves from their competitors and win customers. This paper attempts to study the significance of sustainable competitive advantage from the information service firms' perspective. The paper argues that service firms can distinguish themselves and attain competitive advantage by performing well on operational performance elements that lead to customer satisfaction, loyalty and ultimately to profitability. Particularly, the paper empirically investigates the importance of dependability and quality in driving customer satisfaction and customer loyalty. The analysis shows that dependability is a key driver of customer satisfaction and customer loyalty. Thus, information service firms should focus more on improving the reliability of their services to achieve competitive advantage and later that may lead to a sustainable competitive advantage.

Keywords: Customer loyalty, Customer satisfaction, Competitive advantage, Dependability, Quality, Path analysis.

1 Introduction

In the current competitive climate, achieving sustainable competitive advantage is a key to survival for any small or large service organisation. Therefore, organisations around the globe are continuously seeking ways of improving their operational performances, quality, competitiveness, and profitability that ultimately leads to sustainable competitive advantage. It is well evident that that once dominated by manufacturing industries the economy has, nowadays, shifted more towards a service based economy. This is a result of rapid growth of services in last few decades and is evident from the contribution of services to the Gross Domestic Product (GDP) [1] of

---

* Corresponding author.

V. Prabhu, M. Taisch, and D. Kiritsis (Eds.): APMS 2013, Part I, IFIP AICT 414, pp. 493–500, 2013.

most of the developed economies such as the U.S. (80%), UK (75%), Japan (74%), France (73%) and Germany (68%). In recent years, the information service sector has emerged as a strong contributor to the GDP with the rapid advancement in modern internet and communication technologies across the world [2]. Despite the growth, services appear not to have received sufficient attention from researchers, while manufacturing-oriented research has so far dominated [2]. In addition, there is plenty of research surrounding sustainability issues; however, customer centric view of sustainability has been seldom addressed in research [3]. In services, quality and dependability are normally regarded as critical factors that differentiate them from others. Often these are also referred as the elements of the technical service quality. How well a service firm performs on these dimensions can lead to a source of competitive advantage. Research evidences show that by performing well on customer satisfaction and loyalty dimensions, organisations can enhance their performance and achieve sustainable competitive advantage [4]. Although, the literature on sustainable competitive advantage is vast, this paper primarily focuses on the investigation of the interrelationship between dependability, quality, customer satisfaction, and customer loyalty that are source of competitive advantage. The objective of the study is also to identify whether dependability is a key driver of satisfaction and loyalty.

Research indicates that there are two critical dimensions to service performance: performance relative to operational elements and performance relative to relational elements [5]. However, service operations management views services from customer and operational perspectives [6, 7]. Literature on service quality tends to advocate relational aspects and puts less emphasis on the operational aspects. This research, therefore, also attempts of fill this gap and highlights the importance of operational elements. This research emphasises that performing well on operational elements leads to satisfied and loyal customers. Operational indicators such as dependability, quality, and speed have been of interest for operations management researchers [5, 8]. This research is primarily focused on two operational elements of the service performance-dependability and quality that have widely argued in service quality literature [9, 10, 11]. The research investigates their linkages with customer satisfaction and loyalty in a new context of information intensive services.

The rest of the paper is organised as follows. The next section provides a brief literature review around sustainable competitive advantage, operational performance elements, and their linkages. Sections 3 and 4 discuss the research objectives, research methodology, and propose the research framework that is investigated in this research. The finding of this research is discussed in section 5. Finally, conclusions and implications are discussed in section 6. This section also proposes some future research directions.

2   Research Background

Service organisations are currently going through an era of rapid transformation and intense competition that continuously questions their survival. As a result, achieving sustainability is today regarded as a critical business goal by multiple stakeholders, including investors, customers and policymakers [11, 12]. The willingness and ability of service managers in organisation to respond to the on-going changes in economy determines whether their own organisation will survive and prosper [13]. Rapid innovation has further increased the intensity of competition and in such conditions customer satisfaction and retention has emerged as a source of sustainable competitive advantage [4]. In a resource based model competitive advantage is viewed from the perspective of 'distinctive competencies' that give a firm an edge over its competitors [14]. From service firms perspective the ability of the firm to distinguish itself from other competitors in terms of its service delivery and exceed the customer expectation level can act as a source of competitive advantage. And if the service firm continues to distinguish itself by exceeding customer expectations of service performance levels, it can lead to a sustainable competitive advantage. One of the ways the service firms can meet or exceed customer expectation is by performing well on operational performance aspects (such as quality, dependability, speed etc.) which ultimately leads to customer satisfaction and customer loyalty.

Customer satisfaction is generally measured as a gap between the customer's expectations and actual perceived services [15] whereas customer loyalty is defined as the customer's long-term commitment to repurchase and willingness to use the service repeatedly [5]. The link between customer satisfaction, loyalty, and profitability is well explained through the Service Profit Chain (SPC) framework developed by [16]. The fact that customer satisfaction is of fundamental importance and potentially offers a broad range of benefits for any organisation is well established in literature. Previous studies reveal that a satisfied customer is more likely to repurchase, leading to increased sales and market share [17, 18]. Thus, improving customer satisfaction service firms can lead to a path of sustainable competitive advantage. Eggert and Ulaga [19] pointed out that customer satisfaction is a strong predictor of behavioural variables, such as customer loyalty, word of mouth, and repurchase intentions. This was also supported in the work of [20] and others. These studies indicate a strong link between the two performance-outcome measures; customer satisfaction and customer loyalty.

Gonzalez et al. [11] highlighted the positive relationship between perceived service quality and customer satisfaction. They found that perceived service quality is an antecedent of satisfaction. Chiou et al. [21] showed that the attribute of satisfaction and interactive service quality generate overall satisfaction and trust. These studies show a strong link between customer satisfaction and service quality. This relationship between service quality and customer satisfaction can be further understood through the service concept model [2, 22]. Johnson and Sirikit [13] in their study of the Thai telecommunication industry showed that performing well on service quality dimension leads to a sustainable competitive advantage.

Another important operational indicator, dependability and its relationship to customer satisfaction and loyalty has also been addressed by several researchers, such as [20], and [23]. In a study by [23], he discussed dependability as a performance factor that affects customer satisfaction. This view was also supported in the work of [23] who, demonstrate that perceived dependability affects user satisfaction positively. Rosenzweig and Roth [24] also identified an interrelationship between dependability and quality, as they hypothesized that enhanced conformance to quality has a direct influence on improvements in reliable delivery. They further provided an empirical evidence of their impact in driving business performance (i.e. profitability). A number of researchers have identified dependability as a key operational indicator [5, 23, 25]. However, there is a lack of empirical evidence in literature that addresses the link between dependability, quality, customer satisfaction and customer loyalty in the information service firms. Therefore, this paper sets out a background to explore this interrelationship to assist managers to plan their service strategies and focus on the operational element of prime importance that can help firms to achieve sustainable competitive advantage.

3   Research Objectives and Framework

The literature review highlights operations performance indicators, particularly quality and dependability that affect customer satisfaction and loyalty. This study is a confirmatory study which aims to test the findings of service operations management and service quality literature, particularly in the context of information service settings. However, this study also looks beyond the operational performance and performance outcome link. The study emphasises that performing well on operations performance dimension can assist service firms to achieve distinctive advantage and ultimately lead to a sustainable competitive advantage. Since the study does not encapsulate any variable to measure the competitive advantage, this study can be treated as a preliminary study that primarily focuses on identifying the importance of dependability and quality that forms the foundation for achieving sustainable competitive advantage. The investigation involves assessing these relationships in two large information intensive firms operating in the UK. This research sets out to test the following in the context of information service settings:

- Dependability and quality affect customer satisfaction and customer loyalty
- Dependability is a key indicator/driver of customer satisfaction and customer loyalty
- An interrelationship exists between dependability and quality

The research framework tested in this research comprises of two critical performance indicators; quality and dependability that are usually present in a service delivery system. The literature linking these individual operational indicators and customer loyalty through mediating variable customer satisfaction is available in abundance [5,16,25]. However, empirical studies assessing this relationship in information intensive service firms are limited. The propositions derived from the framework reflect key relationships that were described in the literature review. This case study tests four prepositions:

P1: Customer Loyalty is positively correlated with Customer Satisfaction
P2: Customer Satisfaction is positively correlated with Dependability
P3: Customer Satisfaction is positively correlated with Quality
P4: Dependability and Quality are positively correlated

The next section details the methods for data collection employed in this study.

4   Methodology

The paper studies two large information intensive service firms operating in the UK. The first case study is based on the data collected from a large telecommunication firm. In this research the data for the broadband installation process is collected. The second case is based on the data collected from a large utility firm operating in the UK. The longitudinal data for the telecommunication and utility firm collected through telephonic interviews comprised monthly measurements (total 48 data points) of variables considered as proxies for quality, dependability, customer satisfaction, and customer loyalty in a four-year time frame.

In this research, dependability is referred as an ability to perform the promised service dependably and accurately, including time commitments. Both the service firms studied in this research used a single scale item with the understanding that dependability means fulfilling promises including time commitment. Both the firms also did not employ SERVQUAL scale to measure the quality construct. However, the measures used by the firm resemble to some of the items of the SERVQUAL scale including the empathy, access, assurance, and responsiveness dimensions. Customer satisfaction and customer loyalty constructs were also operationalised as a single item measure. Customer satisfaction was measured as overall satisfaction with the level of services provided and customer loyalty was measured as the likelihood of recommendation of the service to others. The constructs studied in this study conform to the reliability and validity tests.

5   Research Findings

The correlation analysis of the first case study (telecommunication) shows a moderate and positive correlation (0.53) between dependability and customer satisfaction at p <0.01 level. There was also a strong and positive correlation between customer satisfaction and customer loyalty. Correlation between quality and dependability as well as between quality and customer satisfaction was not significant. Similarly, for case II (utility) a strong and positive correlation (0.88) was found between dependability and customer satisfaction at p <0.01 level. A strong and positive correlation was also evident between customer satisfaction and customer loyalty. Interestingly no significant correlation was found between quality and dependability as well as quality and customer satisfaction. Thus, the findings show support for the proposition 1 and 2. However, correlation analysis does not support proposition 3 and 4. To further verify the results of correlation analysis regressions were carried out. Regressions were performed to verify the findings of the correlation analysis. Regression shows that quality and dependability in total explain around 62.4% (Adj. R2 value) and 76.6% (Adj. R2 value) of the unexplained variance respectively for case I and II. However, only the dependability coefficient was found to be significant at 1% level. The correlation analysis results are shown in Figure 1.

Thus, the findings indicate that dependability is a key indicator of customer satisfaction and customer satisfaction is strongly linked with customer loyalty.

However, both studies failed to provide support for propositions 3 and 4. To explore the interrelationship, i.e., causality among the variables, path analysis method was employed. The resultant path model for both cases supported the findings of correlation analysis and indicated a positive causal relationship between dependability and customer satisfaction as well between customer satisfaction and customer loyalty. Path analysis also showed that quality and customer satisfaction share a positive causal relationship thus supporting proposition 4. Additionally, it also showed that quality and dependability share a negative causal relationship that suggest that improvement in one performance indicator is only possible at the expense of the other though this further needs investigation.

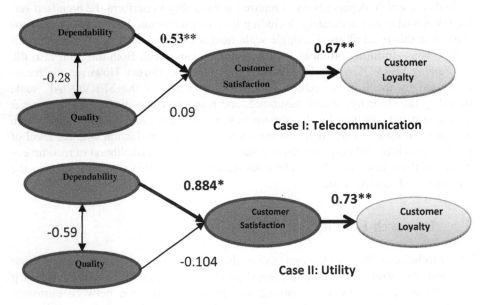

**Correlation is significant at the 0.01 level (2-tailed).

Fig. 1. Correlation analysis result of Case I & II

6   Conclusions and Future Research

The paper provides a brief overview of the significance of achieving sustainable competitive advantage and highlights the importance of customer satisfaction and customer loyalty. This research also argues that for service firms performing well on operational performance elements is a key to achieving sustainable competitive advantage. The paper studies two cases from different information intensive service firms operating in the UK. The analysis of the data showed that dependability is a key driver of customer satisfaction. Both cases further investigated the relative impact of dependability and quality and shows that for information service a firm's dependability is more important as opposed to SERVQUAL literature findings, where traditional priority is afforded to quality. Additionally, the data analysis showed that a negative relationship exists between dependability and quality. Therefore, service firms looking to achieve competitive advantage must focus on improving their dependability/reliability of their service offerings. This is not to say that quality is not important rather it suggests that service firms should first focus on improving their dependability of the service and when a certain level is reached that meets or exceeds the customer expectation level then focus should move on improving the next operational performance element such as quality or speed while still improving dependability. In the current intense competitive environment developing a distinct competence has become a norm for survival and service firms need to differentiate themselves by using and realigning their existing resources and competencies in way their competitors cannot match. By learning to perform well on operational performance dimension can help service companies to achieve their goal of sustainable competitive advantage.

This study is limited to two case studies from the information service firms operating in the UK. For generalisation of the findings more cases are required to be studied, particularly cross-country cases. Though, this research indicates that operational performance elements are important for customer satisfaction and loyalty, and argues their importance for competitive advantage, but the research does not study any variable that measures the competitive advantage. This study is a preliminary step towards the understanding of dependability as a critical factor in achieving competitive advantage. Therefore, future research studies should be aimed at empirically studying a proxy to measure the competitive advantage together with the operational performance and performance outcome indicators.

References

1. Lovelock, C., Wirtz, J.: Services Marketing: People, Technology, Strategy, 6th edn. Pearson Prentice Hall, US (2007)
2. Kumar, V.: An Empirical Investigation of the Linkage between Dependability, Quality and Customer Satisfaction in Information Intensive Service Firms. PhD Thesis, Exeter University (2011)
3. Sheth, J.N., Sethia, N.K., Srinivas, S.: Mindful Consumption: A Customer-centric Approach to Sustainability. Journal of the Academy of Marketing Science 39(1), 21–39 (2011)
4. Verona, G., Prandelli, E.: A Dynamic Model of Customer Loyalty to Sustain Competitive Advantage on the Web. European Management Journal 20(3), 299–309 (2002)
5. Stank, T.P., Goldsby, T.J., Vicekry, S.K.: Effect of Service Supplier Performance on Satisfaction and Loyalty of Store Managers in the Fast Food Industry. Journal of Operations Management 4, 429–447 (1999)
6. Sampson, S.E.: Understanding service businesses: Applying Principles of the Unified Services Theory, 2nd edn. John Wiley & Sons, New York (2001)
7. Sampson, S.E., Froehle, C.M.: Foundation and Implication of a Proposed Unified Services Theory. Production and Operations Management 15(2), 329–343 (2006)
8. Slack, N., Chambers, S., Johnston, R.: Operations Management, 4th edn. Prentice Hall FT, Harlow (2004)

9. Zeithaml, V.A., Parasuraman, A., Berry, L.L.: Delivering Quality Service: Balancing Customer Perceptions and Expectations. Free Press, New York (1990)
10. Parasuraman, A.: Refinement and Reassessment of the SERVQUAL Scale. Journal of Retailing 67(4), 420–450 (1991)
11. Gonzalez, A.E.M., Comesana, R.L., Brea, F.A.J.C.: Assessing Tourist Behavioural Intensions through Perceived Service Quality and Customer Satisfaction. Journal of Business Research 60(2), 153–160 (2007)
12. Pfeffer, J.: Building Sustainable Organizations: The Human Factor. Academy of Management Perspectives 24(1), 34–45 (2010)
13. Johnson, W.C., Sirikit, A.: Service Quality in a Thai Telecommunication Industry: a Tool for Achieving Sustainable Competitive Advantage. Management Decision 40(7), 693–701 (2002)
14. Ghemawat, P.: Sustainable Advantage. Harvard Business Review, 53–58 (September-October 1986)
15. Grönroos, C.: From Scientific Management to Service Management: a Management Perspective for the Age of Service Competition. International Journal of Service Industry Management 5(1), 5–20 (1994)
16. Heskett, J.L., Jones, T.O., Loveman, G.W., Sasser Jr., W.E., Schlesinger, L.A.: Putting the Service-profit Chain to Work. Harvard Business Review, 164–174 (March-April 1994)
17. Cronin, J.J., Morris, M.H.: Satisfying Customer Expectations: the Effect on Conflict and Repurchase Intentions in Industrial Marketing Channels. Journal of the Academy of Marketing Science 17(1), 41–49 (1989)
18. Innis, D.E., La Londe, B.J.: Customer Service: the Key to Customer Satisfaction, Customer Loyalty, and Market Share. Journal of Business Logistics 15(1), 1–27 (1994)
19. Eggert, A., Ulaga, W.: Customer Perceived Value: a Substitute for Satisfaction in Business Markets? Journal of Business and Industrial Marketing 17(2/3), 107–118 (2002)
20. Parasuraman, A., Berry, L.L., Zeithaml, A.V.: SERVQUAL: A Multiple Item Scale for Measuring Customer Perception of Service Quality. Journal of Retailing 64(1), 12–40 (1988)
21. Chiou, J.S., Droge, C., Hanvanich, S.: Does Customer Knowledge Affect How Loyalty is Formed? Journal of Service Research 5(2), 113–124 (2002)
22. Goldstein, S.M., Johnston, R., Duffy, J., Rao, J.: The Service Concept: The Missing Link in Service Design Research? Journal of Operations Management 20(2), 121–134 (2002)
23. Lai, J.Y., Yang, C.C.: Effects of employees perceived dependability on success of enterprise applications in e-business. Industrial Marketing Management 38(3), 263–274 (2009)
24. Rosenzweig, E.D., Roth, A.V.: Towards a Theory of Competitive Progression: Evidence from High-Tech Manufacturing. Production and Operations Management 13(4), 354–368 (2004)
25. Kumar, V., Batista, L., Maull, R.: The Impact of Operations Performance on Customer Loyalty. Service Science 3(2), 158–171 (2011)

Selection and Ranking of Low Cost Countries for Outsourcing and Offshoring in the Manufacturing Sector

Rahul Ulhas Pai[1,2], Sujit Banerji[2], Jose Arturo Garza-Reyes[3], Ming Lim[3], and Vikas Kumar[4]

[1] Cummins Ltd, Darlington, UK
pai.rahul@cummins.com
[2] Warwick Manufacturing Group, The University of Warwick, Coventry, UK
S.Banerji@warwick.ac.uk
[3] Centre for Supply Chain Improvement, The University of Derby, Derby, UK
{J.Reyes,M.Lim}@derby.ac.uk
[4] Dublin City University Business School, Dublin City University, Dublin, ROI
vikas.kumar@dcu.ie

Abstract. With the advent of globalisation, there is a need for companies to gain and sustain a competitive advantage. Outsourcing and offshoring are strategies often employed by organisations to sustain and gain such competitive advantage. This paper focuses on evaluating the factors that influence the selection of Low Cost Countries (LCCs) for outsourcing and offshoring. It also ranks a group of seven LCCs to determine the best locations to emigrate manufacturing operations. To do this, the most influential factors for outsourcing and offshoring are identified and weighted based on their importance. Then, these factors are evaluated based on the degree of development in the studied LCCs. The study indicates that Taiwan, Indian and China are the best top options for manufacturing organisations to outsource/offshore their operations.

Keywords: Globalisation, Low cost countries, Manufacturing sector, Offshoring, Outsourcing.

1   Introduction

In this era of globalisation every organisation is striving hard to be competitive. Competitive advantage can be achieved in a number of ways, for example, by creating technological and product monopolies, providing high quality and/or low cost products, devising aggressive marketing and promotional activities, offering value added services, creating a wide and loyal customer base, etc. In particular, companies are experiencing immense pressure from customers to provide good quality products at reduced costs. At the same time, organisations have to increase their revenues and boost or sustain their profit margins to provide appropriate returns on investment to their shareholders.

One of the initiatives that global companies have undertaken to be competitive and meet the expectations of the customers and shareholders is by developing a sourcing

V. Prabhu, M. Taisch, and D. Kiritsis (Eds.): APMS 2013, Part I, IFIP AICT 414, pp. 501–512, 2013.

strategy that lays emphasis on outsourcing components/products from or offshoring manufacturing operations to Low Cost Countries (LCCs). In recent years, manufacturing companies have identified outsourcing and offshoring to emerging economies as a competitive business strategy to create value for their organisation. In order to sustain and overcome the competitive pressures occurring from globalisation, manufacturing firms, especially in developed countries, look at outsourcing and offshoring to LCCs as a viable option [1]. Globalisation has brought countries closer, thus allowing companies to carry out business not only limited to their home country but also in other parts of the world. Thus, many American and European companies have resorted to outsourcing products and components from vendors in LCCs. Sourcing products from LCCs allows the procuring company to reduce cost on purchased materials and services. For this reason, LCC sourcing has become a strong business trend in the recent years [2-5].

Looking at the increasing trend in outsourcing and offshoring especially to emerging economies, it is of vital importance to understand the factors driving outsourcing and offshoring decisions pertaining to country selection. Country selection plays an important role in outsourcing and offshoring decisions as most of the factors influencing country selection are not in the control of the organisation. The organisation can only evaluate these factors by comparing them with those of other countries and then make the right decision on country selection. Hence this paper focuses on evaluating the factors influencing country selection decisions. After evaluating the factors, the paper rates them against each of the LCCs selected for study. Therefore, the purpose of this paper is to provide a selection and ranking of LCCs for outsourcing and offshoring in the manufacturing sector, and to evaluate the factors affecting the selection and ranking of LCCs for outsourcing and offshoring in the manufacturing sector.

2   Literature Review on Outsourcing, Offshoring and Low Cost Countries

According to [6], sourcing can be defined as a process by virtue of which tasks are contracted or delegated to an external or internal agency rather than doing them in-house. Two dimensions of sourcing are outsourcing and offshoring. Outsourcing refers to the arrangement wherein an organisation contracts or delegates a business process, or a part of it, to an outside entity whereas offshoring implies the transfer or relocation of some of the organisational activities to another country [6]. Berry [7] comments that outsourcing and offshoring are often incorrectly used as interchangeable terms. Researchers differentiate outsourcing and offshoring on the basis of two things: 1) whether the business functions are carried out in-house or they are outsourced, and 2) the geographical location of the business processes to be performed [8]. For example, offshoring takes place when a company transfers jobs which were earlier carried out in its home country to another country, preferably to a LCC. On the other hand, outsourcing is limited to procurement of products or services from a third party service provider or vendor based in the procuring company's home country or abroad. Thus it can be said that offshoring is a subset of outsourcing [7].

There may be numerous reasons for manufacturing organisations to integrate outsourcing or offshoring as part of their overall business strategy. According to [9], some of these reasons include: 1) to acquire new skills and a 2) more effective management, 3) to focus on core business functions and products, 4) to avoid capital investment, and 5) to reduce cost. The freeing up of world markets has caused companies to become immensely cost competitive. Thus, cost reduction can arguably be considered the primary reason for manufacturing organisations to seek the "emigration" of their operations to LCCs. In manufacturing terms, Crnlc et al. [10] consider LCCs as those developing countries that posses an strong manufacturing base but where the cost of living and labour is lower than those of developed countries. For the purpose of this paper, the following LCCs were considered due to the relevance and importance they currently present as main choices for outsourcing and offshoring activities: China, India, Thailand, Taiwan, Philippines, Indonesia, and Nigeria.

The intensive cost competition experienced by organisations in the international market has compelled them to concentrate all their efforts on their core competencies and pay special attention on outsourcing and offshoring decisions. As rightly mentioned by [11-12], out of the total production cost of a product, 60 to 70 percent are procurement costs (i.e. the cost of buying the subcomponents from vendors). Thus, it is evident that supply part costs constitute a major portion of the overall cost of the product. Also it can be said that cost reductions obtained from optimisation and improvement in production processes are limited and that cost reduction throughout the supply chain is necessary to stay competitive. Therefore, outsourcing and offshoring decisions have obtained more importance than before and the purchasing/sourcing department that earlier used to be a mere operational business function has now assumed strategic importance. A study conducted by [13] shows that cost savings of 1% on procured materials increase the profitability of the company by 11% in the engineering sector.

Global reach and presence enables companies to be competitive by procuring and manufacturing cost effective products from emerging economies. Thus LCCs play a vital role in achieving considerable cost savings [14-15]. Companies have identified the potential of these emerging economies and are exploiting them to reap benefits to stay competitive in the market. LCCs in emerging economies offer excellent sourcing opportunities in the form of cost reduction on procured and manufactured products and potential for sales in the local markets [16-17].

3   Factors Affecting the Selection of LCCs

Outsourcing and offshoring decisions are greatly influenced by the selection of the right location. Location refers to the country in which the company plans to outsource or offshore. The decision making process of outsourcing/offshoring to a third party vendor by setting up a subsidiary mostly depends on the attractiveness of countries as sourcing destinations. The attractiveness of these countries keep on changing depending upon the economical, political, cultural, social, technological, etc. environment in that country. The above mentioned factors are pretty dynamic in nature and hence the country attractiveness also keeps on changing. Hence it is necessary to understand the impact of these factors from a long term strategic business perspective [6]. Ample literature is available on Brazil, Russia, India and China, their attractiveness, and the factors influencing their attractiveness as outsourcing and offshoring destinations for information technology (IT) and business process outsourcing industries [6, 18].

Different frameworks are available that help organisations in exploring the attractiveness of countries for outsourcing and offshoring. One of these frameworks is the Carmel's "oval model" of country selection [19], see Figure 1.

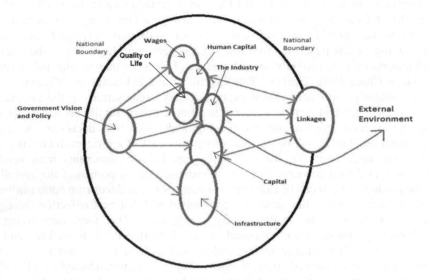

Fig. 1. Carmel's "oval model" of country selection [19]

According to Carmel's model, there are eight factors that lead to the success of nations exploring, particularly IT software. Though these factors are discussed from an IT perspective, they can also be used to explore the factors leading to attractiveness of countries as destinations for outsourcing and offshoring in the manufacturing sector.

A different approach that may be used to determine the attractiveness of countries for outsourcing and offshoring is to consider the factors influencing the competitiveness of a country. The World Economic Forum identifies eleven pillars (see Figure 2), or factors, leading to a country's competitiveness. These factors, according to the World Economic Forum, are also divided into sub-factors that present a more detailed overview of the main eleven pillars. For example, the "Institutions" factor is further divided into five sub-factors that include: 1) intellectual property rights, 2) burden of government regulations, 3) efficiency of legal system, 4) transparency of government policy making, and 5) influence of terrorism on business activities. Similarly, the "Infrastructure" factor is divided into two sub-factors such as 1) quality of overall infrastructure and 2) quality of electricity supply. The rest of the factors are also divided into some sub-factors.

3.1 Selection of Factors Influencing Country Selection for Outsourcing and Offshoring

The authors consider that the competitiveness of a country is a key determinant for organisations to select an appropriate country for outsourcing and offshoring.

However, although the competitiveness of a country stimulates outsourcing/ offshoring activities and attracts foreign direct investment (FDI), the researchers consider that not all the eleven factors have the same importance or consideration while taking outsourcing or offshoring decisions. Hence this paper analyses and discusses the influence of top four factors important from the outsourcing and offshoring decision's point of view. The factors which the authors concentrate on are shown in the Figure 3.

Fig. 2. Pillars of Country Competitiveness

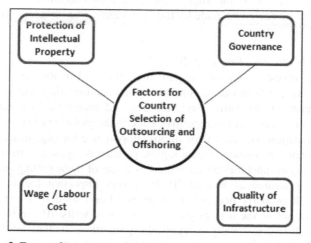

Fig. 3. Factors for country selection for outsourcing and offshoring

The reason behind choosing these four factors for ranking the LCCs studied (i.e. China, India, Thailand, Taiwan, Philippines, Indonesia, and Nigeria) is that, these are not in control of the outsourcing or offshoring organisation. The organisation cannot play a direct role in improving these factors for any country. These are developed within the country itself by the governing bodies with a view to facilitate the overall growth of the country and for the betterment of its citizens. As a matter of fact, organisations outsource or offshore in certain countries because they get ready access to these factors in that particular country. Favourable presence of these factors increases the attractiveness of the country towards any outsourcing or offshoring opportunity and FDI.

3.2   Weighting and Importance of the Factors for Ranking the Countries

The primary purpose of this paper is to rank the LCCs studied as apt locations for outsourcing or offshoring. In order to do this, the authors weighted the four factors under consideration as per their importance in the outsourcing or offshoring decision making process. Weighting the factors helped to prioritise their influence, thus stressing the importance of each one of them while making outsourcing and offshoring decisions. The factors were weighted on a scale of 10 to 50. A weight of 10 depicted least importance of a particular factor and a weight of 50 represented highest importance of a particular factor for country selection. The weighting scale of 10 to 50 was randomly selected by the authors, just to signify the prominence of the factors. The scale may be modified to suit individual requirements, but the key is to appropriately weight the factors as per their importance in decision making.

After weighting the factors as per their importance, the seven LCCs were individually rated against the four factors, based on the performance of each country in relation to each of the factors. This rating was done on a scale of 1 to 7. A rating of 1 meant, the country ranks unfavourably in a particular factor and a rating of 7 implied favourable conditions of the factor in that country. The rating assigned was based on the analysis of the individual factors in relation to every country, the extensive literature reviewed made by the first author, and instances from professional experience of the authors.

Protection of Intellectual Property (IP)
Organisations invest a lot of human and financial resources in research and development. Research and development in the manufacturing sector is necessary for the development of innovative technologies and products. New technologies and products give organisations a competitive edge in the global market, thus strengthening their market position. Hence it is of utmost importance for organisations to safeguard their confidential information, technologies, product designs, etc. from the rest of the world, especially competitors because there is a fear of these getting leaked or illegally copied. This is termed as loss of IP. It is very important for an organisation to safeguard its IP property because, if it accessed and used by others unethically, it deprives the owner of the honorary and monetary benefits. IP can be safeguarded by patenting it with internationally recognised organisations such as USPTO, WIPO, etc. Since it requires a lot of investment for patenting, organisations usually do not resort to this option, unless and until it is a high-tech product, design or technology which is strategically important for a company's survival in the market. Other intellectual property such as part drawings, basic manufacturing process parameters, manufacturing process sheets, costing information, other management data, etc. may not be considered as important, but still play a significant role at operational level.

IP protection is governed by the law of the country where it has been filed, which has provisions to handle such cases. The legal system of the country should also be sensitive enough to the offence of breach of IP and should have stringent enforcement laws which should be efficient enough to give quick results. Different countries have different laws and regulations for handling IP breach cases. The laws in some countries are efficient while in some others they are not.

Having discussed the importance of IP in detail, it is evident that it is one of the decisive factors for organisations to make outsourcing and offshoring decisions. But in comparison with the other three factors under consideration in this paper, it can be seen that IP protection is predominantly an internal factor due to its governance is within the control of the company to a certain extent. If the outsourcing or offshoring organisations take necessary precautions to protect their IP rights at organisational level, instances of IP breach can be controlled without having to raise the issue to the level of law suit.

Hence on a weighting scale of 10 to 50, IP protection has been given a weight of 20. It is important to remember that this weighting has been done purely on comparative basis with respect to the other three factors. If compared with different assessing factors, the weighting may change depending upon the importance of other factors with respect to IP protection.

Country Governance

Country governance is an important macro-level factor that influences an organisation's decision about outsourcing and offshoring to a particular country. Governance plays an important role in the economic development of a country because other micro-level factors are directly or indirectly dependent on the policies and regulations formulated by the government of such country. Country governance includes factors like political stability, accountability towards the citizens, formulating policies for political, economical, social, technological, environmental and legal development of the country, efficiency of enforcement of these policies, citizens security, etc. Irrespectively of the type of governance, these factors play an important role in developing the competitiveness of a country.

The seven LCCs considered in this paper are governed differently by their respective governing bodies. Hence the ideology and vision around which the macro-level policies are made and implemented are also distinct. These seven countries follow distinct political systems and hence operate differently in their own respect. For instance, China follows a communist political system wherein the citizens of the country have little or no role to play in the government selection process. But even then, China has experienced immense economic growth over the past years. This is because the communist party in China is committed towards the country's overall development. Since it does not follow a parliamentary form of government, it can formulate and implement policies without much opposition or debate. Hence the time taken to implement the policies is fast. But this type of governance also has its ill-effects such as citizens being unsatisfied with the way in which the country is being currently run, which may lead to a violent revolt to overthrow the current government. This type of incident happened in Thailand in 2010. But China is an exception because the communist type of governance is deeply rooted in the political system of the country. As opposed to China, India is a democratic country and the second largest emerging economy after China. India has its share of drawbacks, given the democratic political system it follows. Policy formulation and implementation in India is time consuming since it has to be approved by the other members of the parliament with majority. The two main political parties in the country follow completely different social and religious ideologies, but share similar views about the economic and overall development of the country. The drawback of India's political system is that it is plagued with corruption and bureaucracy. India also faces terrorism threats from its neighbouring country Pakistan along with some cross border issue with China. The other LCCs Philippines, Nigeria, Thailand, Indonesia and Taiwan also have similar advantages and disadvantages in their own governance systems.

On a weighting scale of 10 to 50, country governance has been given a maximum weight of 50 as compared to the other factors. This is because all development actions in any country are driven by its governance efficiency. The economic development of a country immensely depends on its governance. Any corporate policies and regulations are formulated on the lines of governance policies to ensure compliance to the legal system.

Wage / Labour Cost
There are various reasons behind organisations taking outsourcing and offshoring decisions. These include focus on core competencies, to avoid investment in capital, to get access to world class skills of service providers, etc. But in the real world, the primary reason for any outsourcing or offshoring decision is cost reduction. In the global competitive market, there are persistent pressures by customers to get low cost products at higher quality. With a view to achieve this objective, organisations try to focus on their core competencies by outsourcing or offshoring the non-core functions to a service provider who excels in the same. In a manufacturing industry, 60 to 70 percent of the parts in a product are procured from outside suppliers and the manufacturing company only assembles it and sells it to the customers. In case of manufacturing of engineering products such as automobiles, industrial products, etc. most of the assembly work is labour intense rather an automated. Hence labour wages form an important component of the unit cost of the product.

Countries in the emerging economies offer a low cost environment, predominantly because they have capable workforce abundantly available at low cost as compared to developed countries. Availability of cheap labour gives them a competitive edge over other developed countries. Hence there is a trend in the industry that most manufacturing organisations are sourcing products from or starting new operations in these LCCs.

But this trend in the labour wages seems to be changing over the past few years. This is due to the worldwide uncertain economic conditions which have resulted in unemployment, high inflation rates, etc. Also, due to rapid economic development in the emerging economies, especially in the Asian countries, the standard of living of the people has increased. This has inflated the labour costs further. Also over the past few years there has been a major change in the mentality of the senior management of organisations to not only focus on the product cost, but look at the bigger picture of Total Cost of Ownership (TCO) when making outsourcing and offshoring decisions. Also cost is no more the only decisive factor for making outsourcing and offshoring decisions, but companies look at it from a strategic perspective to develop business opportunities in the emerging economies. China and India are the two most populous countries in the world offering an advantage of becoming a huge local market for products being produced in their respective countries. Also most of the manufacturing of electronic products is done in South-East Asian countries like Taiwan, China, Thailand, etc. Asia has become the factory for the world.

Hence owing to the reasons stated above, labour wages have been given a weight factor of 40 as compared to the other three factors. Labour wages have been given a lower weight than country governance because, in most countries the minimum wages to be received by a labourer is fixed by the government and the organisation is liable to comply with this requirement.

Infrastructure

Infrastructure plays an important role in the development of the manufacturing sector. The development of the manufacturing sector within a country largely depends upon the commitment of the government towards increasing the competitiveness of the country, thus making it an attractive destination for FDI and outsourcing/offshoring. This can be done by having a well developed infrastructure conducive to support business activities in the manufacturing sector. Sound infrastructure includes well developed network of roadways, railways, waterways, airways that can enable logistics support to the manufacturing sector which increases the efficiency of import-export and local trading. Industrial areas are developed at specific locations in a country, where there is ample space available for the construction of large factories. Industrial areas are usually developed aloof from the residential areas so as to minimize the adverse effects such as noise and environmental pollution. Infrastructure is not only limited to efficient network, but it also encompasses the quality and capacity of roads, railways, ports and airports to handle cargo and human traffic.

Infrastructure has been given a weight of 30 on a scale of 10 to 50 based on the comparative importance of this factor with respect to the other three. This factor was weighted lower than country governance and labour cost because, infrastructure development is dependent upon the government policies and budget allocated to its development. Hence if a government has suitable policies and efficient implementation plans it will suffice the purpose of good infrastructure as well. Even though a particular LCC may have good infrastructure, the cost factor overtakes its importance because a company has to make profits to sustain its business and give appropriate returns to its stakeholders.

Table 1 summaries the weight assigned to the four factors identified as critical for the effective selection of LCC for outsourcing and offshoring.

Table 1. Weighting of factors – scale 10 to 50

	Factors affecting outsourcing and offshoring decisions	Weights
1	Intellectual Property Protection	20
2	Country Governance	50
3	Labour Wages	40
4	Infrastructure	30

4   Rating and Ranking of LCCs

Based on the discussion carried out in section 3.2, the seven LCCs were rated on a scale of 1 to 7 depending upon the favourable and unfavourable presence, in each country, of the four factors considered in this study. The rating was influenced by a detailed country analysis, the authors' knowledge and professional experience and current political, legal and economic situation and trends in the respective countries.

Table 2 shows the rating of the seven LCCs studied as apt locations for outsourcing and offshoring. According to the rating, Taiwan emerges as the most attractive destination for outsourcing and offshoring in the manufacturing sector with the highest score of 690. Second position is secured by India predominantly due to its democratic governance system and low labour costs. India's score is 670. China ranks third with a score of 600, mostly due to its extremely efficient infrastructure that supports the manufacturing sector. Thailand, Indonesia, Philippines and Nigeria ranked in fourth, fifth, sixth and seventh position respectively.

Table 2. Rating of the LCCs studied

Factors for outsourcing and offshoring decisions	Factor Weight (W)	Philippines		Nigeria		Thailand		India		Indonesia		China		Taiwan		Min Rate	Max Rate	County Mean
		PH$_1$	PH$_1$xW	NG$_2$	NG$_2$xW	TH$_3$	TH$_3$xW	IND$_4$	IND$_4$xW	INO$_5$	INO$_5$xW	CH$_5$	CH$_5$xW	TA$_6$	TA$_6$xW			
IP Protection	20	3	60	1	20	4	80	5	100	2	40	5	100	7	140			3.9
Country Governance	40	2	100	1	50	3	150	5	250	2	100	4	200	6	300	1	7	3.3
Labour Wages	50	4	160	6	240	2	80	5	200	5	200	3	120	1	40			3.7
Infrastructure	30	2	50	1	30	5	150	4	120	3	90	6	180	7	210			4.0
Total			380		340		460		670		430		600		690			

PH$_1$ = Philippines; NG$_2$ = Nigeria; TH$_3$ = Thailand; IND$_4$ = India; INO$_5$ = Indonesia; CH$_5$ = China; TA$_6$ = Taiwan

5   Conclusions

Outsourcing and offshoring are a key business aspect, important from a strategic view point for organisations. Organisations use outsourcing and offshoring as business model to gain and sustain a long term competitive advantage. When making outsourcing or offshoring decisions, there are various factors that need to be considered, for example, which process or product to outsource, selection of service provider, contract management, etc.

Arguably, the most important factor is that of country selection, because not all factors influencing the selection of an appropriate country are in control of the organisation. An organisation has to evaluate the important factors influencing country selection, based on their outsourcing and offshoring vision.

For the purpose of this study, the authors selected four key factors for country selection that were important for the manufacturing sector. These were: 1) Protection of IP, 2) Country Governance, 3) Labour Wages, and 4) Infrastructure.

Since the countries considered were all LCCs, exhibiting similar positive and negative aspects for the above factors, the authors evaluated and studied the prominence and presence of each factor in detail. Based on this and after weighting the factors the LCCs studied were ranked as apt locations for outsourcing and offshoring in the manufacturing sector.

In terms of this study's limitations, the authors selected four factors to consider based on target sector, extensive literature review and personal experience. Different sourcing managers may have different requirements when selecting countries for outsourcing and offshoring. Hence, the selection of factors is greatly influenced by the choice of the person making the outsourcing and offshoring decision. Also the weighting of factors is influenced by the involvement of a human aspect, because different sourcing managers may weight the same factors differently as per their outsourcing objectives. In addition, the scope of this study is limited to the manufacturing sector only. Hence the selection of the factors and its analysis and discussions are focused on this sector only. For example, the infrastructure required for IT sector may be completely different from that of manufacturing sector.

Further research can be carried out on this topic by undertaking a real case scenario in an outsourcing company, wherein the practical implications of factors on country selection can be explored. Also, future work on this topic can be done by selecting a different sector such as IT, fast moving customer goods, etc. and analysing the factors influencing country selection pertaining to that particular sector.

References

1. Javalgi, R., Dixit, A., Scherer, R.: Outsourcing to Emerging Markets: Theoretical Perspectives and Policy Implications. Journal of International Management 15(2), 156–168 (2009)
2. Byrne, P.: Global Sourcing: Opportunities and Approaches for the 21st Century. Logistics Management 44(1), 27–28 (2005)
3. Matteo, M.: Sourcing in China. Chinese Business Review, 30–54 (September-October 2003)
4. Fang, T., Axelsson, B.: Strategic Change towards Global Sourcing: Developing Sourcing Capabilities. John Wiley & Sons, Chichester (2005)
5. Trent, R., Monczka, R.: Achieving Excellence in Global Sourcing. MIT Sloan Management Review, 24–32 (October 2005)
6. Oshri, I., Kotlarsky, J., Willcocks, L.: The Handbook of Global Outsourcing and Offshoring. Palgrave Macmillan, Hampshire (2009)
7. Berry, J.: Offshoring Opportunities: Strategies and Tactics for Global Competitiveness. John Wiley & Sons, New Jersey (2006)
8. Domberger, S.: The Contracting Organizations: A Strategic Guide to Outsourcing. Oxford University Press, Oxford (1998)
9. Brown, D., Wilson, S.: The Black Book of Outsourcing: How to Manage the Changes, Challenges and Opportunities. John Wiley & Sons, New Jersey (2005)
10. Crnlc, F., Kleemann, U., Selder, C.: Low Cost Country Sourcing can benefit a company's bottom line, http://www.gregbrennan.com/pdfs/IBM%20Low%20Cost%20Country%20Sourcing.pdf
11. Chapman, T., Demsey, J., Ramsdell, G., Reopel, M.: Purchasing - No Time for Long Rangers. The McKinsey Quarterly, 30–40 (May 1997)

512   R.U. Pai et al.

12. Heberling, M., Carter, J., Hoagland, J.: An Investigation of Purchases by American Business and Governments. International Journal of Purchasing and Materials Management 28(4), 39–45 (1992)
13. Bain and Company: Einkaufsstrategien - Herausforderungen für Top Manager, http://www.bain.com/bainweb/PDFs/cms/Public/Munich_Results_ Einkaufsstrategien_Herausforderungen.pdf
14. Fitzgerald, K.: Big Savings, But Lost of Risk. Supply Chain Management Review 9(9), 16–20 (2005)
15. Hemerling, J., Lee, D.: Sourcing from China - Lessons from the Leaders. Boston Consulting Group, Boston (2007)
16. Vlcek, J.: Risk Management for Buisness with Low Cost Countries (LCC). European Centre for Research in Purchasing and Supply, Vienna (2006)
17. Piontek, J.: Global Sourcing. R. Oldenbourgh, Munich (1997)
18. Kobayashi-Hillary, M.: Building a Future with BRICs - The Next Decade for Offshoring. Springer, London (2008)
19. Carmel, E.: The New Software Exporting Nations: Success Factors. The Electronic Journal of Information Systems in Developing Countries 13(4), 1–12 (2003)

Author Index